D1246889

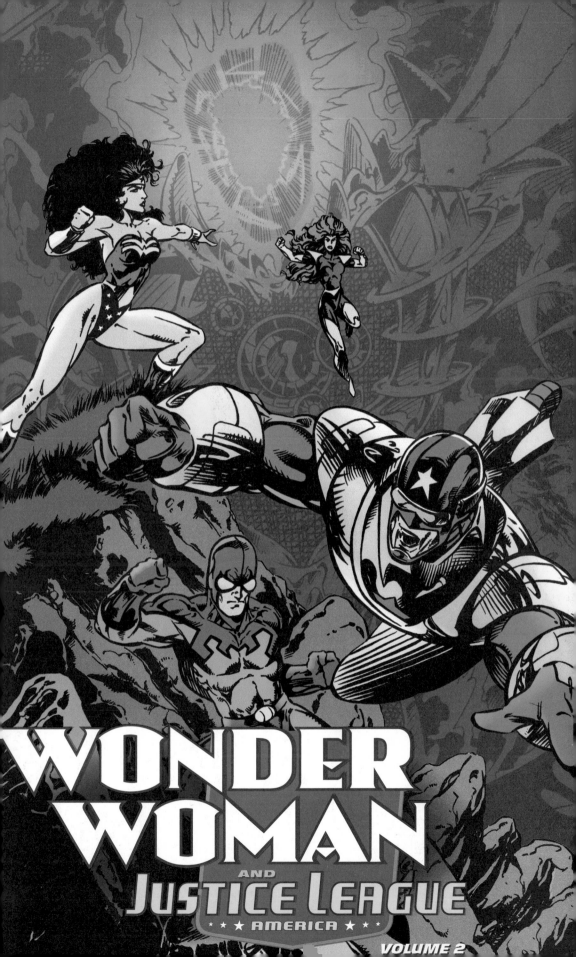

WONDER WOMAN

AND JUSTICE LEAGUE
★ ★ ★ AMERICA ★ ★ ★

VOLUME 2

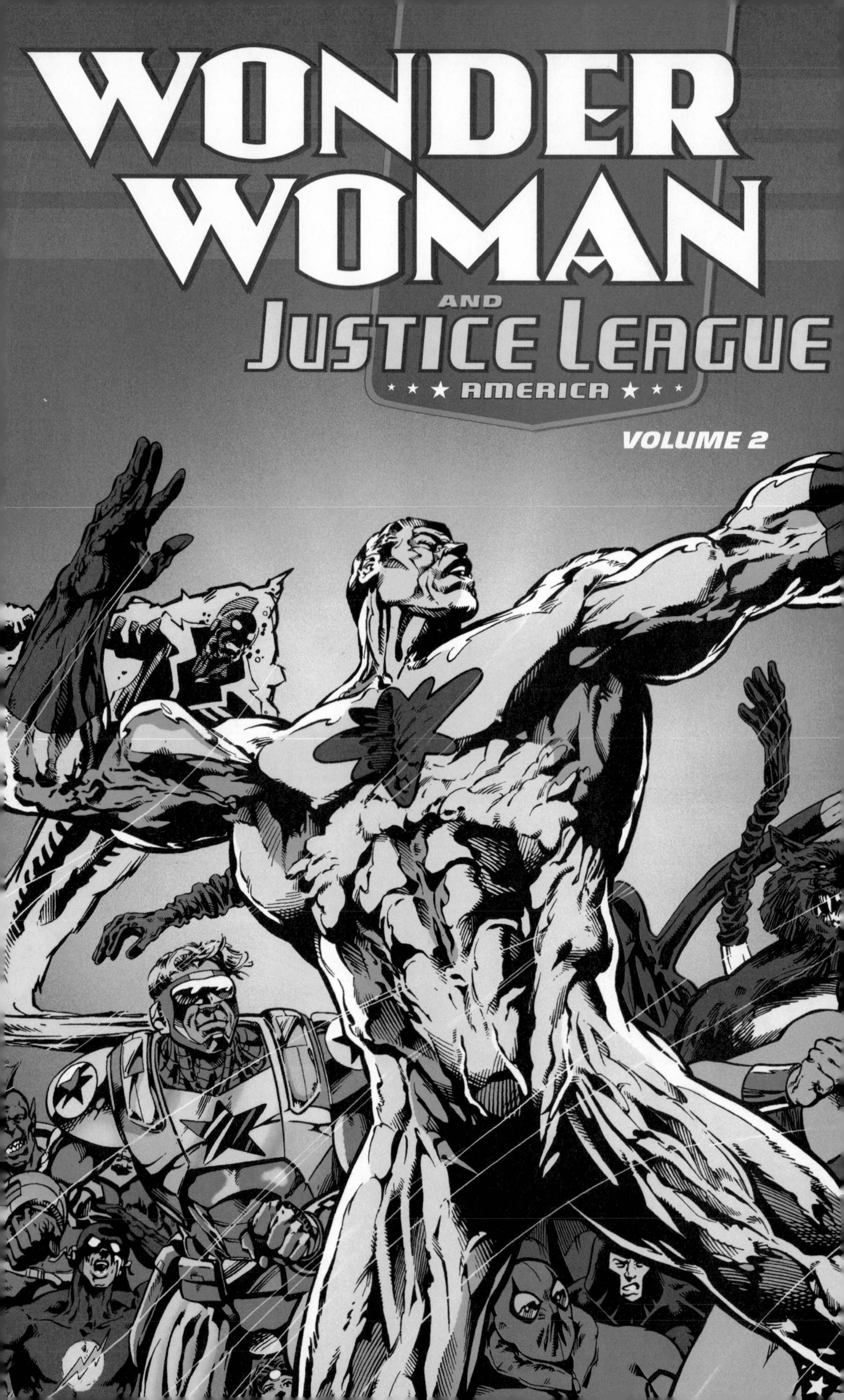
WONDER WOMAN
AND
JUSTICE LEAGUE
AMERICA
VOLUME 2

DAN VADO
GERARD JONES
MARK WAID
WRITERS

MARC CAMPOS
CHUCK WOJTKIEWICZ
SAL VELLUTO
PENCILLERS

KEN BRANCH
KEVIN CONRAD
BOB DVORAK
ROBERT JONES
RICH RANKIN
JEFF ALBRECHT
INKERS

GENE D'ANGELO
GLENN WHITMORE
COLORISTS

CLEM ROBINS
KEVIN CUNNINGHAM
BOB PINAHA
LETTERERS

TOM GRUMMETT
COLLECTION COVER ART

WONDER WOMAN
CREATED BY
WILLIAM MOULTON MARSTON

BRIAN AUGUSTYN Editor – Original Series
RUBEN DIAZ Assistant Editor – Original Series
JEB WOODARD Group Editor – Collected Editions
PAUL SANTOS Editor – Collected Edition
STEVE COOK Design Director – Books
CURTIS KING JR. Publication Design
BOB HARRAS Senior VP – Editor-in-Chief, DC Comics
PAT McCALLUM Executive Editor, DC Comics

DIANE NELSON President
DAN DiDIO Publisher
JIM LEE Publisher
GEOFF JOHNS President & Chief Creative Officer
AMIT DESAI Executive VP – Business & Marketing Strategy,
    Direct to Consumer & Global Franchise Management
SAM ADES Senior VP – Direct to Consumer
BOBBIE CHASE VP – Talent Development
MARK CHIARELLO Senior VP – Art, Design & Collected Editions
JOHN CUNNINGHAM Senior VP – Sales & Trade Marketing
ANNE DePIES Senior VP – Business Strategy, Finance & Administration
DON FALLETTI VP – Manufacturing Operations
LAWRENCE GANEM VP – Editorial Administration & Talent Relations
ALISON GILL Senior VP – Manufacturing & Operations
HANK KANALZ Senior VP – Editorial Strategy & Administration
JAY KOGAN VP – Legal Affairs
JACK MAHAN VP – Business Affairs
NICK J. NAPOLITANO VP – Manufacturing Administration
EDDIE SCANNELL VP – Consumer Marketing
COURTNEY SIMMONS Senior VP – Publicity & Communications
JIM (SKI) SOKOLOWSKI VP – Comic Book Specialty Sales & Trade Marketing
NANCY SPEARS VP – Mass, Book, Digital Sales & Trade Marketing
MICHELE R. WELLS VP – Content Strategy

**WONDER WOMAN AND
JUSTICE LEAGUE AMERICA VOL. 2**

Published by DC Comics. Compilation Copyright
© 2017 DC Comics. All Rights Reserved. Originally
published in single magazine form in JUSTICE
LEAGUE AMERICA 86-91, JUSTICE LEAGUE
INTERNATIONAL 65-66, and JUSTICE LEAGUE
TASK FORCE 13-14. Copyright © 1994 DC Comics.
All Rights Reserved. All characters, their distinctive
likenesses and related elements featured in this
publication are trademarks of DC Comics. The
stories, characters and incidents featured in this
publication are entirely fictional. DC Comics does
not read or accept unsolicited submissions of ideas,
stories or artwork.

DC Comics,
2900 West Alameda Avenue,
Burbank, CA 91505

Printed by LSC Communications,
Owensville, MO, USA. 9/1/17. First Printing.
ISBN: 978-1-4012-7400-9

Library of Congress
Cataloging-in-Publication Data is available.

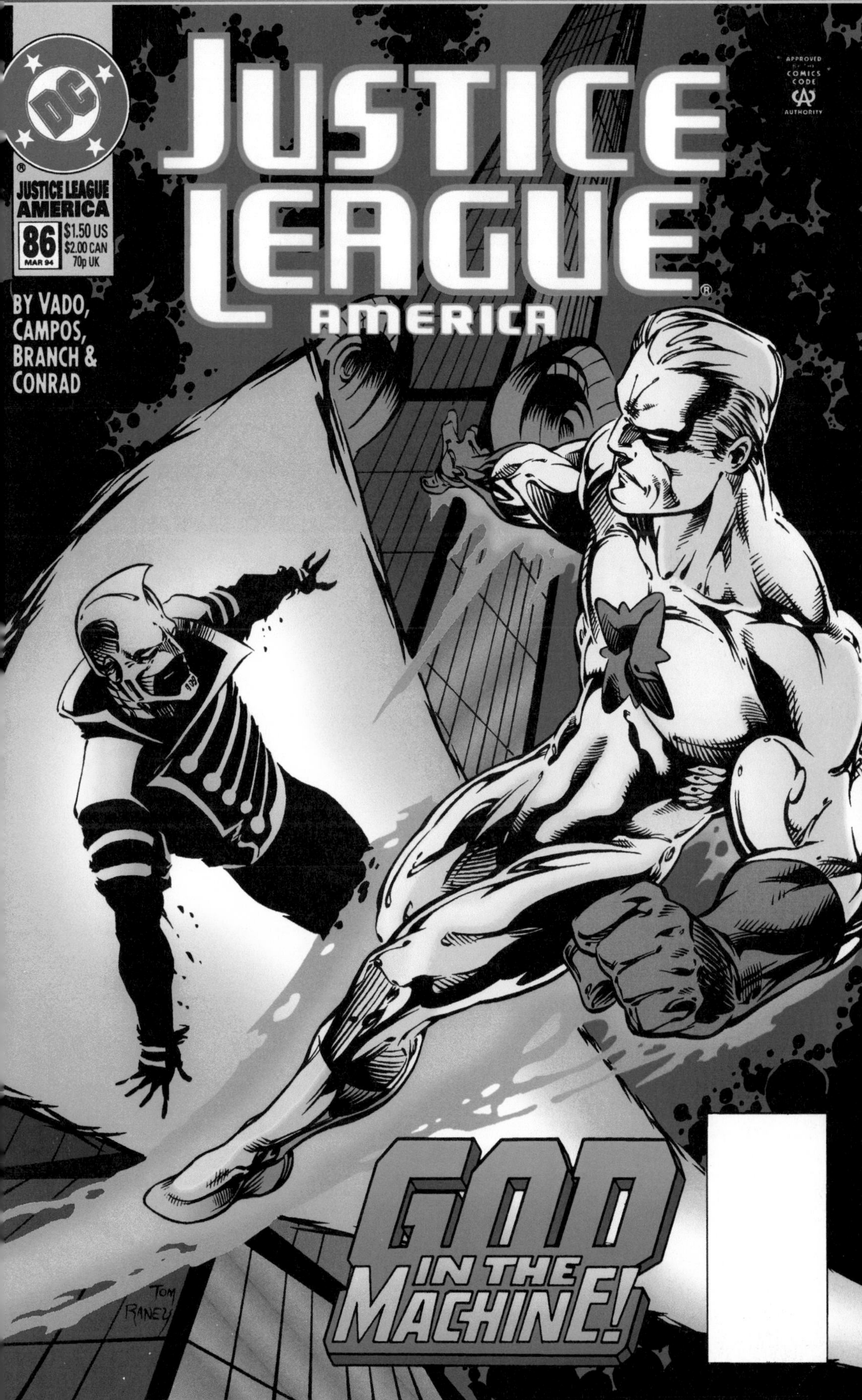
JUSTICE LEAGUE AMERICA
86
MAR 94
$1.50 US
$2.00 CAN
70p UK
JUSTICE LEAGUE
AMERICA
BY VADO, CAMPOS, BRANCH & CONRAD
APPROVED BY THE COMICS CODE AUTHORITY
TOM RANEY
GOD IN THE MACHINE!

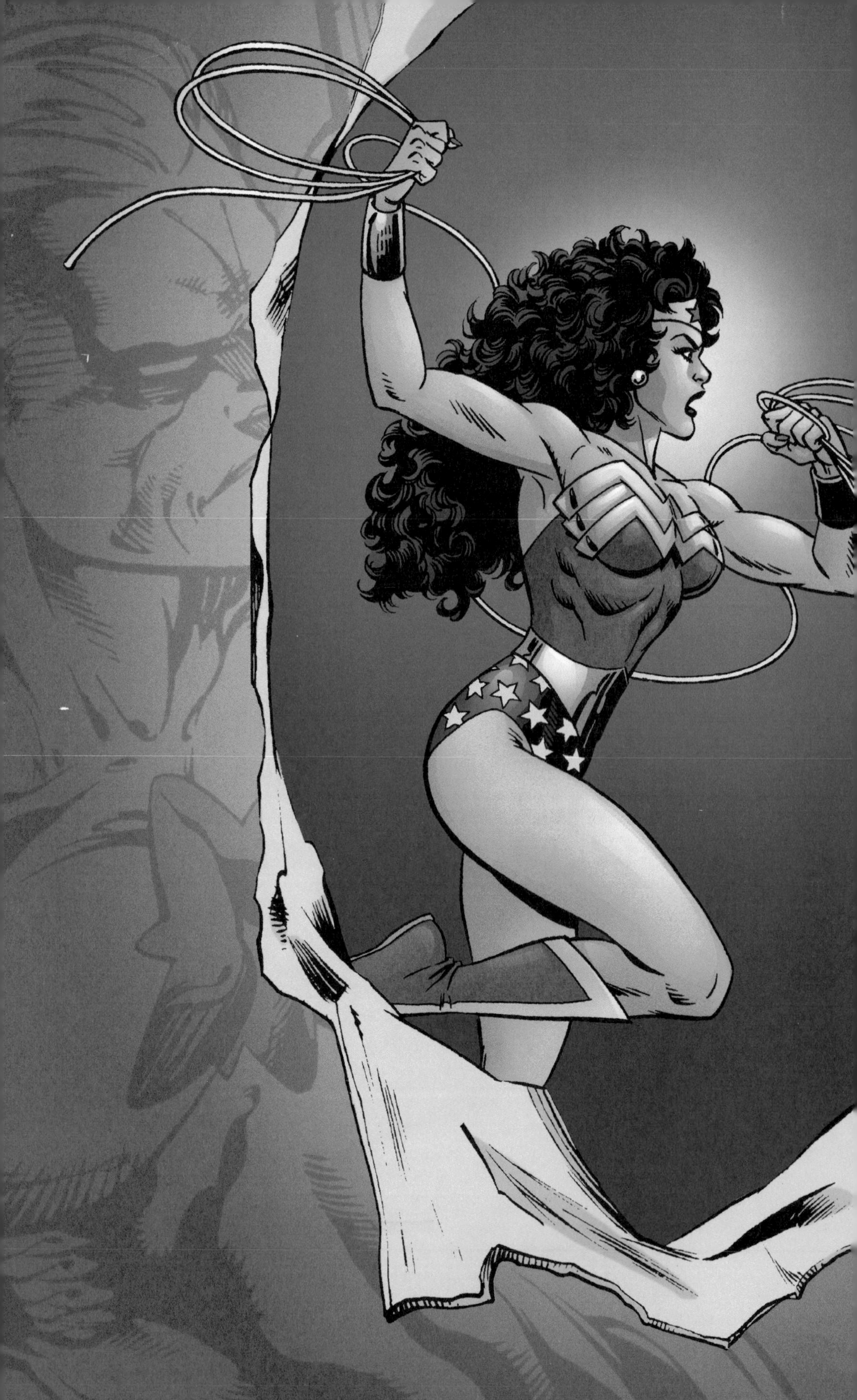

Cover art by **TOM RANEY**

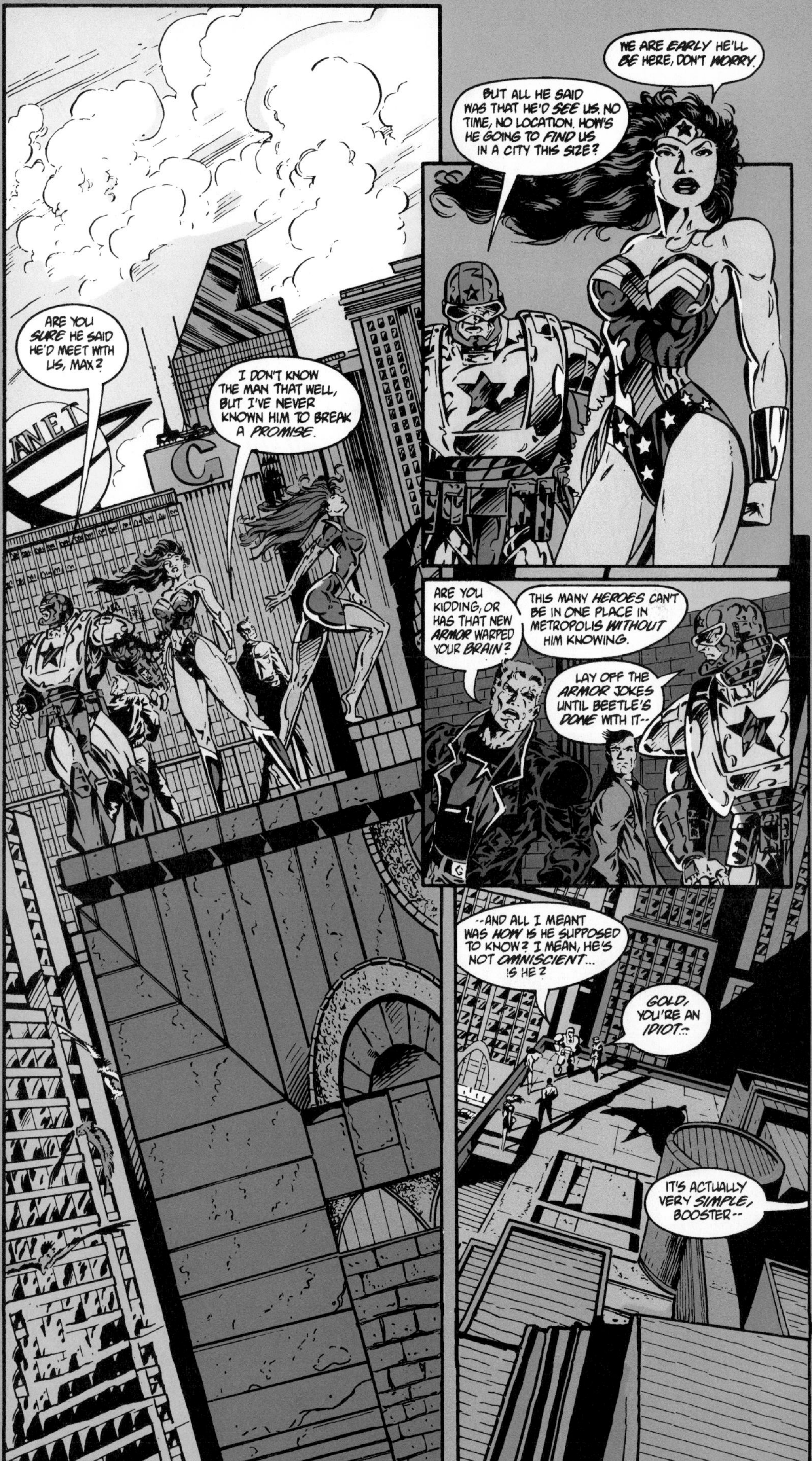
ARE YOU SURE HE SAID HE'D MEET WITH US, MAX?
I DON'T KNOW THE MAN THAT WELL, BUT I'VE NEVER KNOWN HIM TO BREAK A PROMISE.
BUT ALL HE SAID WAS THAT HE'D SEE US. NO TIME, NO LOCATION. HOW'S HE GOING TO FIND US IN A CITY THIS SIZE?
WE ARE EARLY HE'LL BE HERE, DON'T WORRY.
ARE YOU KIDDING, OR HAS THAT NEW ARMOR WARPED YOUR BRAIN?
THIS MANY HEROES CAN'T BE IN ONE PLACE IN METROPOLIS WITHOUT HIM KNOWING.
LAY OFF THE ARMOR JOKES UNTIL BEETLE'S DONE WITH IT--
--AND ALL I MEANT WAS HOW IS HE SUPPOSED TO KNOW? I MEAN, HE'S NOT OMNISCIENT... IS HE?
GOLD, YOU'RE AN IDIOT--
IT'S ACTUALLY VERY SIMPLE, BOOSTER--

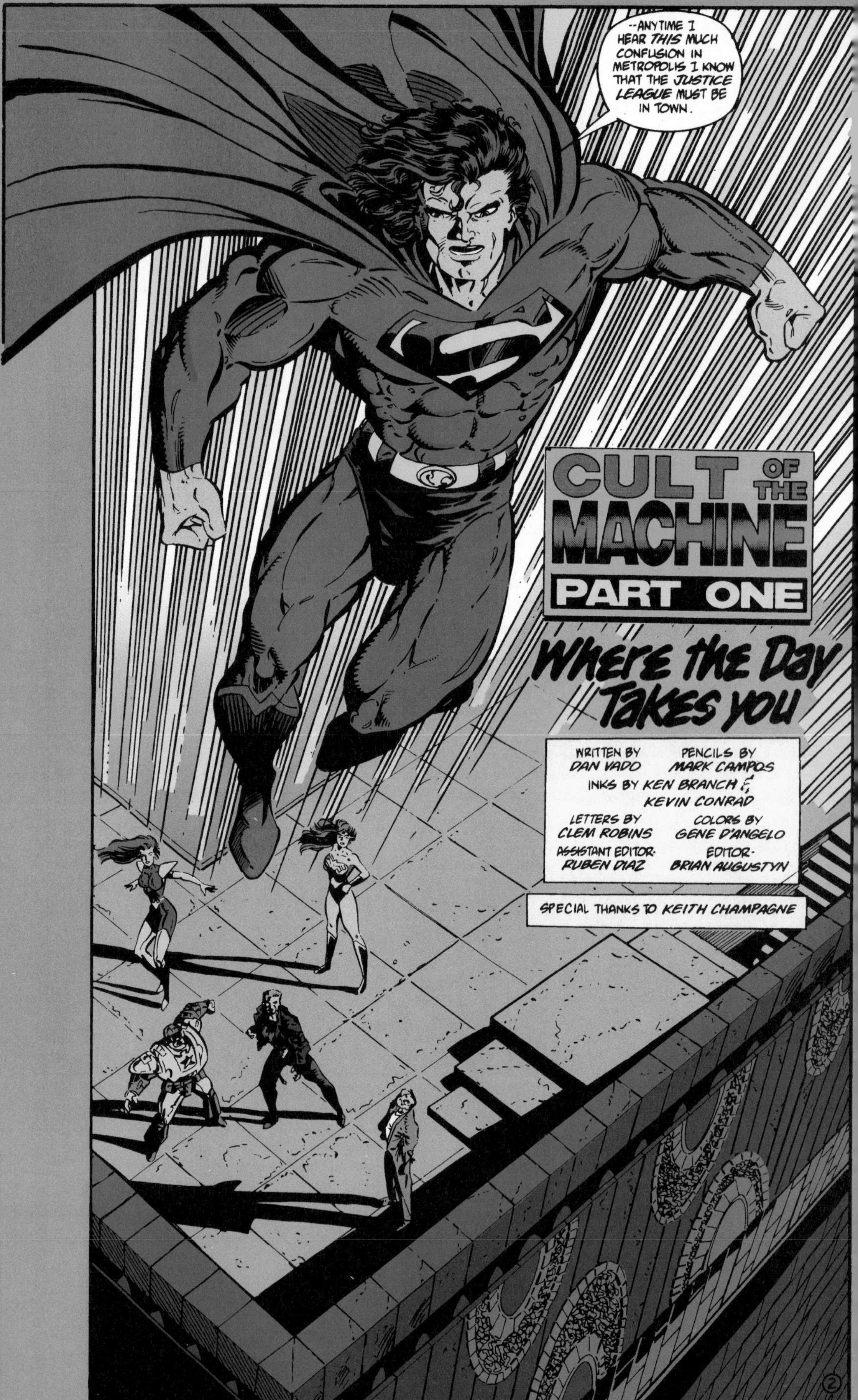
--ANYTIME I HEAR THIS MUCH CONFUSION IN METROPOLIS I KNOW THAT THE JUSTICE LEAGUE MUST BE IN TOWN.
CULT OF THE MACHINE
PART ONE
Where the Day Takes you
WRITTEN BY DAN VADO
PENCILS BY MARK CAMPOS
INKS BY KEN BRANCH & KEVIN CONRAD
LETTERS BY CLEM ROBINS
COLORS BY GENE D'ANGELO
ASSISTANT EDITOR· RUBEN DIAZ
EDITOR· BRIAN AUGUSTYN
SPECIAL THANKS TO KEITH CHAMPAGNE
2

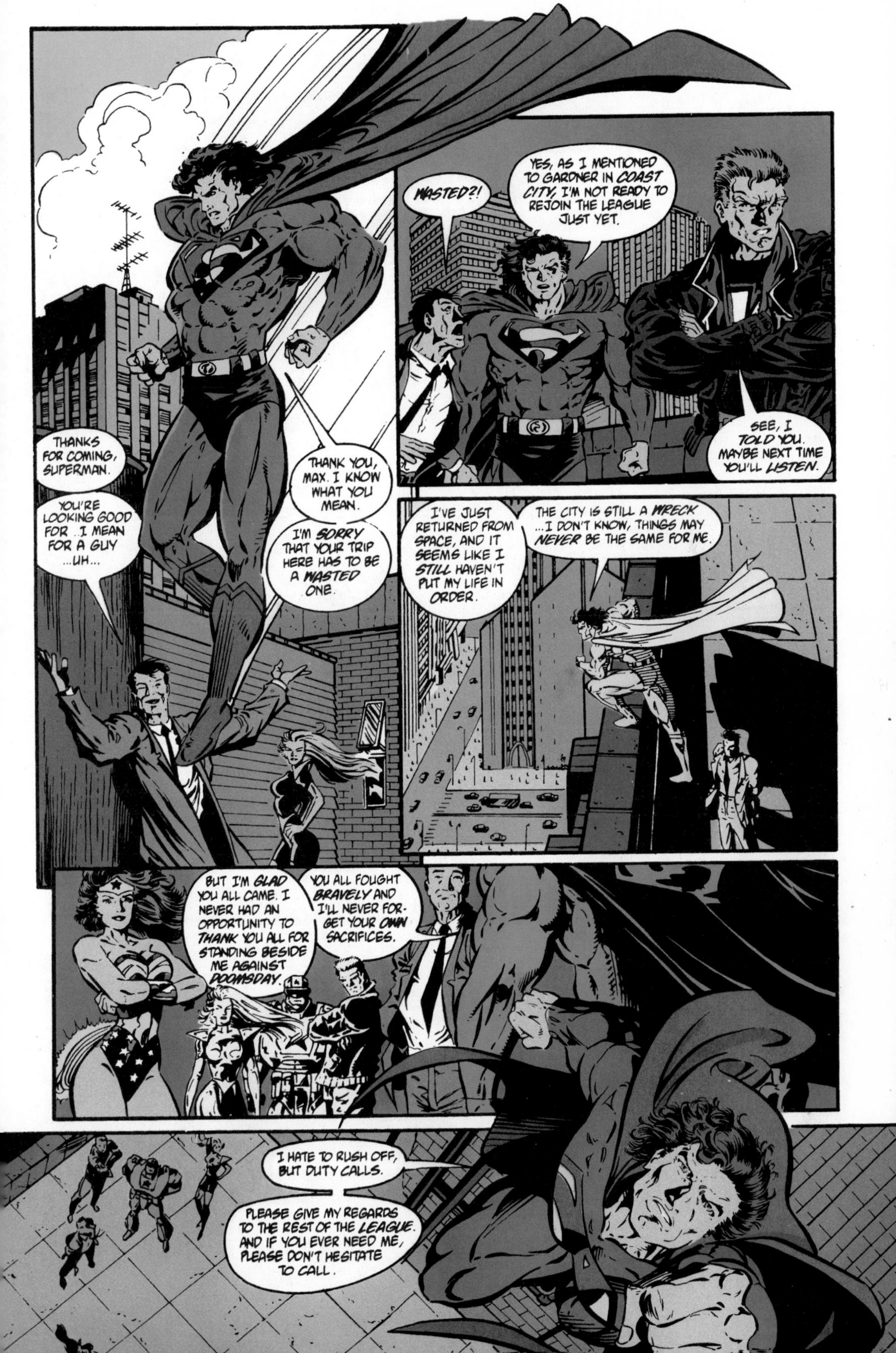

THANKS FOR COMING, SUPERMAN.
YOU'RE LOOKING GOOD FOR ..I MEAN FOR A GUY ...UH...
THANK YOU, MAX. I KNOW WHAT YOU MEAN.
I'M SORRY THAT YOUR TRIP HERE HAS TO BE A WASTED ONE.
WASTED?!
YES, AS I MENTIONED TO GARDNER IN COAST CITY, I'M NOT READY TO REJOIN THE LEAGUE JUST YET.
SEE, I TOLD YOU. MAYBE NEXT TIME YOU'LL LISTEN.
I'VE JUST RETURNED FROM SPACE, AND IT SEEMS LIKE I STILL HAVEN'T PUT MY LIFE IN ORDER.
THE CITY IS STILL A WRECK ...I DON'T KNOW, THINGS MAY NEVER BE THE SAME FOR ME.
BUT I'M GLAD YOU ALL CAME. I NEVER HAD AN OPPORTUNITY TO THANK YOU ALL FOR STANDING BESIDE ME AGAINST DOOMSDAY.
YOU ALL FOUGHT BRAVELY AND I'LL NEVER FORGET YOUR OWN SACRIFICES.
I HATE TO RUSH OFF, BUT DUTY CALLS.
PLEASE GIVE MY REGARDS TO THE REST OF THE LEAGUE. AND IF YOU EVER NEED ME, PLEASE DON'T HESITATE TO CALL.

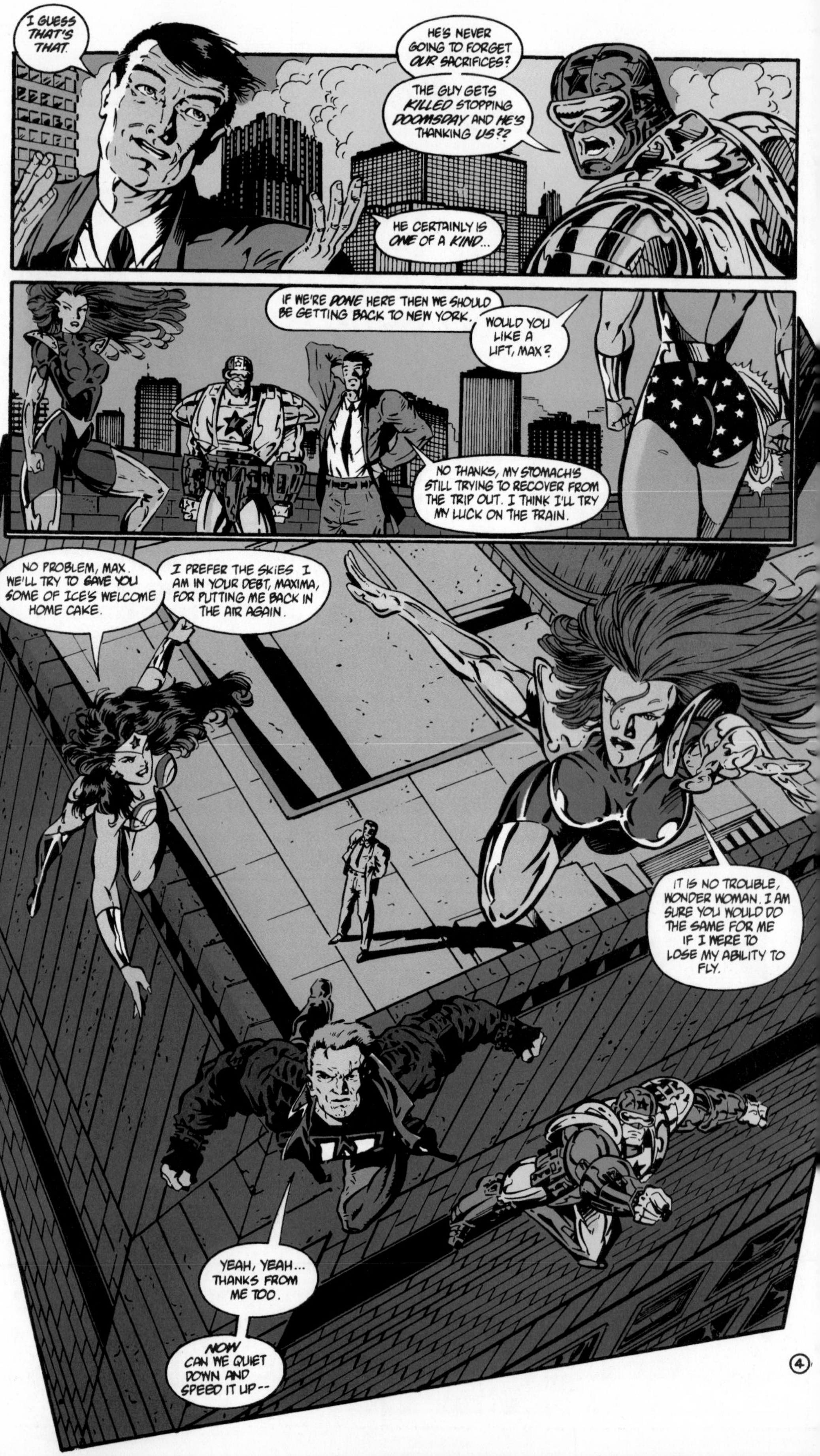
I GUESS THAT'S THAT.
HE'S NEVER GOING TO FORGET OUR SACRIFICES?
THE GUY GETS KILLED STOPPING DOOMSDAY AND HE'S THANKING US??
HE CERTAINLY IS ONE OF A KIND...
IF WE'RE DONE HERE THEN WE SHOULD BE GETTING BACK TO NEW YORK.
WOULD YOU LIKE A LIFT, MAX?
NO THANKS, MY STOMACH'S STILL TRYING TO RECOVER FROM THE TRIP OUT. I THINK I'LL TRY MY LUCK ON THE TRAIN.
NO PROBLEM, MAX. WE'LL TRY TO SAVE YOU SOME OF ICE'S WELCOME HOME CAKE.
I PREFER THE SKIES. I AM IN YOUR DEBT, MAXIMA, FOR PUTTING ME BACK IN THE AIR AGAIN.
IT IS NO TROUBLE, WONDER WOMAN. I AM SURE YOU WOULD DO THE SAME FOR ME IF I WERE TO LOSE MY ABILITY TO FLY.
YEAH, YEAH... THANKS FROM ME TOO.
NOW CAN WE QUIET DOWN AND SPEED IT UP--

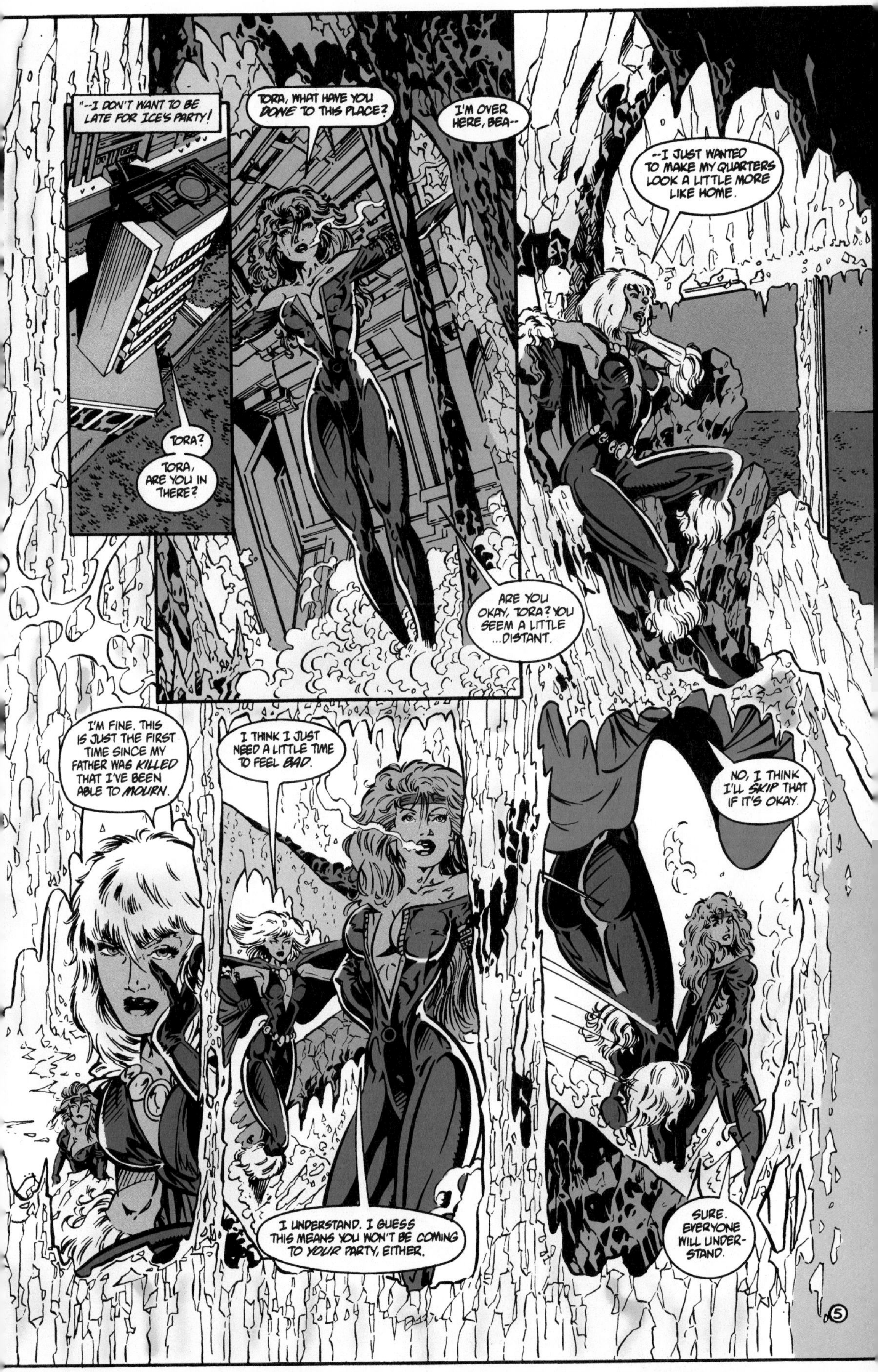
"--I DON'T WANT TO BE LATE FOR ICE'S PARTY!
TORA? TORA, ARE YOU IN THERE?
TORA, WHAT HAVE YOU DONE TO THIS PLACE?
I'M OVER HERE, BEA--
--I JUST WANTED TO MAKE MY QUARTERS LOOK A LITTLE MORE LIKE HOME.
ARE YOU OKAY, TORA? YOU SEEM A LITTLE ...DISTANT.
I'M FINE. THIS IS JUST THE FIRST TIME SINCE MY FATHER WAS KILLED THAT I'VE BEEN ABLE TO MOURN.
I THINK I JUST NEED A LITTLE TIME TO FEEL BAD.
I UNDERSTAND. I GUESS THIS MEANS YOU WON'T BE COMING TO YOUR PARTY, EITHER.
NO, I THINK I'LL SKIP THAT IF IT'S OKAY.
SURE. EVERYONE WILL UNDER-STAND.

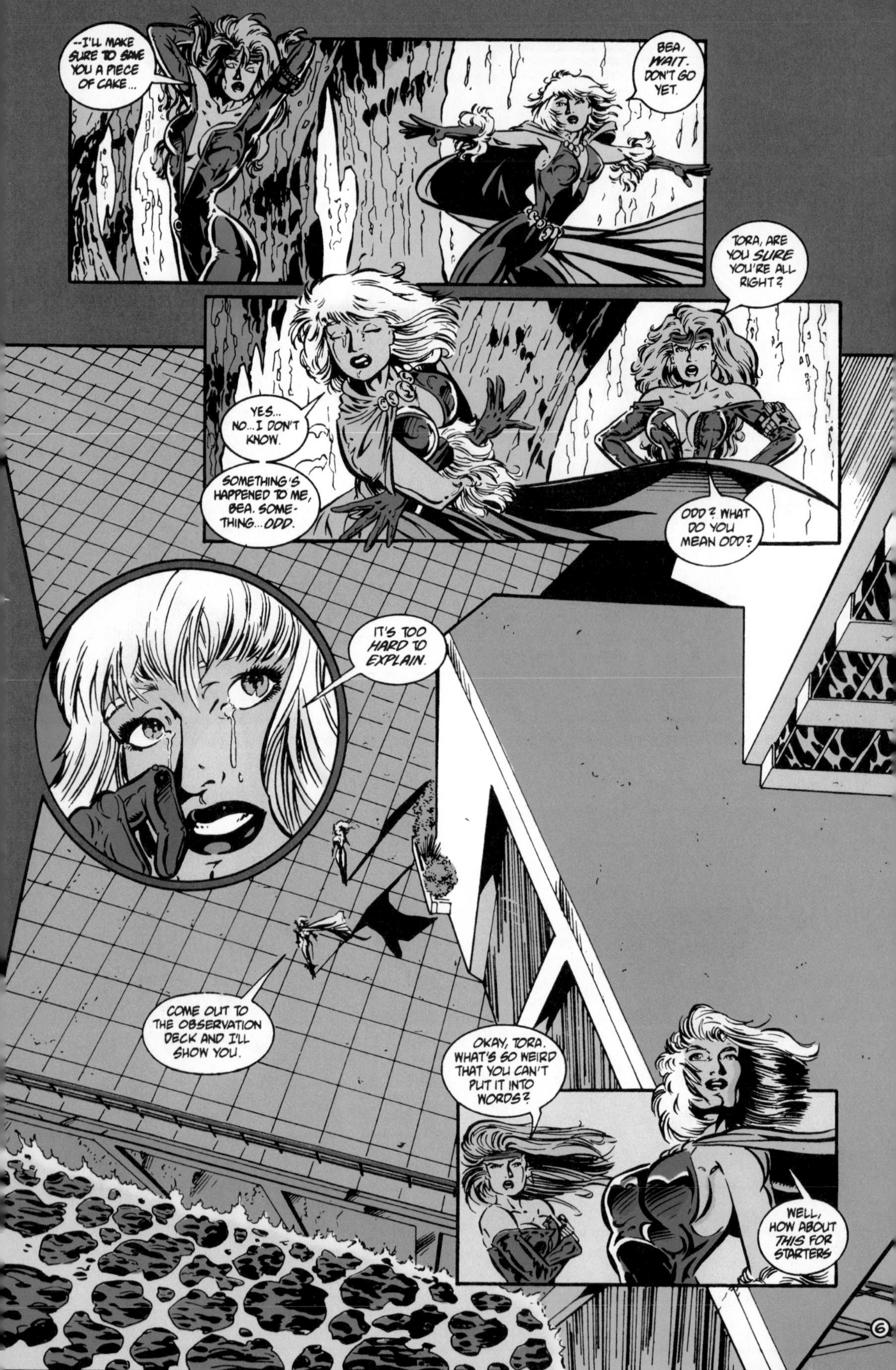
--I'LL MAKE SURE TO SAVE YOU A PIECE OF CAKE...
BEA, WAIT. DON'T GO YET.
TORA, ARE YOU SURE YOU'RE ALL RIGHT?
YES... NO...I DON'T KNOW.
SOMETHING'S HAPPENED TO ME, BEA. SOME-THING...ODD.
ODD? WHAT DO YOU MEAN ODD?
IT'S TOO HARD TO EXPLAIN.
COME OUT TO THE OBSERVATION DECK AND I'LL SHOW YOU.
OKAY, TORA. WHAT'S SO WEIRD THAT YOU CAN'T PUT IT INTO WORDS?
WELL, HOW ABOUT THIS FOR STARTERS

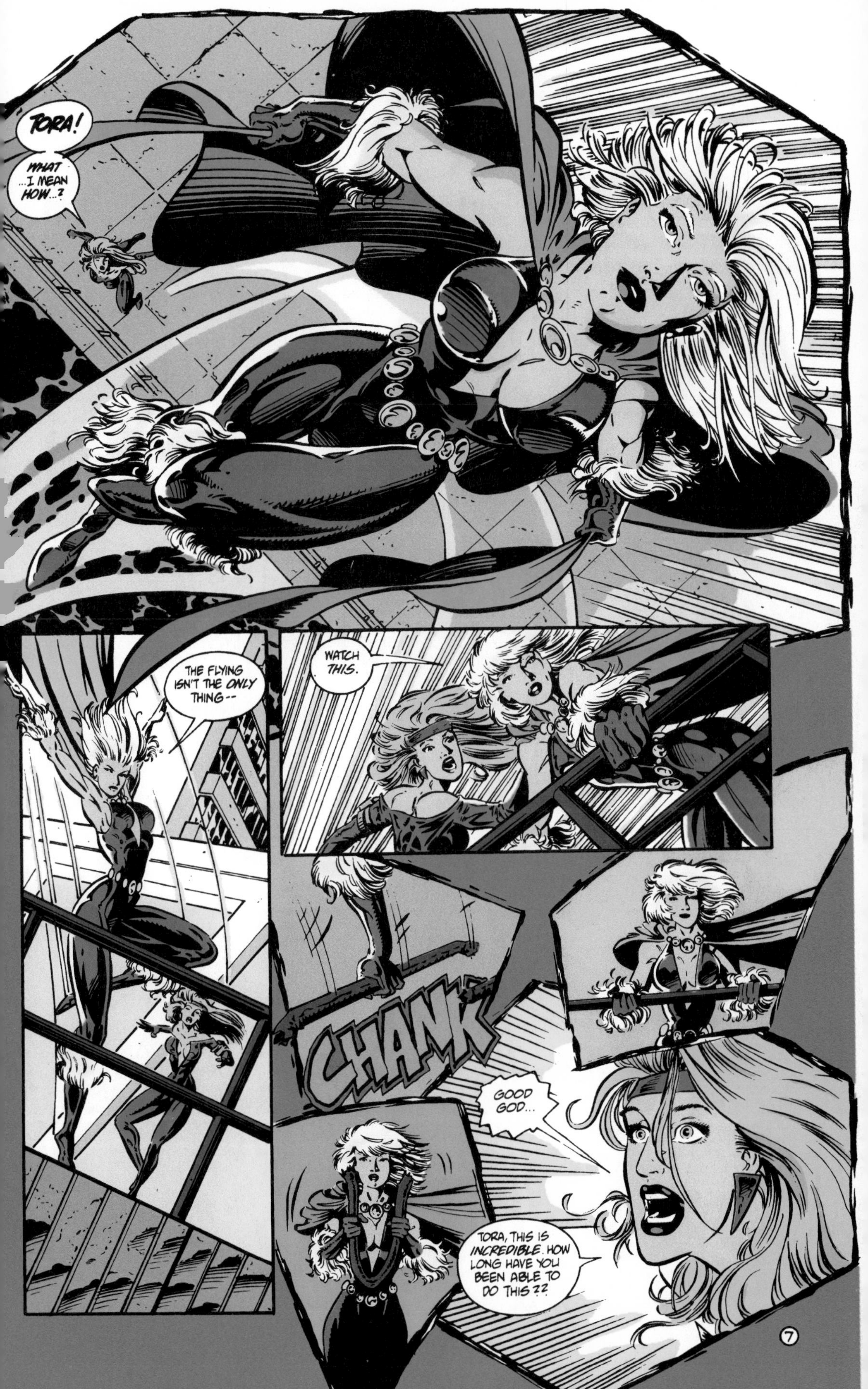
TORA!
WHAT ...I MEAN HOW...?
THE FLYING ISN'T THE ONLY THING--
WATCH THIS.
CHANK
GOOD GOD...
TORA, THIS IS INCREDIBLE. HOW LONG HAVE YOU BEEN ABLE TO DO THIS??

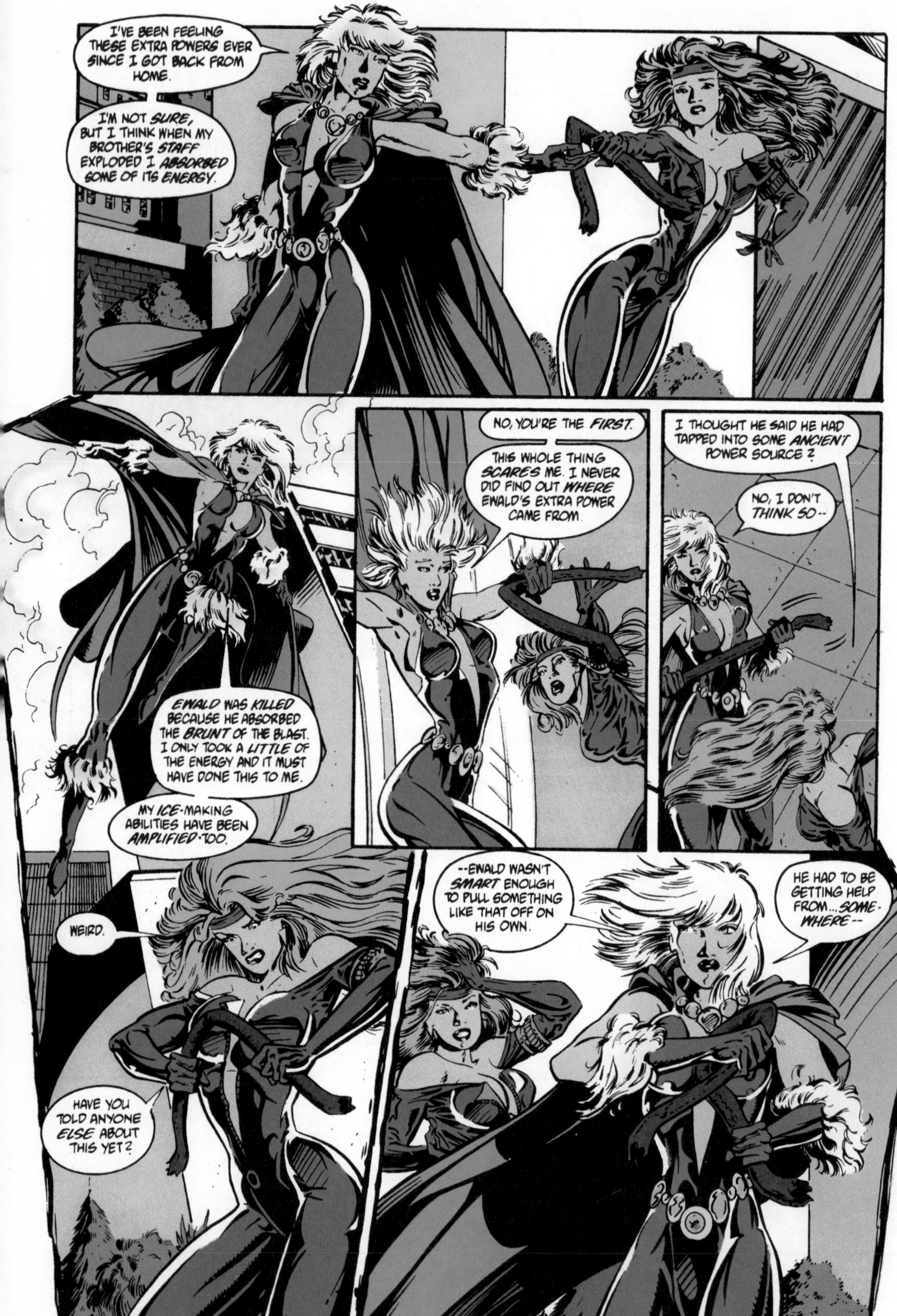
I'VE BEEN FEELING THESE EXTRA POWERS EVER SINCE I GOT BACK FROM HOME.
I'M NOT SURE, BUT I THINK WHEN MY BROTHER'S STAFF EXPLODED I ABSORBED SOME OF ITS ENERGY.
EWALD WAS KILLED BECAUSE HE ABSORBED THE BRUNT OF THE BLAST. I ONLY TOOK A LITTLE OF THE ENERGY AND IT MUST HAVE DONE THIS TO ME.
MY ICE-MAKING ABILITIES HAVE BEEN AMPLIFIED TOO.
NO, YOU'RE THE FIRST.
THIS WHOLE THING SCARES ME. I NEVER DID FIND OUT WHERE EWALD'S EXTRA POWER CAME FROM.
I THOUGHT HE SAID HE HAD TAPPED INTO SOME ANCIENT POWER SOURCE?
NO, I DON'T THINK SO--
WEIRD.
HAVE YOU TOLD ANYONE ELSE ABOUT THIS YET?
--EWALD WASN'T SMART ENOUGH TO PULL SOMETHING LIKE THAT OFF ON HIS OWN.
HE HAD TO BE GETTING HELP FROM... SOME-WHERE--

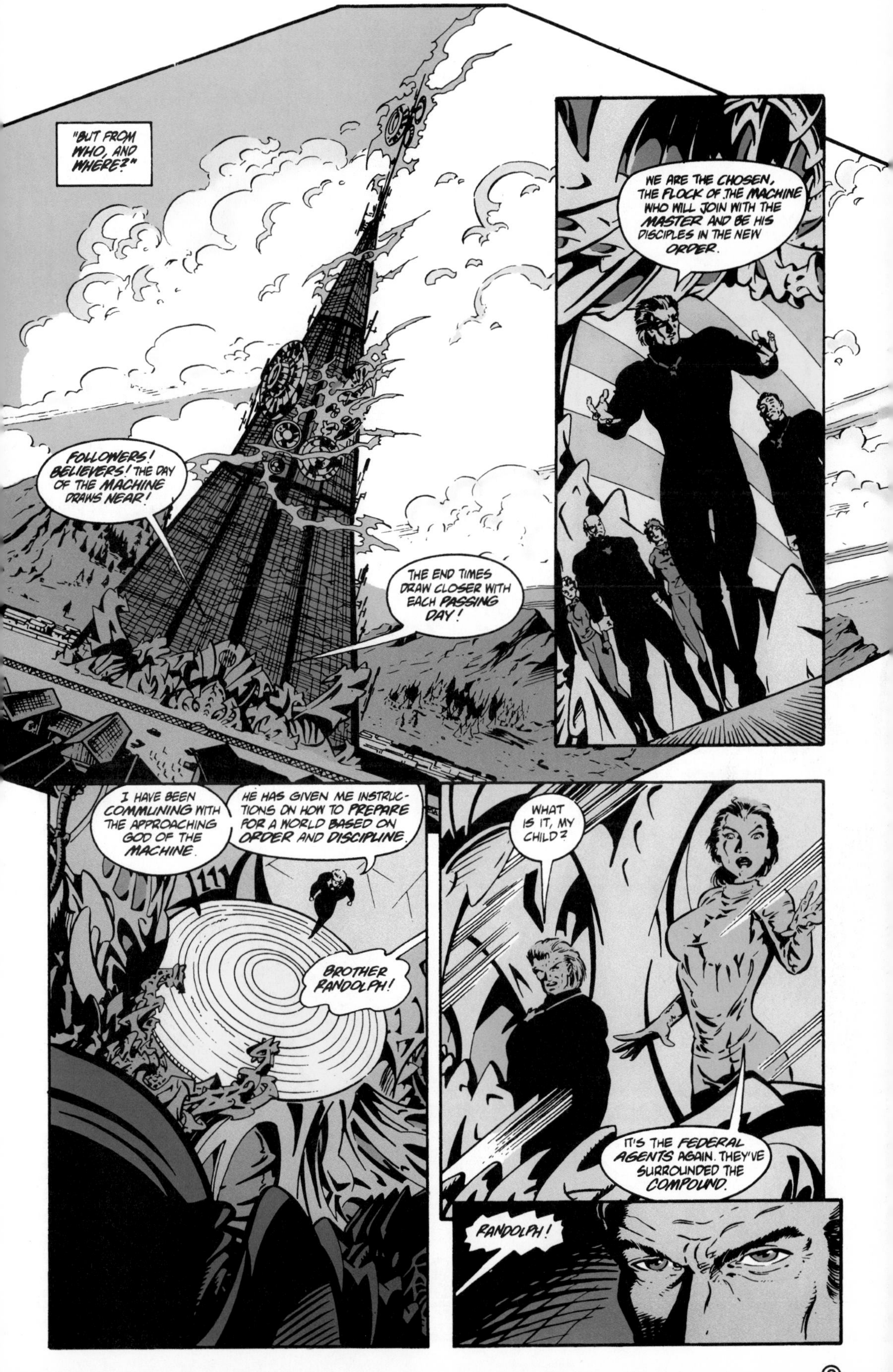
"BUT FROM WHO, AND WHERE?"
FOLLOWERS! BELIEVERS! THE DAY OF THE MACHINE DRAWS NEAR!
THE END TIMES DRAW CLOSER WITH EACH PASSING DAY!
WE ARE THE CHOSEN, THE FLOCK OF THE MACHINE WHO WILL JOIN WITH THE MASTER AND BE HIS DISCIPLES IN THE NEW ORDER.
I HAVE BEEN COMMUNING WITH THE APPROACHING GOD OF THE MACHINE.
HE HAS GIVEN ME INSTRUCTIONS ON HOW TO PREPARE FOR A WORLD BASED ON ORDER AND DISCIPLINE.
BROTHER RANDOLPH!
WHAT IS IT, MY CHILD?
IT'S THE FEDERAL AGENTS AGAIN. THEY'VE SURROUNDED THE COMPOUND.
RANDOLPH!

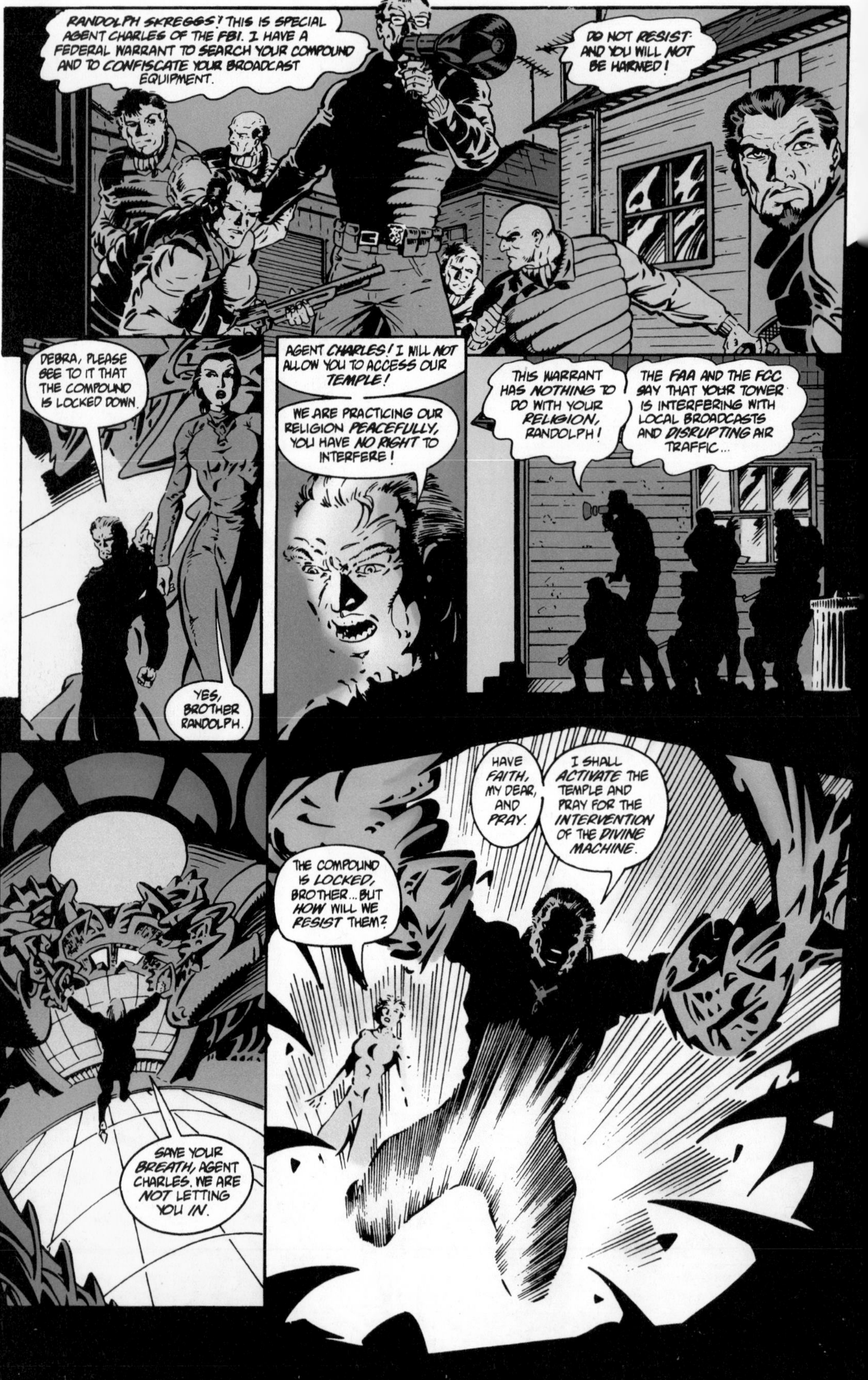
RANDOLPH SKRESSS? THIS IS SPECIAL AGENT CHARLES OF THE FBI. I HAVE A FEDERAL WARRANT TO SEARCH YOUR COMPOUND AND TO CONFISCATE YOUR BROADCAST EQUIPMENT.
DO NOT RESIST AND YOU WILL NOT BE HARMED!
DEBRA, PLEASE SEE TO IT THAT THE COMPOUND IS LOCKED DOWN.
YES, BROTHER RANDOLPH.
AGENT CHARLES! I WILL NOT ALLOW YOU TO ACCESS OUR TEMPLE!
WE ARE PRACTICING OUR RELIGION PEACEFULLY, YOU HAVE NO RIGHT TO INTERFERE!
THIS WARRANT HAS NOTHING TO DO WITH YOUR RELIGION, RANDOLPH!
THE FAA AND THE FCC SAY THAT YOUR TOWER IS INTERFERING WITH LOCAL BROADCASTS AND DISRUPTING AIR TRAFFIC...
SAVE YOUR BREATH, AGENT CHARLES. WE ARE NOT LETTING YOU IN.
THE COMPOUND IS LOCKED, BROTHER... BUT HOW WILL WE RESIST THEM?
HAVE FAITH, MY DEAR, AND PRAY.
I SHALL ACTIVATE THE TEMPLE AND PRAY FOR THE INTERVENTION OF THE DIVINE MACHINE.

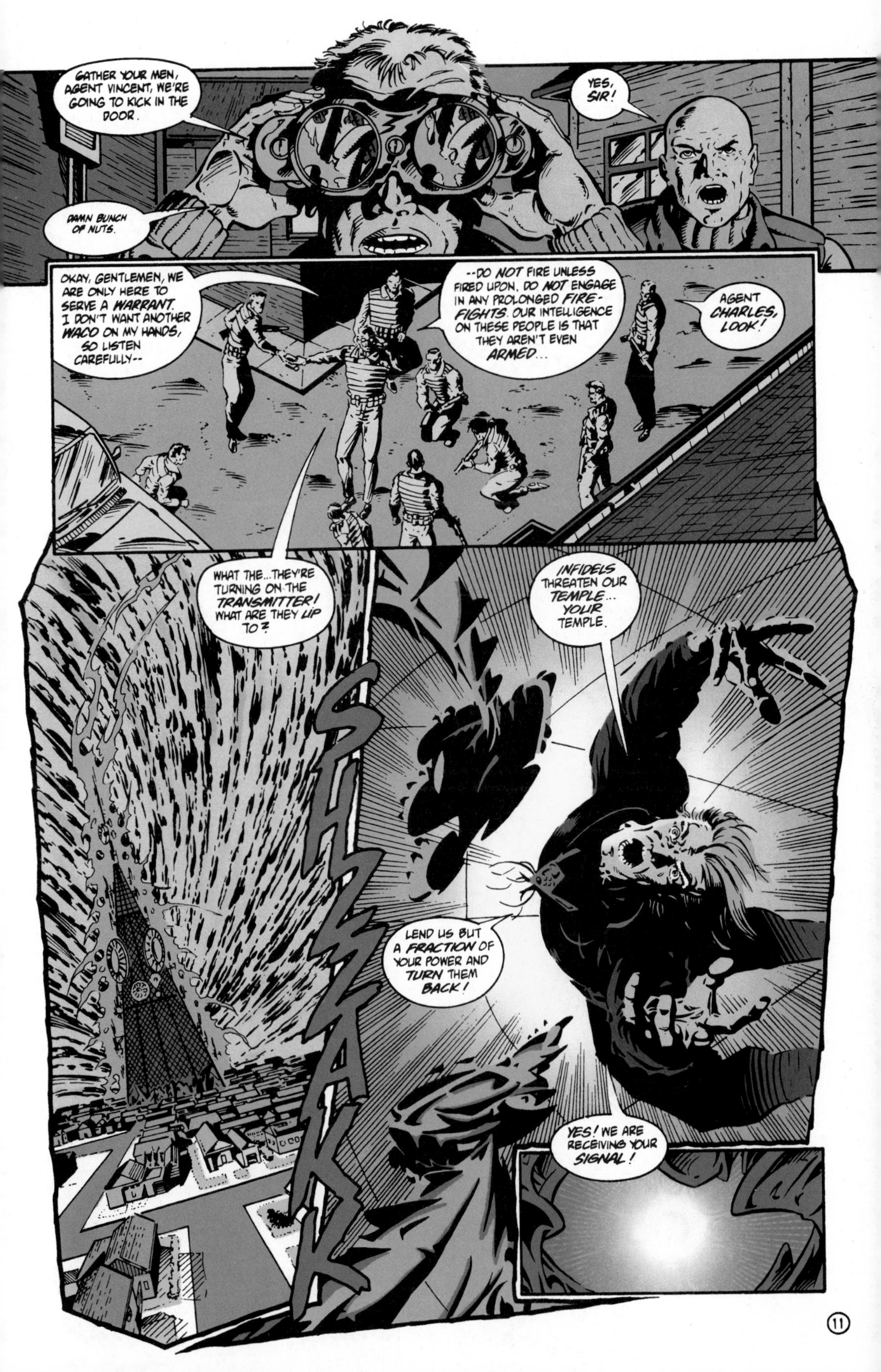
GATHER YOUR MEN, AGENT VINCENT, WE'RE GOING TO KICK IN THE DOOR.
DAMN BUNCH OF NUTS.
YES, SIR!
OKAY, GENTLEMEN, WE ARE ONLY HERE TO SERVE A WARRANT. I DON'T WANT ANOTHER WACO ON MY HANDS, SO LISTEN CAREFULLY--
--DO NOT FIRE UNLESS FIRED UPON. DO NOT ENGAGE IN ANY PROLONGED FIRE-FIGHTS. OUR INTELLIGENCE ON THESE PEOPLE IS THAT THEY AREN'T EVEN ARMED...
AGENT CHARLES, LOOK!
WHAT THE... THEY'RE TURNING ON THE TRANSMITTER! WHAT ARE THEY UP TO?
INFIDELS THREATEN OUR TEMPLE... YOUR TEMPLE.
SHHWAKK
LEND US BUT A FRACTION OF YOUR POWER AND TURN THEM BACK!
YES! WE ARE RECEIVING YOUR SIGNAL!

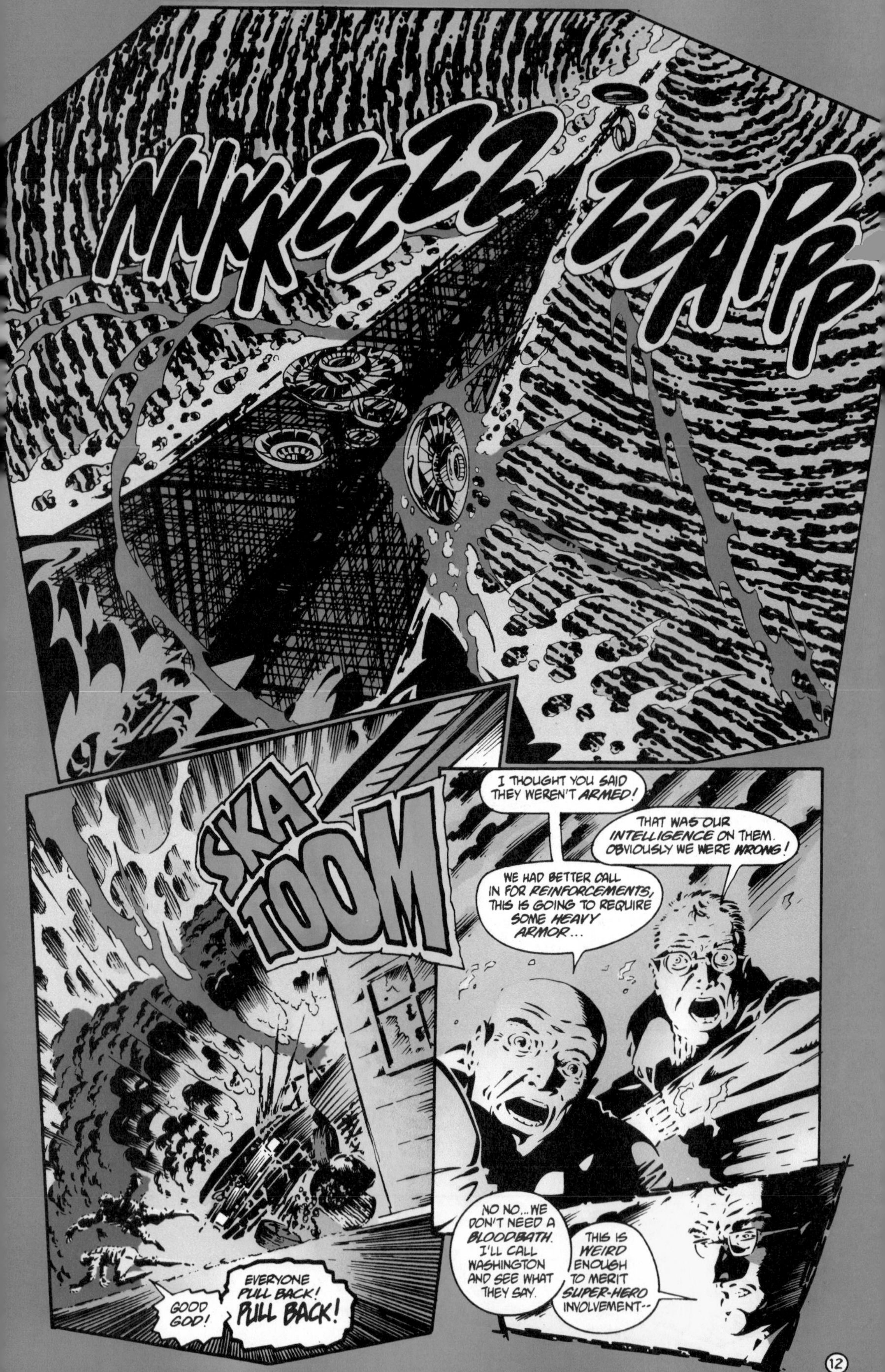
MNKKZZZZ ZZAPP
SKA-TOOM
GOOD GOD!
EVERYONE PULL BACK! PULL BACK!
I THOUGHT YOU SAID THEY WEREN'T ARMED!
THAT WAS OUR INTELLIGENCE ON THEM. OBVIOUSLY WE WERE WRONG!
WE HAD BETTER CALL IN FOR REINFORCEMENTS, THIS IS GOING TO REQUIRE SOME HEAVY ARMOR...
NO NO...WE DON'T NEED A BLOODBATH. I'LL CALL WASHINGTON AND SEE WHAT THEY SAY.
THIS IS WEIRD ENOUGH TO MERIT SUPER-HERO INVOLVEMENT--

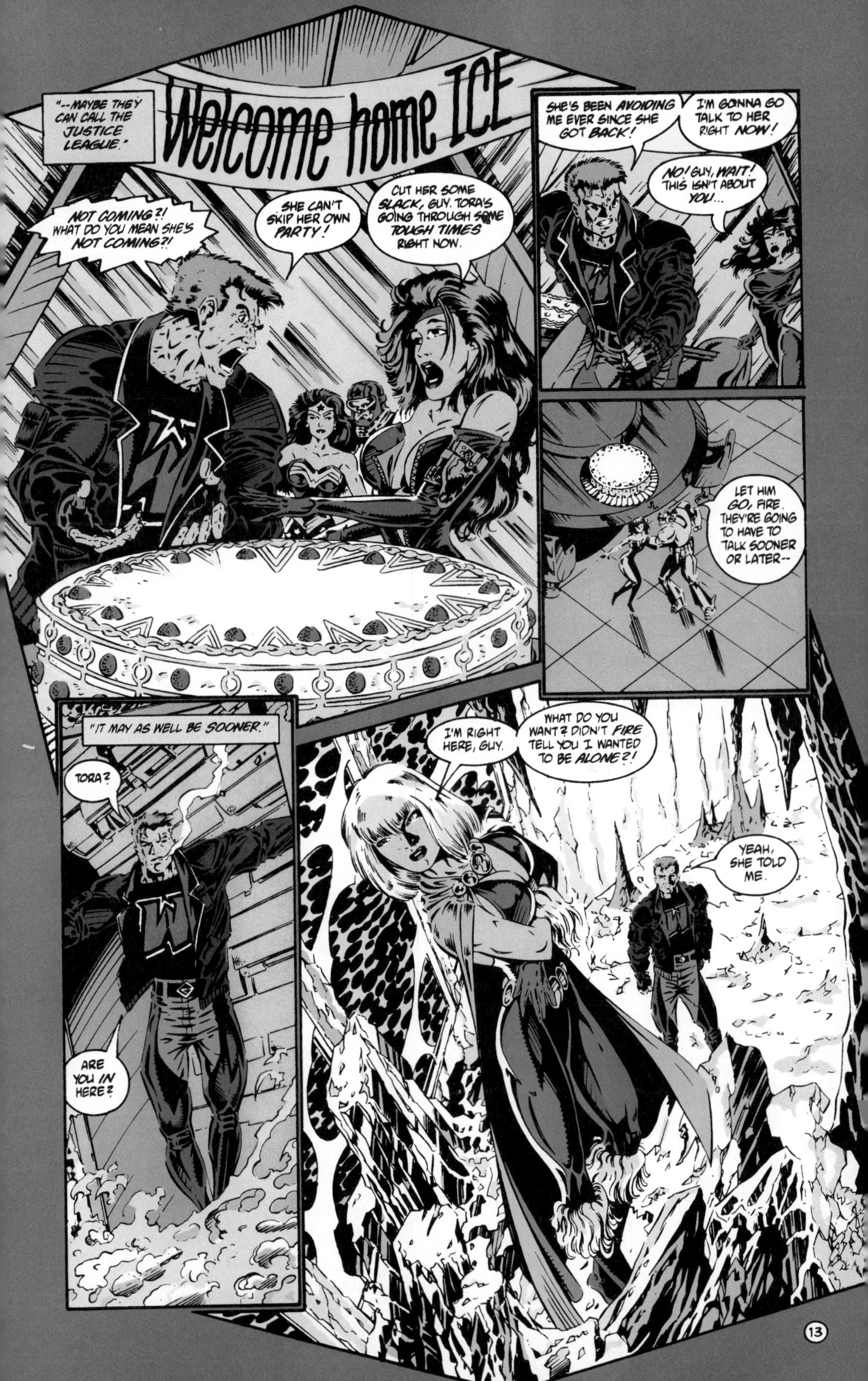
"--MAYBE THEY CAN CALL THE JUSTICE LEAGUE."
Welcome home ICE
NOT COMING?! WHAT DO YOU MEAN SHE'S NOT COMING?!
SHE CAN'T SKIP HER OWN PARTY!
CUT HER SOME SLACK, GUY. TORA'S GOING THROUGH SOME TOUGH TIMES RIGHT NOW.
SHE'S BEEN AVOIDING ME EVER SINCE SHE GOT BACK!
I'M GONNA GO TALK TO HER RIGHT NOW!
NO! GUY, WAIT! THIS ISN'T ABOUT YOU...
LET HIM GO, FIRE. THEY'RE GOING TO HAVE TO TALK SOONER OR LATER--
"IT MAY AS WELL BE SOONER."
TORA?
ARE YOU IN HERE?
I'M RIGHT HERE, GUY.
WHAT DO YOU WANT? DIDN'T FIRE TELL YOU I WANTED TO BE ALONE?!
YEAH, SHE TOLD ME.

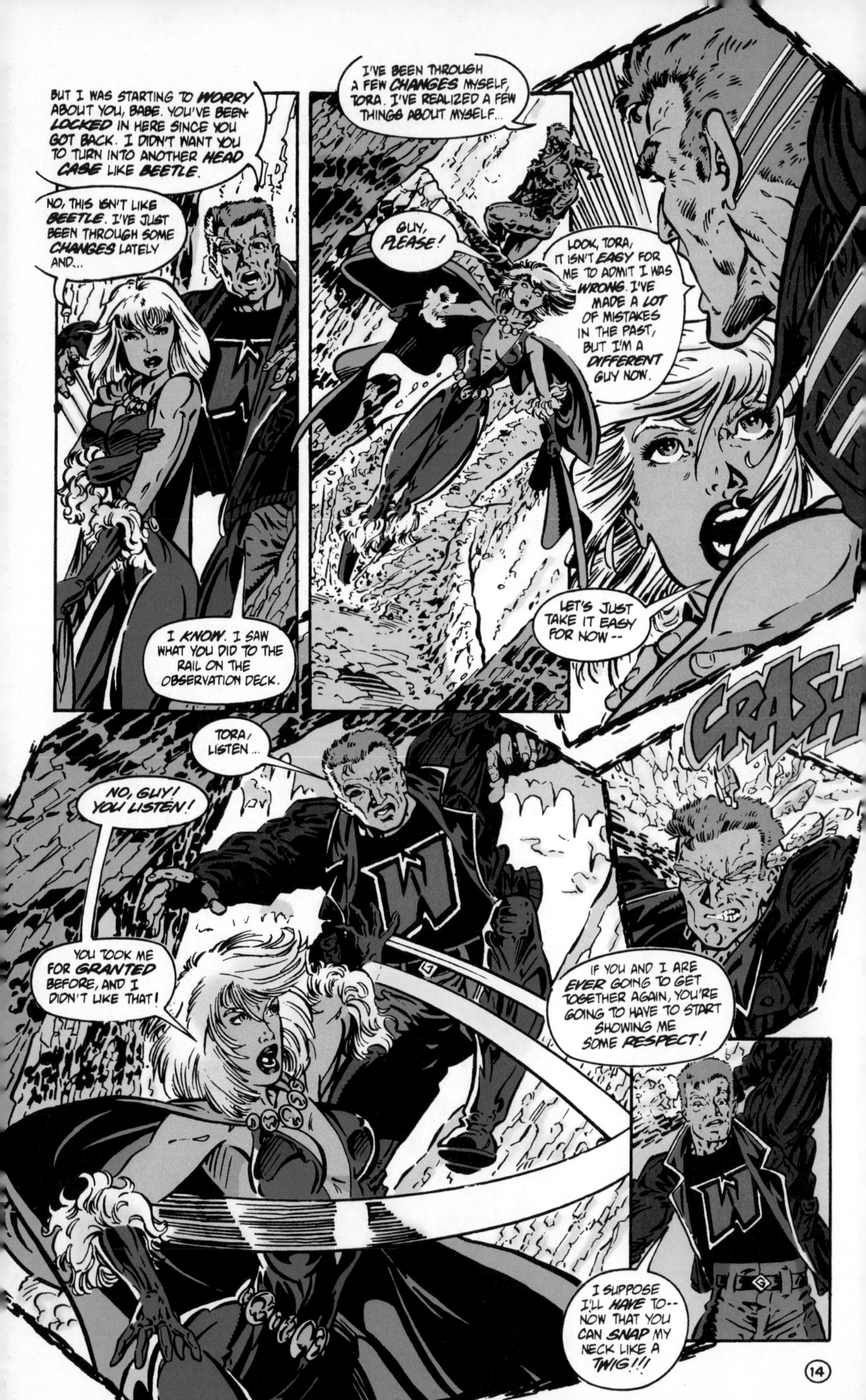

BUT I WAS STARTING TO WORRY ABOUT YOU, BABE. YOU'VE BEEN LOCKED IN HERE SINCE YOU GOT BACK. I DIDN'T WANT YOU TO TURN INTO ANOTHER HEAD CASE LIKE BEETLE.
NO, THIS ISN'T LIKE BEETLE. I'VE JUST BEEN THROUGH SOME CHANGES LATELY AND...
I KNOW. I SAW WHAT YOU DID TO THE RAIL ON THE OBSERVATION DECK.
I'VE BEEN THROUGH A FEW CHANGES MYSELF, TORA. I'VE REALIZED A FEW THINGS ABOUT MYSELF...
GUY, PLEASE!
LOOK, TORA, IT ISN'T EASY FOR ME TO ADMIT I WAS WRONG. I'VE MADE A LOT OF MISTAKES IN THE PAST, BUT I'M A DIFFERENT GUY NOW.
LET'S JUST TAKE IT EASY FOR NOW --
CRASH
TORA, LISTEN...
NO, GUY! YOU LISTEN!
YOU TOOK ME FOR GRANTED BEFORE, AND I DIDN'T LIKE THAT!
IF YOU AND I ARE EVER GOING TO GET TOGETHER AGAIN, YOU'RE GOING TO HAVE TO START SHOWING ME SOME RESPECT!
I SUPPOSE I'LL HAVE TO-- NOW THAT YOU CAN SNAP MY NECK LIKE A TWIG!!!

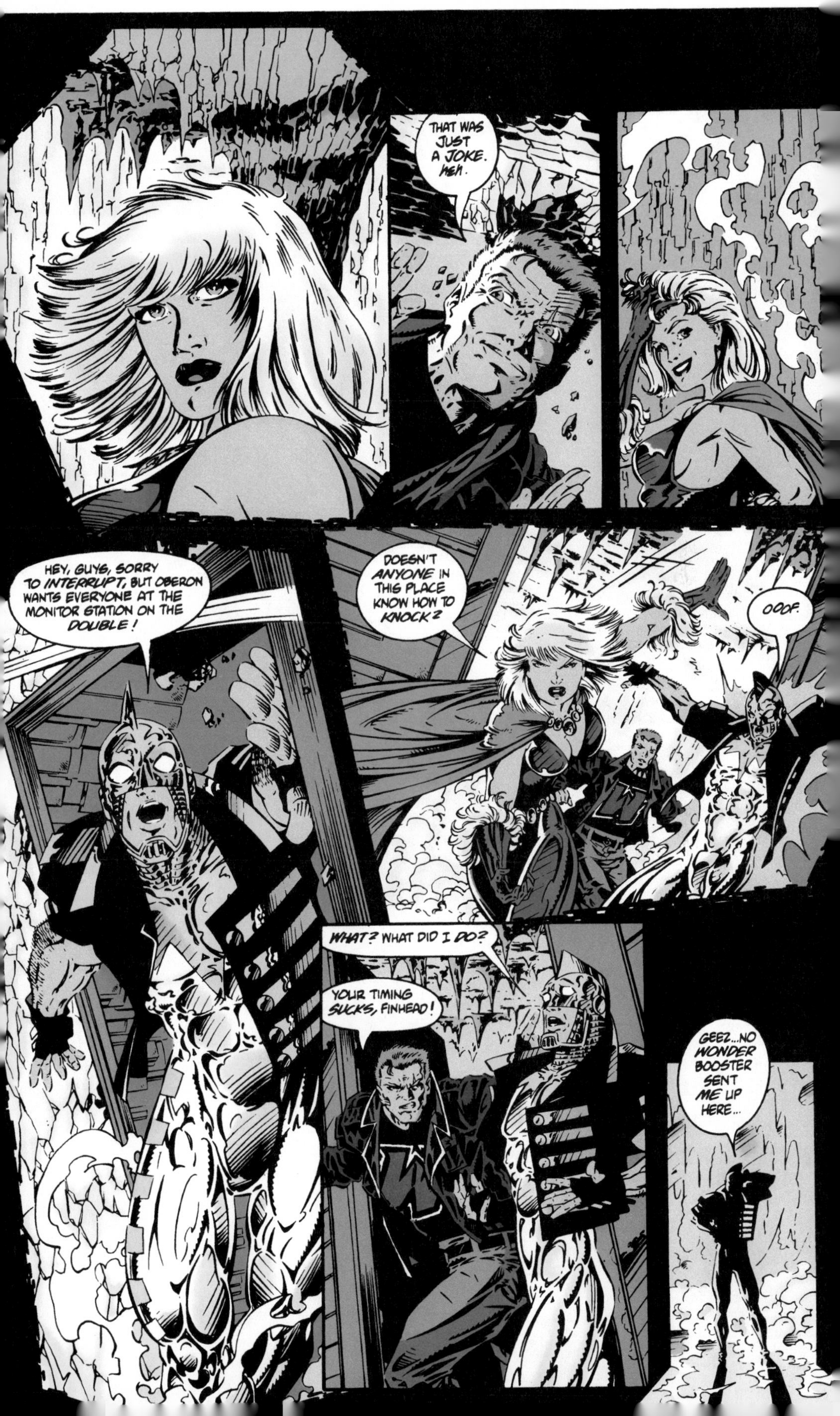
THAT WAS JUST A JOKE. HEH.
HEY, GUYS, SORRY TO INTERRUPT, BUT OBERON WANTS EVERYONE AT THE MONITOR STATION ON THE DOUBLE!
DOESN'T ANYONE IN THIS PLACE KNOW HOW TO KNOCK?
OOOF.
WHAT? WHAT DID I DO?
YOUR TIMING SUCKS, FINHEAD!
GEEZ...NO WONDER BOOSTER SENT ME UP HERE...

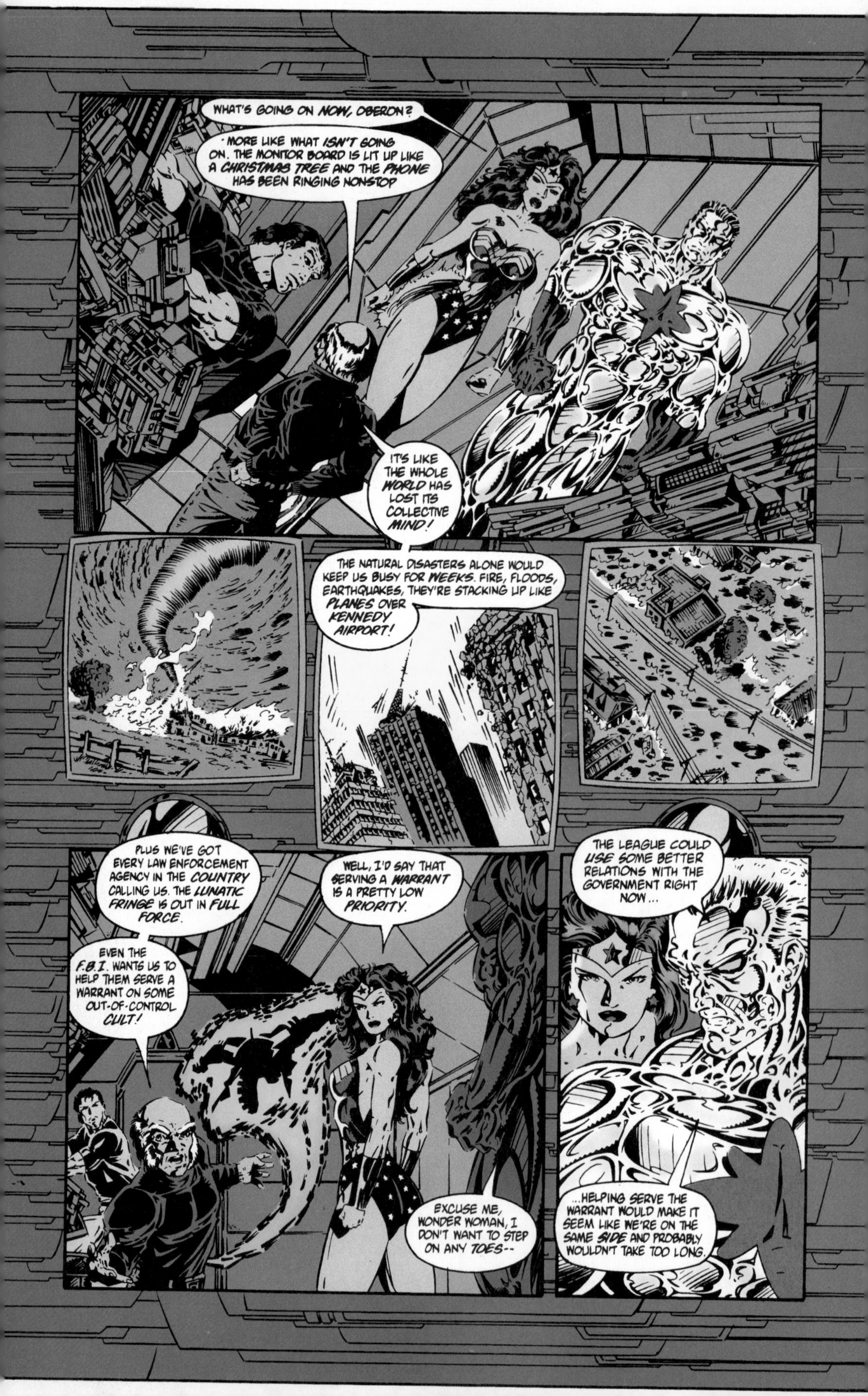
WHAT'S GOING ON NOW, OBERON?
...MORE LIKE WHAT ISN'T GOING ON. THE MONITOR BOARD IS LIT UP LIKE A CHRISTMAS TREE AND THE PHONE HAS BEEN RINGING NONSTOP
IT'S LIKE THE WHOLE WORLD HAS LOST ITS COLLECTIVE MIND!
THE NATURAL DISASTERS ALONE WOULD KEEP US BUSY FOR WEEKS. FIRE, FLOODS, EARTHQUAKES, THEY'RE STACKING UP LIKE PLANES OVER KENNEDY AIRPORT!
PLUS WE'VE GOT EVERY LAW ENFORCEMENT AGENCY IN THE COUNTRY CALLING US. THE LUNATIC FRINGE IS OUT IN FULL FORCE.
EVEN THE F.B.I. WANTS US TO HELP THEM SERVE A WARRANT ON SOME OUT-OF-CONTROL CULT!
WELL, I'D SAY THAT SERVING A WARRANT IS A PRETTY LOW PRIORITY.
EXCUSE ME, WONDER WOMAN, I DON'T WANT TO STEP ON ANY TOES--
THE LEAGUE COULD USE SOME BETTER RELATIONS WITH THE GOVERNMENT RIGHT NOW...
...HELPING SERVE THE WARRANT WOULD MAKE IT SEEM LIKE WE'RE ON THE SAME SIDE AND PROBABLY WOULDN'T TAKE TOO LONG.

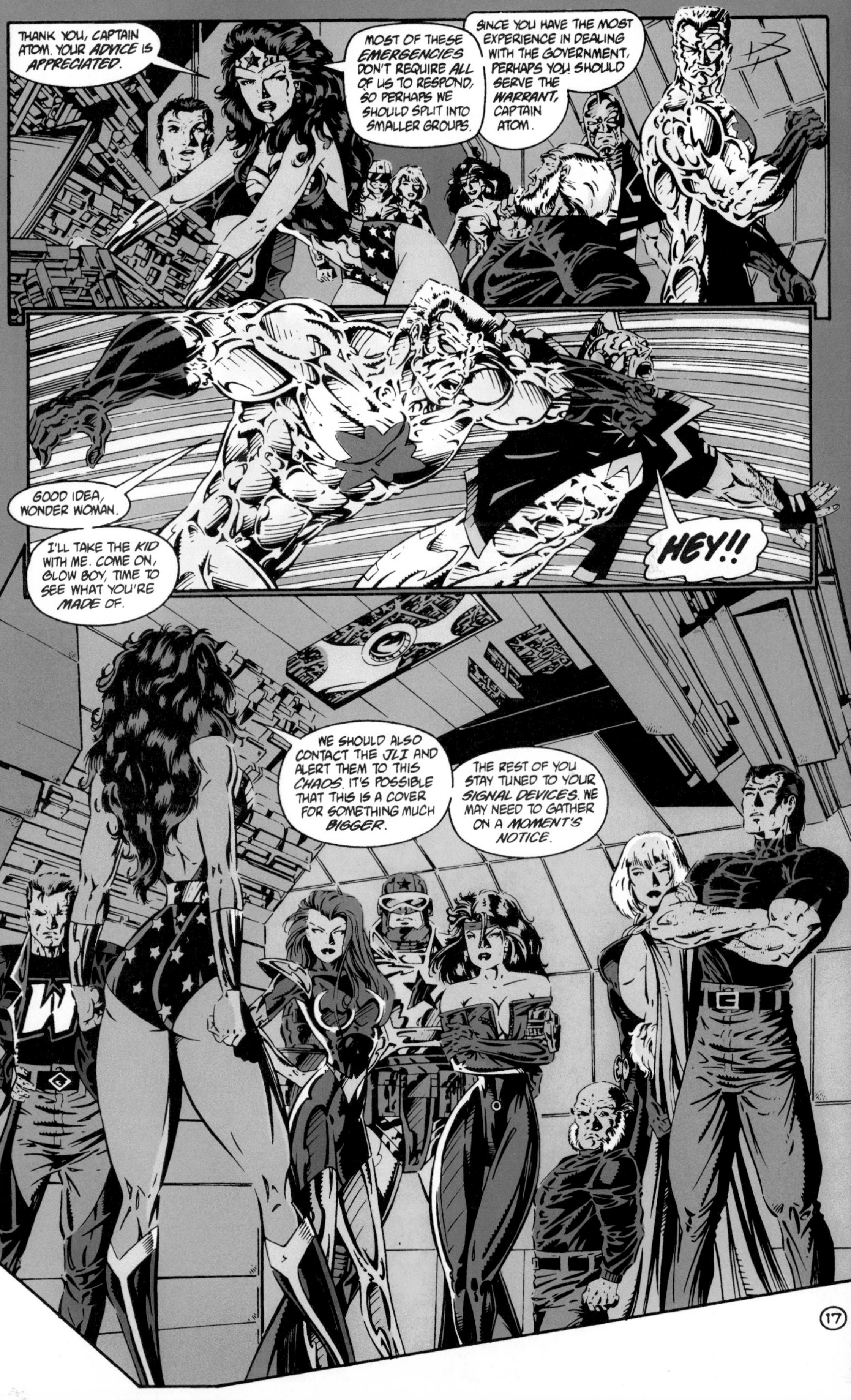

THANK YOU, CAPTAIN ATOM. YOUR ADVICE IS APPRECIATED.
MOST OF THESE EMERGENCIES DON'T REQUIRE ALL OF US TO RESPOND, SO PERHAPS WE SHOULD SPLIT INTO SMALLER GROUPS.
SINCE YOU HAVE THE MOST EXPERIENCE IN DEALING WITH THE GOVERNMENT, PERHAPS YOU SHOULD SERVE THE WARRANT, CAPTAIN ATOM.
GOOD IDEA, WONDER WOMAN.
I'LL TAKE THE KID WITH ME. COME ON, GLOW BOY, TIME TO SEE WHAT YOU'RE MADE OF.
HEY!!
WE SHOULD ALSO CONTACT THE JLI AND ALERT THEM TO THIS CHAOS. IT'S POSSIBLE THAT THIS IS A COVER FOR SOMETHING MUCH BIGGER.
THE REST OF YOU STAY TUNED TO YOUR SIGNAL DEVICES. WE MAY NEED TO GATHER ON A MOMENT'S NOTICE.

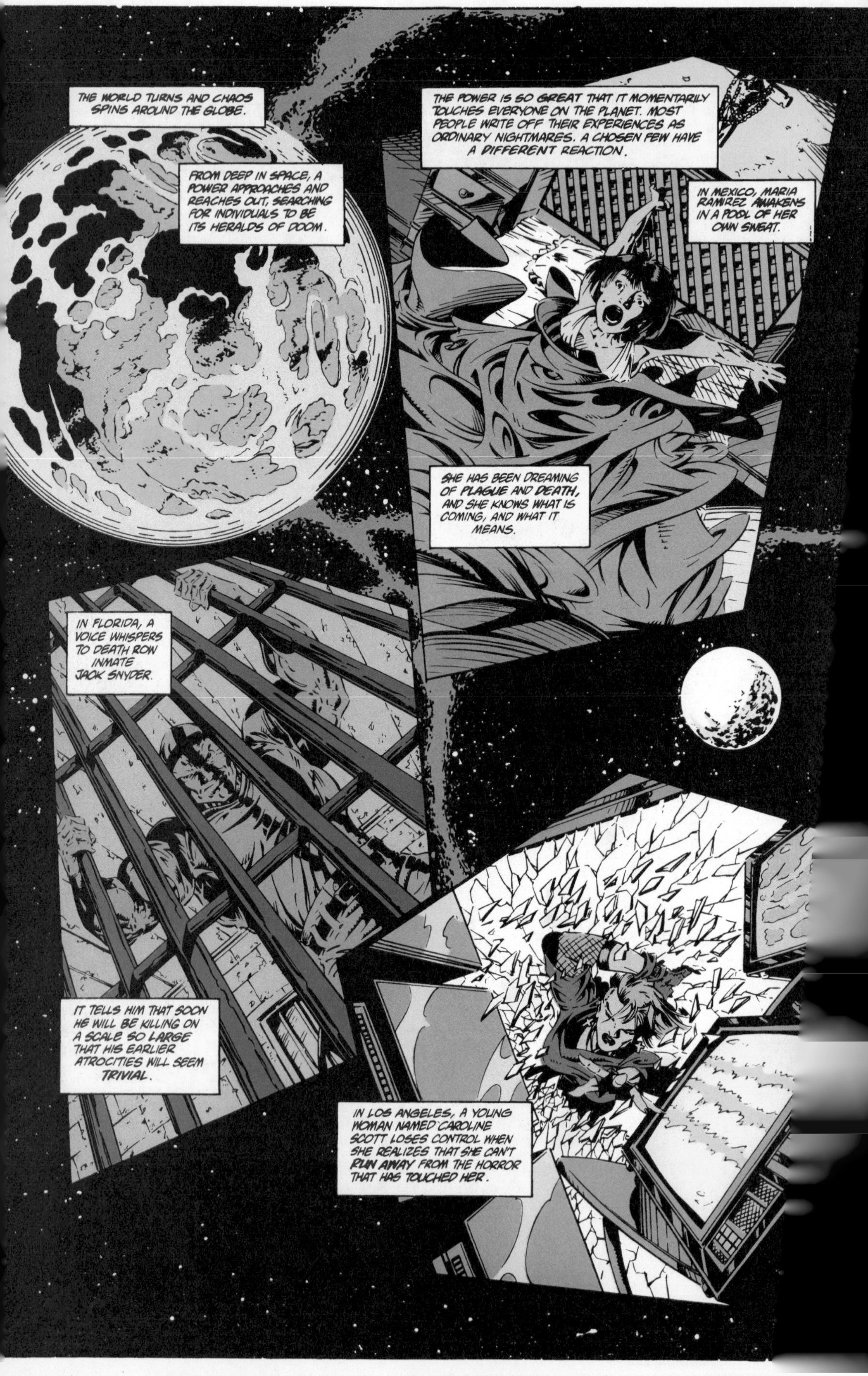
THE WORLD TURNS AND CHAOS SPINS AROUND THE GLOBE.
FROM DEEP IN SPACE, A POWER APPROACHES AND REACHES OUT, SEARCHING FOR INDIVIDUALS TO BE ITS HERALDS OF DOOM.
THE POWER IS SO GREAT THAT IT MOMENTARILY TOUCHES EVERYONE ON THE PLANET. MOST PEOPLE WRITE OFF THEIR EXPERIENCES AS ORDINARY NIGHTMARES. A CHOSEN FEW HAVE A DIFFERENT REACTION.
IN MEXICO, MARIA RAMIREZ AWAKENS IN A POOL OF HER OWN SWEAT.
SHE HAS BEEN DREAMING OF PLAGUE AND DEATH, AND SHE KNOWS WHAT IS COMING, AND WHAT IT MEANS.
IN FLORIDA, A VOICE WHISPERS TO DEATH ROW INMATE JACK SNYDER.
IT TELLS HIM THAT SOON HE WILL BE KILLING ON A SCALE SO LARGE THAT HIS EARLIER ATROCITIES WILL SEEM TRIVIAL.
IN LOS ANGELES, A YOUNG WOMAN NAMED CAROLINE SCOTT LOSES CONTROL WHEN SHE REALIZES THAT SHE CAN'T RUN AWAY FROM THE HORROR THAT HAS TOUCHED HER.

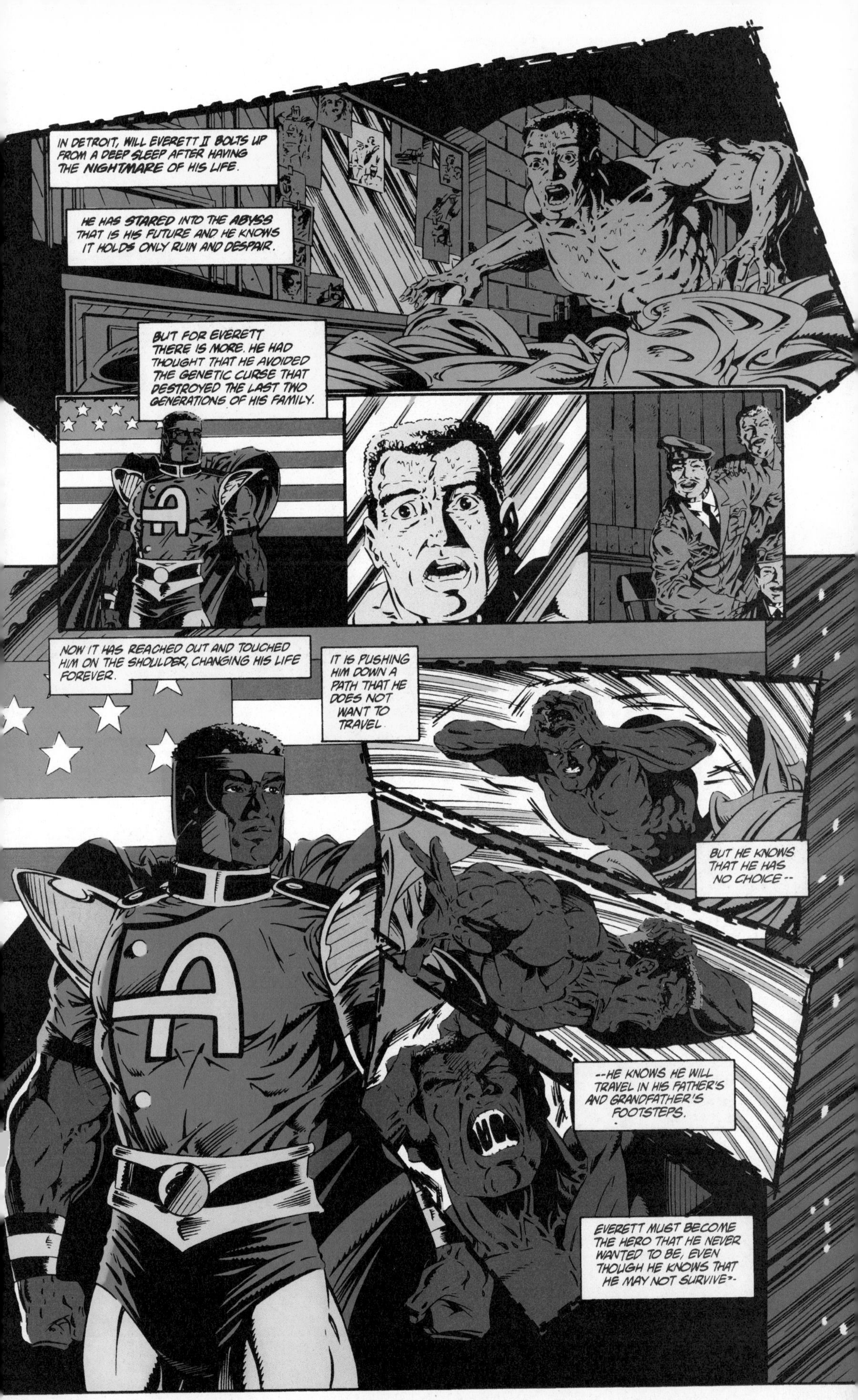
IN DETROIT, WILL EVERETT II BOLTS UP FROM A DEEP SLEEP AFTER HAVING THE NIGHTMARE OF HIS LIFE.
HE HAS STARED INTO THE ABYSS THAT IS HIS FUTURE AND HE KNOWS IT HOLDS ONLY RUIN AND DESPAIR.
BUT FOR EVERETT THERE IS MORE. HE HAD THOUGHT THAT HE AVOIDED THE GENETIC CURSE THAT DESTROYED THE LAST TWO GENERATIONS OF HIS FAMILY.
NOW IT HAS REACHED OUT AND TOUCHED HIM ON THE SHOULDER, CHANGING HIS LIFE FOREVER.
IT IS PUSHING HIM DOWN A PATH THAT HE DOES NOT WANT TO TRAVEL.
BUT HE KNOWS THAT HE HAS NO CHOICE--
--HE KNOWS HE WILL TRAVEL IN HIS FATHER'S AND GRANDFATHER'S FOOTSTEPS.
EVERETT MUST BECOME THE HERO THAT HE NEVER WANTED TO BE, EVEN THOUGH HE KNOWS THAT HE MAY NOT SURVIVE?-

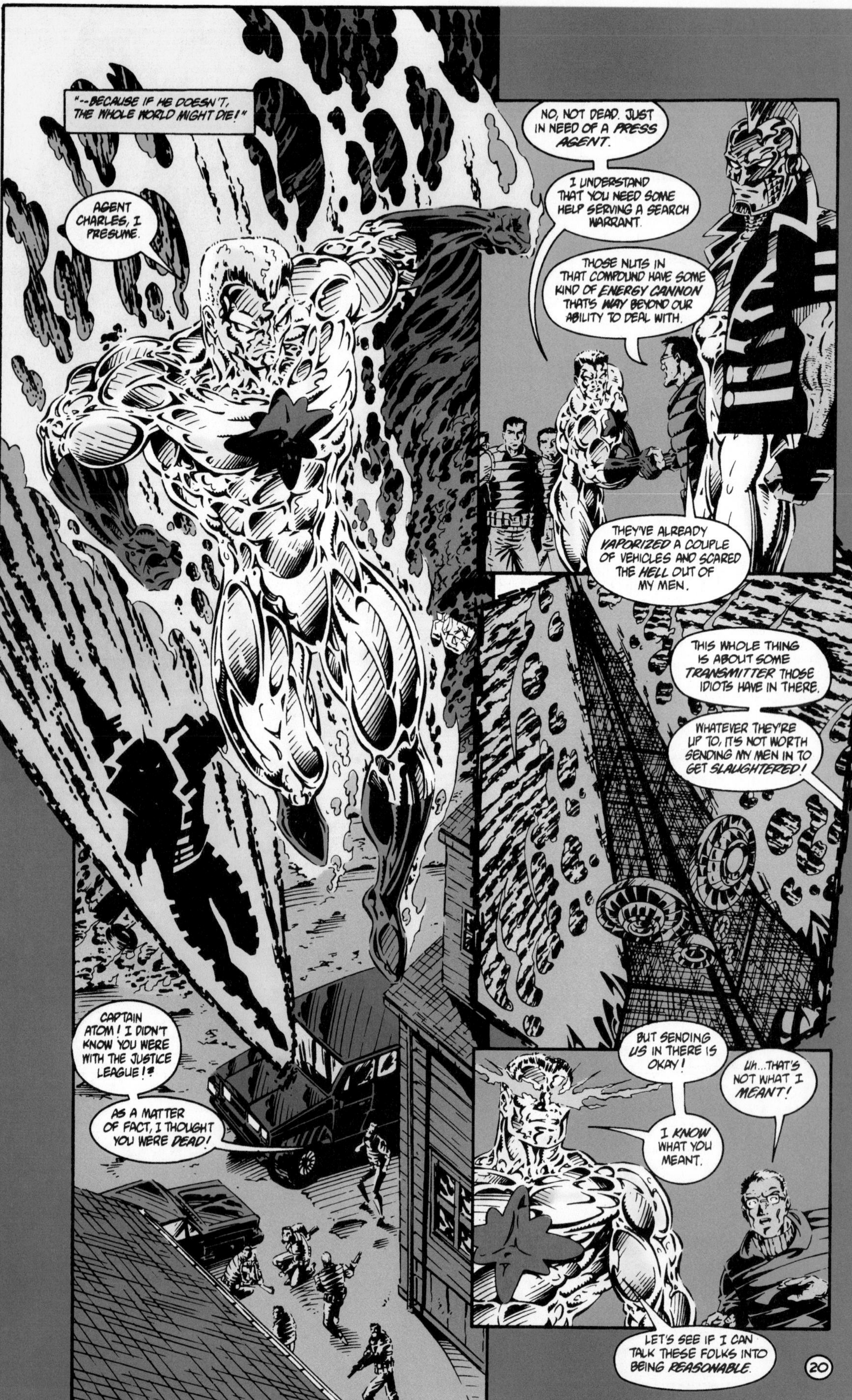
"--BECAUSE IF HE DOESN'T, THE WHOLE WORLD MIGHT DIE!"
AGENT CHARLES, I PRESUME.
NO, NOT DEAD. JUST IN NEED OF A PRESS AGENT.
I UNDERSTAND THAT YOU NEED SOME HELP SERVING A SEARCH WARRANT.
THOSE NUTS IN THAT COMPOUND HAVE SOME KIND OF ENERGY CANNON THAT'S WAY BEYOND OUR ABILITY TO DEAL WITH.
THEY'VE ALREADY VAPORIZED A COUPLE OF VEHICLES AND SCARED THE HELL OUT OF MY MEN.
THIS WHOLE THING IS ABOUT SOME TRANSMITTER THOSE IDIOTS HAVE IN THERE.
WHATEVER THEY'RE UP TO, IT'S NOT WORTH SENDING MY MEN IN TO GET SLAUGHTERED!
CAPTAIN ATOM! I DIDN'T KNOW YOU WERE WITH THE JUSTICE LEAGUE!
AS A MATTER OF FACT, I THOUGHT YOU WERE DEAD!
BUT SENDING US IN THERE IS OKAY!
UH...THAT'S NOT WHAT I MEANT!
I KNOW WHAT YOU MEANT.
LET'S SEE IF I CAN TALK THESE FOLKS INTO BEING REASONABLE.

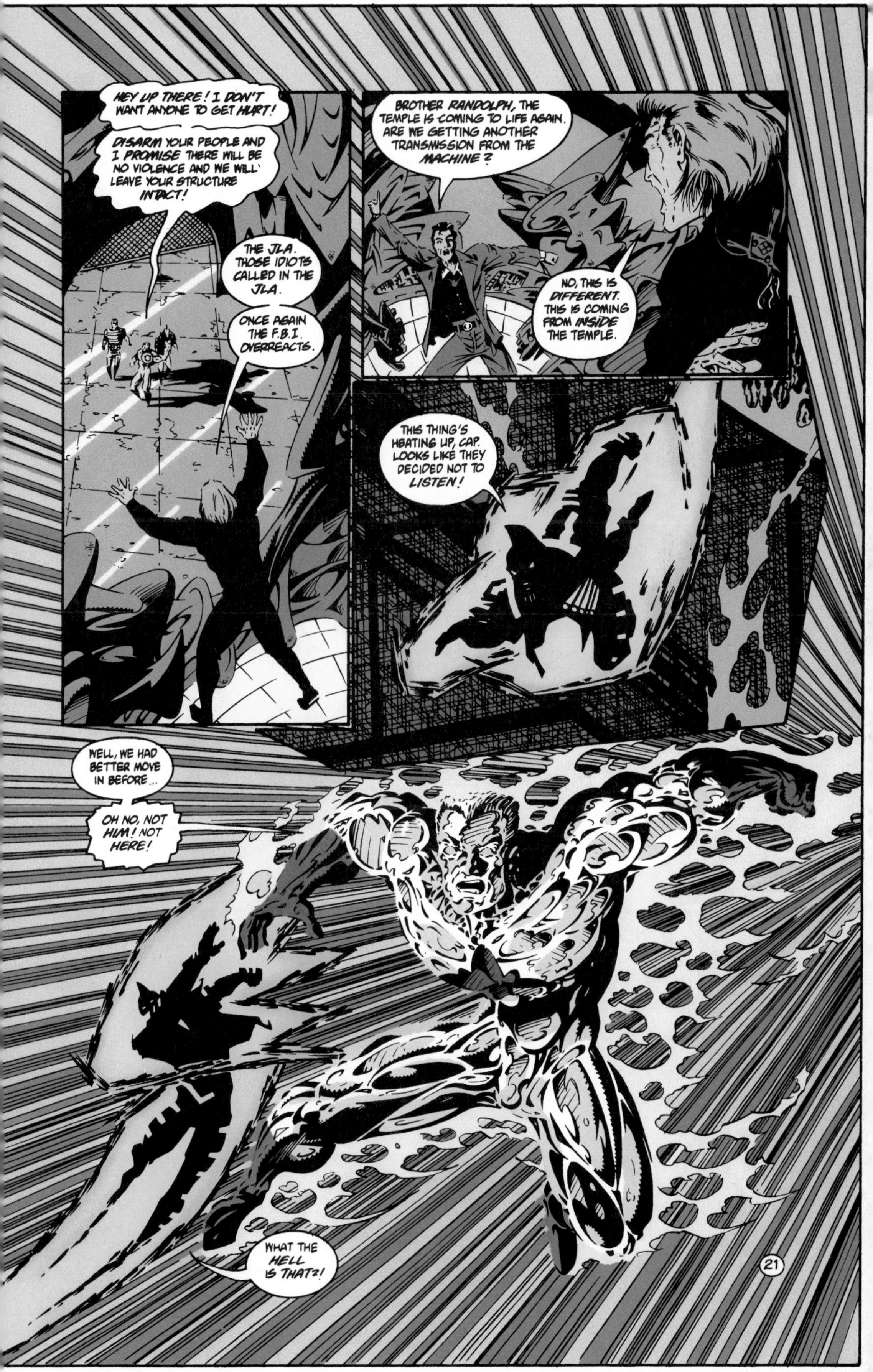
HEY UP THERE! I DON'T WANT ANYONE TO GET HURT!
DISARM YOUR PEOPLE AND I PROMISE THERE WILL BE NO VIOLENCE AND WE WILL LEAVE YOUR STRUCTURE INTACT!
THE JLA. THOSE IDIOTS CALLED IN THE JLA.
ONCE AGAIN THE F.B.I. OVERREACTS.
BROTHER RANDOLPH, THE TEMPLE IS COMING TO LIFE AGAIN. ARE WE GETTING ANOTHER TRANSMISSION FROM THE MACHINE?
NO, THIS IS DIFFERENT. THIS IS COMING FROM INSIDE THE TEMPLE.
THIS THING'S HEATING UP, CAP. LOOKS LIKE THEY DECIDED NOT TO LISTEN!
WELL, WE HAD BETTER MOVE IN BEFORE...
OH NO, NOT HIM! NOT HERE!
WHAT THE HELL IS THAT?!

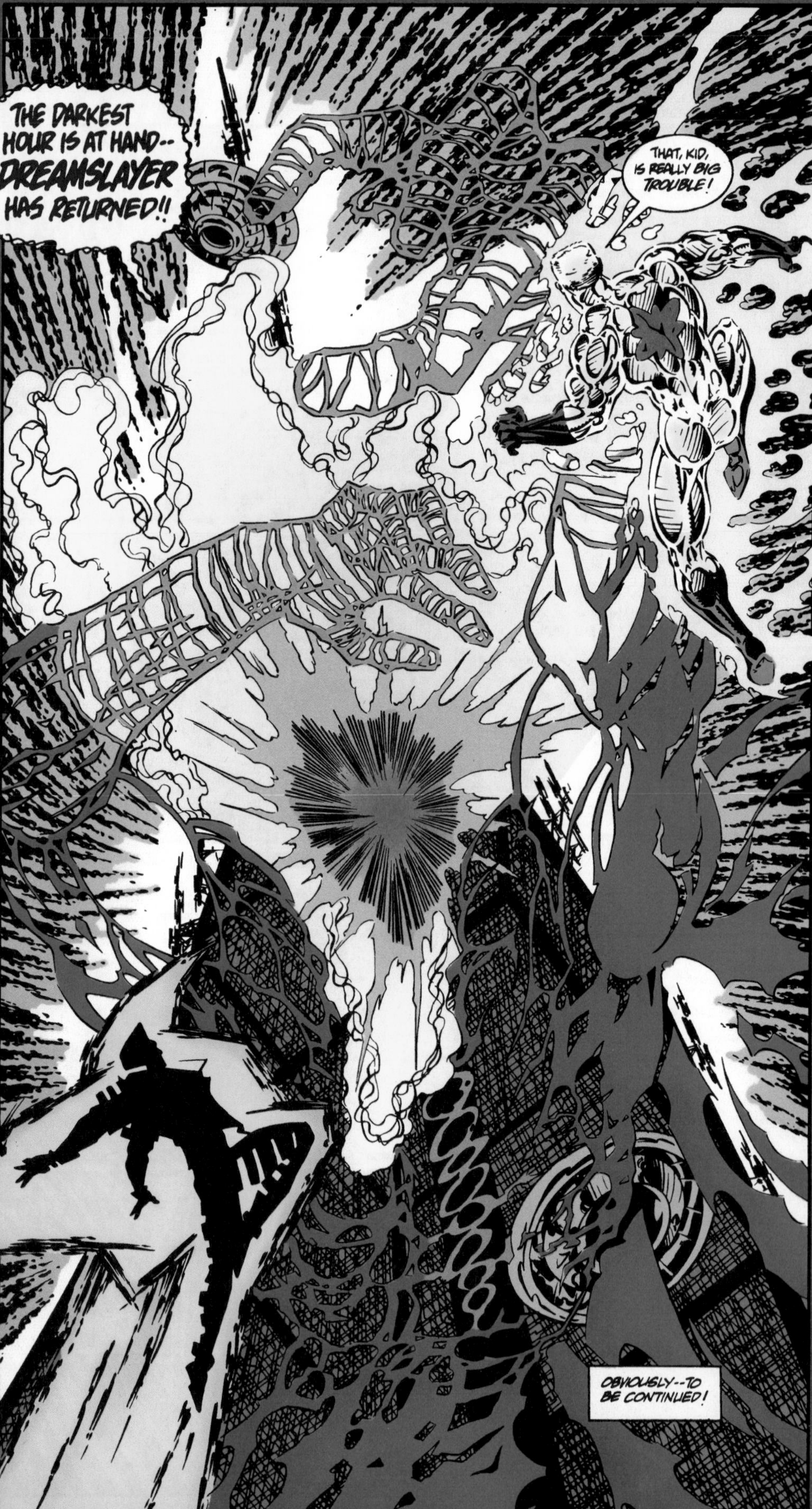
THE DARKEST HOUR IS AT HAND--
DREAMSLAYER HAS RETURNED!!
THAT, KID, IS REALLY BIG TROUBLE!
OBVIOUSLY--TO BE CONTINUED!

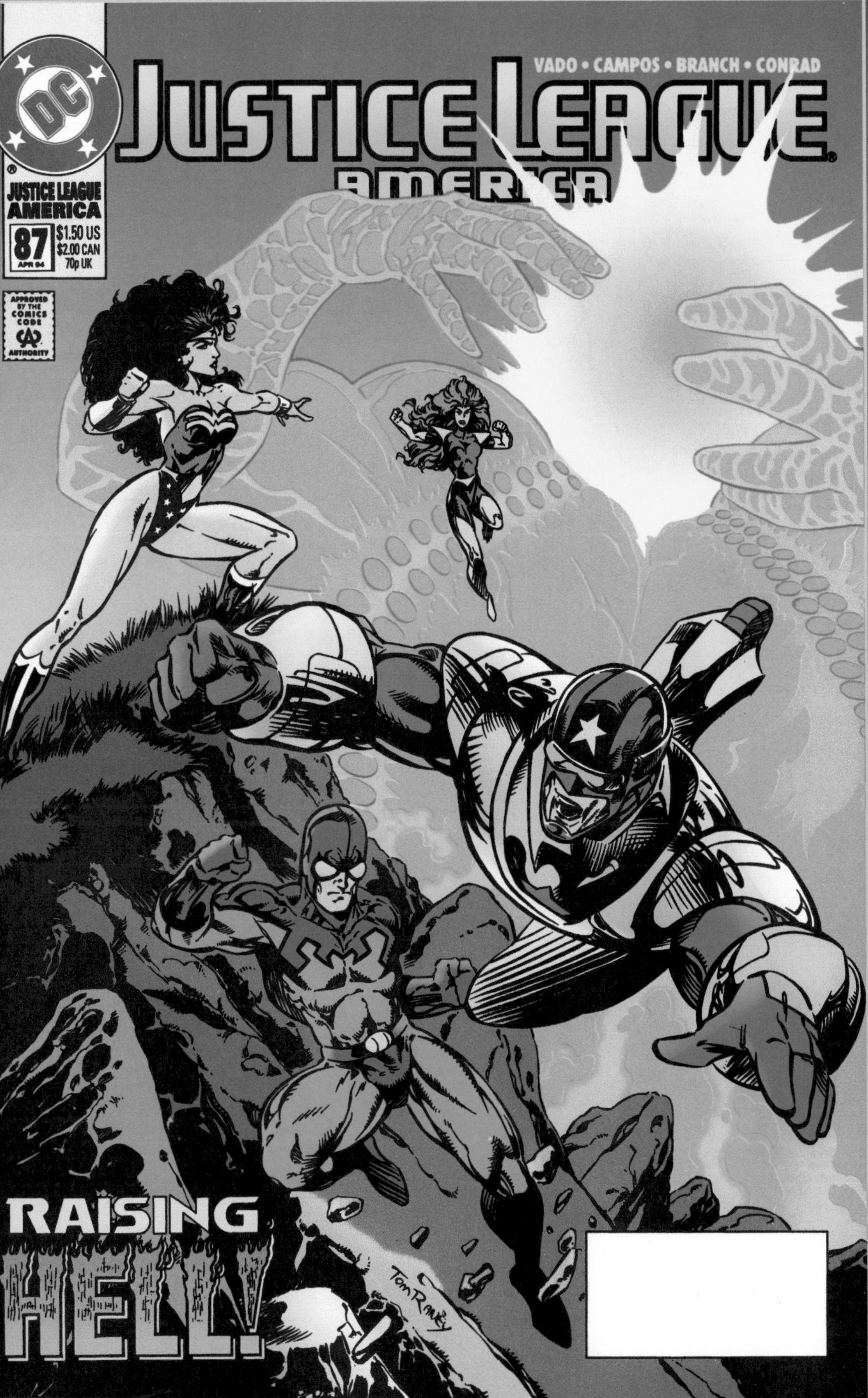

VADO • CAMPOS • BRANCH • CONRAD
JUSTICE LEAGUE
AMERICA
JUSTICE LEAGUE AMERICA
87
APR 94
$1.50 US
$2.00 CAN
70p UK
APPROVED BY THE COMICS CODE AUTHORITY
RAISING
HELL!
TOM RANEY

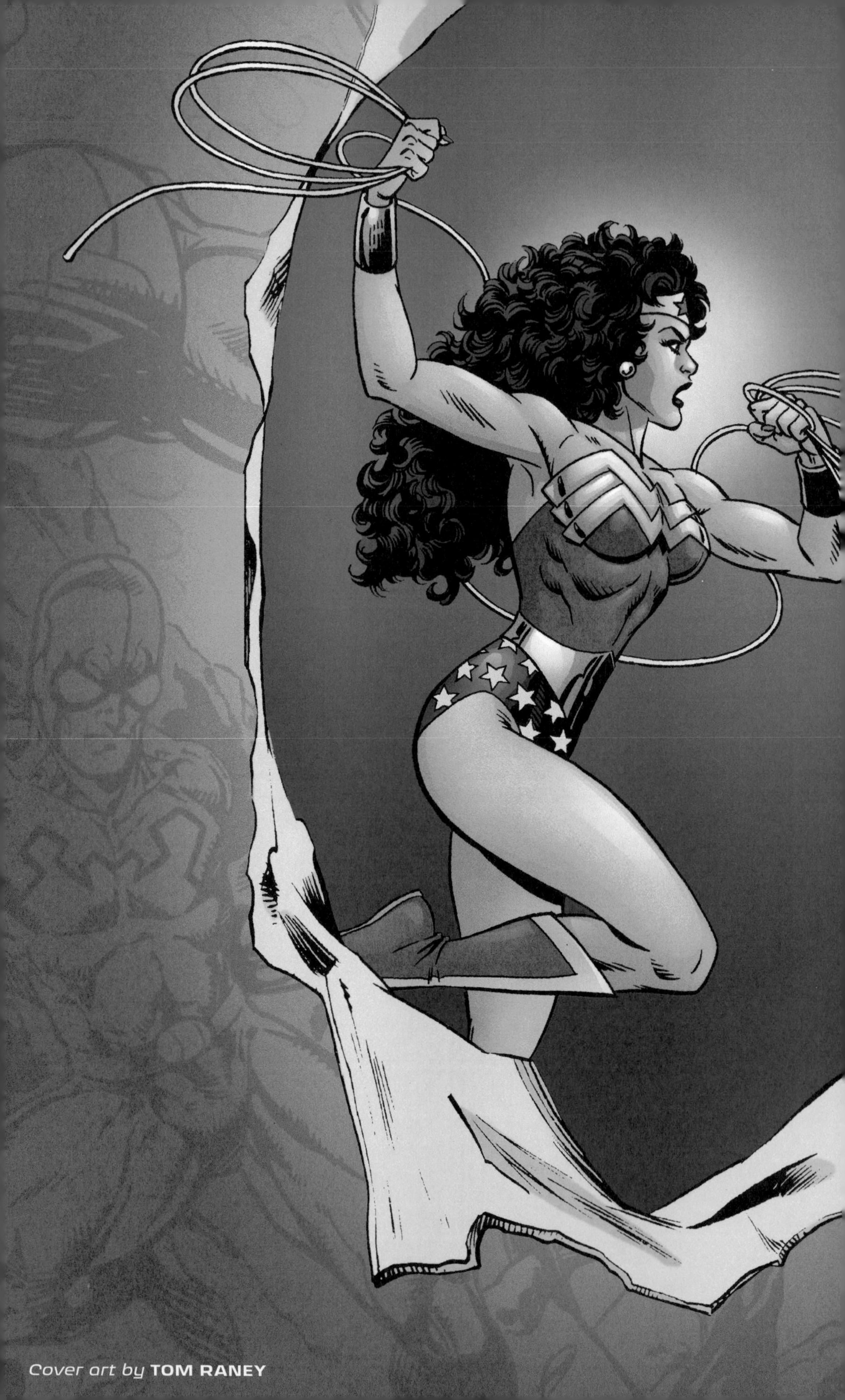

Cover art by **TOM RANEY**

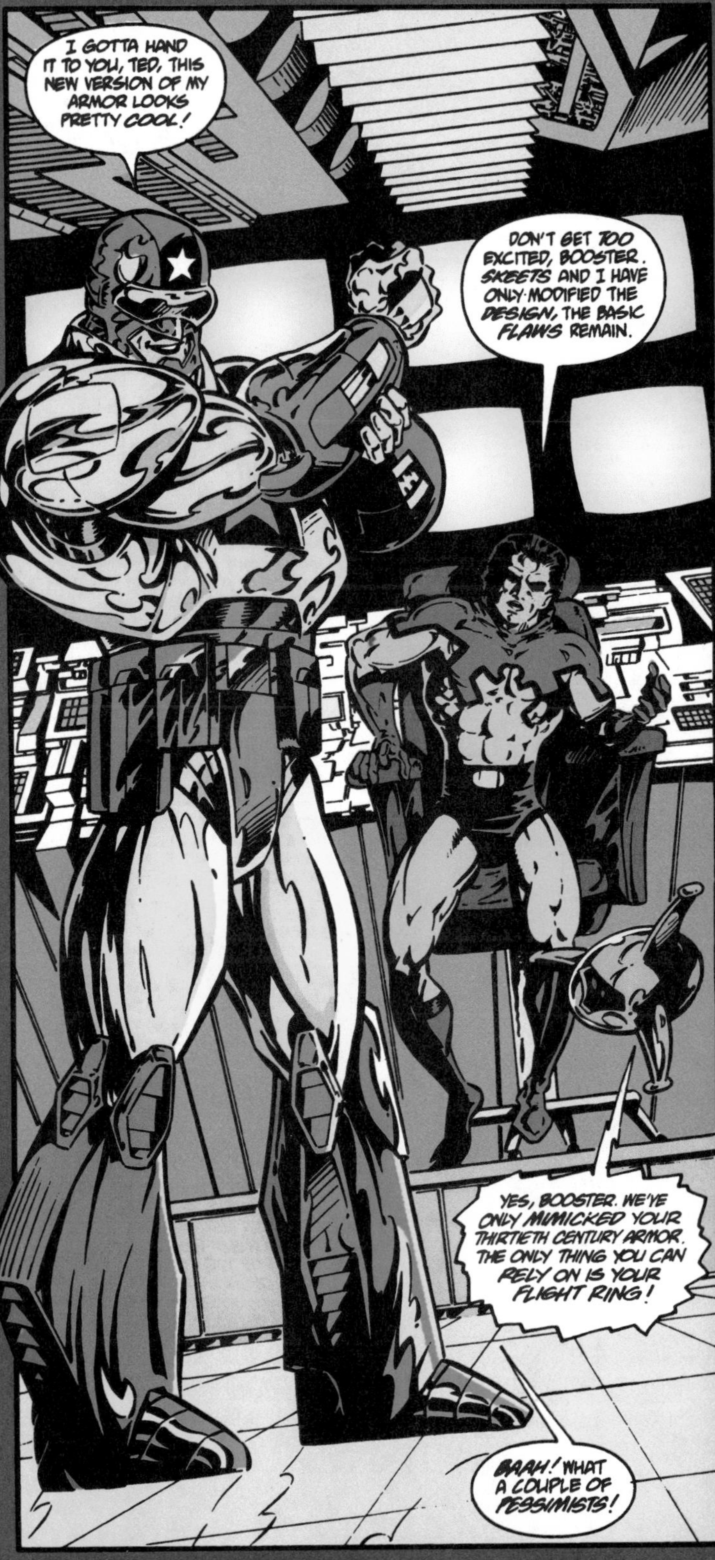
I GOTTA HAND IT TO YOU, TED, THIS NEW VERSION OF MY ARMOR LOOKS PRETTY COOL!
DON'T GET TOO EXCITED, BOOSTER. SKEETS AND I HAVE ONLY MODIFIED THE DESIGN. THE BASIC FLAWS REMAIN.
YES, BOOSTER. WE'VE ONLY MIMICKED YOUR THIRTIETH CENTURY ARMOR. THE ONLY THING YOU CAN RELY ON IS YOUR FLIGHT RING!
BAAH! WHAT A COUPLE OF PESSIMISTS!

CULT OF THE MACHINE PART II:

GOD IN THE MACHINE

WRITER DAN VADO

PENCILLER MARK CAMPOS

INKERS KEN BRANCH & KEVIN CONRAD

COLORIST GENE D'ANGELO

LETTERER CLEM ROBINS

ASSISTANT EDITOR RUBEN DIAZ

EDITOR BRIAN AUGUSTYN

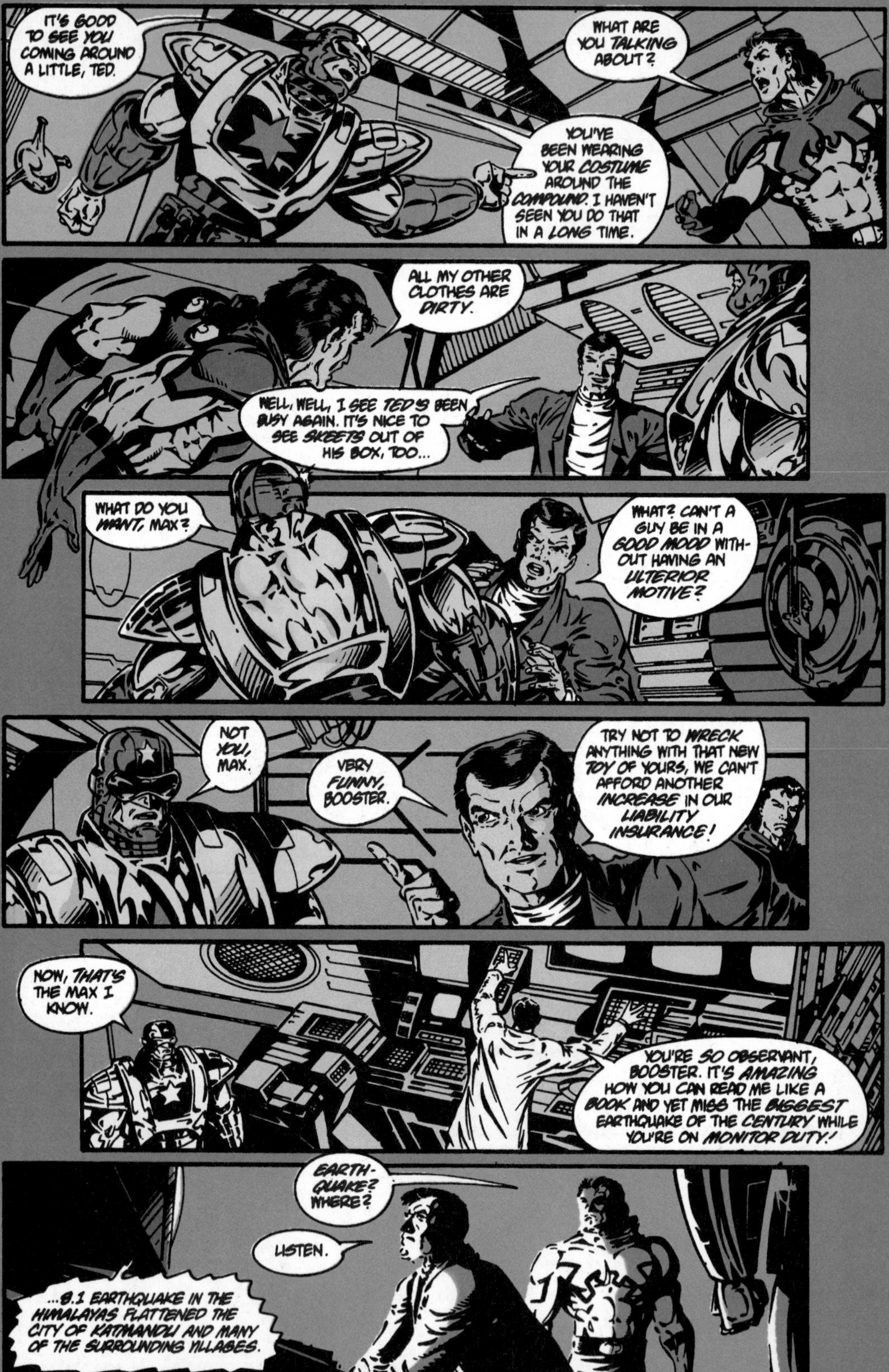

IT'S GOOD TO SEE YOU COMING AROUND A LITTLE, TED.
WHAT ARE YOU TALKING ABOUT?
YOU'VE BEEN WEARING YOUR COSTUME AROUND THE COMPOUND. I HAVEN'T SEEN YOU DO THAT IN A LONG TIME.
ALL MY OTHER CLOTHES ARE DIRTY.
WELL, WELL, I SEE TED'S BEEN BUSY AGAIN. IT'S NICE TO SEE SKEETS OUT OF HIS BOX, TOO...
WHAT DO YOU WANT, MAX?
WHAT? CAN'T A GUY BE IN A GOOD MOOD WITHOUT HAVING AN ULTERIOR MOTIVE?
NOT YOU, MAX.
VERY FUNNY, BOOSTER.
TRY NOT TO WRECK ANYTHING WITH THAT NEW TOY OF YOURS, WE CAN'T AFFORD ANOTHER INCREASE IN OUR LIABILITY INSURANCE!
NOW, THAT'S THE MAX I KNOW.
YOU'RE SO OBSERVANT, BOOSTER. IT'S AMAZING HOW YOU CAN READ ME LIKE A BOOK AND YET MISS THE BIGGEST EARTHQUAKE OF THE CENTURY WHILE YOU'RE ON MONITOR DUTY!
EARTHQUAKE? WHERE?
LISTEN.
...8.1 EARTHQUAKE IN THE HIMALAYAS FLATTENED THE CITY OF KATMANDU AND MANY OF THE SURROUNDING VILLAGES.

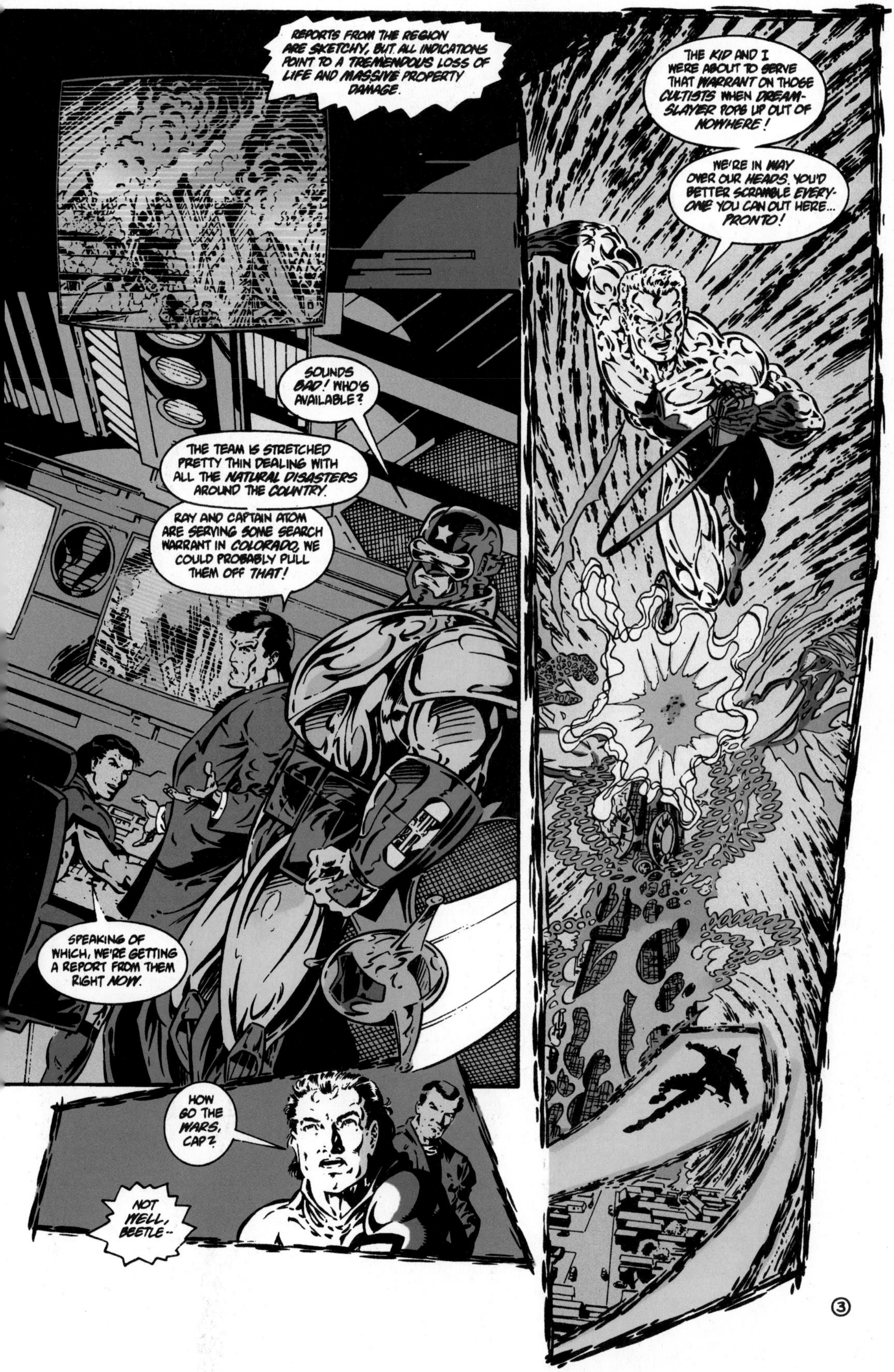
REPORTS FROM THE REGION ARE SKETCHY, BUT ALL INDICATIONS POINT TO A TREMENDOUS LOSS OF LIFE AND MASSIVE PROPERTY DAMAGE.
SOUNDS BAD! WHO'S AVAILABLE?
THE TEAM IS STRETCHED PRETTY THIN DEALING WITH ALL THE NATURAL DISASTERS AROUND THE COUNTRY.
RAY AND CAPTAIN ATOM ARE SERVING SOME SEARCH WARRANT IN COLORADO, WE COULD PROBABLY PULL THEM OFF THAT!
SPEAKING OF WHICH, WE'RE GETTING A REPORT FROM THEM RIGHT NOW.
HOW GO THE WARS, CAP?
NOT WELL, BEETLE--
THE KID AND I WERE ABOUT TO SERVE THAT WARRANT ON THOSE CULTISTS WHEN DREAM-SLAYER POPS UP OUT OF NOWHERE!
WE'RE IN WAY OVER OUR HEADS. YOU'D BETTER SCRAMBLE EVERY-ONE YOU CAN OUT HERE... PRONTO!

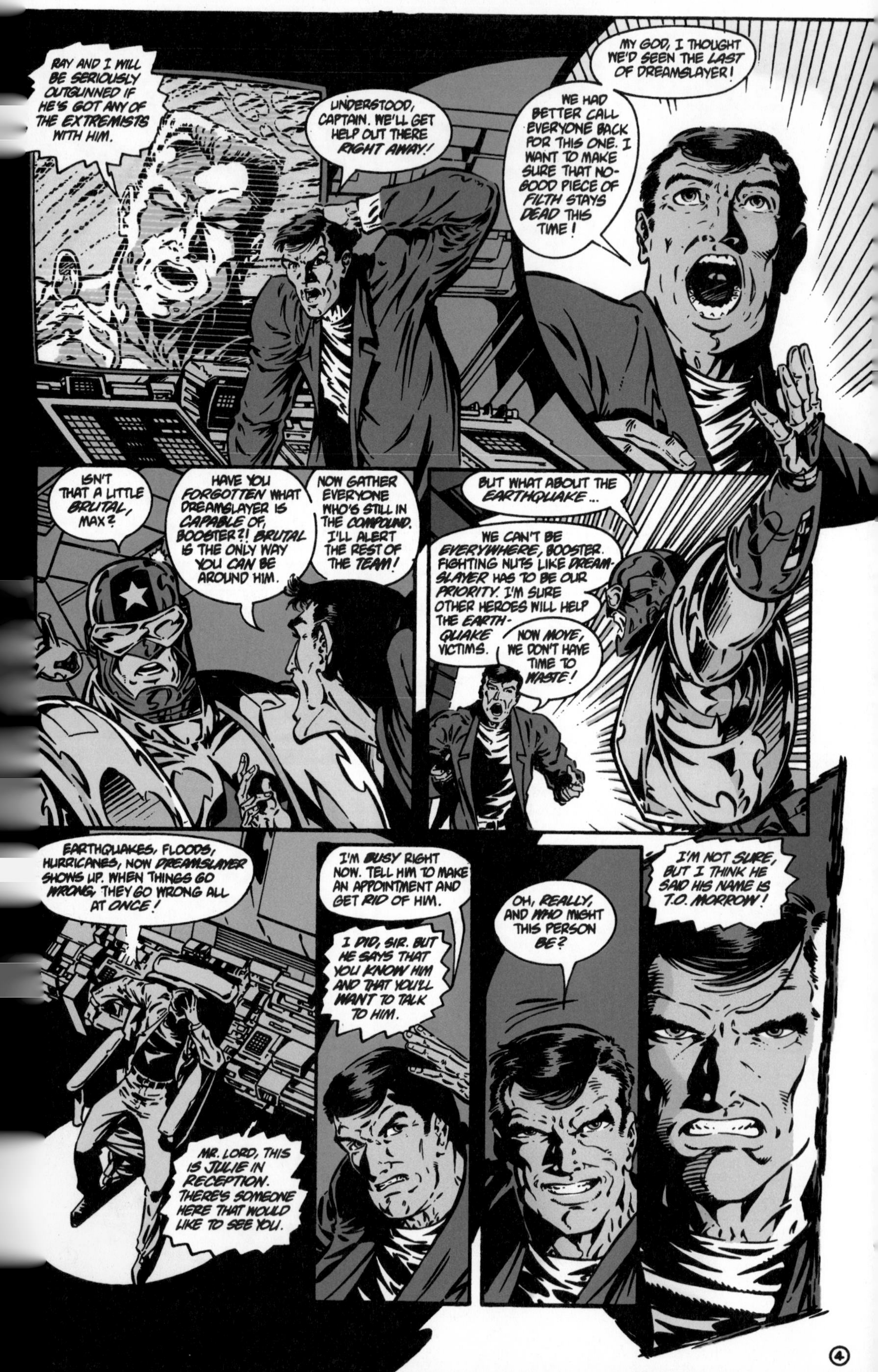

RAY AND I WILL BE SERIOUSLY OUTGUNNED IF HE'S GOT ANY OF THE EXTREMISTS WITH HIM.
UNDERSTOOD, CAPTAIN. WE'LL GET HELP OUT THERE RIGHT AWAY!
MY GOD, I THOUGHT WE'D SEEN THE LAST OF DREAMSLAYER!
WE HAD BETTER CALL EVERYONE BACK FOR THIS ONE. I WANT TO MAKE SURE THAT NO-GOOD PIECE OF FILTH STAYS DEAD THIS TIME!
ISN'T THAT A LITTLE BRUTAL, MAX?
HAVE YOU FORGOTTEN WHAT DREAMSLAYER IS CAPABLE OF, BOOSTER?! BRUTAL IS THE ONLY WAY YOU CAN BE AROUND HIM.
NOW GATHER EVERYONE WHO'S STILL IN THE COMPOUND. I'LL ALERT THE REST OF THE TEAM!
BUT WHAT ABOUT THE EARTHQUAKE...
WE CAN'T BE EVERYWHERE, BOOSTER. FIGHTING NUTS LIKE DREAMSLAYER HAS TO BE OUR PRIORITY. I'M SURE OTHER HEROES WILL HELP THE EARTHQUAKE VICTIMS.
NOW MOVE, WE DON'T HAVE TIME TO WASTE!
EARTHQUAKES, FLOODS, HURRICANES, NOW DREAMSLAYER SHOWS UP. WHEN THINGS GO WRONG, THEY GO WRONG ALL AT ONCE!
MR. LORD, THIS IS JULIE IN RECEPTION. THERE'S SOMEONE HERE THAT WOULD LIKE TO SEE YOU.
I'M BUSY RIGHT NOW. TELL HIM TO MAKE AN APPOINTMENT AND GET RID OF HIM.
I DID, SIR. BUT HE SAYS THAT YOU KNOW HIM AND THAT YOU'LL WANT TO TALK TO HIM.
OH, REALLY, AND WHO MIGHT THIS PERSON BE?
I'M NOT SURE, BUT I THINK HE SAID HIS NAME IS T.O. MORROW!

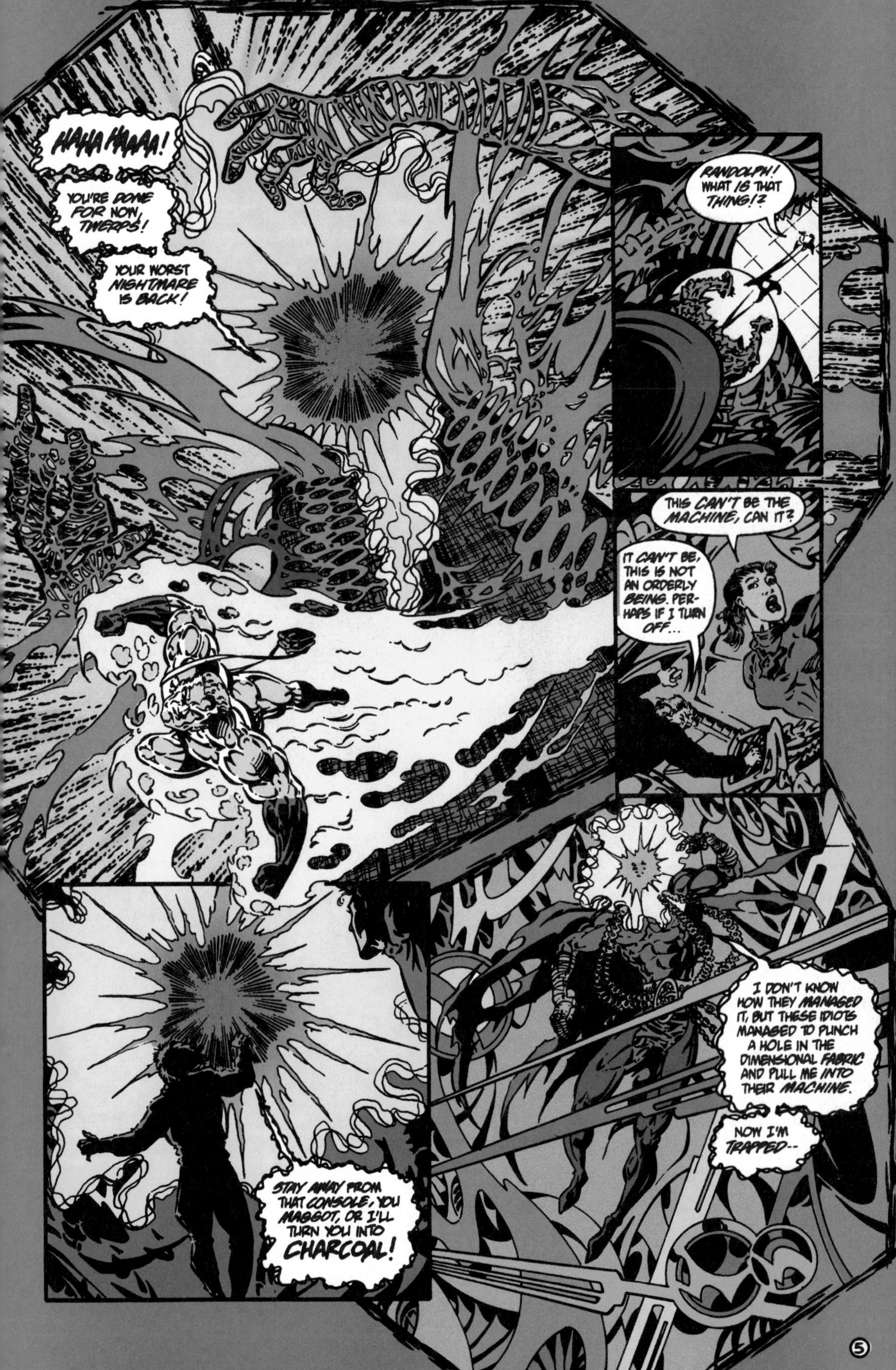
HAHA HAAAA!
YOU'RE DONE FOR NOW, TWERPS!
YOUR WORST NIGHTMARE IS BACK!
RANDOLPH! WHAT IS THAT THING!?
THIS CAN'T BE THE MACHINE, CAN IT?
IT CAN'T BE. THIS IS NOT AN ORDERLY BEING. PERHAPS IF I TURN OFF...
STAY AWAY FROM THAT CONSOLE, YOU MAGGOT, OR I'LL TURN YOU INTO CHARCOAL!
I DON'T KNOW HOW THEY MANAGED IT, BUT THESE IDIOTS MANAGED TO PUNCH A HOLE IN THE DIMENSIONAL FABRIC AND PULL ME INTO THEIR MACHINE.
NOW I'M TRAPPED--

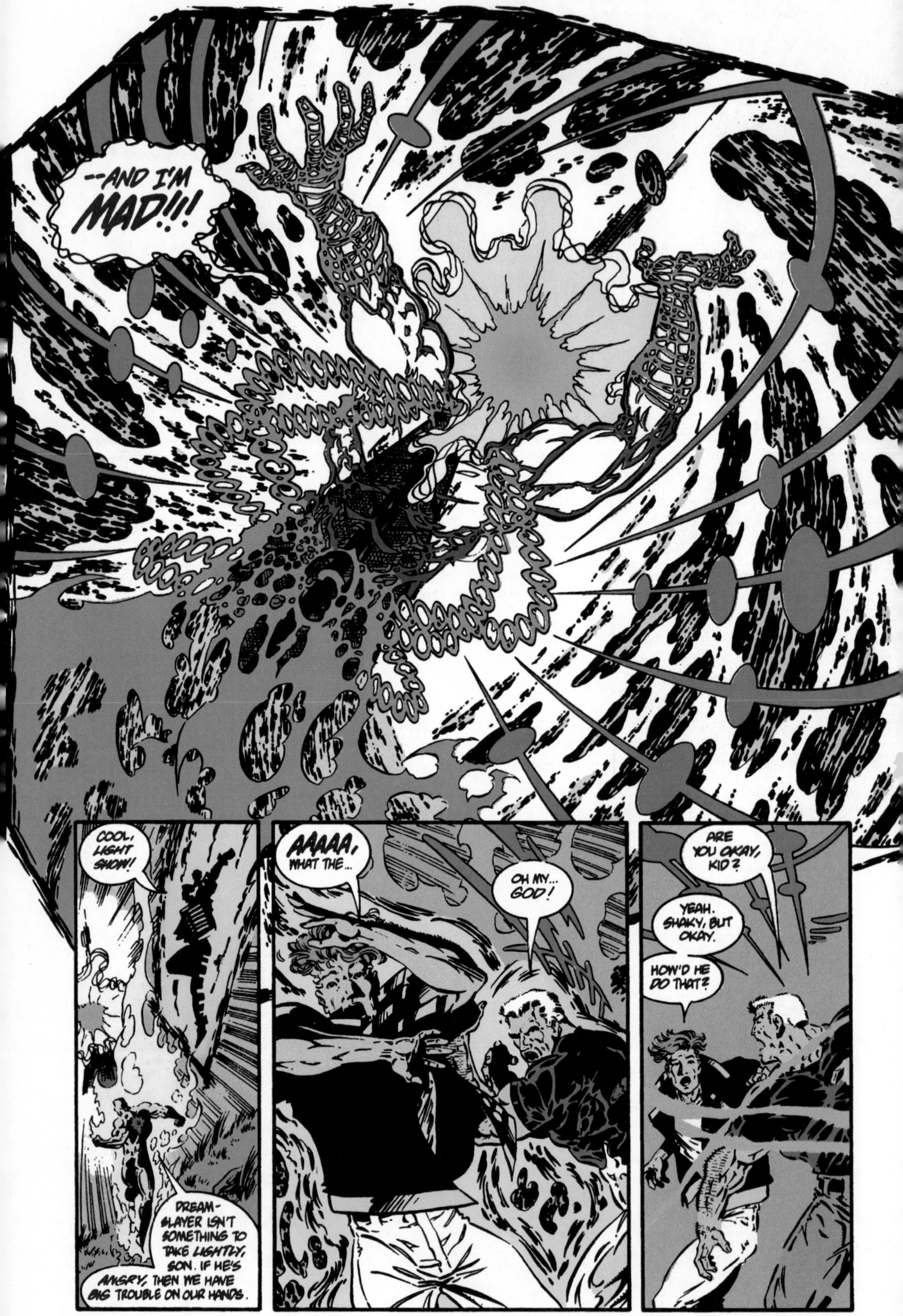
--AND I'M MAD!!!
COOL, LIGHT SHOW!
DREAM-SLAYER ISN'T SOMETHING TO TAKE LIGHTLY, SON. IF HE'S ANGRY, THEN WE HAVE BIG TROUBLE ON OUR HANDS.
AAAAA, WHAT THE...
OH MY... GOD!
ARE YOU OKAY, KID?
YEAH. SHAKY, BUT OKAY.
HOW'D HE DO THAT?

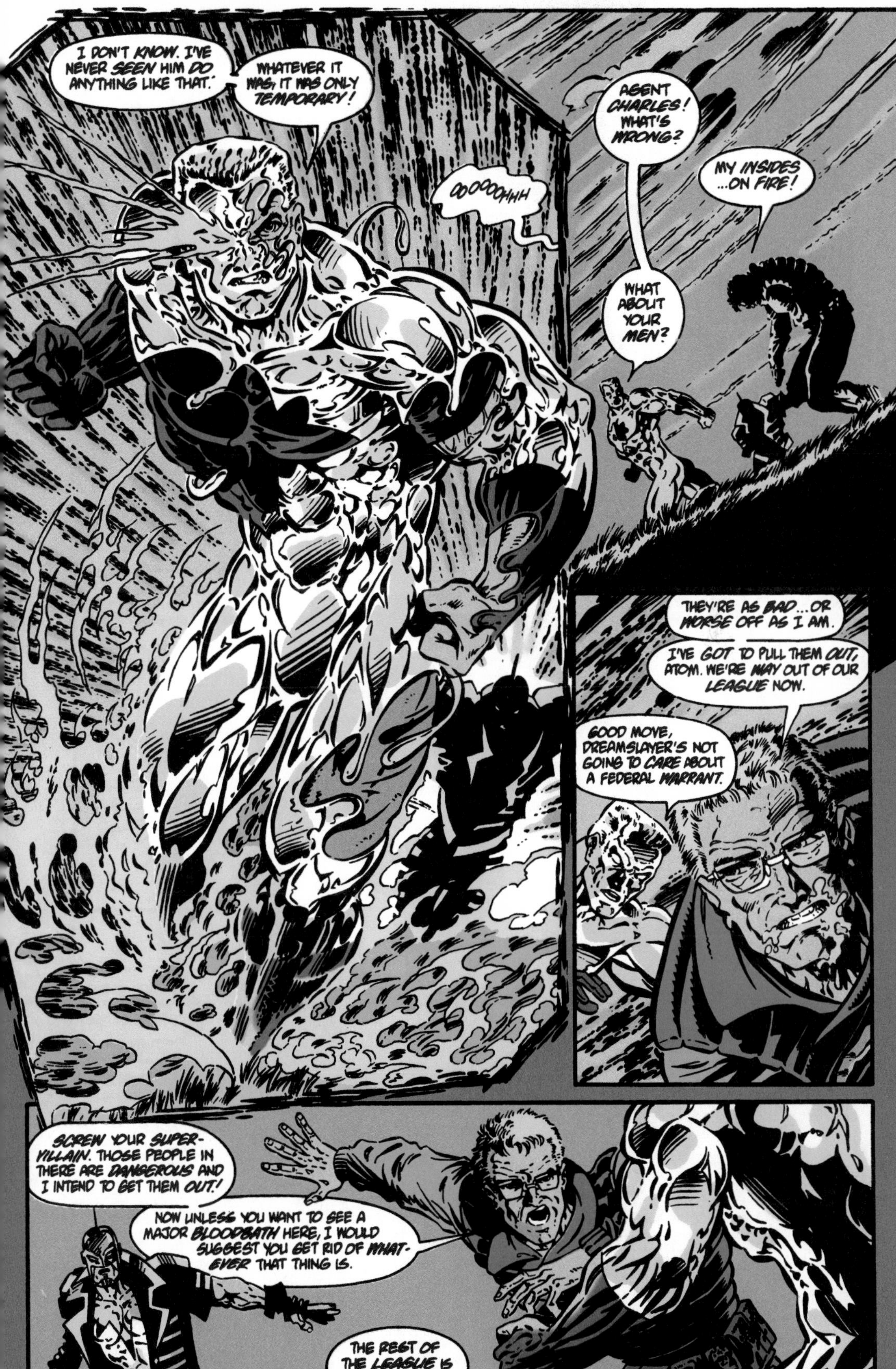
I DON'T KNOW. I'VE NEVER SEEN HIM DO ANYTHING LIKE THAT.
WHATEVER IT WAS, IT WAS ONLY TEMPORARY!
OOOOOOHHH
AGENT CHARLES! WHAT'S WRONG?
MY INSIDES ...ON FIRE!
WHAT ABOUT YOUR MEN?
THEY'RE AS BAD...OR WORSE OFF AS I AM.
I'VE GOT TO PULL THEM OUT, ATOM. WE'RE WAY OUT OF OUR LEAGUE NOW.
GOOD MOVE, DREAMSLAYER'S NOT GOING TO CARE ABOUT A FEDERAL WARRANT.
SCREW YOUR SUPER-VILLAIN. THOSE PEOPLE IN THERE ARE DANGEROUS AND I INTEND TO GET THEM OUT!
NOW UNLESS YOU WANT TO SEE A MAJOR BLOODBATH HERE, I WOULD SUGGEST YOU GET RID OF WHAT-EVER THAT THING IS.
THE REST OF THE LEAGUE IS ON ITS WAY--

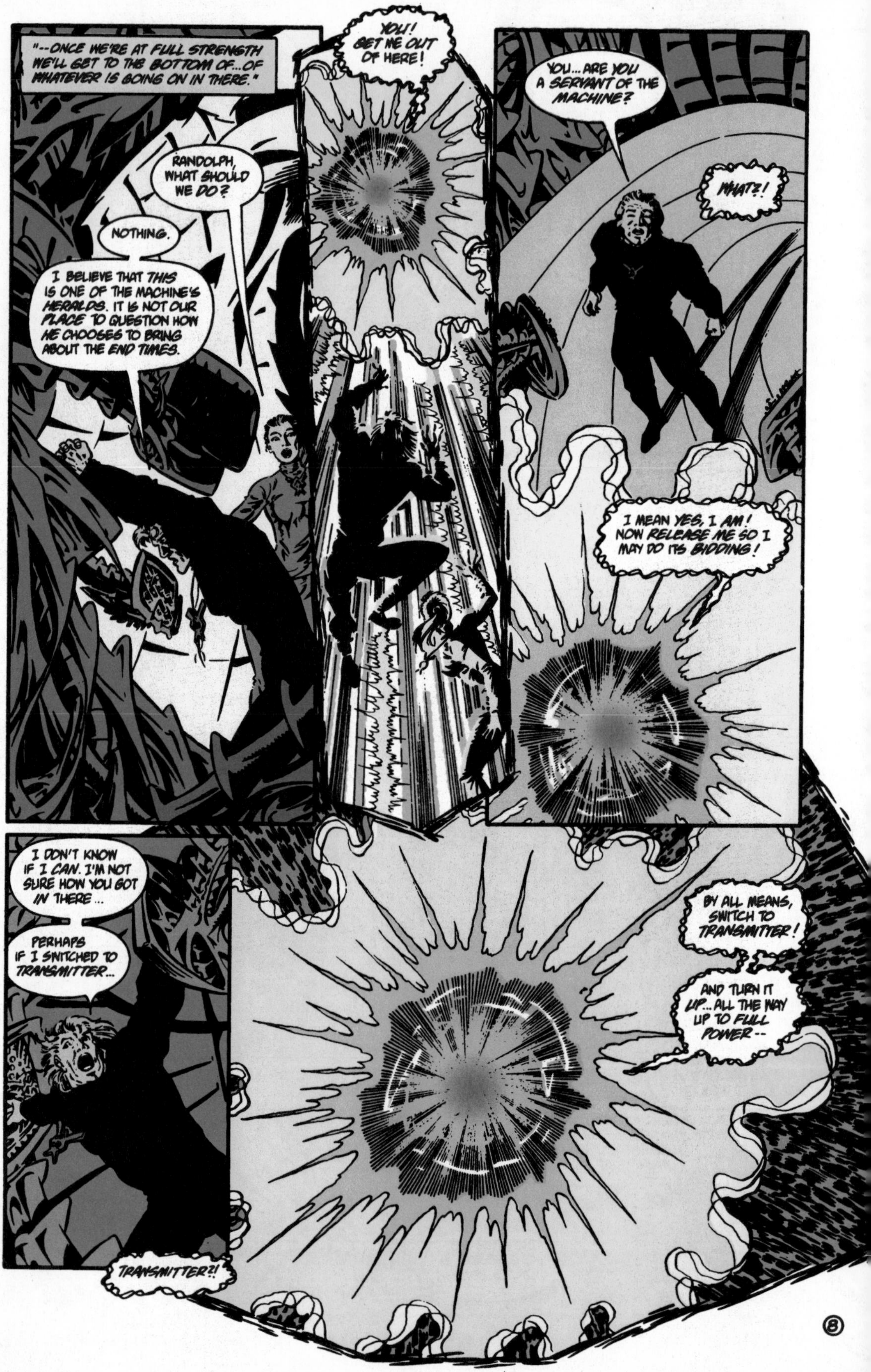

"--ONCE WE'RE AT FULL STRENGTH WE'LL GET TO THE BOTTOM OF...OF WHATEVER IS GOING ON IN THERE."
RANDOLPH, WHAT SHOULD WE DO?
NOTHING.
I BELIEVE THAT THIS IS ONE OF THE MACHINE'S HERALDS. IT IS NOT OUR PLACE TO QUESTION HOW HE CHOOSES TO BRING ABOUT THE END TIMES.
YOU! GET ME OUT OF HERE!
YOU...ARE YOU A SERVANT OF THE MACHINE?
WHAT?!
I MEAN YES, I AM! NOW RELEASE ME SO I MAY DO ITS BIDDING!
I DON'T KNOW IF I CAN. I'M NOT SURE HOW YOU GOT IN THERE...
PERHAPS IF I SWITCHED TO TRANSMITTER...
TRANSMITTER?!
BY ALL MEANS, SWITCH TO TRANSMITTER!
AND TURN IT UP...ALL THE WAY UP TO FULL POWER--

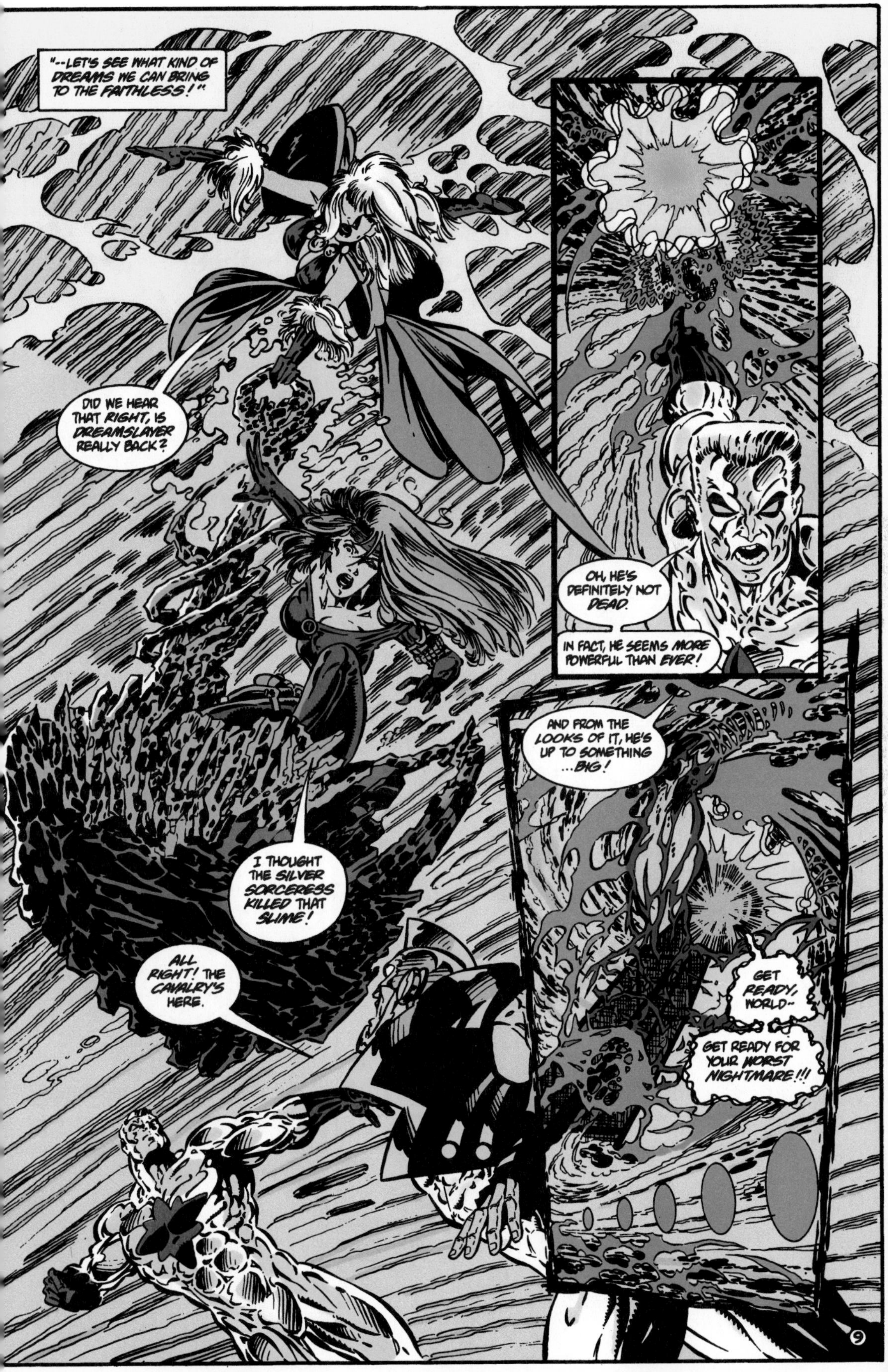
"--LET'S SEE WHAT KIND OF DREAMS WE CAN BRING TO THE FAITHLESS!"
DID WE HEAR THAT RIGHT, IS DREAMSLAYER REALLY BACK?
OH, HE'S DEFINITELY NOT DEAD.
IN FACT, HE SEEMS MORE POWERFUL THAN EVER!
AND FROM THE LOOKS OF IT, HE'S UP TO SOMETHING ...BIG!
I THOUGHT THE SILVER SORCERESS KILLED THAT SLIME!
ALL RIGHT! THE CAVALRY'S HERE.
GET READY, WORLD--
GET READY FOR YOUR WORST NIGHTMARE!!!

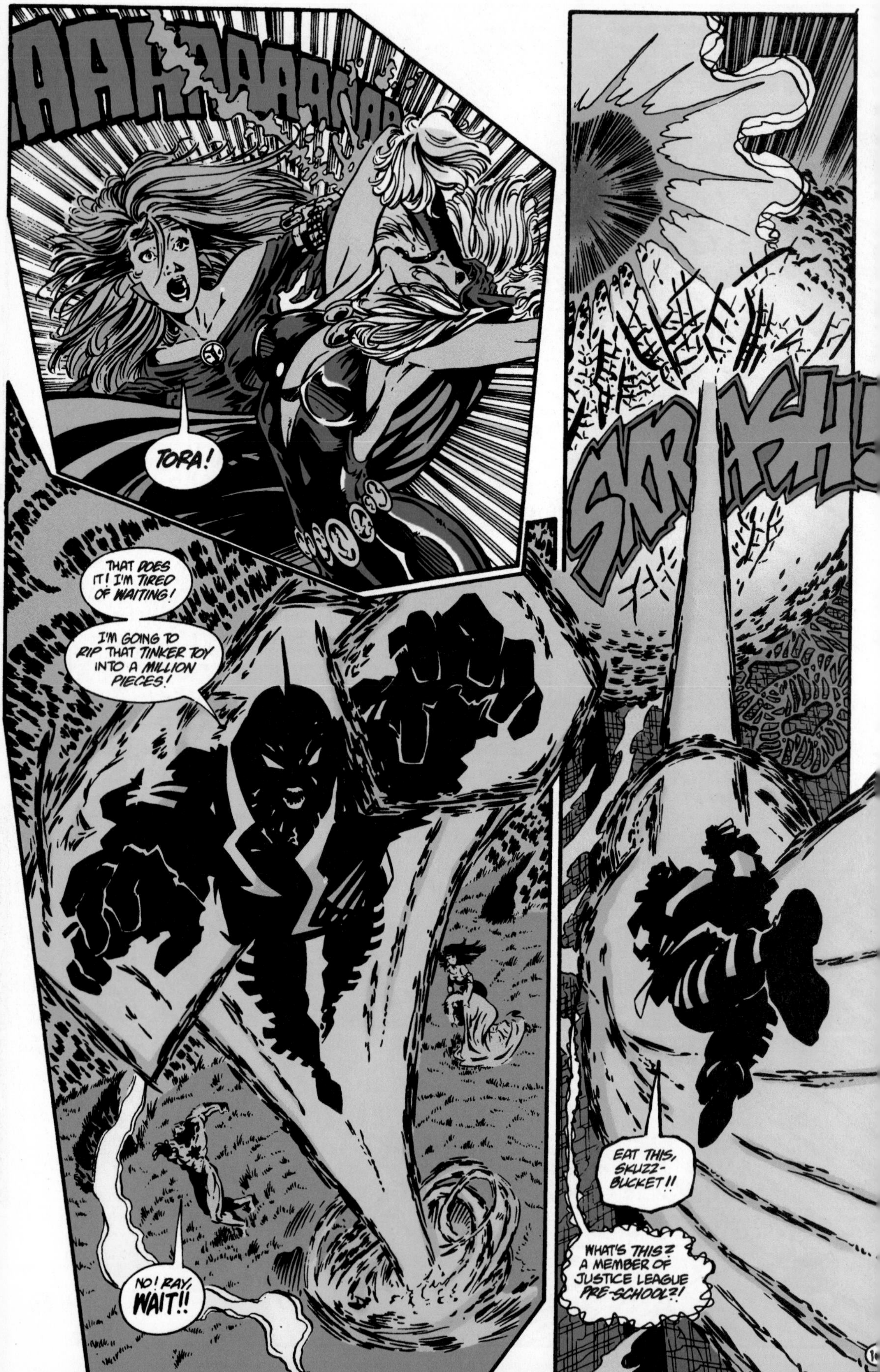

TORA!
THAT DOES IT! I'M TIRED OF WAITING!
I'M GOING TO RIP THAT TINKER TOY INTO A MILLION PIECES!
NO! RAY, WAIT!!
EAT THIS, SKUZZ-BUCKET!!
WHAT'S THIS? A MEMBER OF JUSTICE LEAGUE PRE-SCHOOL?!

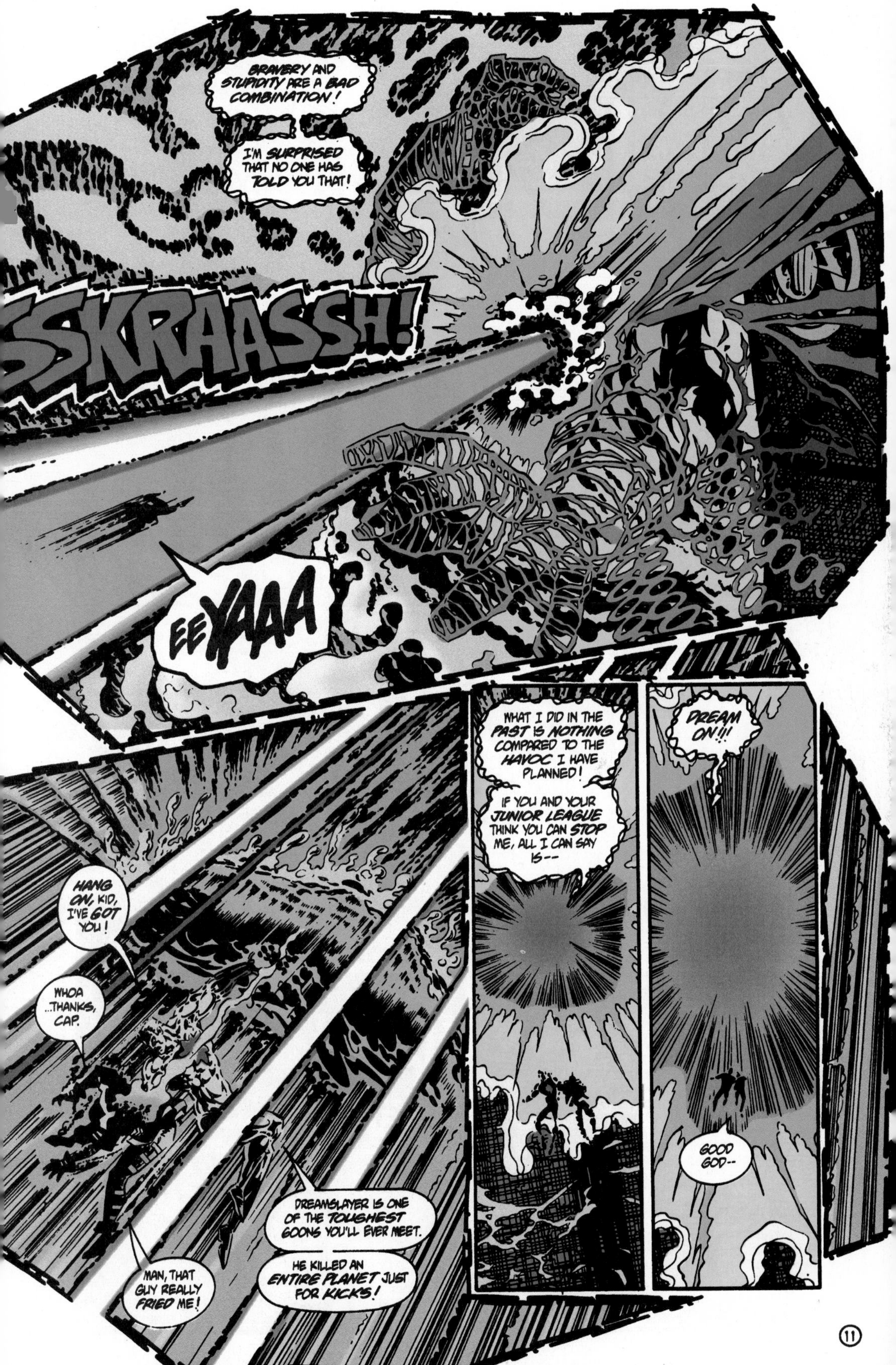
BRAVERY AND STUPIDITY ARE A BAD COMBINATION!
I'M SURPRISED THAT NO ONE HAS TOLD YOU THAT!
SSKRAASSH!
EEYAAA
WHAT I DID IN THE PAST IS NOTHING COMPARED TO THE HAVOC I HAVE PLANNED!
IF YOU AND YOUR JUNIOR LEAGUE THINK YOU CAN STOP ME, ALL I CAN SAY IS--
DREAM ON!!!
HANG ON, KID, I'VE GOT YOU!
WHOA ...THANKS, CAP.
GOOD GOD--
DREAMSLAYER IS ONE OF THE TOUGHEST GOONS YOU'LL EVER MEET.
HE KILLED AN ENTIRE PLANET JUST FOR KICKS!
MAN, THAT GUY REALLY FRIED ME!

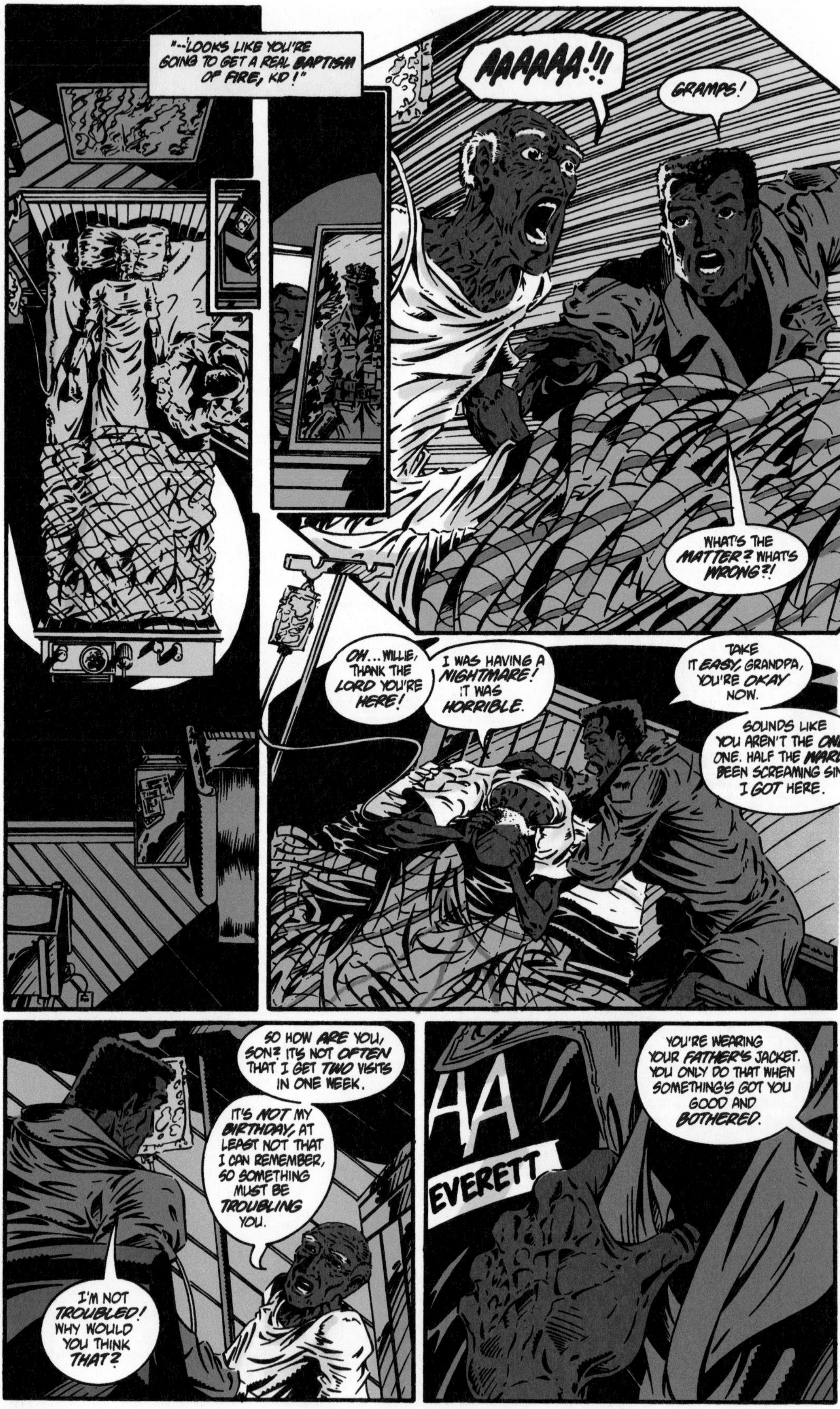
"--LOOKS LIKE YOU'RE GOING TO GET A REAL BAPTISM OF FIRE, KID!"
AAAAAA!!!
GRAMPS!
WHAT'S THE MATTER? WHAT'S WRONG?!
OH... WILLIE, THANK THE LORD YOU'RE HERE!
I WAS HAVING A NIGHTMARE! IT WAS HORRIBLE.
TAKE IT EASY, GRANDPA, YOU'RE OKAY NOW.
SOUNDS LIKE YOU AREN'T THE ONLY ONE. HALF THE WARD'S BEEN SCREAMING SINCE I GOT HERE.
SO HOW ARE YOU, SON? IT'S NOT OFTEN THAT I GET TWO VISITS IN ONE WEEK.
IT'S NOT MY BIRTHDAY, AT LEAST NOT THAT I CAN REMEMBER, SO SOMETHING MUST BE TROUBLING YOU.
I'M NOT TROUBLED! WHY WOULD YOU THINK THAT?
YOU'RE WEARING YOUR FATHER'S JACKET. YOU ONLY DO THAT WHEN SOMETHING'S GOT YOU GOOD AND BOTHERED.
4A
EVERETT

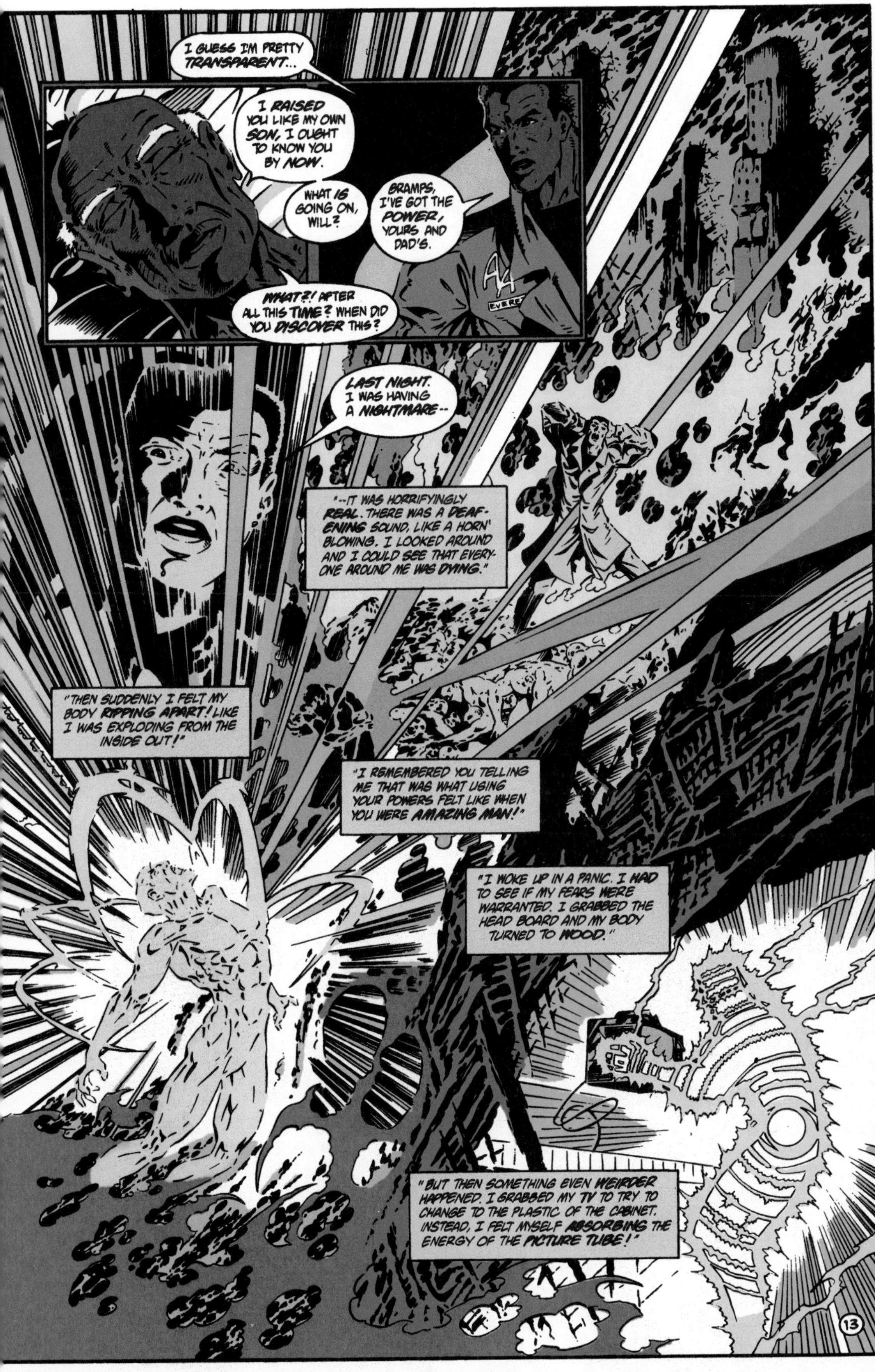

I GUESS I'M PRETTY TRANSPARENT...
I RAISED YOU LIKE MY OWN SON, I OUGHT TO KNOW YOU BY NOW.
WHAT IS GOING ON, WILL?
BRAMPS, I'VE GOT THE POWER, YOURS AND DAD'S.
WHAT?! AFTER ALL THIS TIME? WHEN DID YOU DISCOVER THIS?
LAST NIGHT. I WAS HAVING A NIGHTMARE--
"--IT WAS HORRIFYINGLY REAL. THERE WAS A DEAF-ENING SOUND, LIKE A HORN BLOWING. I LOOKED AROUND AND I COULD SEE THAT EVERY-ONE AROUND ME WAS DYING."
"THEN SUDDENLY I FELT MY BODY RIPPING APART! LIKE I WAS EXPLODING FROM THE INSIDE OUT!"
"I REMEMBERED YOU TELLING ME THAT WAS WHAT USING YOUR POWERS FELT LIKE WHEN YOU WERE AMAZING MAN!"
"I WOKE UP IN A PANIC. I HAD TO SEE IF MY FEARS WERE WARRANTED. I GRABBED THE HEAD BOARD AND MY BODY TURNED TO WOOD."
"BUT THEN SOMETHING EVEN WEIRDER HAPPENED. I GRABBED MY TV TO TRY TO CHANGE TO THE PLASTIC OF THE CABINET. INSTEAD, I FELT MYSELF ABSORBING THE ENERGY OF THE PICTURE TUBE!"

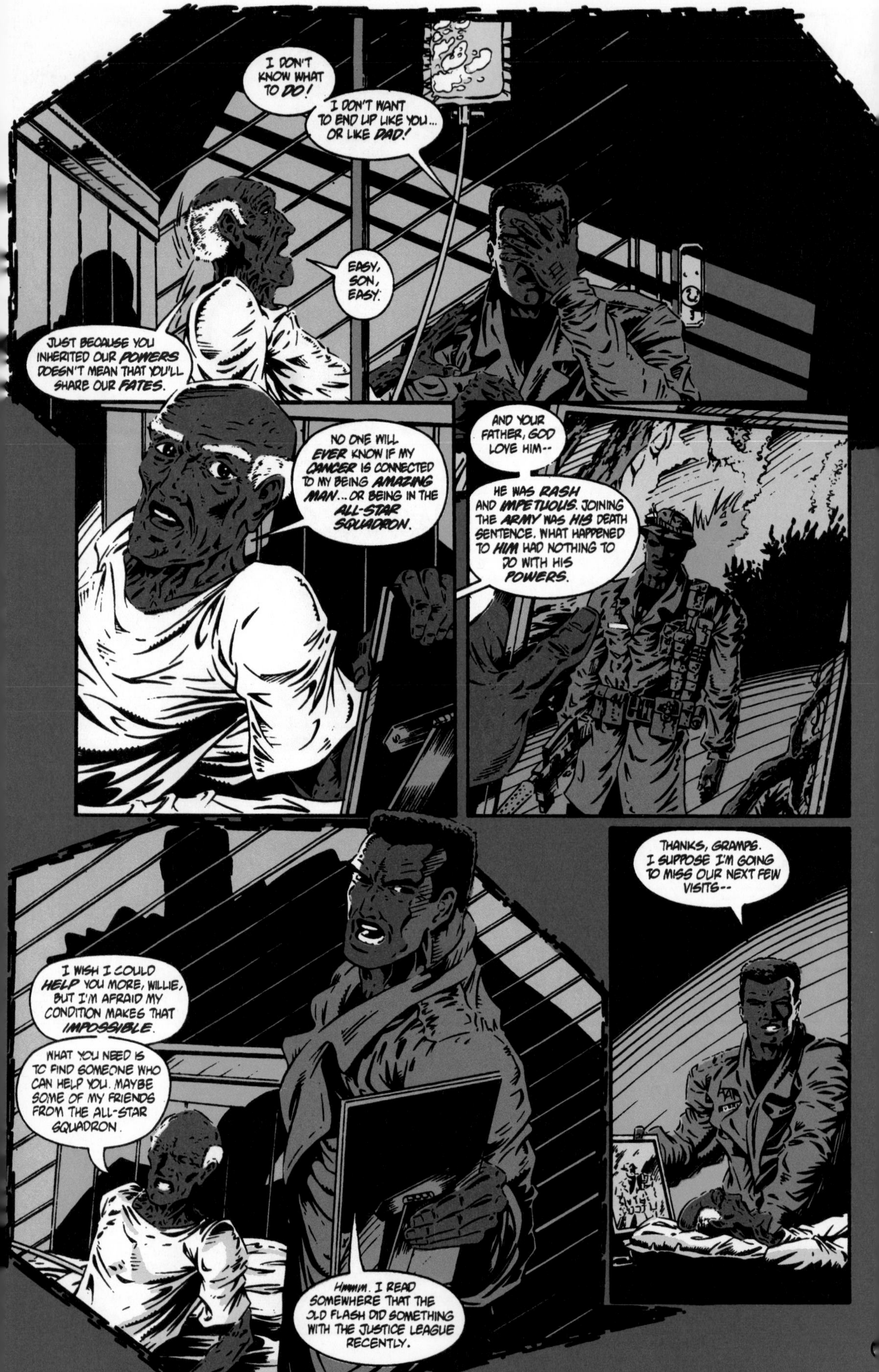
I DON'T KNOW WHAT TO DO!
I DON'T WANT TO END UP LIKE YOU... OR LIKE DAD!
EASY, SON, EASY.
JUST BECAUSE YOU INHERITED OUR POWERS DOESN'T MEAN THAT YOU'LL SHARE OUR FATES.
NO ONE WILL EVER KNOW IF MY CANCER IS CONNECTED TO MY BEING AMAZING MAN... OR BEING IN THE ALL-STAR SQUADRON.
AND YOUR FATHER, GOD LOVE HIM--
HE WAS RASH AND IMPETUOUS. JOINING THE ARMY WAS HIS DEATH SENTENCE. WHAT HAPPENED TO HIM HAD NOTHING TO DO WITH HIS POWERS.
I WISH I COULD HELP YOU MORE, WILLIE, BUT I'M AFRAID MY CONDITION MAKES THAT IMPOSSIBLE.
WHAT YOU NEED IS TO FIND SOMEONE WHO CAN HELP YOU. MAYBE SOME OF MY FRIENDS FROM THE ALL-STAR SQUADRON.
HMMM. I READ SOMEWHERE THAT THE OLD FLASH DID SOMETHING WITH THE JUSTICE LEAGUE RECENTLY.
THANKS, GRAMPS. I SUPPOSE I'M GOING TO MISS OUR NEXT FEW VISITS--

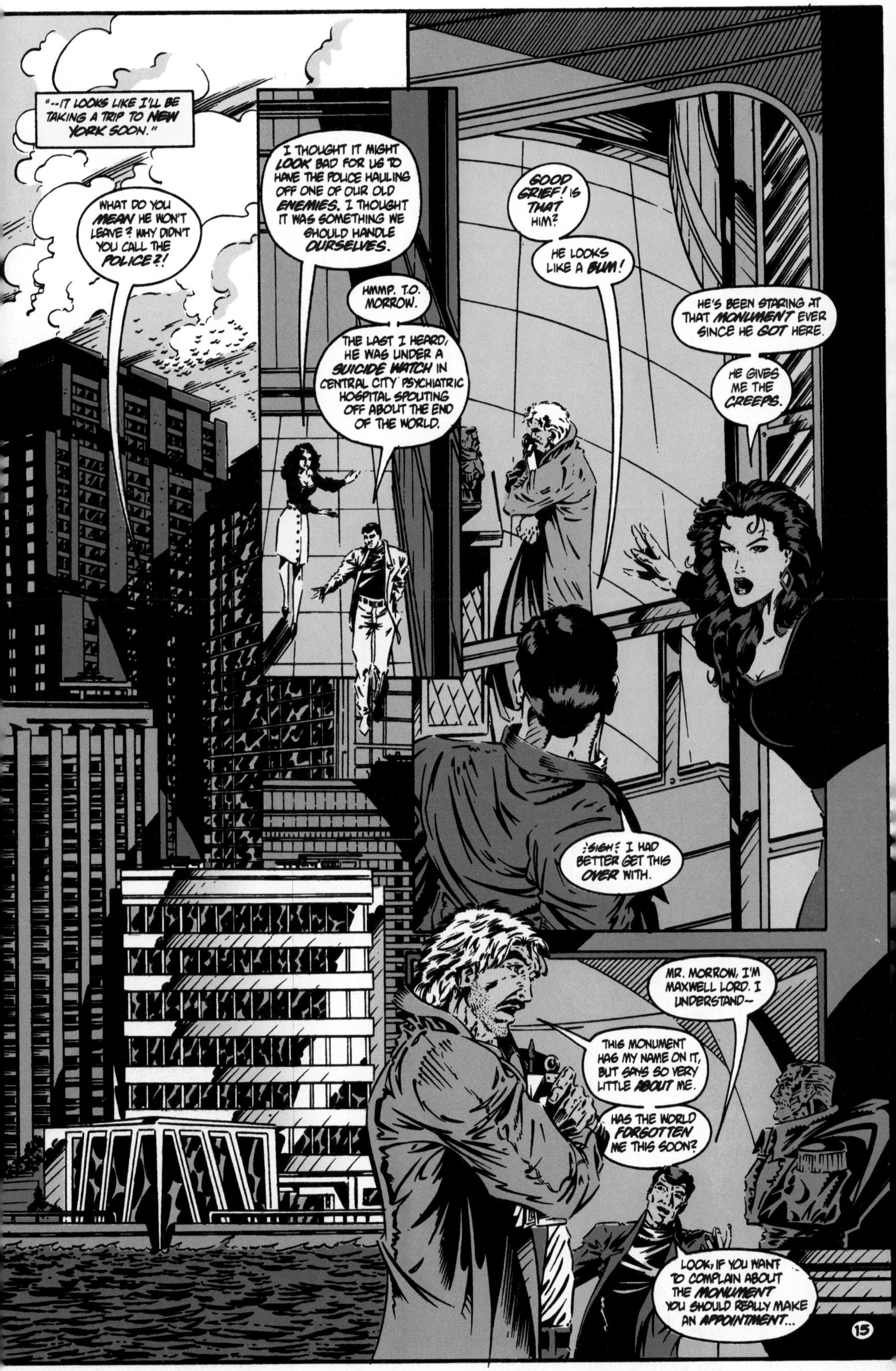
"--IT LOOKS LIKE I'LL BE TAKING A TRIP TO NEW YORK SOON."
WHAT DO YOU MEAN HE WON'T LEAVE? WHY DIDN'T YOU CALL THE POLICE?!
I THOUGHT IT MIGHT LOOK BAD FOR US TO HAVE THE POLICE HAULING OFF ONE OF OUR OLD ENEMIES. I THOUGHT IT WAS SOMETHING WE SHOULD HANDLE OURSELVES.
HMMP. T.O. MORROW.
THE LAST I HEARD, HE WAS UNDER A SUICIDE WATCH IN CENTRAL CITY PSYCHIATRIC HOSPITAL SPOUTING OFF ABOUT THE END OF THE WORLD.
GOOD GRIEF! IS THAT HIM?
HE LOOKS LIKE A BUM!
HE'S BEEN STARING AT THAT MONUMENT EVER SINCE HE GOT HERE.
HE GIVES ME THE CREEPS.
:SIGH: I HAD BETTER GET THIS OVER WITH.
MR. MORROW, I'M MAXWELL LORD. I UNDERSTAND--
THIS MONUMENT HAS MY NAME ON IT, BUT SAYS SO VERY LITTLE ABOUT ME.
HAS THE WORLD FORGOTTEN ME THIS SOON?
LOOK, IF YOU WANT TO COMPLAIN ABOUT THE MONUMENT YOU SHOULD REALLY MAKE AN APPOINTMENT...

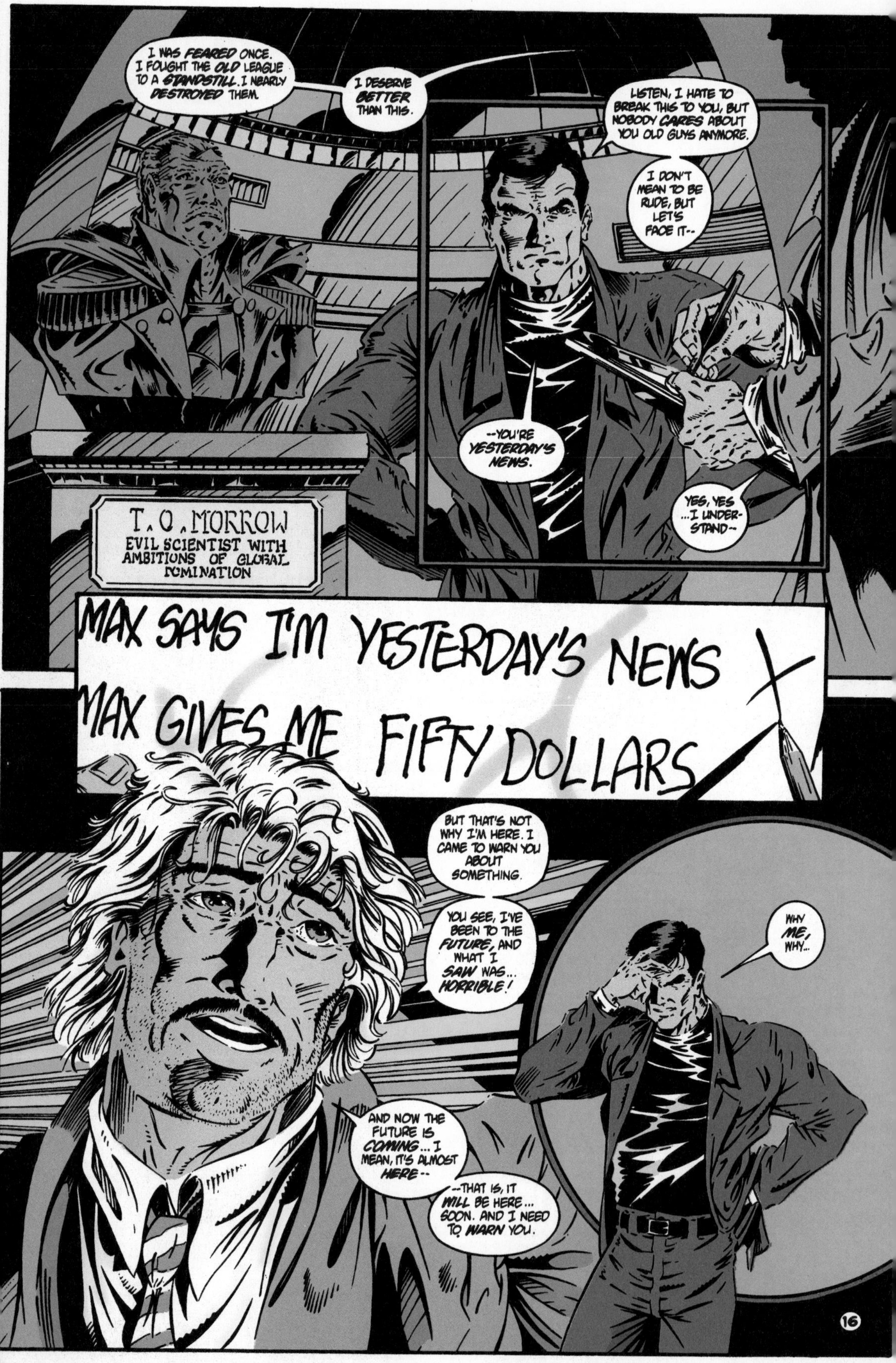
I WAS FEARED ONCE. I FOUGHT THE OLD LEAGUE TO A STANDSTILL. I NEARLY DESTROYED THEM.
I DESERVE BETTER THAN THIS.
LISTEN, I HATE TO BREAK THIS TO YOU, BUT NOBODY CARES ABOUT YOU OLD GUYS ANYMORE.
I DON'T MEAN TO BE RUDE, BUT LET'S FACE IT--
--YOU'RE YESTERDAY'S NEWS.
YES, YES ...I UNDERSTAND--
T. O. MORROW
EVIL SCIENTIST WITH AMBITIONS OF GLOBAL DOMINATION
MAX SAYS I'M YESTERDAY'S NEWS
MAX GIVES ME FIFTY DOLLARS
BUT THAT'S NOT WHY I'M HERE. I CAME TO WARN YOU ABOUT SOMETHING.
YOU SEE, I'VE BEEN TO THE FUTURE, AND WHAT I SAW WAS... HORRIBLE!
WHY ME, WHY...
AND NOW THE FUTURE IS COMING... I MEAN, IT'S ALMOST HERE--
--THAT IS, IT WILL BE HERE... SOON. AND I NEED TO WARN YOU.

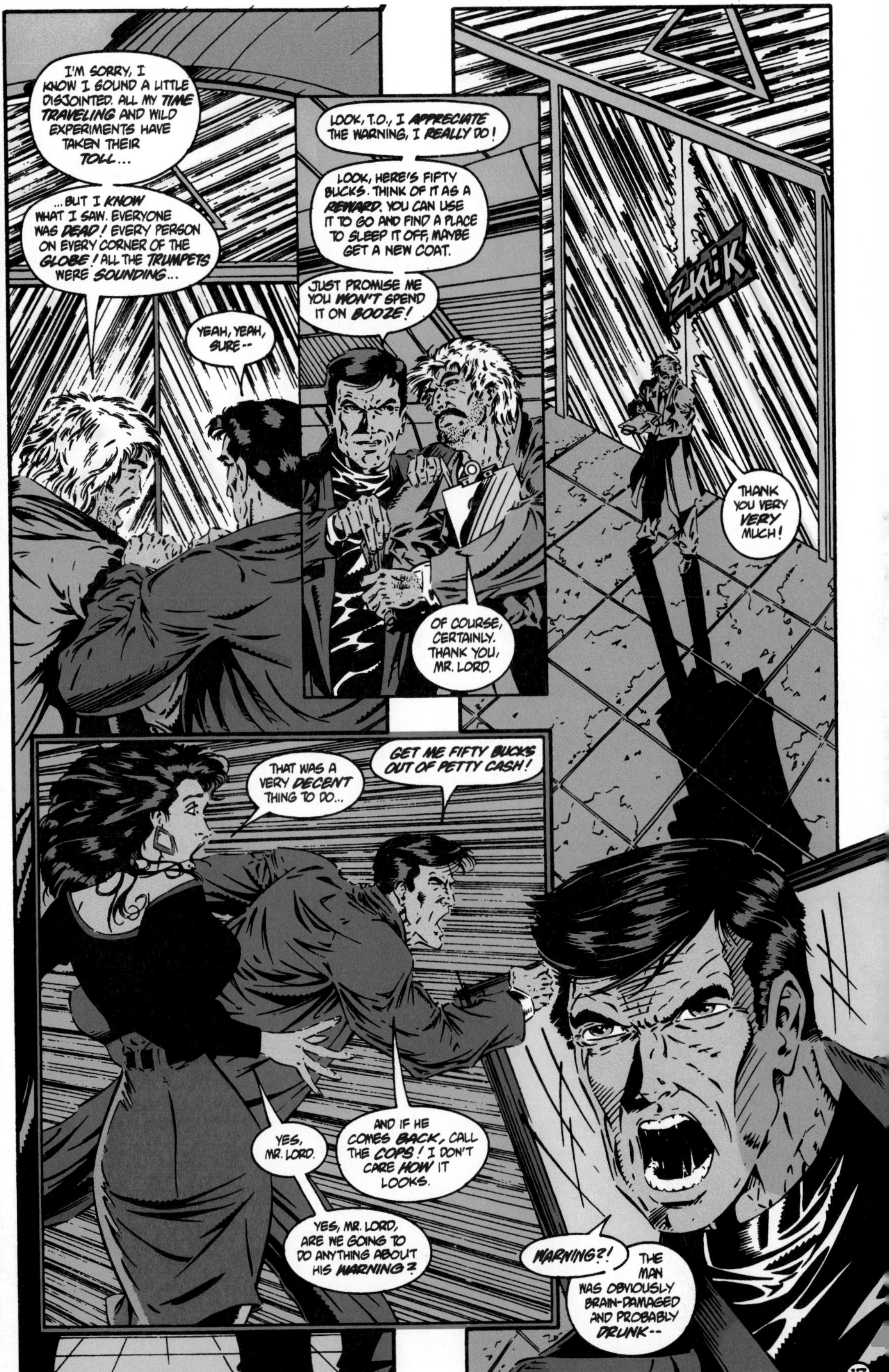
I'M SORRY, I KNOW I SOUND A LITTLE DISJOINTED. ALL MY TIME TRAVELING AND WILD EXPERIMENTS HAVE TAKEN THEIR TOLL...
...BUT I KNOW WHAT I SAW. EVERYONE WAS DEAD! EVERY PERSON ON EVERY CORNER OF THE GLOBE! ALL THE TRUMPETS WERE SOUNDING...
YEAH, YEAH, SURE--
LOOK, T.O., I APPRECIATE THE WARNING, I REALLY DO!
LOOK, HERE'S FIFTY BUCKS. THINK OF IT AS A REWARD. YOU CAN USE IT TO GO AND FIND A PLACE TO SLEEP IT OFF, MAYBE GET A NEW COAT.
JUST PROMISE ME YOU WON'T SPEND IT ON BOOZE!
OF COURSE, CERTAINLY. THANK YOU, MR. LORD.
ZKLIK
THANK YOU VERY VERY MUCH!
THAT WAS A VERY DECENT THING TO DO...
GET ME FIFTY BUCKS OUT OF PETTY CASH!
YES, MR. LORD.
AND IF HE COMES BACK, CALL THE COPS! I DON'T CARE HOW IT LOOKS.
YES, MR. LORD, ARE WE GOING TO DO ANYTHING ABOUT HIS WARNING?
WARNING?!
THE MAN WAS OBVIOUSLY BRAIN-DAMAGED AND PROBABLY DRUNK--

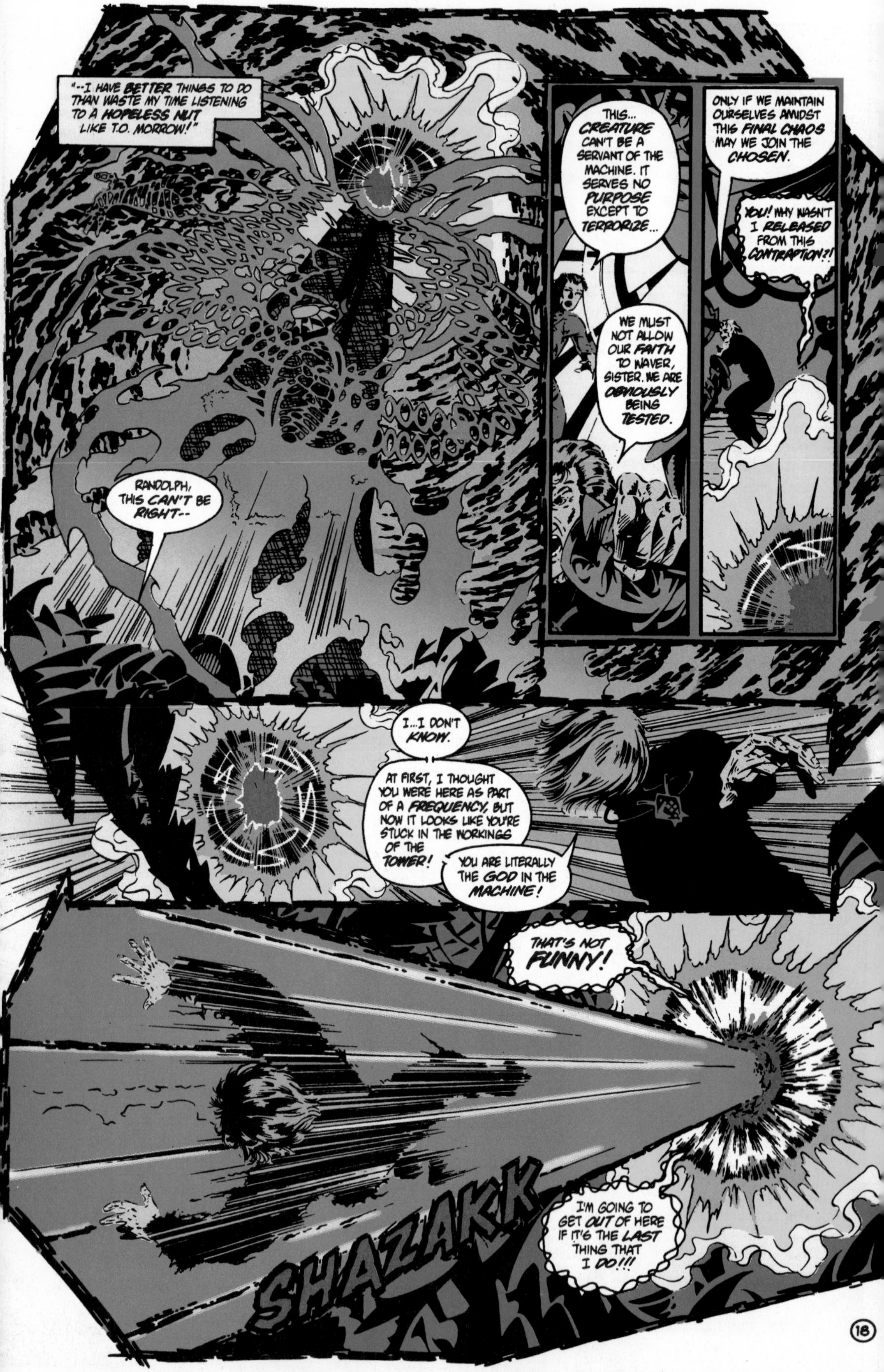
"--I HAVE BETTER THINGS TO DO THAN WASTE MY TIME LISTENING TO A HOPELESS NUT LIKE T.O. MORROW!"
THIS... CREATURE CAN'T BE A SERVANT OF THE MACHINE. IT SERVES NO PURPOSE EXCEPT TO TERRORIZE...
WE MUST NOT ALLOW OUR FAITH TO WAVER, SISTER. WE ARE OBVIOUSLY BEING TESTED.
ONLY IF WE MAINTAIN OURSELVES AMIDST THIS FINAL CHAOS MAY WE JOIN THE CHOSEN.
YOU! WHY WASN'T I RELEASED FROM THIS CONTRAPTION?!
RANDOLPH, THIS CAN'T BE RIGHT--
I...I DON'T KNOW.
AT FIRST, I THOUGHT YOU WERE HERE AS PART OF A FREQUENCY, BUT NOW IT LOOKS LIKE YOU'RE STUCK IN THE WORKINGS OF THE TOWER!
YOU ARE LITERALLY THE GOD IN THE MACHINE!
THAT'S NOT FUNNY!
I'M GOING TO GET OUT OF HERE IF IT'S THE LAST THING THAT I DO!!!
SHAZAKK

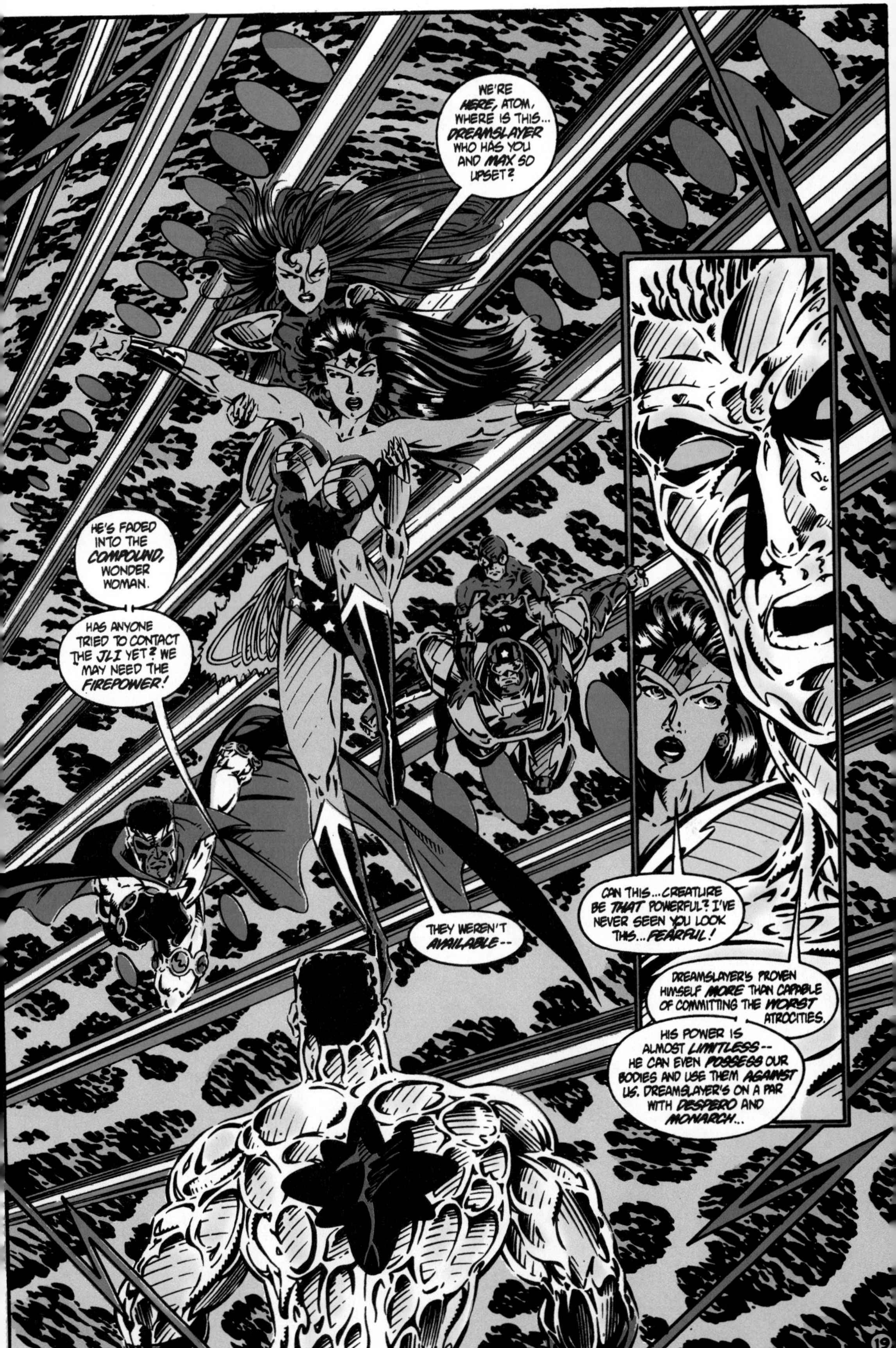

WE'RE HERE, ATOM, WHERE IS THIS... DREAMSLAYER WHO HAS YOU AND MAX SO UPSET?
HE'S FADED INTO THE COMPOUND, WONDER WOMAN.
HAS ANYONE TRIED TO CONTACT THE JLI YET? WE MAY NEED THE FIREPOWER!
THEY WEREN'T AVAILABLE--
CAN THIS...CREATURE BE THAT POWERFUL? I'VE NEVER SEEN YOU LOOK THIS...FEARFUL!
DREAMSLAYER'S PROVEN HIMSELF MORE THAN CAPABLE OF COMMITTING THE WORST ATROCITIES.
HIS POWER IS ALMOST LIMITLESS-- HE CAN EVEN POSSESS OUR BODIES AND USE THEM AGAINST US. DREAMSLAYER'S ON A PAR WITH DESPERO AND MONARCH...

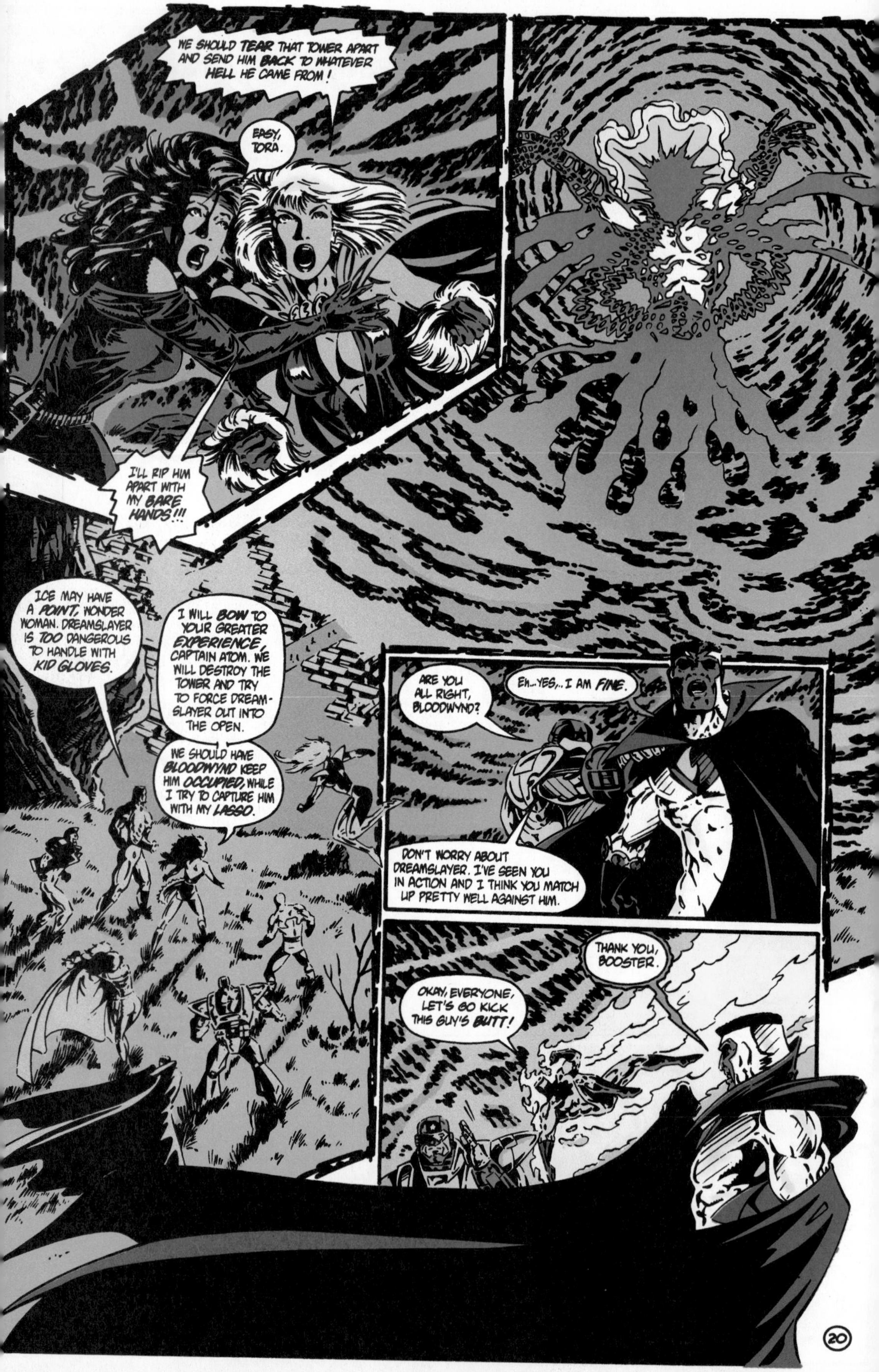

WE SHOULD TEAR THAT TOWER APART AND SEND HIM BACK TO WHATEVER HELL HE CAME FROM!
EASY, TORA.
I'LL RIP HIM APART WITH MY BARE HANDS!!!
ICE MAY HAVE A POINT, WONDER WOMAN. DREAMSLAYER IS TOO DANGEROUS TO HANDLE WITH KID GLOVES.
I WILL BOW TO YOUR GREATER EXPERIENCE, CAPTAIN ATOM. WE WILL DESTROY THE TOWER AND TRY TO FORCE DREAMSLAYER OUT INTO THE OPEN.
WE SHOULD HAVE BLOODWYND KEEP HIM OCCUPIED, WHILE I TRY TO CAPTURE HIM WITH MY LASSO.
ARE YOU ALL RIGHT, BLOODWYND?
Eh...YES... I AM FINE.
DON'T WORRY ABOUT DREAMSLAYER. I'VE SEEN YOU IN ACTION AND I THINK YOU MATCH UP PRETTY WELL AGAINST HIM.
THANK YOU, BOOSTER.
OKAY, EVERYONE, LET'S GO KICK THIS GUY'S BUTT!

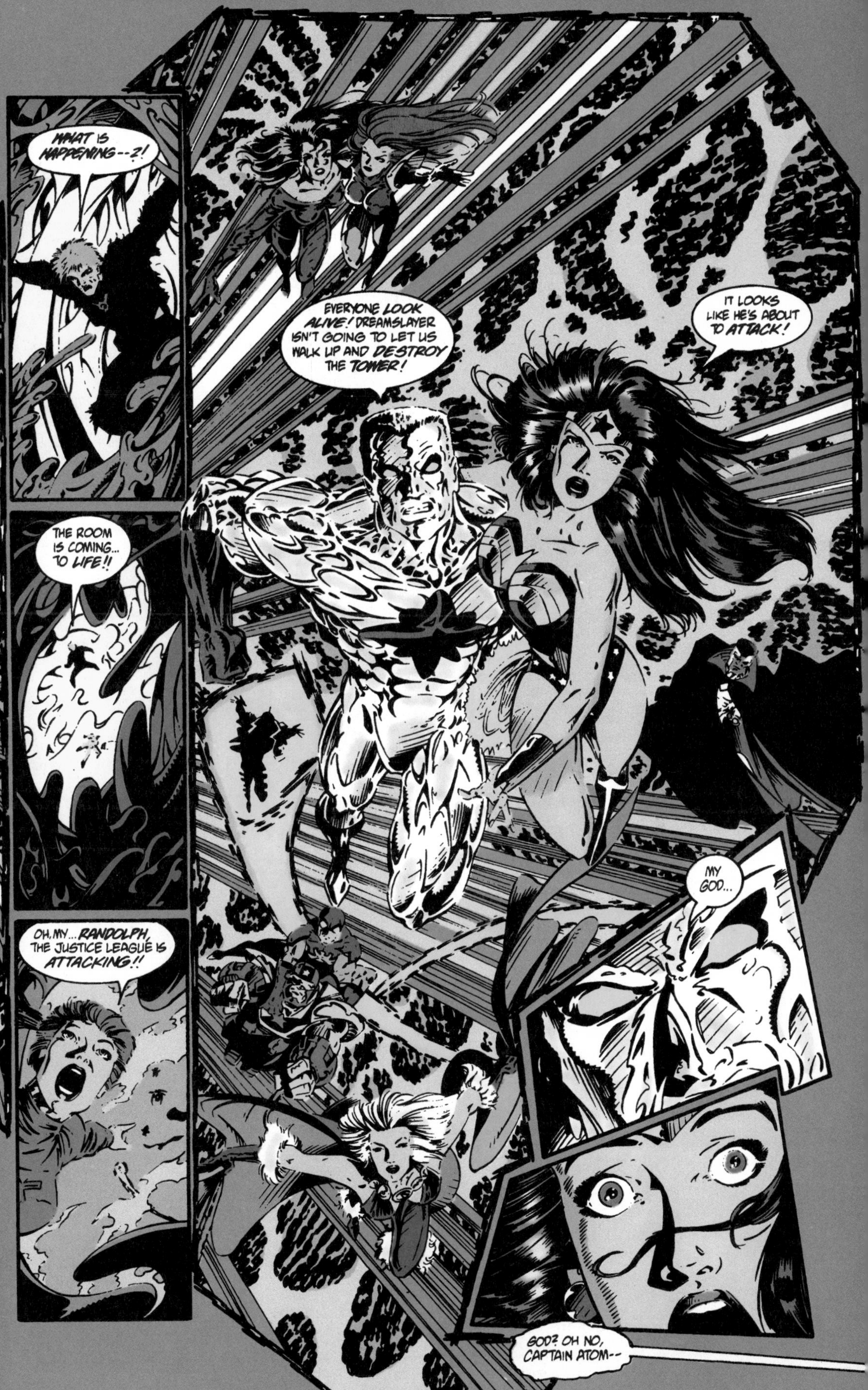
WHAT IS HAPPENING--?!
THE ROOM IS COMING... TO LIFE!!
OH, MY... RANDOLPH, THE JUSTICE LEAGUE IS ATTACKING!!
EVERYONE LOOK ALIVE! DREAMSLAYER ISN'T GOING TO LET US WALK UP AND DESTROY THE TOWER!
IT LOOKS LIKE HE'S ABOUT TO ATTACK!
MY GOD...
GOD? OH NO, CAPTAIN ATOM--

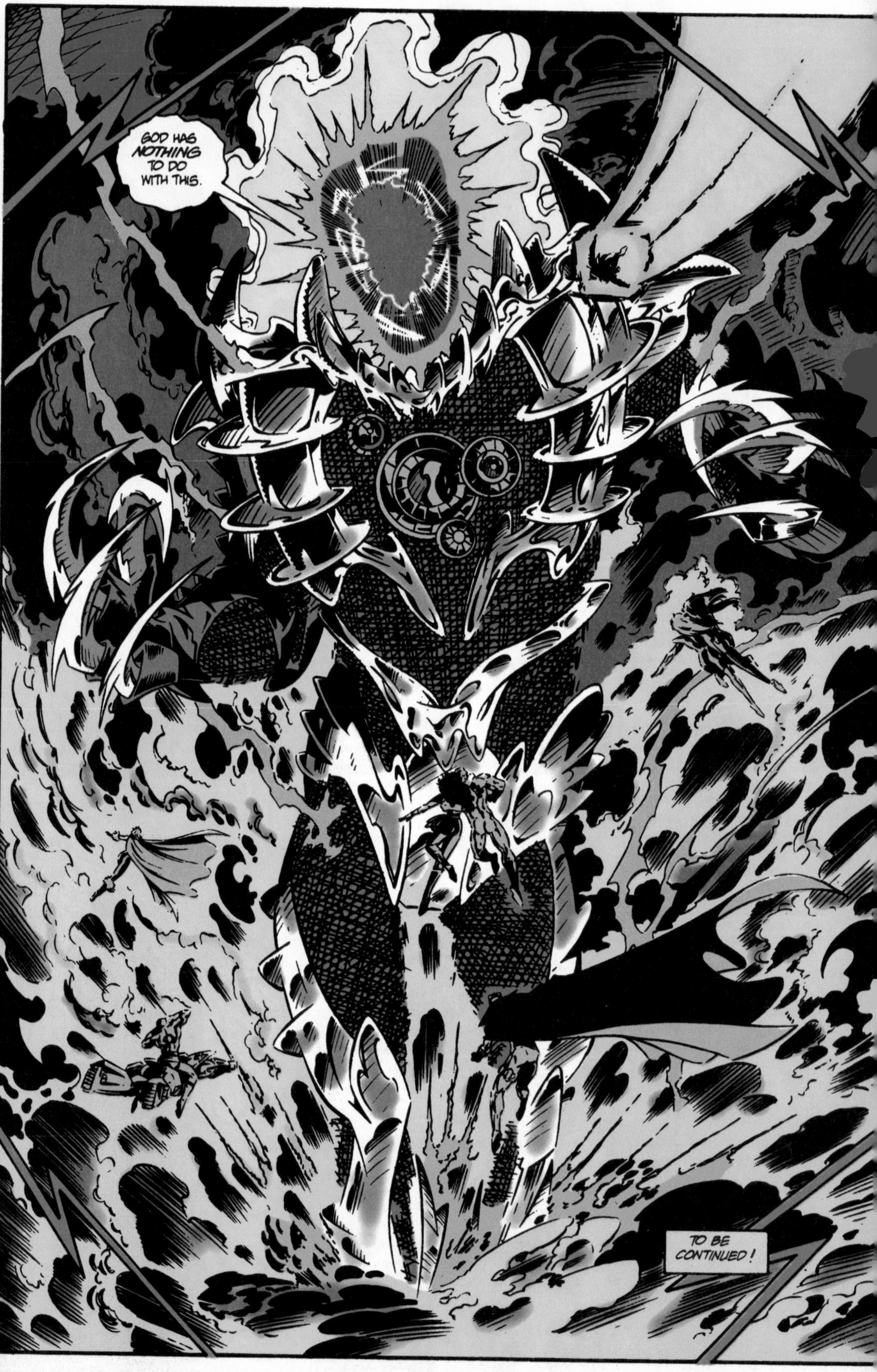
GOD HAS *NOTHING* TO DO WITH THIS.
TO BE CONTINUED!

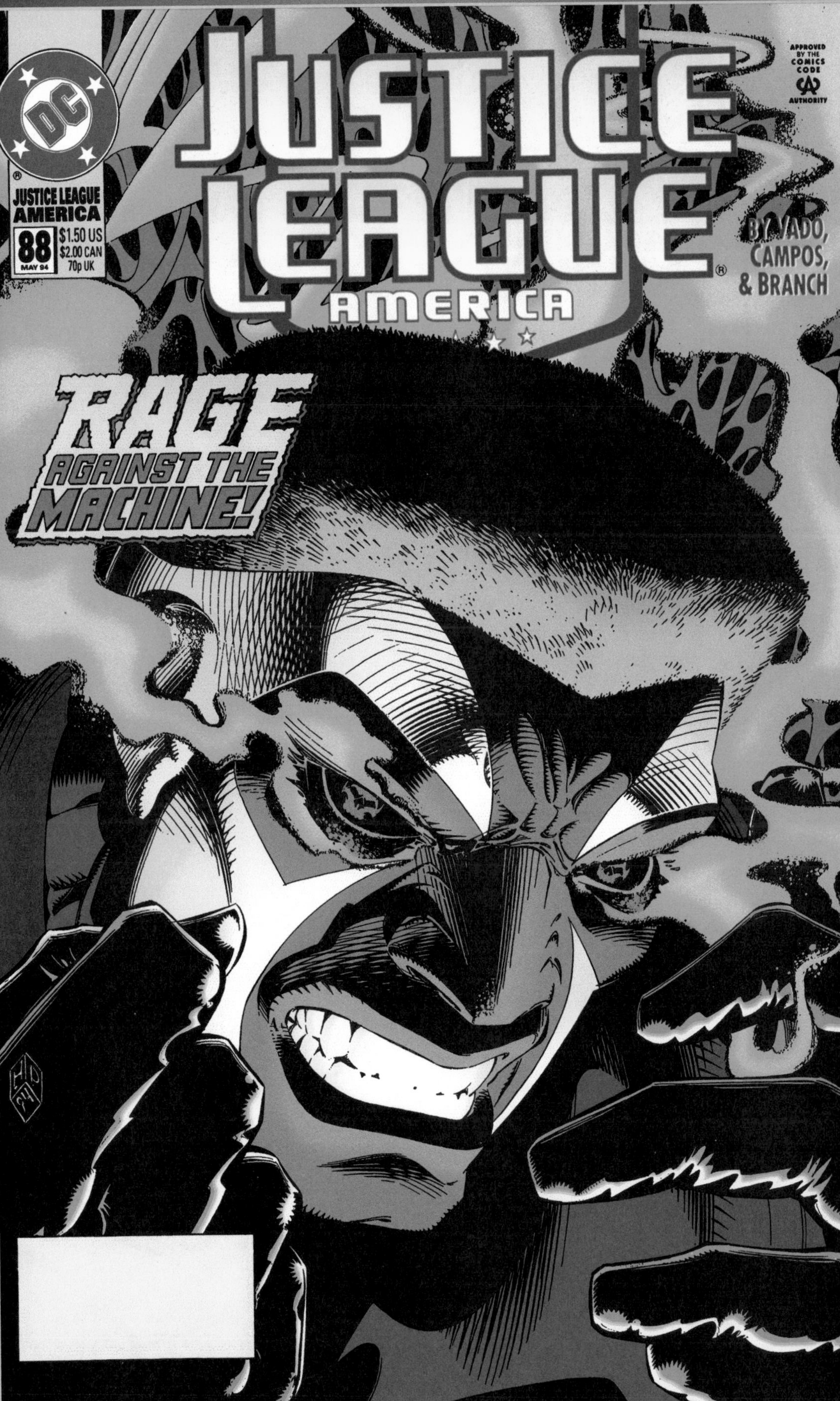

DC
JUSTICE LEAGUE AMERICA
88
MAY 94
$1.50 US
$2.00 CAN
70p UK
JUSTICE LEAGUE AMERICA
APPROVED BY THE COMICS CODE AUTHORITY
BY VADO, CAMPOS, & BRANCH
RAGE AGAINST THE MACHINE!

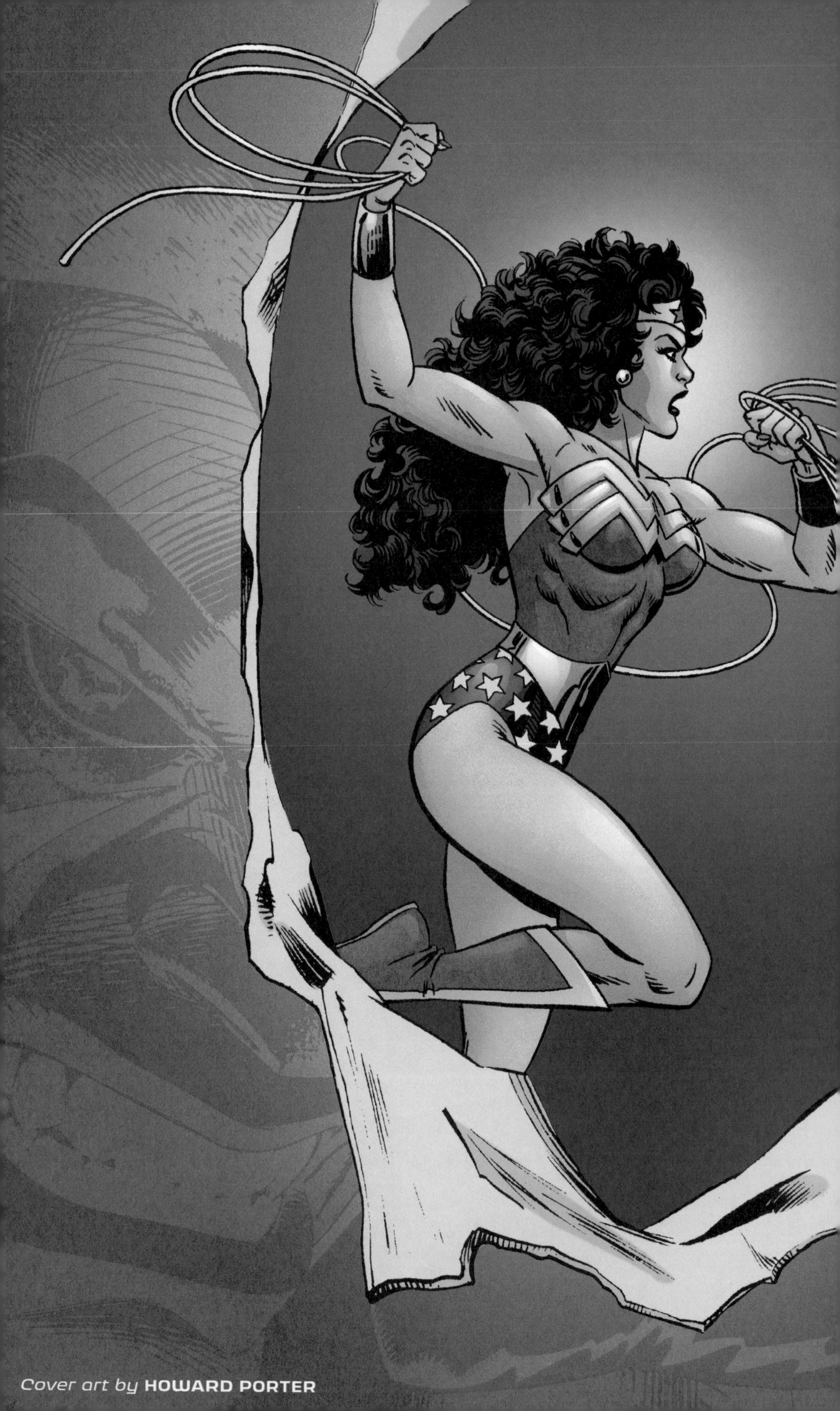

Cover art by **HOWARD PORTER**

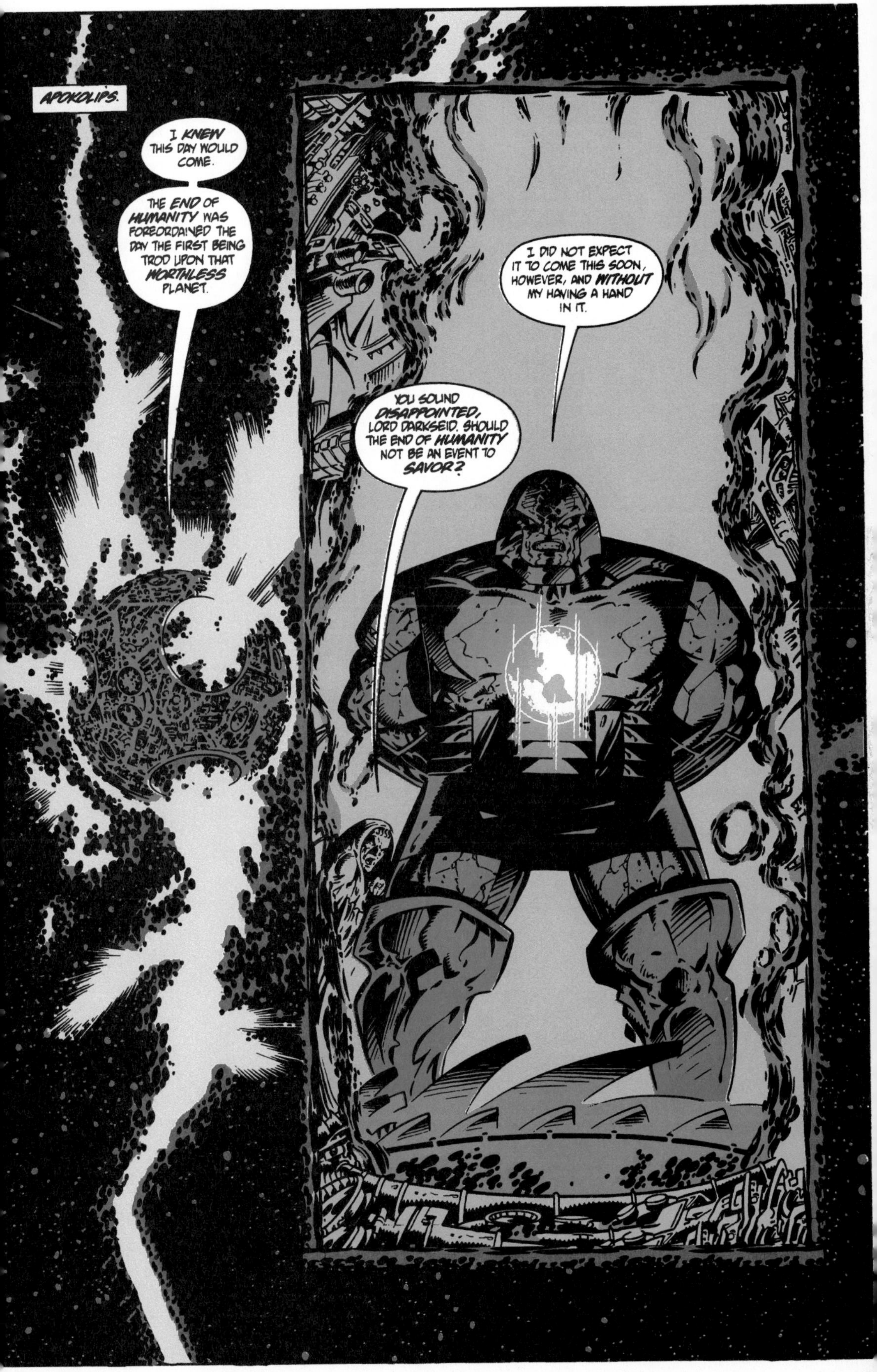
APOKOLIPS.
I KNEW THIS DAY WOULD COME.
THE END OF HUMANITY WAS FOREORDAINED THE DAY THE FIRST BEING TROD UPON THAT WORTHLESS PLANET.
I DID NOT EXPECT IT TO COME THIS SOON, HOWEVER, AND WITHOUT MY HAVING A HAND IN IT.
YOU SOUND DISAPPOINTED, LORD DARKSEID. SHOULD THE END OF HUMANITY NOT BE AN EVENT TO SAVOR?

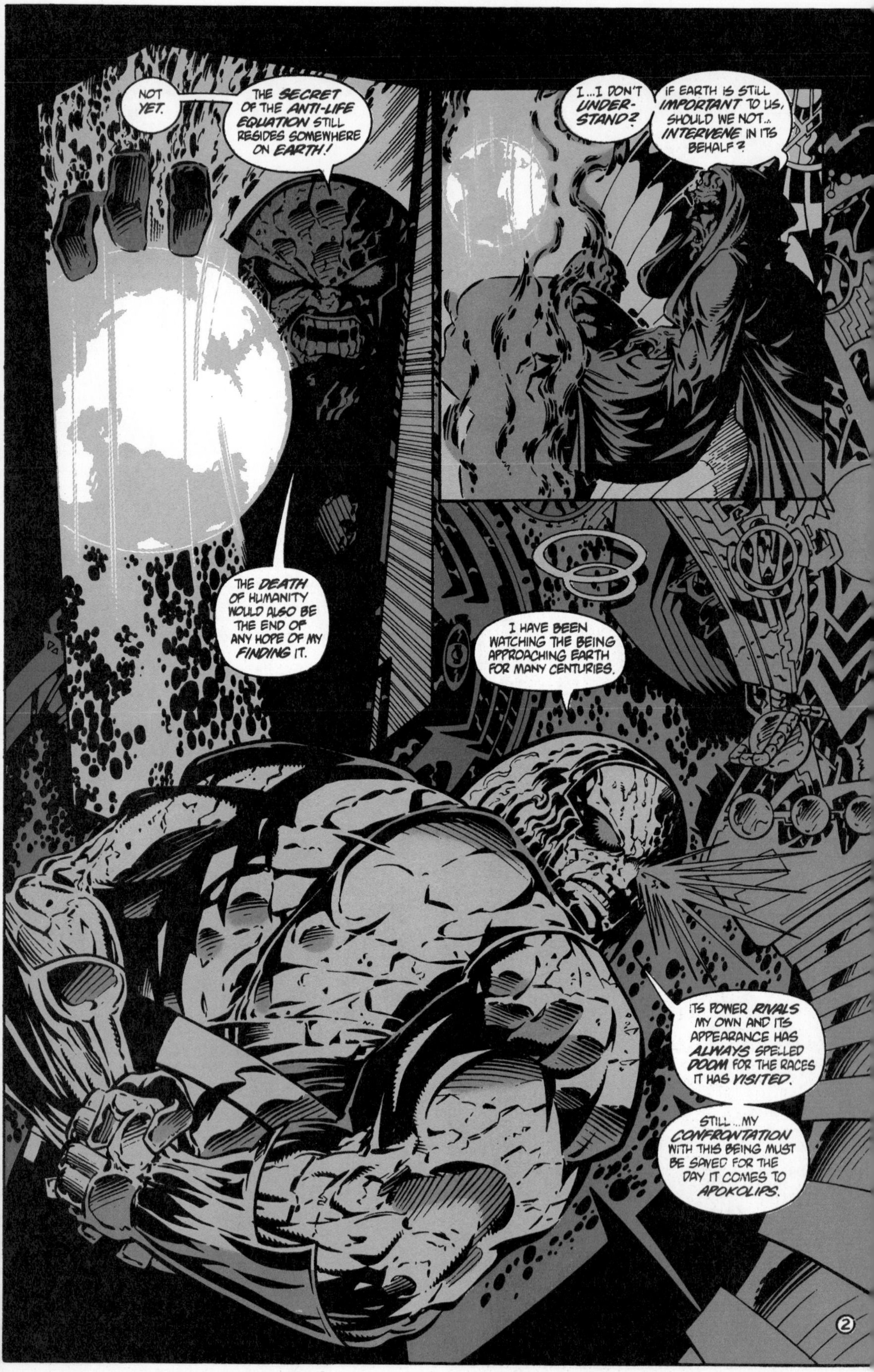
NOT YET.
THE SECRET OF THE ANTI-LIFE EQUATION STILL RESIDES SOMEWHERE ON EARTH!
I...I DON'T UNDER-STAND?
IF EARTH IS STILL IMPORTANT TO US, SHOULD WE NOT... INTERVENE IN ITS BEHALF?
THE DEATH OF HUMANITY WOULD ALSO BE THE END OF ANY HOPE OF MY FINDING IT.
I HAVE BEEN WATCHING THE BEING APPROACHING EARTH FOR MANY CENTURIES.
ITS POWER RIVALS MY OWN AND ITS APPEARANCE HAS ALWAYS SPELLED DOOM FOR THE RACES IT HAS VISITED.
STILL...MY CONFRONTATION WITH THIS BEING MUST BE SAVED FOR THE DAY IT COMES TO APOKOLIPS.

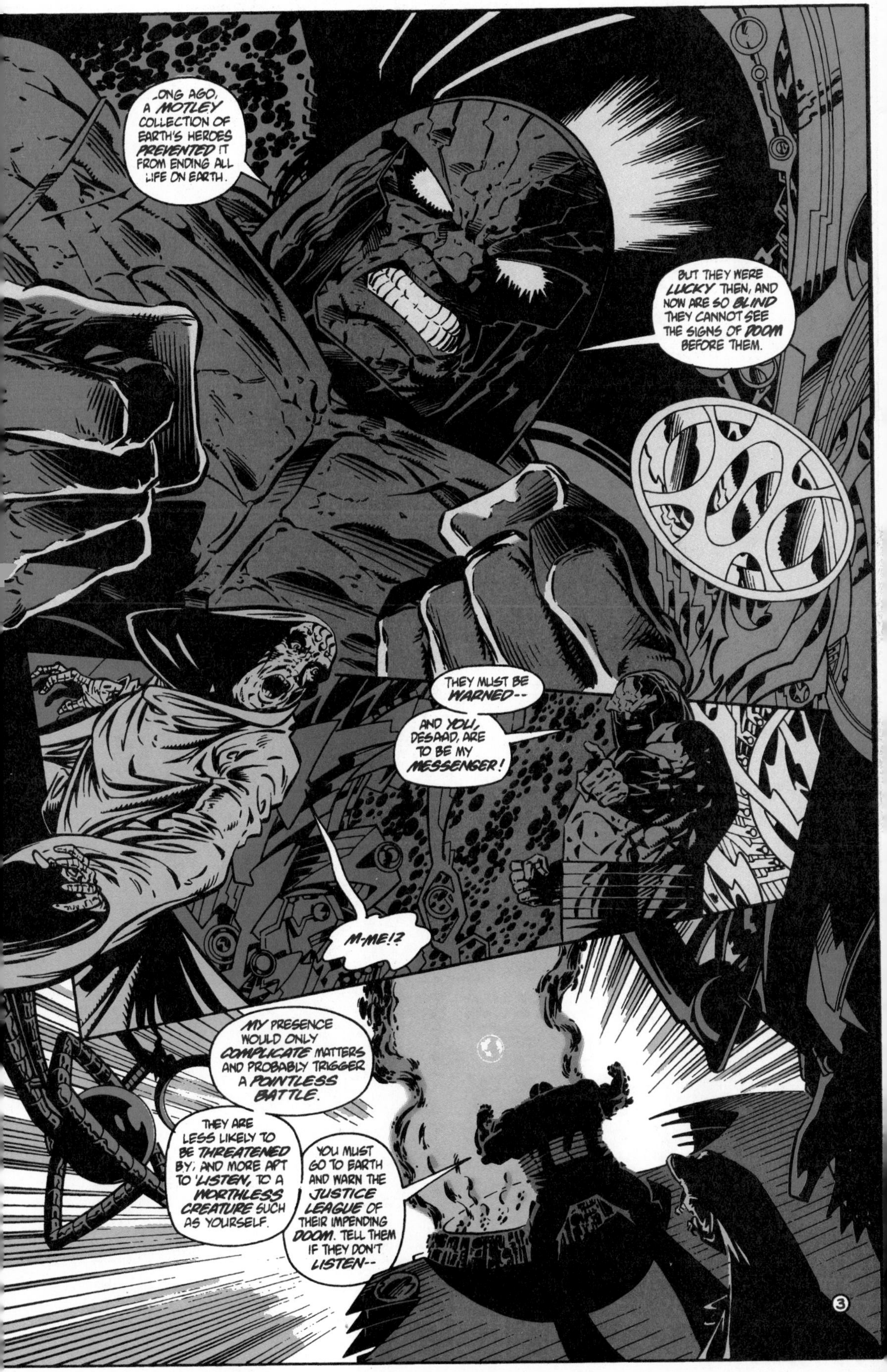

-ONG AGO, A MOTLEY COLLECTION OF EARTH'S HEROES PREVENTED IT FROM ENDING ALL LIFE ON EARTH.
BUT THEY WERE LUCKY THEN, AND NOW ARE SO BLIND THEY CANNOT SEE THE SIGNS OF DOOM BEFORE THEM.
THEY MUST BE WARNED--
AND YOU, DESAAD, ARE TO BE MY MESSENGER!
M-ME!?
MY PRESENCE WOULD ONLY COMPLICATE MATTERS AND PROBABLY TRIGGER A POINTLESS BATTLE.
THEY ARE LESS LIKELY TO BE THREATENED BY, AND MORE APT TO 'LISTEN,' TO A WORTHLESS CREATURE SUCH AS YOURSELF.
YOU MUST GO TO EARTH AND WARN THE JUSTICE LEAGUE OF THEIR IMPENDING DOOM. TELL THEM IF THEY DON'T LISTEN--

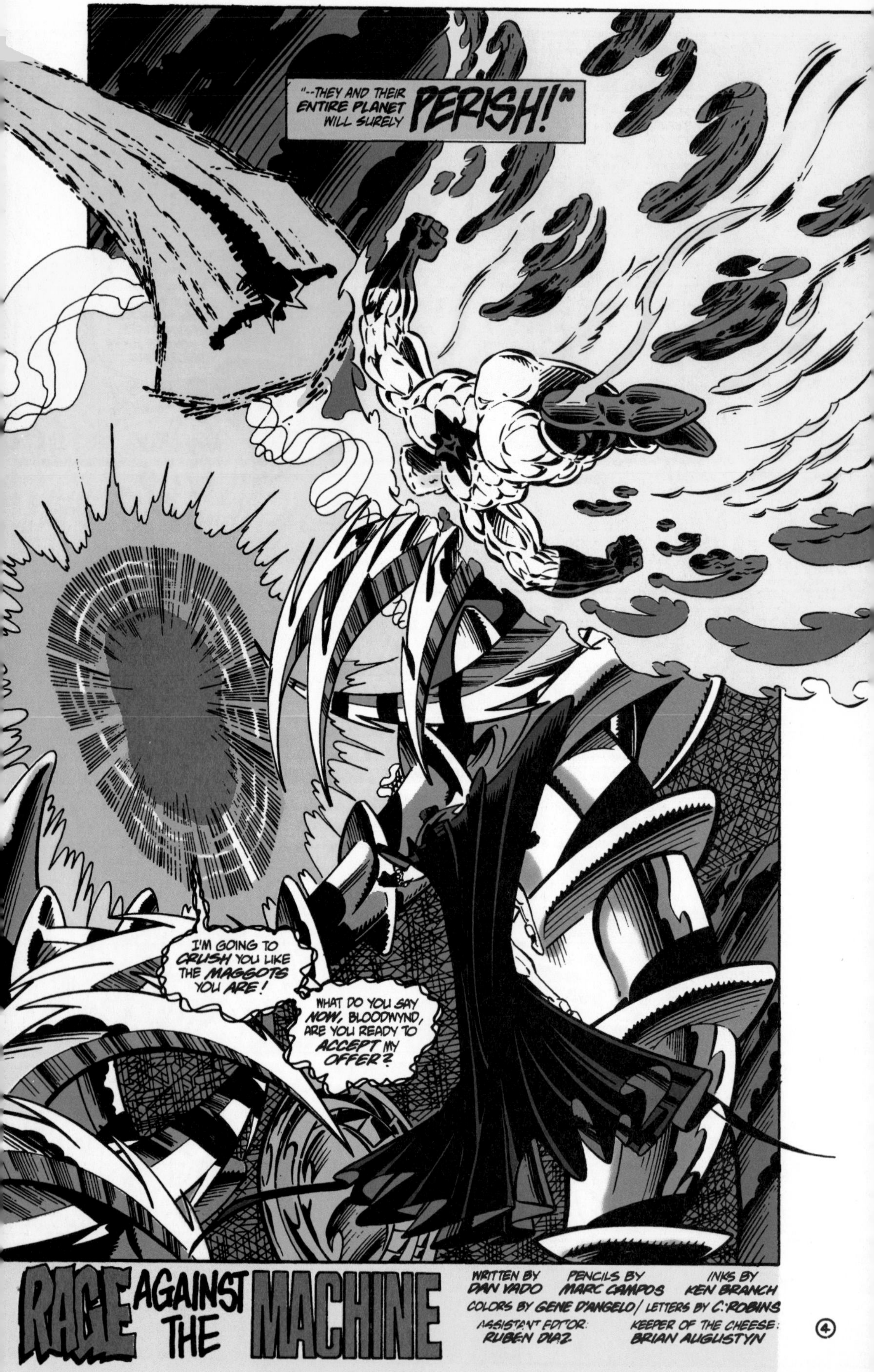
"--THEY AND THEIR ENTIRE PLANET WILL SURELY PERISH!"
I'M GOING TO CRUSH YOU LIKE THE MAGGOTS YOU ARE!
WHAT DO YOU SAY NOW, BLOODWYND, ARE YOU READY TO ACCEPT MY OFFER?
RAGE AGAINST THE MACHINE
WRITTEN BY DAN VADO
PENCILS BY MARC CAMPOS
INKS BY KEN BRANCH
COLORS BY GENE D'ANGELO / LETTERS BY C. ROBINS
ASSISTANT EDITOR: RUBEN DIAZ
KEEPER OF THE CHEESE: BRIAN AUGUSTYN

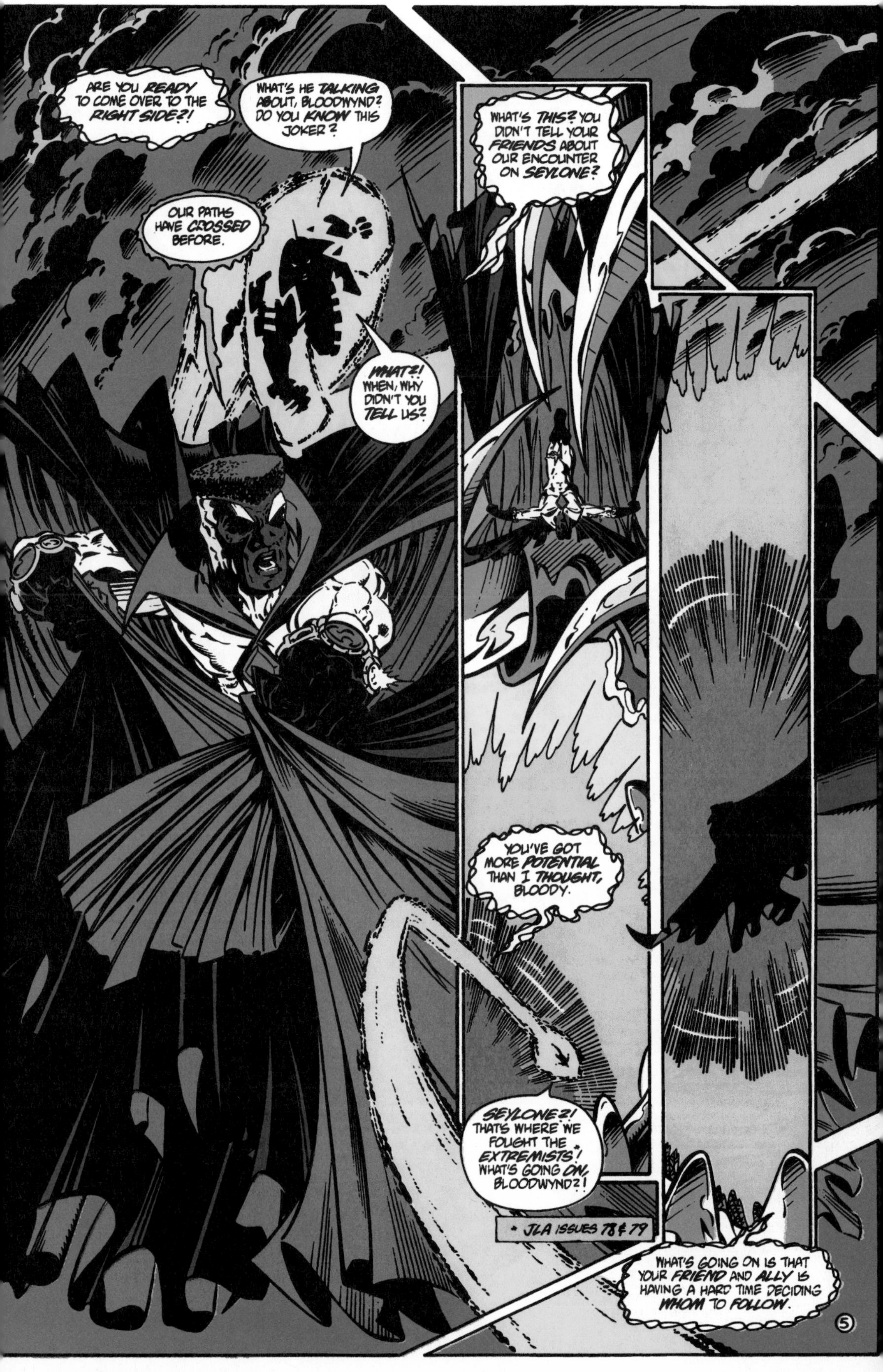
ARE YOU READY TO COME OVER TO THE RIGHT SIDE?!
WHAT'S HE TALKING ABOUT, BLOODWYND? DO YOU KNOW THIS JOKER?
OUR PATHS HAVE CROSSED BEFORE.
WHAT?! WHEN, WHY DIDN'T YOU TELL US?
WHAT'S THIS? YOU DIDN'T TELL YOUR FRIENDS ABOUT OUR ENCOUNTER ON SEYLONE?
YOU'VE GOT MORE POTENTIAL THAN I THOUGHT, BLOODY.
SEYLONE?! THAT'S WHERE WE FOUGHT THE EXTREMISTS*! WHAT'S GOING ON, BLOODWYND?!
* JLA ISSUES 78 & 79
WHAT'S GOING ON IS THAT YOUR FRIEND AND ALLY IS HAVING A HARD TIME DECIDING WHOM TO FOLLOW.

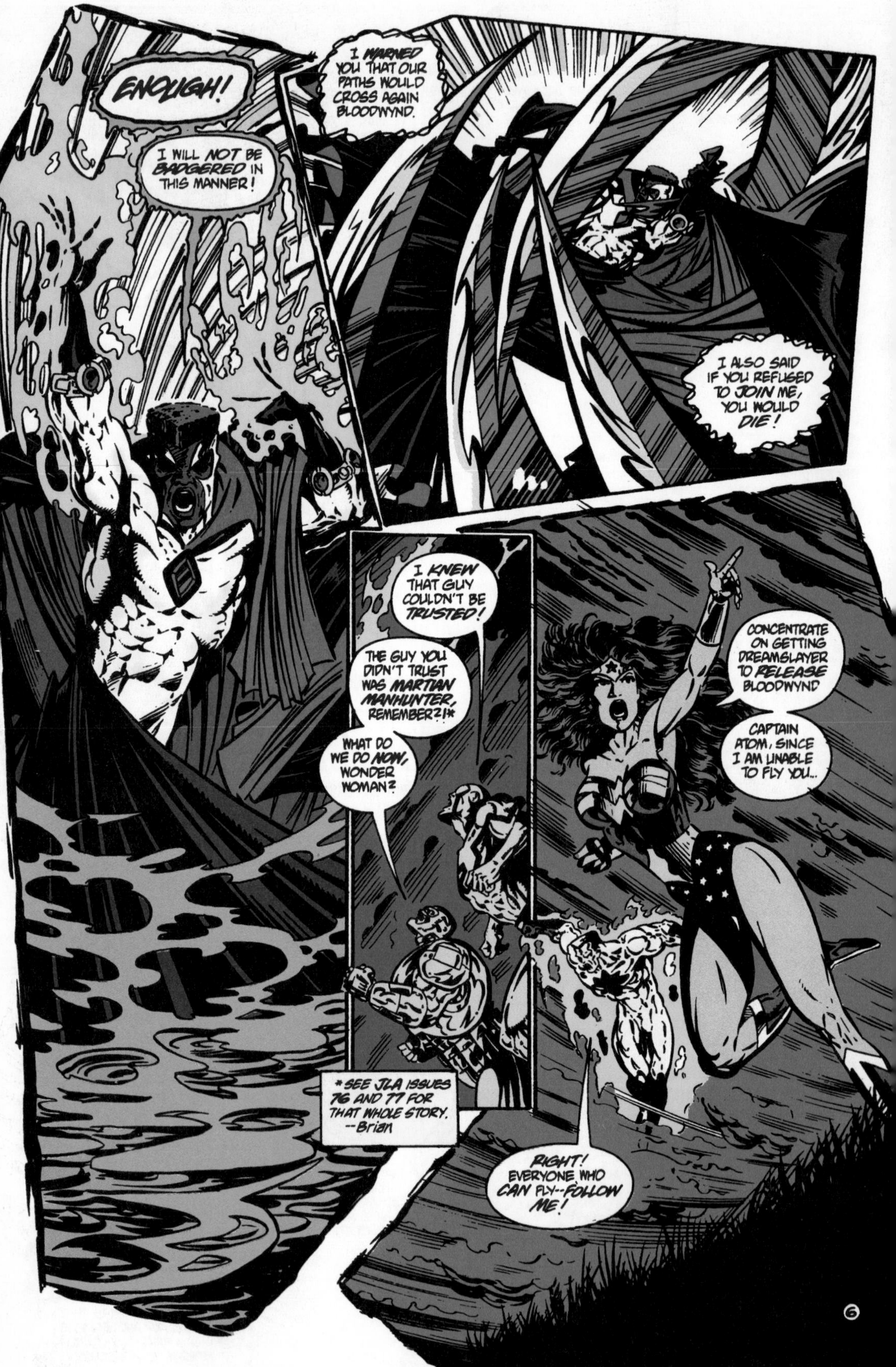
ENOUGH!
I WILL NOT BE BADGERED IN THIS MANNER!
I WARNED YOU THAT OUR PATHS WOULD CROSS AGAIN BLOODWYND.
I ALSO SAID IF YOU REFUSED TO JOIN ME, YOU WOULD DIE!
I KNEW THAT GUY COULDN'T BE TRUSTED!
THE GUY YOU DIDN'T TRUST WAS MARTIAN MANHUNTER, REMEMBER?!*
WHAT DO WE DO NOW, WONDER WOMAN?
CONCENTRATE ON GETTING DREAMSLAYER TO RELEASE BLOODWYND
CAPTAIN ATOM, SINCE I AM UNABLE TO FLY YOU...
*SEE JLA ISSUES 76 AND 77 FOR THAT WHOLE STORY. --Brian
RIGHT! EVERYONE WHO CAN FLY--FOLLOW ME!
6

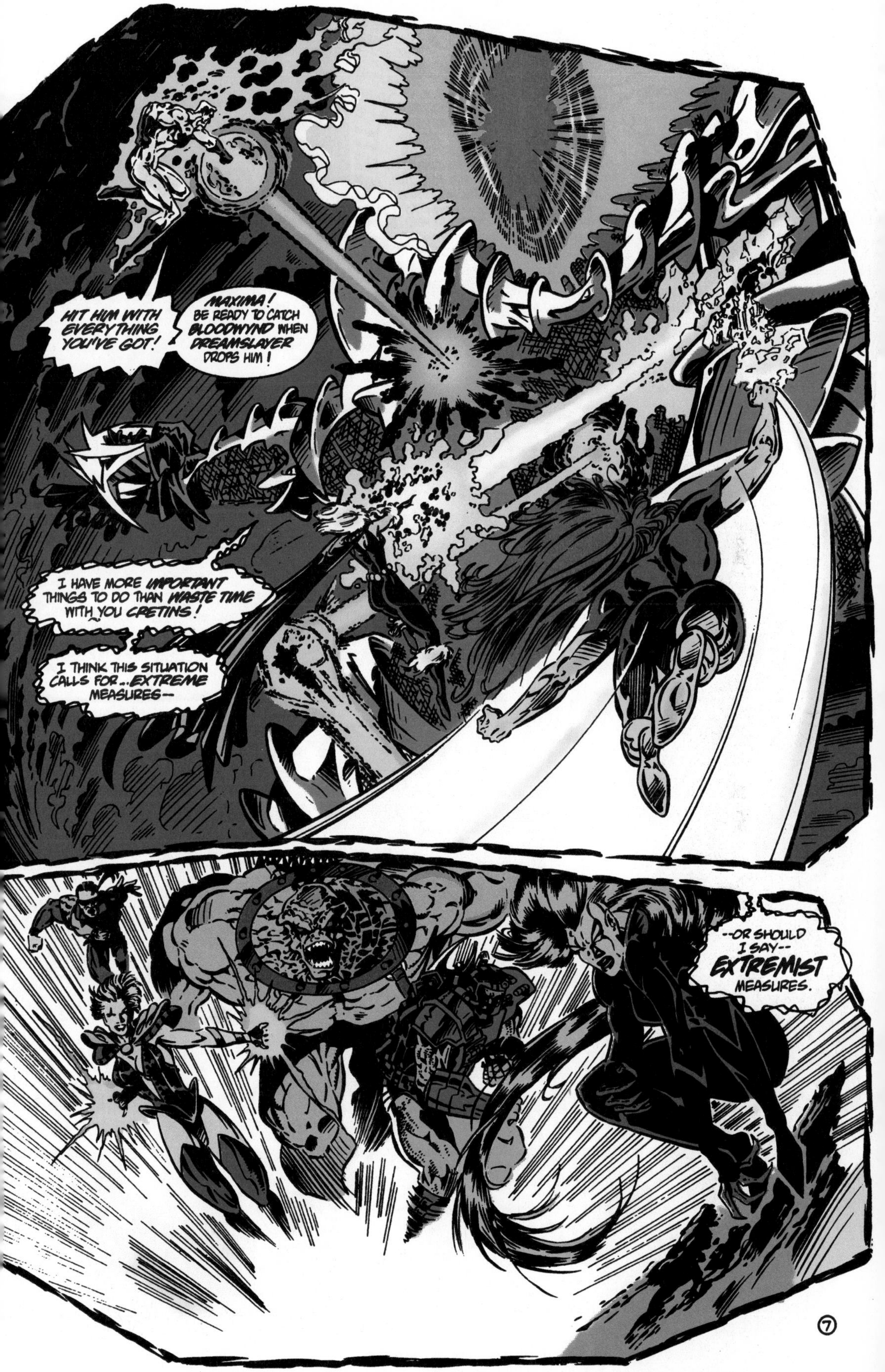
HIT HIM WITH EVERYTHING YOU'VE GOT!
MAXIMA! BE READY TO CATCH BLOODWYND WHEN DREAMSLAYER DROPS HIM!
I HAVE MORE IMPORTANT THINGS TO DO THAN WASTE TIME WITH YOU CRETINS!
I THINK THIS SITUATION CALLS FOR...EXTREME MEASURES--
--OR SHOULD I SAY-- EXTREMIST MEASURES.

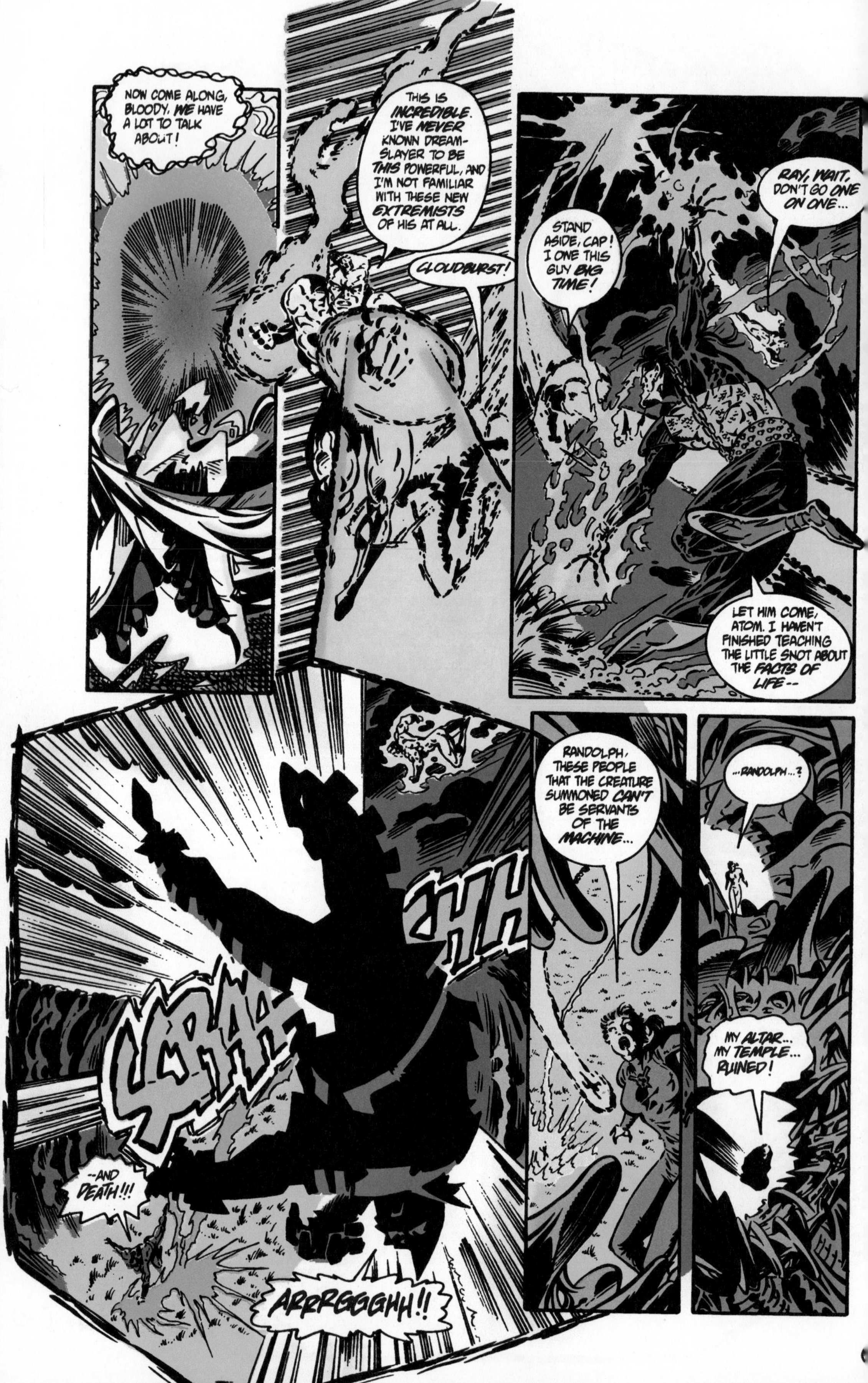
NOW COME ALONG, BLOODY. WE HAVE A LOT TO TALK ABOUT!
THIS IS INCREDIBLE. I'VE NEVER KNOWN DREAMSLAYER TO BE THIS POWERFUL, AND I'M NOT FAMILIAR WITH THESE NEW EXTREMISTS OF HIS AT ALL.
CLOUDBURST!
STAND ASIDE, CAP! I ONE THIS GUY BIG TIME!
RAY, WAIT, DON'T GO ONE ON ONE...
LET HIM COME, ATOM. I HAVEN'T FINISHED TEACHING THE LITTLE SNOT ABOUT THE FACTS OF LIFE--
--AND DEATH!!!
ARRRGGGHH!!
RANDOLPH, THESE PEOPLE THAT THE CREATURE SUMMONED CAN'T BE SERVANTS OF THE MACHINE...
...RANDOLPH...?
MY ALTAR... MY TEMPLE... RUINED!

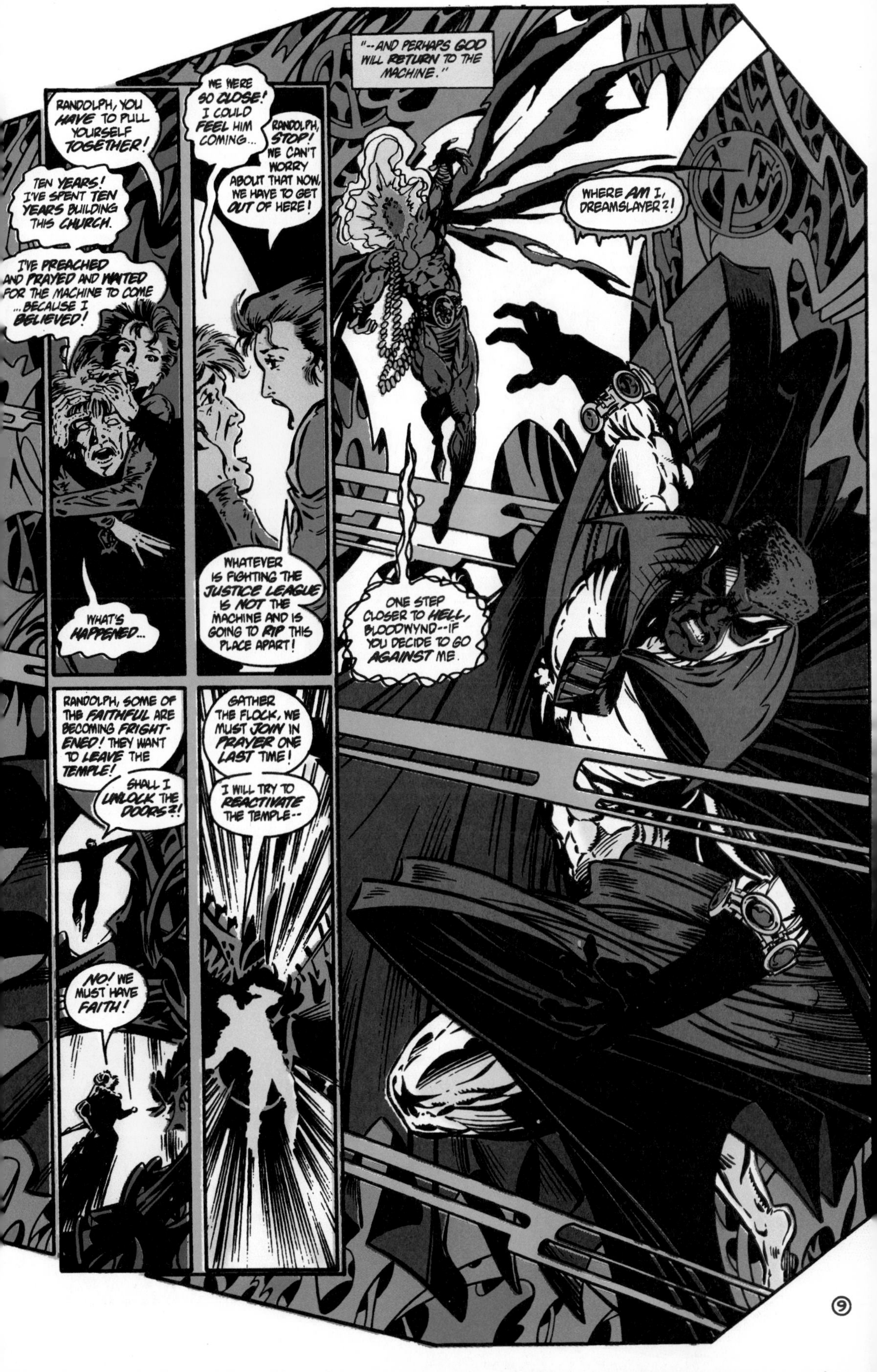
"--AND PERHAPS GOD WILL RETURN TO THE MACHINE."
RANDOLPH, YOU HAVE TO PULL YOURSELF TOGETHER!
TEN YEARS! I'VE SPENT TEN YEARS BUILDING THIS CHURCH.
I'VE PREACHED AND PRAYED AND WAITED FOR THE MACHINE TO COME ...BECAUSE I BELIEVED!
WHAT'S HAPPENED...
WE WERE SO CLOSE! I COULD FEEL HIM COMING...
RANDOLPH, STOP! WE CAN'T WORRY ABOUT THAT NOW, WE HAVE TO GET OUT OF HERE!
WHATEVER IS FIGHTING THE JUSTICE LEAGUE IS NOT THE MACHINE AND IS GOING TO RIP THIS PLACE APART!
RANDOLPH, SOME OF THE FAITHFUL ARE BECOMING FRIGHT-ENED! THEY WANT TO LEAVE THE TEMPLE!
SHALL I UNLOCK THE DOORS?!
NO! WE MUST HAVE FAITH!
GATHER THE FLOCK, WE MUST JOIN IN PRAYER ONE LAST TIME!
I WILL TRY TO REACTIVATE THE TEMPLE--
WHERE AM I, DREAMSLAYER?!
ONE STEP CLOSER TO HELL, BLOODWYND--IF YOU DECIDE TO GO AGAINST ME.

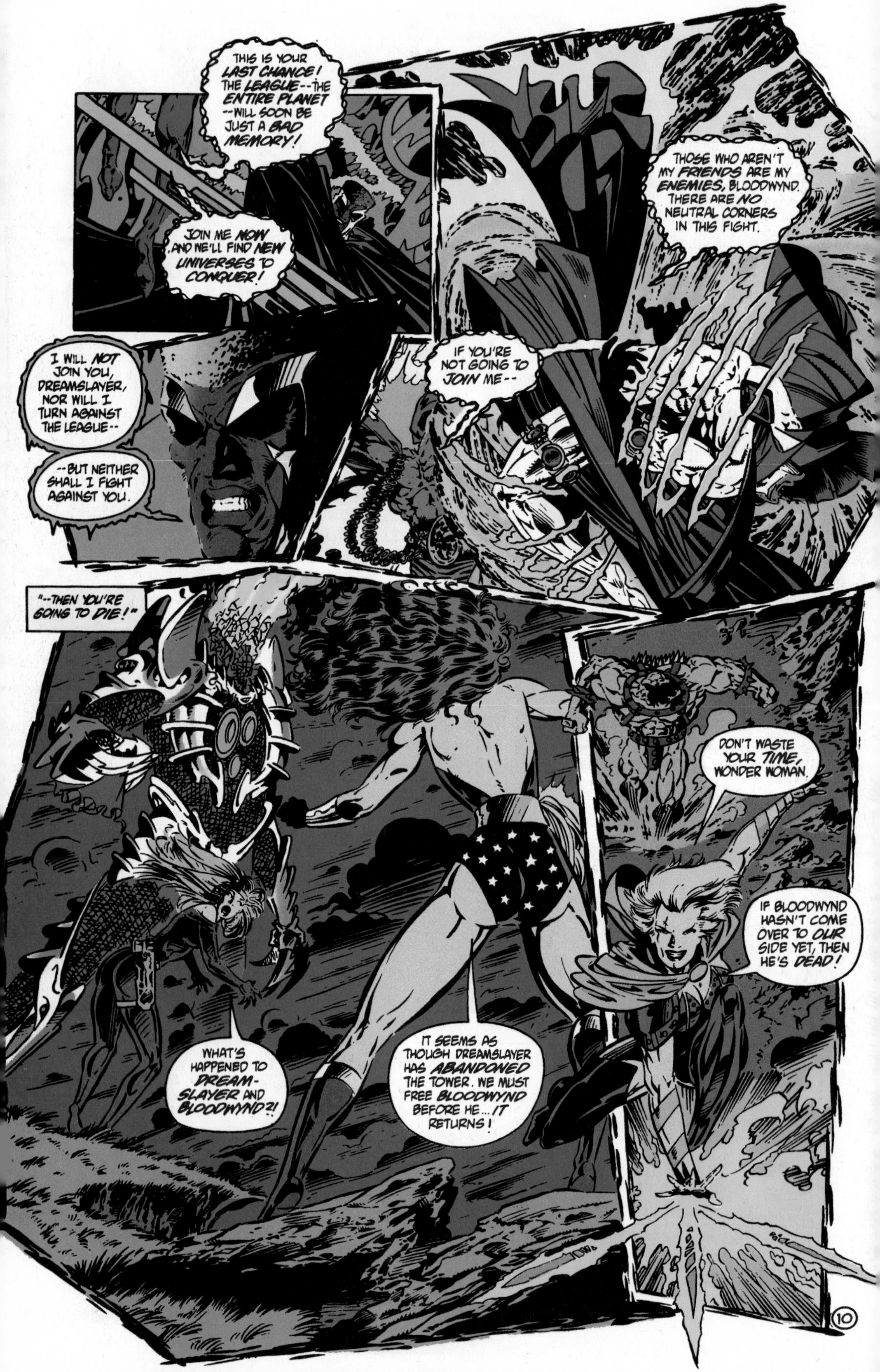
THIS IS YOUR LAST CHANCE! THE LEAGUE--THE ENTIRE PLANET --WILL SOON BE JUST A BAD MEMORY!
JOIN ME NOW AND WE'LL FIND NEW UNIVERSES TO CONQUER!
THOSE WHO AREN'T MY FRIENDS ARE MY ENEMIES, BLOODWYND. THERE ARE NO NEUTRAL CORNERS IN THIS FIGHT.
I WILL NOT JOIN YOU, DREAMSLAYER, NOR WILL I TURN AGAINST THE LEAGUE--
--BUT NEITHER SHALL I FIGHT AGAINST YOU.
IF YOU'RE NOT GOING TO JOIN ME--
"--THEN YOU'RE GOING TO DIE!"
DON'T WASTE YOUR TIME, WONDER WOMAN.
IF BLOODWYND HASN'T COME OVER TO OUR SIDE YET, THEN HE'S DEAD!
WHAT'S HAPPENED TO DREAM-SLAYER AND BLOODWYND?!
IT SEEMS AS THOUGH DREAMSLAYER HAS ABANDONED THE TOWER. WE MUST FREE BLOODWYND BEFORE HE... IT RETURNS!
10

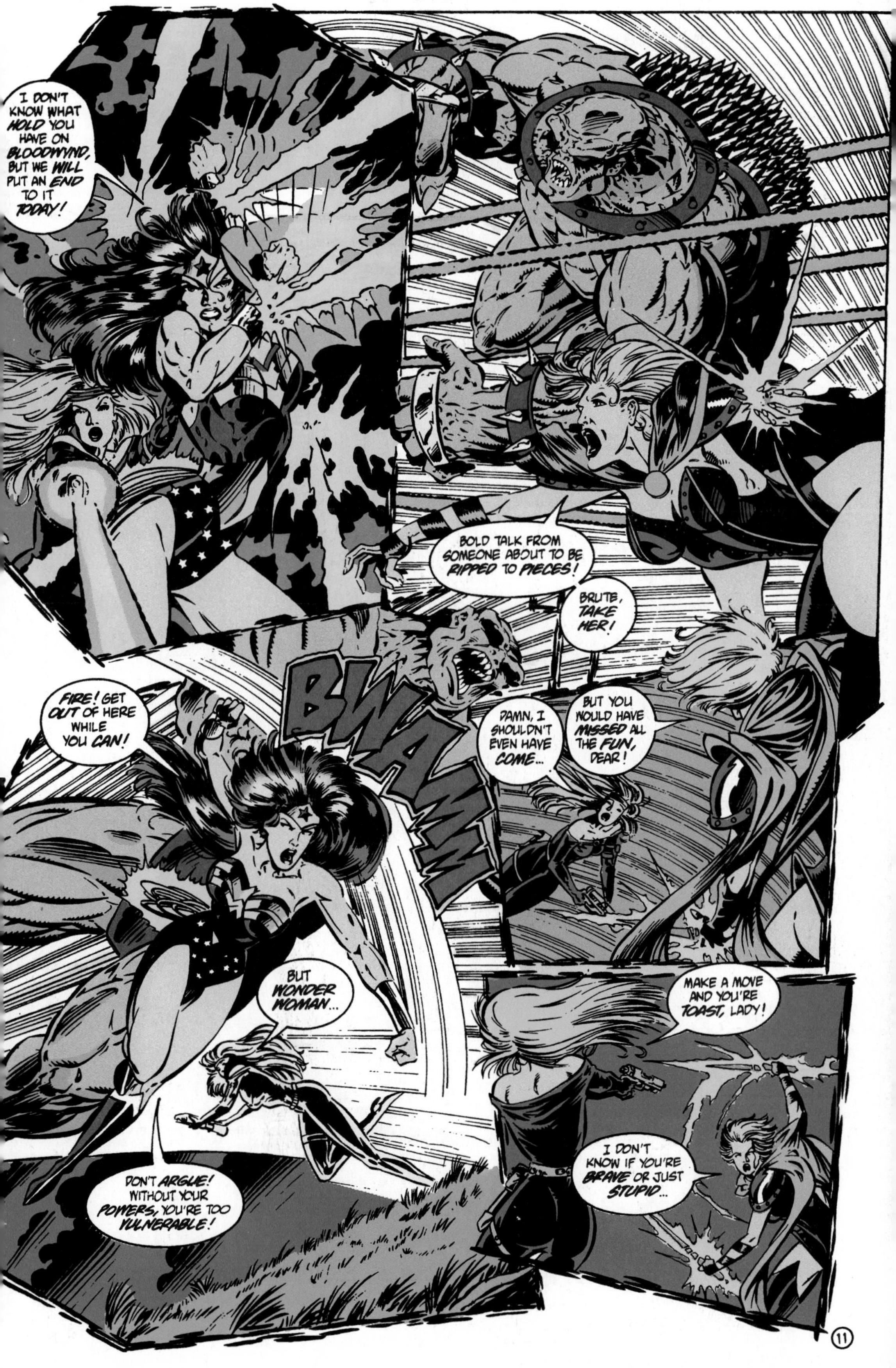

I DON'T KNOW WHAT HOLD YOU HAVE ON BLOODWYND, BUT WE WILL PUT AN END TO IT TODAY!
BOLD TALK FROM SOMEONE ABOUT TO BE RIPPED TO PIECES!
BRUTE, TAKE HER!
BWAAM
FIRE! GET OUT OF HERE WHILE YOU CAN!
DAMN, I SHOULDN'T EVEN HAVE COME...
BUT YOU WOULD HAVE MISSED ALL THE FUN, DEAR!
BUT WONDER WOMAN...
DON'T ARGUE! WITHOUT YOUR POWERS, YOU'RE TOO VULNERABLE!
MAKE A MOVE AND YOU'RE TOAST, LADY!
I DON'T KNOW IF YOU'RE BRAVE OR JUST STUPID...

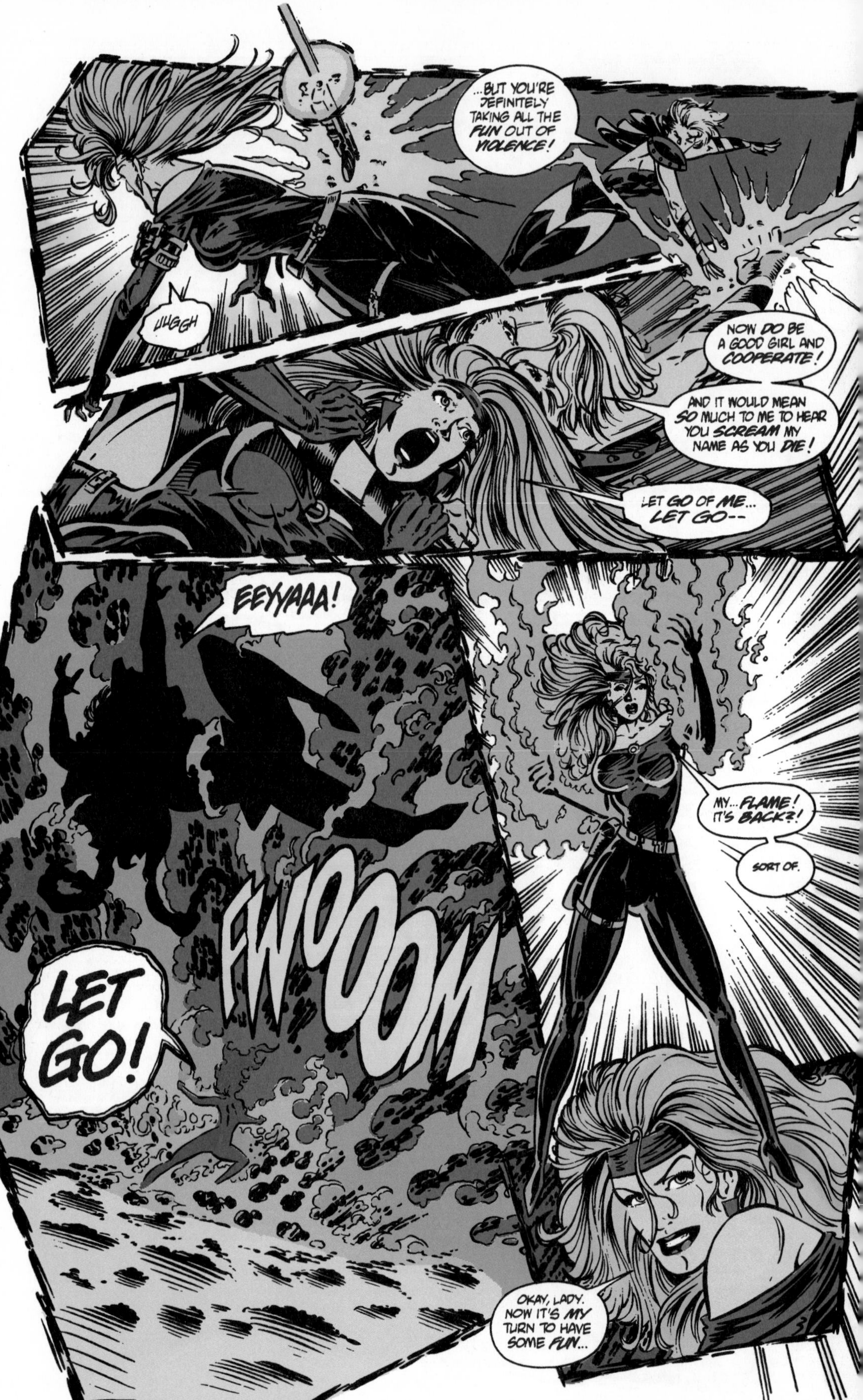
...BUT YOU'RE DEFINITELY TAKING ALL THE FUN OUT OF VIOLENCE!
UUGGH
NOW DO BE A GOOD GIRL AND COOPERATE!
AND IT WOULD MEAN SO MUCH TO ME TO HEAR YOU SCREAM MY NAME AS YOU DIE!
LET GO OF ME... LET GO--
EEYYAAA!
LET GO!
FWOOOM
MY... FLAME! IT'S BACK?!
SORT OF.
OKAY, LADY. NOW IT'S MY TURN TO HAVE SOME FUN...

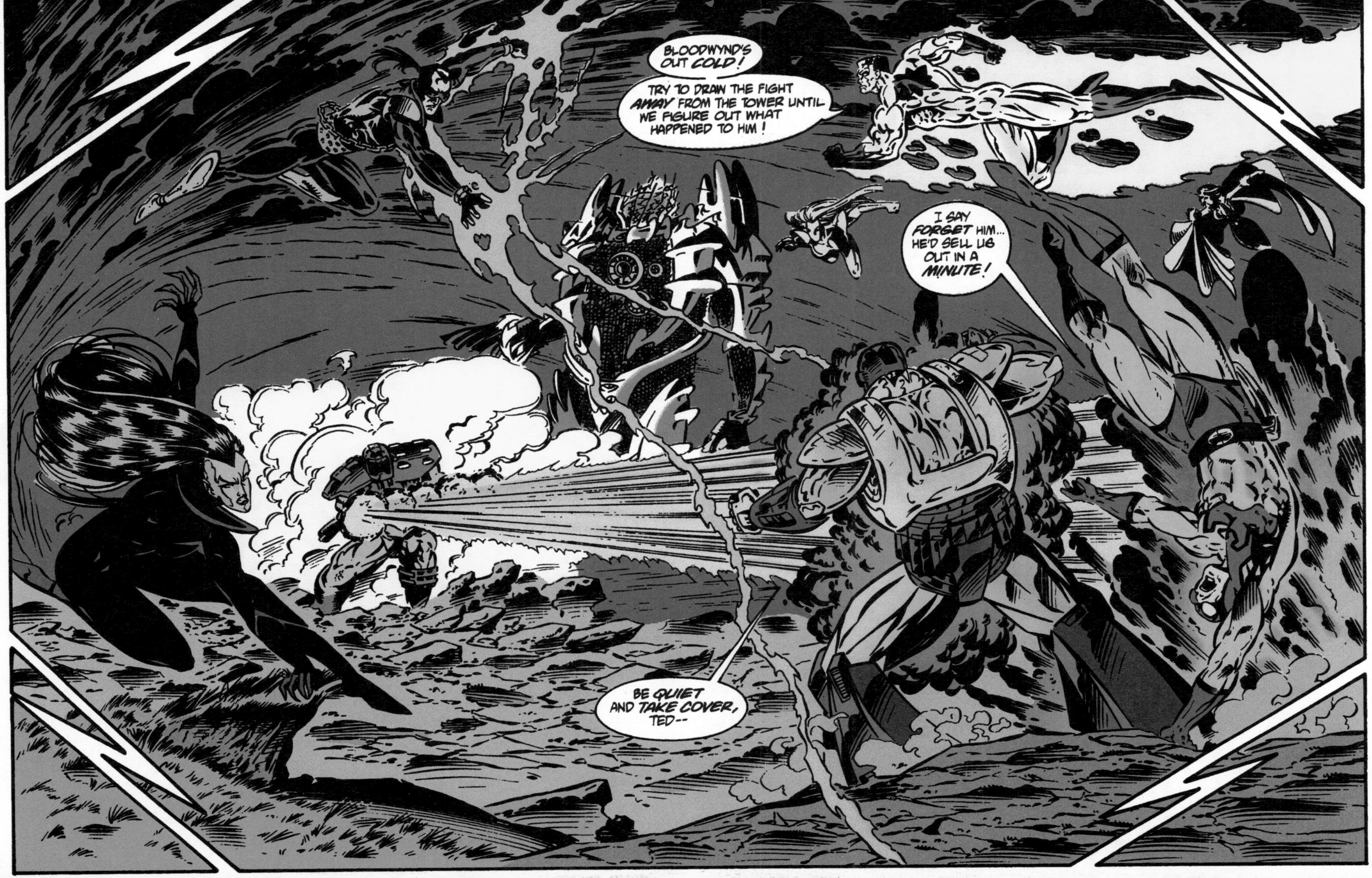
BLOODWYND'S OUT COLD!
TRY TO DRAW THE FIGHT AWAY FROM THE TOWER UNTIL WE FIGURE OUT WHAT HAPPENED TO HIM!
I SAY FORGET HIM... HE'D SELL US OUT IN A MINUTE!
BE QUIET AND TAKE COVER, TED--

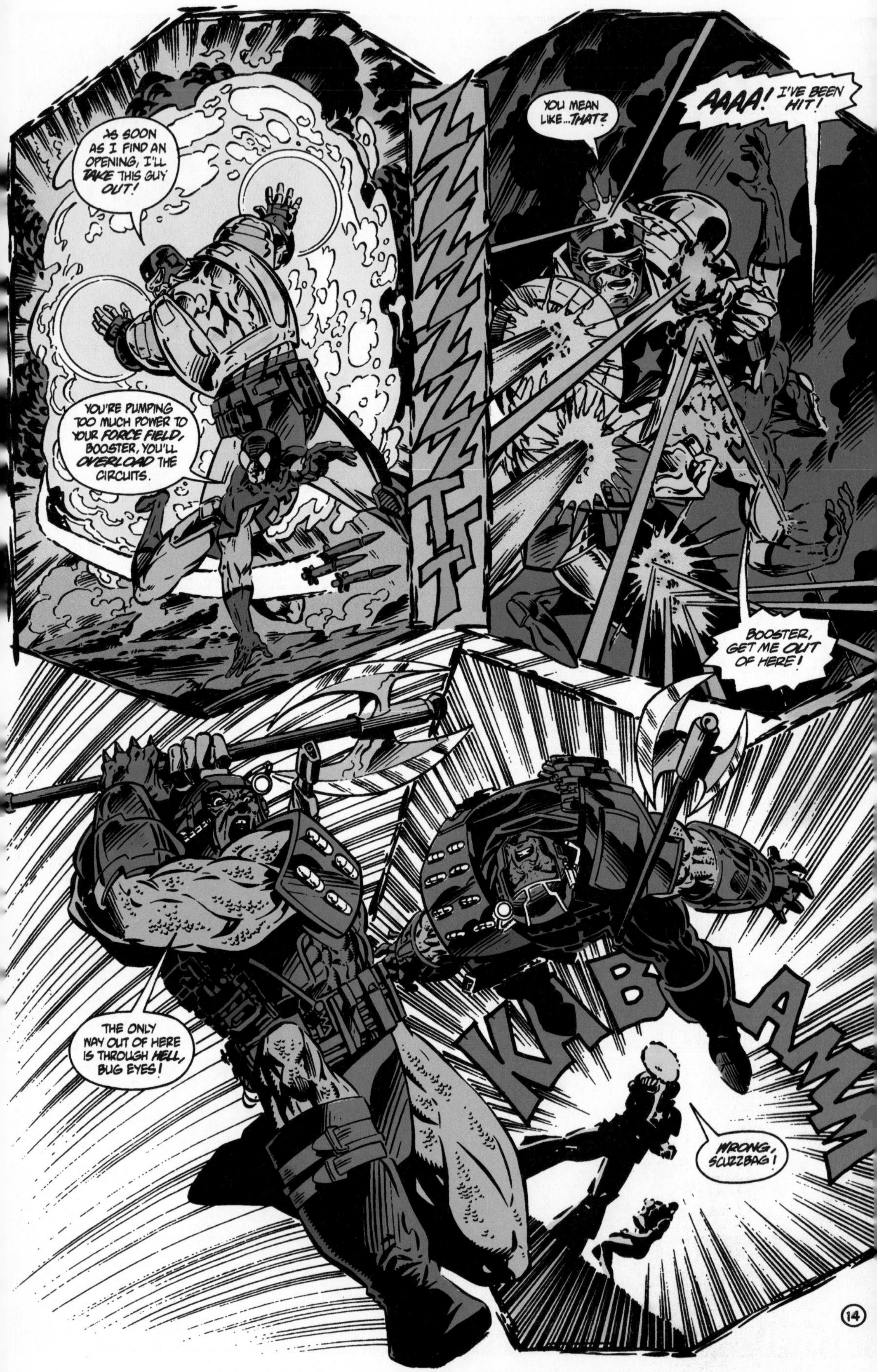
AS SOON AS I FIND AN OPENING, I'LL TAKE THIS GUY OUT!
YOU'RE PUMPING TOO MUCH POWER TO YOUR FORCE FIELD, BOOSTER. YOU'LL OVERLOAD THE CIRCUITS.
ZZZZZZZTTT
YOU MEAN LIKE...THAT?
AAAA! I'VE BEEN HIT!
BOOSTER, GET ME OUT OF HERE!
THE ONLY WAY OUT OF HERE IS THROUGH HELL, BUG EYES!
KABLAMM
WRONG, SCUZZBAG!

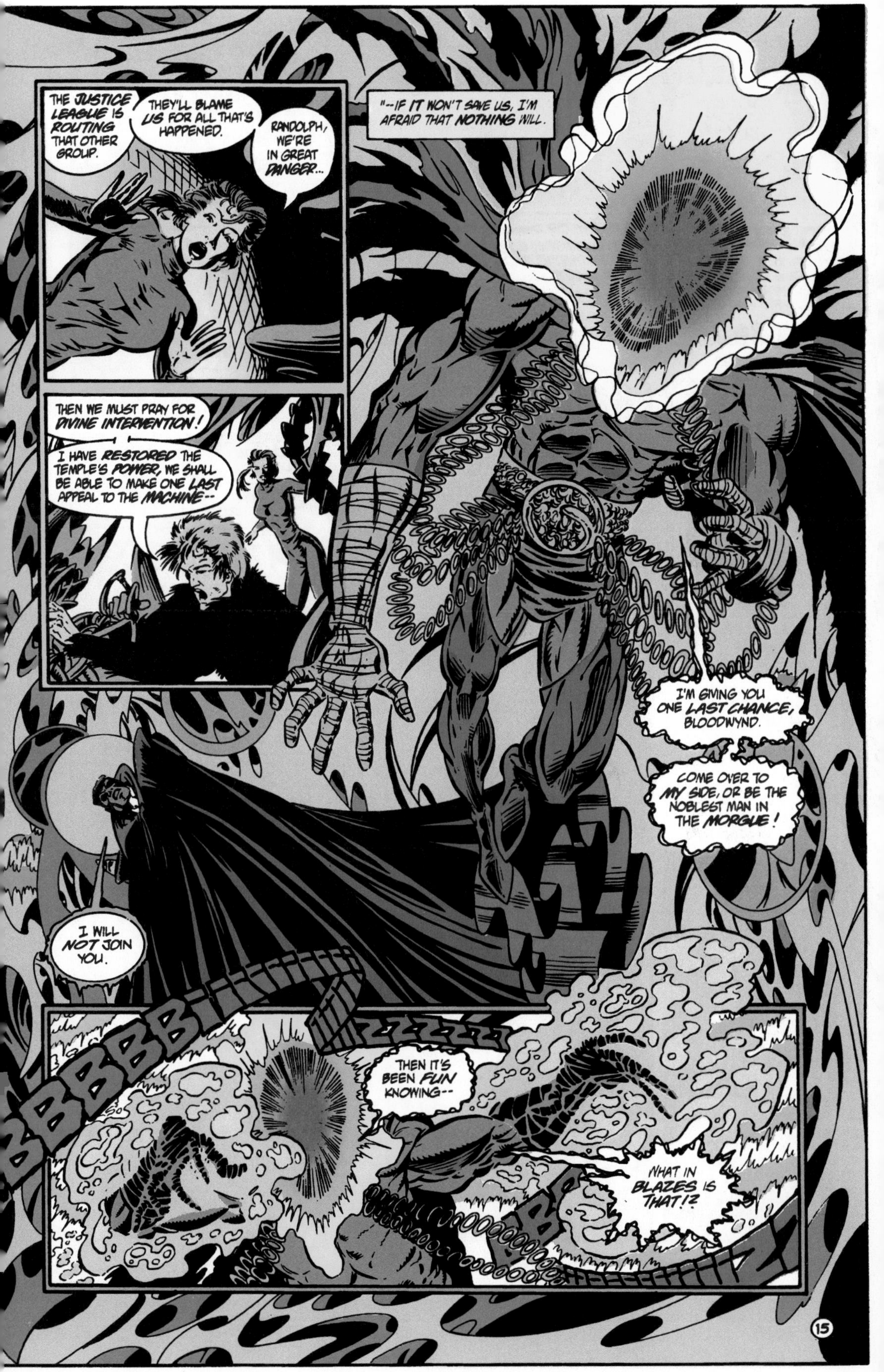

THE JUSTICE LEAGUE IS ROUTING THAT OTHER GROUP.
THEY'LL BLAME US FOR ALL THAT'S HAPPENED.
RANDOLPH, WE'RE IN GREAT DANGER...
"--IF IT WON'T SAVE US, I'M AFRAID THAT NOTHING WILL.
THEN WE MUST PRAY FOR DIVINE INTERVENTION!
I HAVE RESTORED THE TEMPLE'S POWER, WE SHALL BE ABLE TO MAKE ONE LAST APPEAL TO THE MACHINE--
I'M GIVING YOU ONE LAST CHANCE, BLOODWYND.
COME OVER TO MY SIDE, OR BE THE NOBLEST MAN IN THE MORGUE!
I WILL NOT JOIN YOU.
BBBBBZZZZZZZ
THEN IT'S BEEN FUN KNOWING--
WHAT IN BLAZES IS THAT!?

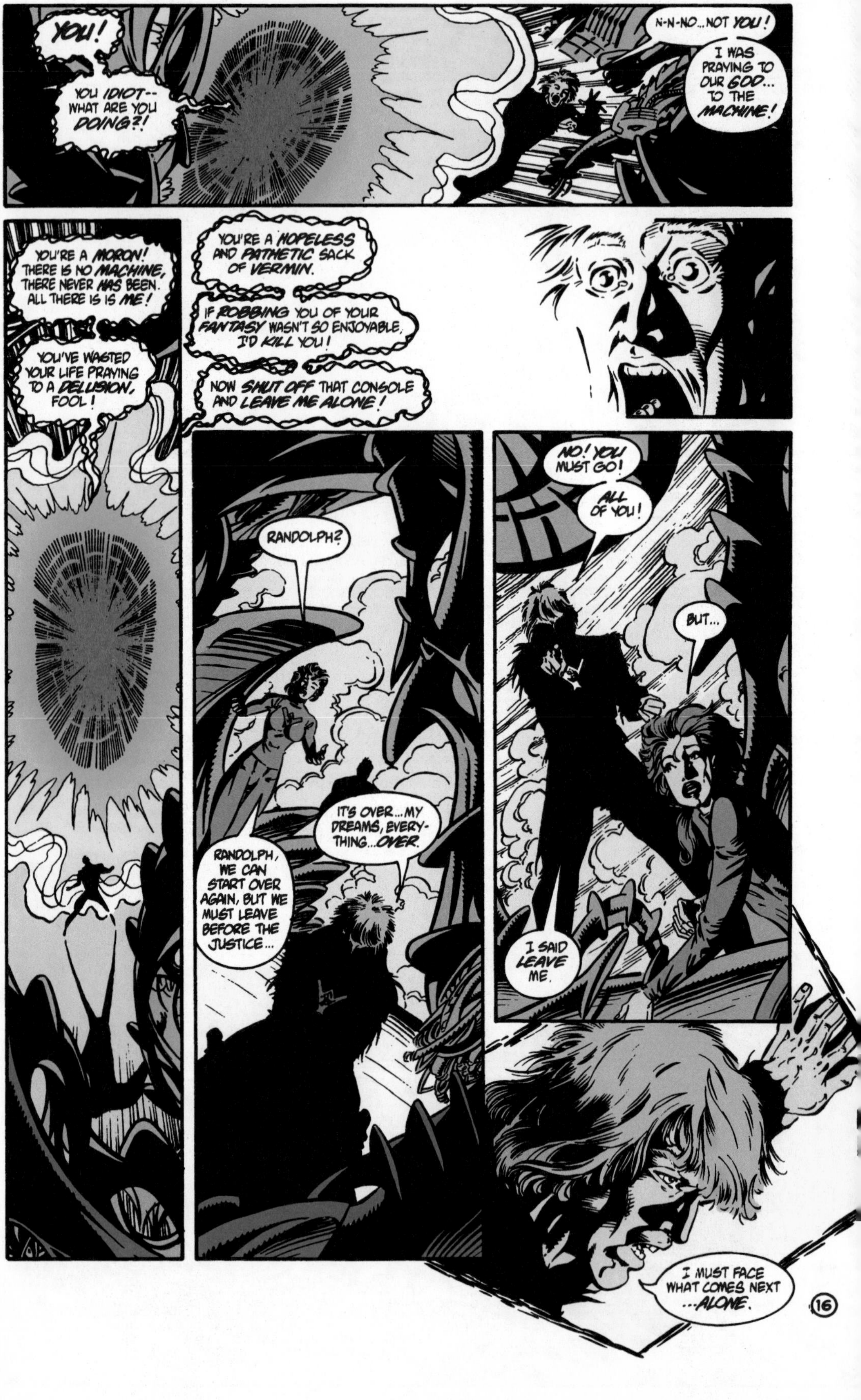
YOU!
YOU IDIOT-- WHAT ARE YOU DOING?!
N-N-NO...NOT YOU!
I WAS PRAYING TO OUR GOD... TO THE MACHINE!
YOU'RE A MORON! THERE IS NO MACHINE, THERE NEVER HAS BEEN. ALL THERE IS IS ME!
YOU'VE WASTED YOUR LIFE PRAYING TO A DELUSION, FOOL!
YOU'RE A HOPELESS AND PATHETIC SACK OF VERMIN.
IF ROBBING YOU OF YOUR FANTASY WASN'T SO ENJOYABLE, I'D KILL YOU!
NOW SHUT OFF THAT CONSOLE AND LEAVE ME ALONE!
RANDOLPH?
IT'S OVER...MY DREAMS, EVERYTHING...OVER.
RANDOLPH, WE CAN START OVER AGAIN, BUT WE MUST LEAVE BEFORE THE JUSTICE...
NO! YOU MUST GO!
ALL OF YOU!
BUT...
I SAID LEAVE ME.
I MUST FACE WHAT COMES NEXT ...ALONE.

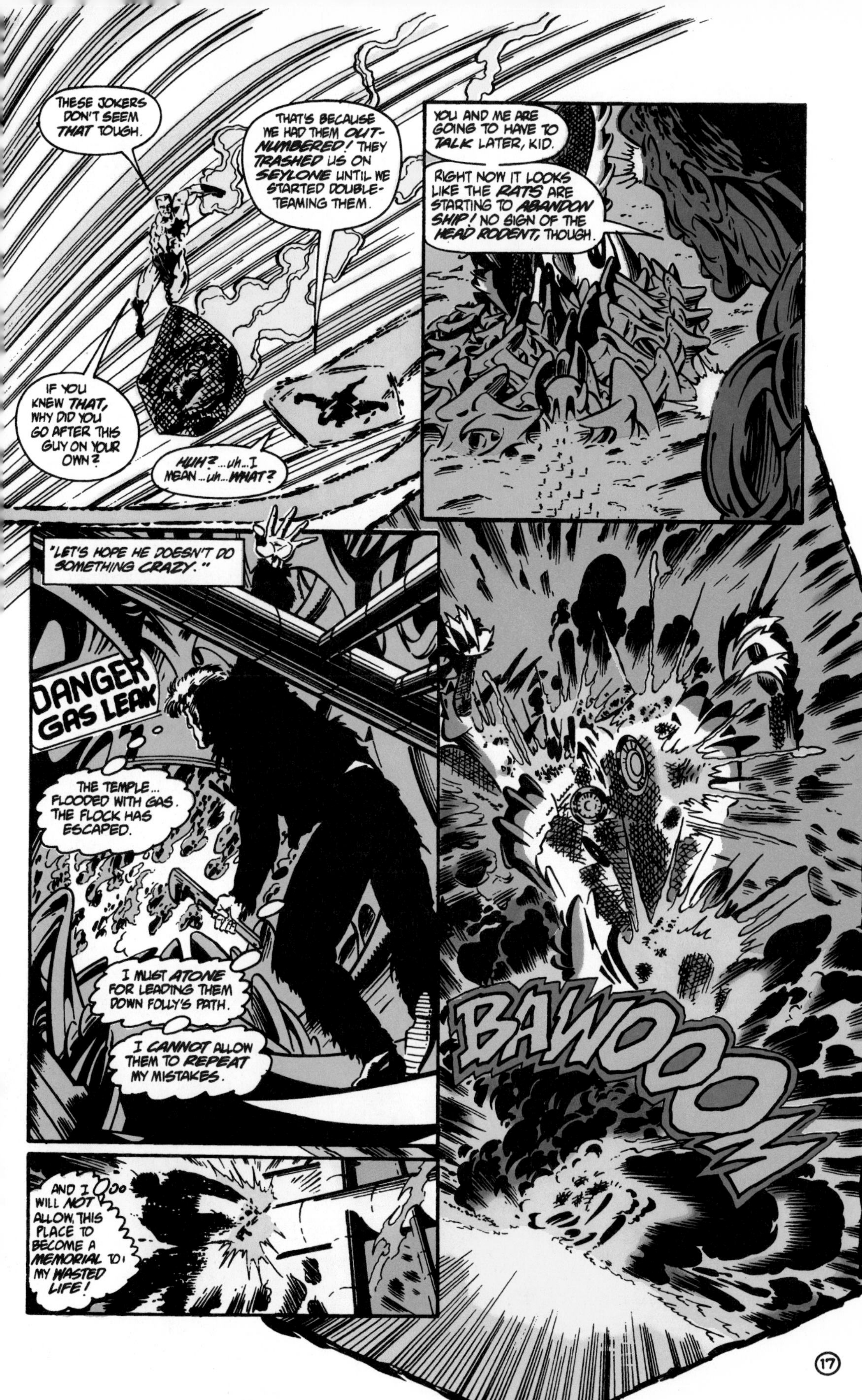

THESE JOKERS DON'T SEEM THAT TOUGH.
THAT'S BECAUSE WE HAD THEM OUT-NUMBERED! THEY TRASHED US ON SEYLONE UNTIL WE STARTED DOUBLE-TEAMING THEM.
IF YOU KNEW THAT, WHY DID YOU GO AFTER THIS GUY ON YOUR OWN?
HUH?...uh...I MEAN...uh...WHAT?
YOU AND ME ARE GOING TO HAVE TO TALK LATER, KID.
RIGHT NOW IT LOOKS LIKE THE RATS ARE STARTING TO ABANDON SHIP! NO SIGN OF THE HEAD RODENT, THOUGH.
"LET'S HOPE HE DOESN'T DO SOMETHING CRAZY."
DANGER GAS LEAK
THE TEMPLE... FLOODED WITH GAS. THE FLOCK HAS ESCAPED.
I MUST ATONE FOR LEADING THEM DOWN FOLLY'S PATH.
I CANNOT ALLOW THEM TO REPEAT MY MISTAKES.
AND I WILL NOT ALLOW THIS PLACE TO BECOME A MEMORIAL TO MY WASTED LIFE!
BAWOOOM

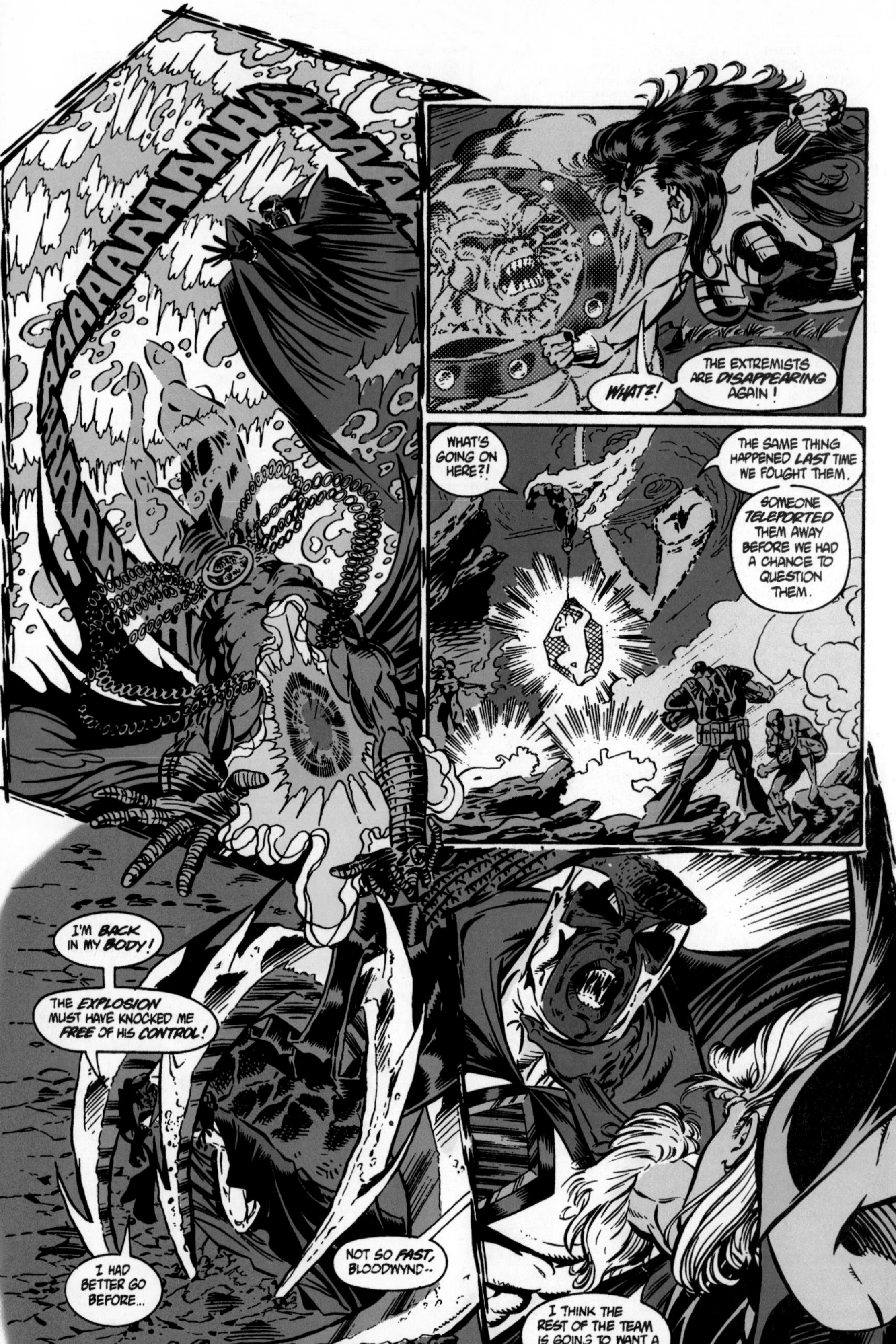

AAAAAAAAAAAAAAAAAAAAAAAAAAAAAAAAAAAAAAAAAAAAAAAAAAAAAAAAAAAAAAAAAAAAAAAAAAAAAAAAAAAAAAAAAAAAAAAAAAAAAAAAAAAAAAAAAAAAAAAAAAAAAAAA
THE EXTREMISTS ARE DISAPPEARING AGAIN!
WHAT?!
WHAT'S GOING ON HERE?!
THE SAME THING HAPPENED LAST TIME WE FOUGHT THEM.
SOMEONE TELEPORTED THEM AWAY BEFORE WE HAD A CHANCE TO QUESTION THEM.
I'M BACK IN MY BODY!
THE EXPLOSION MUST HAVE KNOCKED ME FREE OF HIS CONTROL!
I HAD BETTER GO BEFORE...
NOT SO FAST, BLOODWYND--
I THINK THE REST OF THE TEAM IS GOING TO WANT A WORD WITH YOU!

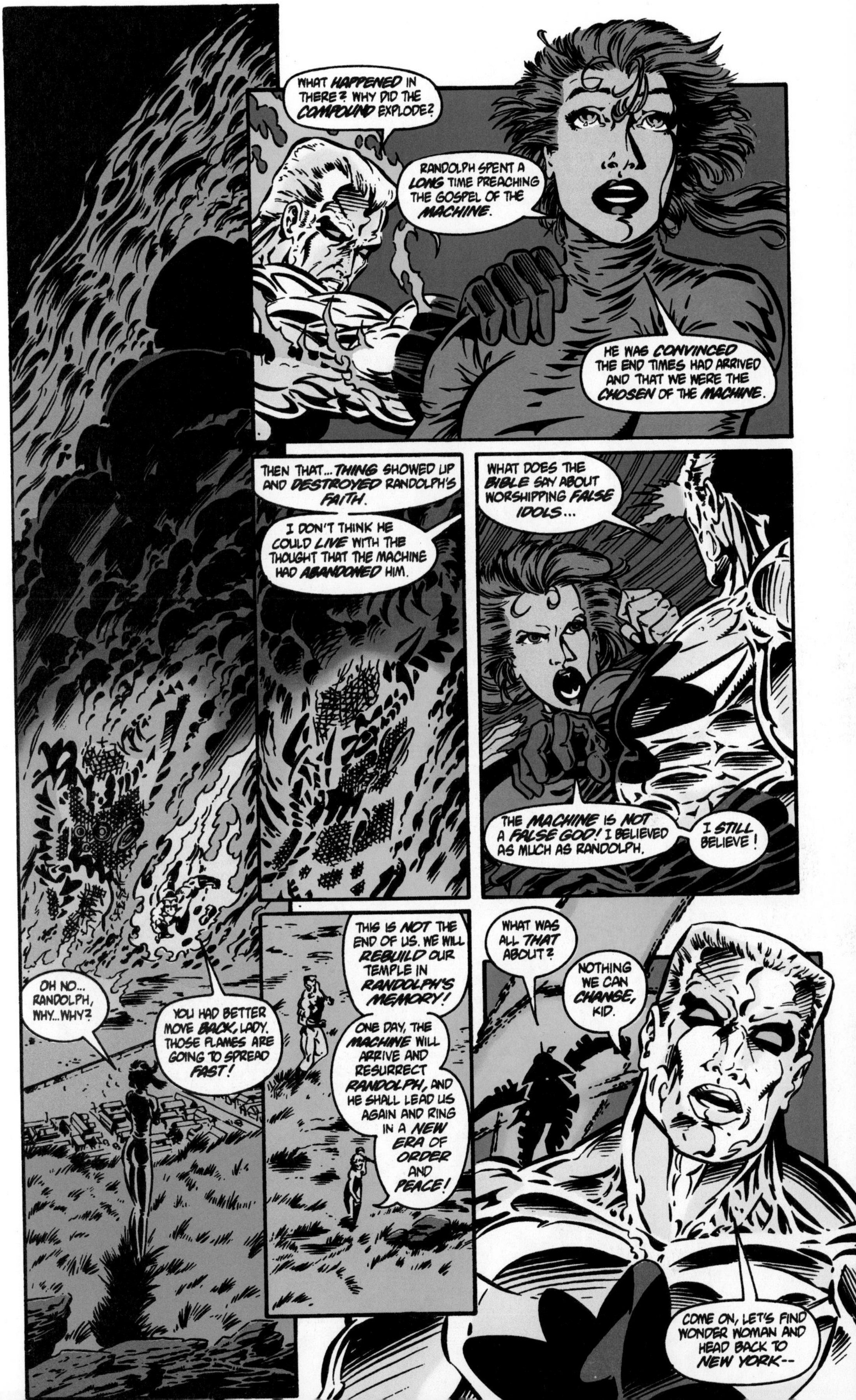

WHAT HAPPENED IN THERE? WHY DID THE COMPOUND EXPLODE?
RANDOLPH SPENT A LONG TIME PREACHING THE GOSPEL OF THE MACHINE.
HE WAS CONVINCED THE END TIMES HAD ARRIVED AND THAT WE WERE THE CHOSEN OF THE MACHINE.
THEN THAT... THING SHOWED UP AND DESTROYED RANDOLPH'S FAITH.
I DON'T THINK HE COULD LIVE WITH THE THOUGHT THAT THE MACHINE HAD ABANDONED HIM.
WHAT DOES THE BIBLE SAY ABOUT WORSHIPPING FALSE IDOLS...
THE MACHINE IS NOT A FALSE GOD! I BELIEVED AS MUCH AS RANDOLPH.
I STILL BELIEVE!
OH NO... RANDOLPH, WHY... WHY?
YOU HAD BETTER MOVE BACK, LADY. THOSE FLAMES ARE GOING TO SPREAD FAST!
THIS IS NOT THE END OF US. WE WILL REBUILD OUR TEMPLE IN RANDOLPH'S MEMORY!
ONE DAY, THE MACHINE WILL ARRIVE AND RESURRECT RANDOLPH, AND HE SHALL LEAD US AGAIN AND RING IN A NEW ERA OF ORDER AND PEACE!
WHAT WAS ALL THAT ABOUT?
NOTHING WE CAN CHANGE, KID.
COME ON, LET'S FIND WONDER WOMAN AND HEAD BACK TO NEW YORK--

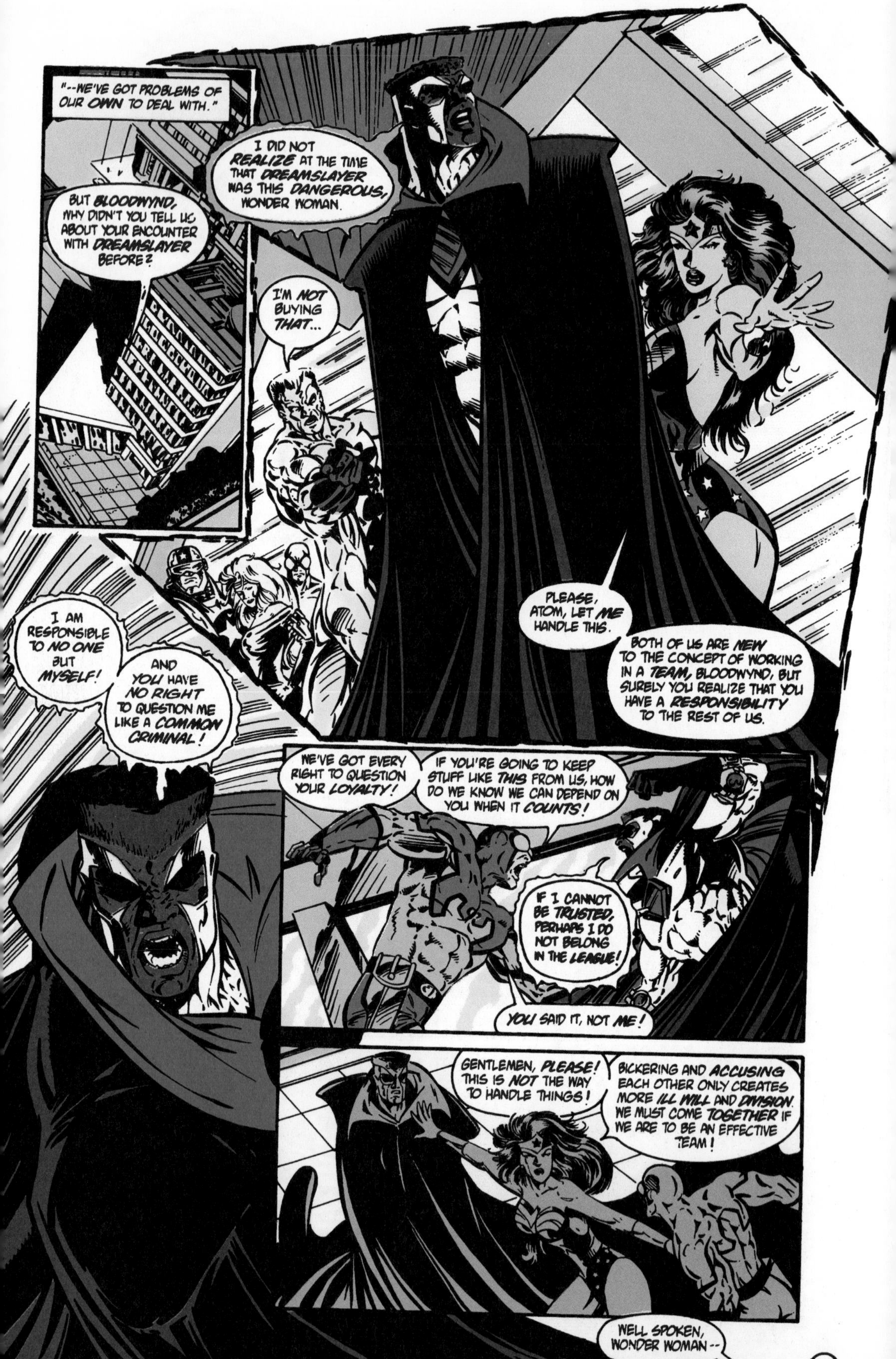
"--WE'VE GOT PROBLEMS OF OUR OWN TO DEAL WITH."
I DID NOT REALIZE AT THE TIME THAT DREAMSLAYER WAS THIS DANGEROUS, WONDER WOMAN.
BUT BLOODWYND, WHY DIDN'T YOU TELL US ABOUT YOUR ENCOUNTER WITH DREAMSLAYER BEFORE?
I'M NOT BUYING THAT...
PLEASE, ATOM, LET ME HANDLE THIS.
BOTH OF US ARE NEW TO THE CONCEPT OF WORKING IN A TEAM, BLOODWYND, BUT SURELY YOU REALIZE THAT YOU HAVE A RESPONSIBILITY TO THE REST OF US.
I AM RESPONSIBLE TO NO ONE BUT MYSELF!
AND YOU HAVE NO RIGHT TO QUESTION ME LIKE A COMMON CRIMINAL!
WE'VE GOT EVERY RIGHT TO QUESTION YOUR LOYALTY!
IF YOU'RE GOING TO KEEP STUFF LIKE THIS FROM US, HOW DO WE KNOW WE CAN DEPEND ON YOU WHEN IT COUNTS!
IF I CANNOT BE TRUSTED, PERHAPS I DO NOT BELONG IN THE LEAGUE!
YOU SAID IT, NOT ME!
GENTLEMEN, PLEASE! THIS IS NOT THE WAY TO HANDLE THINGS!
BICKERING AND ACCUSING EACH OTHER ONLY CREATES MORE ILL WILL AND DIVISION. WE MUST COME TOGETHER IF WE ARE TO BE AN EFFECTIVE TEAM!
WELL SPOKEN, WONDER WOMAN--

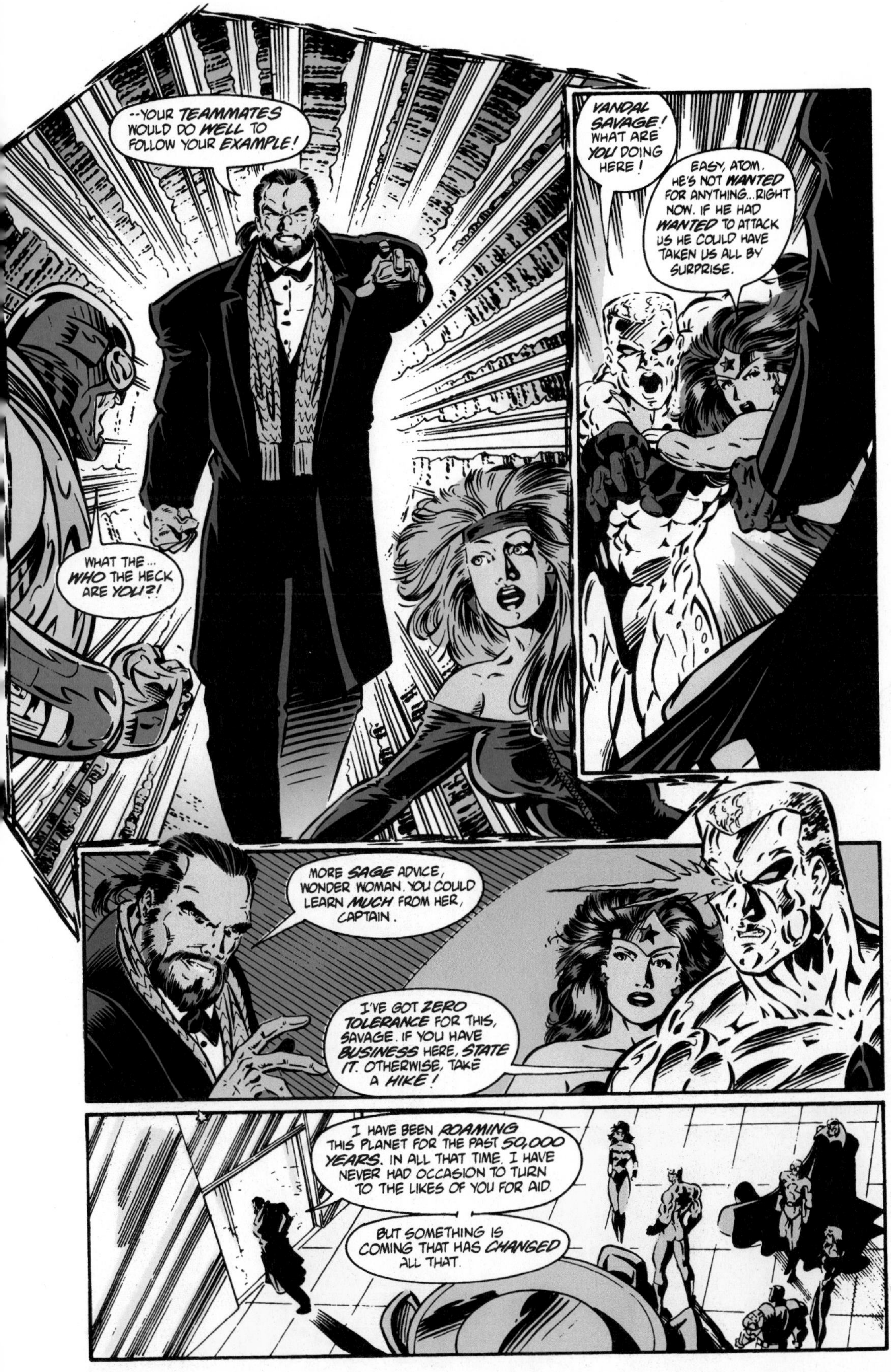
--YOUR TEAMMATES WOULD DO WELL TO FOLLOW YOUR EXAMPLE!
VANDAL SAVAGE! WHAT ARE YOU DOING HERE!
EASY, ATOM. HE'S NOT WANTED FOR ANYTHING...RIGHT NOW. IF HE HAD WANTED TO ATTACK US HE COULD HAVE TAKEN US ALL BY SURPRISE.
WHAT THE... WHO THE HECK ARE YOU?!
MORE SAGE ADVICE, WONDER WOMAN. YOU COULD LEARN MUCH FROM HER, CAPTAIN.
I'VE GOT ZERO TOLERANCE FOR THIS, SAVAGE. IF YOU HAVE BUSINESS HERE, STATE IT. OTHERWISE, TAKE A HIKE!
I HAVE BEEN ROAMING THIS PLANET FOR THE PAST 50,000 YEARS. IN ALL THAT TIME, I HAVE NEVER HAD OCCASION TO TURN TO THE LIKES OF YOU FOR AID.
BUT SOMETHING IS COMING THAT HAS CHANGED ALL THAT.

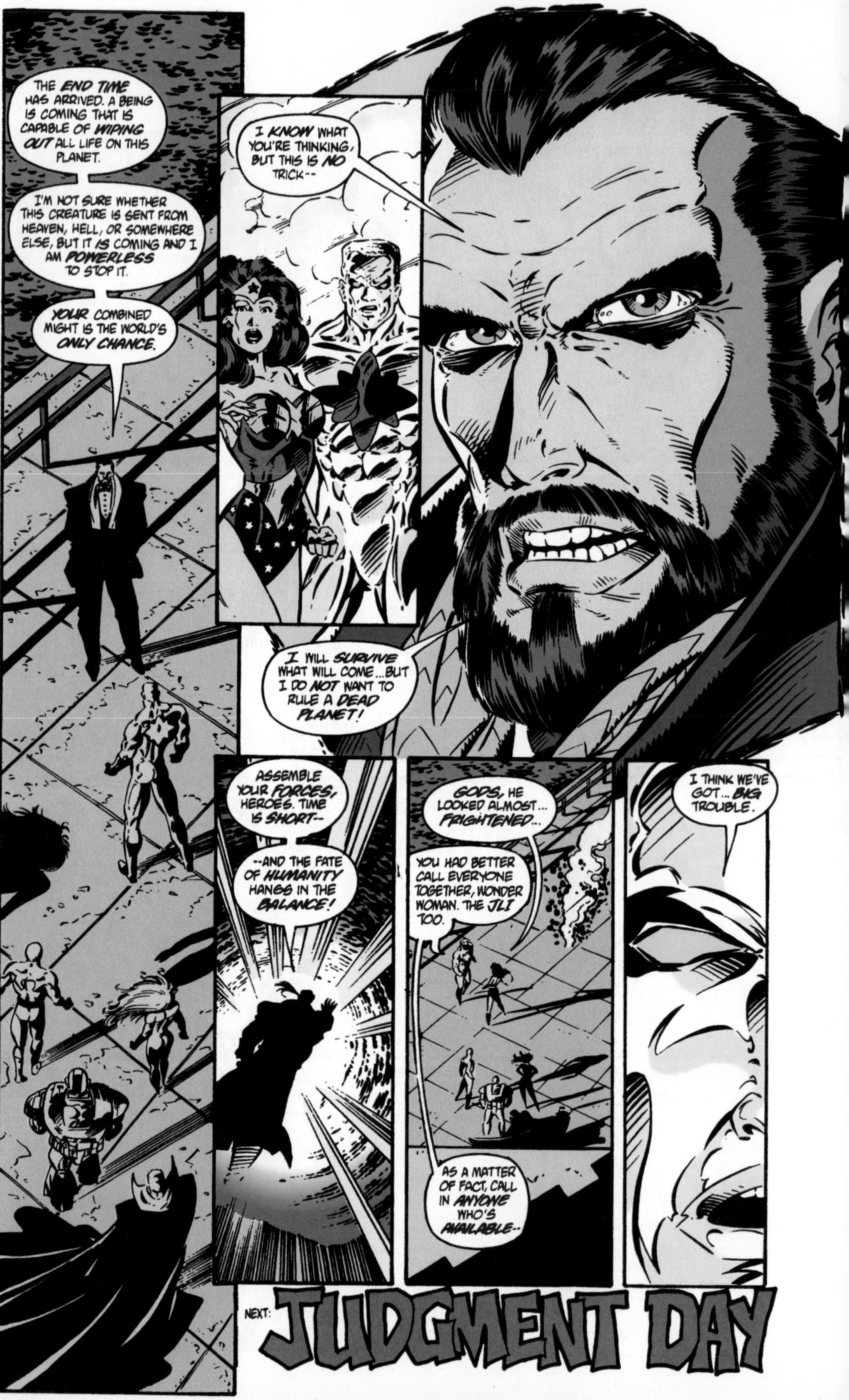
THE END TIME HAS ARRIVED. A BEING IS COMING THAT IS CAPABLE OF WIPING OUT ALL LIFE ON THIS PLANET.
I'M NOT SURE WHETHER THIS CREATURE IS SENT FROM HEAVEN, HELL, OR SOMEWHERE ELSE, BUT IT IS COMING AND I AM POWERLESS TO STOP IT.
YOUR COMBINED MIGHT IS THE WORLD'S ONLY CHANCE.
I KNOW WHAT YOU'RE THINKING, BUT THIS IS NO TRICK--
I WILL SURVIVE WHAT WILL COME...BUT I DO NOT WANT TO RULE A DEAD PLANET!
ASSEMBLE YOUR FORCES, HEROES. TIME IS SHORT--
--AND THE FATE OF HUMANITY HANGS IN THE BALANCE!
GODS, HE LOOKED ALMOST... FRIGHTENED...
YOU HAD BETTER CALL EVERYONE TOGETHER, WONDER WOMAN. THE JLI TOO.
AS A MATTER OF FACT, CALL IN ANYONE WHO'S AVAILABLE..
I THINK WE'VE GOT... BIG TROUBLE.
NEXT: JUDGMENT DAY

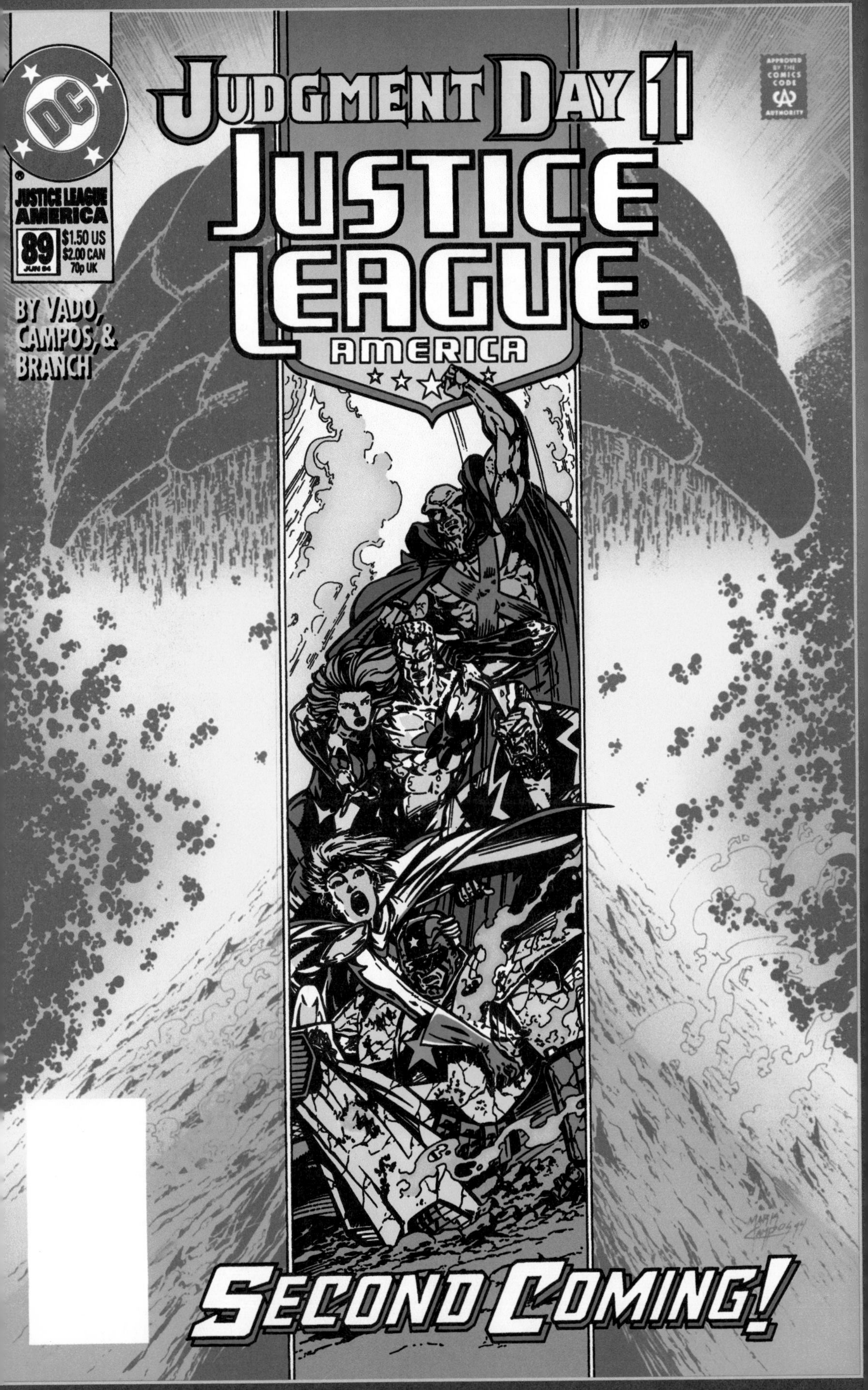
JUDGMENT DAY 1
JUSTICE LEAGUE AMERICA
JUSTICE LEAGUE AMERICA
89
JUN 94
$1.50 US
$2.00 CAN
70p UK
APPROVED BY THE COMICS CODE AUTHORITY
BY VADO, CAMPOS, & BRANCH
SECOND COMING!

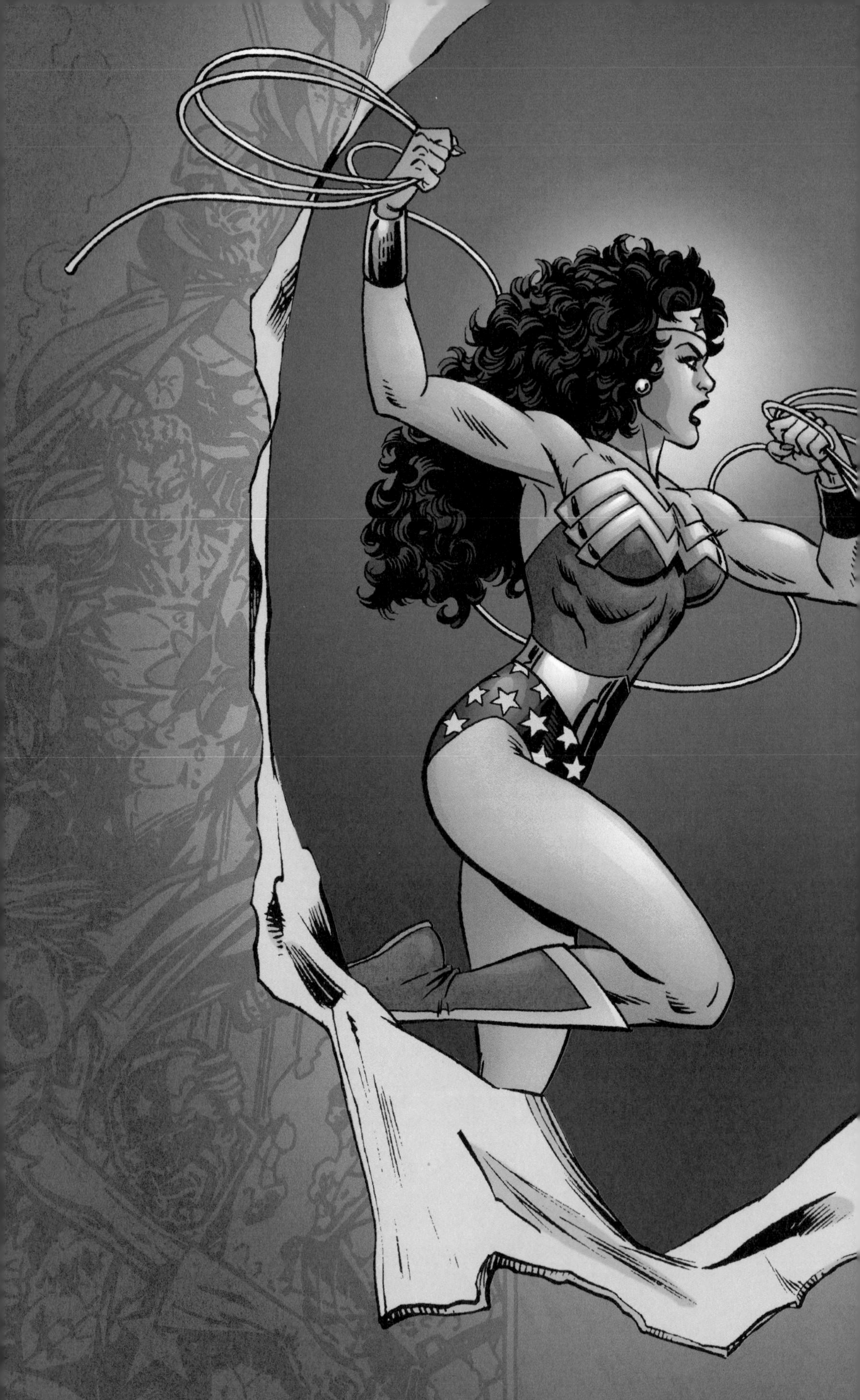

Cover art by **MARC CAMPOS**

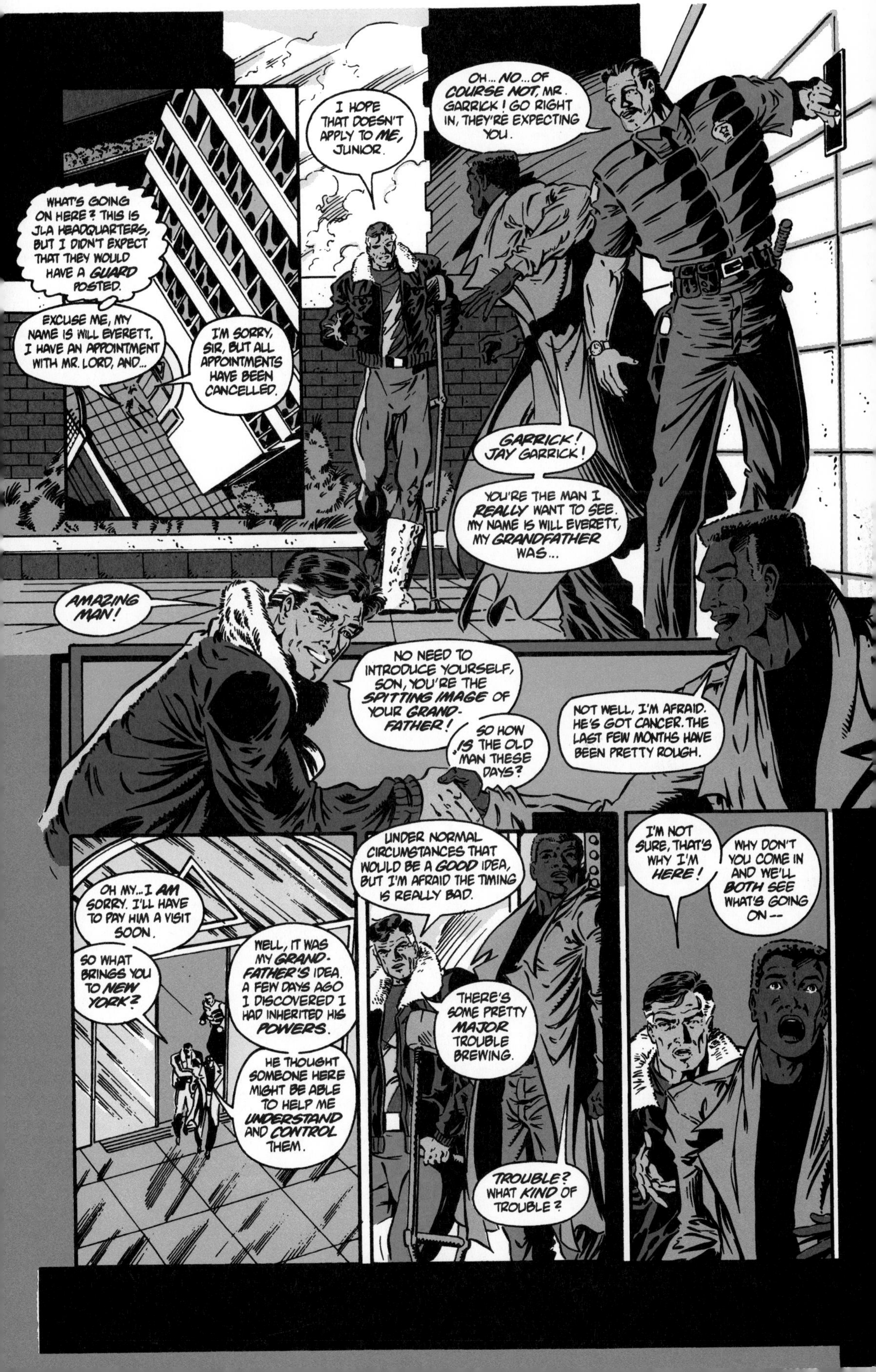
WHAT'S GOING ON HERE? THIS IS JLA HEADQUARTERS, BUT I DIDN'T EXPECT THAT THEY WOULD HAVE A GUARD POSTED.
EXCUSE ME, MY NAME IS WILL EVERETT. I HAVE AN APPOINTMENT WITH MR. LORD, AND...
I'M SORRY, SIR, BUT ALL APPOINTMENTS HAVE BEEN CANCELLED.
I HOPE THAT DOESN'T APPLY TO ME, JUNIOR.
OH... NO... OF COURSE NOT, MR. GARRICK! GO RIGHT IN, THEY'RE EXPECTING YOU.
GARRICK! JAY GARRICK!
YOU'RE THE MAN I REALLY WANT TO SEE. MY NAME IS WILL EVERETT, MY GRANDFATHER WAS...
AMAZING MAN!
NO NEED TO INTRODUCE YOURSELF, SON, YOU'RE THE SPITTING IMAGE OF YOUR GRANDFATHER!
SO HOW IS THE OLD MAN THESE DAYS?
NOT WELL, I'M AFRAID. HE'S GOT CANCER. THE LAST FEW MONTHS HAVE BEEN PRETTY ROUGH.
OH MY... I AM SORRY. I'LL HAVE TO PAY HIM A VISIT SOON.
SO WHAT BRINGS YOU TO NEW YORK?
WELL, IT WAS MY GRANDFATHER'S IDEA. A FEW DAYS AGO I DISCOVERED I HAD INHERITED HIS POWERS.
HE THOUGHT SOMEONE HERE MIGHT BE ABLE TO HELP ME UNDERSTAND AND CONTROL THEM.
UNDER NORMAL CIRCUMSTANCES THAT WOULD BE A GOOD IDEA, BUT I'M AFRAID THE TIMING IS REALLY BAD.
THERE'S SOME PRETTY MAJOR TROUBLE BREWING.
TROUBLE? WHAT KIND OF TROUBLE?
I'M NOT SURE, THAT'S WHY I'M HERE!
WHY DON'T YOU COME IN AND WE'LL BOTH SEE WHAT'S GOING ON--

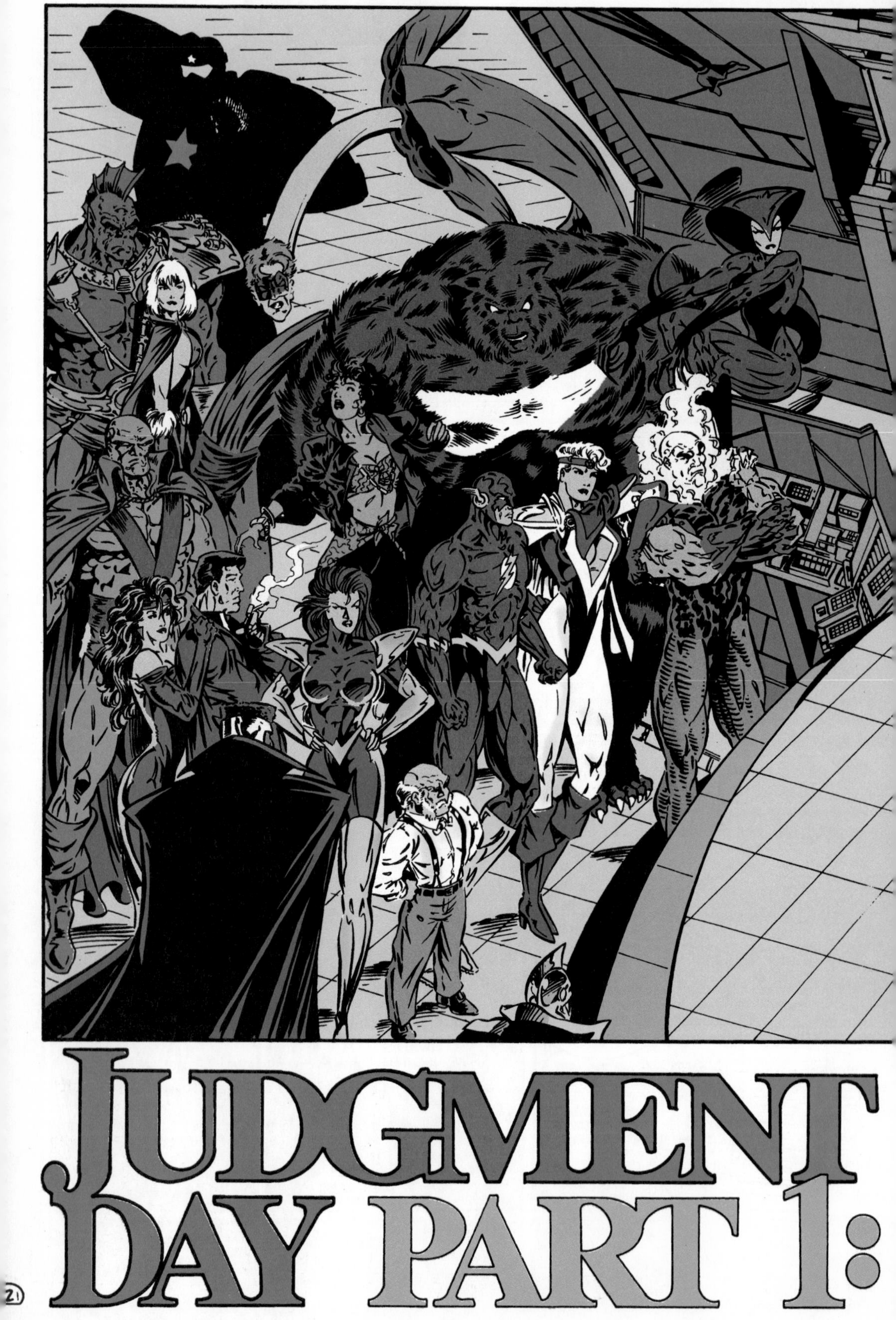

JUDGMENT DAY PART 1:

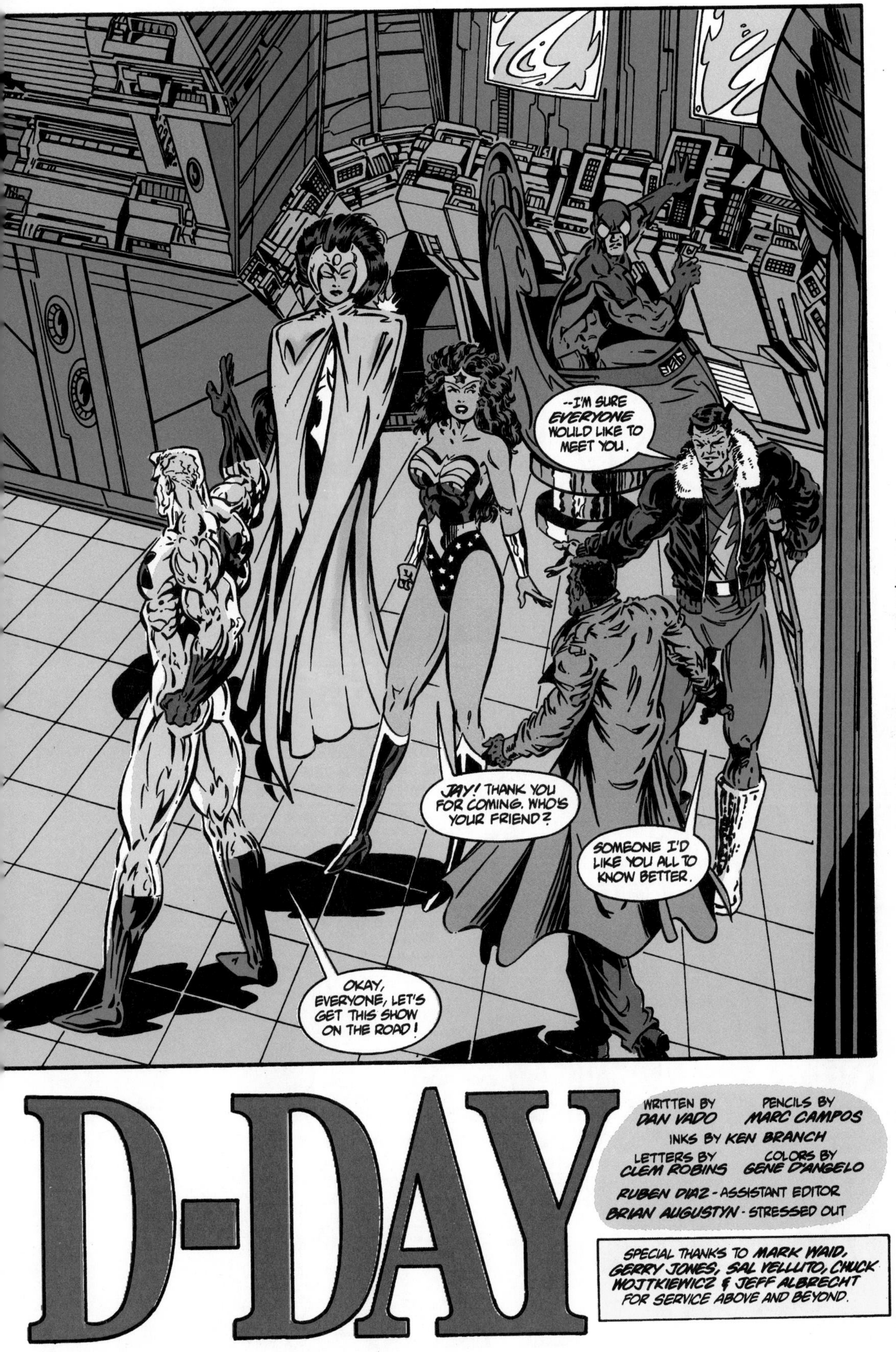
JAY! THANK YOU FOR COMING. WHO'S YOUR FRIEND?
SOMEONE I'D LIKE YOU ALL TO KNOW BETTER.
--I'M SURE EVERYONE WOULD LIKE TO MEET YOU.
OKAY, EVERYONE, LET'S GET THIS SHOW ON THE ROAD!

D-DAY

WRITTEN BY DAN VADO
PENCILS BY MARC CAMPOS
INKS BY KEN BRANCH
LETTERS BY CLEM ROBINS
COLORS BY GENE D'ANGELO
RUBEN DIAZ - ASSISTANT EDITOR
BRIAN AUGUSTYN - STRESSED OUT

SPECIAL THANKS TO MARK WAID, GERRY JONES, SAL VELLUTO, CHUCK WOJTKIEWICZ & JEFF ALBRECHT FOR SERVICE ABOVE AND BEYOND.

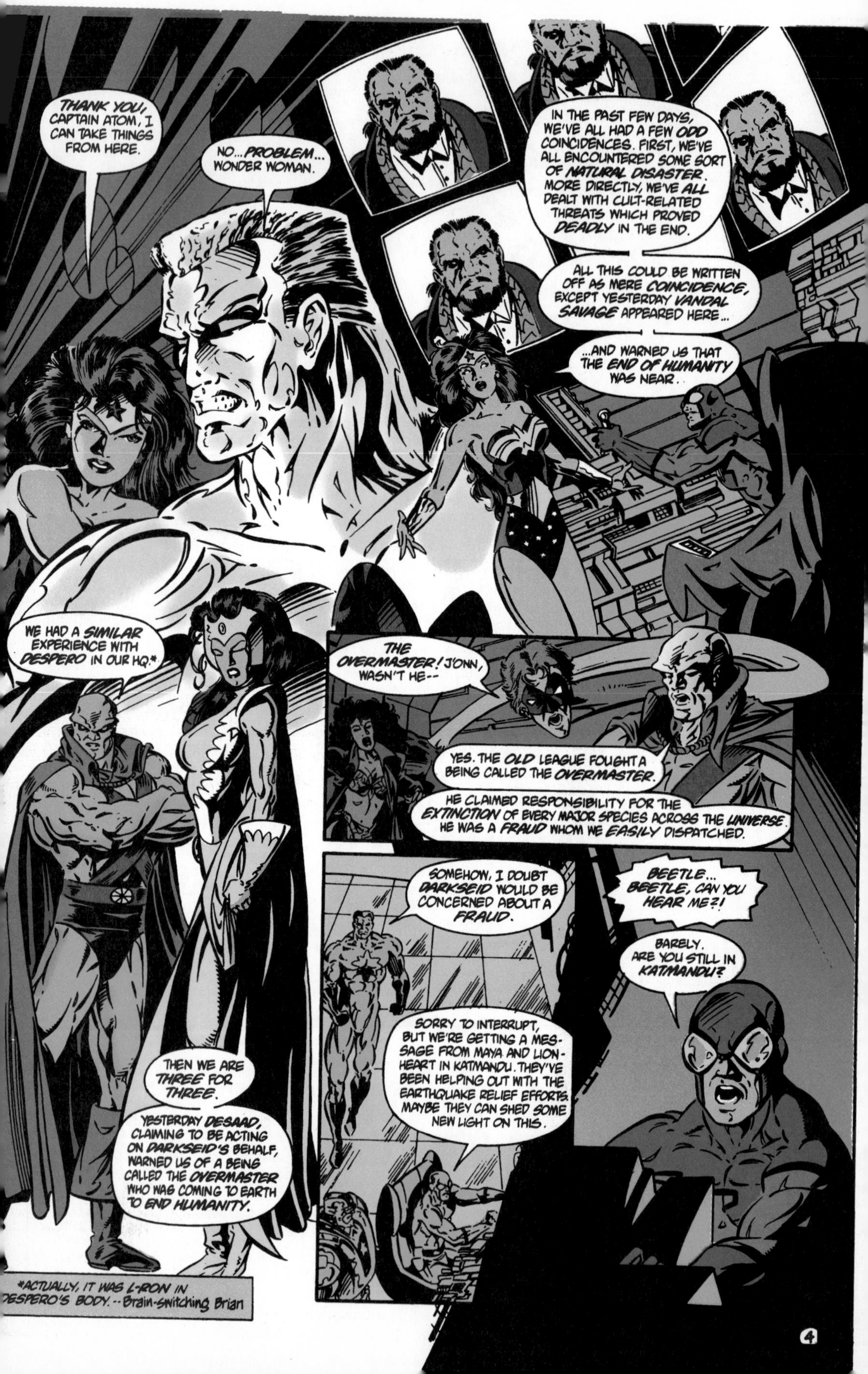
THANK YOU, CAPTAIN ATOM, I CAN TAKE THINGS FROM HERE.
NO... PROBLEM... WONDER WOMAN.
IN THE PAST FEW DAYS, WE'VE ALL HAD A FEW ODD COINCIDENCES. FIRST, WE'VE ALL ENCOUNTERED SOME SORT OF NATURAL DISASTER. MORE DIRECTLY, WE'VE ALL DEALT WITH CULT-RELATED THREATS WHICH PROVED DEADLY IN THE END.
ALL THIS COULD BE WRITTEN OFF AS MERE COINCIDENCE, EXCEPT YESTERDAY VANDAL SAVAGE APPEARED HERE...
...AND WARNED US THAT THE END OF HUMANITY WAS NEAR.
WE HAD A SIMILAR EXPERIENCE WITH DESPERO IN OUR HQ.*
THEN WE ARE THREE FOR THREE.
YESTERDAY DESAAD, CLAIMING TO BE ACTING ON DARKSEID'S BEHALF, WARNED US OF A BEING CALLED THE OVERMASTER WHO WAS COMING TO EARTH TO END HUMANITY.
THE OVERMASTER! J'ONN, WASN'T HE--
YES. THE OLD LEAGUE FOUGHT A BEING CALLED THE OVERMASTER.
HE CLAIMED RESPONSIBILITY FOR THE EXTINCTION OF EVERY MAJOR SPECIES ACROSS THE UNIVERSE. HE WAS A FRAUD WHOM WE EASILY DISPATCHED.
SOMEHOW, I DOUBT DARKSEID WOULD BE CONCERNED ABOUT A FRAUD.
SORRY TO INTERRUPT, BUT WE'RE GETTING A MES-SAGE FROM MAYA AND LION-HEART IN KATMANDU. THEY'VE BEEN HELPING OUT WITH THE EARTHQUAKE RELIEF EFFORTS. MAYBE THEY CAN SHED SOME NEW LIGHT ON THIS.
BEETLE... BEETLE, CAN YOU HEAR ME?!
BARELY. ARE YOU STILL IN KATMANDU?
*ACTUALLY, IT WAS L-RON IN DESPERO'S BODY. --Brain-switching Brian

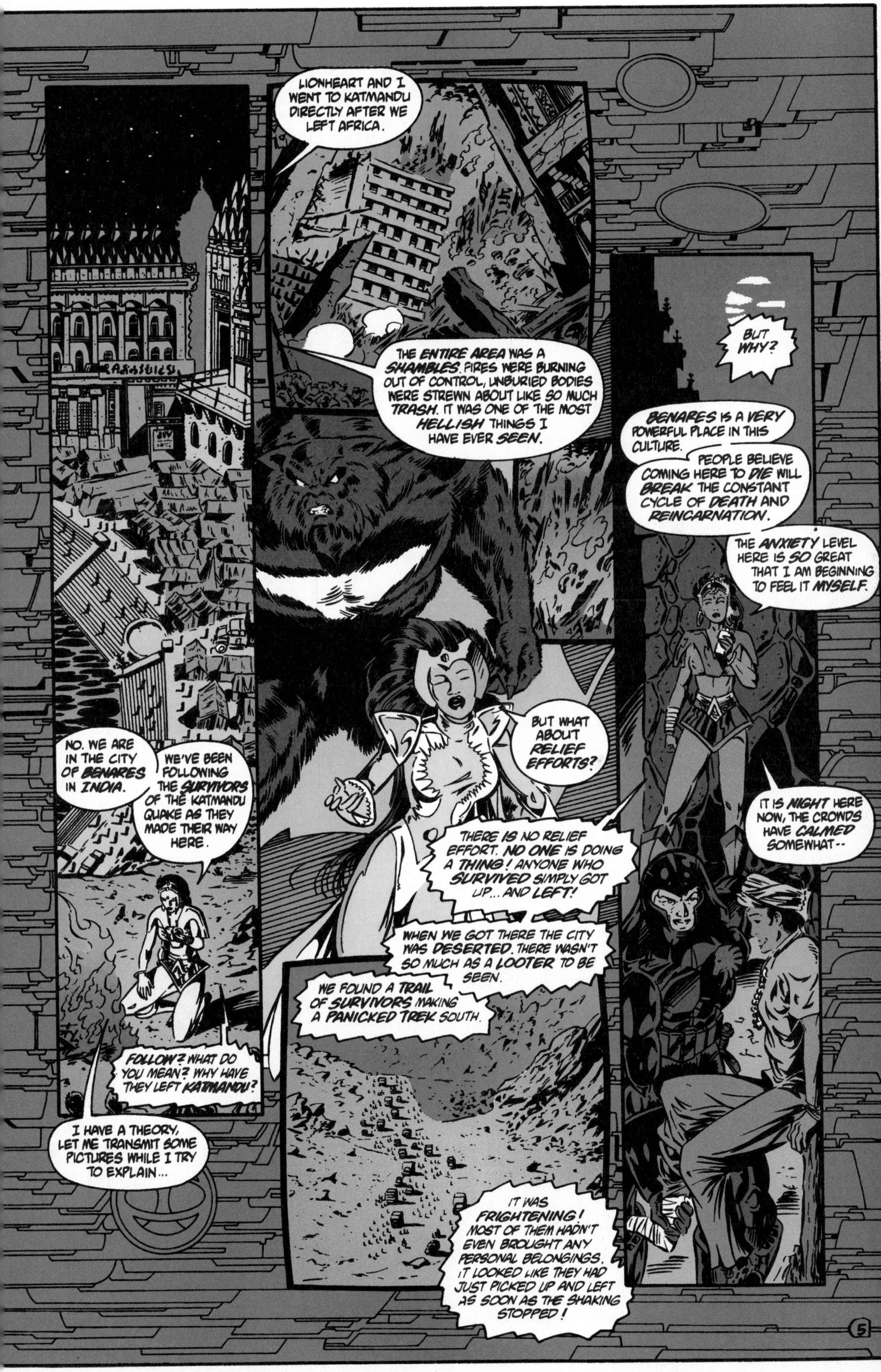
LIONHEART AND I WENT TO KATMANDU DIRECTLY AFTER WE LEFT AFRICA.
THE ENTIRE AREA WAS A SHAMBLES. FIRES WERE BURNING OUT OF CONTROL, UNBURIED BODIES WERE STREWN ABOUT LIKE SO MUCH TRASH. IT WAS ONE OF THE MOST HELLISH THINGS I HAVE EVER SEEN.
BUT WHAT ABOUT RELIEF EFFORTS?
THERE IS NO RELIEF EFFORT. NO ONE IS DOING A THING! ANYONE WHO SURVIVED SIMPLY GOT UP... AND LEFT!
WHEN WE GOT THERE THE CITY WAS DESERTED. THERE WASN'T SO MUCH AS A LOOTER TO BE SEEN.
WE FOUND A TRAIL OF SURVIVORS MAKING A PANICKED TREK SOUTH.
IT WAS FRIGHTENING! MOST OF THEM HADN'T EVEN BROUGHT ANY PERSONAL BELONGINGS. IT LOOKED LIKE THEY HAD JUST PICKED UP AND LEFT AS SOON AS THE SHAKING STOPPED!
NO. WE ARE IN THE CITY OF BENARES IN INDIA.
WE'VE BEEN FOLLOWING THE SURVIVORS OF THE KATMANDU QUAKE AS THEY MADE THEIR WAY HERE.
FOLLOW? WHAT DO YOU MEAN? WHY HAVE THEY LEFT KATMANDU?
I HAVE A THEORY, LET ME TRANSMIT SOME PICTURES WHILE I TRY TO EXPLAIN...
BUT WHY?
BENARES IS A VERY POWERFUL PLACE IN THIS CULTURE.
PEOPLE BELIEVE COMING HERE TO DIE WILL BREAK THE CONSTANT CYCLE OF DEATH AND REINCARNATION.
THE ANXIETY LEVEL HERE IS SO GREAT THAT I AM BEGINNING TO FEEL IT MYSELF.
IT IS NIGHT HERE NOW, THE CROWDS HAVE CALMED SOMEWHAT--

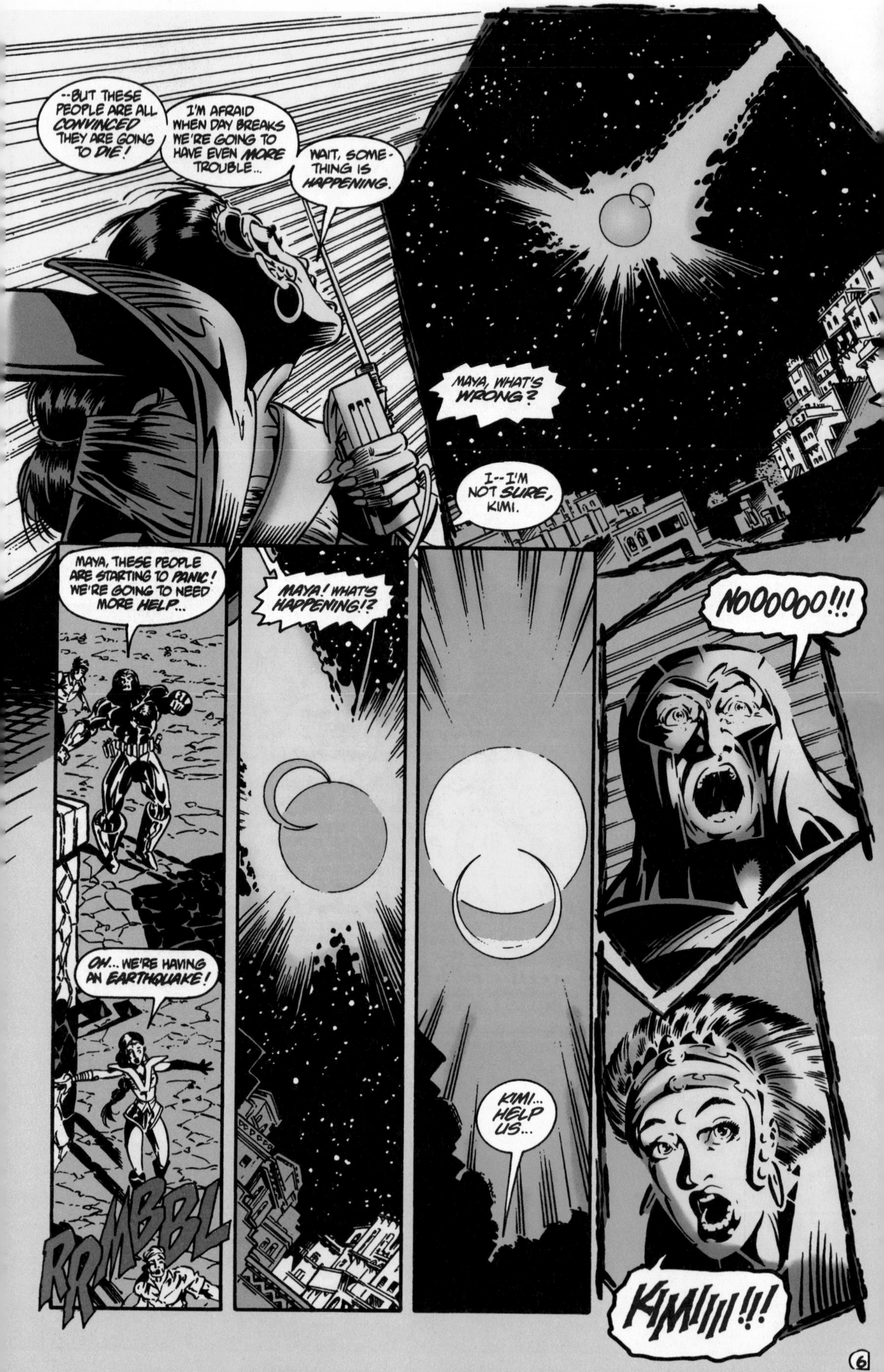
--BUT THESE PEOPLE ARE ALL CONVINCED THEY ARE GOING TO DIE!
I'M AFRAID WHEN DAY BREAKS WE'RE GOING TO HAVE EVEN MORE TROUBLE...
WAIT, SOMETHING IS HAPPENING.
MAYA, WHAT'S WRONG?
I--I'M NOT SURE, KIMI.
MAYA, THESE PEOPLE ARE STARTING TO PANIC! WE'RE GOING TO NEED MORE HELP...
OH... WE'RE HAVING AN EARTHQUAKE!
RRMBBL
MAYA! WHAT'S HAPPENING!?
KIMI... HELP US...
NOOOOOO!!!
KIMIIII!!!

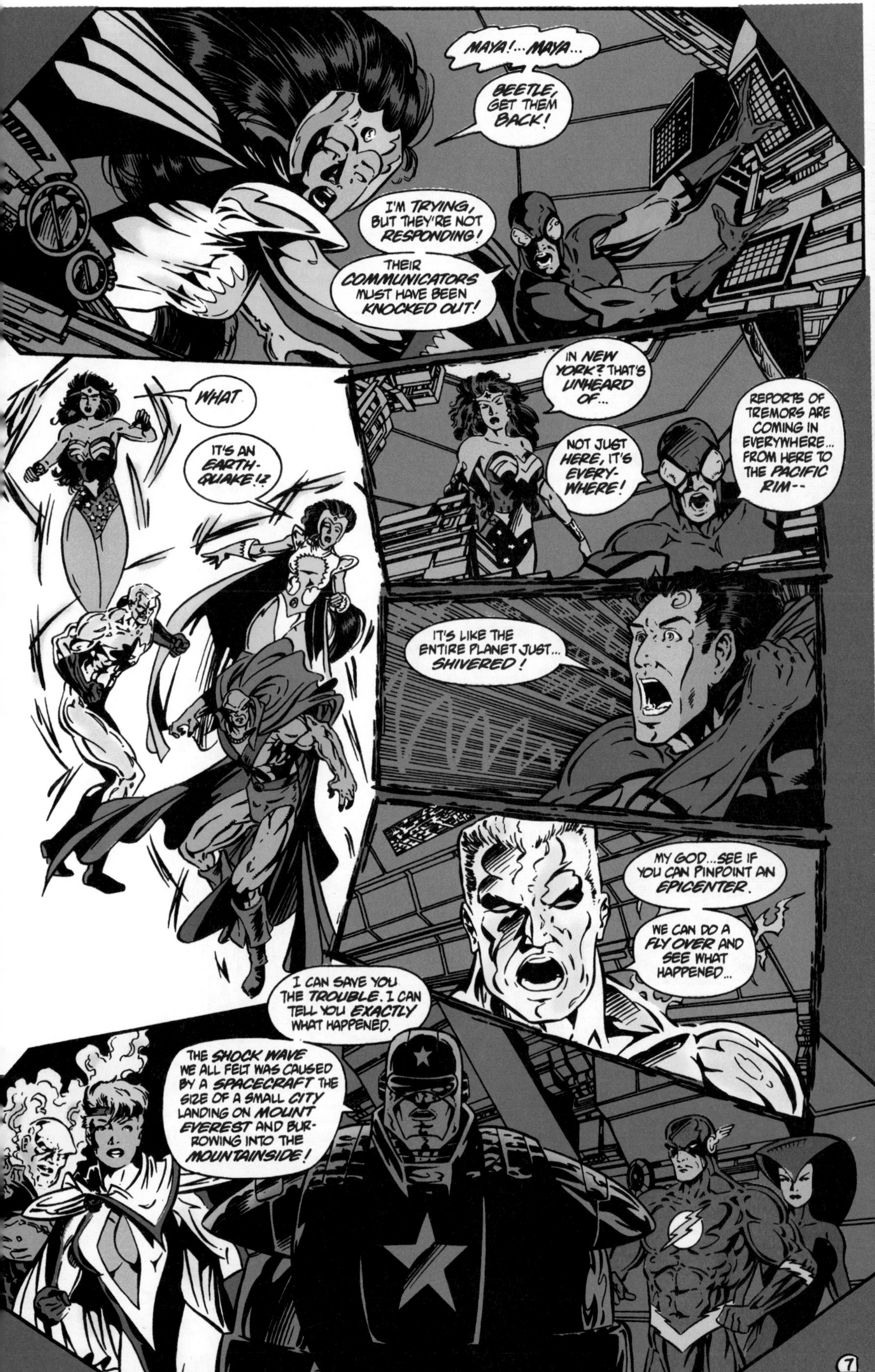
MAYA!... MAYA...
BEETLE, GET THEM BACK!
I'M TRYING, BUT THEY'RE NOT RESPONDING!
THEIR COMMUNICATORS MUST HAVE BEEN KNOCKED OUT!
WHAT
IT'S AN EARTH-QUAKE!?
IN NEW YORK? THAT'S UNHEARD OF...
NOT JUST HERE, IT'S EVERY-WHERE!
REPORTS OF TREMORS ARE COMING IN EVERYWHERE... FROM HERE TO THE PACIFIC RIM--
IT'S LIKE THE ENTIRE PLANET JUST... SHIVERED!
MY GOD...SEE IF YOU CAN PINPOINT AN EPICENTER.
WE CAN DO A FLY OVER AND SEE WHAT HAPPENED...
I CAN SAVE YOU THE TROUBLE. I CAN TELL YOU EXACTLY WHAT HAPPENED.
THE SHOCK WAVE WE ALL FELT WAS CAUSED BY A SPACECRAFT THE SIZE OF A SMALL CITY LANDING ON MOUNT EVEREST AND BUR-ROWING INTO THE MOUNTAINSIDE!

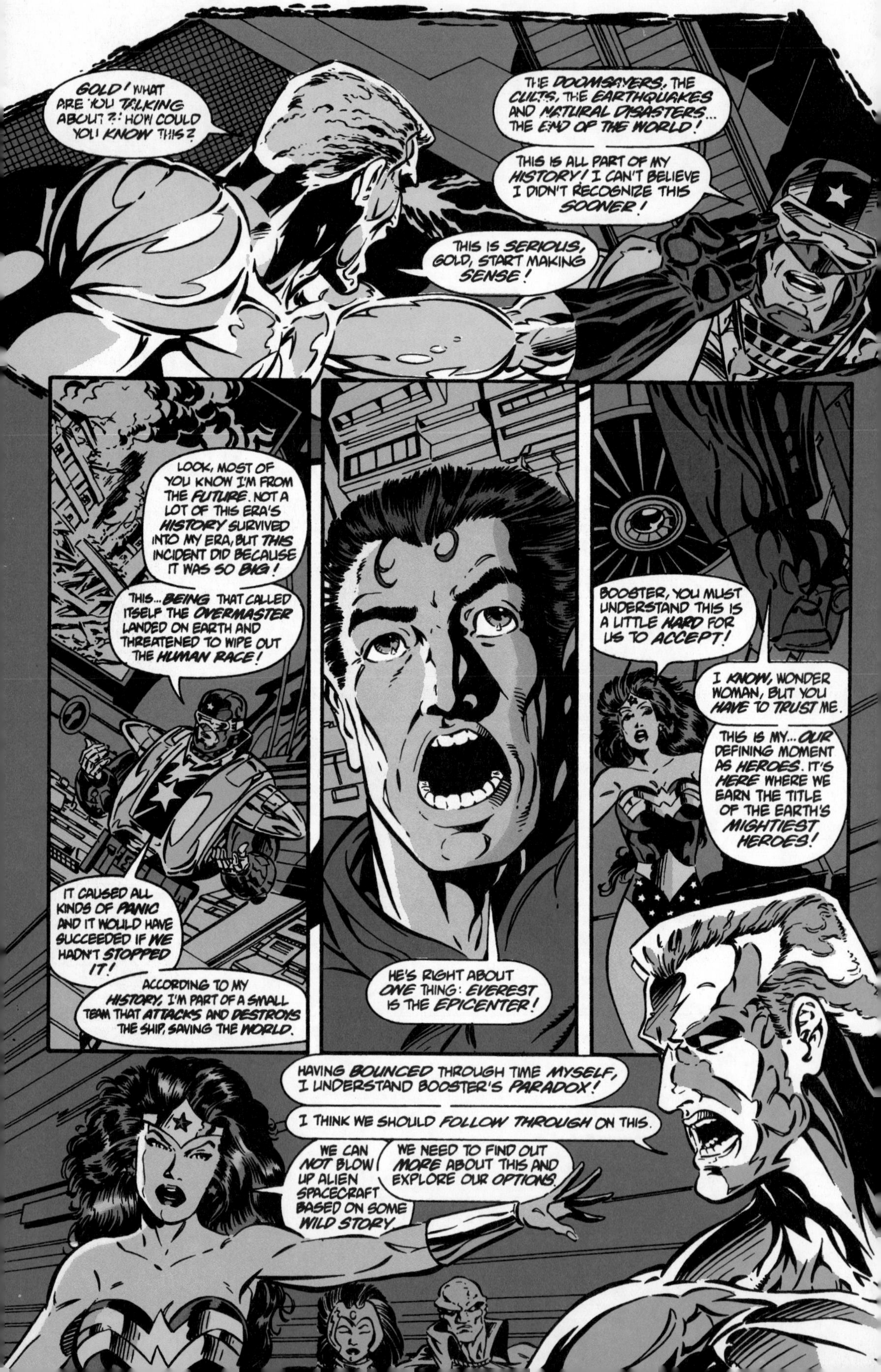
GOLD! WHAT ARE YOU TALKING ABOUT?! HOW COULD YOU KNOW THIS?
THE DOOMSAYERS, THE CULTS, THE EARTHQUAKES AND NATURAL DISASTERS... THE END OF THE WORLD!
THIS IS ALL PART OF MY HISTORY! I CAN'T BELIEVE I DIDN'T RECOGNIZE THIS SOONER!
THIS IS SERIOUS, GOLD, START MAKING SENSE!
LOOK, MOST OF YOU KNOW I'M FROM THE FUTURE. NOT A LOT OF THIS ERA'S HISTORY SURVIVED INTO MY ERA, BUT THIS INCIDENT DID BECAUSE IT WAS SO BIG!
THIS... BEING THAT CALLED ITSELF THE OVERMASTER LANDED ON EARTH AND THREATENED TO WIPE OUT THE HUMAN RACE!
IT CAUSED ALL KINDS OF PANIC AND IT WOULD HAVE SUCCEEDED IF WE HADN'T STOPPED IT!
ACCORDING TO MY HISTORY, I'M PART OF A SMALL TEAM THAT ATTACKS AND DESTROYS THE SHIP, SAVING THE WORLD.
HE'S RIGHT ABOUT ONE THING: EVEREST IS THE EPICENTER!
BOOSTER, YOU MUST UNDERSTAND THIS IS A LITTLE HARD FOR US TO ACCEPT!
I KNOW, WONDER WOMAN, BUT YOU HAVE TO TRUST ME.
THIS IS MY... OUR DEFINING MOMENT AS HEROES. IT'S HERE WHERE WE EARN THE TITLE OF THE EARTH'S MIGHTIEST HEROES!
HAVING BOUNCED THROUGH TIME MYSELF, I UNDERSTAND BOOSTER'S PARADOX!
I THINK WE SHOULD FOLLOW THROUGH ON THIS.
WE CAN NOT BLOW UP ALIEN SPACECRAFT BASED ON SOME WILD STORY.
WE NEED TO FIND OUT MORE ABOUT THIS AND EXPLORE OUR OPTIONS.

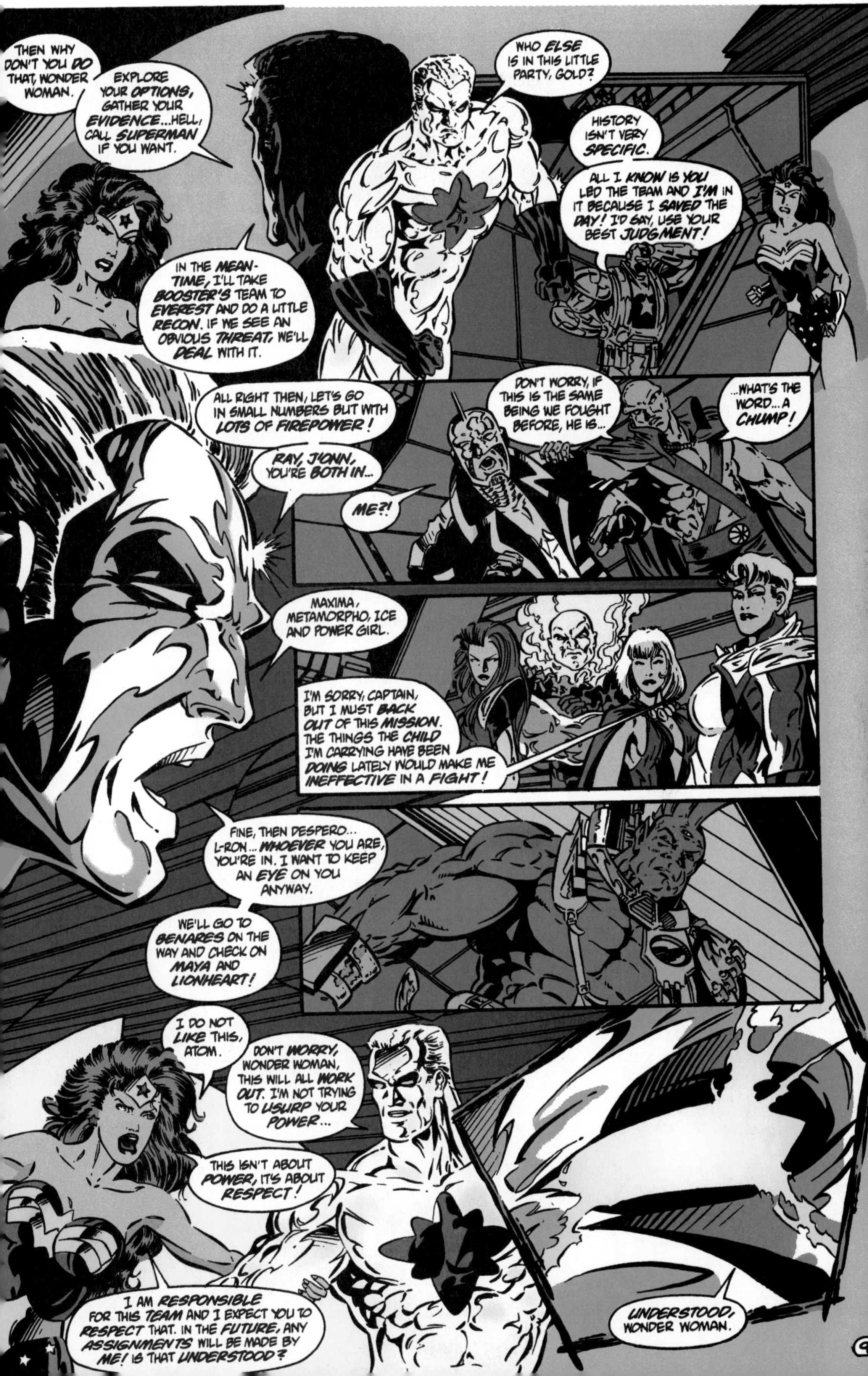
THEN WHY DON'T YOU DO THAT, WONDER WOMAN.
EXPLORE YOUR OPTIONS, GATHER YOUR EVIDENCE...HELL, CALL SUPERMAN IF YOU WANT.
WHO ELSE IS IN THIS LITTLE PARTY, GOLD?
HISTORY ISN'T VERY SPECIFIC.
ALL I KNOW IS YOU LED THE TEAM AND I'M IN IT BECAUSE I SAVED THE DAY! I'D SAY, USE YOUR BEST JUDGMENT!
IN THE MEAN-TIME, I'LL TAKE BOOSTER'S TEAM TO EVEREST AND DO A LITTLE RECON. IF WE SEE AN OBVIOUS THREAT, WE'LL DEAL WITH IT.
ALL RIGHT THEN, LET'S GO IN SMALL NUMBERS BUT WITH LOTS OF FIREPOWER!
DON'T WORRY, IF THIS IS THE SAME BEING WE FOUGHT BEFORE, HE IS...
...WHAT'S THE WORD...A CHUMP!
RAY, J'ONN, YOU'RE BOTH IN...
ME?!
MAXIMA, METAMORPHO, ICE AND POWER GIRL.
I'M SORRY, CAPTAIN, BUT I MUST BACK OUT OF THIS MISSION. THE THINGS THE CHILD I'M CARRYING HAVE BEEN DOING LATELY WOULD MAKE ME INEFFECTIVE IN A FIGHT!
FINE, THEN DESPERO... L-RON... WHOEVER YOU ARE, YOU'RE IN. I WANT TO KEEP AN EYE ON YOU ANYWAY.
WE'LL GO TO BENARES ON THE WAY AND CHECK ON MAYA AND LIONHEART!
I DO NOT LIKE THIS, ATOM.
DON'T WORRY, WONDER WOMAN, THIS WILL ALL WORK OUT. I'M NOT TRYING TO USURP YOUR POWER...
THIS ISN'T ABOUT POWER, IT'S ABOUT RESPECT!
I AM RESPONSIBLE FOR THIS TEAM AND I EXPECT YOU TO RESPECT THAT. IN THE FUTURE, ANY ASSIGNMENTS WILL BE MADE BY ME! IS THAT UNDERSTOOD?
UNDERSTOOD, WONDER WOMAN.

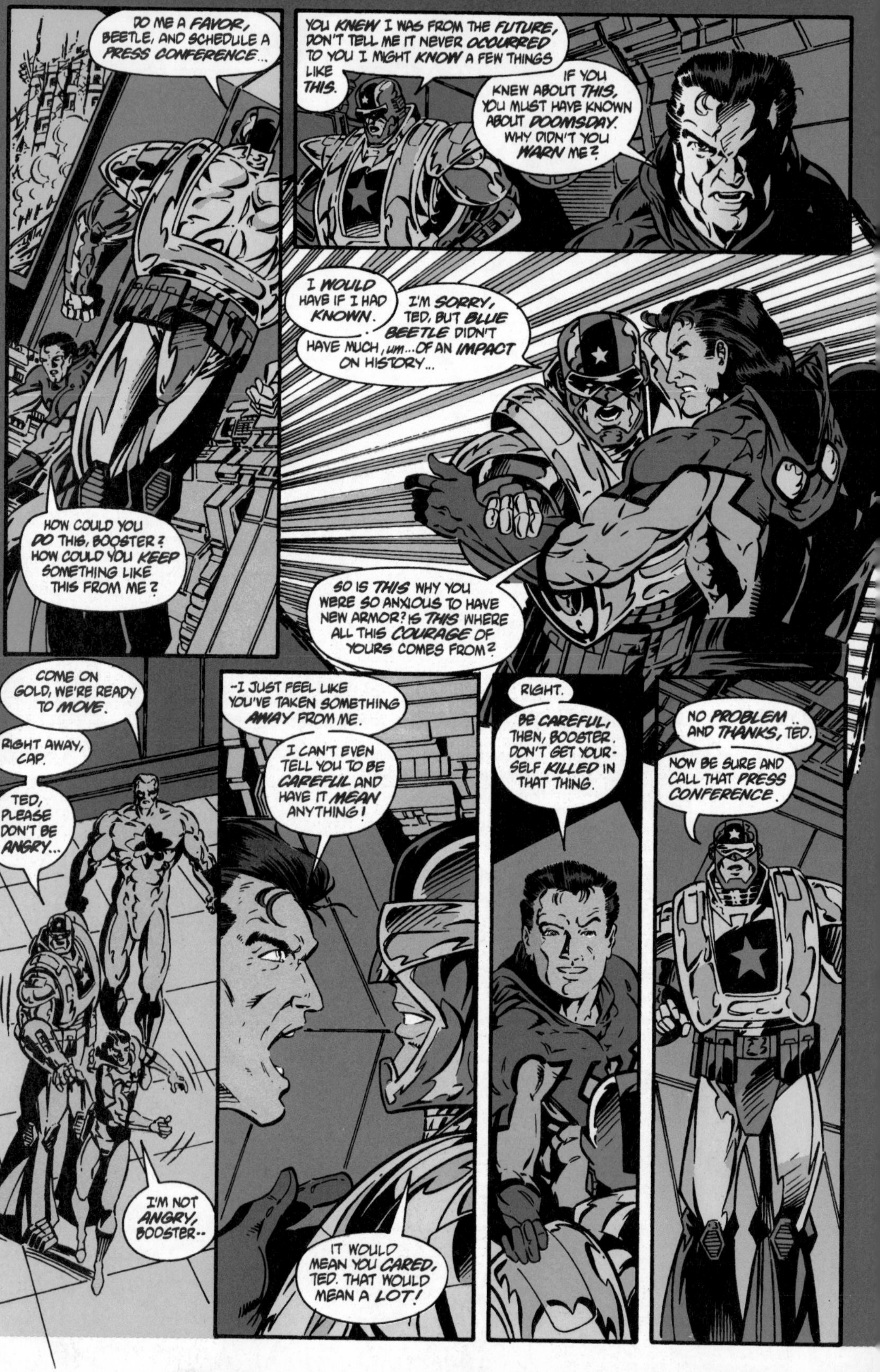
DO ME A FAVOR, BEETLE, AND SCHEDULE A PRESS CONFERENCE...
HOW COULD YOU DO THIS, BOOSTER? HOW COULD YOU KEEP SOMETHING LIKE THIS FROM ME?
YOU KNEW I WAS FROM THE FUTURE, DON'T TELL ME IT NEVER OCCURRED TO YOU I MIGHT KNOW A FEW THINGS LIKE THIS.
IF YOU KNEW ABOUT THIS, YOU MUST HAVE KNOWN ABOUT DOOMSDAY. WHY DIDN'T YOU WARN ME?
I WOULD HAVE IF I HAD KNOWN.
I'M SORRY, TED, BUT BLUE BEETLE DIDN'T HAVE MUCH, um...OF AN IMPACT ON HISTORY...
SO IS THIS WHY YOU WERE SO ANXIOUS TO HAVE NEW ARMOR? IS THIS WHERE ALL THIS COURAGE OF YOURS COMES FROM?
COME ON GOLD, WE'RE READY TO MOVE.
RIGHT AWAY, CAP.
TED, PLEASE DON'T BE ANGRY...
I'M NOT ANGRY, BOOSTER--
--I JUST FEEL LIKE YOU'VE TAKEN SOMETHING AWAY FROM ME.
I CAN'T EVEN TELL YOU TO BE CAREFUL AND HAVE IT MEAN ANYTHING!
IT WOULD MEAN YOU CARED, TED. THAT WOULD MEAN A LOT!
RIGHT.
BE CAREFUL, THEN, BOOSTER. DON'T GET YOUR-SELF KILLED IN THAT THING.
NO PROBLEM AND THANKS, TED.
NOW BE SURE AND CALL THAT PRESS CONFERENCE.

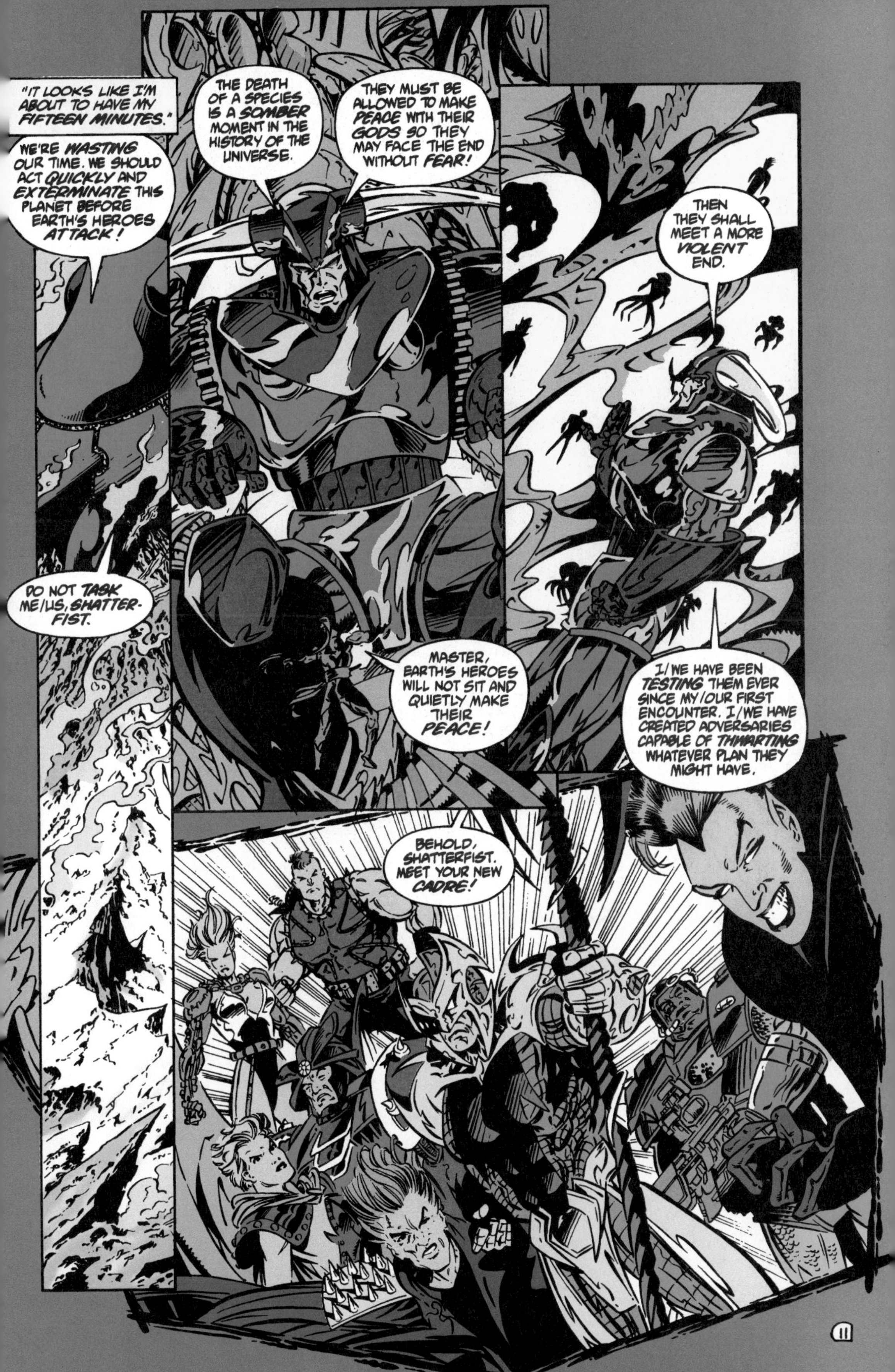
"IT LOOKS LIKE I'M ABOUT TO HAVE MY FIFTEEN MINUTES."
WE'RE WASTING OUR TIME. WE SHOULD ACT QUICKLY AND EXTERMINATE THIS PLANET BEFORE EARTH'S HEROES ATTACK!
THE DEATH OF A SPECIES IS A SOMBER MOMENT IN THE HISTORY OF THE UNIVERSE.
THEY MUST BE ALLOWED TO MAKE PEACE WITH THEIR GODS SO THEY MAY FACE THE END WITHOUT FEAR!
THEN THEY SHALL MEET A MORE VIOLENT END.
DO NOT TASK ME/US, SHATTER-FIST.
MASTER, EARTH'S HEROES WILL NOT SIT AND QUIETLY MAKE THEIR PEACE!
I/WE HAVE BEEN TESTING THEM EVER SINCE MY/OUR FIRST ENCOUNTER. I/WE HAVE CREATED ADVERSARIES CAPABLE OF THWARTING WHATEVER PLAN THEY MIGHT HAVE.
BEHOLD, SHATTERFIST. MEET YOUR NEW CADRE!

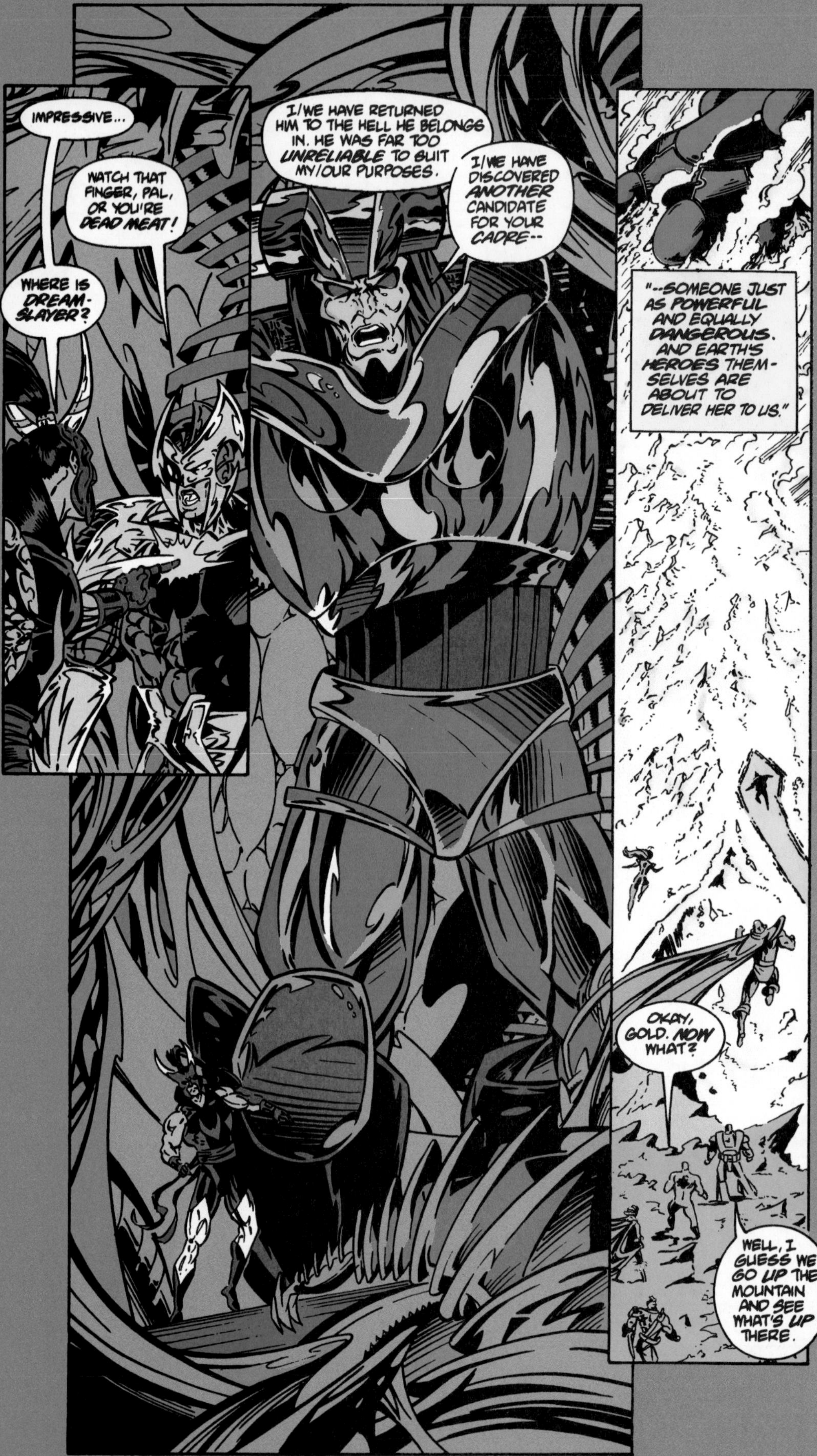
IMPRESSIVE...
WATCH THAT FINGER, PAL, OR YOU'RE DEAD MEAT!
WHERE IS DREAM-SLAYER?
I/WE HAVE RETURNED HIM TO THE HELL HE BELONGS IN. HE WAS FAR TOO UNRELIABLE TO SUIT MY/OUR PURPOSES.
I/WE HAVE DISCOVERED ANOTHER CANDIDATE FOR YOUR CADRE--
"--SOMEONE JUST AS POWERFUL AND EQUALLY DANGEROUS. AND EARTH'S HEROES THEM-SELVES ARE ABOUT TO DELIVER HER TO US."
OKAY, GOLD. NOW WHAT?
WELL, I GUESS WE GO UP THE MOUNTAIN AND SEE WHAT'S UP THERE.

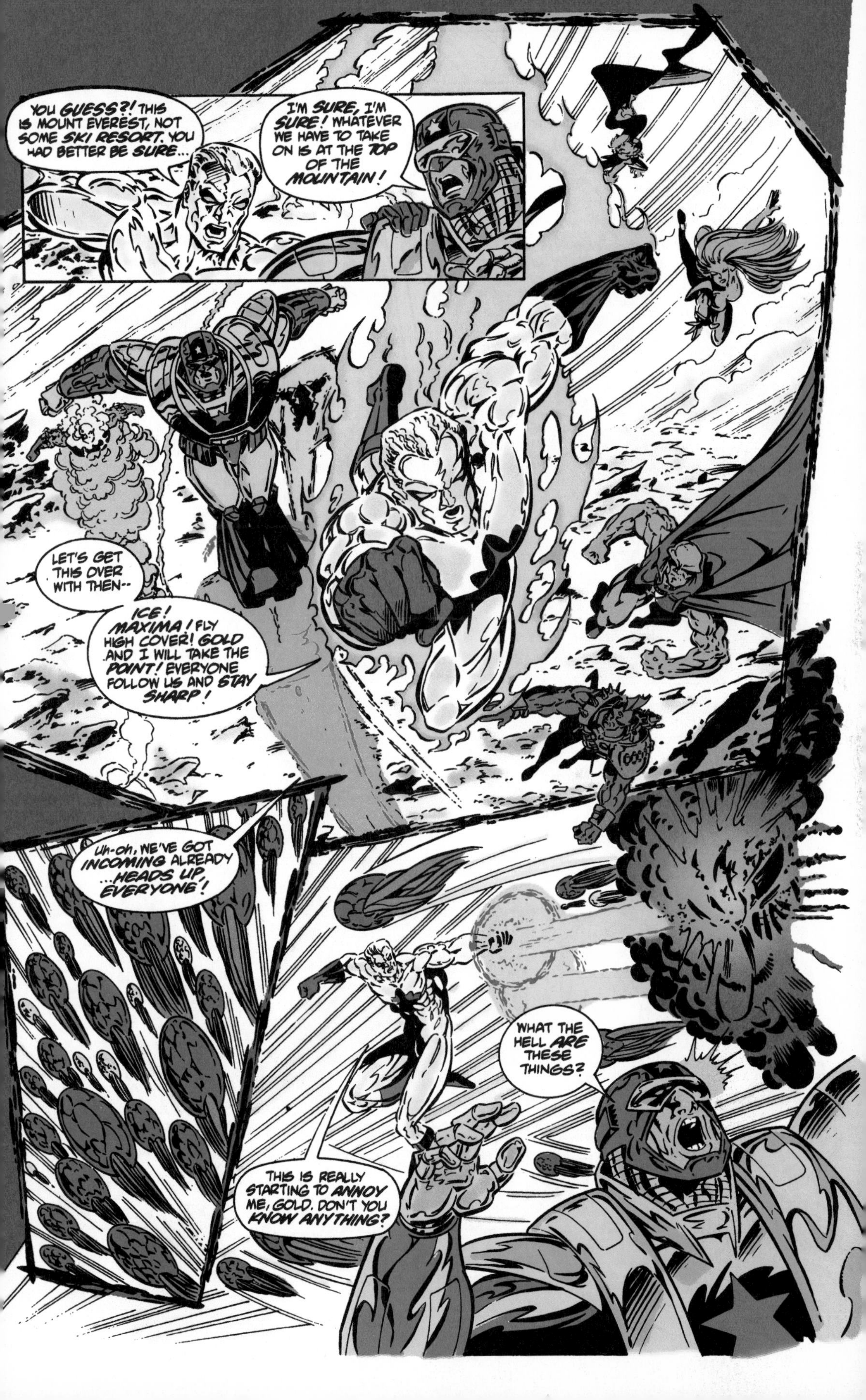
YOU GUESS?! THIS IS MOUNT EVEREST, NOT SOME SKI RESORT. YOU HAD BETTER BE SURE...
I'M SURE, I'M SURE! WHATEVER WE HAVE TO TAKE ON IS AT THE TOP OF THE MOUNTAIN!
LET'S GET THIS OVER WITH THEN--
ICE! MAXIMA! FLY HIGH COVER! GOLD AND I WILL TAKE THE POINT! EVERYONE FOLLOW US AND STAY SHARP!
Uh-oh, WE'VE GOT INCOMING ALREADY ...HEADS UP, EVERYONE!
WHAT THE HELL ARE THESE THINGS?
THIS IS REALLY STARTING TO ANNOY ME, GOLD. DON'T YOU KNOW ANYTHING?

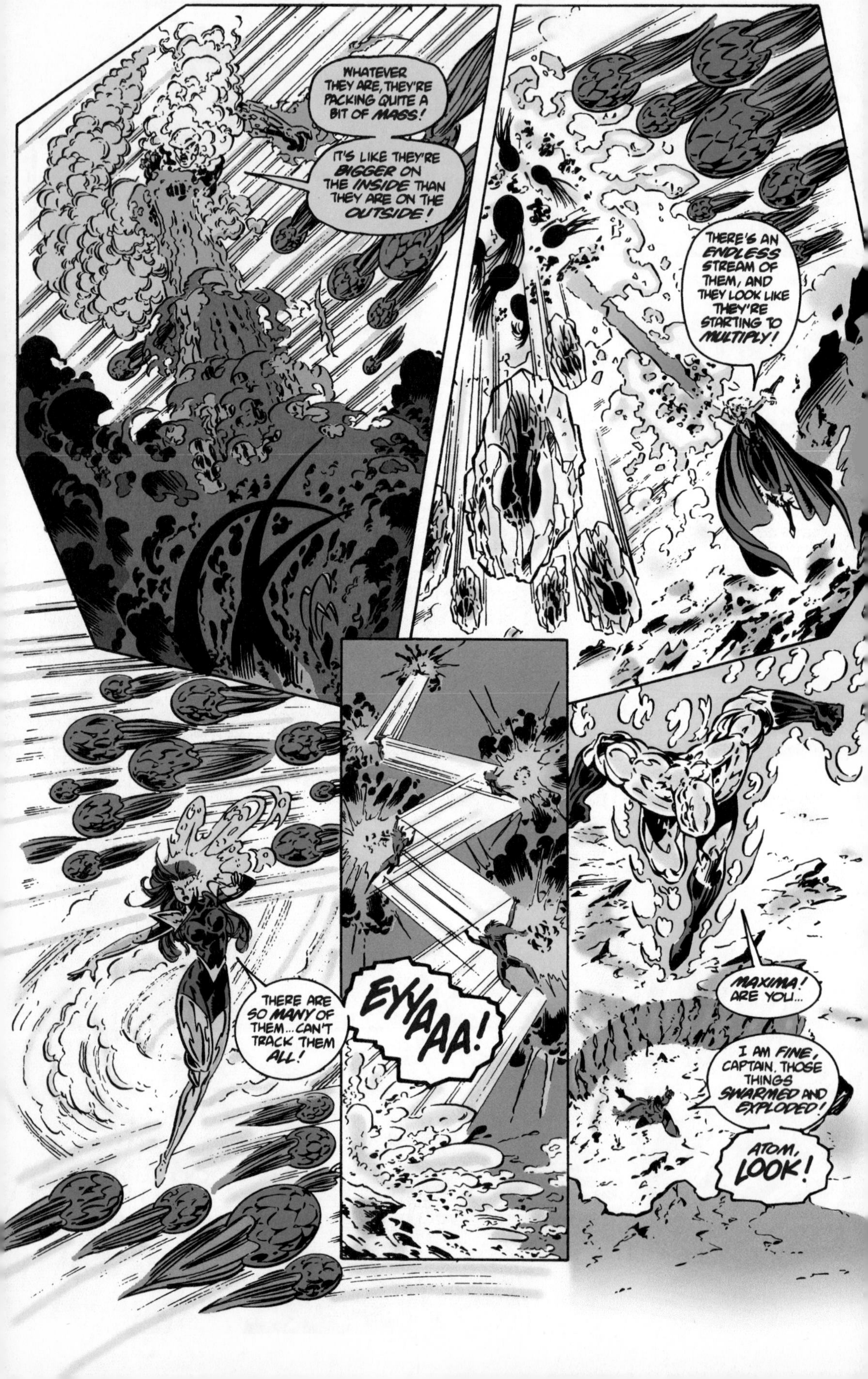
WHATEVER THEY ARE, THEY'RE PACKING QUITE A BIT OF MASS!
IT'S LIKE THEY'RE BIGGER ON THE INSIDE THAN THEY ARE ON THE OUTSIDE!
THERE'S AN ENDLESS STREAM OF THEM, AND THEY LOOK LIKE THEY'RE STARTING TO MULTIPLY!
THERE ARE SO MANY OF THEM... CAN'T TRACK THEM ALL!
EYYAAA!
MAXIMA! ARE YOU...
I AM FINE, CAPTAIN. THOSE THINGS SWARMED AND EXPLODED!
ATOM, LOOK!

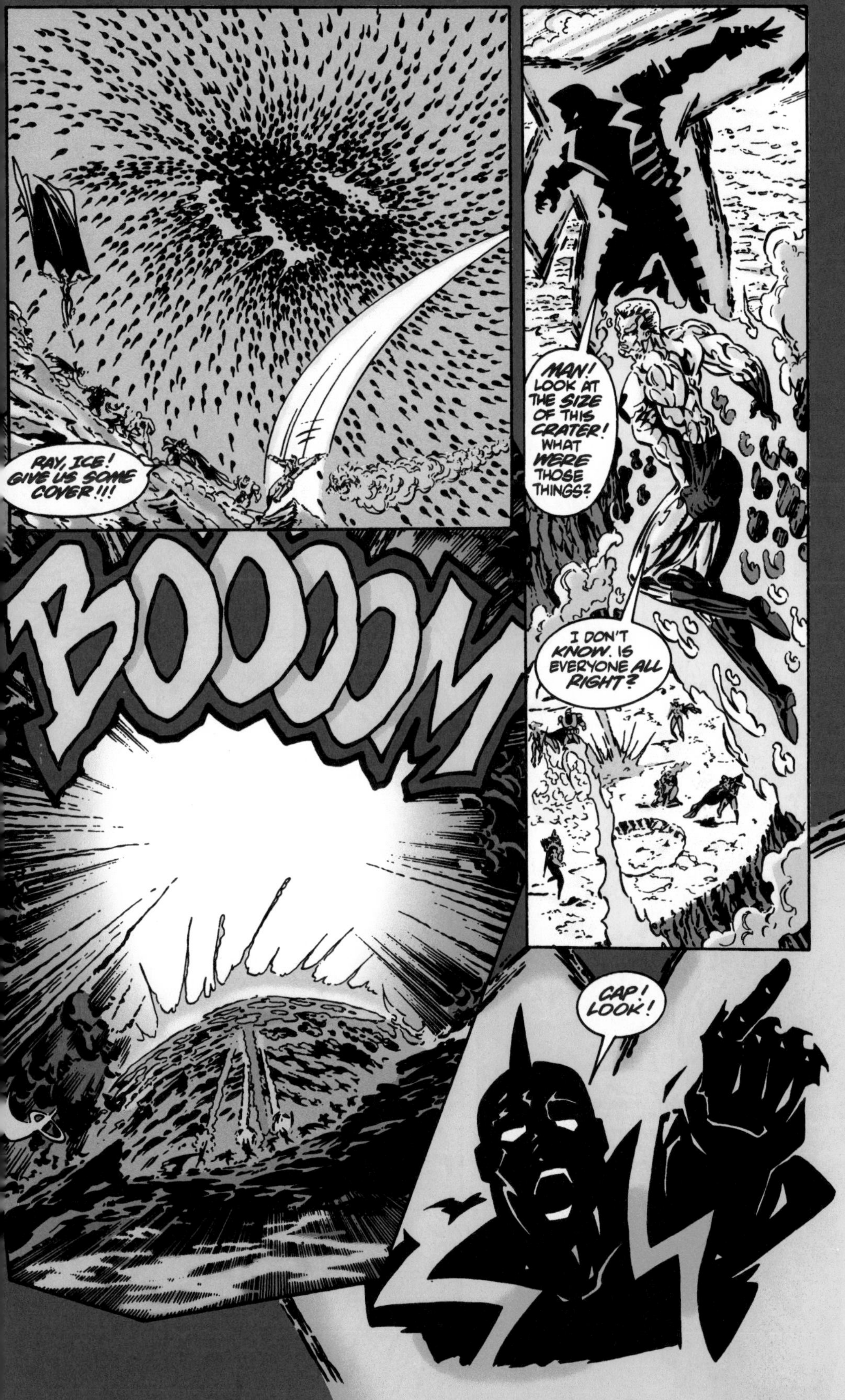
RAY, ICE! GIVE US SOME COVER!!!
MAN! LOOK AT THE SIZE OF THIS CRATER! WHAT WERE THOSE THINGS?
I DON'T KNOW. IS EVERYONE ALL RIGHT?
BOOOOM
CAP! LOOK!

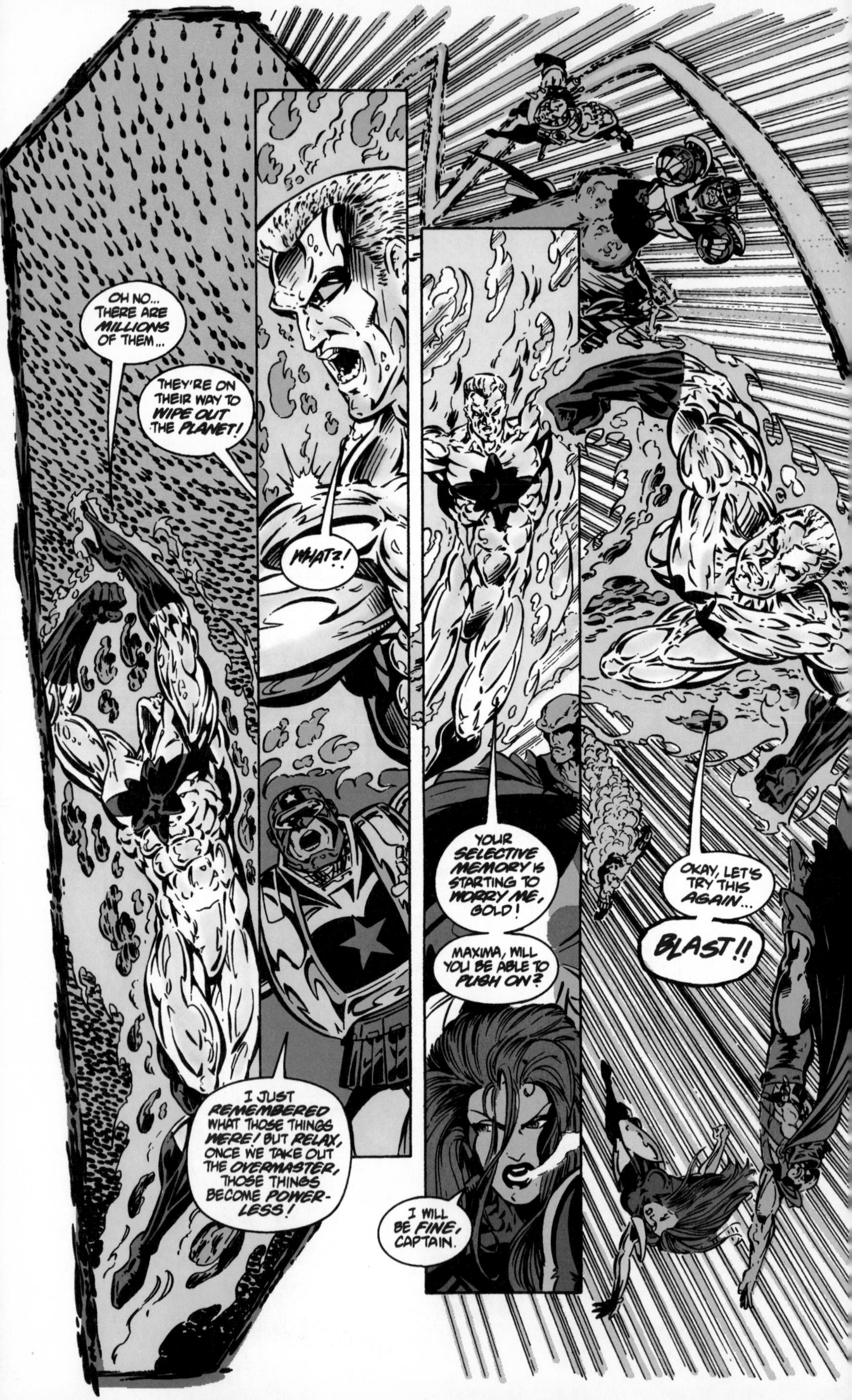

OH NO... THERE ARE MILLIONS OF THEM...
THEY'RE ON THEIR WAY TO WIPE OUT THE PLANET!
WHAT?!
YOUR SELECTIVE MEMORY IS STARTING TO WORRY ME, GOLD!
OKAY, LET'S TRY THIS AGAIN...
BLAST!!
MAXIMA, WILL YOU BE ABLE TO PUSH ON?
I JUST REMEMBERED WHAT THOSE THINGS WERE! BUT RELAX, ONCE WE TAKE OUT THE OVERMASTER, THOSE THINGS BECOME POWERLESS!
I WILL BE FINE, CAPTAIN.

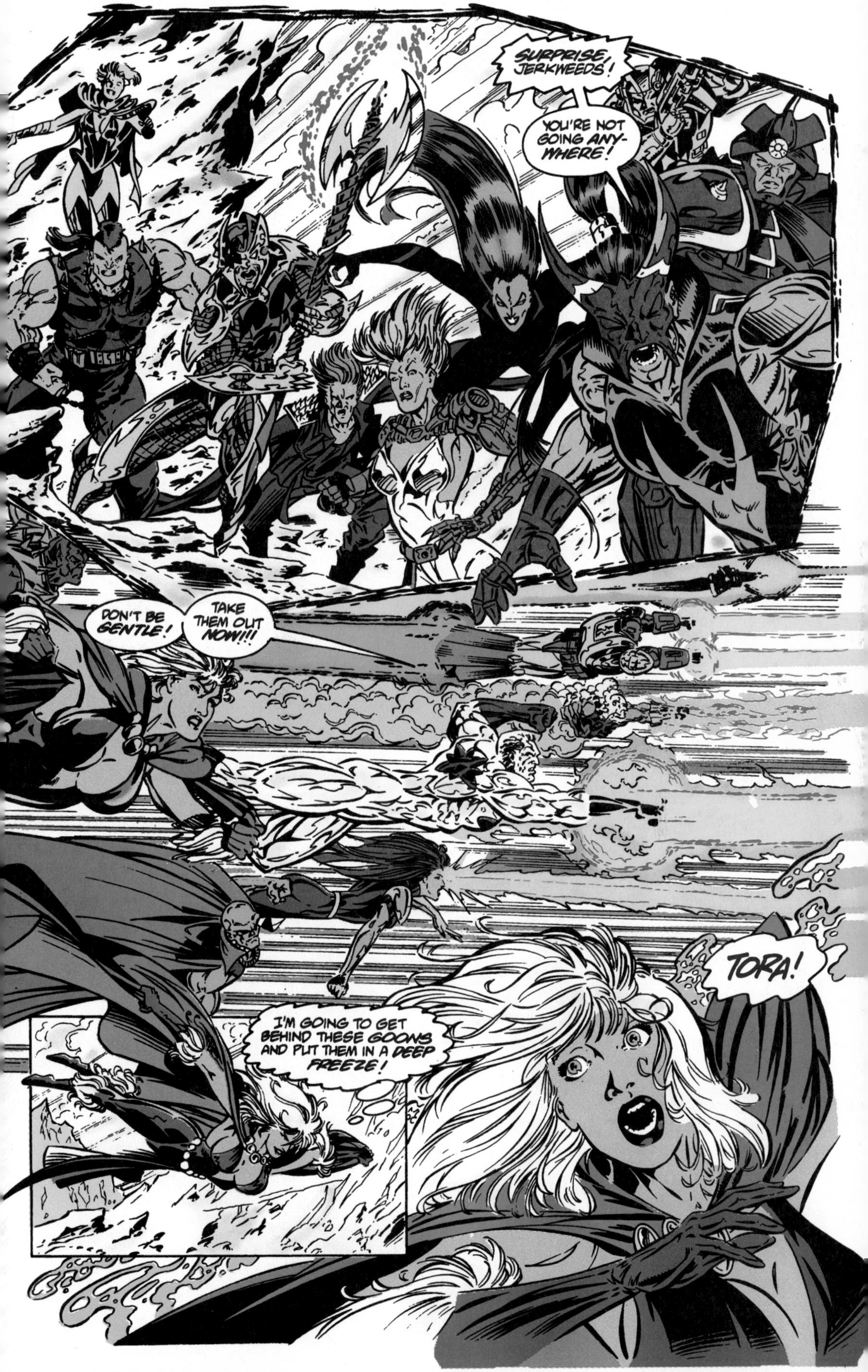
SURPRISE, JERKWEEDS!
YOU'RE NOT GOING ANY-WHERE!
DON'T BE GENTLE!
TAKE THEM OUT NOW!!!
TORA!
I'M GOING TO GET BEHIND THESE GOONS AND PUT THEM IN A DEEP FREEZE!

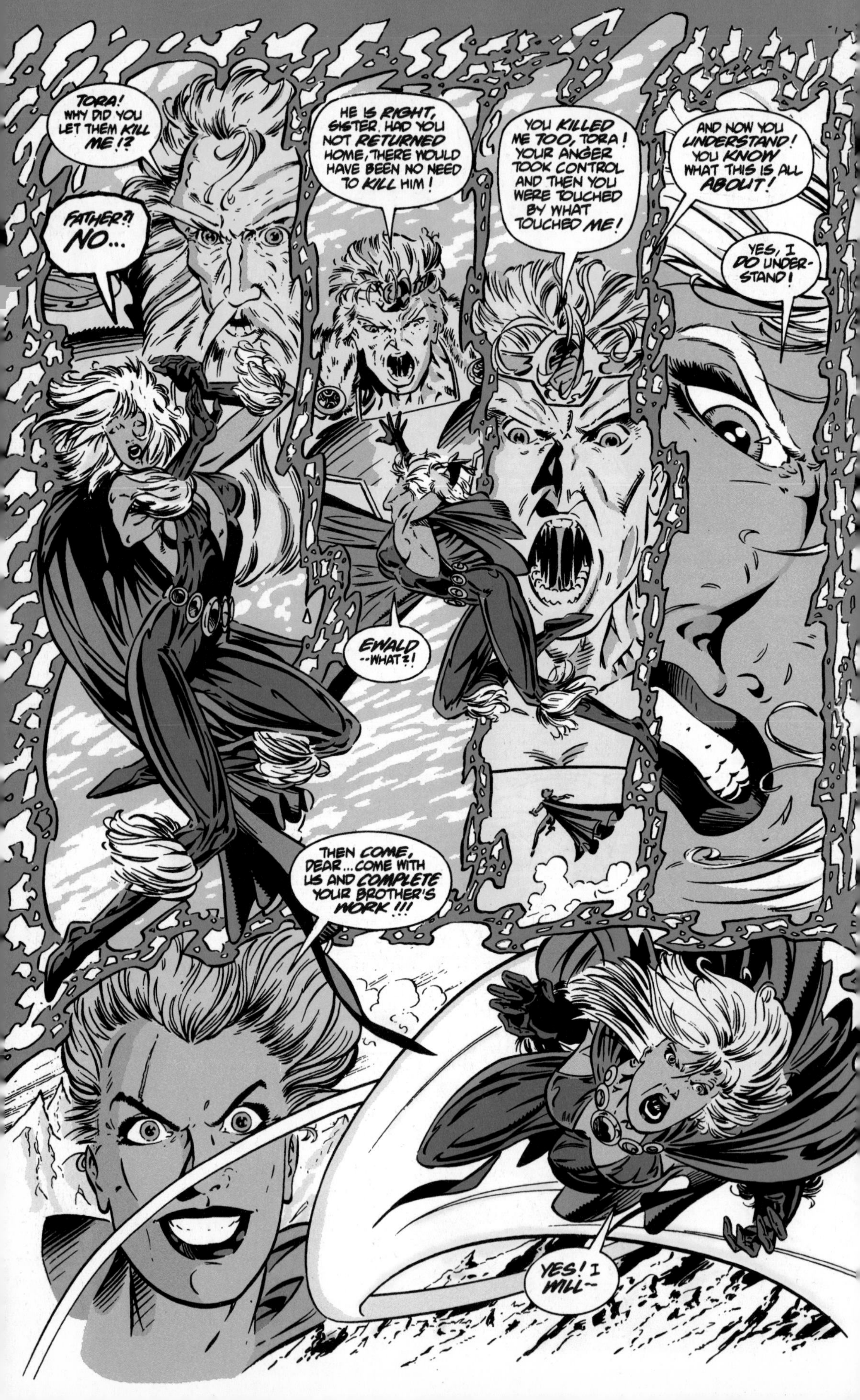
TORA! WHY DID YOU LET THEM KILL ME!?
FATHER?! NO...
HE IS RIGHT, SISTER. HAD YOU NOT RETURNED HOME, THERE WOULD HAVE BEEN NO NEED TO KILL HIM!
EWALD --WHAT?!
YOU KILLED ME TOO, TORA! YOUR ANGER TOOK CONTROL AND THEN YOU WERE TOUCHED BY WHAT TOUCHED ME!
AND NOW YOU UNDERSTAND! YOU KNOW WHAT THIS IS ALL ABOUT!
YES, I DO UNDER-STAND!
THEN COME, DEAR... COME WITH US AND COMPLETE YOUR BROTHER'S WORK!!!
YES! I WILL--

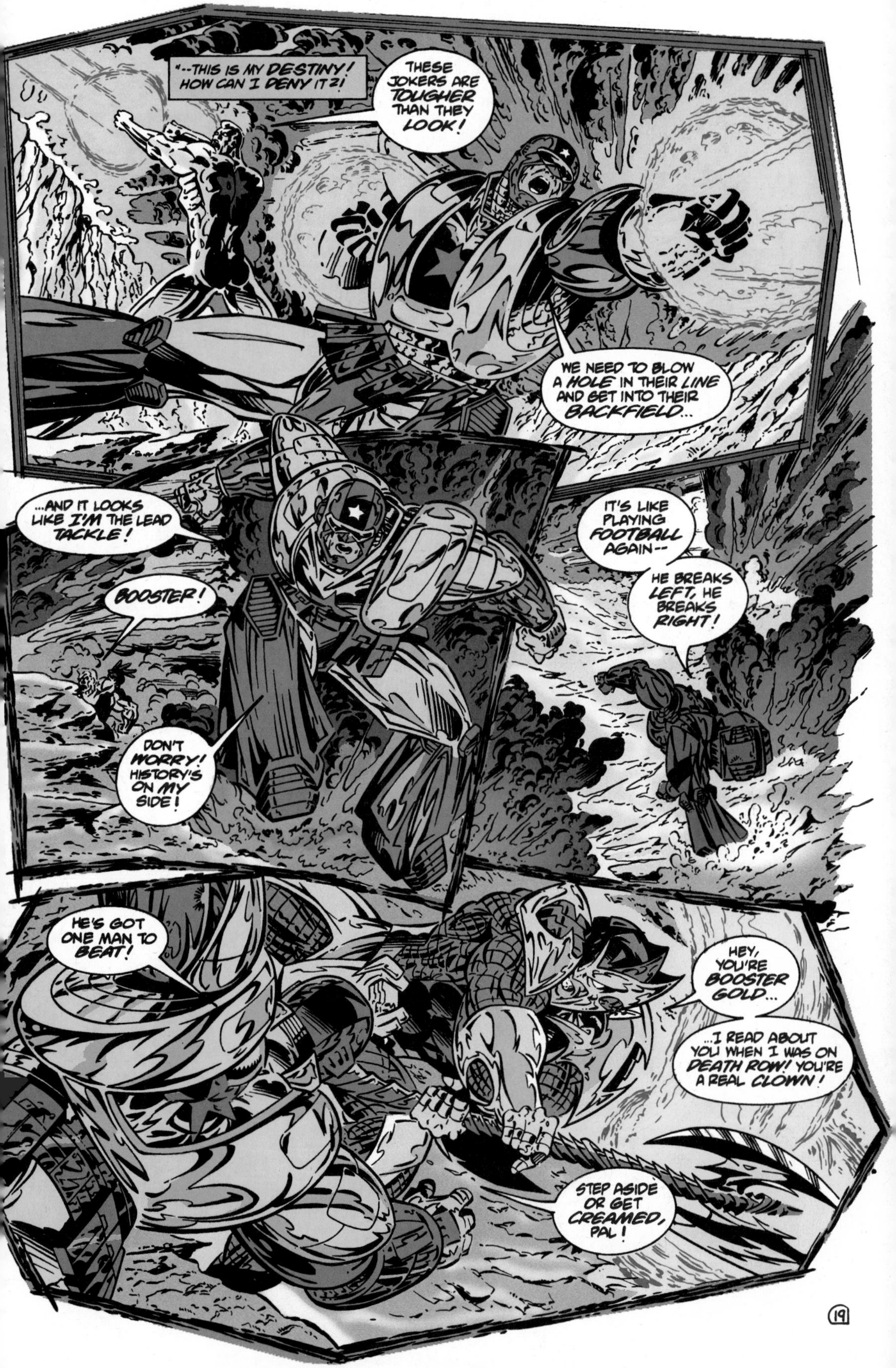
"--THIS IS MY DESTINY! HOW CAN I DENY IT?!
THESE JOKERS ARE TOUGHER THAN THEY LOOK!
WE NEED TO BLOW A HOLE IN THEIR LINE AND GET INTO THEIR BACKFIELD...
...AND IT LOOKS LIKE I'M THE LEAD TACKLE!
IT'S LIKE PLAYING FOOTBALL AGAIN--
HE BREAKS LEFT, HE BREAKS RIGHT!
BOOSTER!
DON'T WORRY! HISTORY'S ON MY SIDE!
HE'S GOT ONE MAN TO BEAT!
HEY, YOU'RE BOOSTER GOLD...
...I READ ABOUT YOU WHEN I WAS ON DEATH ROW! YOU'RE A REAL CLOWN!
STEP ASIDE OR GET CREAMED, PAL!

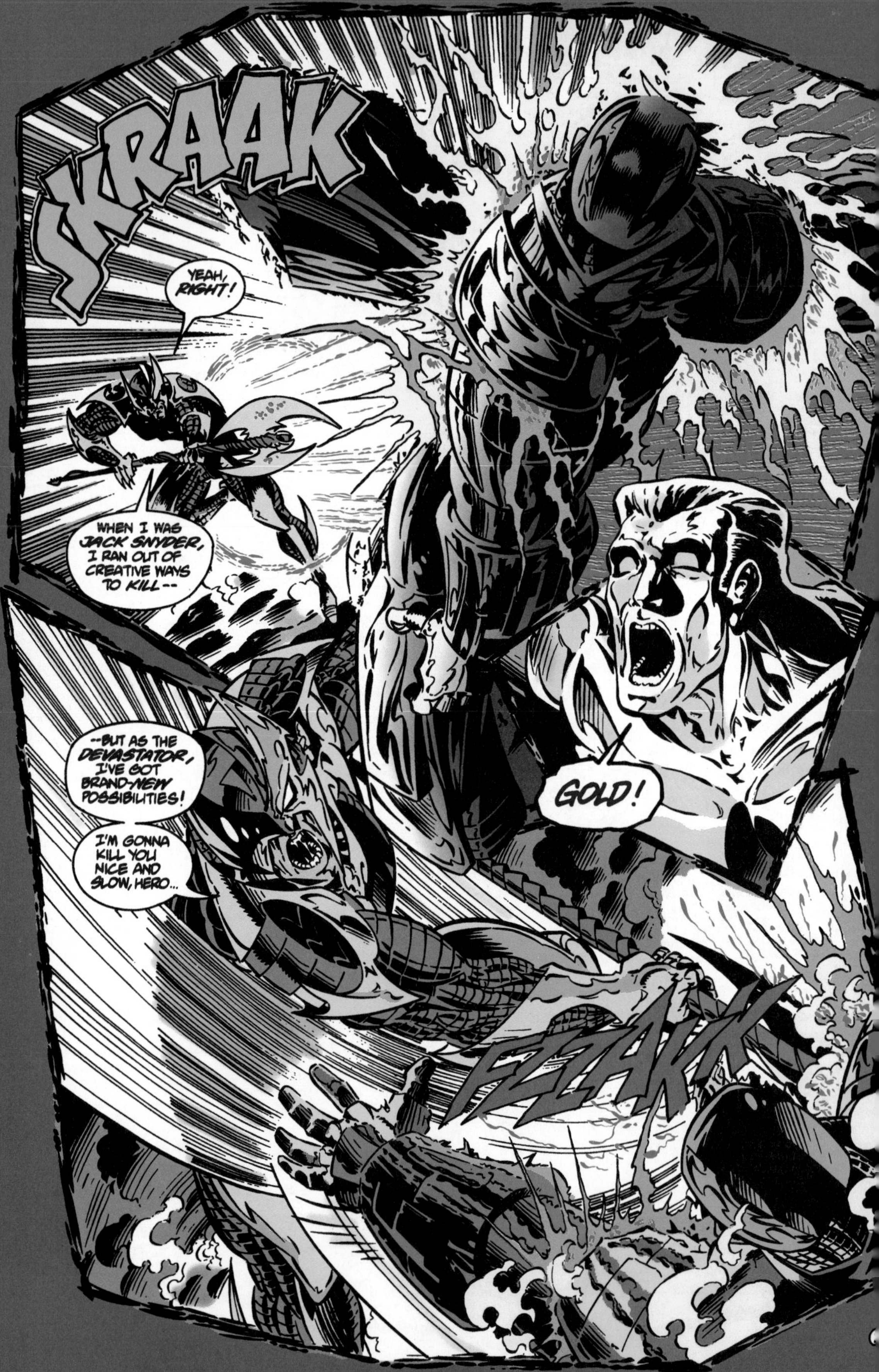
KRAAK
YEAH, RIGHT!
WHEN I WAS JACK SNYDER, I RAN OUT OF CREATIVE WAYS TO KILL--
--BUT AS THE DEVASTATOR, I'VE GOT BRAND-NEW POSSIBILITIES!
I'M GONNA KILL YOU NICE AND SLOW, HERO...
GOLD!

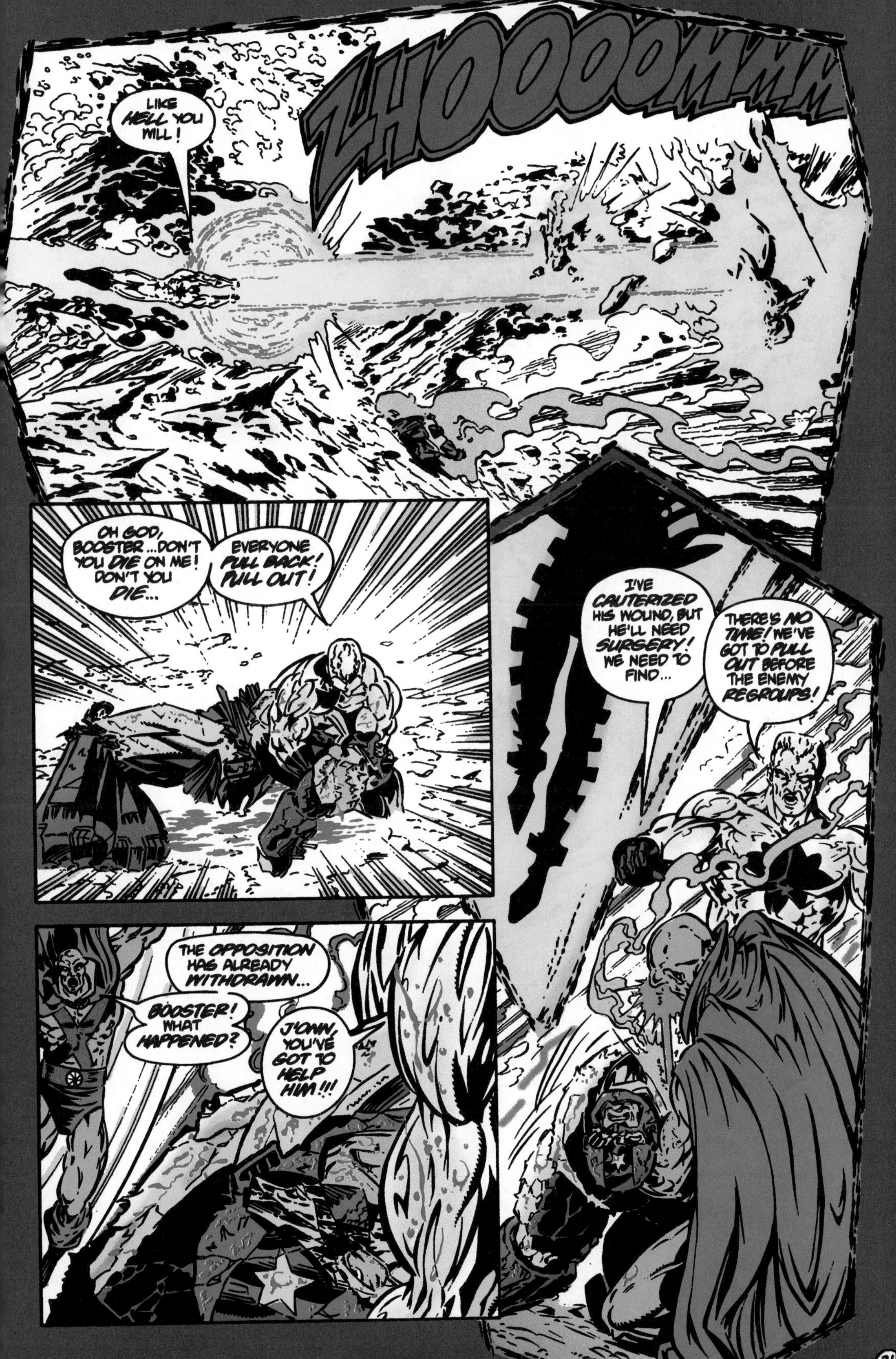
LIKE HELL YOU WILL!
ZHOOOOOMMM
OH GOD, BOOSTER...DON'T YOU DIE ON ME! DON'T YOU DIE...
EVERYONE PULL BACK! PULL OUT!
I'VE CAUTERIZED HIS WOUND, BUT HE'LL NEED SURGERY! WE NEED TO FIND...
THERE'S NO TIME! WE'VE GOT TO PULL OUT BEFORE THE ENEMY REGROUPS!
THE OPPOSITION HAS ALREADY WITHDRAWN...
BOOSTER! WHAT HAPPENED?
J'ONN, YOU'VE GOT TO HELP HIM!!!

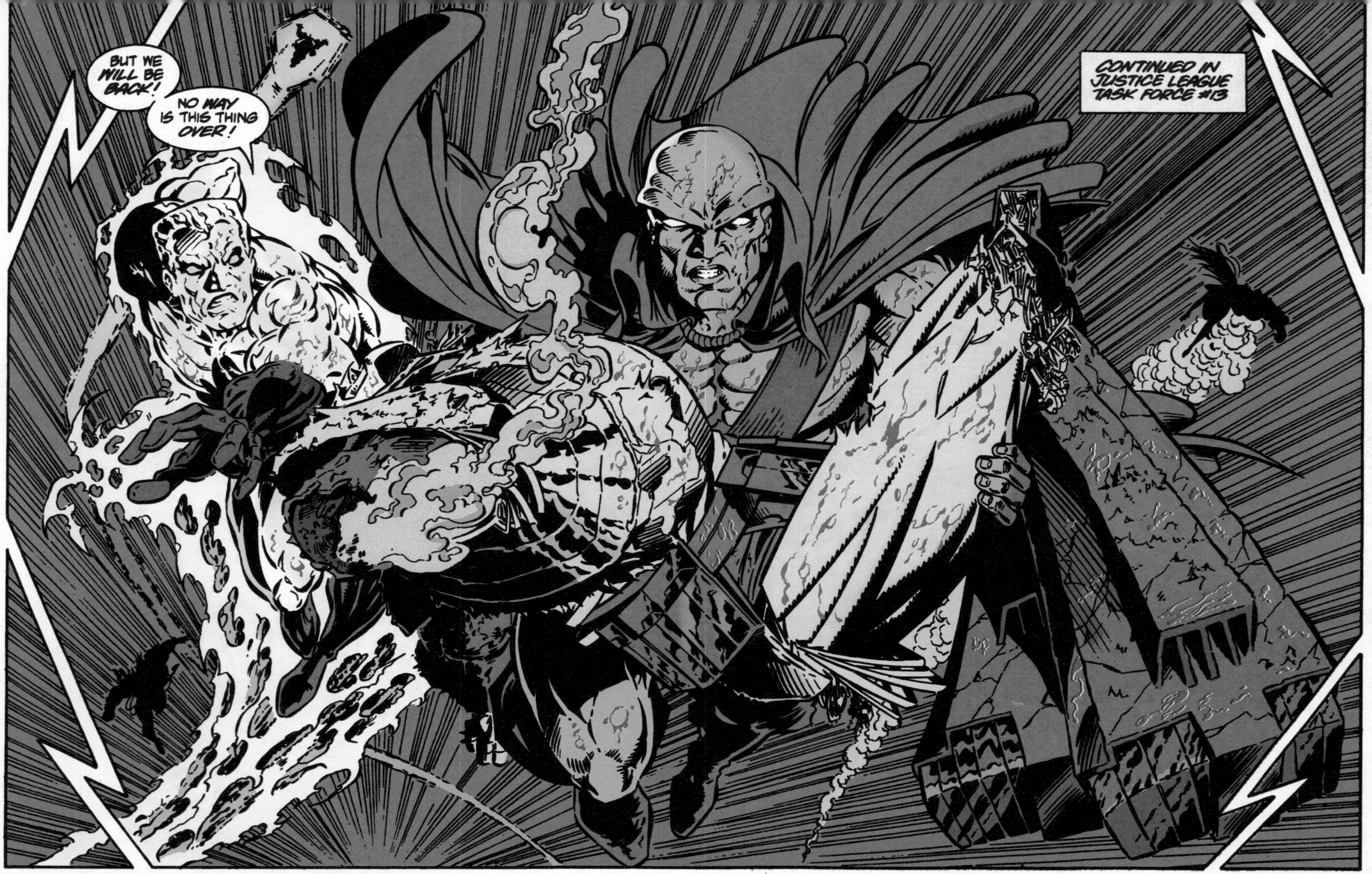
BUT WE WILL BE BACK!
NO WAY IS THIS THING OVER!
CONTINUED IN JUSTICE LEAGUE TASK FORCE #13

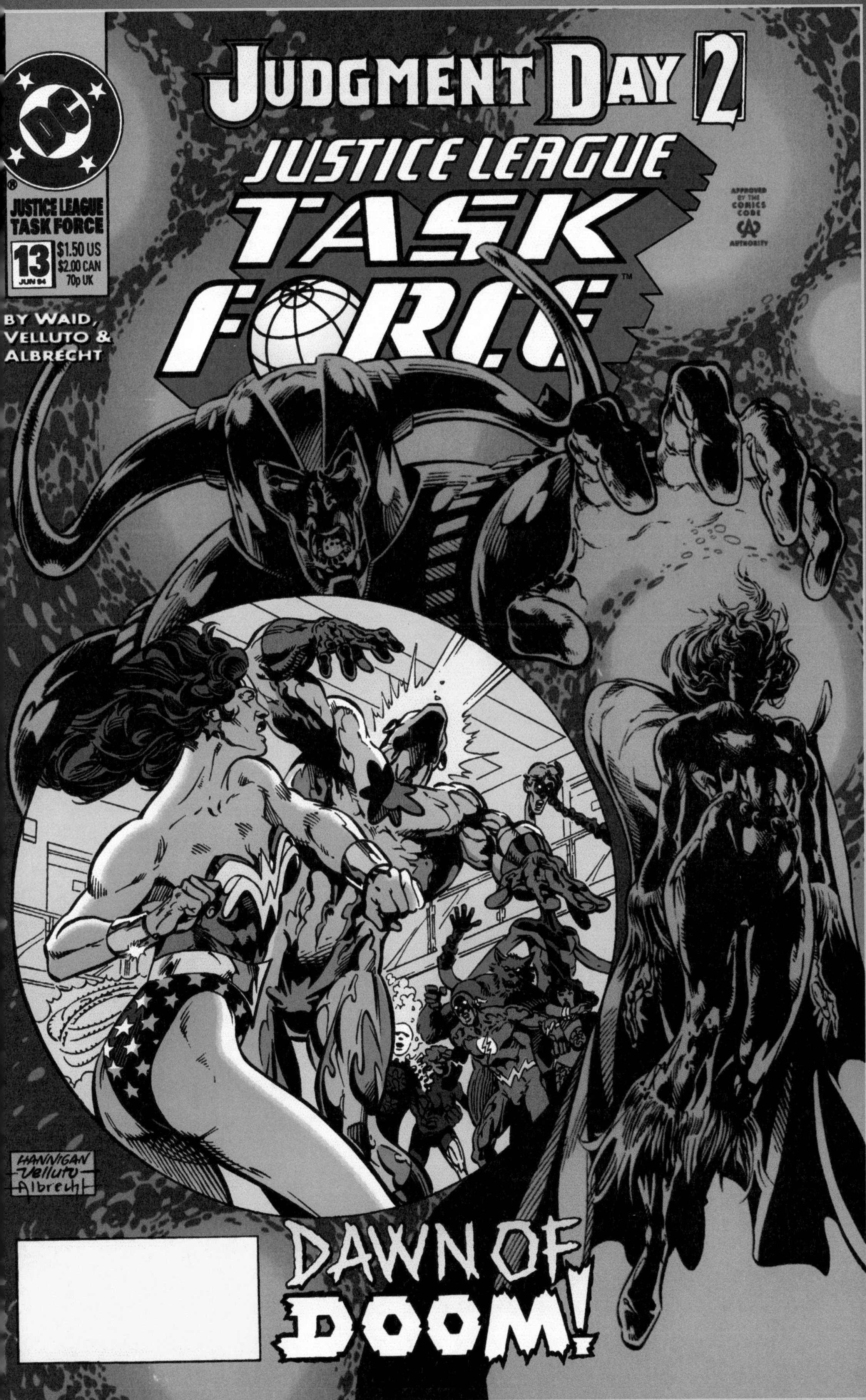

JUDGMENT DAY 2
JUSTICE LEAGUE
TASK FORCE
JUSTICE LEAGUE TASK FORCE
13
JUN 94
$1.50 US
$2.00 CAN
70p UK
APPROVED BY THE COMICS CODE AUTHORITY
BY WAID, VELLUTO & ALBRECHT
HANNIGAN
Velluto
Albrecht
DAWN OF DOOM!

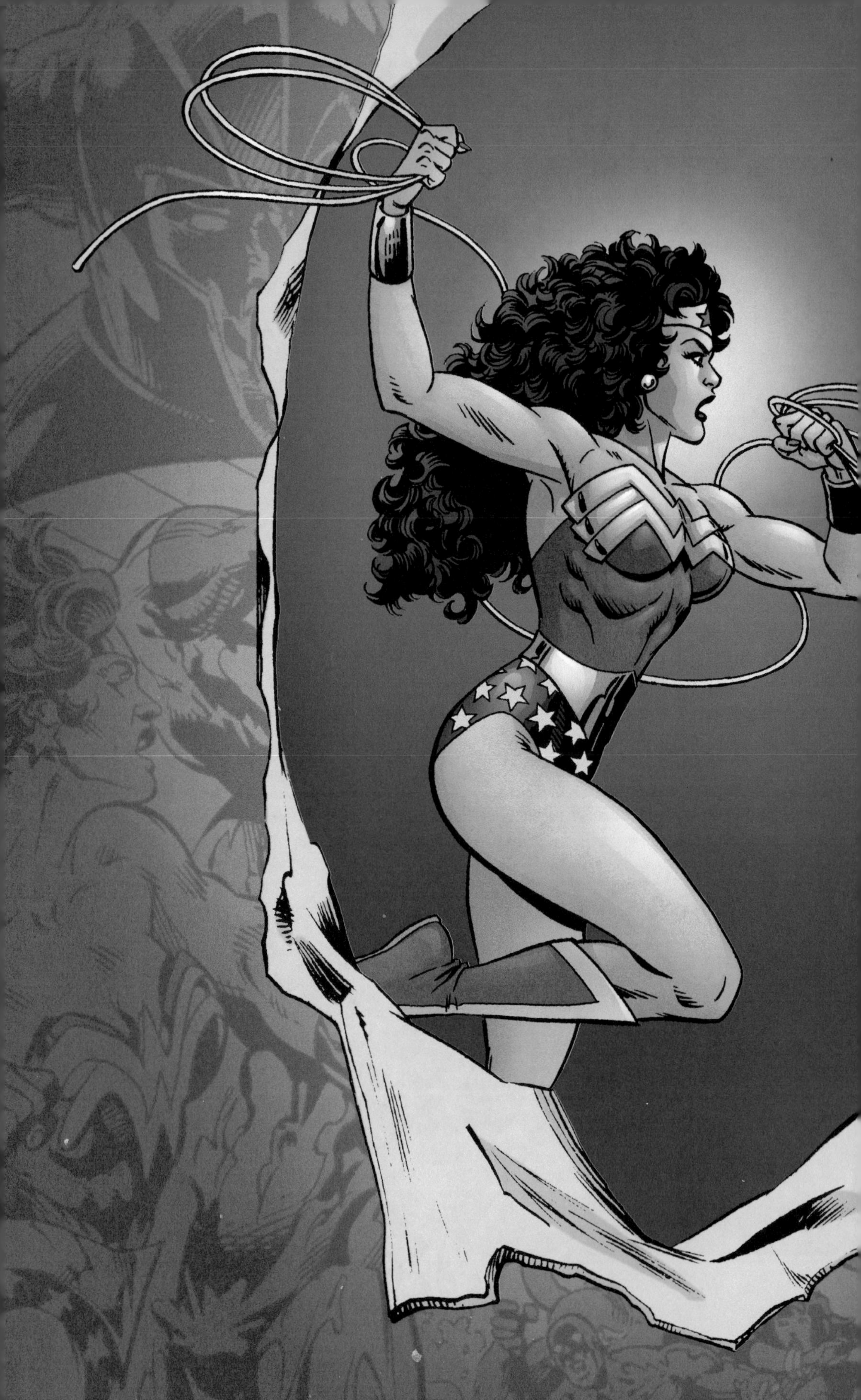

Cover art by **SAL VELLUTO, ED HANNIGAN and JEFF ALBRECHT**

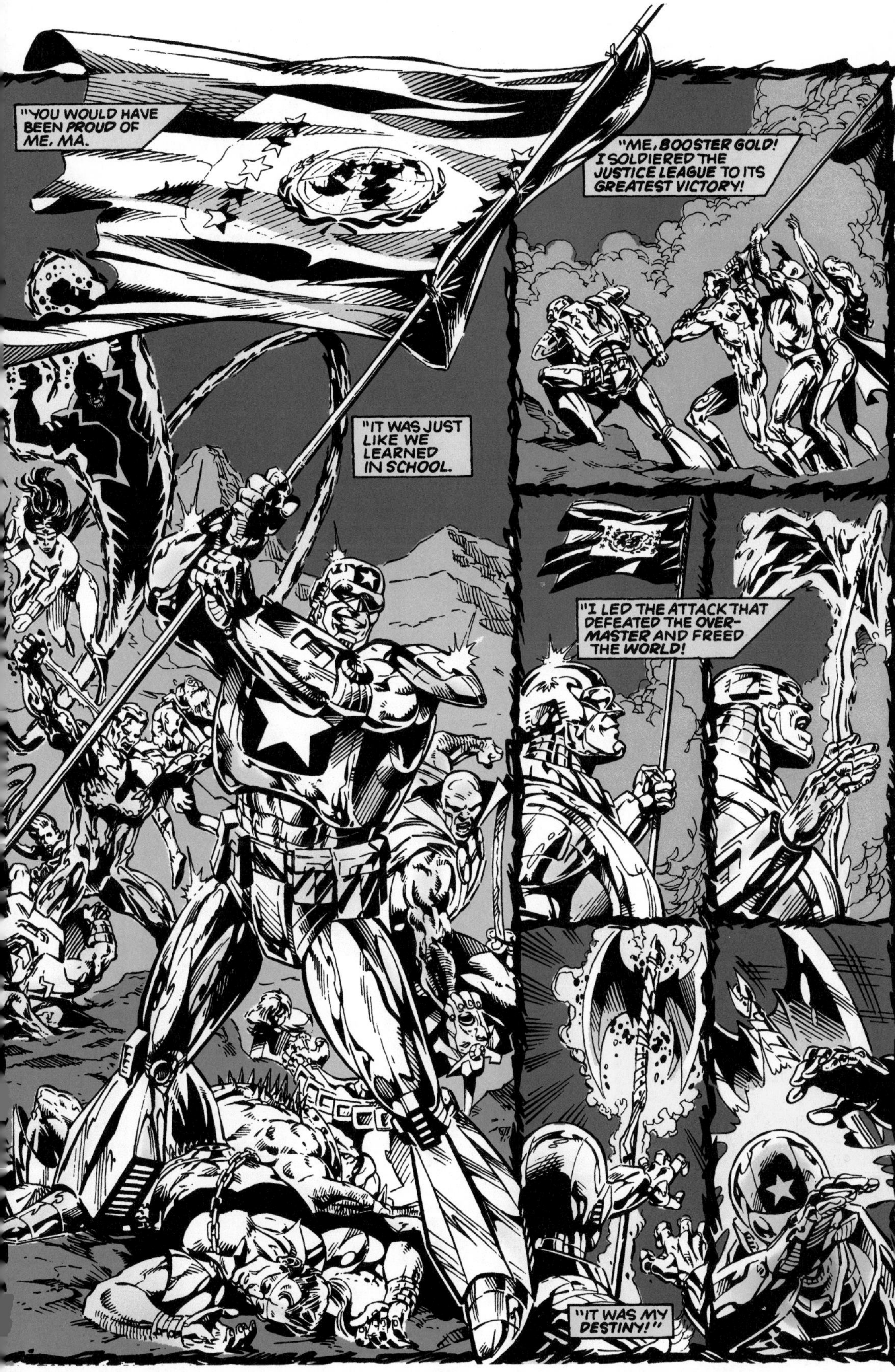
"YOU WOULD HAVE BEEN PROUD OF ME, MA.
"ME, BOOSTER GOLD! I SOLDIERED THE JUSTICE LEAGUE TO ITS GREATEST VICTORY!
"IT WAS JUST LIKE WE LEARNED IN SCHOOL.
"I LED THE ATTACK THAT DEFEATED THE OVER-MASTER AND FREED THE WORLD!
"IT WAS MY DESTINY!"

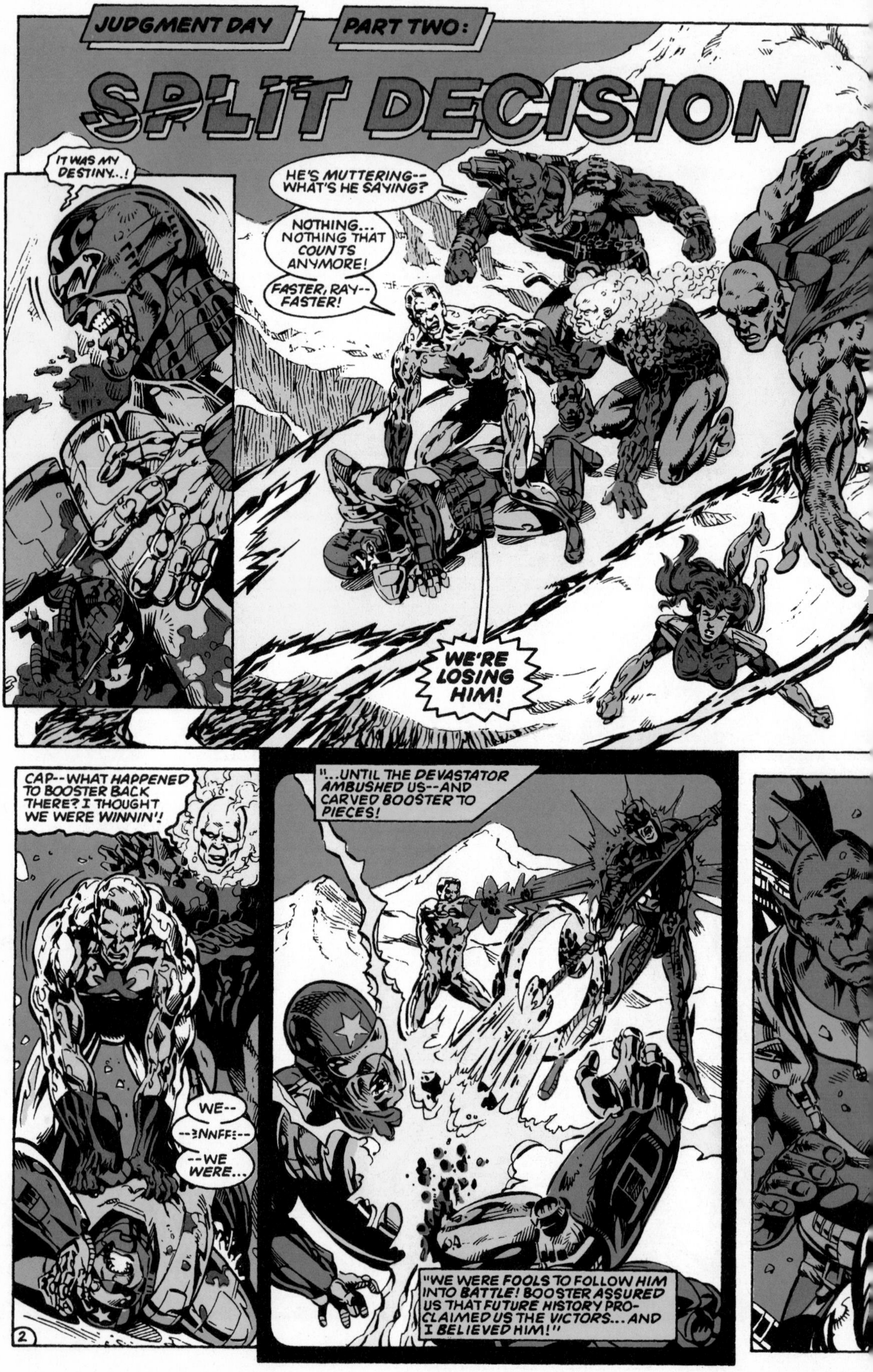
JUDGMENT DAY
PART TWO:
SPLIT DECISION
IT WAS MY DESTINY...!
HE'S MUTTERING-- WHAT'S HE SAYING?
NOTHING... NOTHING THAT COUNTS ANYMORE!
FASTER, RAY-- FASTER!
WE'RE LOSING HIM!
CAP--WHAT HAPPENED TO BOOSTER BACK THERE? I THOUGHT WE WERE WINNIN'!
WE--
--UNNFF--
--WE WERE...
"...UNTIL THE DEVASTATOR AMBUSHED US--AND CARVED BOOSTER TO PIECES!
"WE WERE FOOLS TO FOLLOW HIM INTO BATTLE! BOOSTER ASSURED US THAT FUTURE HISTORY PROCLAIMED US THE VICTORS... AND I BELIEVED HIM!"

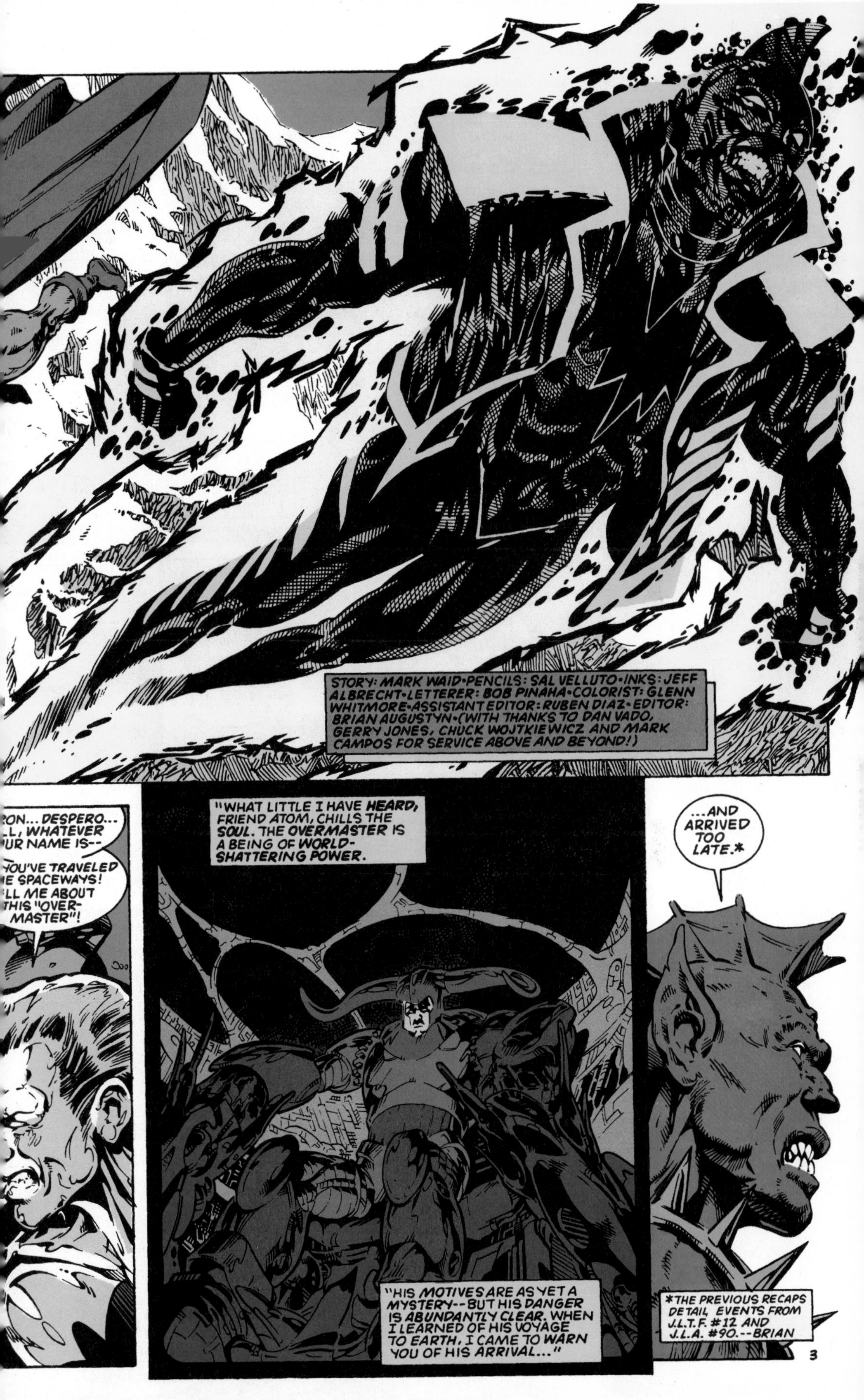

STORY: MARK WAID•PENCILS: SAL VELLUTO•INKS: JEFF ALBRECHT•LETTERER: BOB PINAHA•COLORIST: GLENN WHITMORE•ASSISTANT EDITOR: RUBEN DIAZ•EDITOR: BRIAN AUGUSTYN•(WITH THANKS TO DAN VADO, GERRY JONES, CHUCK WOJTKIEWICZ AND MARK CAMPOS FOR SERVICE ABOVE AND BEYOND!)
DESPERO... WHATEVER NAME IS--
YOU'VE TRAVELED SPACEWAYS! ME ABOUT THIS "OVER-MASTER"!
"WHAT LITTLE I HAVE HEARD, FRIEND ATOM, CHILLS THE SOUL. THE OVERMASTER IS A BEING OF WORLD-SHATTERING POWER.
"HIS MOTIVES ARE AS YET A MYSTERY--BUT HIS DANGER IS ABUNDANTLY CLEAR. WHEN I LEARNED OF HIS VOYAGE TO EARTH, I CAME TO WARN YOU OF HIS ARRIVAL..."
...AND ARRIVED TOO LATE.*
*THE PREVIOUS RECAPS DETAIL EVENTS FROM J.L.T.F. #12 AND J.L.A. #90.--BRIAN

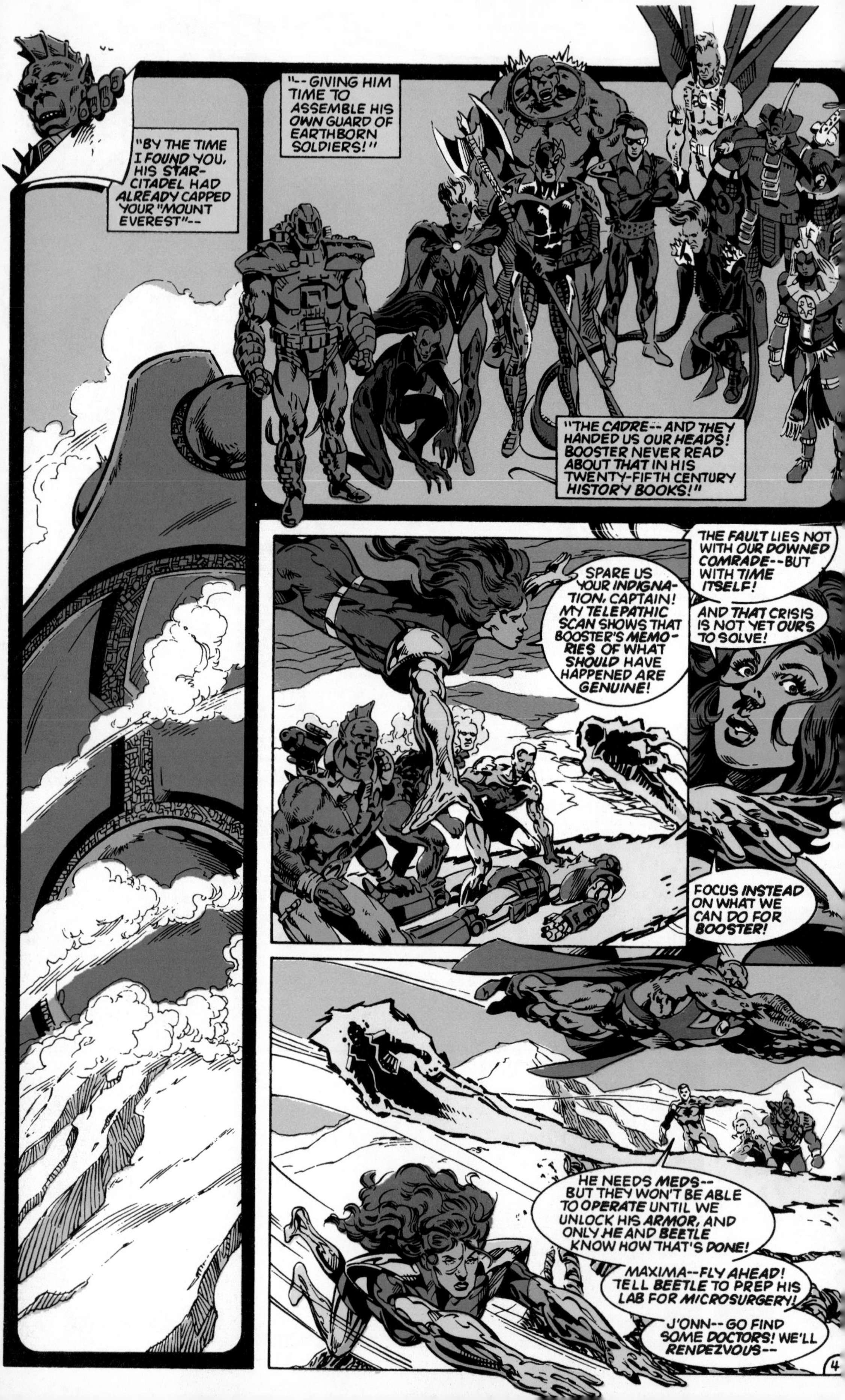
"BY THE TIME I FOUND YOU, HIS STAR-CITADEL HAD ALREADY CAPPED YOUR "MOUNT EVEREST"--
"--GIVING HIM TIME TO ASSEMBLE HIS OWN GUARD OF EARTHBORN SOLDIERS!"
"THE CADRE-- AND THEY HANDED US OUR HEADS! BOOSTER NEVER READ ABOUT THAT IN HIS TWENTY-FIFTH CENTURY HISTORY BOOKS!"
SPARE US YOUR INDIGNATION, CAPTAIN! MY TELEPATHIC SCAN SHOWS THAT BOOSTER'S MEMORIES OF WHAT SHOULD HAVE HAPPENED ARE GENUINE!
THE FAULT LIES NOT WITH OUR DOWNED COMRADE--BUT WITH TIME ITSELF!
AND THAT CRISIS IS NOT YET OURS TO SOLVE!
FOCUS INSTEAD ON WHAT WE CAN DO FOR BOOSTER!
HE NEEDS MEDS-- BUT THEY WON'T BE ABLE TO OPERATE UNTIL WE UNLOCK HIS ARMOR, AND ONLY HE AND BEETLE KNOW HOW THAT'S DONE!
MAXIMA--FLY AHEAD! TELL BEETLE TO PREP HIS LAB FOR MICROSURGERY!
J'ONN--GO FIND SOME DOCTORS! WE'LL RENDEZVOUS--
4

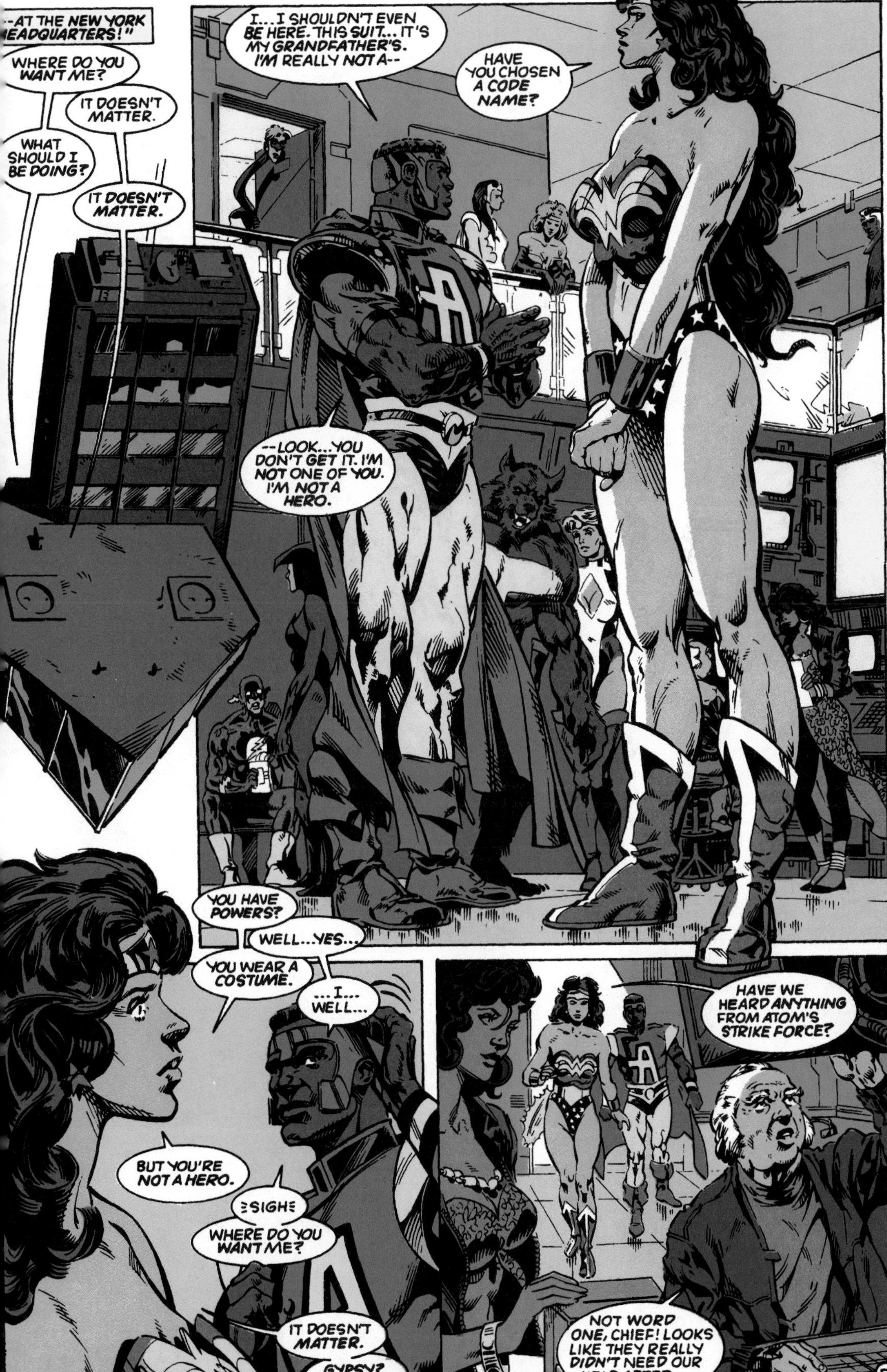
--AT THE NEW YORK HEADQUARTERS!"
WHERE DO YOU WANT ME?
IT DOESN'T MATTER.
WHAT SHOULD I BE DOING?
IT DOESN'T MATTER.
I... I SHOULDN'T EVEN BE HERE. THIS SUIT... IT'S MY GRANDFATHER'S. I'M REALLY NOT A--
HAVE YOU CHOSEN A CODE NAME?
--LOOK... YOU DON'T GET IT. I'M NOT ONE OF YOU. I'M NOT A HERO.
YOU HAVE POWERS?
WELL... YES...
YOU WEAR A COSTUME.
... I... WELL...
BUT YOU'RE NOT A HERO.
SIGH
WHERE DO YOU WANT ME?
IT DOESN'T MATTER.
GYPSY? OBERON?
HAVE WE HEARD ANYTHING FROM ATOM'S STRIKE FORCE?
NOT WORD ONE, CHIEF! LOOKS LIKE THEY REALLY DIDN'T NEED OUR HELP AFTER--
5

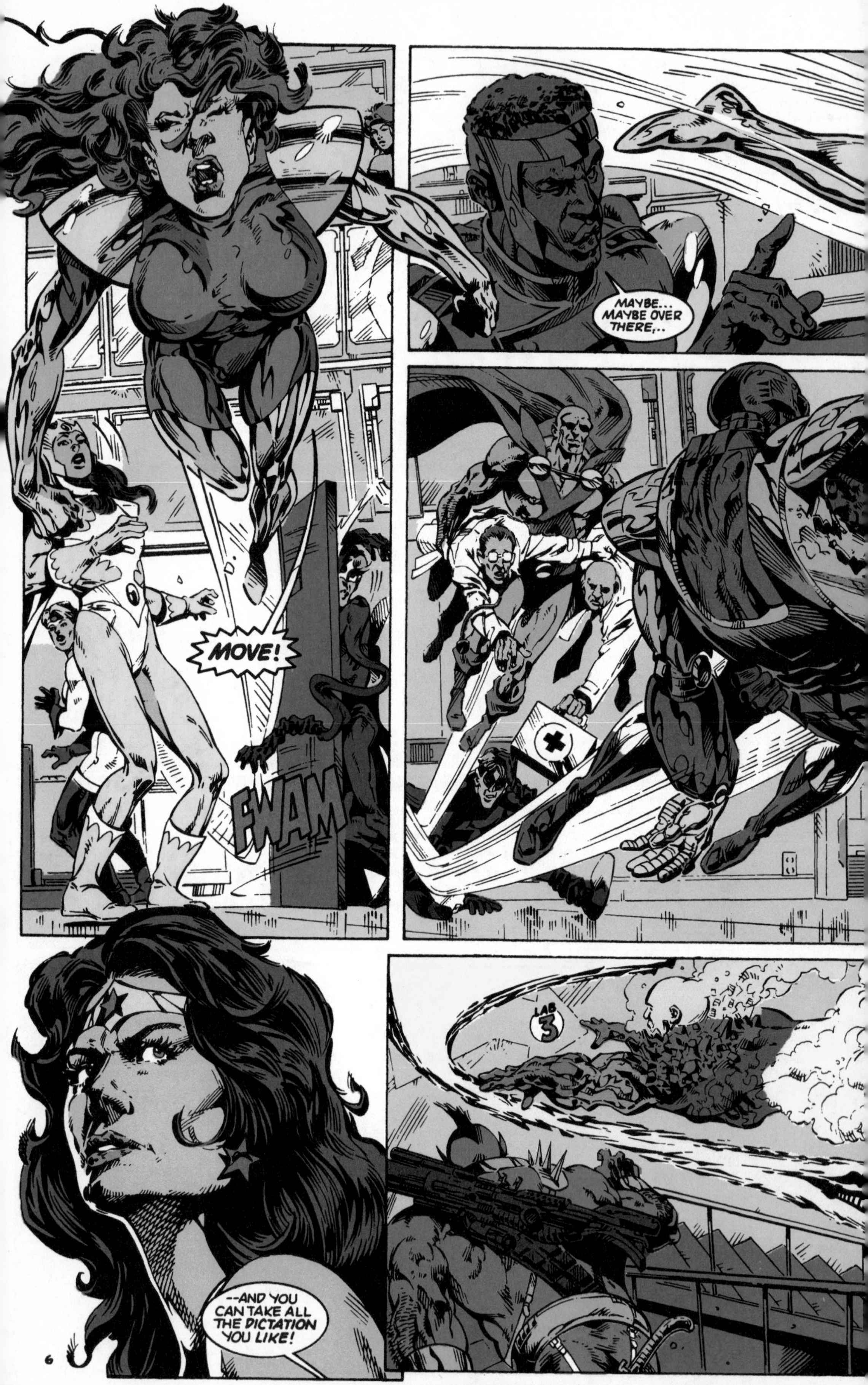
MAYBE... MAYBE OVER THERE,..
MOVE!
FWAM
LAB 3
--AND YOU CAN TAKE ALL THE DICTATION YOU LIKE!

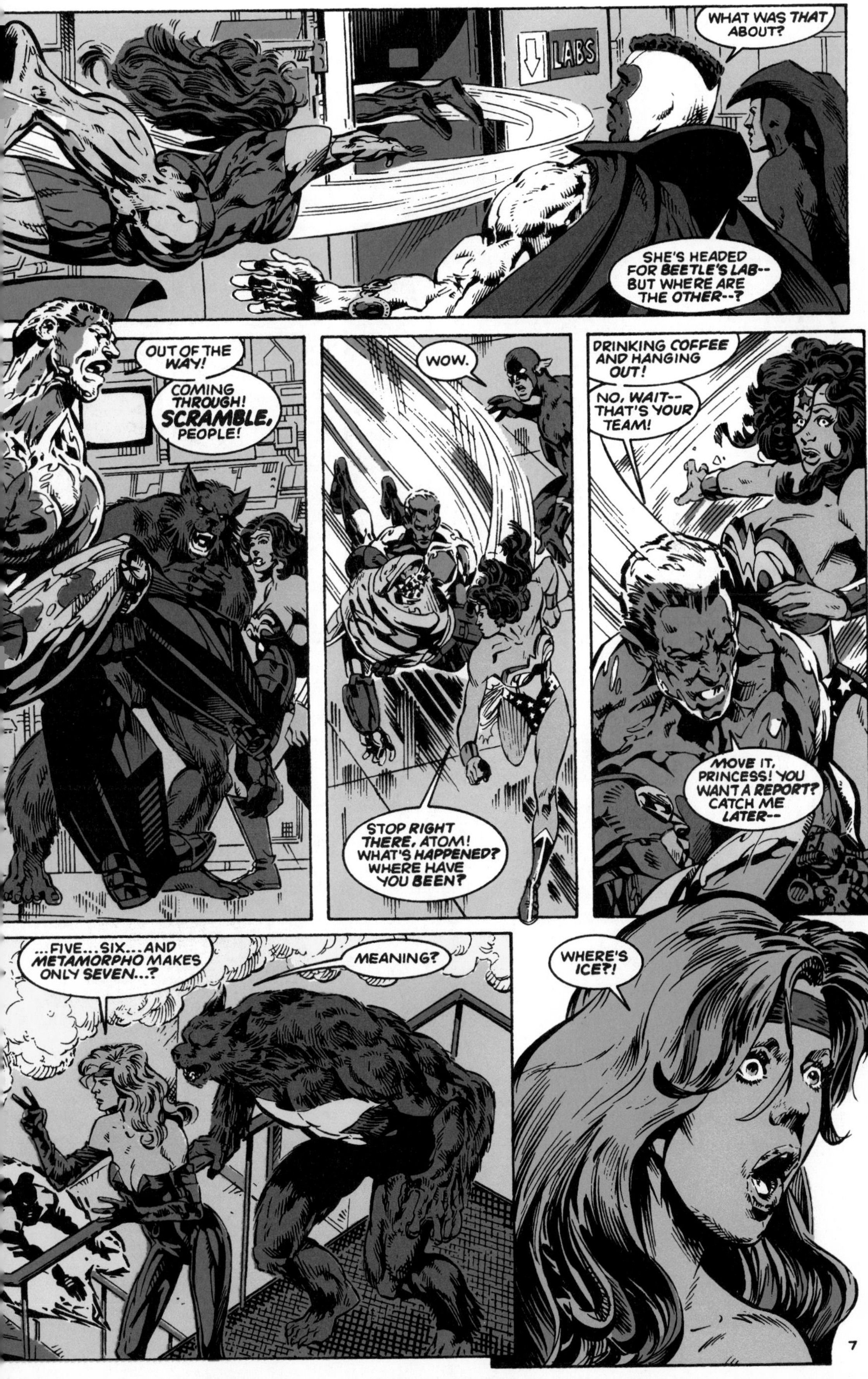

WHAT WAS THAT ABOUT?
LABS
SHE'S HEADED FOR BEETLE'S LAB-- BUT WHERE ARE THE OTHER--?
OUT OF THE WAY!
COMING THROUGH! SCRAMBLE, PEOPLE!
WOW.
STOP RIGHT THERE, ATOM! WHAT'S HAPPENED? WHERE HAVE YOU BEEN?
DRINKING COFFEE AND HANGING OUT!
NO, WAIT-- THAT'S YOUR TEAM!
MOVE IT, PRINCESS! YOU WANT A REPORT? CATCH ME LATER--
...FIVE...SIX...AND METAMORPHO MAKES ONLY SEVEN...?
MEANING?
WHERE'S ICE?!

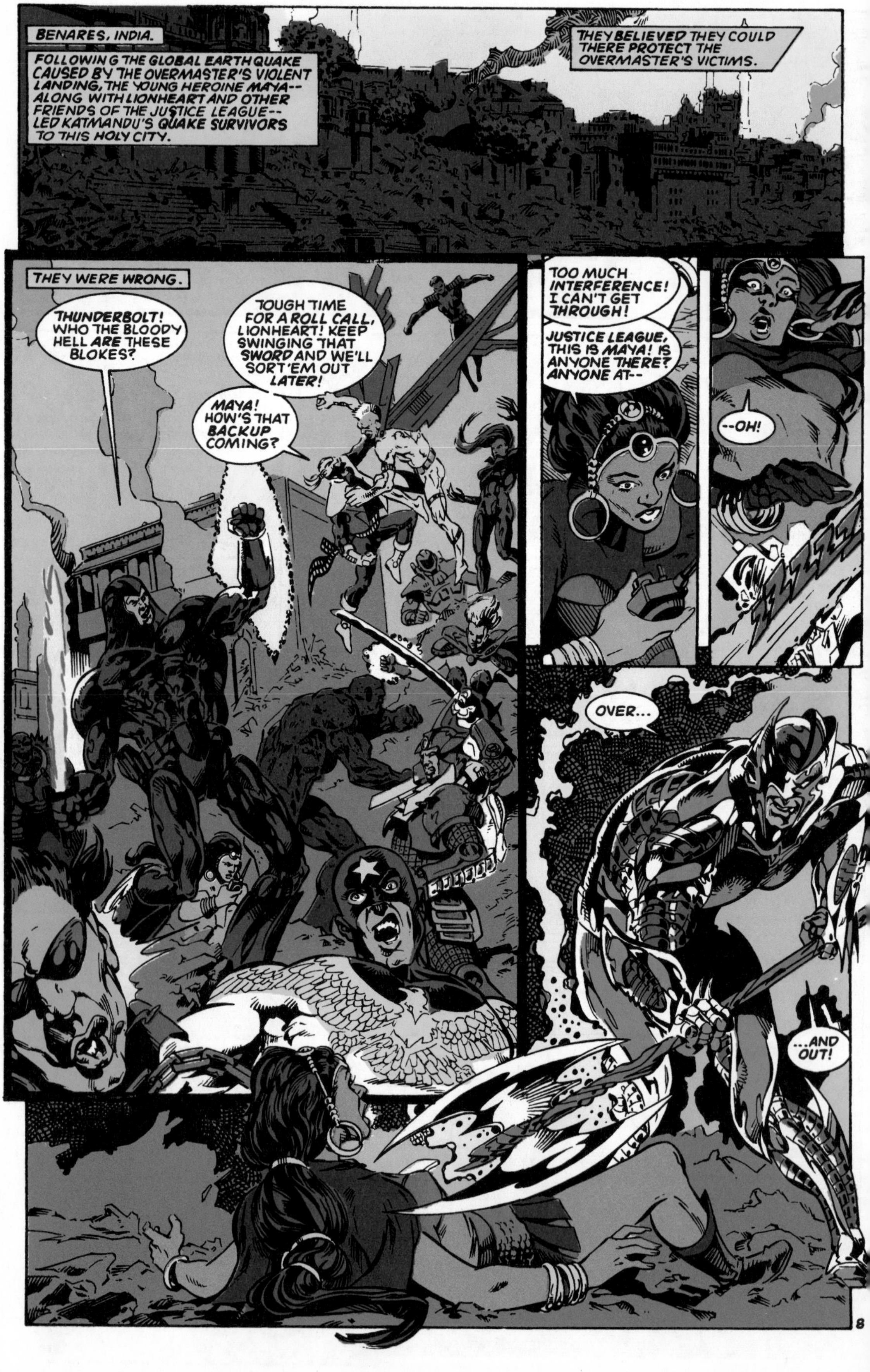
BENARES, INDIA.
FOLLOWING THE GLOBAL EARTHQUAKE CAUSED BY THE OVERMASTER'S VIOLENT LANDING, THE YOUNG HEROINE MAYA--ALONG WITH LIONHEART AND OTHER FRIENDS OF THE JUSTICE LEAGUE--LED KATMANDU'S QUAKE SURVIVORS TO THIS HOLY CITY.
THEY BELIEVED THEY COULD THERE PROTECT THE OVERMASTER'S VICTIMS.
THEY WERE WRONG.
THUNDERBOLT! WHO THE BLOODY HELL ARE THESE BLOKES?
TOUGH TIME FOR A ROLL CALL, LIONHEART! KEEP SWINGING THAT SWORD AND WE'LL SORT 'EM OUT LATER!
MAYA! HOW'S THAT BACKUP COMING?
TOO MUCH INTERFERENCE! I CAN'T GET THROUGH!
JUSTICE LEAGUE, THIS IS MAYA! IS ANYONE THERE? ANYONE AT--
--OH!
OVER...
...AND OUT!

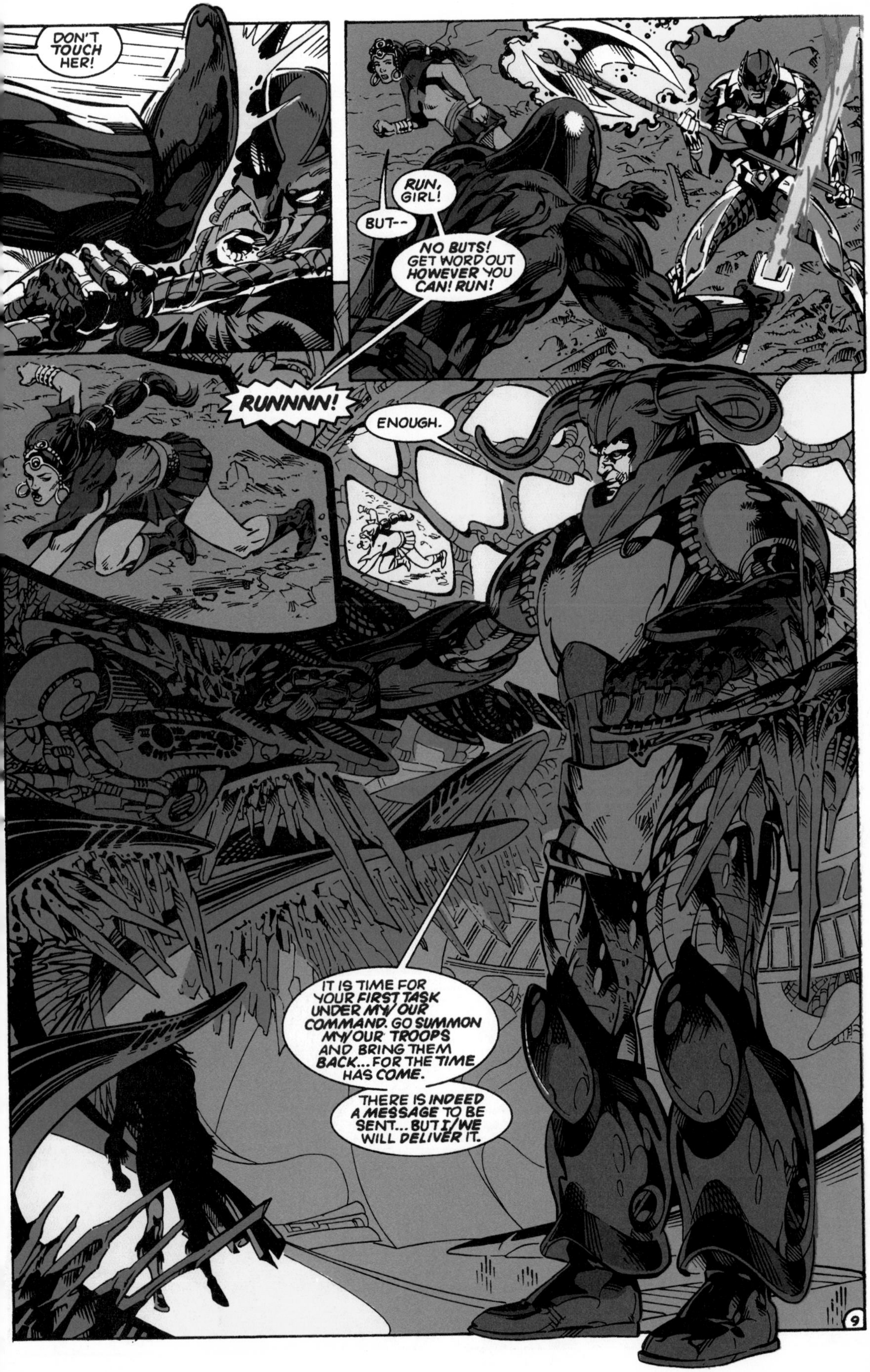

DON'T TOUCH HER!
RUN, GIRL!
BUT--
NO BUTS! GET WORD OUT HOWEVER YOU CAN! RUN!
RUNNNN!
ENOUGH.
IT IS TIME FOR YOUR FIRST TASK UNDER MY/ OUR COMMAND. GO SUMMON MY/OUR TROOPS AND BRING THEM BACK... FOR THE TIME HAS COME.
THERE IS INDEED A MESSAGE TO BE SENT... BUT I/WE WILL DELIVER IT.

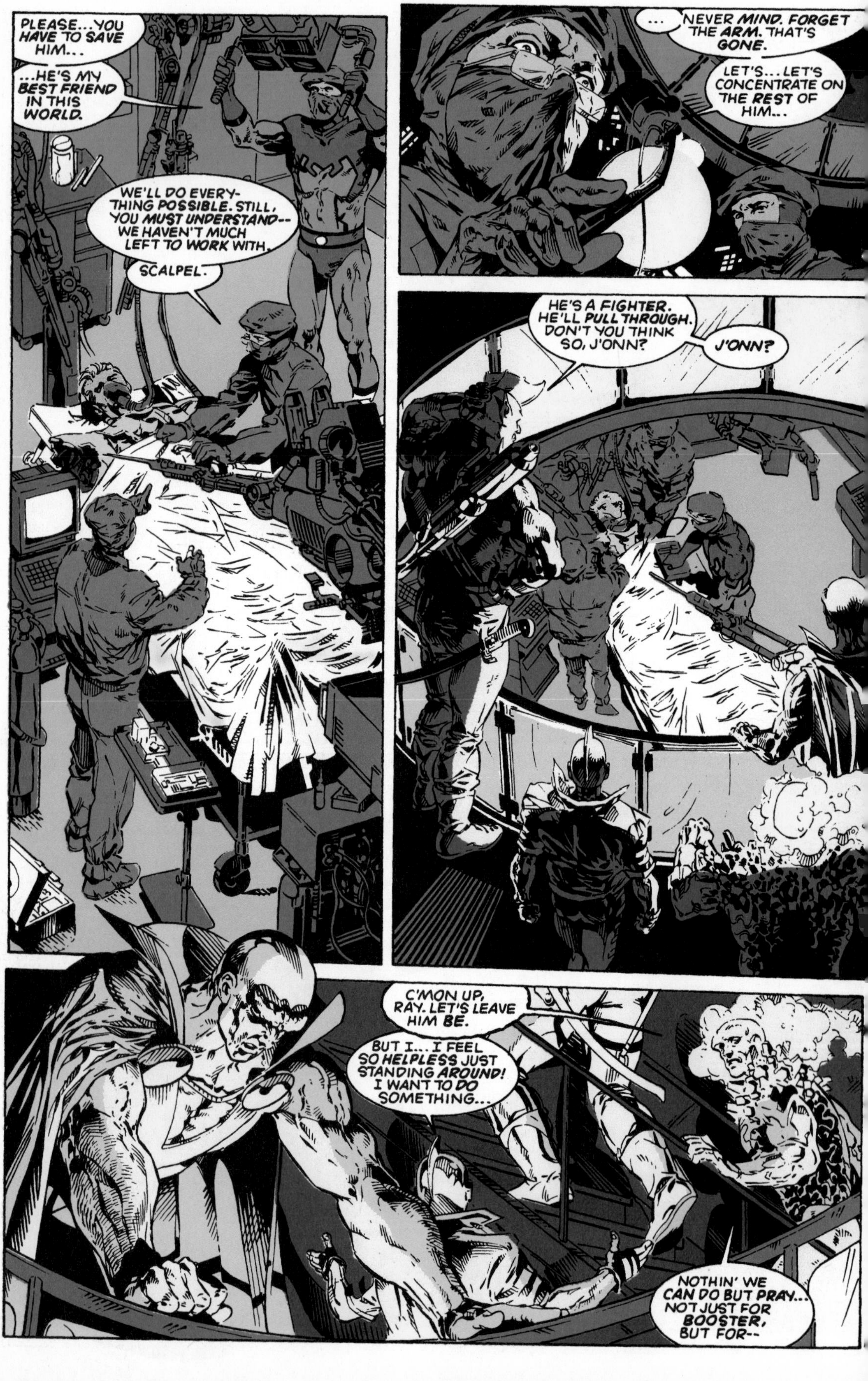
PLEASE... YOU HAVE TO SAVE HIM...
...HE'S MY BEST FRIEND IN THIS WORLD.
WE'LL DO EVERYTHING POSSIBLE. STILL, YOU MUST UNDERSTAND-- WE HAVEN'T MUCH LEFT TO WORK WITH.
SCALPEL.
...
NEVER MIND. FORGET THE ARM. THAT'S GONE.
LET'S... LET'S CONCENTRATE ON THE REST OF HIM...
HE'S A FIGHTER. HE'LL PULL THROUGH. DON'T YOU THINK SO, J'ONN?
J'ONN?
C'MON UP, RAY. LET'S LEAVE HIM BE.
BUT I... I FEEL SO HELPLESS JUST STANDING AROUND! I WANT TO DO SOMETHING...
NOTHIN' WE CAN DO BUT PRAY... NOT JUST FOR BOOSTER, BUT FOR--

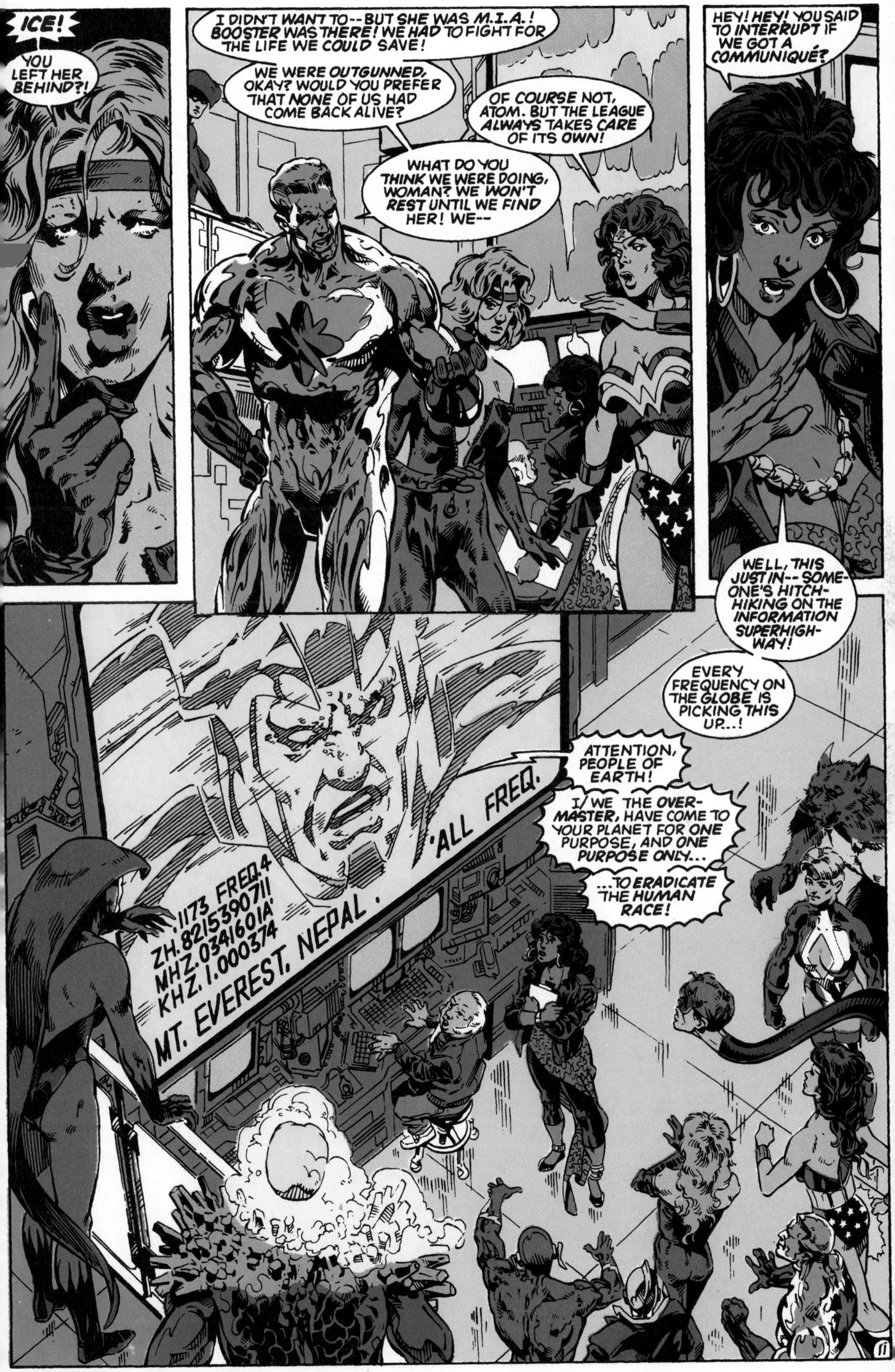
ICE!
YOU LEFT HER BEHIND?!
I DIDN'T WANT TO-- BUT SHE WAS M.I.A.! BOOSTER WAS THERE! WE HAD TO FIGHT FOR THE LIFE WE COULD SAVE!
WE WERE OUTGUNNED, OKAY? WOULD YOU PREFER THAT NONE OF US HAD COME BACK ALIVE?
OF COURSE NOT, ATOM. BUT THE LEAGUE ALWAYS TAKES CARE OF ITS OWN!
WHAT DO YOU THINK WE WERE DOING, WOMAN? WE WON'T REST UNTIL WE FIND HER! WE--
HEY! HEY! YOU SAID TO INTERRUPT IF WE GOT A COMMUNIQUÉ?
WELL, THIS JUST IN-- SOMEONE'S HITCH-HIKING ON THE INFORMATION SUPERHIGHWAY!
EVERY FREQUENCY ON THE GLOBE IS PICKING THIS UP...!
'ALL FREQ.
.1173 FREQ.4
ZH.8215390711
MHZ.0341601A'
KHZ.1.000374
MT. EVEREST. NEPAL.
ATTENTION, PEOPLE OF EARTH!
I/WE THE OVER-MASTER, HAVE COME TO YOUR PLANET FOR ONE PURPOSE, AND ONE PURPOSE ONLY...
...TO ERADICATE THE HUMAN RACE!

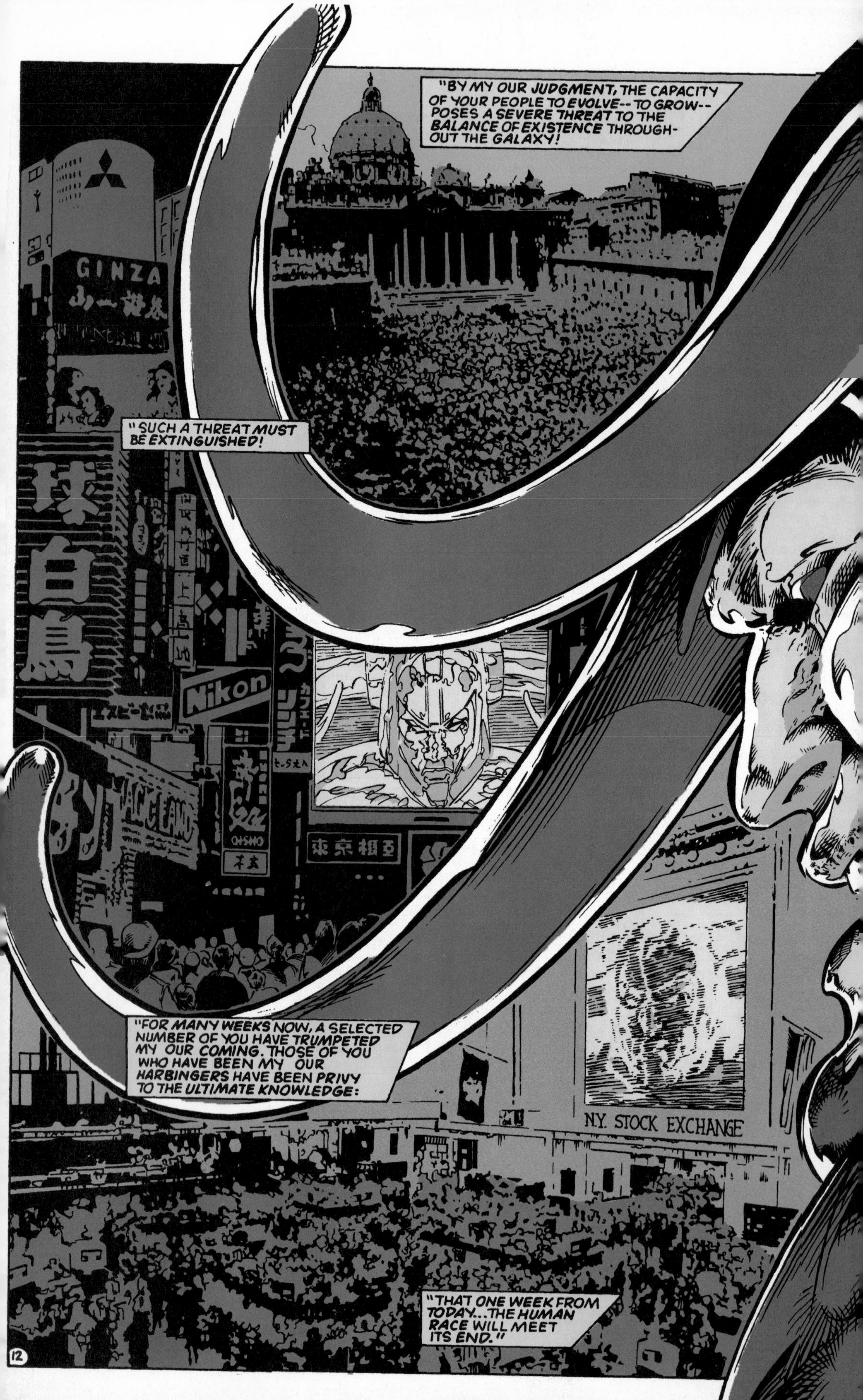
"BY MY OUR JUDGMENT, THE CAPACITY OF YOUR PEOPLE TO EVOLVE-- TO GROW-- POSES A SEVERE THREAT TO THE BALANCE OF EXISTENCE THROUGH-OUT THE GALAXY!
"SUCH A THREAT MUST BE EXTINGUISHED!
GINZA
Nikon
"FOR MANY WEEKS NOW, A SELECTED NUMBER OF YOU HAVE TRUMPETED MY OUR COMING. THOSE OF YOU WHO HAVE BEEN MY OUR HARBINGERS HAVE BEEN PRIVY TO THE ULTIMATE KNOWLEDGE:
N.Y. STOCK EXCHANGE
"THAT ONE WEEK FROM TODAY... THE HUMAN RACE WILL MEET ITS END."

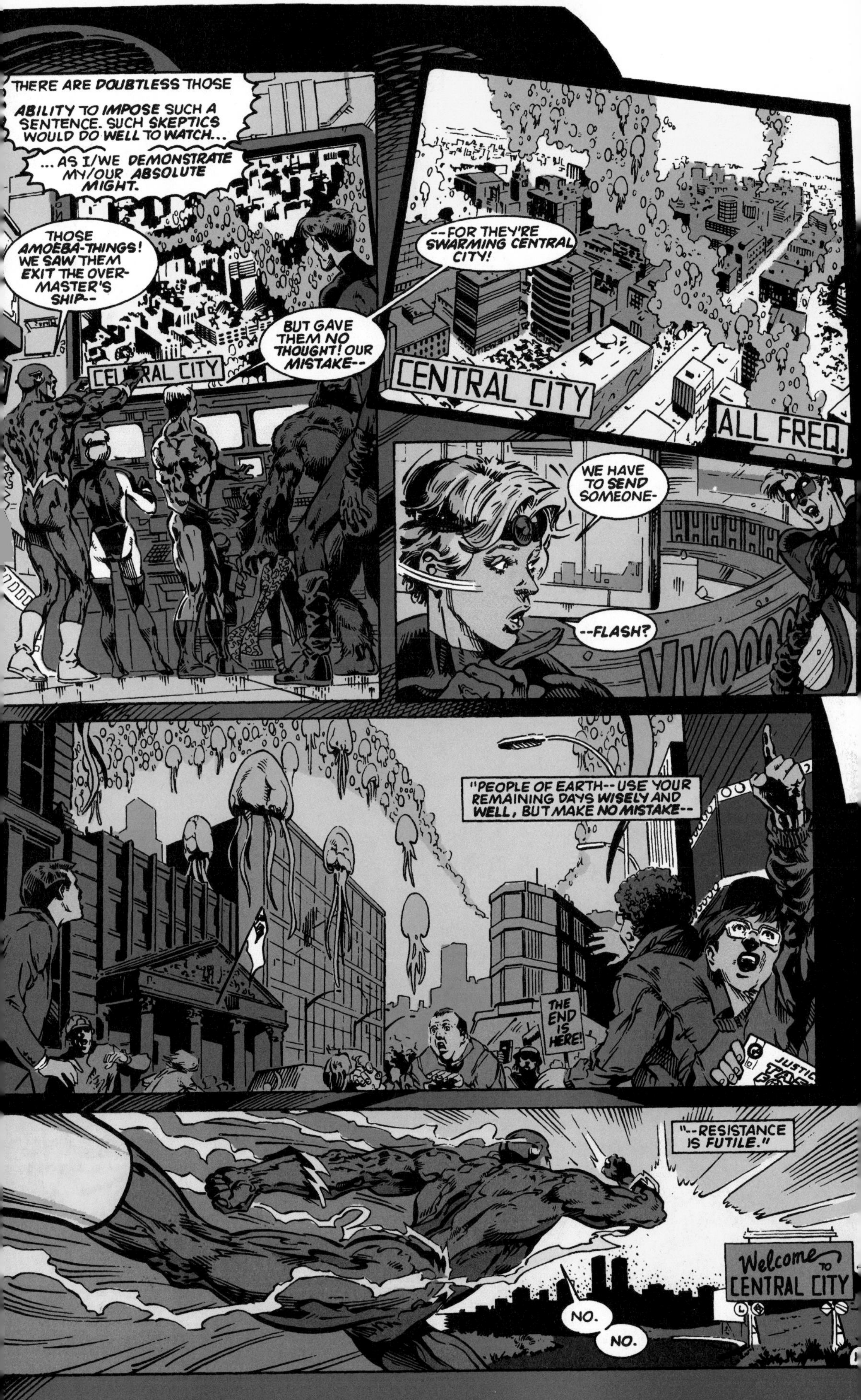
THERE ARE DOUBTLESS THOSE
ABILITY TO IMPOSE SUCH A SENTENCE. SUCH SKEPTICS WOULD DO WELL TO WATCH...
...AS I/WE DEMONSTRATE MY/OUR ABSOLUTE MIGHT.
THOSE AMOEBA-THINGS! WE SAW THEM EXIT THE OVER-MASTER'S SHIP--
BUT GAVE THEM NO THOUGHT! OUR MISTAKE--
--FOR THEY'RE SWARMING CENTRAL CITY!
CENTRAL CITY
CENTRAL CITY
ALL FREQ.
WE HAVE TO SEND SOMEONE-
--FLASH?
VVOOOO
"PEOPLE OF EARTH--USE YOUR REMAINING DAYS WISELY AND WELL, BUT MAKE NO MISTAKE--
THE END IS HERE!
"--RESISTANCE IS FUTILE."
Welcome TO CENTRAL CITY
NO.
NO.

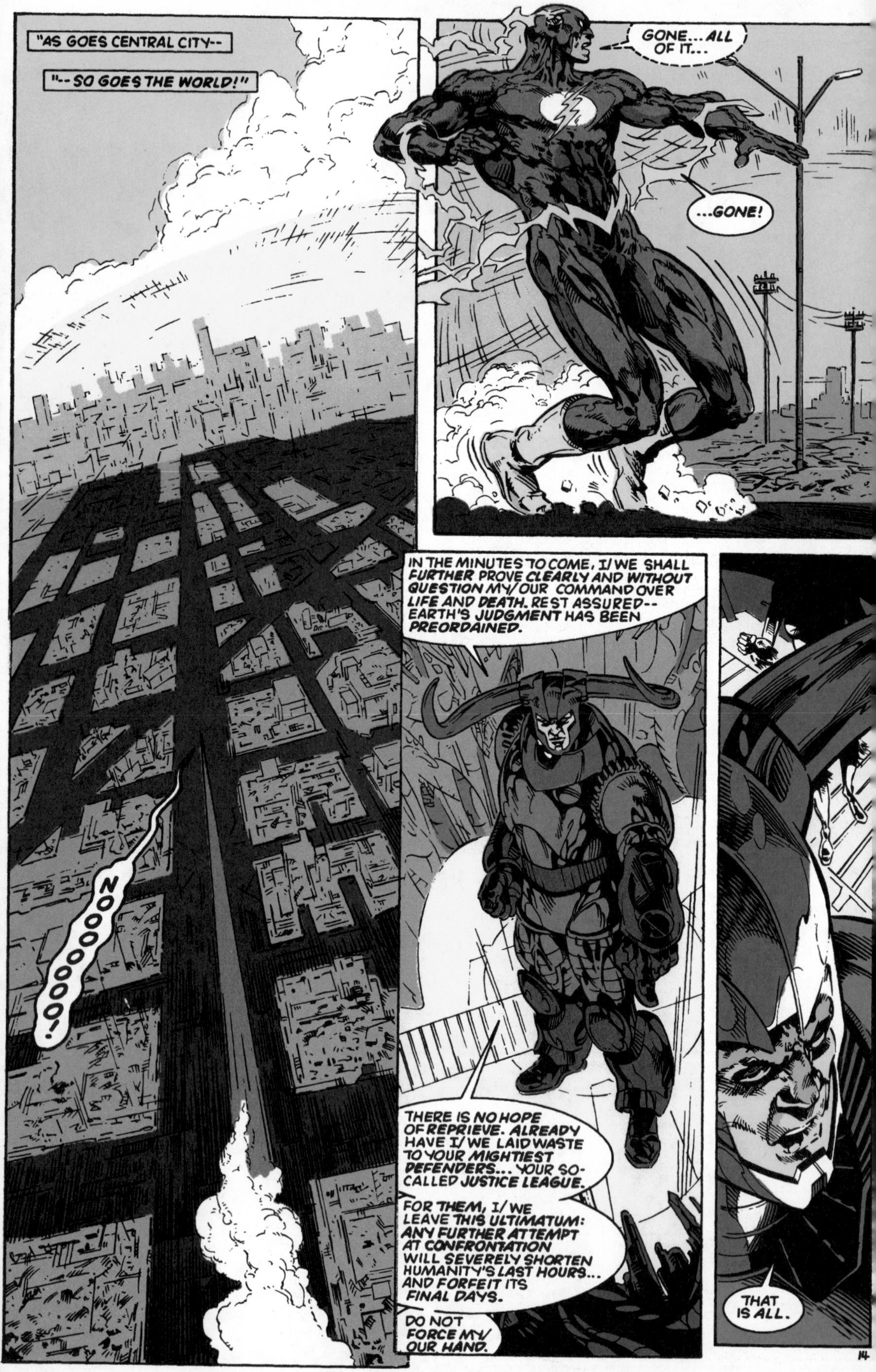
"AS GOES CENTRAL CITY--
"--SO GOES THE WORLD!"
NOOOOOOOO!
GONE... ALL OF IT...
...GONE!
IN THE MINUTES TO COME, I/WE SHALL FURTHER PROVE CLEARLY AND WITHOUT QUESTION MY/OUR COMMAND OVER LIFE AND DEATH. REST ASSURED-- EARTH'S JUDGMENT HAS BEEN PREORDAINED.
THERE IS NO HOPE OF REPRIEVE. ALREADY HAVE I/WE LAID WASTE TO YOUR MIGHTIEST DEFENDERS... YOUR SO-CALLED JUSTICE LEAGUE.
FOR THEM, I/WE LEAVE THIS ULTIMATUM: ANY FURTHER ATTEMPT AT CONFRONTATION WILL SEVERELY SHORTEN HUMANITY'S LAST HOURS... AND FORFEIT ITS FINAL DAYS.
DO NOT FORCE MY/OUR HAND.
THAT IS ALL.

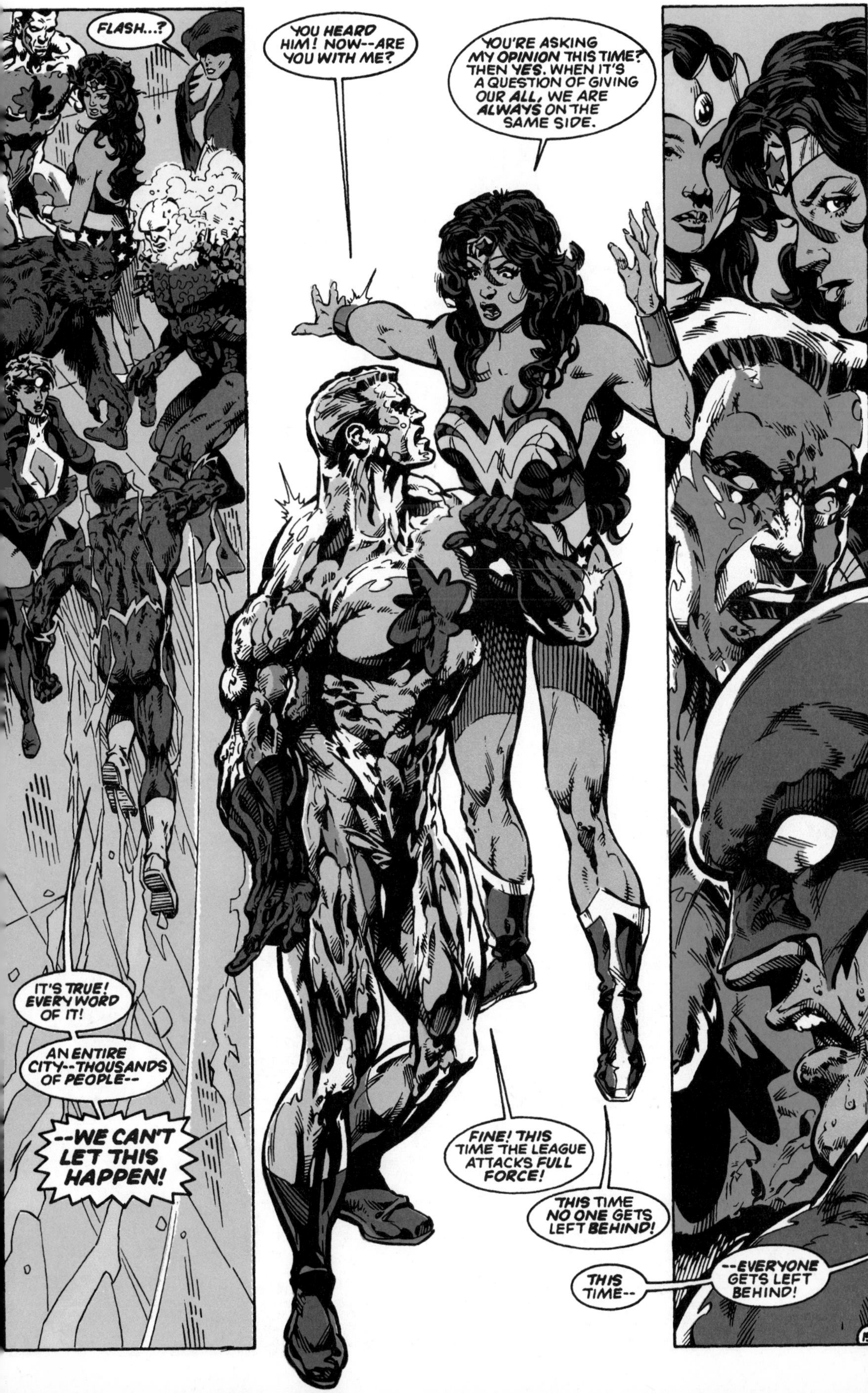
FLASH...?
YOU HEARD HIM! NOW--ARE YOU WITH ME?
YOU'RE ASKING MY OPINION THIS TIME? THEN YES. WHEN IT'S A QUESTION OF GIVING OUR ALL, WE ARE ALWAYS ON THE SAME SIDE.
IT'S TRUE! EVERY WORD OF IT!
AN ENTIRE CITY--THOUSANDS OF PEOPLE--
--WE CAN'T LET THIS HAPPEN!
FINE! THIS TIME THE LEAGUE ATTACKS FULL FORCE!
THIS TIME NO ONE GETS LEFT BEHIND!
THIS TIME--
--EVERYONE GETS LEFT BEHIND!
15

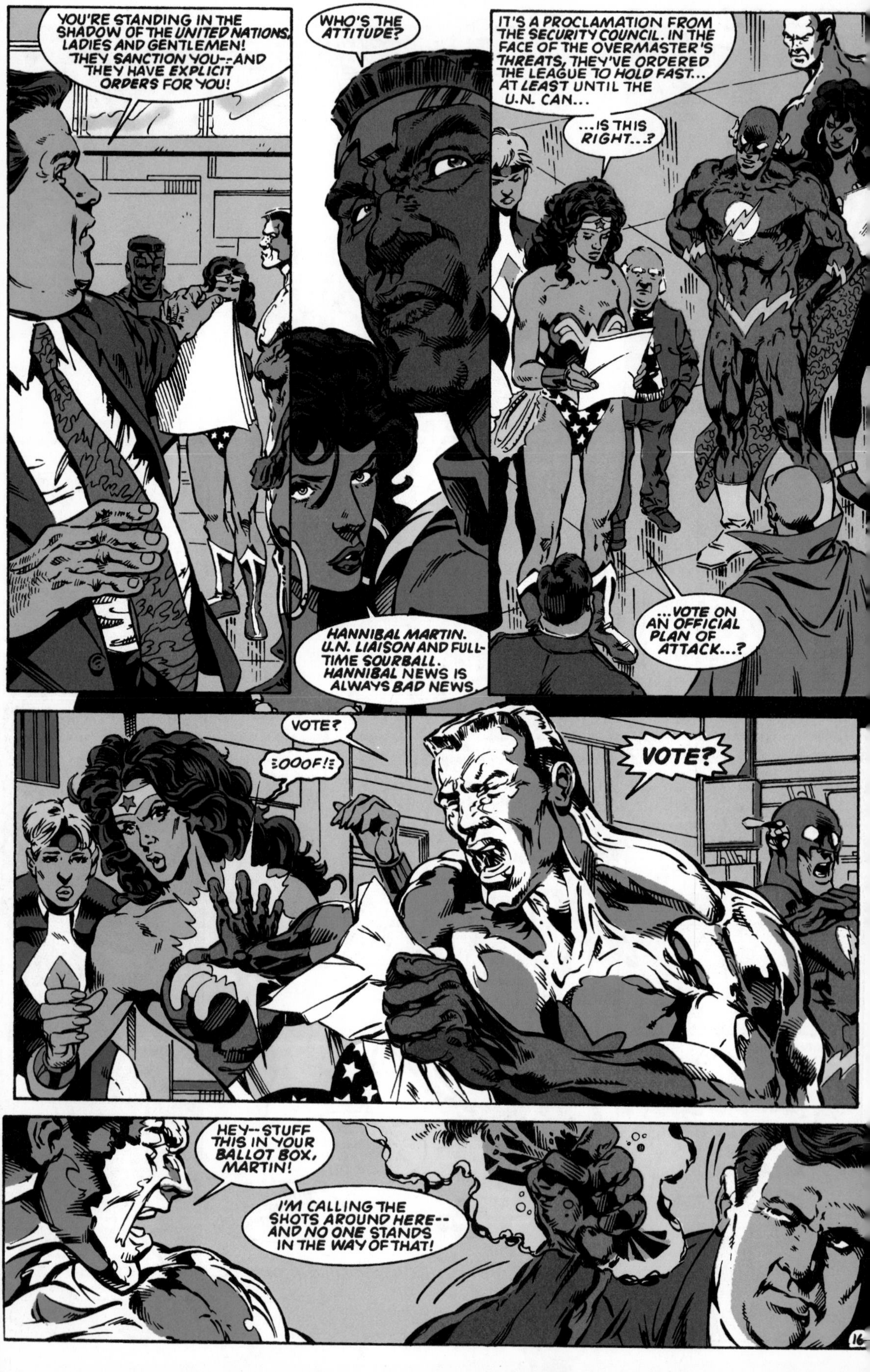
YOU'RE STANDING IN THE SHADOW OF THE UNITED NATIONS, LADIES AND GENTLEMEN! THEY SANCTION YOU--AND THEY HAVE EXPLICIT ORDERS FOR YOU!
WHO'S THE ATTITUDE?
HANNIBAL MARTIN. U.N. LIAISON AND FULL-TIME SOURBALL. HANNIBAL NEWS IS ALWAYS BAD NEWS.
IT'S A PROCLAMATION FROM THE SECURITY COUNCIL. IN THE FACE OF THE OVERMASTER'S THREATS, THEY'VE ORDERED THE LEAGUE TO HOLD FAST... AT LEAST UNTIL THE U.N. CAN...
...IS THIS RIGHT...?
...VOTE ON AN OFFICIAL PLAN OF ATTACK...?
VOTE?
OOOF!
VOTE?
HEY--STUFF THIS IN YOUR BALLOT BOX, MARTIN!
I'M CALLING THE SHOTS AROUND HERE--AND NO ONE STANDS IN THE WAY OF THAT!

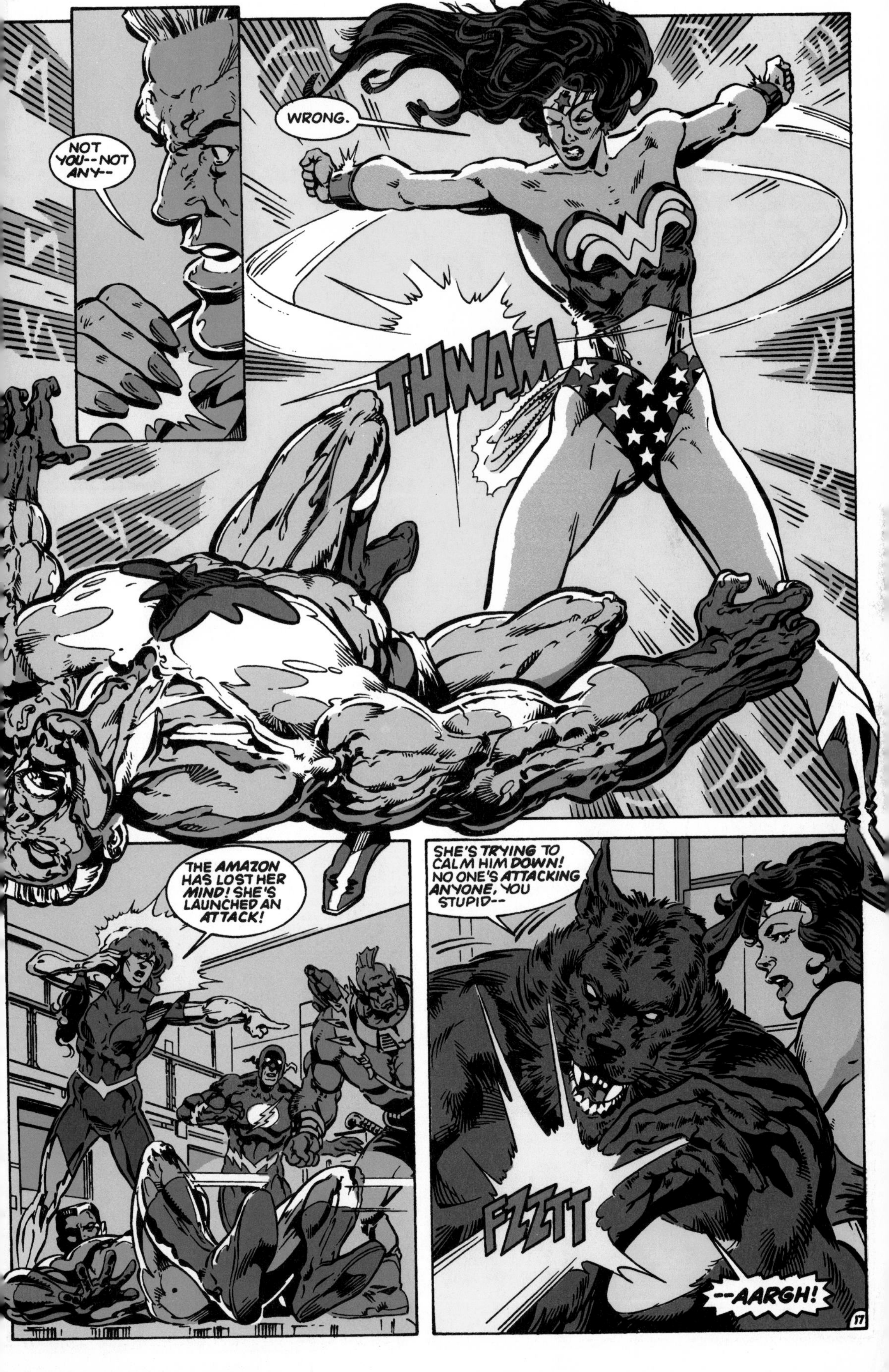
NOT YOU--NOT ANY--
WRONG.
THWAM
THE AMAZON HAS LOST HER MIND! SHE'S LAUNCHED AN ATTACK!
SHE'S TRYING TO CALM HIM DOWN! NO ONE'S ATTACKING ANYONE, YOU STUPID--
FZZTT
--AARGH!

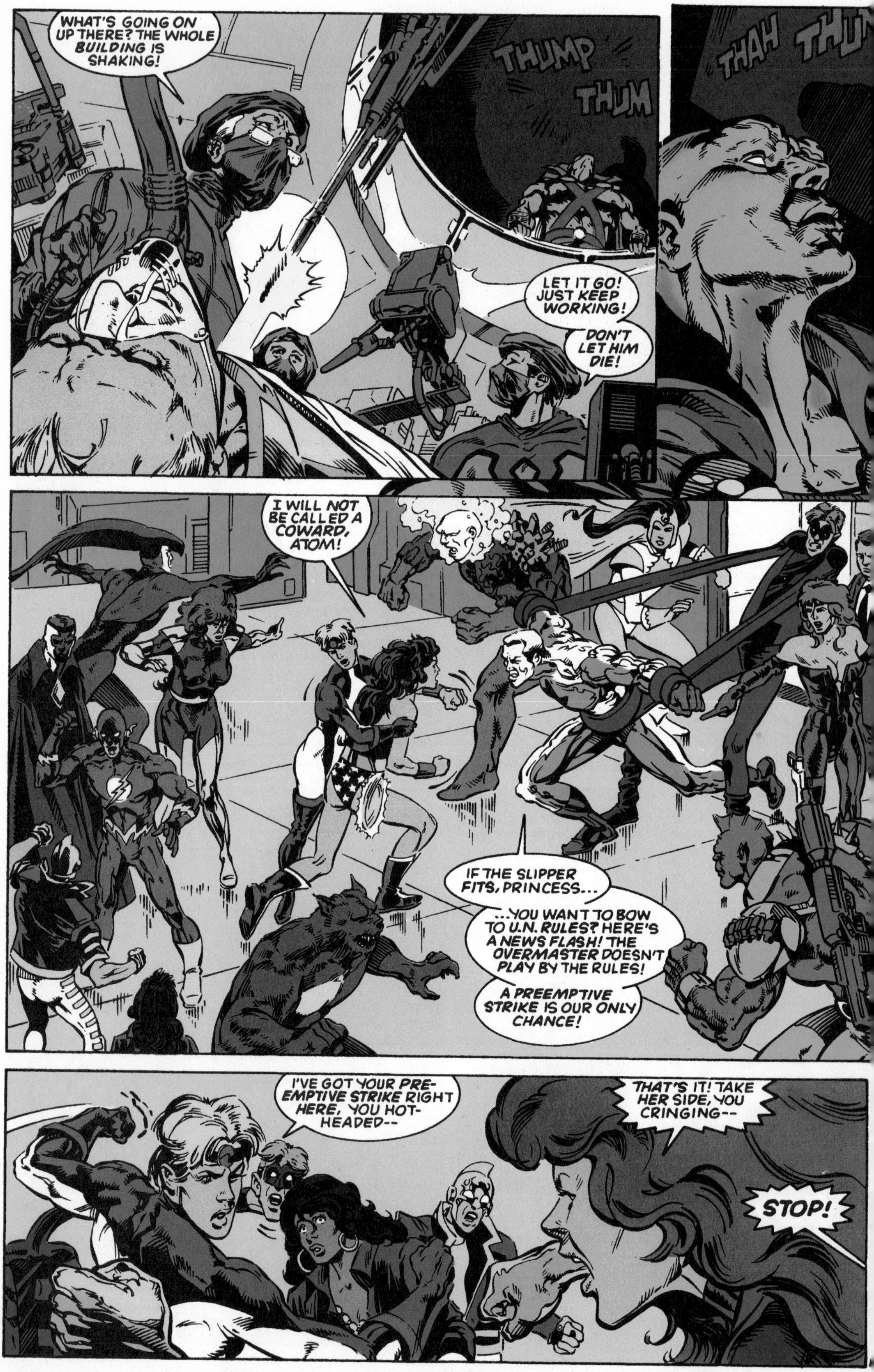

WHAT'S GOING ON UP THERE? THE WHOLE BUILDING IS SHAKING!
THUMP
THUM
LET IT GO! JUST KEEP WORKING!
DON'T LET HIM DIE!
THAH
I WILL NOT BE CALLED A COWARD, ATOM!
IF THE SLIPPER FITS, PRINCESS...
...YOU WANT TO BOW TO U.N. RULES? HERE'S A NEWS FLASH! THE OVERMASTER DOESN'T PLAY BY THE RULES!
A PREEMPTIVE STRIKE IS OUR ONLY CHANCE!
I'VE GOT YOUR PRE-EMPTIVE STRIKE RIGHT HERE, YOU HOT-HEADED--
THAT'S IT! TAKE HER SIDE, YOU CRINGING--
STOP!

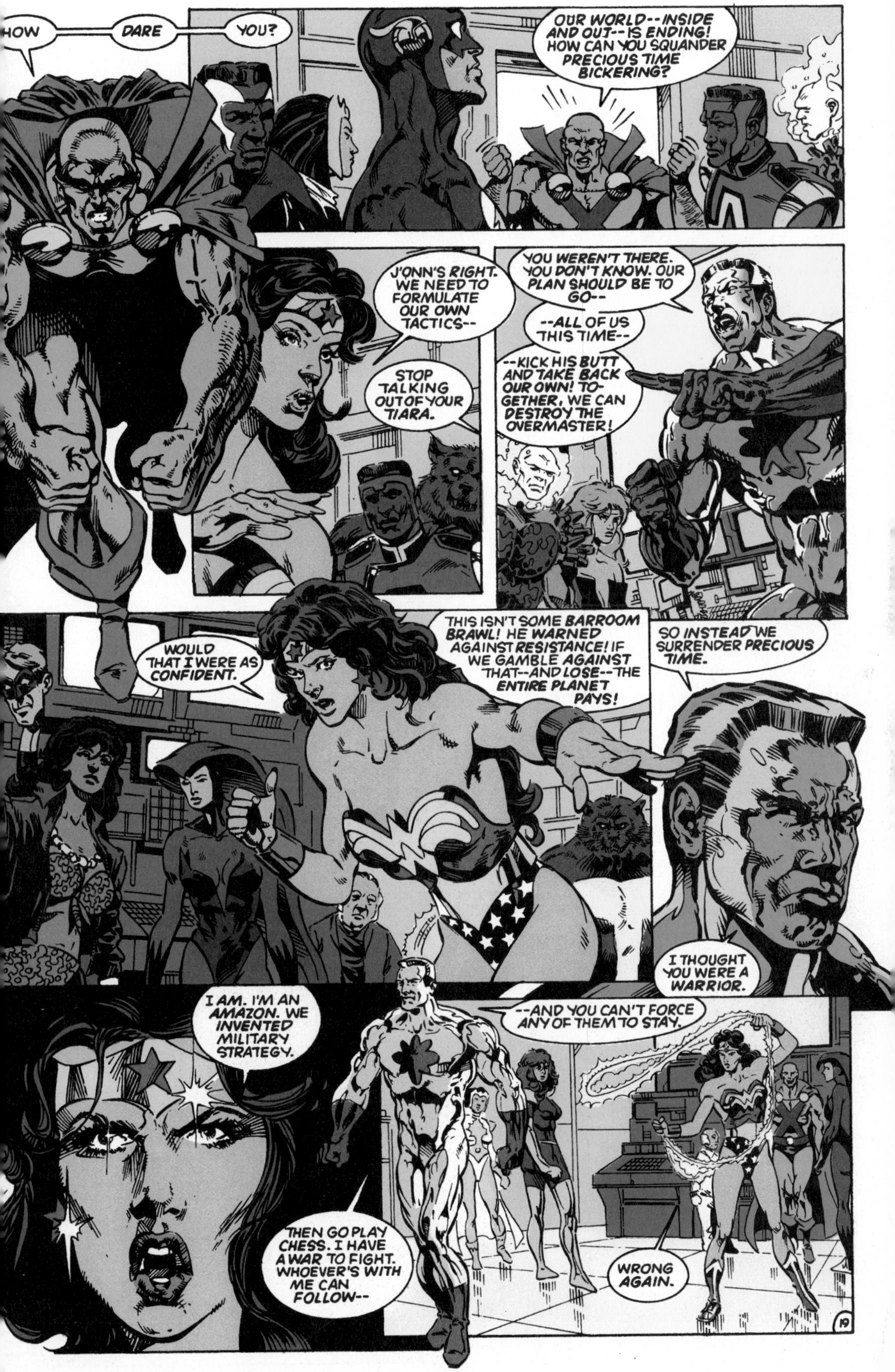
HOW DARE YOU?
OUR WORLD--INSIDE AND OUT--IS ENDING! HOW CAN YOU SQUANDER PRECIOUS TIME BICKERING?
J'ONN'S RIGHT. WE NEED TO FORMULATE OUR OWN TACTICS--
STOP TALKING OUT OF YOUR TIARA.
YOU WEREN'T THERE. YOU DON'T KNOW. OUR PLAN SHOULD BE TO GO--
--ALL OF US THIS TIME--
--KICK HIS BUTT AND TAKE BACK OUR OWN! TOGETHER, WE CAN DESTROY THE OVERMASTER!
WOULD THAT I WERE AS CONFIDENT.
THIS ISN'T SOME BARROOM BRAWL! HE WARNED AGAINST RESISTANCE! IF WE GAMBLE AGAINST THAT--AND LOSE--THE ENTIRE PLANET PAYS!
SO INSTEAD WE SURRENDER PRECIOUS TIME.
I THOUGHT YOU WERE A WARRIOR.
I AM. I'M AN AMAZON. WE INVENTED MILITARY STRATEGY.
THEN GO PLAY CHESS. I HAVE A WAR TO FIGHT. WHOEVER'S WITH ME CAN FOLLOW--
--AND YOU CAN'T FORCE ANY OF THEM TO STAY.
WRONG AGAIN.
19

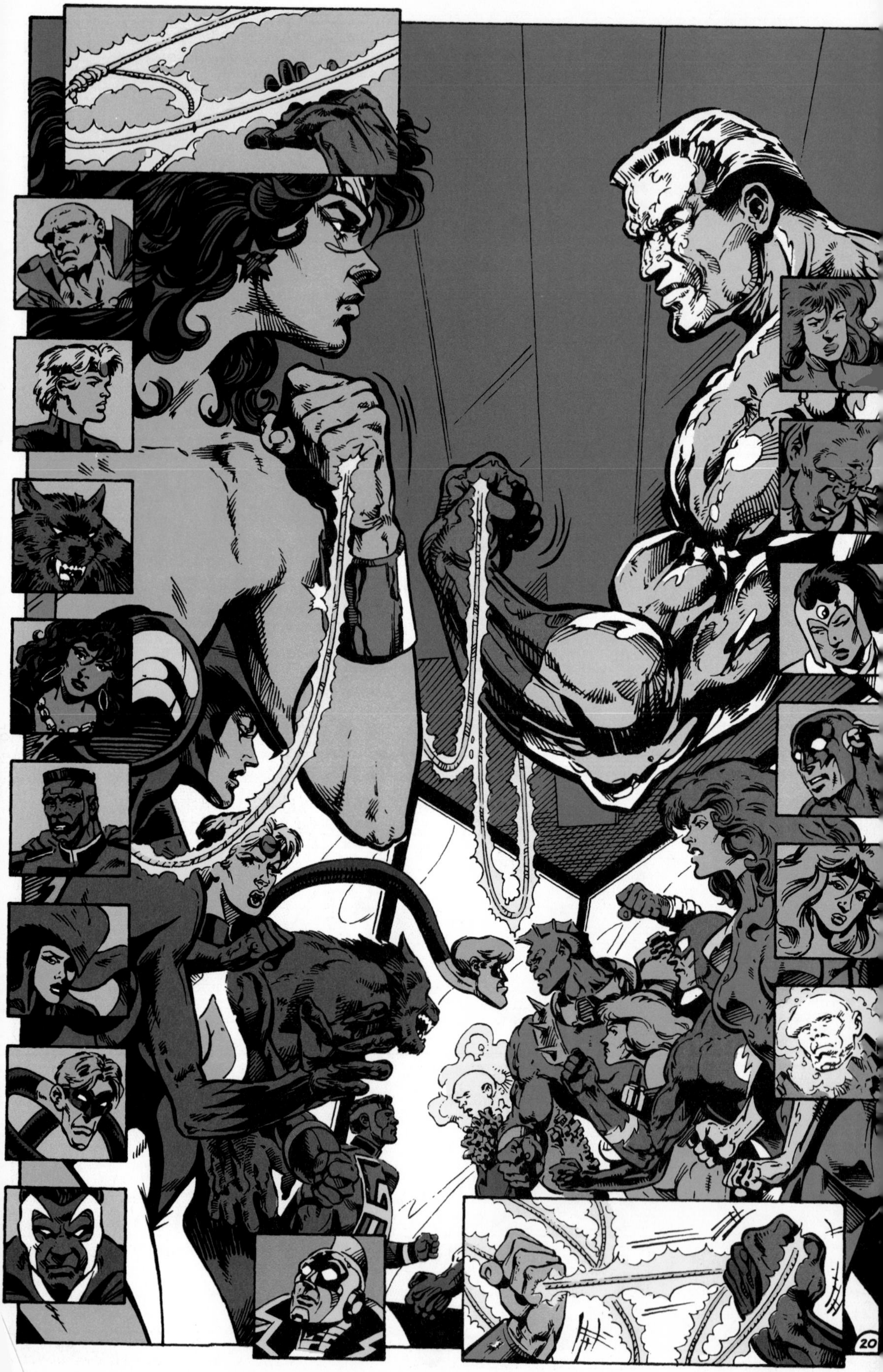

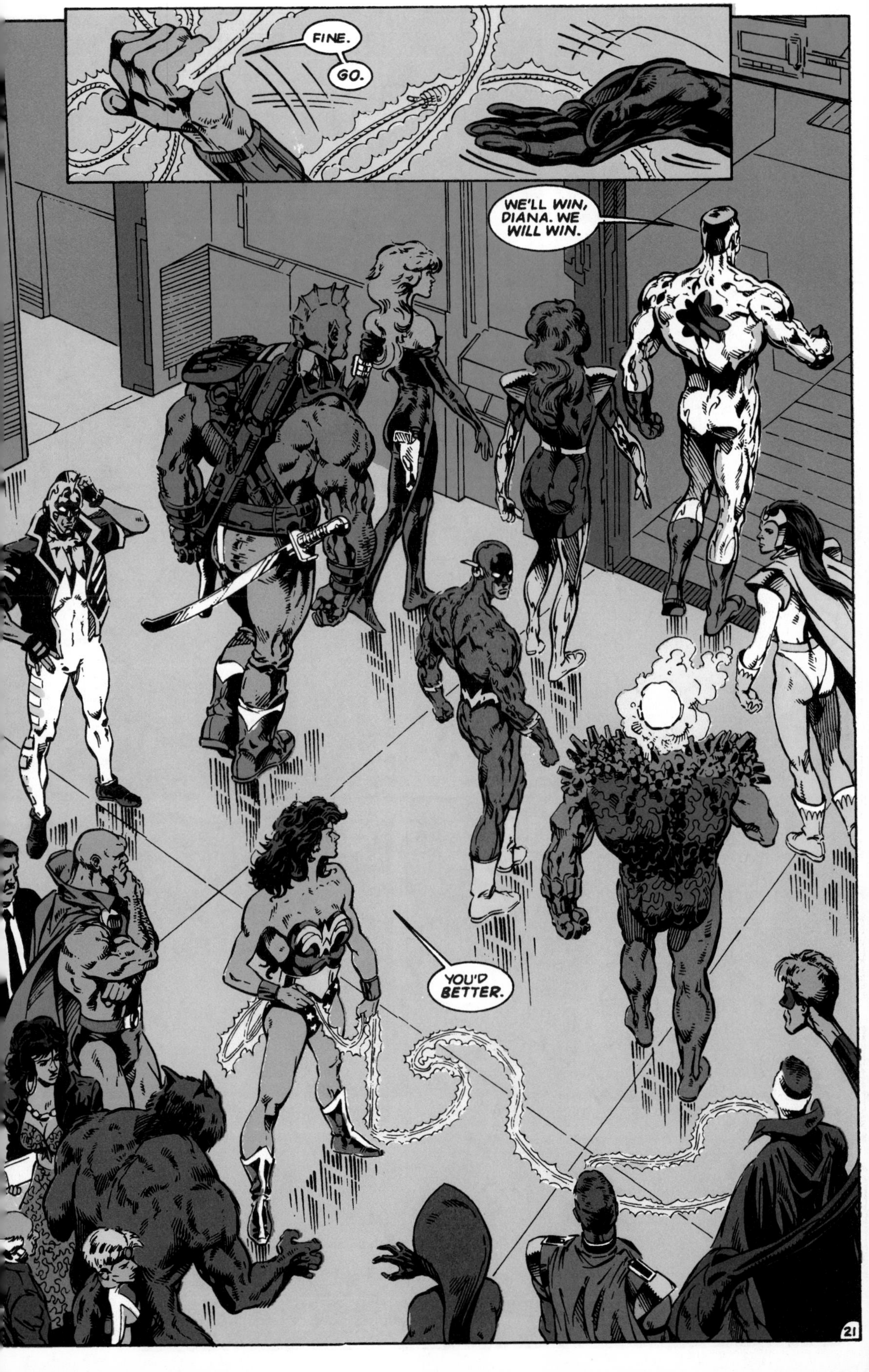
FINE.
GO.
WE'LL WIN, DIANA. WE WILL WIN.
YOU'D BETTER.

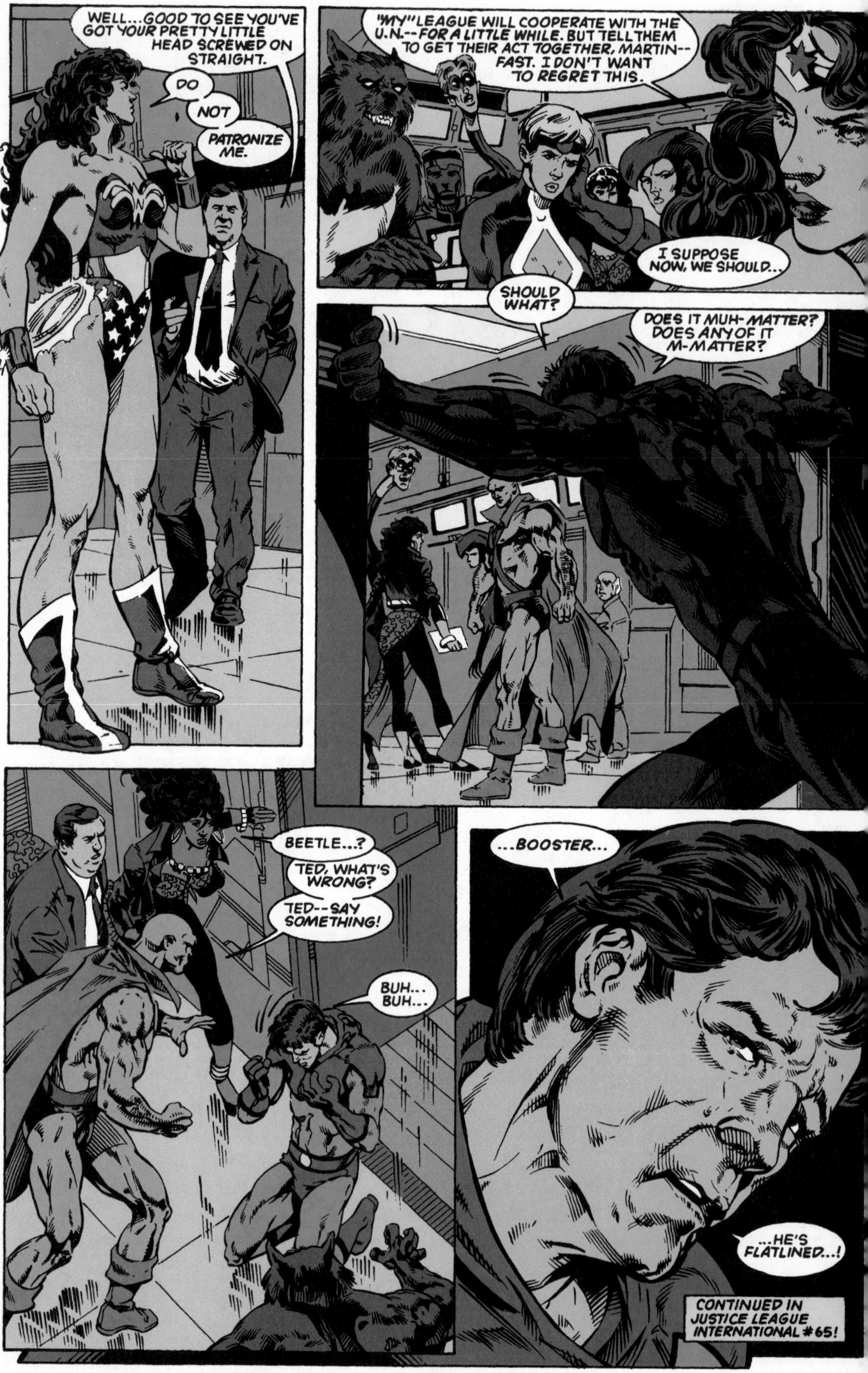
WELL...GOOD TO SEE YOU'VE GOT YOUR PRETTY LITTLE HEAD SCREWED ON STRAIGHT.
DO
NOT
PATRONIZE ME.
"MY" LEAGUE WILL COOPERATE WITH THE U.N.--FOR A LITTLE WHILE. BUT TELL THEM TO GET THEIR ACT TOGETHER, MARTIN--FAST. I DON'T WANT TO REGRET THIS.
I SUPPOSE NOW, WE SHOULD...
SHOULD WHAT?
DOES IT MUH-MATTER? DOES ANY OF IT M-MATTER?
BEETLE...?
TED, WHAT'S WRONG?
TED--SAY SOMETHING!
BUH... BUH...
...BOOSTER...
...HE'S FLATLINED...!
CONTINUED IN JUSTICE LEAGUE INTERNATIONAL #65!

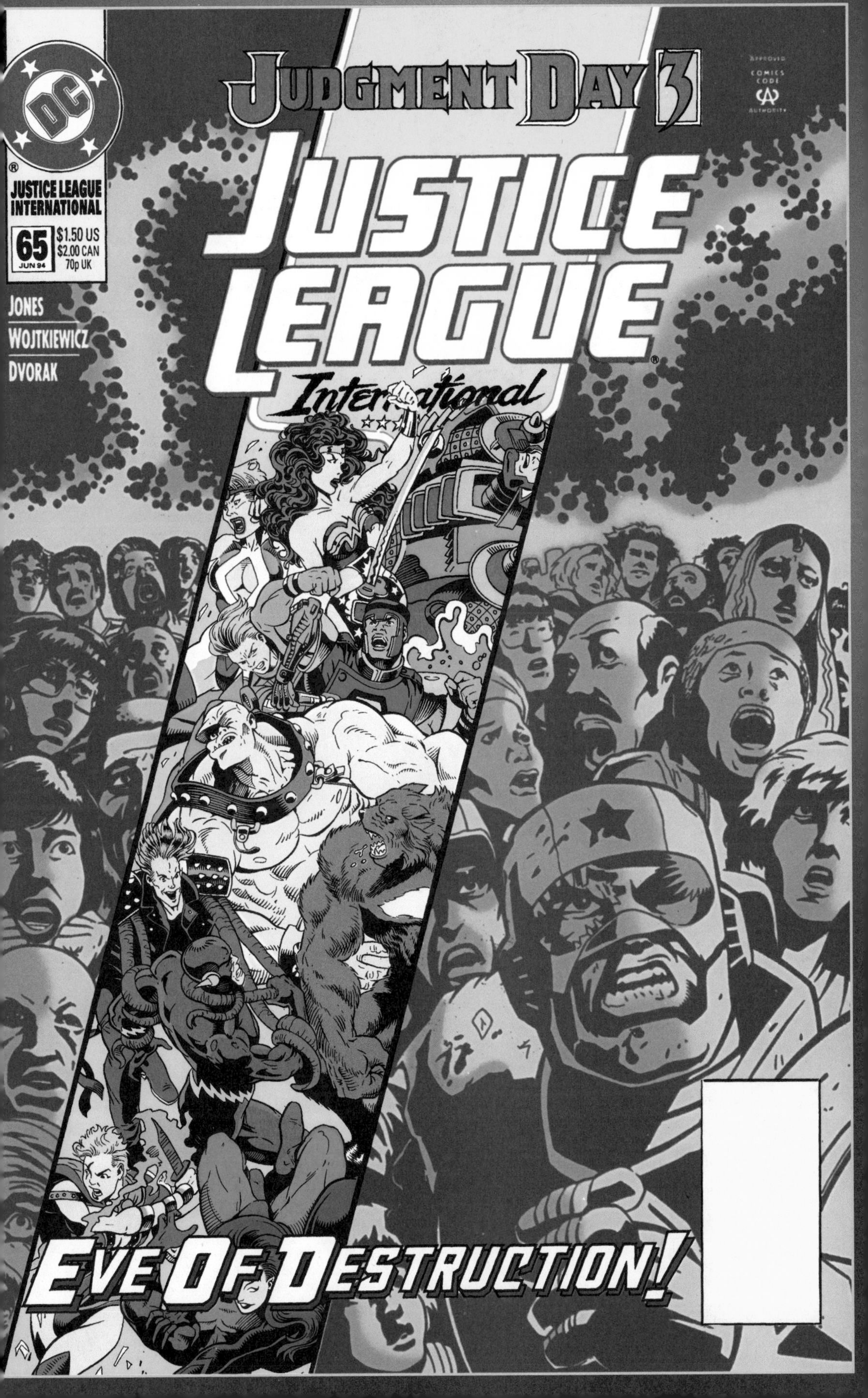
JUDGMENT DAY 3
APPROVED COMICS CODE AUTHORITY
DC
JUSTICE LEAGUE INTERNATIONAL
65 JUN 94
$1.50 US $2.00 CAN 70p UK
JONES
WOJTKIEWICZ
DVORAK
JUSTICE LEAGUE International
EVE OF DESTRUCTION!

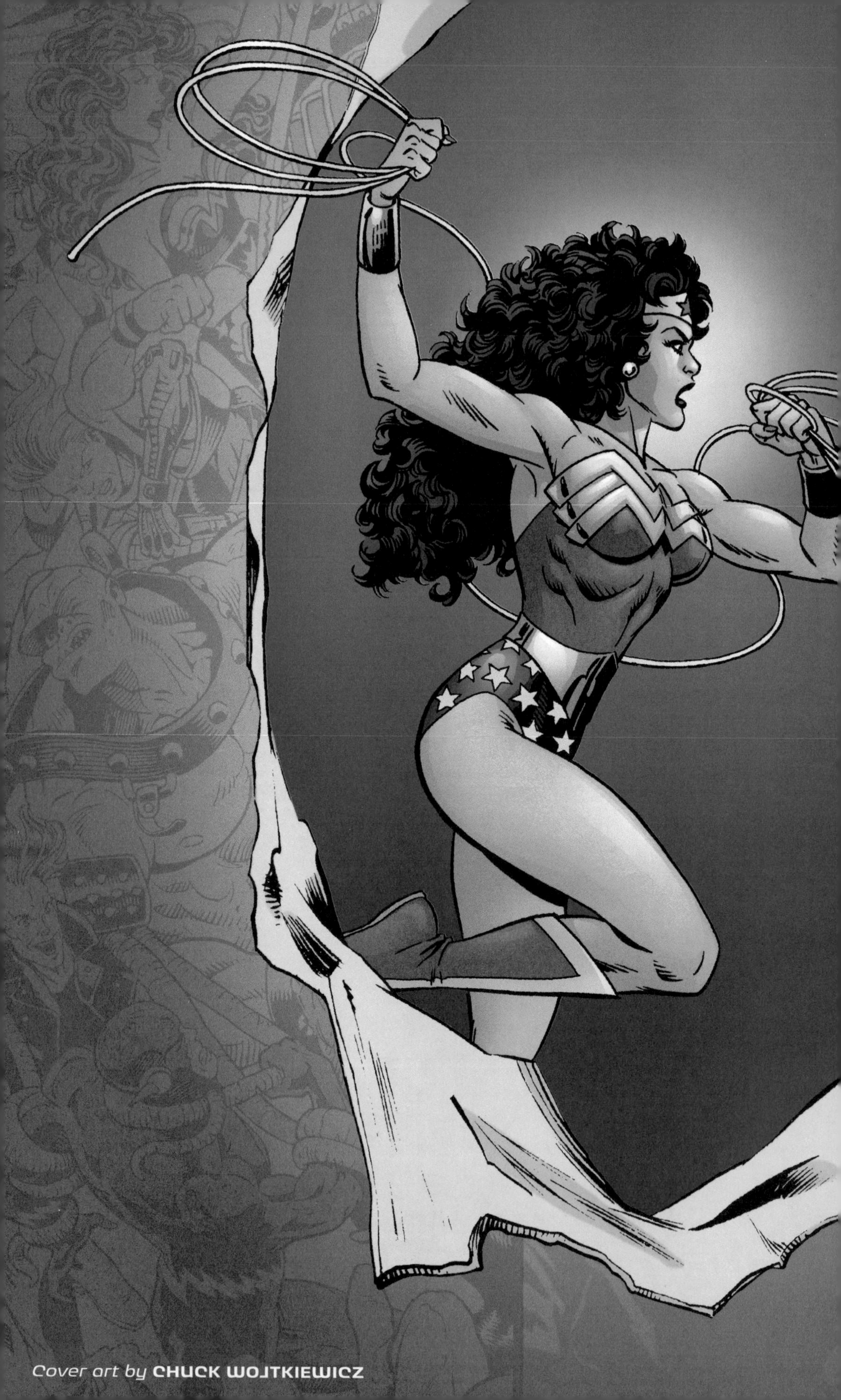

Cover art by **CHUCK WOJTKIEWICZ**

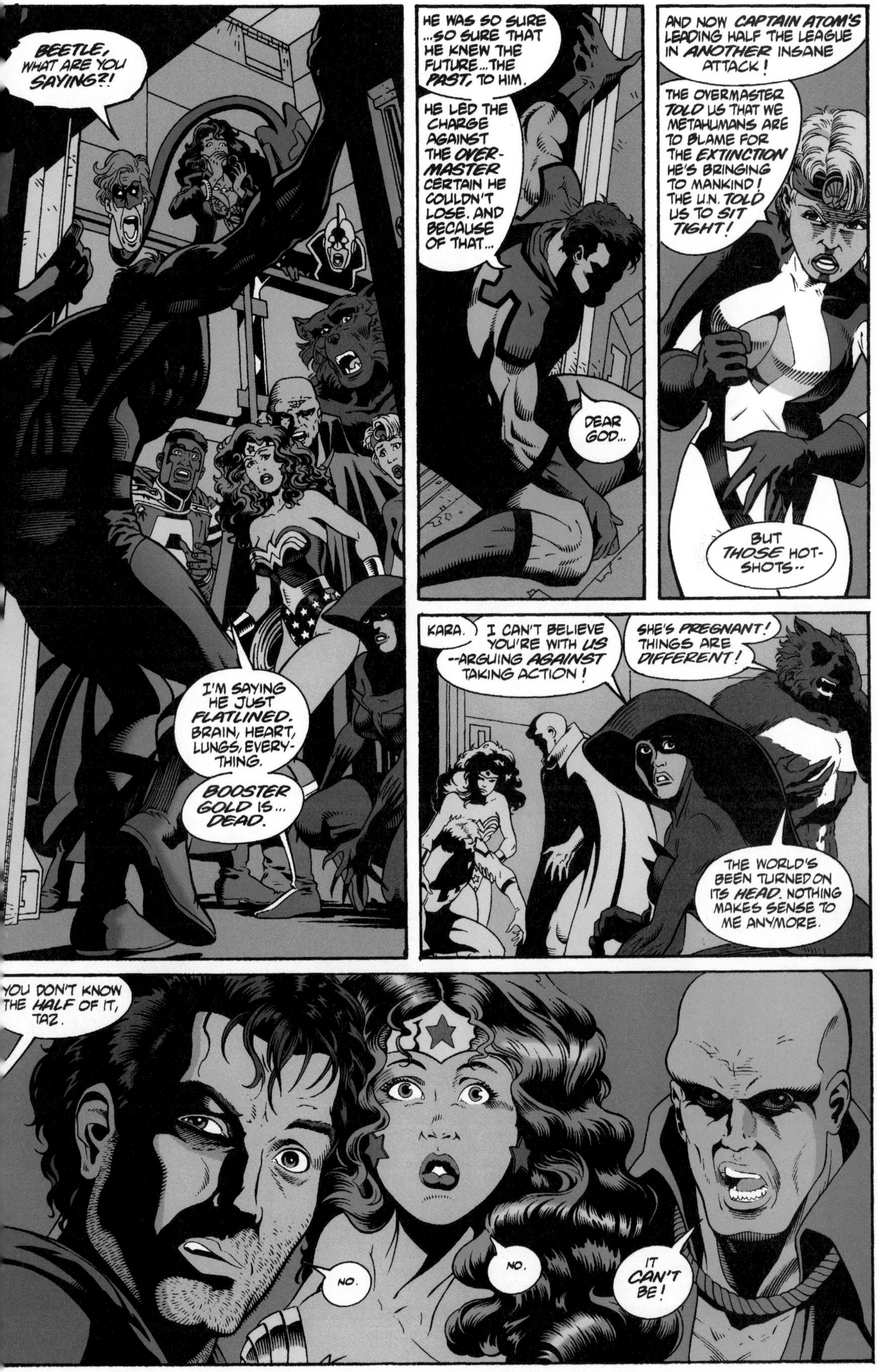
BEETLE, WHAT ARE YOU SAYING?!
I'M SAYING HE JUST FLATLINED. BRAIN, HEART, LUNGS, EVERYTHING.
BOOSTER GOLD IS... DEAD.
HE WAS SO SURE ...SO SURE THAT HE KNEW THE FUTURE... THE PAST, TO HIM.
HE LED THE CHARGE AGAINST THE OVERMASTER CERTAIN HE COULDN'T LOSE. AND BECAUSE OF THAT...
DEAR GOD...
AND NOW CAPTAIN ATOM'S LEADING HALF THE LEAGUE IN ANOTHER INSANE ATTACK!
THE OVERMASTER TOLD US THAT WE METAHUMANS ARE TO BLAME FOR THE EXTINCTION HE'S BRINGING TO MANKIND! THE U.N. TOLD US TO SIT TIGHT!
BUT THOSE HOT-SHOTS--
KARA.
I CAN'T BELIEVE YOU'RE WITH US --ARGUING AGAINST TAKING ACTION!
SHE'S PREGNANT! THINGS ARE DIFFERENT!
THE WORLD'S BEEN TURNED ON ITS HEAD. NOTHING MAKES SENSE TO ME ANYMORE.
YOU DON'T KNOW THE HALF OF IT, TAZ.
NO.
NO.
IT CAN'T BE!

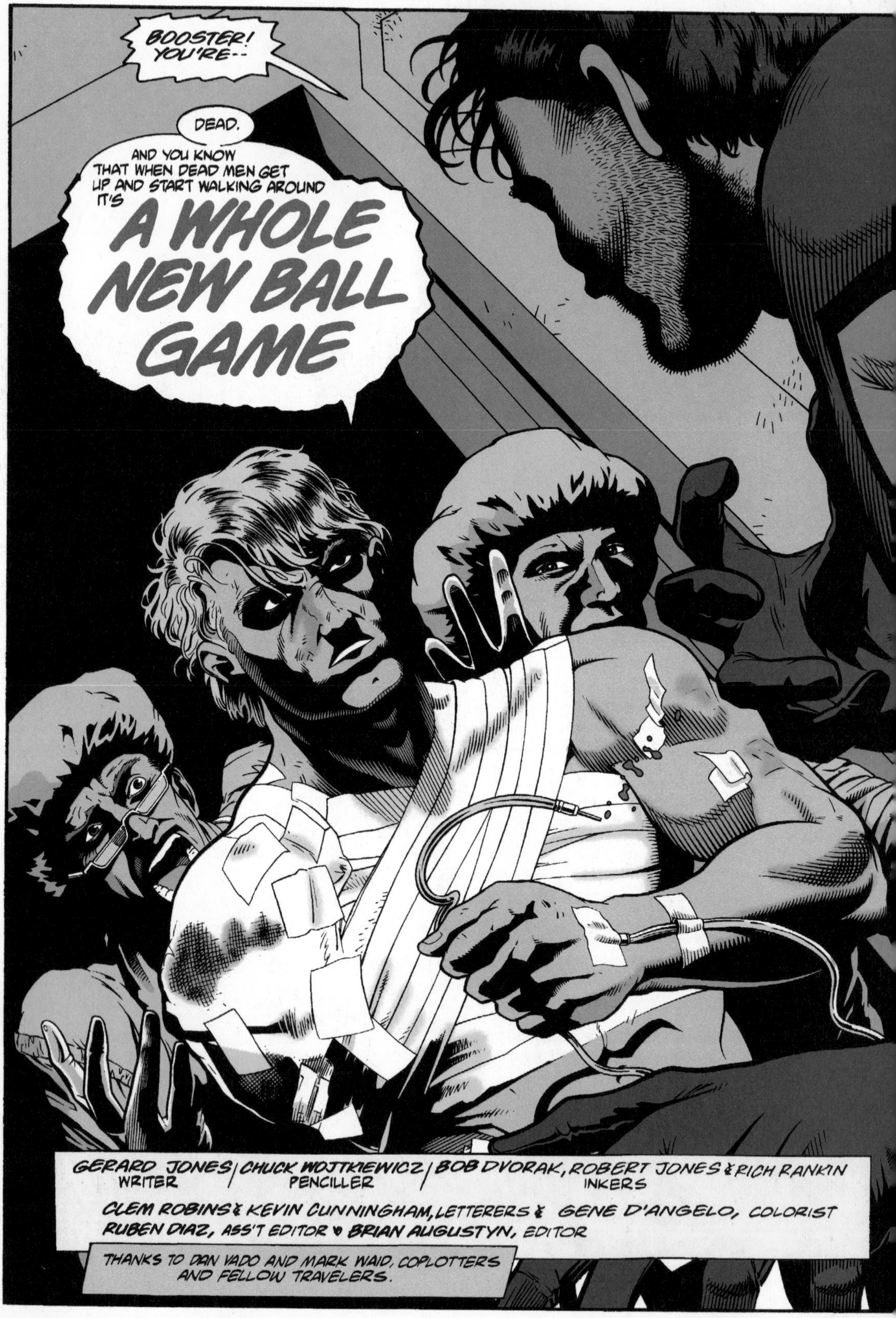
BOOSTER! YOU'RE--
DEAD.
AND YOU KNOW THAT WHEN DEAD MEN GET UP AND START WALKING AROUND IT'S
A WHOLE NEW BALL GAME
GERARD JONES WRITER | CHUCK WOJTKIEWICZ PENCILLER | BOB DVORAK, ROBERT JONES & RICH RANKIN INKERS
CLEM ROBINS & KEVIN CUNNINGHAM, LETTERERS & GENE D'ANGELO, COLORIST
RUBEN DIAZ, ASS'T EDITOR • BRIAN AUGUSTYN, EDITOR
THANKS TO DAN VADO AND MARK WAID, COPLOTTERS AND FELLOW TRAVELERS.

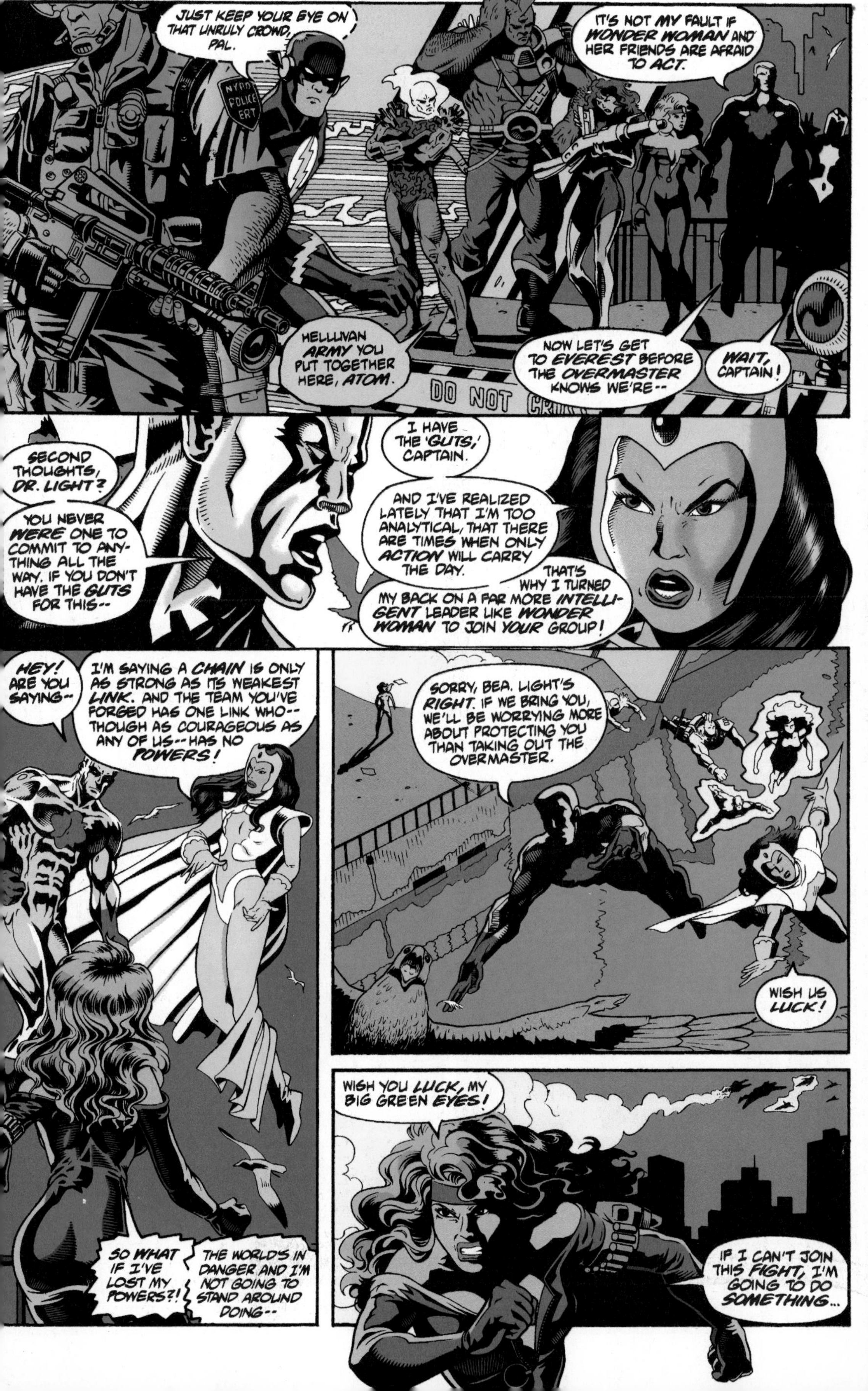
JUST KEEP YOUR EYE ON THAT UNRULY CROWD, PAL.
IT'S NOT MY FAULT IF WONDER WOMAN AND HER FRIENDS ARE AFRAID TO ACT.
NYPD POLICE ERT
HELLUVAN ARMY YOU PUT TOGETHER HERE, ATOM.
NOW LET'S GET TO EVEREST BEFORE THE OVERMASTER KNOWS WE'RE--
WAIT, CAPTAIN!
DO NOT CROSS
SECOND THOUGHTS, DR. LIGHT?
YOU NEVER WERE ONE TO COMMIT TO ANYTHING ALL THE WAY. IF YOU DON'T HAVE THE GUTS FOR THIS--
I HAVE THE 'GUTS,' CAPTAIN.
AND I'VE REALIZED LATELY THAT I'M TOO ANALYTICAL, THAT THERE ARE TIMES WHEN ONLY ACTION WILL CARRY THE DAY.
THAT'S WHY I TURNED MY BACK ON A FAR MORE INTELLIGENT LEADER LIKE WONDER WOMAN TO JOIN YOUR GROUP!
HEY! ARE YOU SAYING--
I'M SAYING A CHAIN IS ONLY AS STRONG AS ITS WEAKEST LINK. AND THE TEAM YOU'VE FORGED HAS ONE LINK WHO--THOUGH AS COURAGEOUS AS ANY OF US--HAS NO POWERS!
SORRY, BEA. LIGHT'S RIGHT. IF WE BRING YOU, WE'LL BE WORRYING MORE ABOUT PROTECTING YOU THAN TAKING OUT THE OVERMASTER.
WISH US LUCK!
SO WHAT IF I'VE LOST MY POWERS?!
THE WORLD'S IN DANGER AND I'M NOT GOING TO STAND AROUND DOING--
WISH YOU LUCK, MY BIG GREEN EYES!
IF I CAN'T JOIN THIS FIGHT, I'M GOING TO DO SOMETHING...

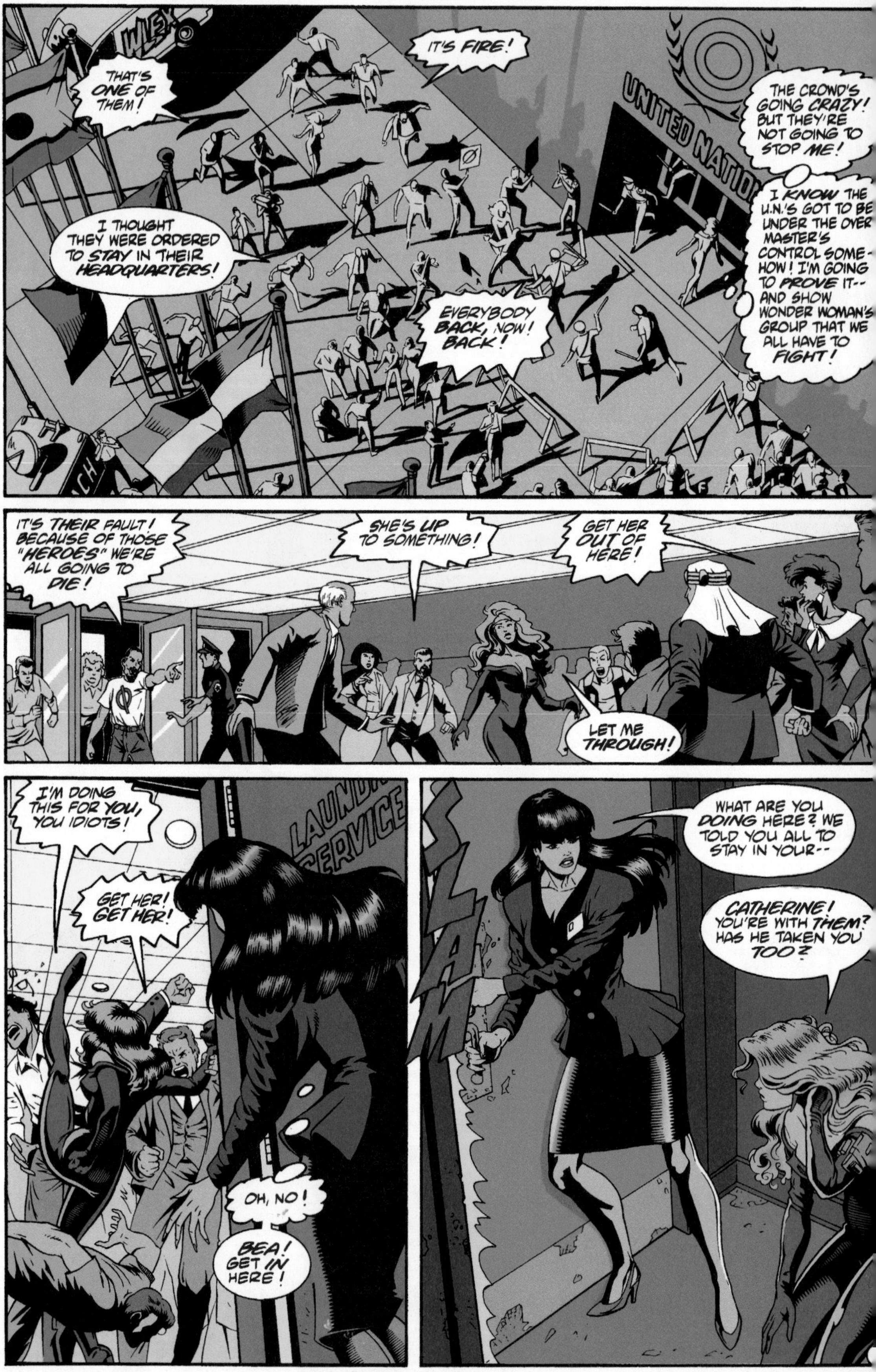
THAT'S ONE OF THEM!
IT'S FIRE!
THE CROWD'S GOING CRAZY! BUT THEY'RE NOT GOING TO STOP ME!
I KNOW THE U.N.'S GOT TO BE UNDER THE OVERMASTER'S CONTROL SOMEHOW! I'M GOING TO PROVE IT-- AND SHOW WONDER WOMAN'S GROUP THAT WE ALL HAVE TO FIGHT!
UNITED NATIO
I THOUGHT THEY WERE ORDERED TO STAY IN THEIR HEADQUARTERS!
EVERYBODY BACK, NOW! BACK!
IT'S THEIR FAULT! BECAUSE OF THOSE "HEROES" WE'RE ALL GOING TO DIE!
SHE'S UP TO SOMETHING!
GET HER OUT OF HERE!
LET ME THROUGH!
I'M DOING THIS FOR YOU, YOU IDIOTS!
GET HER! GET HER!
OH, NO!
BEA! GET IN HERE!
WHAT ARE YOU DOING HERE? WE TOLD YOU ALL TO STAY IN YOUR--
CATHERINE! YOU'RE WITH THEM? HAS HE TAKEN YOU TOO?

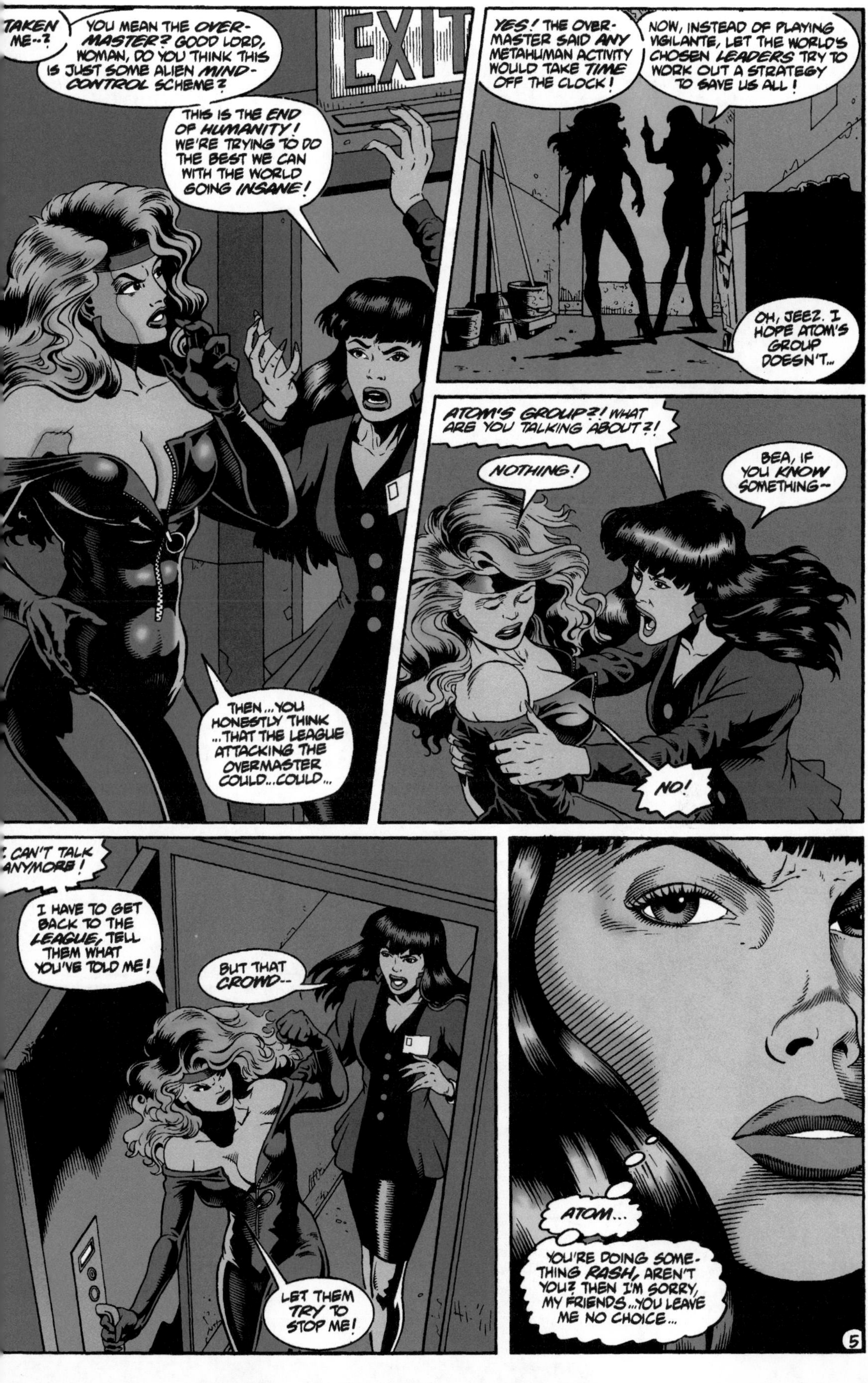
TAKEN ME--?
YOU MEAN THE OVERMASTER? GOOD LORD, WOMAN, DO YOU THINK THIS IS JUST SOME ALIEN MIND-CONTROL SCHEME?
EXIT
THIS IS THE END OF HUMANITY! WE'RE TRYING TO DO THE BEST WE CAN WITH THE WORLD GOING INSANE!
THEN... YOU HONESTLY THINK ...THAT THE LEAGUE ATTACKING THE OVERMASTER COULD...COULD...
YES! THE OVERMASTER SAID ANY METAHUMAN ACTIVITY WOULD TAKE TIME OFF THE CLOCK!
NOW, INSTEAD OF PLAYING VIGILANTE, LET THE WORLD'S CHOSEN LEADERS TRY TO WORK OUT A STRATEGY TO SAVE US ALL!
OH, JEEZ. I HOPE ATOM'S GROUP DOESN'T...
ATOM'S GROUP?! WHAT ARE YOU TALKING ABOUT?!
NOTHING!
BEA, IF YOU KNOW SOMETHING--
NO!
CAN'T TALK ANYMORE!
I HAVE TO GET BACK TO THE LEAGUE, TELL THEM WHAT YOU'VE TOLD ME!
BUT THAT CROWD--
LET THEM TRY TO STOP ME!
ATOM...
YOU'RE DOING SOMETHING RASH, AREN'T YOU? THEN I'M SORRY, MY FRIENDS...YOU LEAVE ME NO CHOICE...

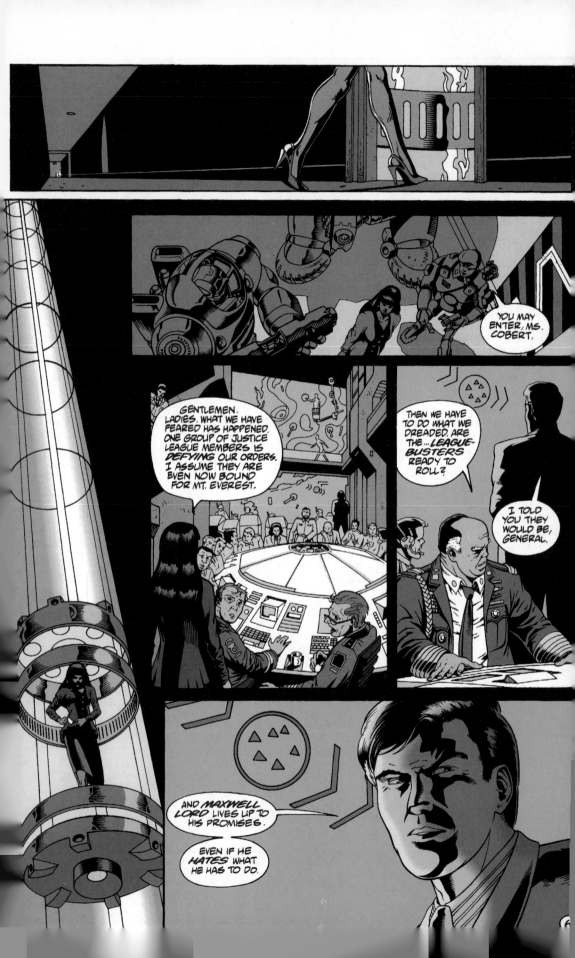

YOU MAY ENTER, MS. COBERT.

GENTLEMEN. LADIES. WHAT WE HAVE FEARED HAS HAPPENED. ONE GROUP OF JUSTICE LEAGUE MEMBERS IS *DEFYING* OUR ORDERS. I ASSUME THEY ARE EVEN NOW BOUND FOR MT. EVEREST.

THEN WE HAVE TO DO WHAT WE DREADED. ARE THE ...*LEAGUE-BUSTERS* READY TO ROLL?

I TOLD YOU THEY WOULD BE, GENERAL.

AND *MAXWELL LORD* LIVES UP TO HIS PROMISES.

EVEN IF HE *HATES* WHAT HE HAS TO DO.

...THEN RIGHT OVER THE HEART OF RUSSIA, THE QUICKEST ROUTE TO EVEREST.

NO, CAPTAIN. WE SHOULD GO THROUGH *BENARES* FIRST--TO ADD *LIONHEART* AND *MAYA* TO OUR RANKS.

JUST WHAT WE NEED. A LIMEY-IN-A-CAN AND A THIRTEEN-YEAR-OLD WHO PLAYS WITH FIRE.

MAYA IS FINDING GREATER AND GREATER POWER WITHIN HERSELF, CAPTAIN. SOON ENOUGH SHE MAY PROVE TO BE THE *MOST POWER-FUL* OF US ALL!

NOW, I HAVE A *DETOUR* TO MAKE. I'LL MEET YOU SOON ...

...IN *BENARES*!

TAKING OVER THE JLI BY *DEFAULT* MUST BE GOING TO HER *HEAD*.

SHE TALKS LIKE SHE'S TAKEN OVER *THIS GROUP*.

SHE'S BEEN SHOWING SOME *SMARTS* LATELY ...AND NOT JUST FOR SCIENCE.

MAYBE HER "*TAKING OVER*" WOULDN'T BE SO BAD.

WE'LL *SETTLE* THAT, FLASH...AFTER EVEREST!

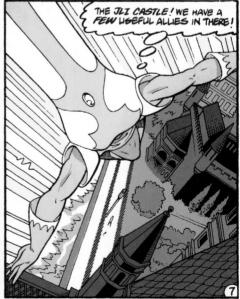

THE *JLI CASTLE*! WE HAVE A *FEW* USEFUL ALLIES IN THERE!

7

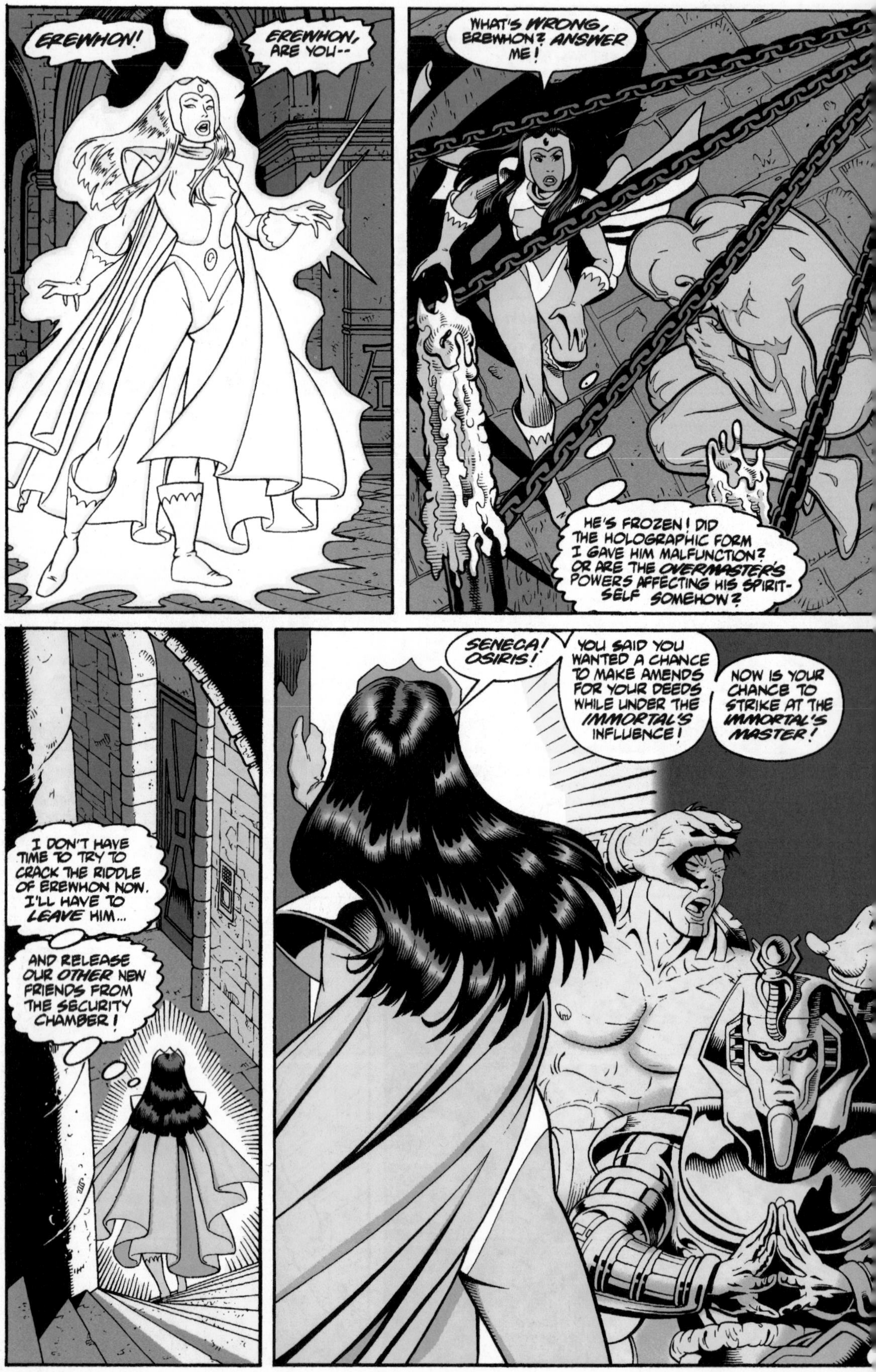
EREWHON!
EREWHON, ARE YOU--
WHAT'S WRONG, EREWHON? ANSWER ME!
HE'S FROZEN! DID THE HOLOGRAPHIC FORM I GAVE HIM MALFUNCTION? OR ARE THE OVERMASTER'S POWERS AFFECTING HIS SPIRIT-SELF SOMEHOW?
I DON'T HAVE TIME TO TRY TO CRACK THE RIDDLE OF EREWHON NOW. I'LL HAVE TO LEAVE HIM...
AND RELEASE OUR OTHER NEW FRIENDS FROM THE SECURITY CHAMBER!
SENECA! OSIRIS!
YOU SAID YOU WANTED A CHANCE TO MAKE AMENDS FOR YOUR DEEDS WHILE UNDER THE IMMORTAL'S INFLUENCE!
NOW IS YOUR CHANCE TO STRIKE AT THE IMMORTAL'S MASTER!

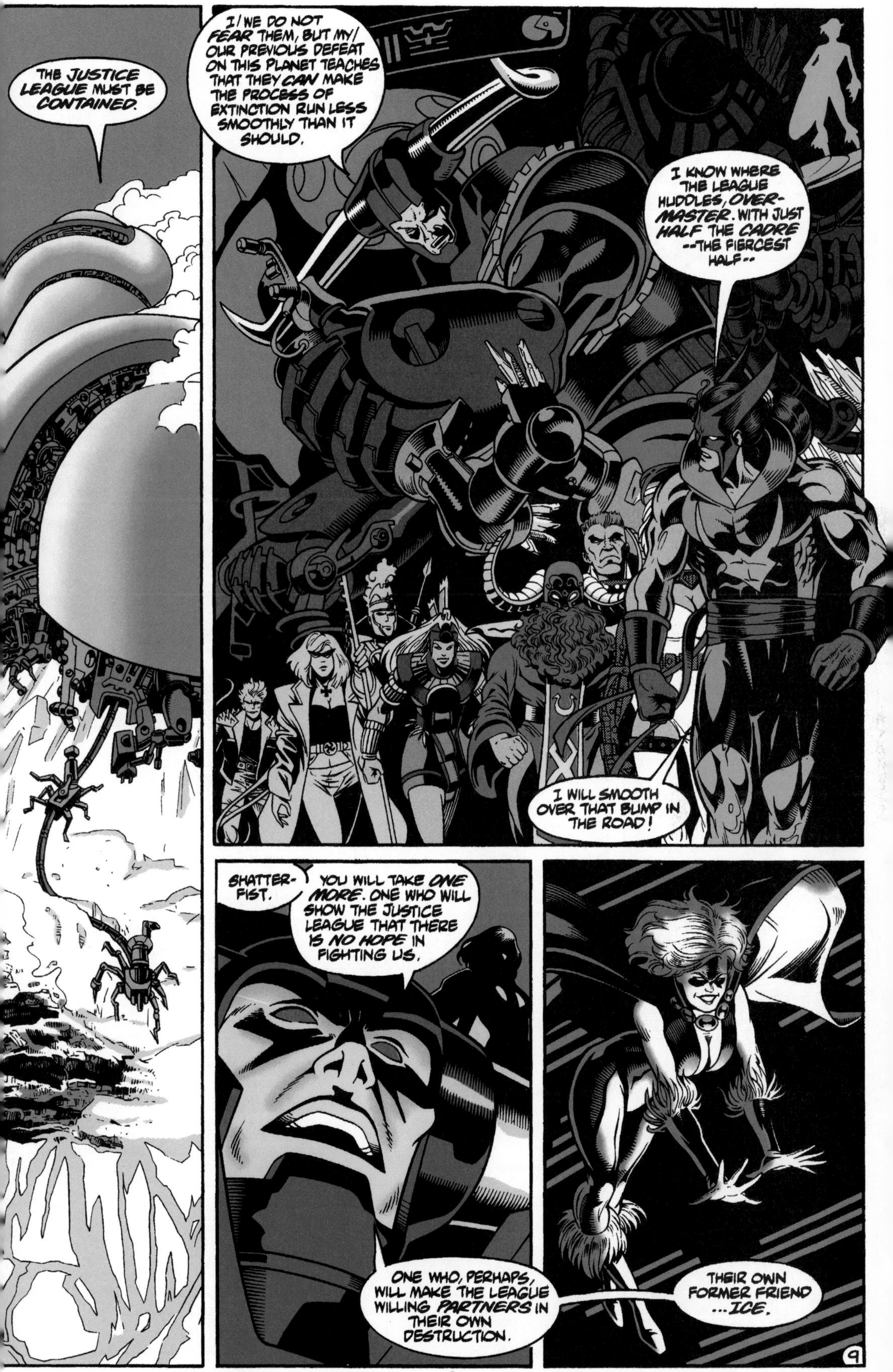
THE JUSTICE LEAGUE MUST BE CONTAINED.
I/WE DO NOT FEAR THEM, BUT MY/OUR PREVIOUS DEFEAT ON THIS PLANET TEACHES THAT THEY CAN MAKE THE PROCESS OF EXTINCTION RUN LESS SMOOTHLY THAN IT SHOULD.
I KNOW WHERE THE LEAGUE HUDDLES, OVERMASTER. WITH JUST HALF THE CADRE --THE FIERCEST HALF--
I WILL SMOOTH OVER THAT BUMP IN THE ROAD!
SHATTER-FIST.
YOU WILL TAKE ONE MORE. ONE WHO WILL SHOW THE JUSTICE LEAGUE THAT THERE IS NO HOPE IN FIGHTING US.
ONE WHO, PERHAPS, WILL MAKE THE LEAGUE WILLING PARTNERS IN THEIR OWN DESTRUCTION.
THEIR OWN FORMER FRIEND ...ICE.
9

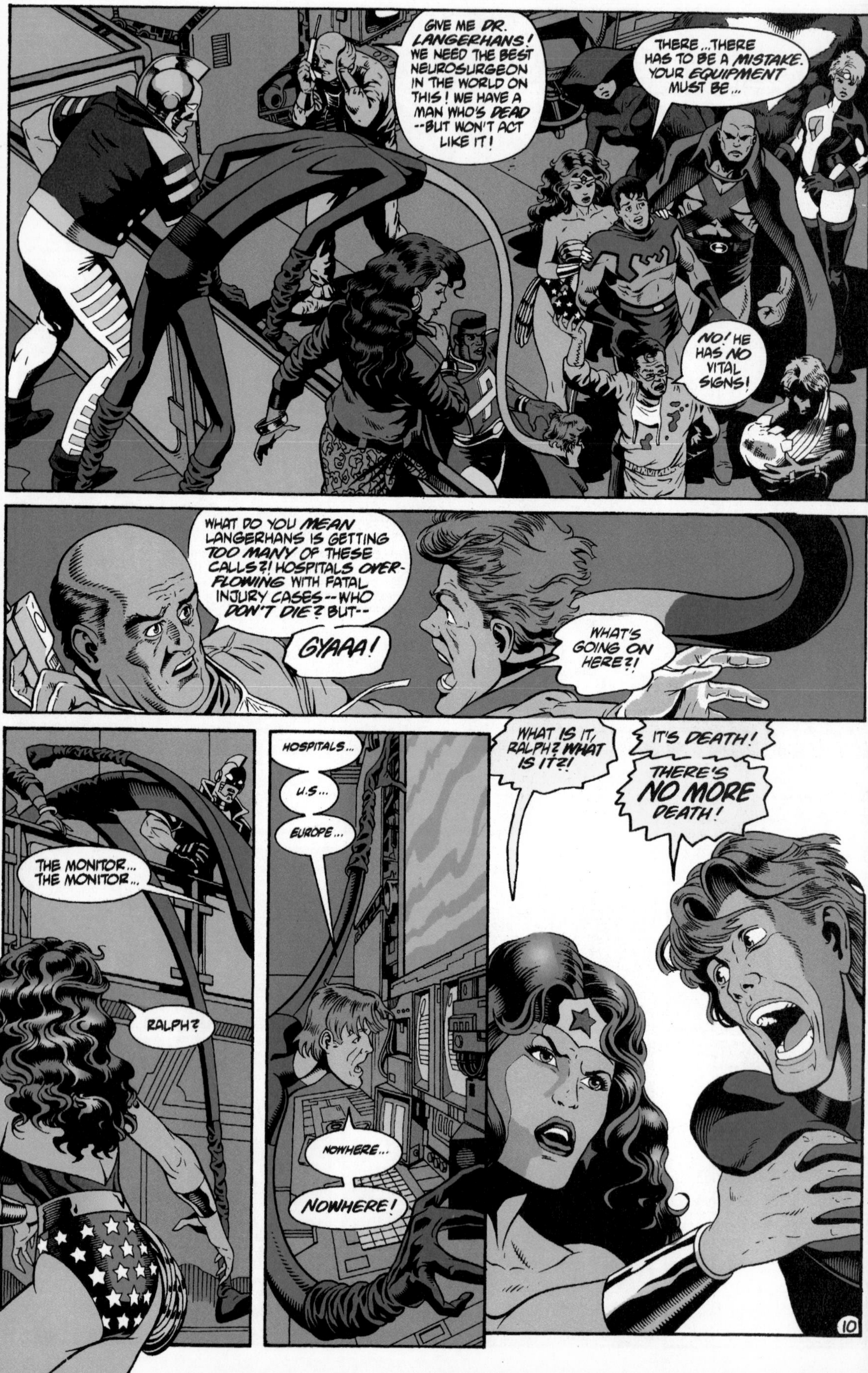
GIVE ME DR. LANGERHANS! WE NEED THE BEST NEUROSURGEON IN THE WORLD ON THIS! WE HAVE A MAN WHO'S DEAD --BUT WON'T ACT LIKE IT!
THERE...THERE HAS TO BE A MISTAKE. YOUR EQUIPMENT MUST BE...
NO! HE HAS NO VITAL SIGNS!
WHAT DO YOU MEAN LANGERHANS IS GETTING TOO MANY OF THESE CALLS?! HOSPITALS OVER-FLOWING WITH FATAL INJURY CASES--WHO DON'T DIE? BUT--
GYAAA!
WHAT'S GOING ON HERE?!
THE MONITOR... THE MONITOR...
RALPH?
HOSPITALS...
U.S...
EUROPE...
NOWHERE...
NOWHERE!
WHAT IS IT, RALPH? WHAT IS IT?!
IT'S DEATH!
THERE'S NO MORE DEATH!
10

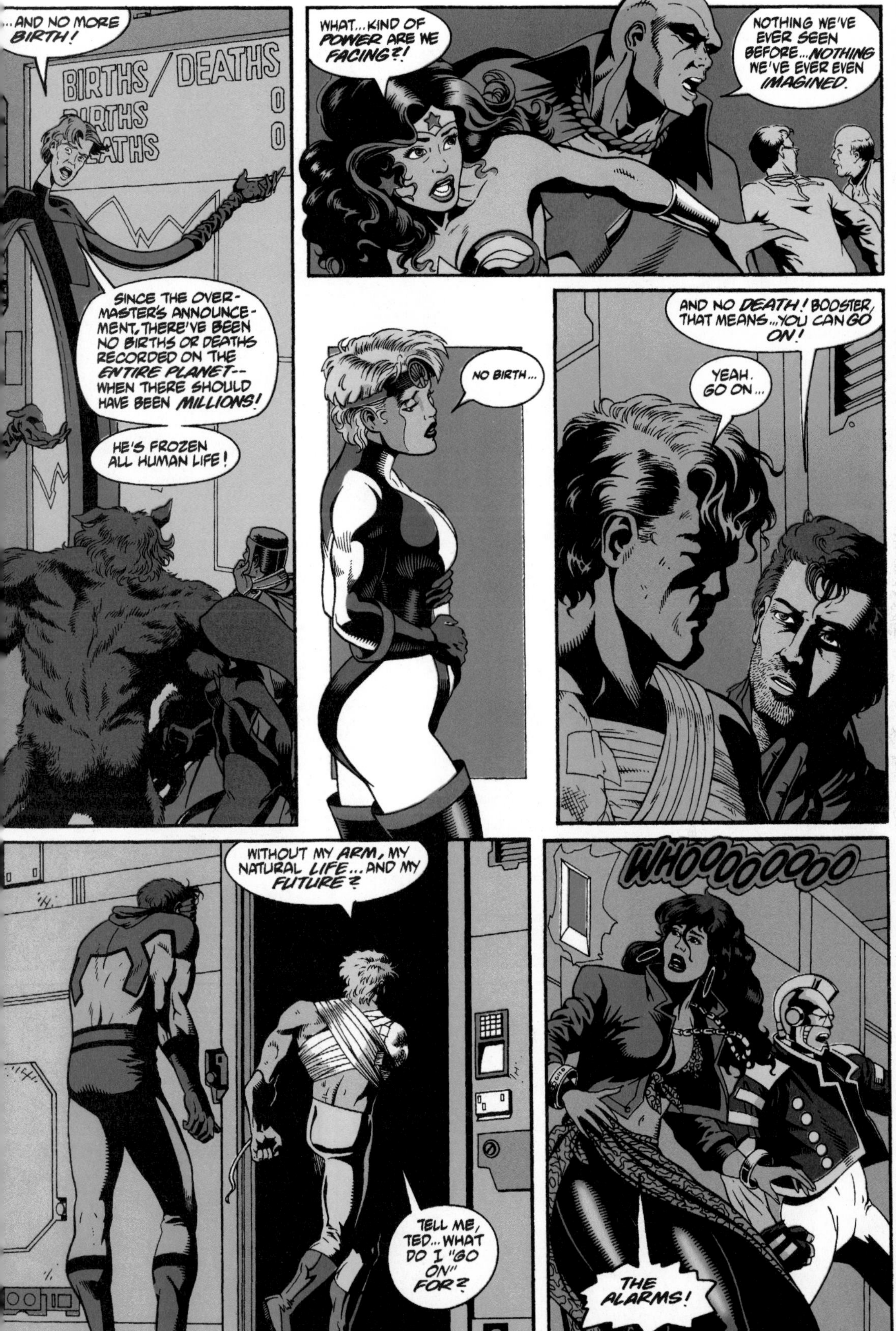
...AND NO MORE BIRTH!
BIRTHS / DEATHS
BIRTHS 0
DEATHS 0
SINCE THE OVER-MASTER'S ANNOUNCE-MENT, THERE'VE BEEN NO BIRTHS OR DEATHS RECORDED ON THE ENTIRE PLANET--WHEN THERE SHOULD HAVE BEEN MILLIONS!
HE'S FROZEN ALL HUMAN LIFE!
WHAT...KIND OF POWER ARE WE FACING?!
NOTHING WE'VE EVER SEEN BEFORE...NOTHING WE'VE EVER EVEN IMAGINED.
NO BIRTH...
AND NO DEATH! BOOSTER, THAT MEANS...YOU CAN GO ON!
YEAH. GO ON...
WITHOUT MY ARM, MY NATURAL LIFE...AND MY FUTURE?
TELL ME, TED...WHAT DO I "GO ON" FOR?
WHOOOOOOOOO
THE ALARMS!

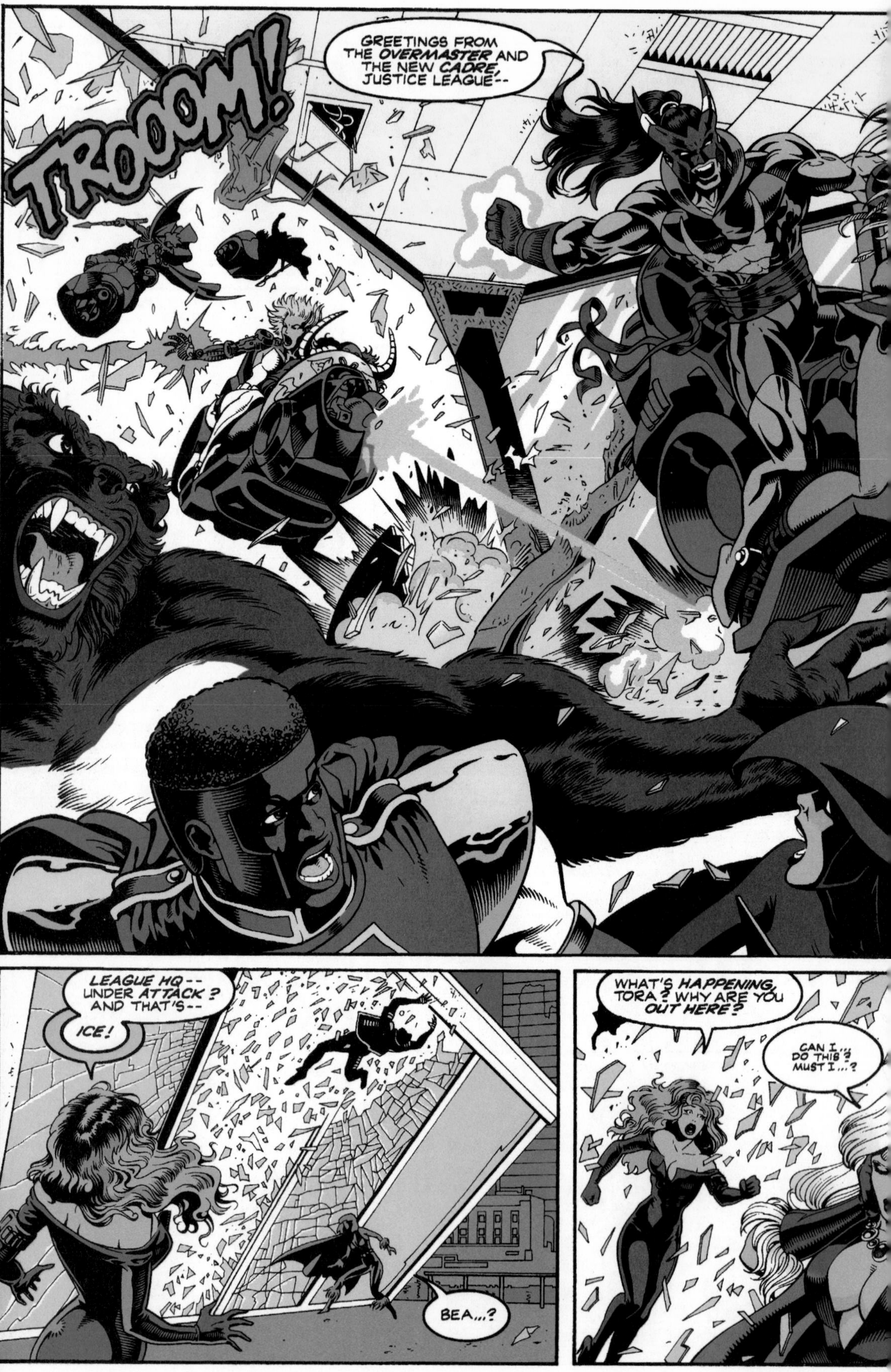
GREETINGS FROM THE OVERMASTER AND THE NEW CADRE, JUSTICE LEAGUE--
TROOOM!
LEAGUE HQ-- UNDER ATTACK? AND THAT'S--
ICE!
BEA...?
WHAT'S HAPPENING, TORA? WHY ARE YOU OUT HERE?
CAN I... DO THIS? MUST I...?

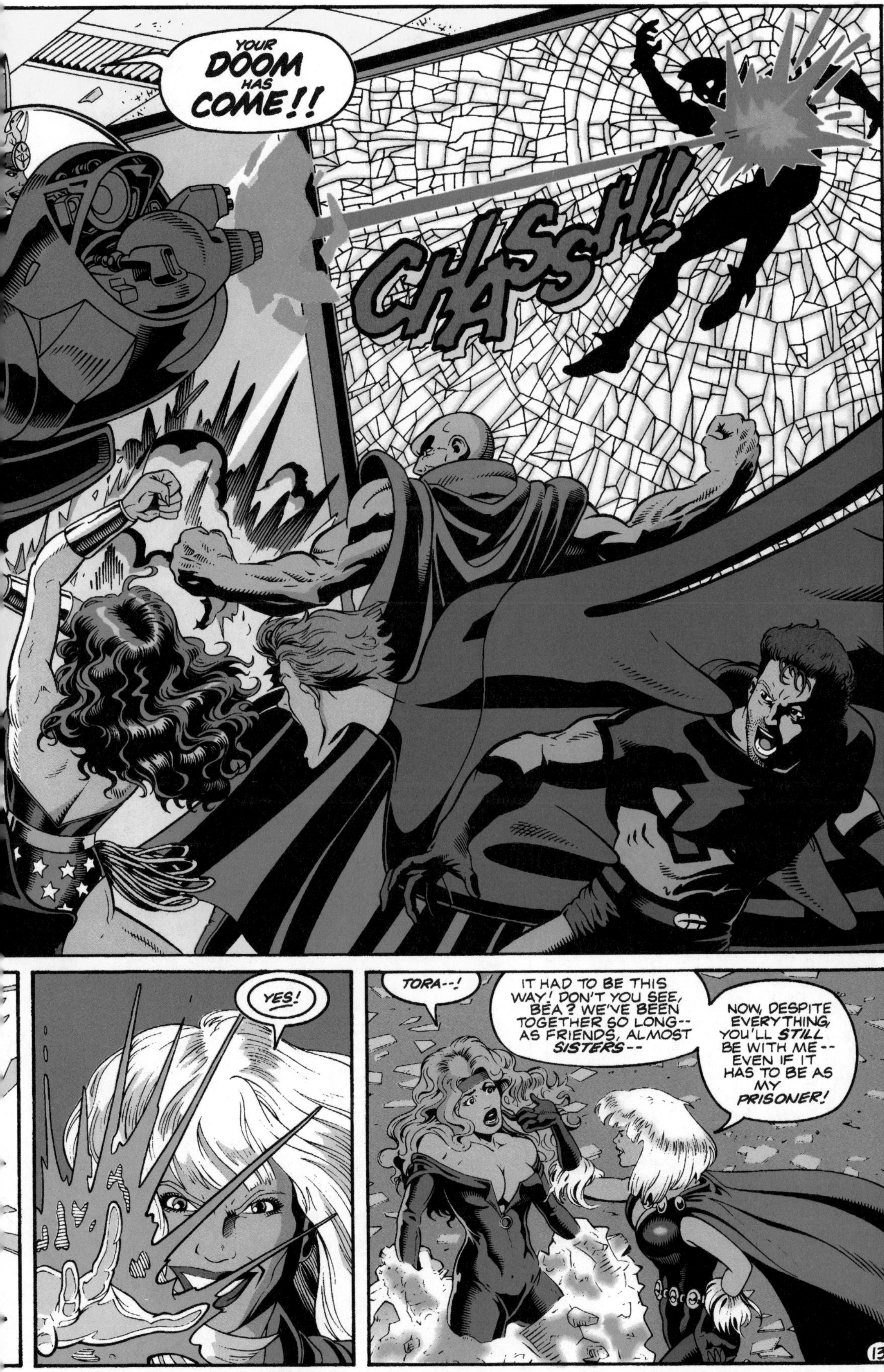
YOUR DOOM HAS COME!!
CHASSH!!
YES!
TORA--!
IT HAD TO BE THIS WAY! DON'T YOU SEE, BEA? WE'VE BEEN TOGETHER SO LONG-- AS FRIENDS, ALMOST SISTERS--
NOW, DESPITE EVERYTHING, YOU'LL STILL BE WITH ME-- EVEN IF IT HAS TO BE AS MY PRISONER!

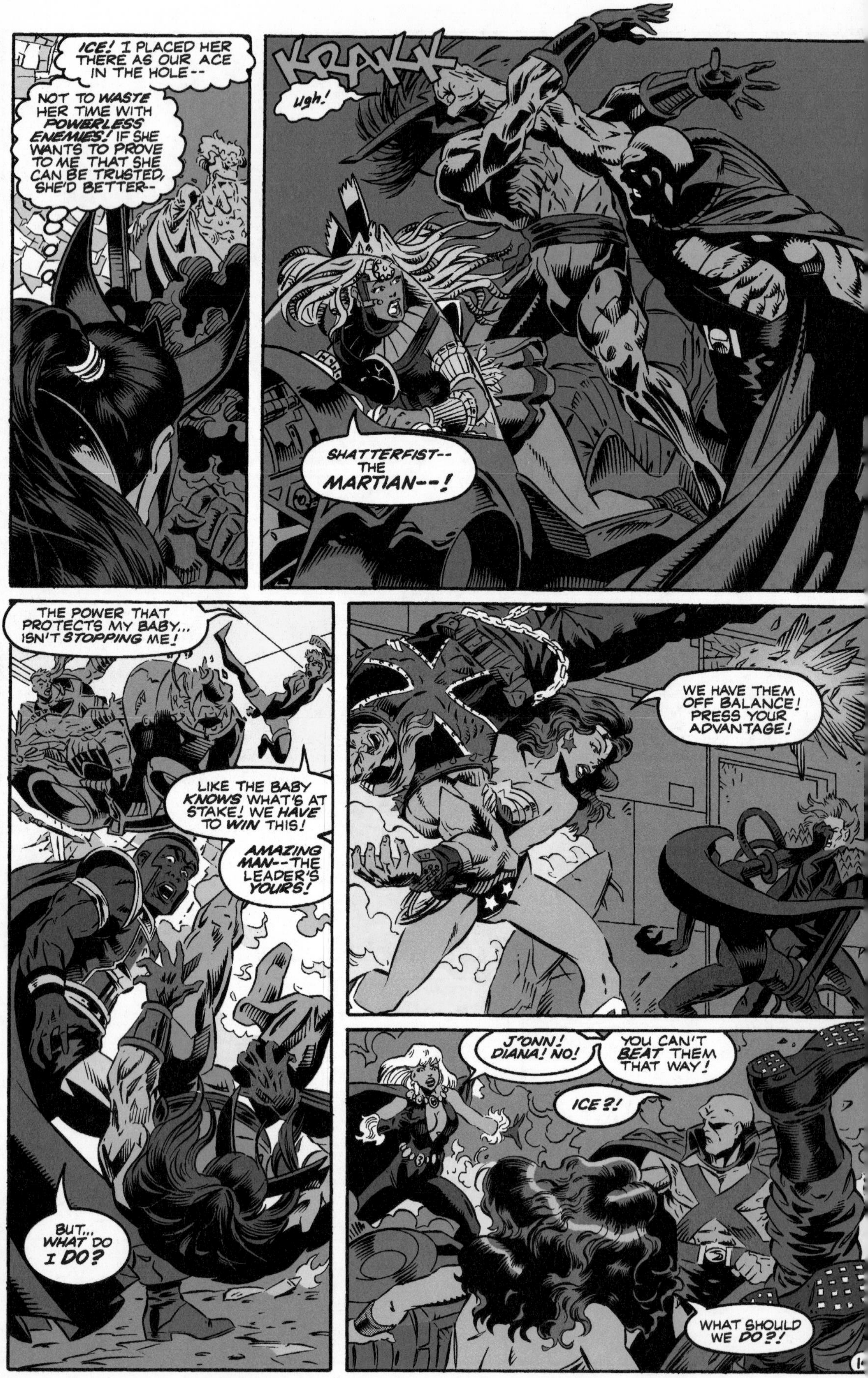
ICE! I PLACED HER THERE AS OUR ACE IN THE HOLE--
NOT TO WASTE HER TIME WITH POWERLESS ENEMIES! IF SHE WANTS TO PROVE TO ME THAT SHE CAN BE TRUSTED, SHE'D BETTER--
KRAKK
ugh!
SHATTERFIST-- THE MARTIAN--!
THE POWER THAT PROTECTS MY BABY... ISN'T STOPPING ME!
LIKE THE BABY KNOWS WHAT'S AT STAKE! WE HAVE TO WIN THIS!
AMAZING MAN--THE LEADER'S YOURS!
BUT... WHAT DO I DO?
WE HAVE THEM OFF BALANCE! PRESS YOUR ADVANTAGE!
J'ONN! DIANA! NO!
YOU CAN'T BEAT THEM THAT WAY!
ICE?!
WHAT SHOULD WE DO?!

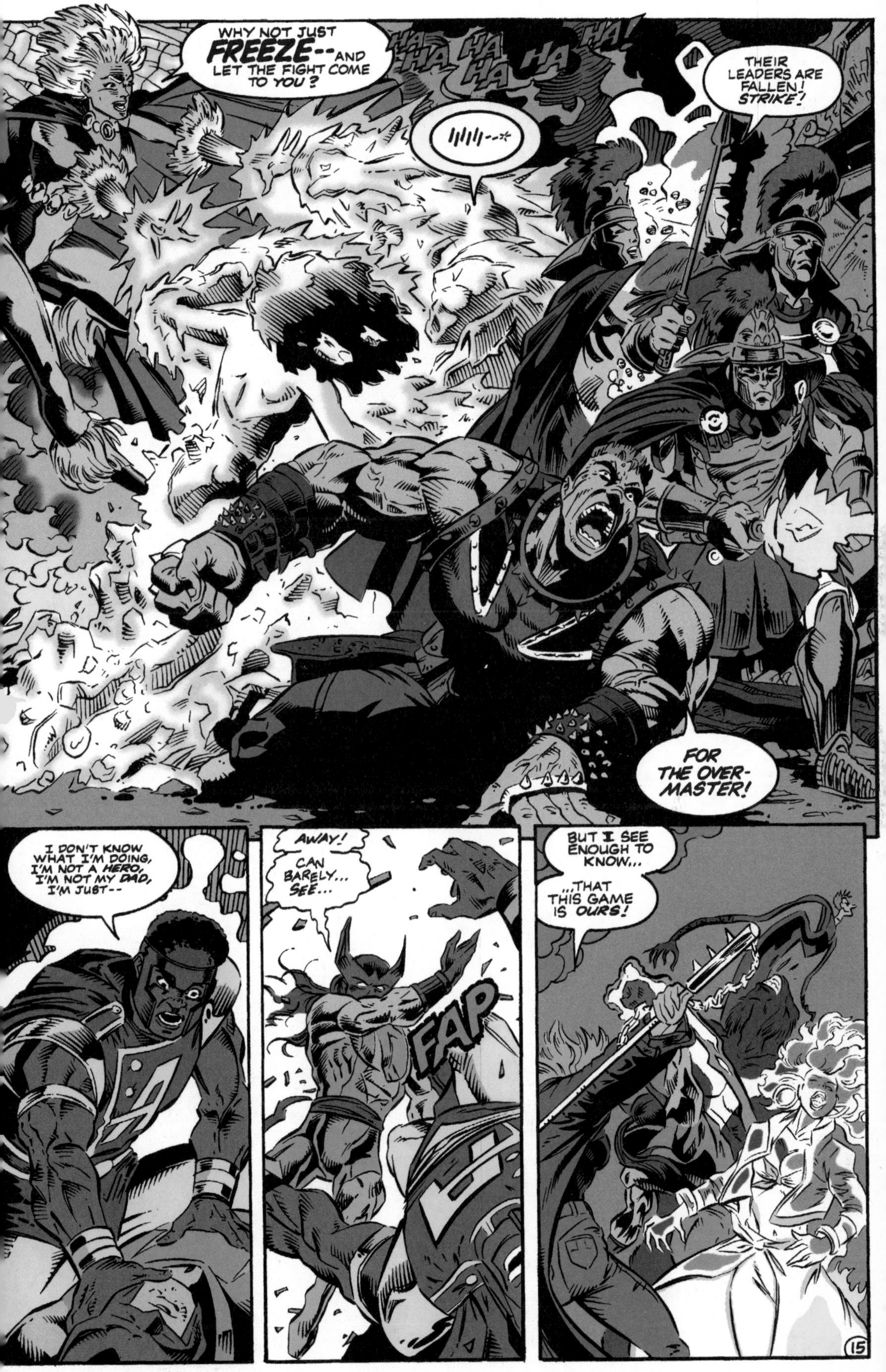
WHY NOT JUST FREEZE--AND LET THE FIGHT COME TO YOU?
HA HA HA HA HA HA HA!
THEIR LEADERS ARE FALLEN! STRIKE!
FOR THE OVER-MASTER!
I DON'T KNOW WHAT I'M DOING, I'M NOT A HERO, I'M NOT MY DAD, I'M JUST--
AWAY!
CAN BARELY... SEE...
FAP
BUT I SEE ENOUGH TO KNOW...
...THAT THIS GAME IS OURS!
15

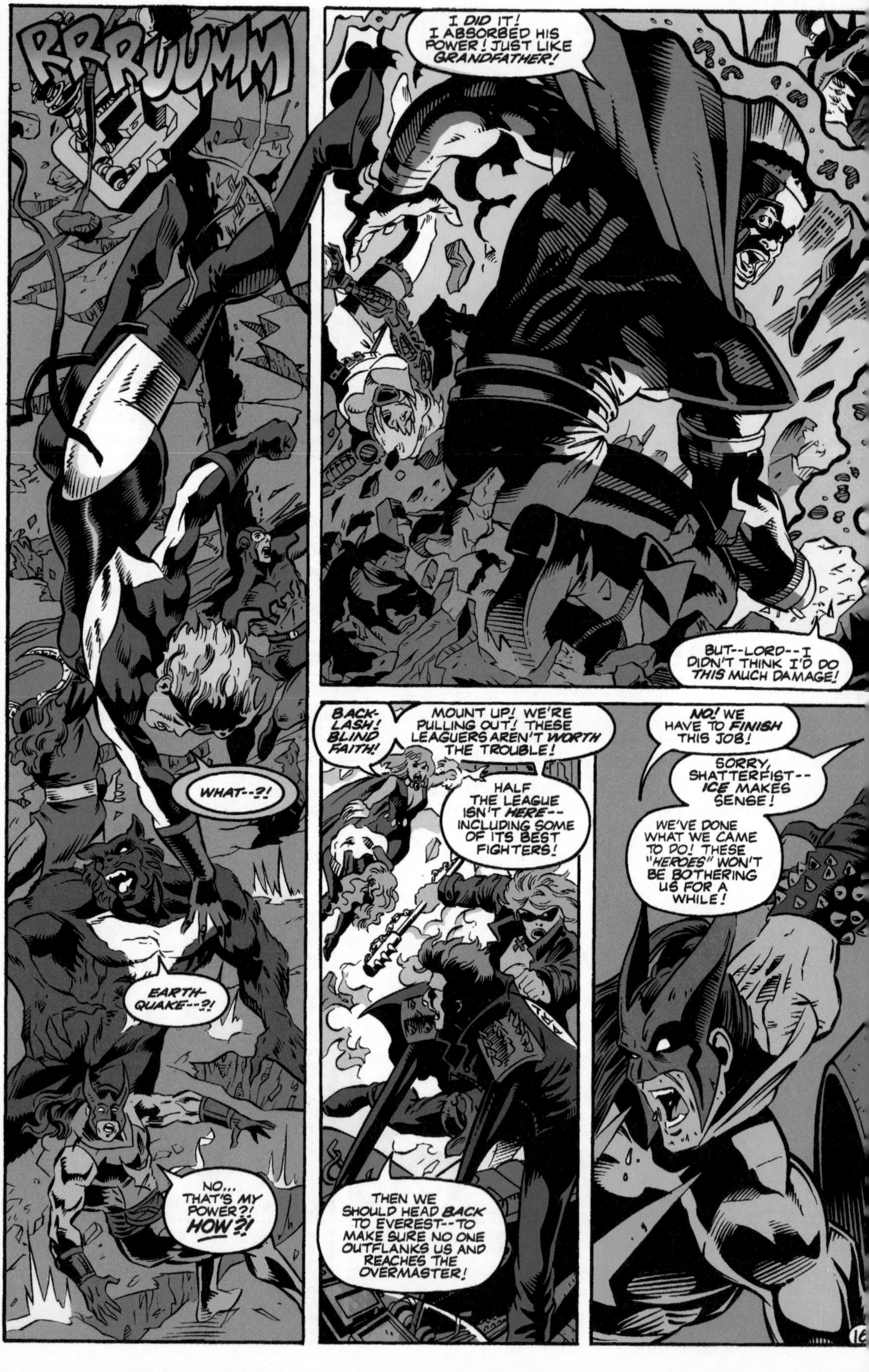
RRRUUMM
WHAT--?!
EARTHQUAKE--?!
NO... THAT'S MY POWER?! HOW?!
I DID IT! I ABSORBED HIS POWER! JUST LIKE GRANDFATHER!
BUT--LORD--I DIDN'T THINK I'D DO THIS MUCH DAMAGE!
BACKLASH! BLIND FAITH!
MOUNT UP! WE'RE PULLING OUT! THESE LEAGUERS AREN'T WORTH THE TROUBLE!
HALF THE LEAGUE ISN'T HERE--INCLUDING SOME OF ITS BEST FIGHTERS!
THEN WE SHOULD HEAD BACK TO EVEREST--TO MAKE SURE NO ONE OUTFLANKS US AND REACHES THE OVERMASTER!
NO! WE HAVE TO FINISH THIS JOB!
SORRY, SHATTERFIST--ICE MAKES SENSE!
WE'VE DONE WHAT WE CAME TO DO! THESE "HEROES" WON'T BE BOTHERING US FOR A WHILE!

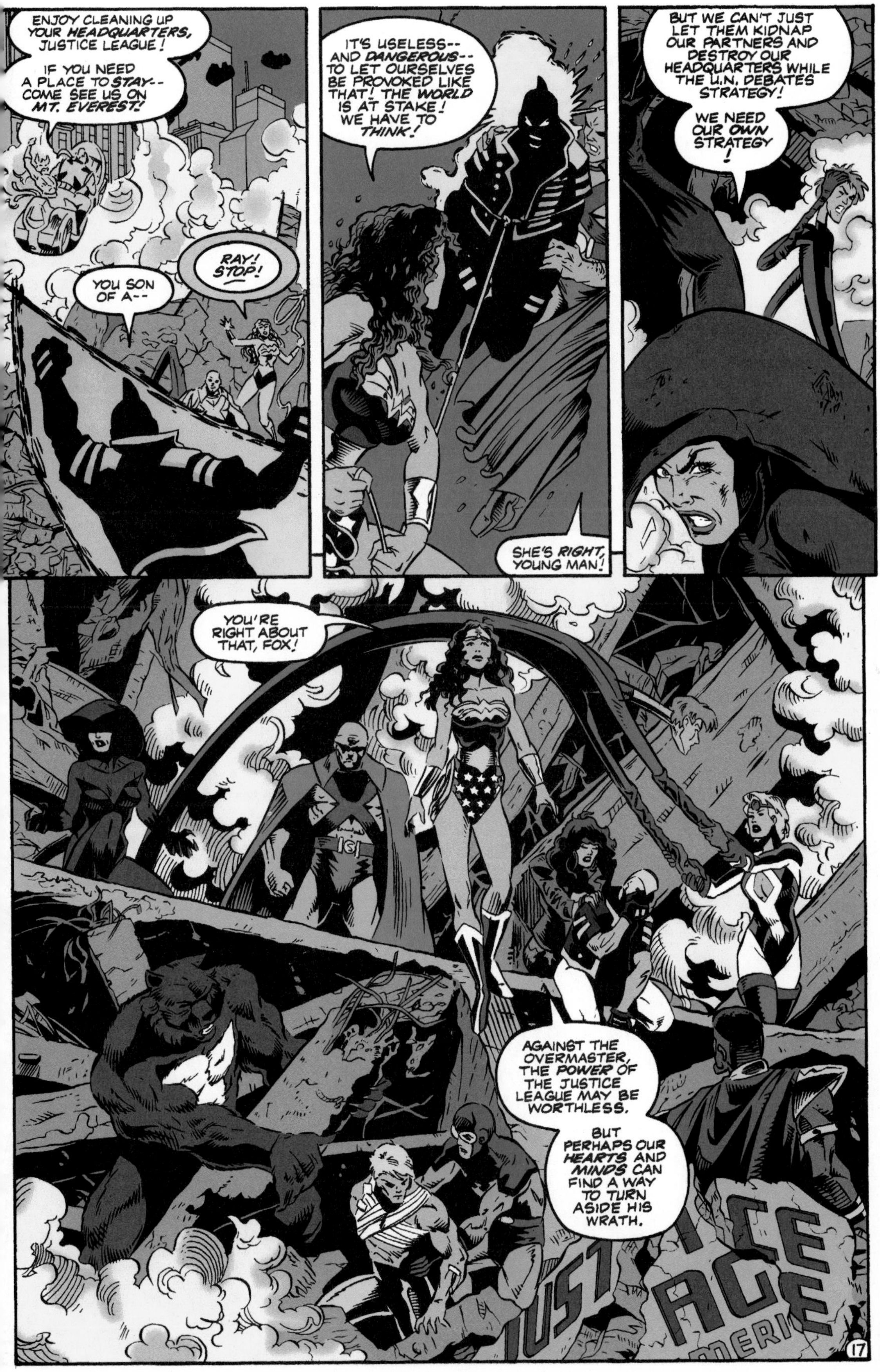
ENJOY CLEANING UP YOUR HEADQUARTERS, JUSTICE LEAGUE!
IF YOU NEED A PLACE TO STAY-- COME SEE US ON MT. EVEREST!
YOU SON OF A--
RAY! STOP!
IT'S USELESS-- AND DANGEROUS-- TO LET OURSELVES BE PROVOKED LIKE THAT! THE WORLD IS AT STAKE! WE HAVE TO THINK!
SHE'S RIGHT, YOUNG MAN!
BUT WE CAN'T JUST LET THEM KIDNAP OUR PARTNERS AND DESTROY OUR HEADQUARTERS WHILE THE U.N. DEBATES STRATEGY!
WE NEED OUR OWN STRATEGY!
YOU'RE RIGHT ABOUT THAT, FOX!
AGAINST THE OVERMASTER, THE POWER OF THE JUSTICE LEAGUE MAY BE WORTHLESS.
BUT PERHAPS OUR HEARTS AND MINDS CAN FIND A WAY TO TURN ASIDE HIS WRATH.

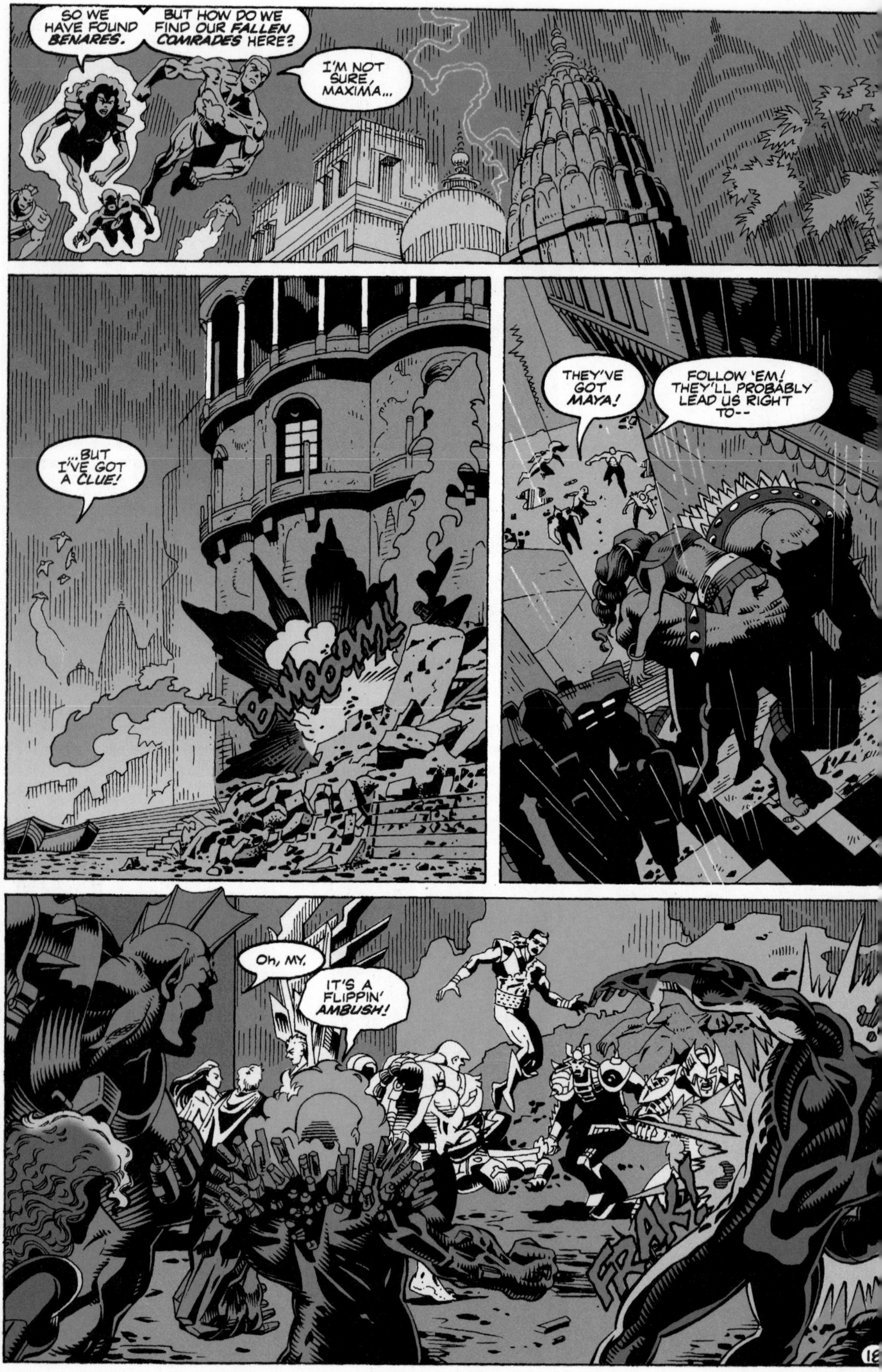
SO WE HAVE FOUND BENARES.
BUT HOW DO WE FIND OUR FALLEN COMRADES HERE?
I'M NOT SURE, MAXIMA...
...BUT I'VE GOT A CLUE!
BWOOOM!
THEY'VE GOT MAYA!
FOLLOW 'EM! THEY'LL PROBABLY LEAD US RIGHT TO--
Oh, MY.
IT'S A FLIPPIN' AMBUSH!
FRAK!

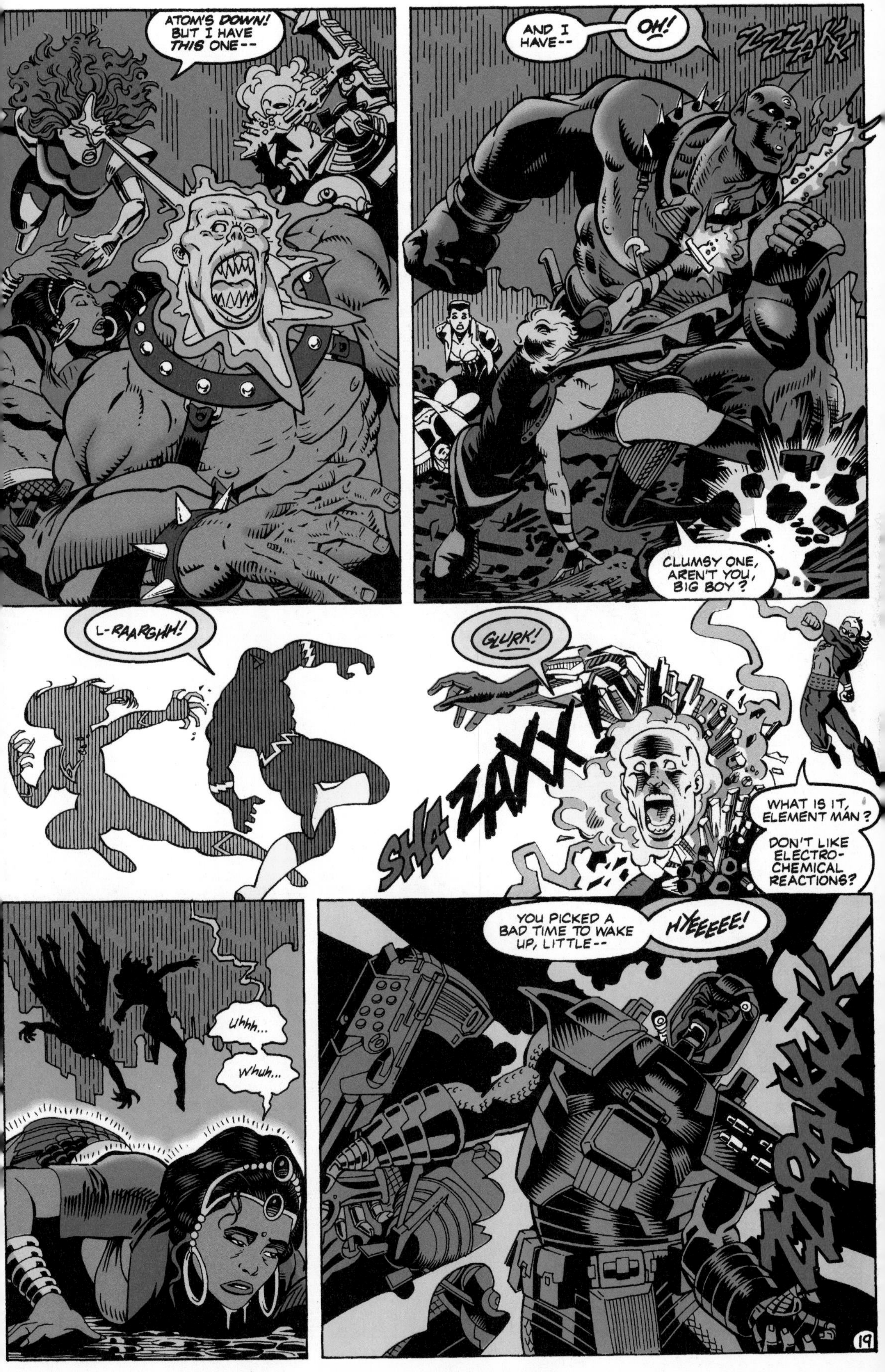
ATOM'S DOWN! BUT I HAVE THIS ONE--
AND I HAVE--
OH!
ZZZAKK
CLUMSY ONE, AREN'T YOU, BIG BOY?
L-RAARGHH!
GLURK!
SHAZAXX
WHAT IS IT, ELEMENT MAN?
DON'T LIKE ELECTRO-CHEMICAL REACTIONS?
Uhhh...
Whuh...
YOU PICKED A BAD TIME TO WAKE UP, LITTLE--
HYEEEEE!
KRAKK
19

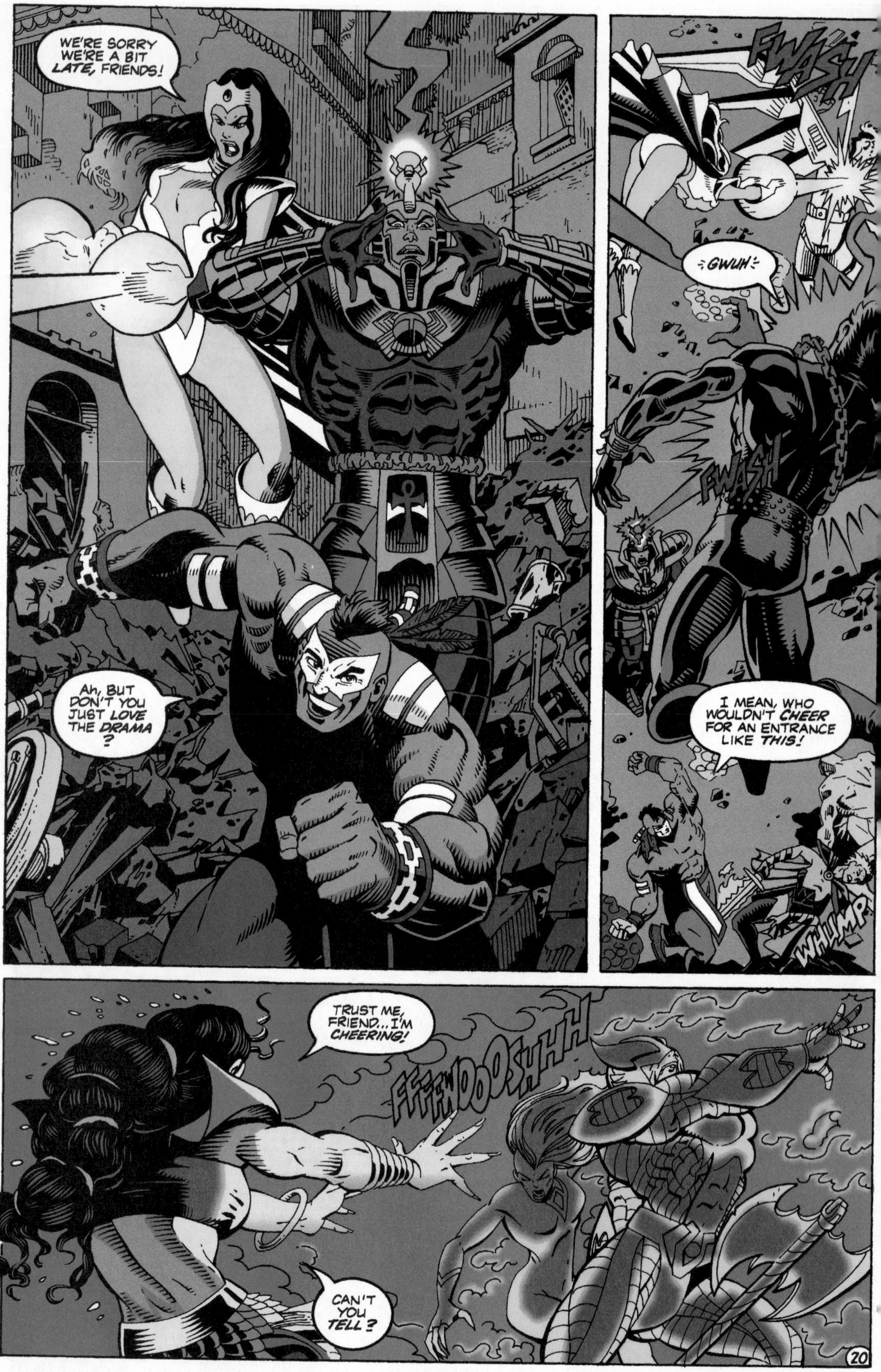

WE'RE SORRY WE'RE A BIT LATE, FRIENDS!
Ah, BUT DON'T YOU JUST LOVE THE DRAMA?
FWASH
GWUH
FWASH
I MEAN, WHO WOULDN'T CHEER FOR AN ENTRANCE LIKE THIS!
WHUMP
TRUST ME, FRIEND... I'M CHEERING!
FFFWOOOSHHH
CAN'T YOU TELL?
20

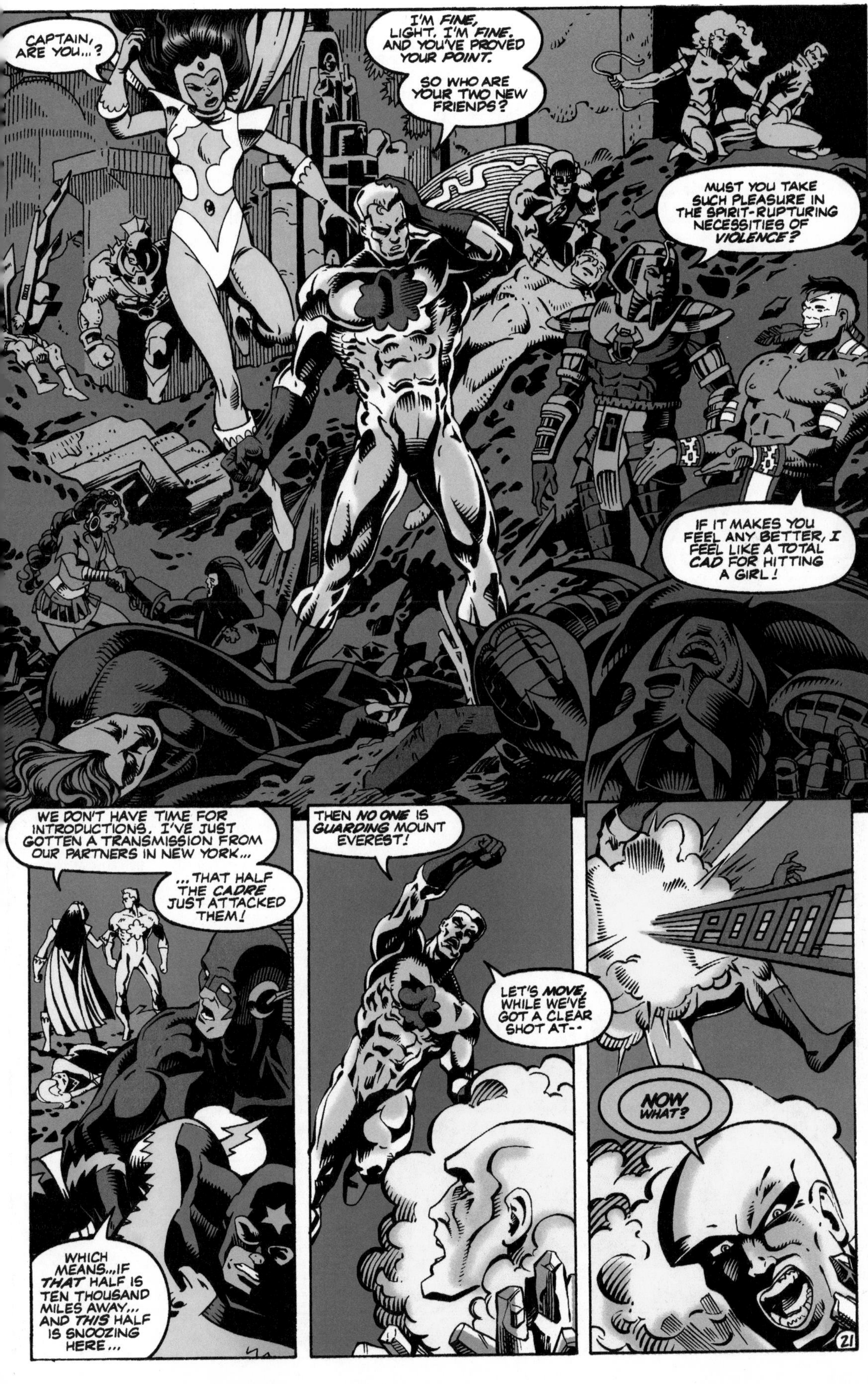

CAPTAIN, ARE YOU...?
I'M FINE, LIGHT. I'M FINE. AND YOU'VE PROVED YOUR POINT.
SO WHO ARE YOUR TWO NEW FRIENDS?
MUST YOU TAKE SUCH PLEASURE IN THE SPIRIT-RUPTURING NECESSITIES OF VIOLENCE?
IF IT MAKES YOU FEEL ANY BETTER, I FEEL LIKE A TOTAL CAD FOR HITTING A GIRL!
WE DON'T HAVE TIME FOR INTRODUCTIONS. I'VE JUST GOTTEN A TRANSMISSION FROM OUR PARTNERS IN NEW YORK...
...THAT HALF THE CADRE JUST ATTACKED THEM!
WHICH MEANS...IF THAT HALF IS TEN THOUSAND MILES AWAY... AND THIS HALF IS SNOOZING HERE...
THEN NO ONE IS GUARDING MOUNT EVEREST!
LET'S MOVE, WHILE WE'VE GOT A CLEAR SHOT AT--
NOW WHAT?

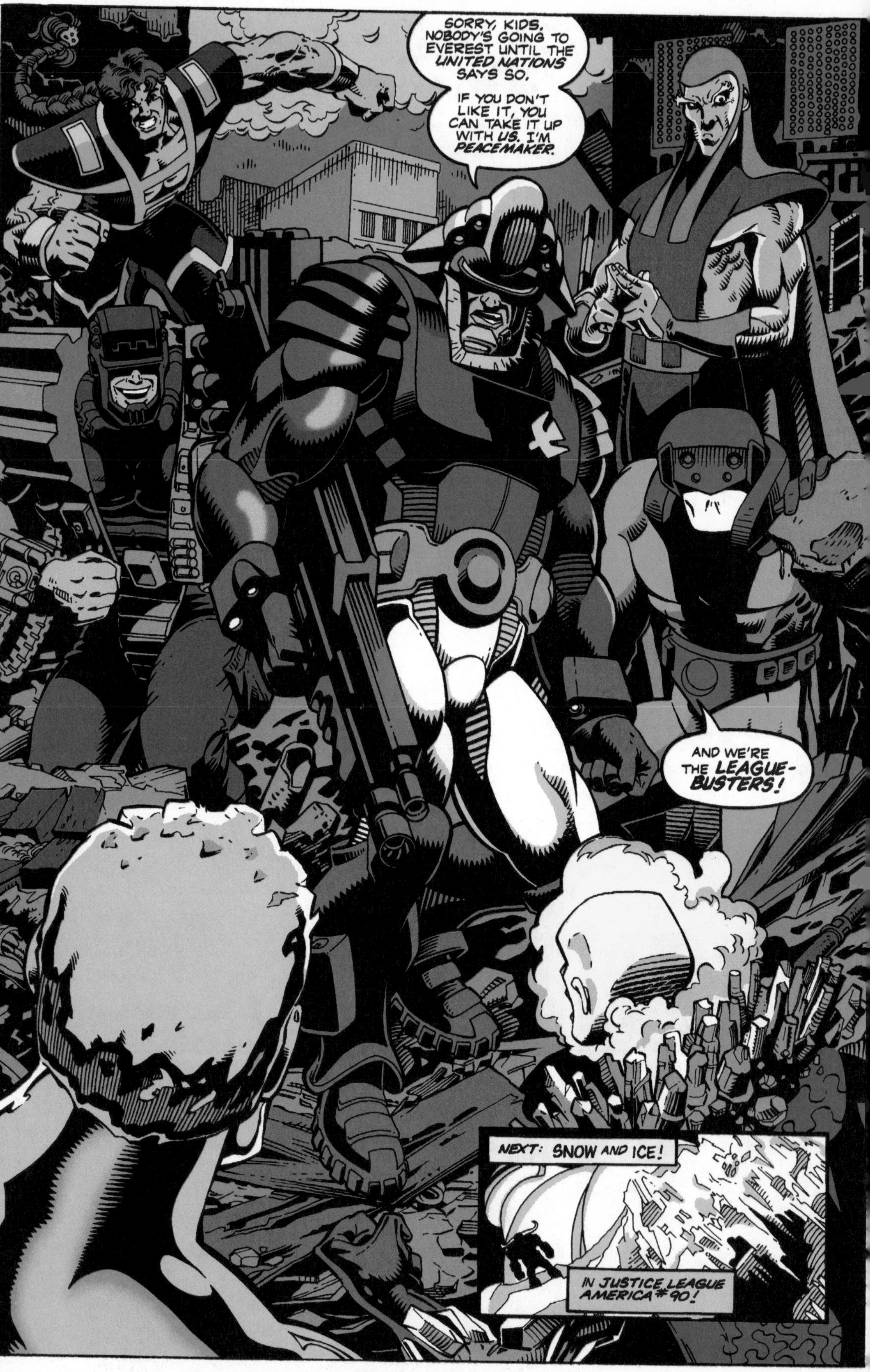
SORRY, KIDS. NOBODY'S GOING TO EVEREST UNTIL THE UNITED NATIONS SAYS SO.
IF YOU DON'T LIKE IT, YOU CAN TAKE IT UP WITH US. I'M PEACEMAKER.
AND WE'RE THE LEAGUE-BUSTERS!
NEXT: SNOW AND ICE!
IN JUSTICE LEAGUE AMERICA #90!

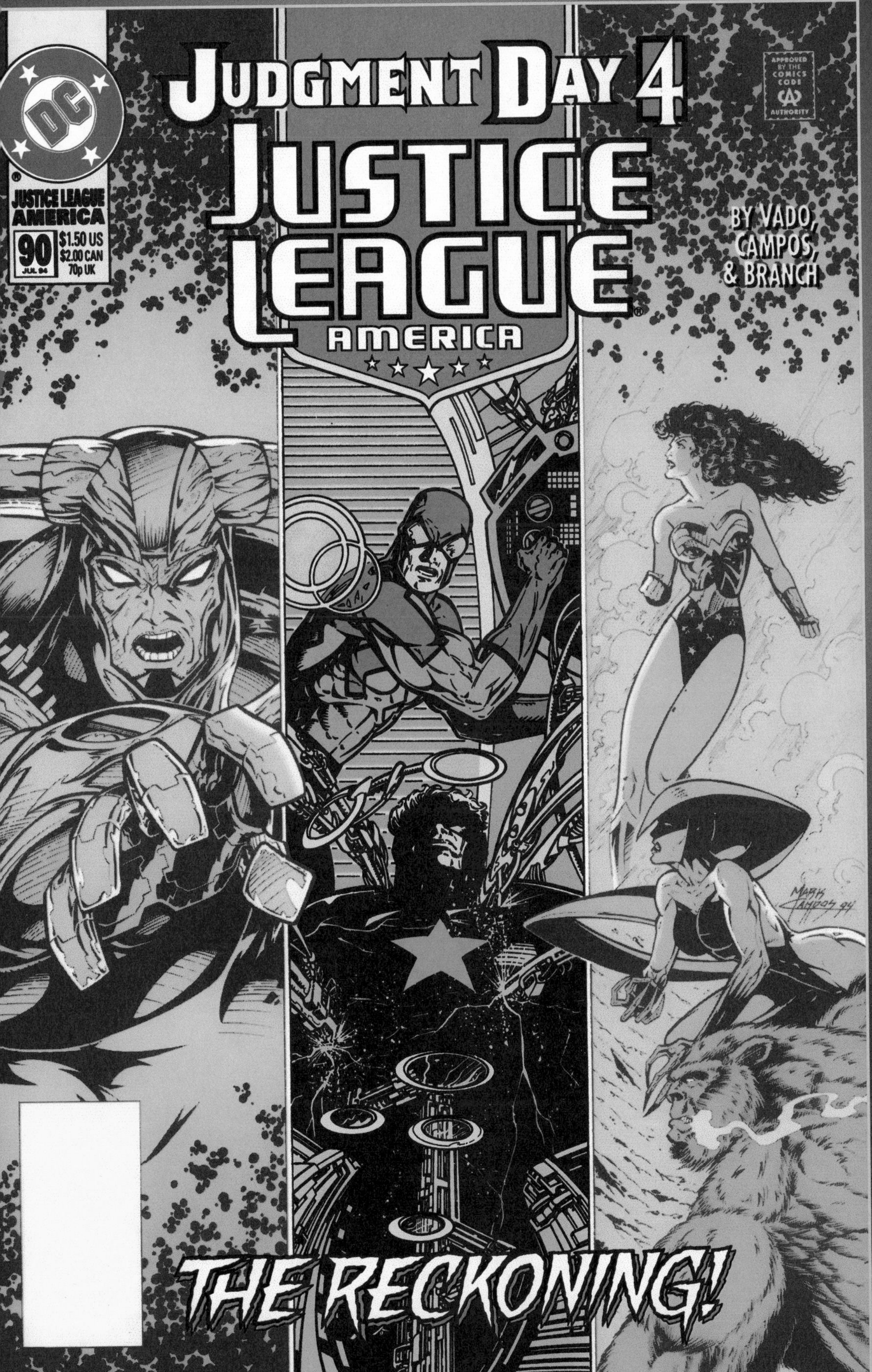

DC
JUSTICE LEAGUE AMERICA
90
JUL 94
$1.50 US
$2.00 CAN
70p UK
JUDGMENT DAY 4
JUSTICE LEAGUE AMERICA
APPROVED BY THE COMICS CODE AUTHORITY
BY VADO, CAMPOS, & BRANCH
THE RECKONING!

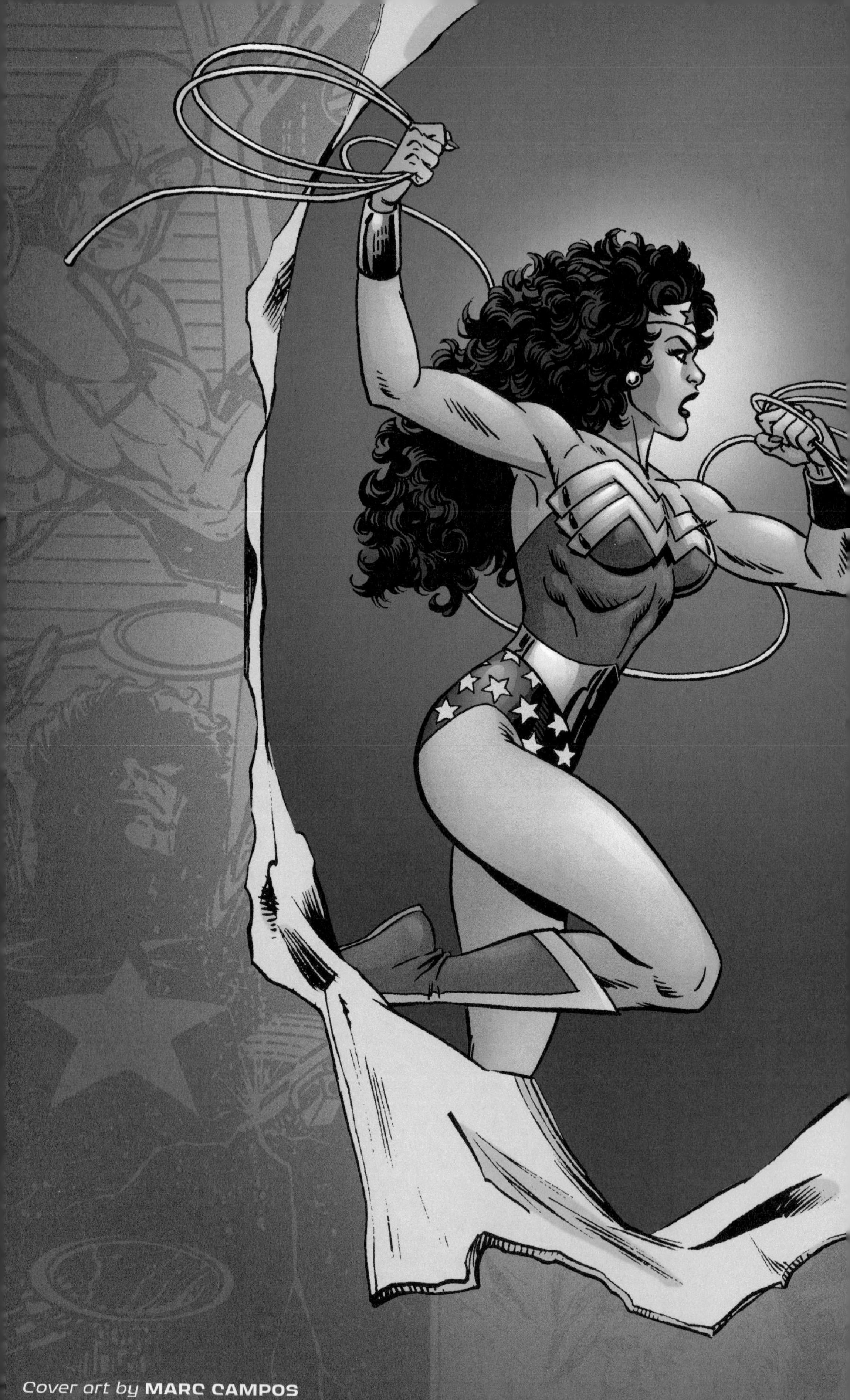

Cover art by **MARC CAMPOS**

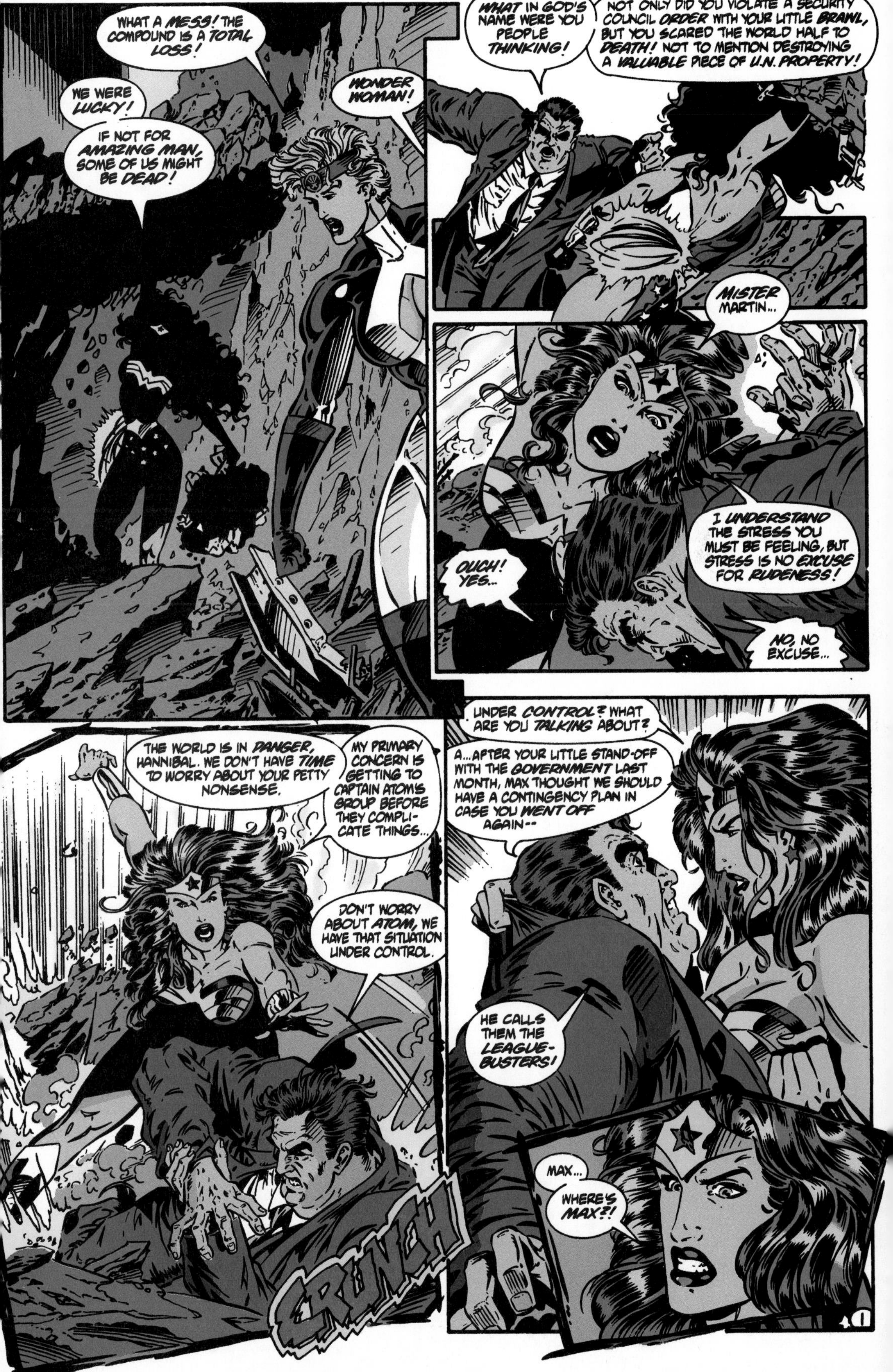

WHAT A MESS! THE COMPOUND IS A TOTAL LOSS!
WE WERE LUCKY!
IF NOT FOR AMAZING MAN, SOME OF US MIGHT BE DEAD!
WONDER WOMAN!
WHAT IN GOD'S NAME WERE YOU PEOPLE THINKING!
NOT ONLY DID YOU VIOLATE A SECURITY COUNCIL ORDER WITH YOUR LITTLE BRAWL, BUT YOU SCARED THE WORLD HALF TO DEATH! NOT TO MENTION DESTROYING A VALUABLE PIECE OF U.N. PROPERTY!
MISTER MARTIN...
I UNDERSTAND THE STRESS YOU MUST BE FEELING, BUT STRESS IS NO EXCUSE FOR RUDENESS!
OUCH! YES...
NO, NO EXCUSE...
THE WORLD IS IN DANGER, HANNIBAL. WE DON'T HAVE TIME TO WORRY ABOUT YOUR PETTY NONSENSE.
MY PRIMARY CONCERN IS GETTING TO CAPTAIN ATOM'S GROUP BEFORE THEY COMPLICATE THINGS...
DON'T WORRY ABOUT ATOM, WE HAVE THAT SITUATION UNDER CONTROL.
CRUNCH
UNDER CONTROL? WHAT ARE YOU TALKING ABOUT?
A...AFTER YOUR LITTLE STAND-OFF WITH THE GOVERNMENT LAST MONTH, MAX THOUGHT WE SHOULD HAVE A CONTINGENCY PLAN IN CASE YOU WENT OFF AGAIN--
HE CALLS THEM THE LEAGUE-BUSTERS!
MAX...
WHERE'S MAX?!

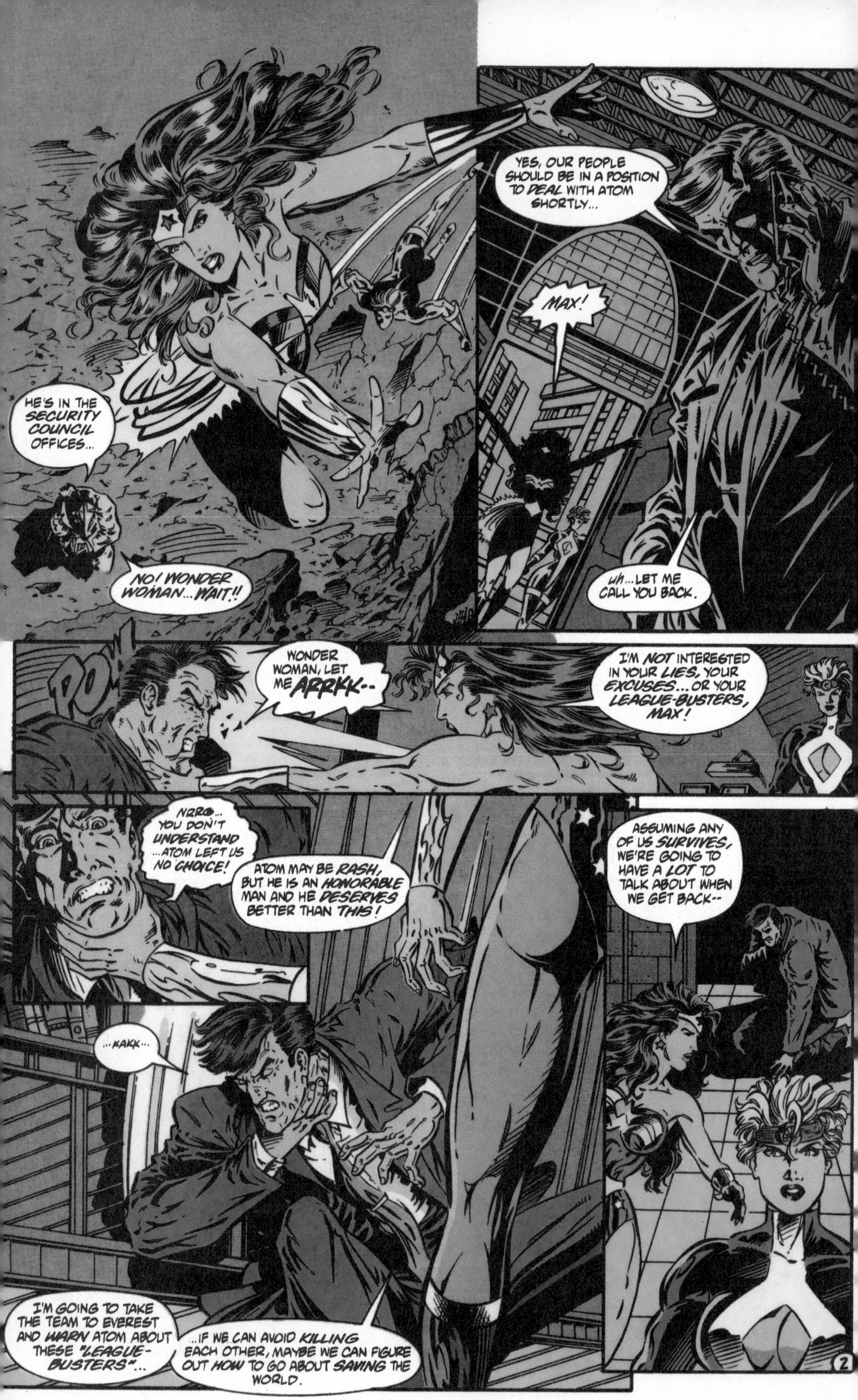

YES, OUR PEOPLE SHOULD BE IN A POSITION TO DEAL WITH ATOM SHORTLY...
MAX!
HE'S IN THE SECURITY COUNCIL OFFICES...
NO! WONDER WOMAN... WAIT!!
uh... LET ME CALL YOU BACK.
POW
WONDER WOMAN, LET ME ARRKK--
I'M NOT INTERESTED IN YOUR LIES, YOUR EXCUSES... OR YOUR LEAGUE-BUSTERS, MAX!
NRRG... YOU DON'T UNDERSTAND ...ATOM LEFT US NO CHOICE!
ATOM MAY BE RASH, BUT HE IS AN HONORABLE MAN AND HE DESERVES BETTER THAN THIS!
ASSUMING ANY OF US SURVIVES, WE'RE GOING TO HAVE A LOT TO TALK ABOUT WHEN WE GET BACK--
...KAKK...
I'M GOING TO TAKE THE TEAM TO EVEREST AND WARN ATOM ABOUT THESE "LEAGUE-BUSTERS"...
...IF WE CAN AVOID KILLING EACH OTHER, MAYBE WE CAN FIGURE OUT HOW TO GO ABOUT SAVING THE WORLD.

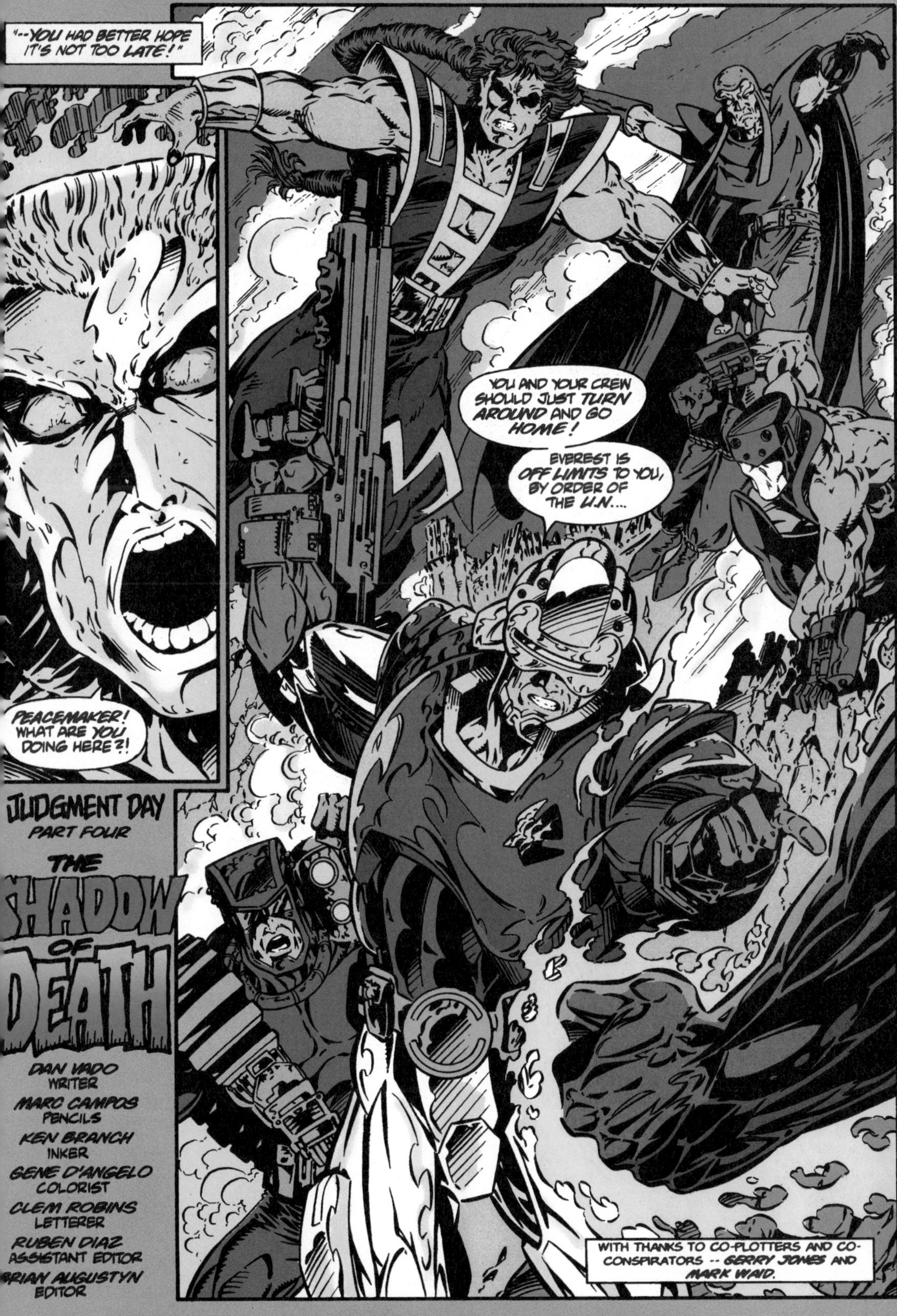

"--YOU HAD BETTER HOPE IT'S NOT TOO LATE!"
PEACEMAKER! WHAT ARE YOU DOING HERE?!
YOU AND YOUR CREW SHOULD JUST TURN AROUND AND GO HOME!
EVEREST IS OFF LIMITS TO YOU, BY ORDER OF THE U.N....
JUDGMENT DAY PART FOUR
THE SHADOW OF DEATH
DAN VADO WRITER
MARC CAMPOS PENCILS
KEN BRANCH INKER
GENE D'ANGELO COLORIST
CLEM ROBINS LETTERER
RUBEN DIAZ ASSISTANT EDITOR
BRIAN AUGUSTYN EDITOR
WITH THANKS TO CO-PLOTTERS AND CO-CONSPIRATORS -- GERRY JONES AND MARK WAID.

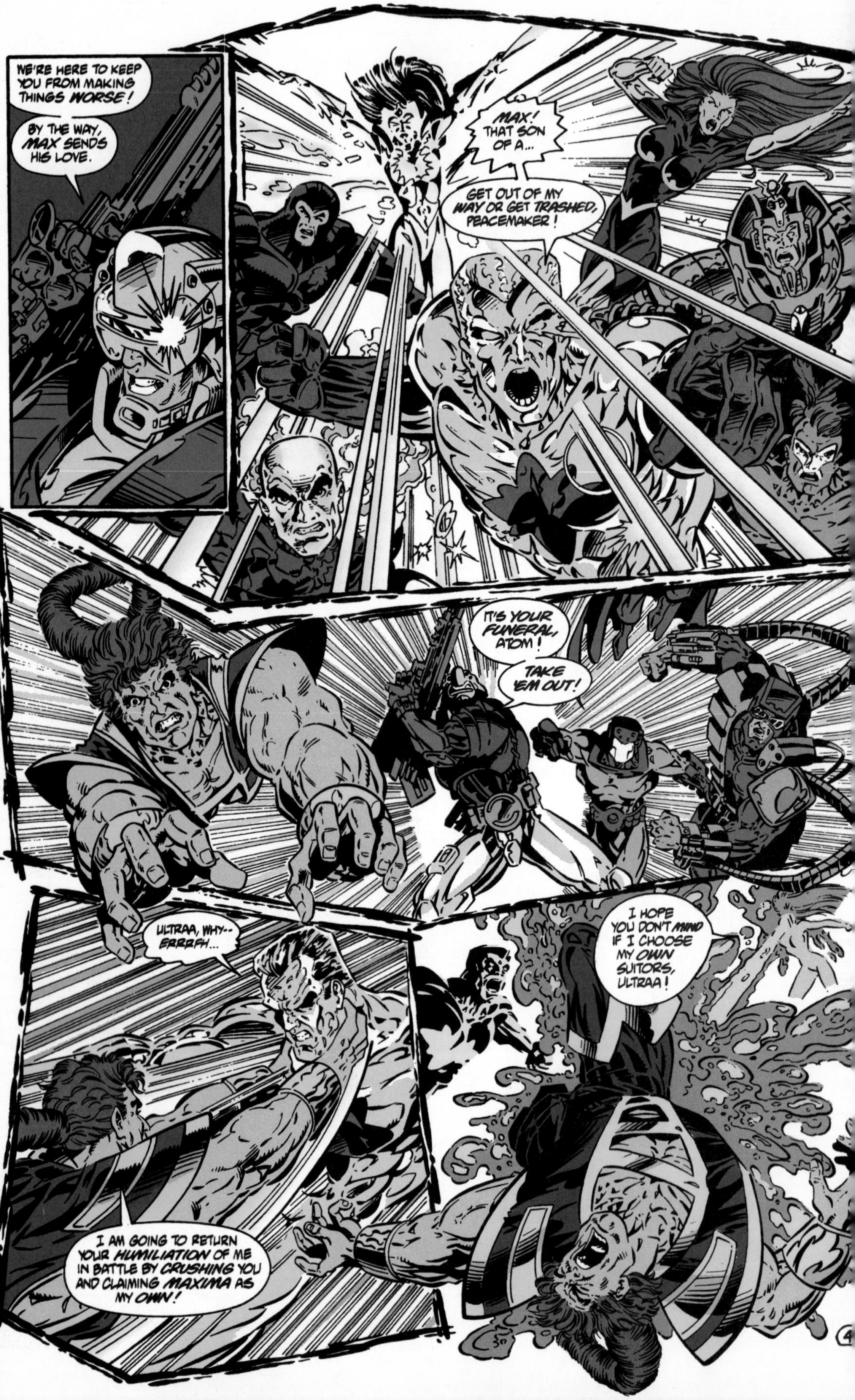
WE'RE HERE TO KEEP YOU FROM MAKING THINGS WORSE!
BY THE WAY, MAX SENDS HIS LOVE.
MAX! THAT SON OF A...
GET OUT OF MY WAY OR GET TRASHED, PEACEMAKER!
IT'S YOUR FUNERAL, ATOM!
TAKE 'EM OUT!
ULTRAA, WHY-- ERRRFH...
I AM GOING TO RETURN YOUR HUMILIATION OF ME IN BATTLE BY CRUSHING YOU AND CLAIMING MAXIMA AS MY OWN!
I HOPE YOU DON'T MIND IF I CHOOSE MY OWN SUITORS, ULTRAA!

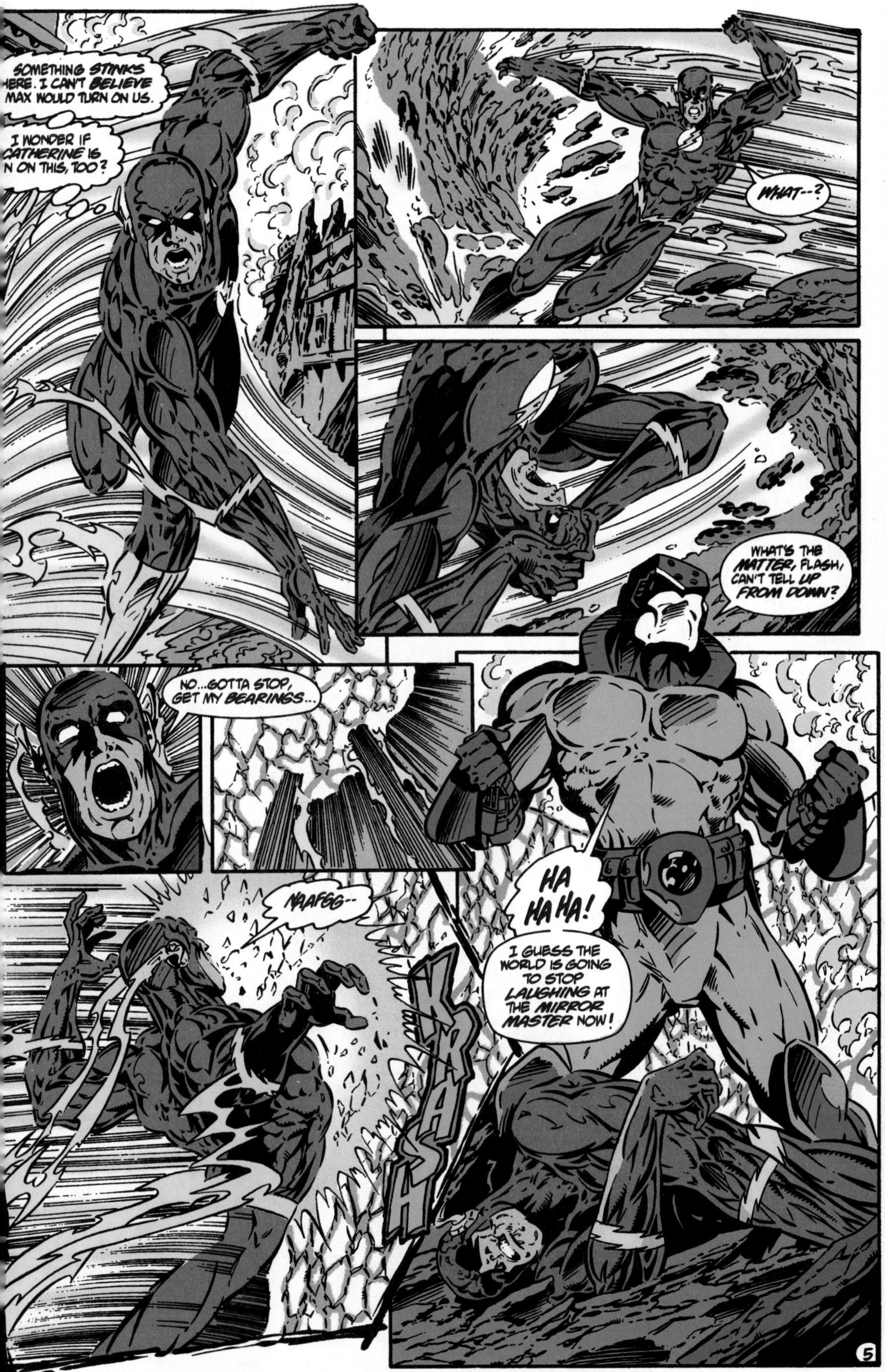
SOMETHING STINKS HERE. I CAN'T BELIEVE MAX WOULD TURN ON US.
I WONDER IF CATHERINE IS IN ON THIS, TOO?
WHAT--?
WHAT'S THE MATTER, FLASH, CAN'T TELL UP FROM DOWN?
NO...GOTTA STOP, GET MY BEARINGS...
HA HA HA!
I GUESS THE WORLD IS GOING TO STOP LAUGHING AT THE MIRROR MASTER NOW!
NAAFGG--
5

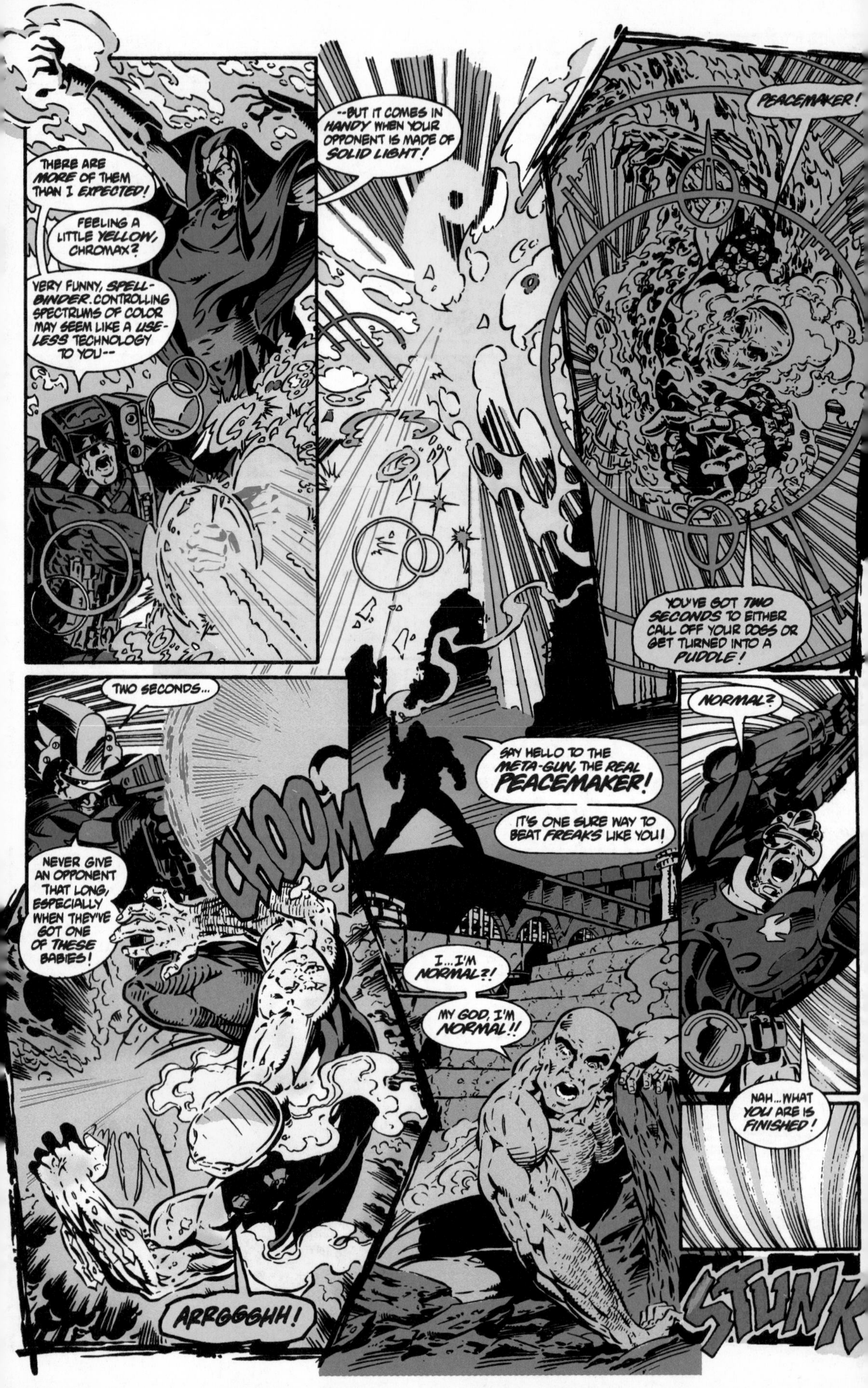
THERE ARE MORE OF THEM THAN I EXPECTED!
FEELING A LITTLE YELLOW, CHROMAX?
VERY FUNNY, SPELLBINDER. CONTROLLING SPECTRUMS OF COLOR MAY SEEM LIKE A USELESS TECHNOLOGY TO YOU--
--BUT IT COMES IN HANDY WHEN YOUR OPPONENT IS MADE OF SOLID LIGHT!
PEACEMAKER!
YOU'VE GOT TWO SECONDS TO EITHER CALL OFF YOUR DOGS OR GET TURNED INTO A PUDDLE!
TWO SECONDS...
NEVER GIVE AN OPPONENT THAT LONG, ESPECIALLY WHEN THEY'VE GOT ONE OF THESE BABIES!
CHOOM
SAY HELLO TO THE META-GUN, THE REAL PEACEMAKER!
IT'S ONE SURE WAY TO BEAT FREAKS LIKE YOU!
ARRGGGHH!
I...I'M NORMAL?!
MY GOD, I'M NORMAL!!
NORMAL?
NAH...WHAT YOU ARE IS FINISHED!
STUNK

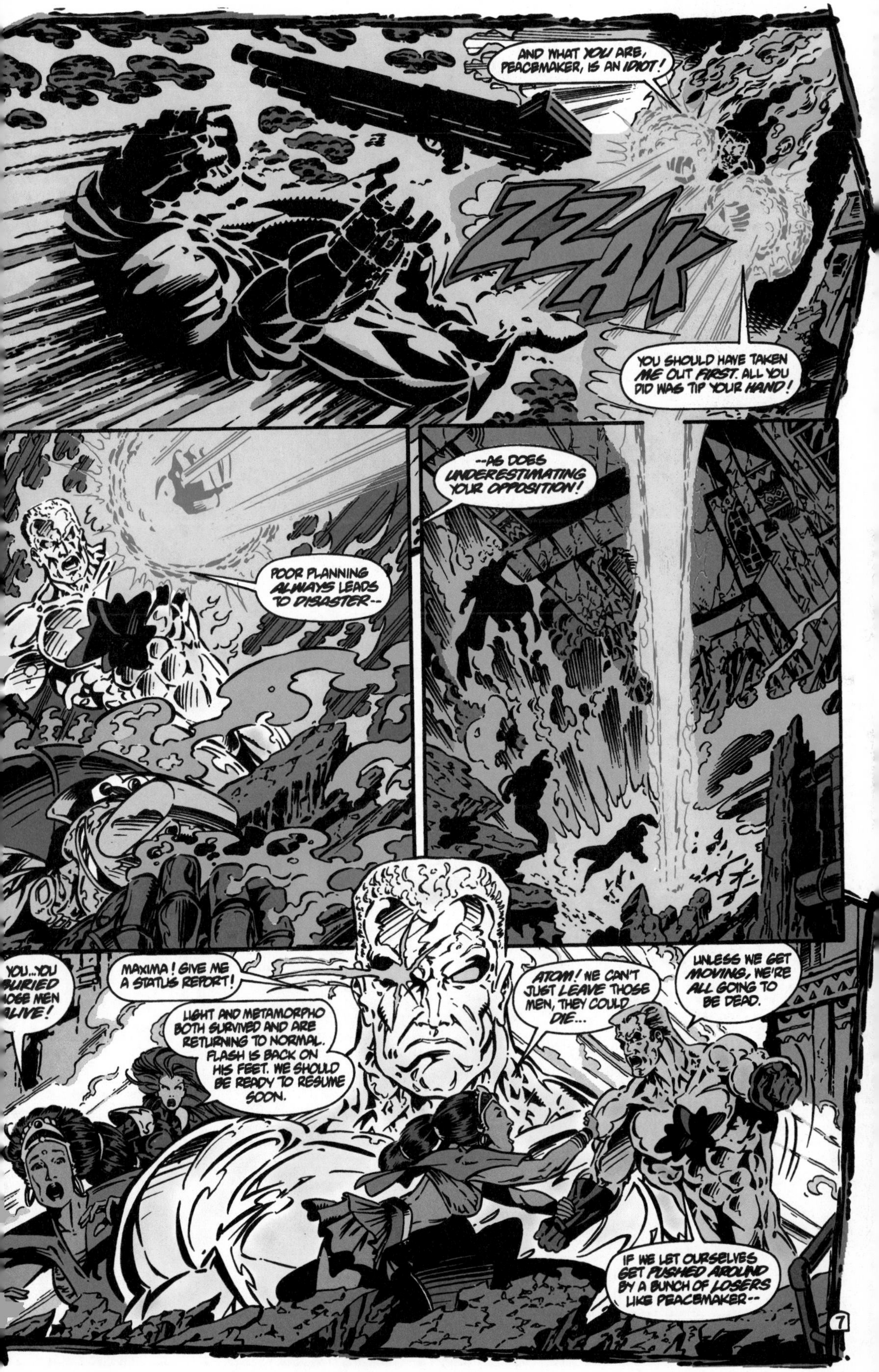
AND WHAT YOU ARE, PEACEMAKER, IS AN IDIOT!
ZZAK
YOU SHOULD HAVE TAKEN ME OUT FIRST. ALL YOU DID WAS TIP YOUR HAND!
POOR PLANNING ALWAYS LEADS TO DISASTER--
--AS DOES UNDERESTIMATING YOUR OPPOSITION!
YOU...YOU BURIED THOSE MEN ALIVE!
MAXIMA! GIVE ME A STATUS REPORT!
LIGHT AND METAMORPHO BOTH SURVIVED AND ARE RETURNING TO NORMAL. FLASH IS BACK ON HIS FEET. WE SHOULD BE READY TO RESUME SOON.
ATOM! WE CAN'T JUST LEAVE THOSE MEN, THEY COULD DIE...
UNLESS WE GET MOVING, WE'RE ALL GOING TO BE DEAD.
IF WE LET OURSELVES GET PUSHED AROUND BY A BUNCH OF LOSERS LIKE PEACEMAKER--

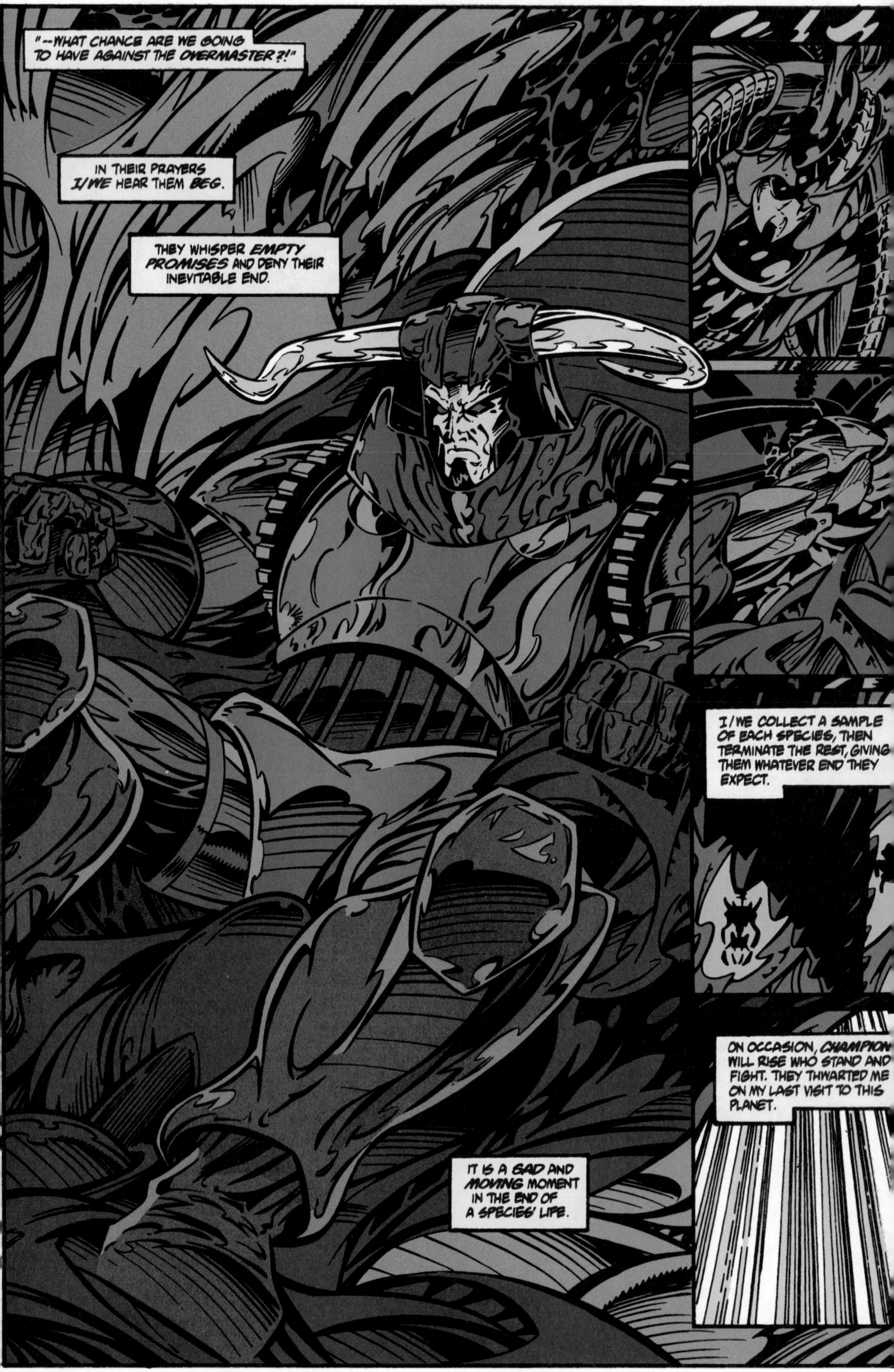
"--WHAT CHANCE ARE WE GOING TO HAVE AGAINST THE OVERMASTER?!"
IN THEIR PRAYERS I/WE HEAR THEM BEG.
THEY WHISPER EMPTY PROMISES AND DENY THEIR INEVITABLE END.
I/WE COLLECT A SAMPLE OF EACH SPECIES, THEN TERMINATE THE REST, GIVING THEM WHATEVER END THEY EXPECT.
ON OCCASION, CHAMPION WILL RISE WHO STAND AND FIGHT. THEY THWARTED ME ON MY LAST VISIT TO THIS PLANET.
IT IS A SAD AND MOVING MOMENT IN THE END OF A SPECIES' LIFE.

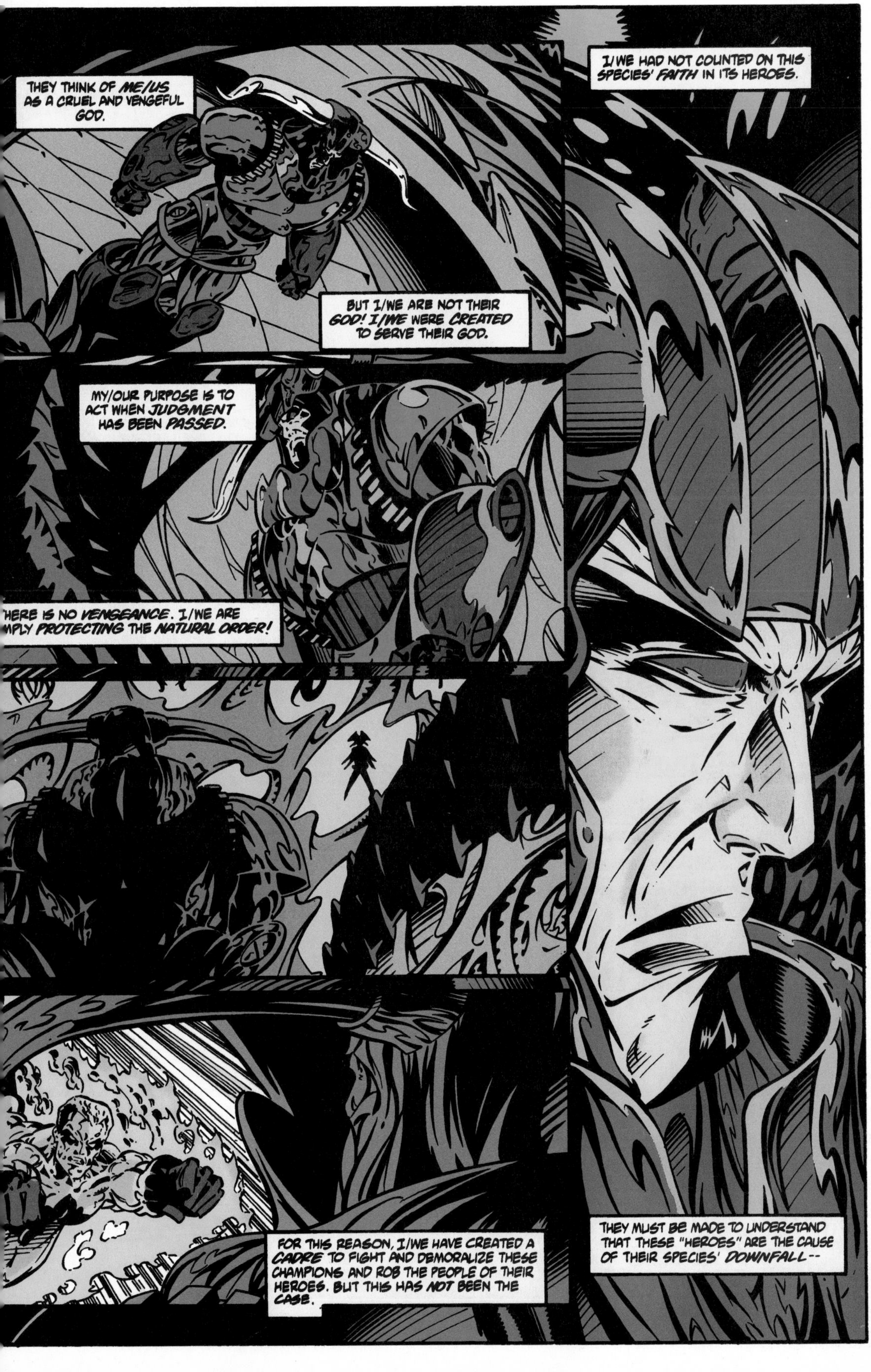

THEY THINK OF ME/US AS A CRUEL AND VENGEFUL GOD.
BUT I/WE ARE NOT THEIR GOD! I/WE WERE CREATED TO SERVE THEIR GOD.
MY/OUR PURPOSE IS TO ACT WHEN JUDGMENT HAS BEEN PASSED.
HERE IS NO VENGEANCE. I/WE ARE
MPLY PROTECTING THE NATURAL ORDER!
FOR THIS REASON, I/WE HAVE CREATED A CADRE TO FIGHT AND DEMORALIZE THESE CHAMPIONS AND ROB THE PEOPLE OF THEIR HEROES. BUT THIS HAS NOT BEEN THE CASE.
I/WE HAD NOT COUNTED ON THIS SPECIES' FAITH IN ITS HEROES.
THEY MUST BE MADE TO UNDERSTAND THAT THESE "HEROES" ARE THE CAUSE OF THEIR SPECIES' DOWNFALL--

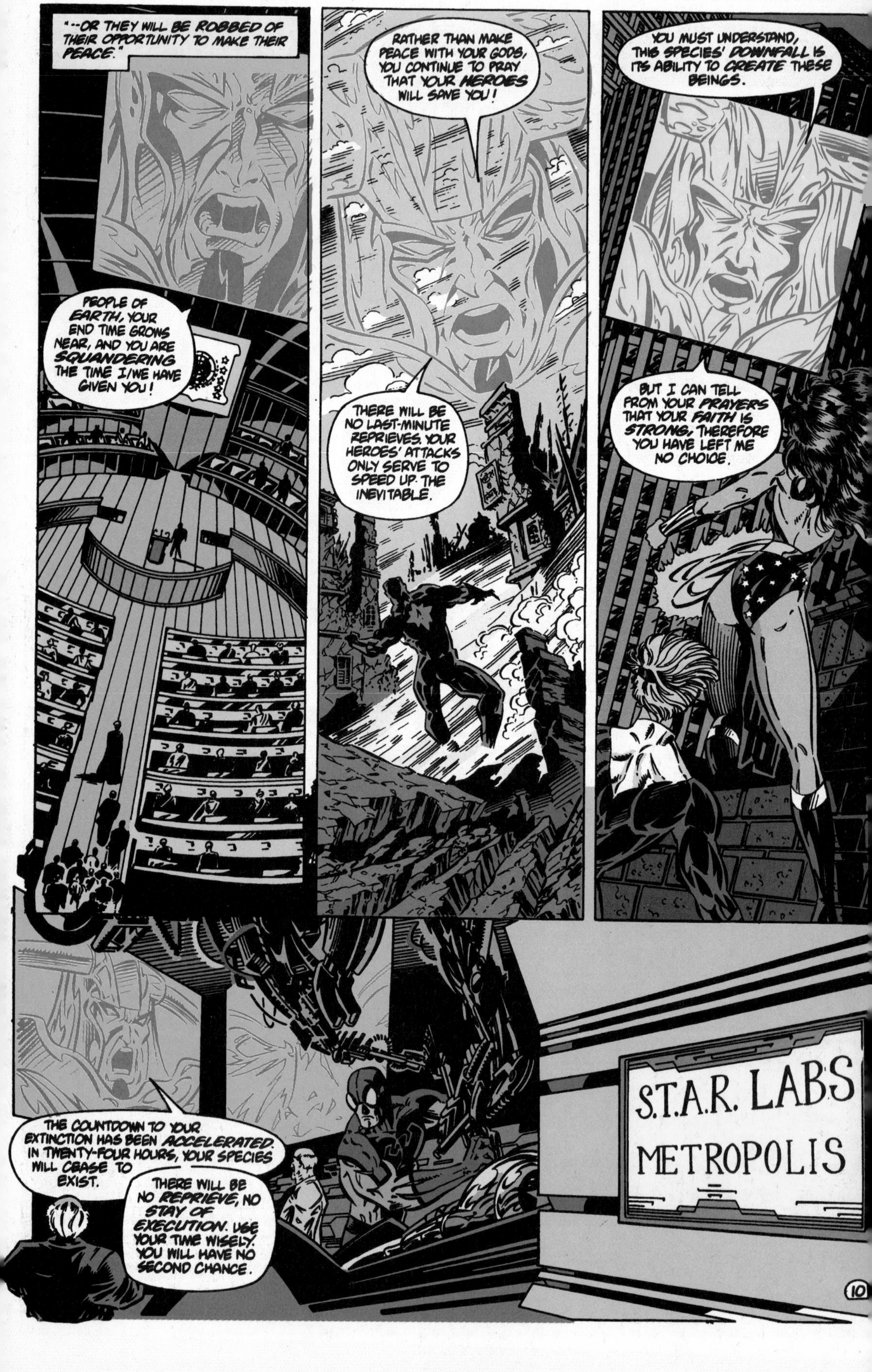
"--OR THEY WILL BE ROBBED OF THEIR OPPORTUNITY TO MAKE THEIR PEACE."
PEOPLE OF EARTH, YOUR END TIME GROWS NEAR, AND YOU ARE SQUANDERING THE TIME I/WE HAVE GIVEN YOU!
RATHER THAN MAKE PEACE WITH YOUR GODS, YOU CONTINUE TO PRAY THAT YOUR HEROES WILL SAVE YOU!
THERE WILL BE NO LAST-MINUTE REPRIEVES. YOUR HEROES' ATTACKS ONLY SERVE TO SPEED UP THE INEVITABLE.
YOU MUST UNDERSTAND, THIS SPECIES' DOWNFALL IS ITS ABILITY TO CREATE THESE BEINGS.
BUT I CAN TELL FROM YOUR PRAYERS THAT YOUR FAITH IS STRONG, THEREFORE YOU HAVE LEFT ME NO CHOICE.
THE COUNTDOWN TO YOUR EXTINCTION HAS BEEN ACCELERATED. IN TWENTY-FOUR HOURS, YOUR SPECIES WILL CEASE TO EXIST.
THERE WILL BE NO REPRIEVE, NO STAY OF EXECUTION. USE YOUR TIME WISELY. YOU WILL HAVE NO SECOND CHANCE.
S.T.A.R. LABS
METROPOLIS

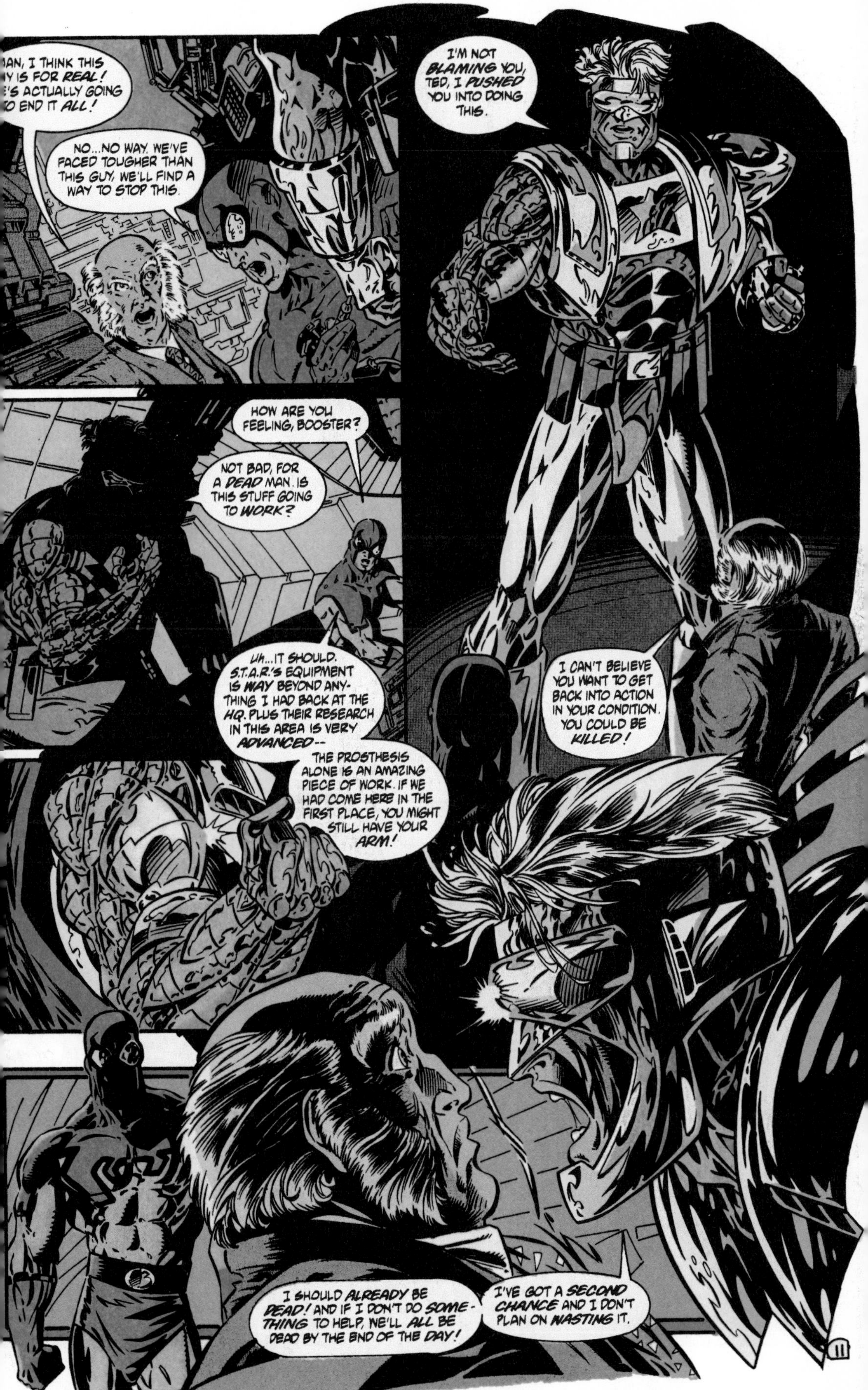

MAN, I THINK THIS
Y IS FOR REAL!
E'S ACTUALLY GOING
O END IT ALL!
NO...NO WAY. WE'VE FACED TOUGHER THAN THIS GUY. WE'LL FIND A WAY TO STOP THIS.
HOW ARE YOU FEELING, BOOSTER?
NOT BAD, FOR A DEAD MAN. IS THIS STUFF GOING TO WORK?
UH...IT SHOULD. S.T.A.R.'S EQUIPMENT IS WAY BEYOND ANY-THING I HAD BACK AT THE HQ. PLUS THEIR RESEARCH IN THIS AREA IS VERY ADVANCED--
THE PROSTHESIS ALONE IS AN AMAZING PIECE OF WORK. IF WE HAD COME HERE IN THE FIRST PLACE, YOU MIGHT STILL HAVE YOUR ARM!
I'M NOT BLAMING YOU, TED. I PUSHED YOU INTO DOING THIS.
I CAN'T BELIEVE YOU WANT TO GET BACK INTO ACTION IN YOUR CONDITION. YOU COULD BE KILLED!
I SHOULD ALREADY BE DEAD! AND IF I DON'T DO SOME-THING TO HELP, WE'LL ALL BE DEAD BY THE END OF THE DAY!
I'VE GOT A SECOND CHANCE AND I DON'T PLAN ON WASTING IT.

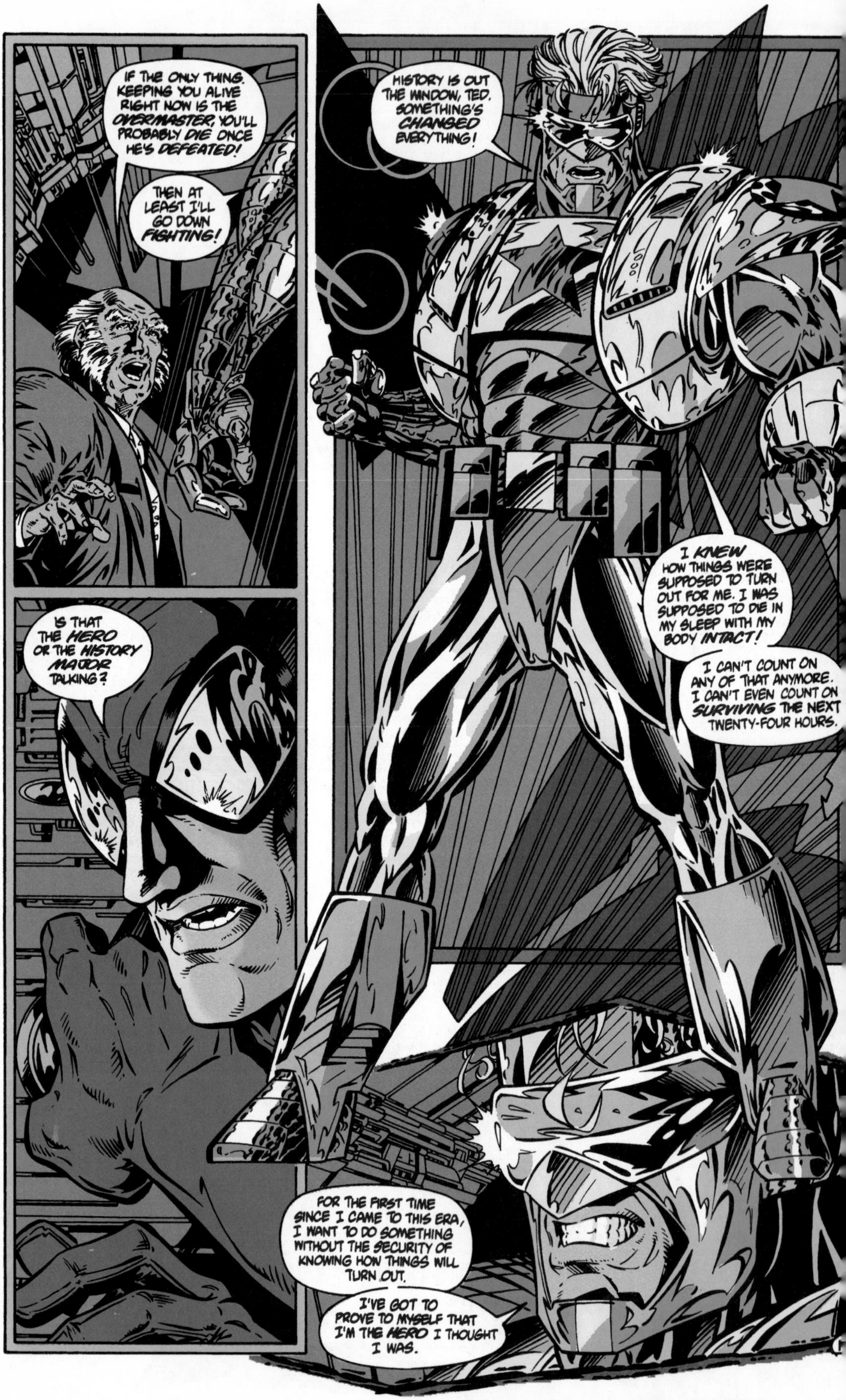
IF THE ONLY THING KEEPING YOU ALIVE RIGHT NOW IS THE OVERMASTER, YOU'LL PROBABLY DIE ONCE HE'S DEFEATED!
THEN AT LEAST I'LL GO DOWN FIGHTING!
HISTORY IS OUT THE WINDOW, TED. SOMETHING'S CHANGED EVERYTHING!
IS THAT THE HERO OR THE HISTORY MAJOR TALKING?
I KNEW HOW THINGS WERE SUPPOSED TO TURN OUT FOR ME. I WAS SUPPOSED TO DIE IN MY SLEEP WITH MY BODY INTACT!
I CAN'T COUNT ON ANY OF THAT ANYMORE. I CAN'T EVEN COUNT ON SURVIVING THE NEXT TWENTY-FOUR HOURS.
FOR THE FIRST TIME SINCE I CAME TO THIS ERA, I WANT TO DO SOMETHING WITHOUT THE SECURITY OF KNOWING HOW THINGS WILL TURN OUT.
I'VE GOT TO PROVE TO MYSELF THAT I'M THE HERO I THOUGHT I WAS.

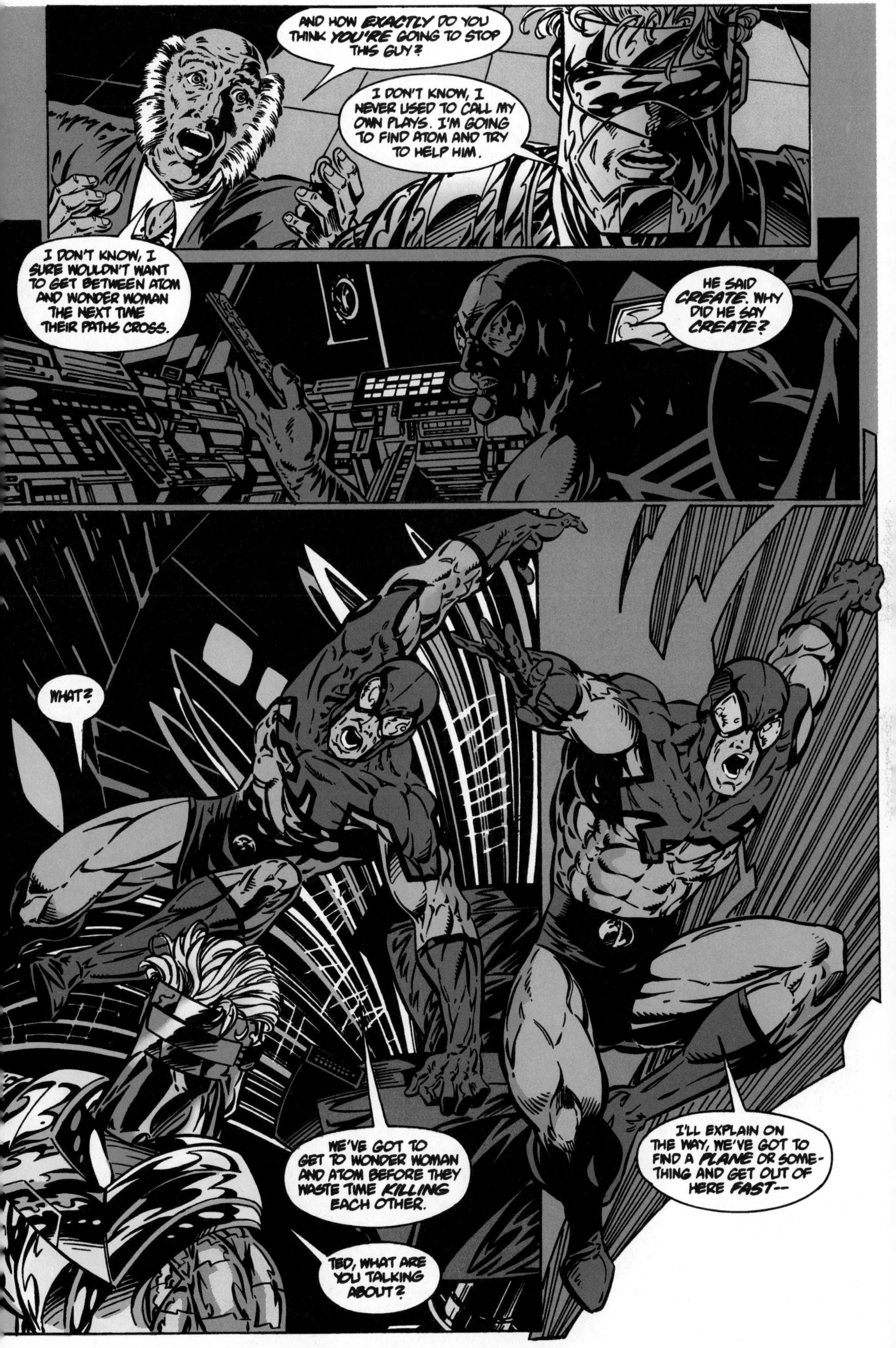
AND HOW EXACTLY DO YOU THINK YOU'RE GOING TO STOP THIS GUY?
I DON'T KNOW, I NEVER USED TO CALL MY OWN PLAYS. I'M GOING TO FIND ATOM AND TRY TO HELP HIM.
I DON'T KNOW, I SURE WOULDN'T WANT TO GET BETWEEN ATOM AND WONDER WOMAN THE NEXT TIME THEIR PATHS CROSS.
HE SAID CREATE. WHY DID HE SAY CREATE?
WHAT?
WE'VE GOT TO GET TO WONDER WOMAN AND ATOM BEFORE THEY WASTE TIME KILLING EACH OTHER.
TED, WHAT ARE YOU TALKING ABOUT?
I'LL EXPLAIN ON THE WAY, WE'VE GOT TO FIND A PLANE OR SOMETHING AND GET OUT OF HERE FAST--

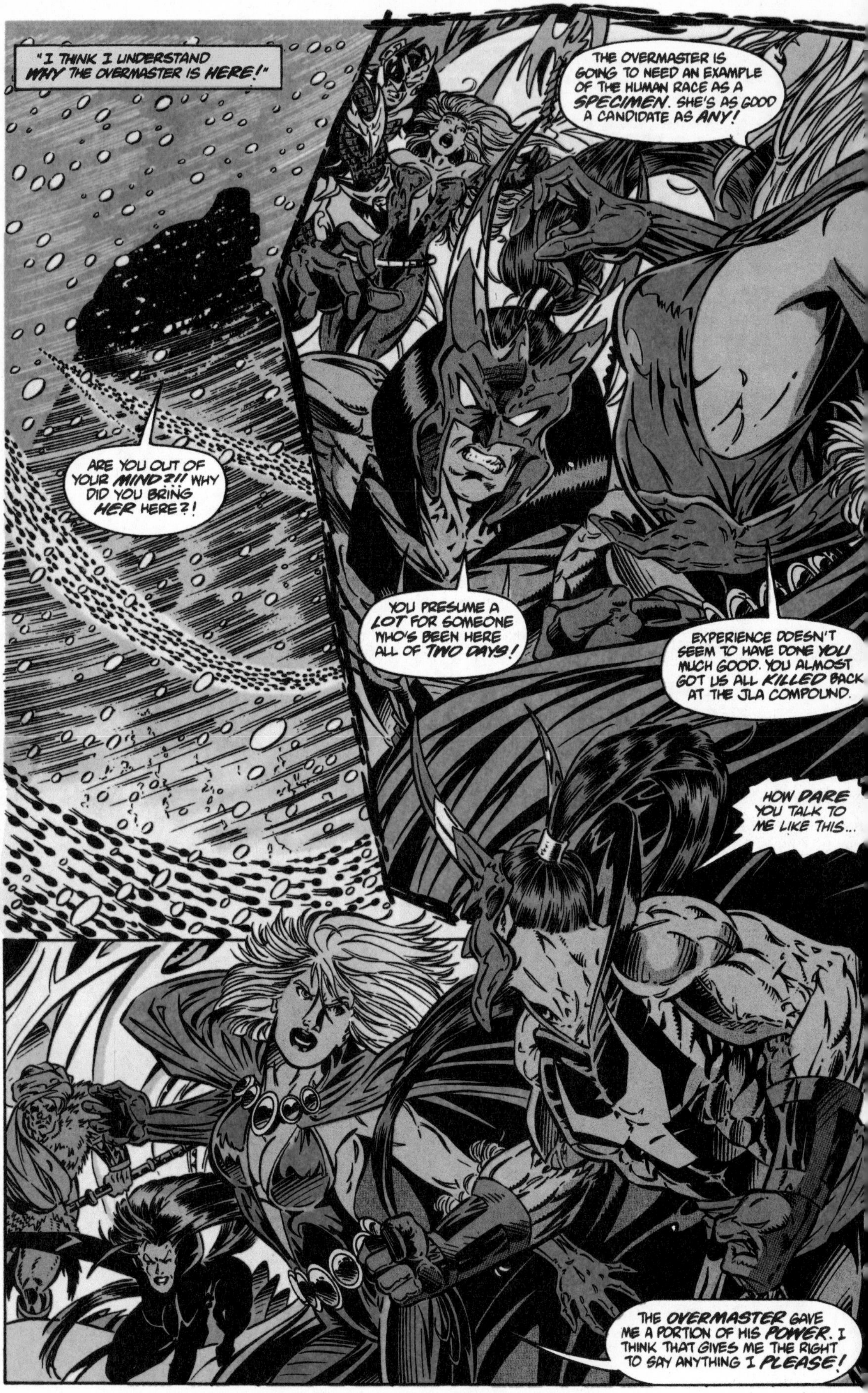
"I THINK I UNDERSTAND WHY THE OVERMASTER IS HERE!"
THE OVERMASTER IS GOING TO NEED AN EXAMPLE OF THE HUMAN RACE AS A SPECIMEN. SHE'S AS GOOD A CANDIDATE AS ANY!
ARE YOU OUT OF YOUR MIND?!! WHY DID YOU BRING HER HERE?!
YOU PRESUME A LOT FOR SOMEONE WHO'S BEEN HERE ALL OF TWO DAYS!
EXPERIENCE DOESN'T SEEM TO HAVE DONE YOU MUCH GOOD. YOU ALMOST GOT US ALL KILLED BACK AT THE JLA COMPOUND.
HOW DARE YOU TALK TO ME LIKE THIS...
THE OVERMASTER GAVE ME A PORTION OF HIS POWER. I THINK THAT GIVES ME THE RIGHT TO SAY ANYTHING I PLEASE!

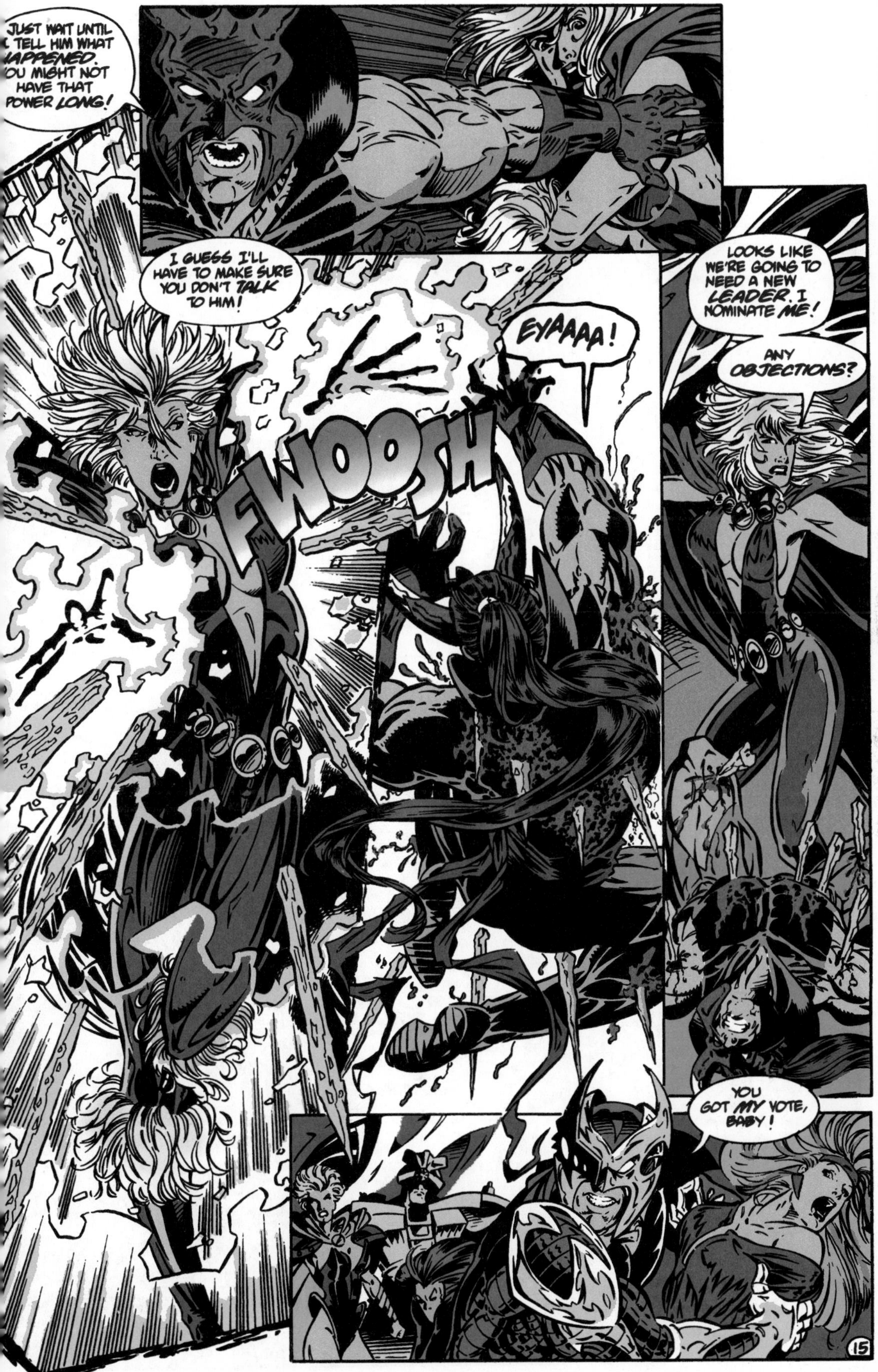

JUST WAIT UNTIL I TELL HIM WHAT HAPPENED. YOU MIGHT NOT HAVE THAT POWER LONG!
I GUESS I'LL HAVE TO MAKE SURE YOU DON'T TALK TO HIM!
EYAAAA!
FWOOSH
LOOKS LIKE WE'RE GOING TO NEED A NEW LEADER. I NOMINATE ME!
ANY OBJECTIONS?
YOU GOT MY VOTE, BABY!

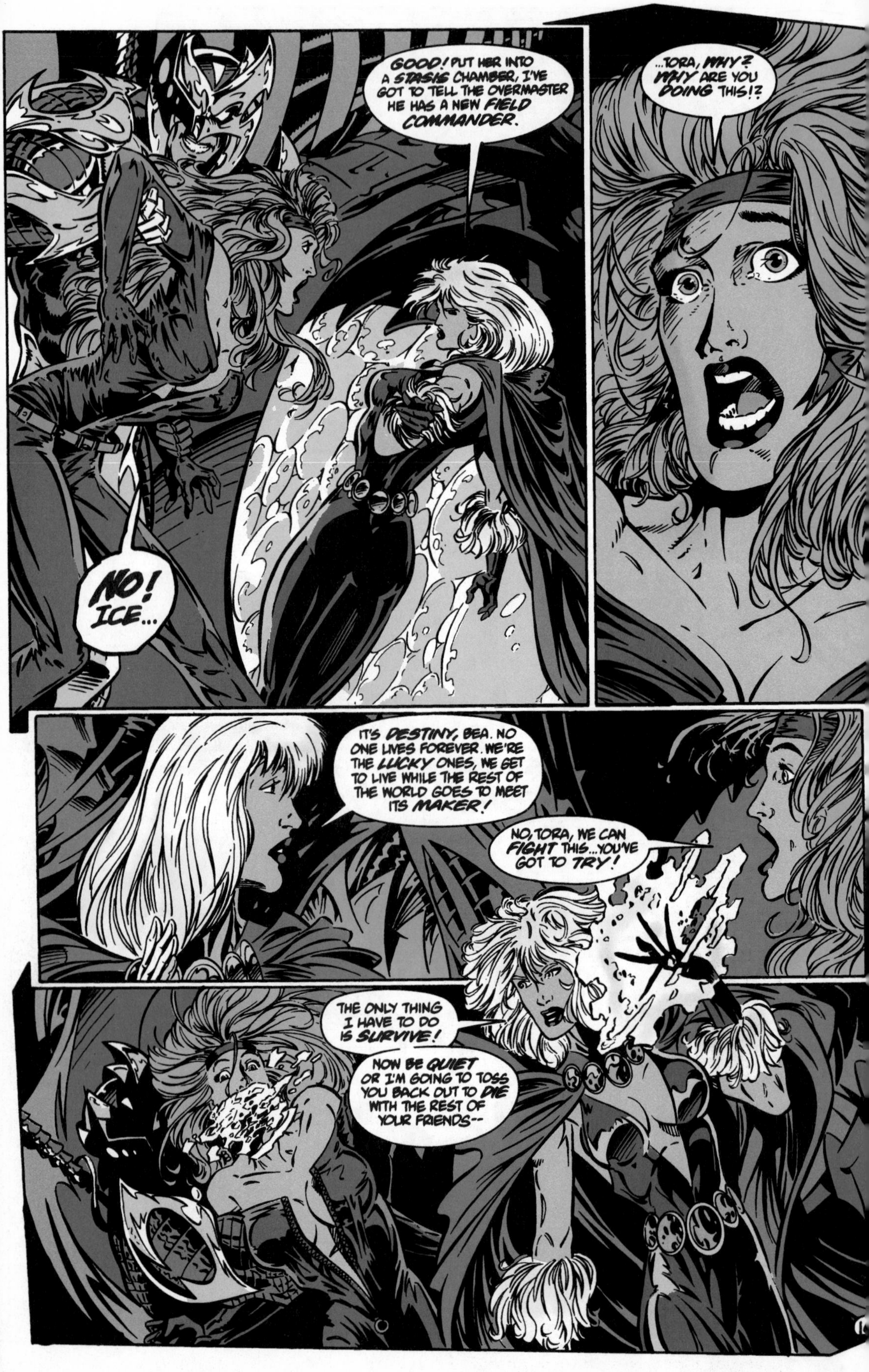
GOOD! PUT HER INTO A STASIS CHAMBER, I'VE GOT TO TELL THE OVERMASTER HE HAS A NEW FIELD COMMANDER.
NO! ICE...
...TORA, WHY? WHY ARE YOU DOING THIS!?
IT'S DESTINY, BEA. NO ONE LIVES FOREVER. WE'RE THE LUCKY ONES, WE GET TO LIVE WHILE THE REST OF THE WORLD GOES TO MEET ITS MAKER!
NO, TORA, WE CAN FIGHT THIS...YOU'VE GOT TO TRY!
THE ONLY THING I HAVE TO DO IS SURVIVE!
NOW BE QUIET OR I'M GOING TO TOSS YOU BACK OUT TO DIE WITH THE REST OF YOUR FRIENDS--

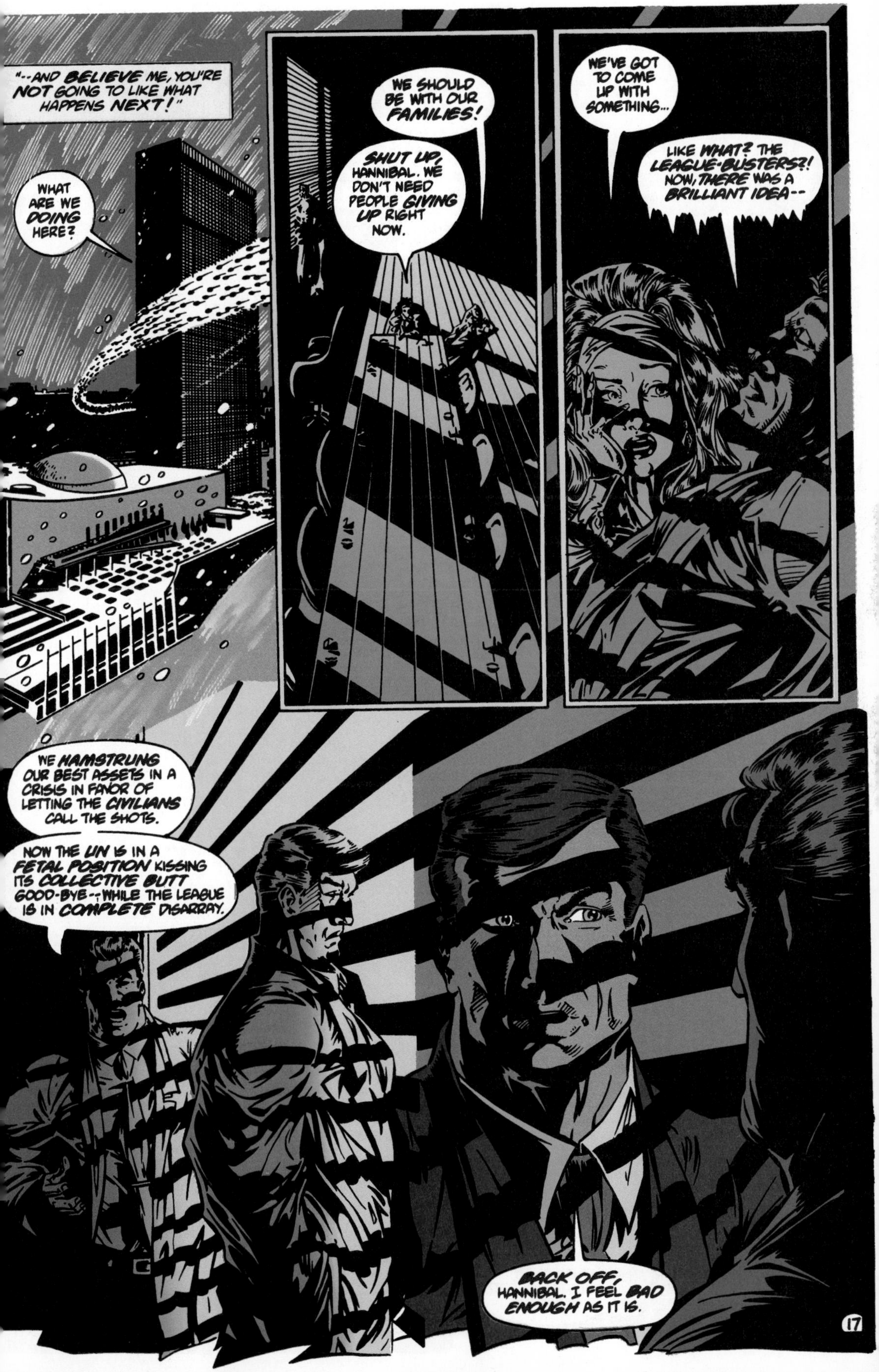
"--AND BELIEVE ME, YOU'RE NOT GOING TO LIKE WHAT HAPPENS NEXT!"
WHAT ARE WE DOING HERE?
WE SHOULD BE WITH OUR FAMILIES!
SHUT UP, HANNIBAL. WE DON'T NEED PEOPLE GIVING UP RIGHT NOW.
WE'VE GOT TO COME UP WITH SOMETHING...
LIKE WHAT? THE LEAGUE-BUSTERS?! NOW, THERE WAS A BRILLIANT IDEA--
WE HAMSTRUNG OUR BEST ASSETS IN A CRISIS IN FAVOR OF LETTING THE CIVILIANS CALL THE SHOTS.
NOW THE UN IS IN A FETAL POSITION KISSING ITS COLLECTIVE BUTT GOOD-BYE--WHILE THE LEAGUE IS IN COMPLETE DISARRAY.
BACK OFF, HANNIBAL. I FEEL BAD ENOUGH AS IT IS.

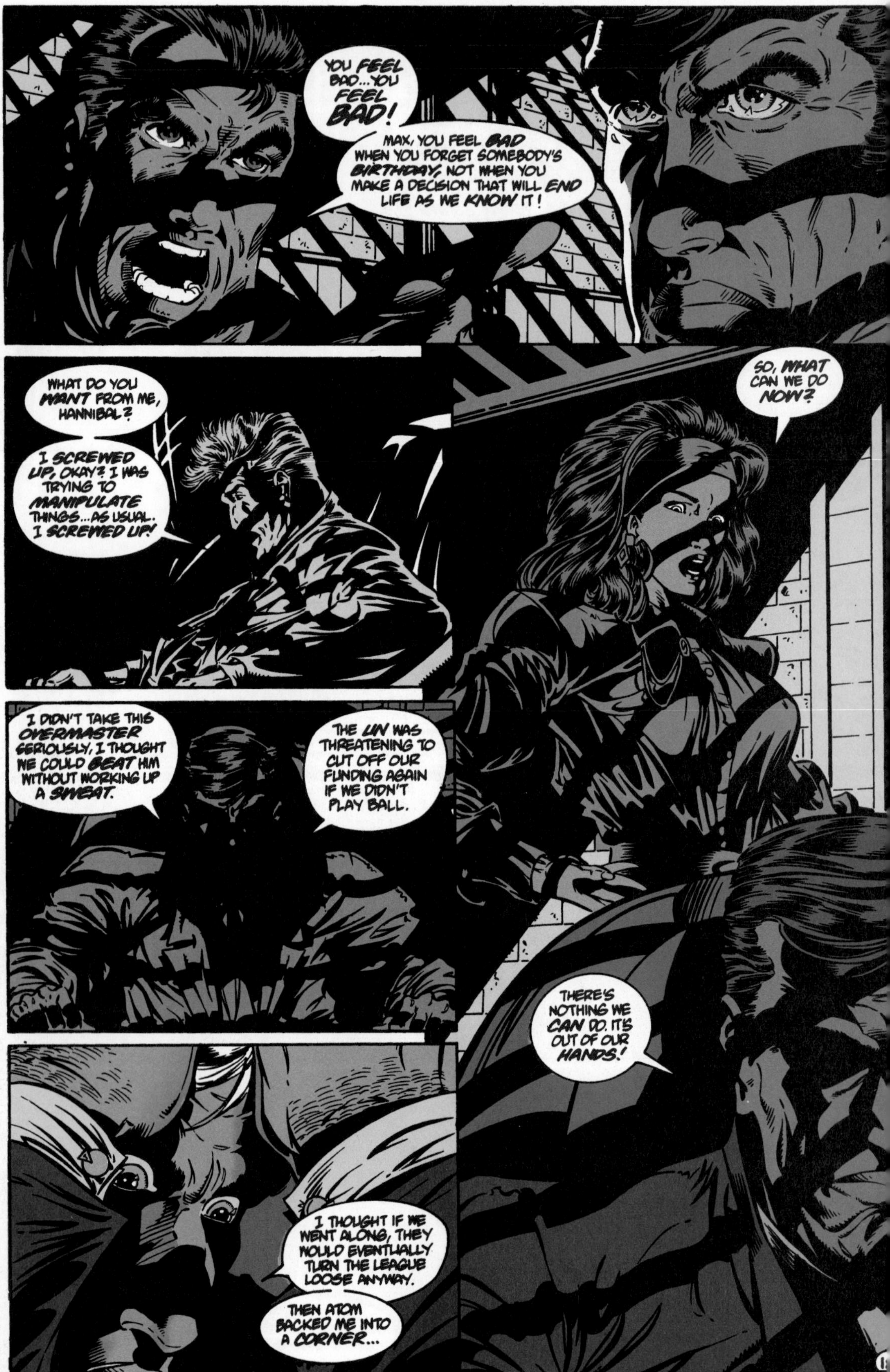
YOU FEEL BAD... YOU FEEL BAD!
MAX, YOU FEEL BAD WHEN YOU FORGET SOMEBODY'S BIRTHDAY, NOT WHEN YOU MAKE A DECISION THAT WILL END LIFE AS WE KNOW IT!
WHAT DO YOU WANT FROM ME, HANNIBAL?
I SCREWED UP, OKAY? I WAS TRYING TO MANIPULATE THINGS...AS USUAL. I SCREWED UP!
SO, WHAT CAN WE DO NOW?
I DIDN'T TAKE THIS OVERMASTER SERIOUSLY, I THOUGHT WE COULD BEAT HIM WITHOUT WORKING UP A SWEAT.
THE UN WAS THREATENING TO CUT OFF OUR FUNDING AGAIN IF WE DIDN'T PLAY BALL.
I THOUGHT IF WE WENT ALONG, THEY WOULD EVENTUALLY TURN THE LEAGUE LOOSE ANYWAY.
THEN ATOM BACKED ME INTO A CORNER...
THERE'S NOTHING WE CAN DO. IT'S OUT OF OUR HANDS!

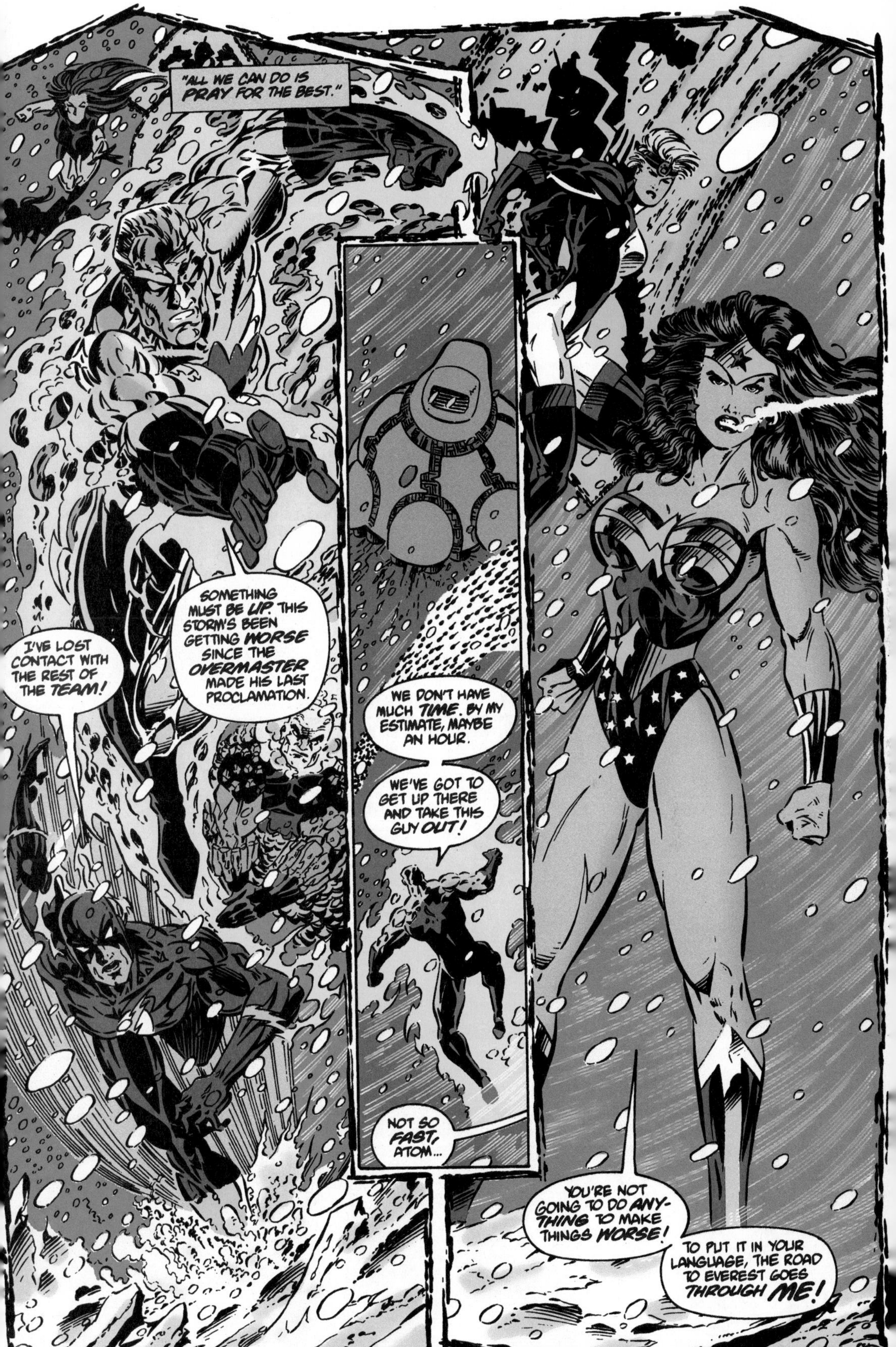
"ALL WE CAN DO IS PRAY FOR THE BEST."
SOMETHING MUST BE UP. THIS STORM'S BEEN GETTING WORSE SINCE THE OVERMASTER MADE HIS LAST PROCLAMATION.
I'VE LOST CONTACT WITH THE REST OF THE TEAM!
WE DON'T HAVE MUCH TIME. BY MY ESTIMATE, MAYBE AN HOUR.
WE'VE GOT TO GET UP THERE AND TAKE THIS GUY OUT!
NOT SO FAST, ATOM...
YOU'RE NOT GOING TO DO ANY-THING TO MAKE THINGS WORSE!
TO PUT IT IN YOUR LANGUAGE, THE ROAD TO EVEREST GOES THROUGH ME!
19

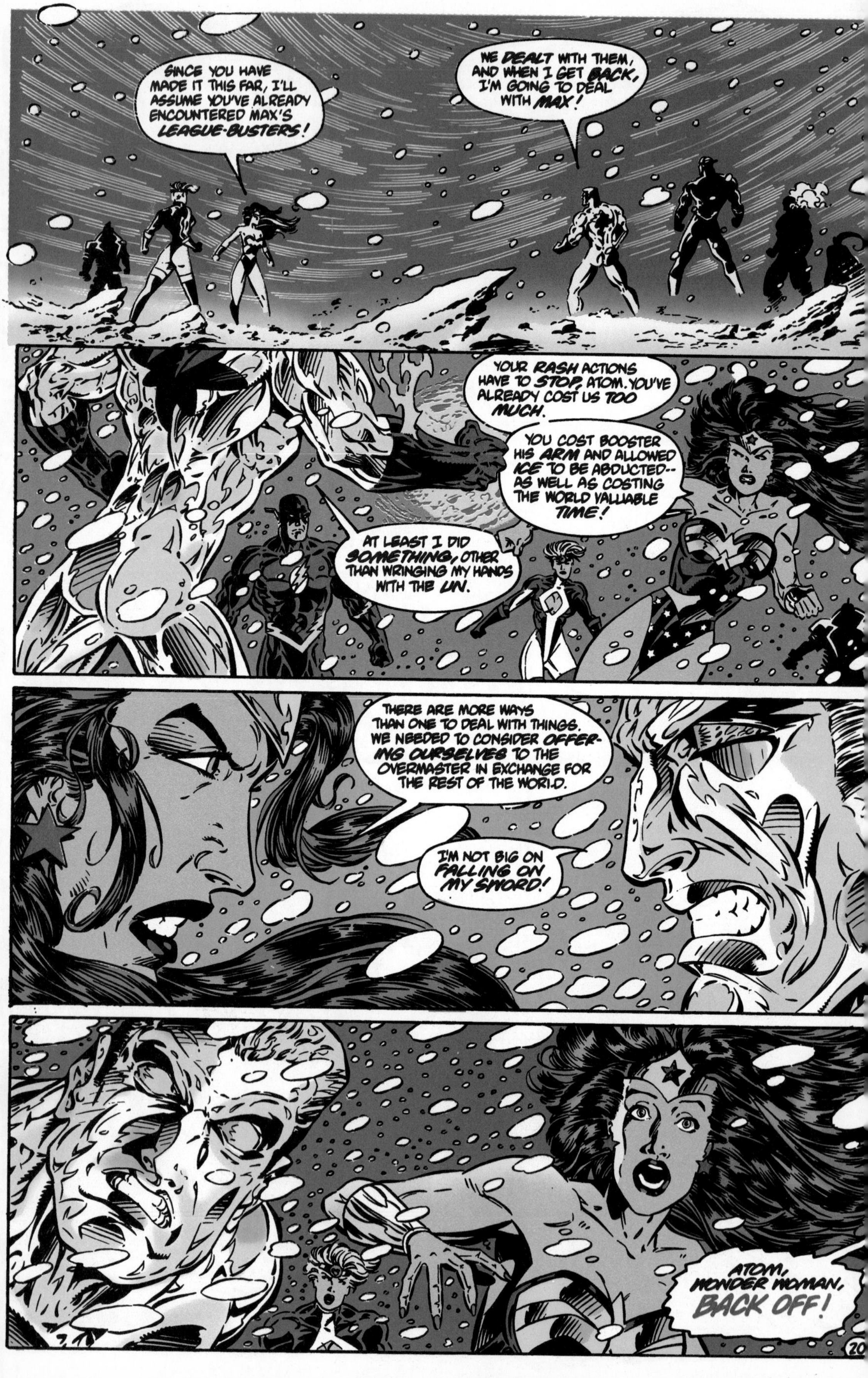
SINCE YOU HAVE MADE IT THIS FAR, I'LL ASSUME YOU'VE ALREADY ENCOUNTERED MAX'S LEAGUE-BUSTERS!
WE DEALT WITH THEM, AND WHEN I GET BACK, I'M GOING TO DEAL WITH MAX!
YOUR RASH ACTIONS HAVE TO STOP, ATOM. YOU'VE ALREADY COST US TOO MUCH.
YOU COST BOOSTER HIS ARM AND ALLOWED ICE TO BE ABDUCTED-- AS WELL AS COSTING THE WORLD VALLIABLE TIME!
AT LEAST I DID SOMETHING, OTHER THAN WRINGING MY HANDS WITH THE UN.
THERE ARE MORE WAYS THAN ONE TO DEAL WITH THINGS. WE NEEDED TO CONSIDER OFFERING OURSELVES TO THE OVERMASTER IN EXCHANGE FOR THE REST OF THE WORLD.
I'M NOT BIG ON FALLING ON MY SWORD!
ATOM, WONDER WOMAN, BACK OFF!

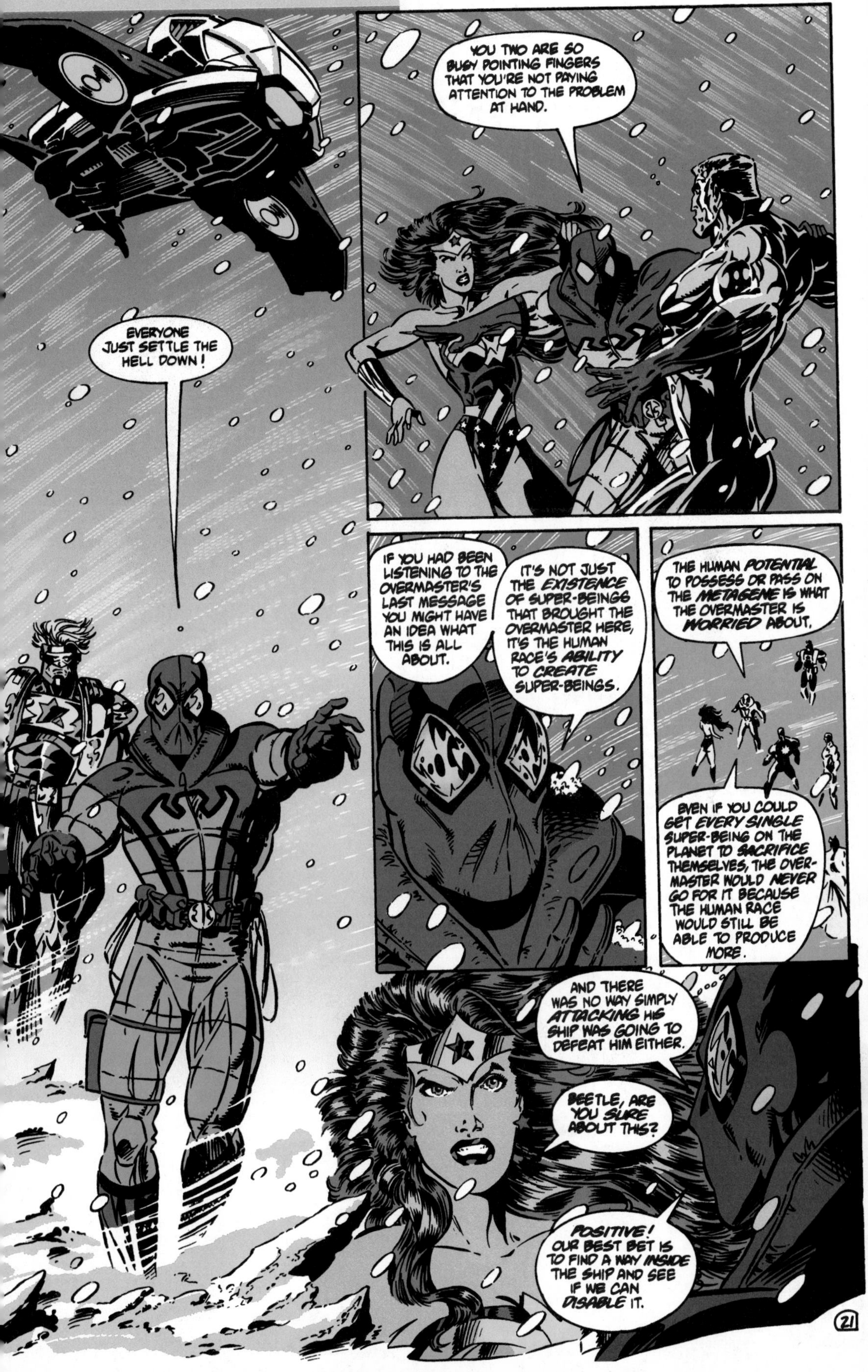

YOU TWO ARE SO BUSY POINTING FINGERS THAT YOU'RE NOT PAYING ATTENTION TO THE PROBLEM AT HAND.
EVERYONE JUST SETTLE THE HELL DOWN!
IF YOU HAD BEEN LISTENING TO THE OVERMASTER'S LAST MESSAGE YOU MIGHT HAVE AN IDEA WHAT THIS IS ALL ABOUT.
IT'S NOT JUST THE *EXISTENCE* OF SUPER-BEINGS THAT BROUGHT THE OVERMASTER HERE, IT'S THE HUMAN RACE'S *ABILITY* TO *CREATE* SUPER-BEINGS.
THE HUMAN *POTENTIAL* TO POSSESS OR PASS ON THE *METAGENE* IS WHAT THE OVERMASTER IS *WORRIED* ABOUT.
EVEN IF YOU COULD GET *EVERY SINGLE* SUPER-BEING ON THE PLANET TO *SACRIFICE* THEMSELVES, THE OVER-MASTER WOULD *NEVER* GO FOR IT BECAUSE THE HUMAN RACE WOULD STILL BE ABLE TO PRODUCE MORE.
AND THERE WAS NO WAY SIMPLY *ATTACKING* HIS SHIP WAS GOING TO DEFEAT HIM EITHER.
BEETLE, ARE YOU *SURE* ABOUT THIS?
POSITIVE! OUR BEST BET IS TO FIND A WAY *INSIDE* THE SHIP AND SEE IF WE CAN *DISABLE* IT.

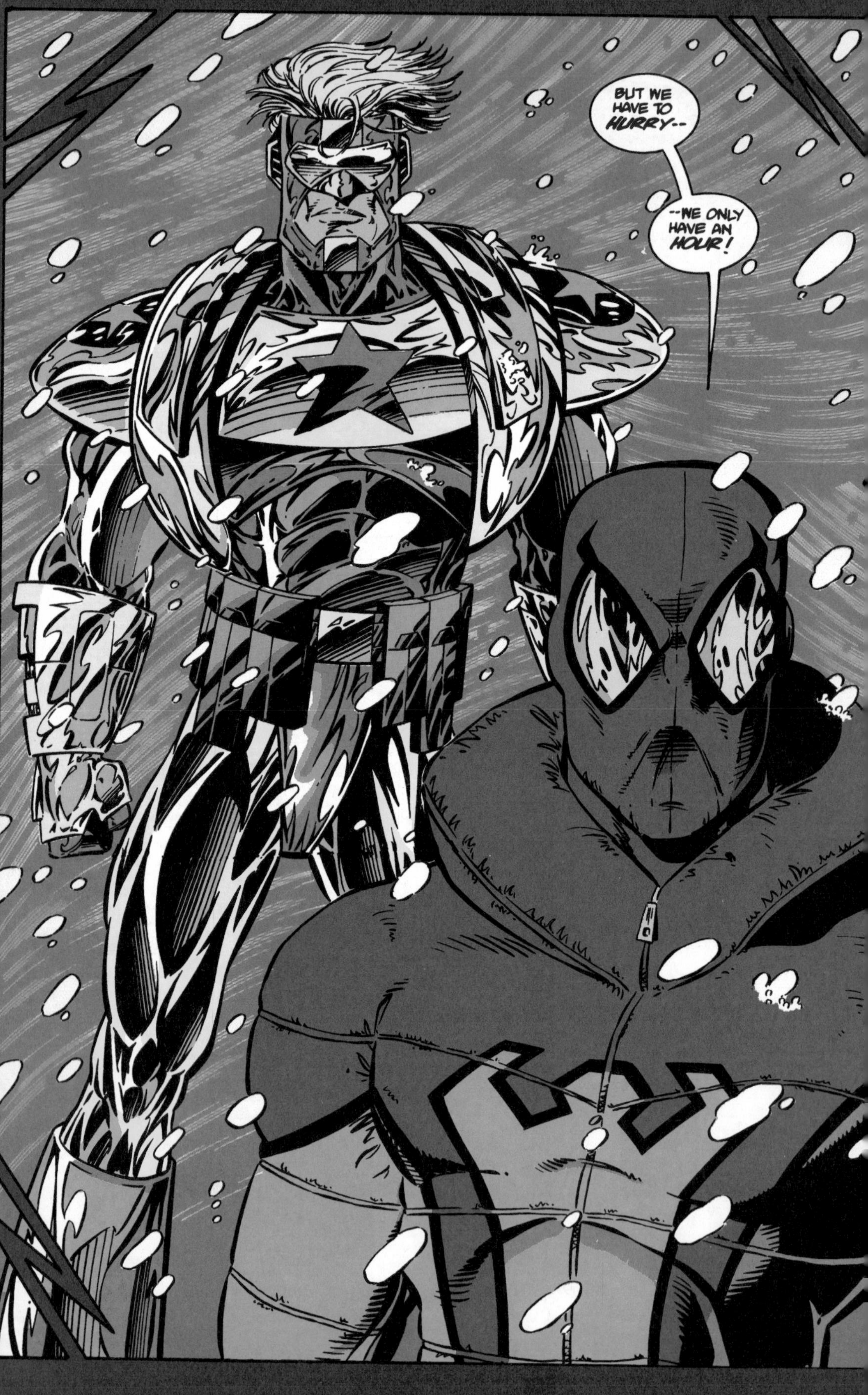
BUT WE HAVE TO HURRY--
--WE ONLY HAVE AN HOUR!

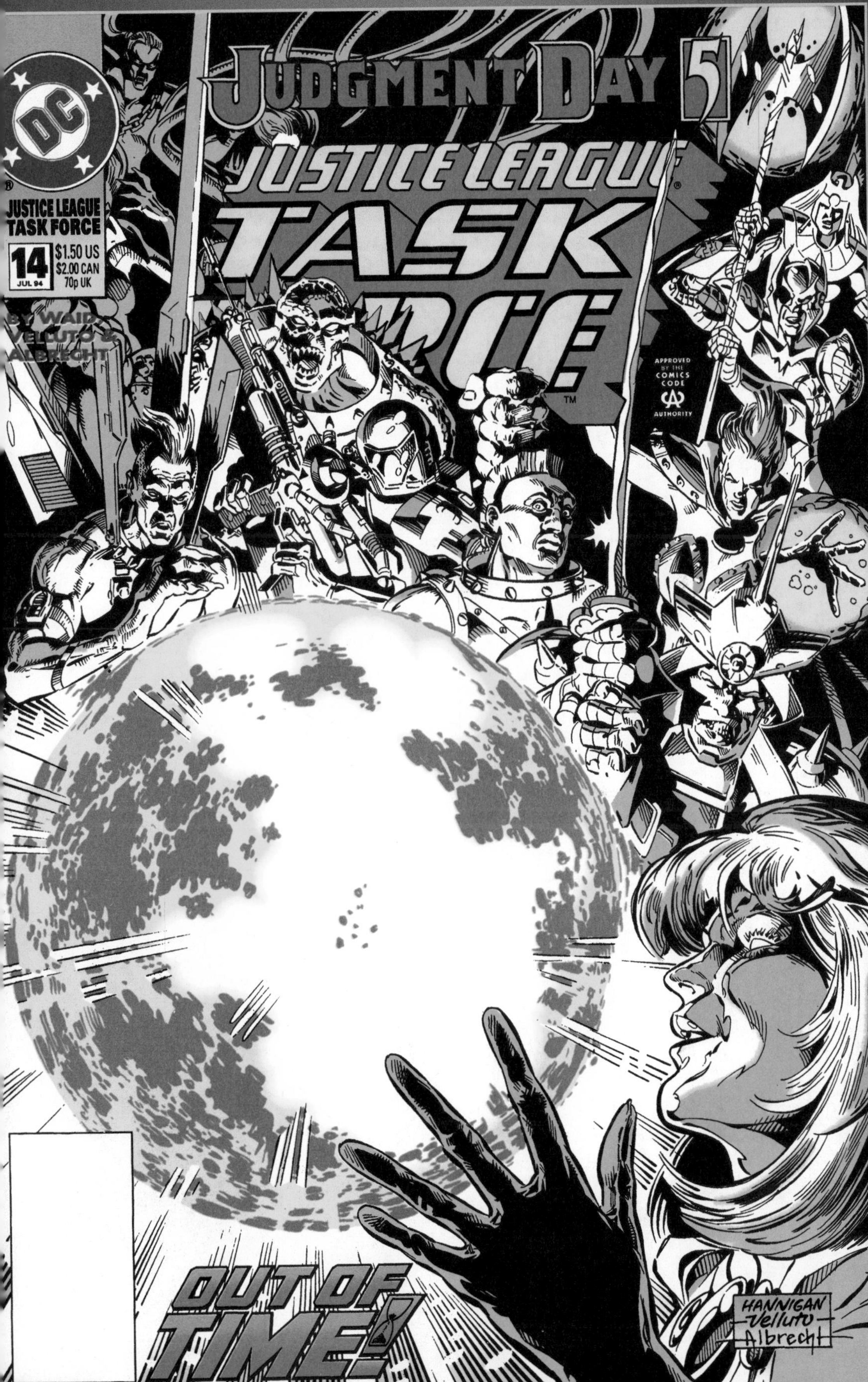
JUDGMENT DAY 5
JUSTICE LEAGUE TASK FORCE
DC
JUSTICE LEAGUE TASK FORCE
14 JUL 94
$1.50 US $2.00 CAN 70p UK
BY WAID, VELLUTO & ALBRECHT
APPROVED BY THE COMICS CODE AUTHORITY
OUT OF TIME!
HANNIGAN Velluto Albrecht

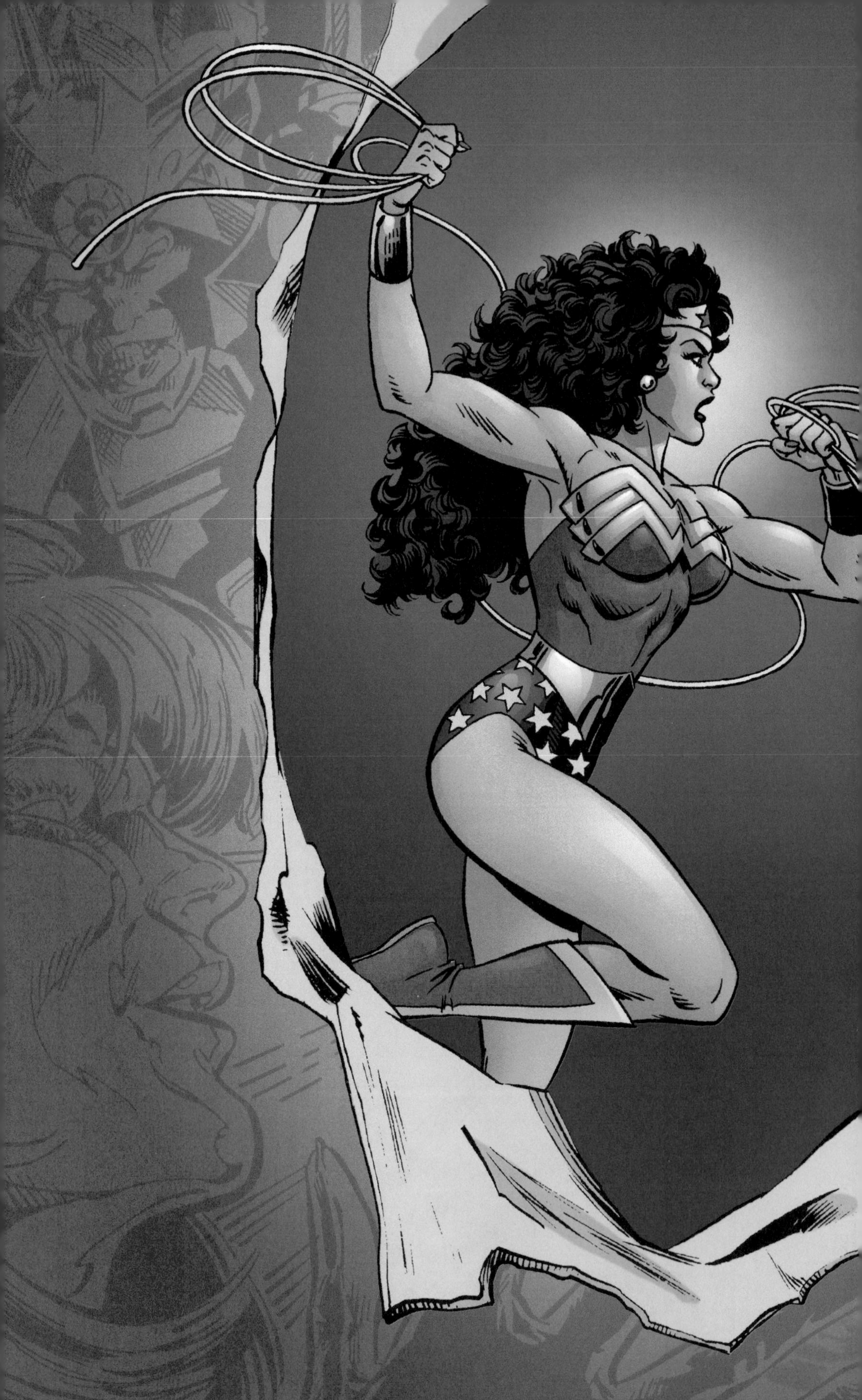

Cover art by **SAL VELLUTO, ED HANNIGAN and JEFF ALBRECHT**

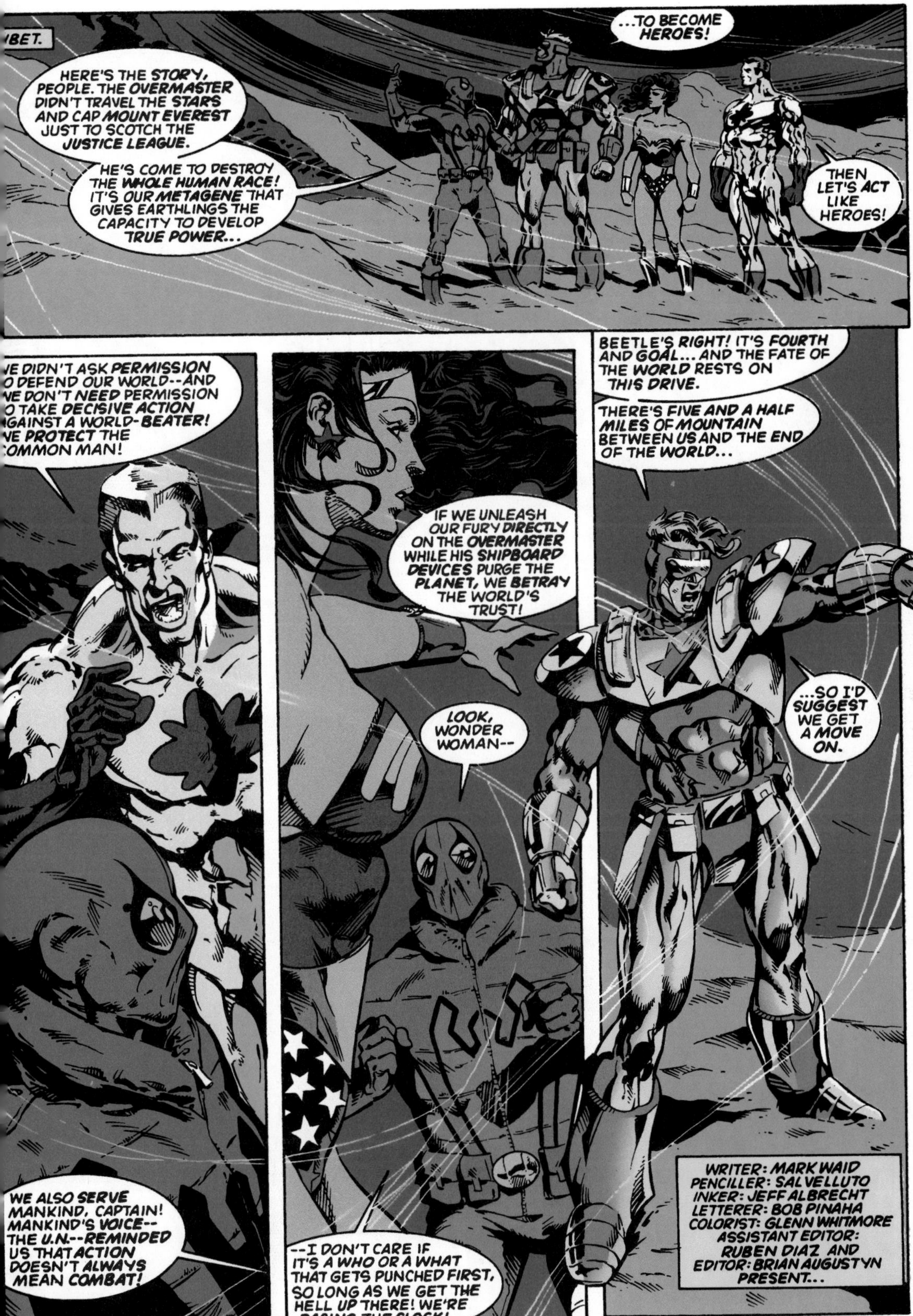

IBET.
HERE'S THE STORY, PEOPLE. THE OVERMASTER DIDN'T TRAVEL THE STARS AND CAP MOUNT EVEREST JUST TO SCOTCH THE JUSTICE LEAGUE.
HE'S COME TO DESTROY THE WHOLE HUMAN RACE! IT'S OUR METAGENE THAT GIVES EARTHLINGS THE CAPACITY TO DEVELOP TRUE POWER...
...TO BECOME HEROES!
THEN LET'S ACT LIKE HEROES!
E DIDN'T ASK PERMISSION O DEFEND OUR WORLD--AND E DON'T NEED PERMISSION O TAKE DECISIVE ACTION GAINST A WORLD-BEATER! E PROTECT THE COMMON MAN!
WE ALSO SERVE MANKIND, CAPTAIN! MANKIND'S VOICE--THE U.N.--REMINDED US THAT ACTION DOESN'T ALWAYS MEAN COMBAT!
IF WE UNLEASH OUR FURY DIRECTLY ON THE OVERMASTER WHILE HIS SHIPBOARD DEVICES PURGE THE PLANET, WE BETRAY THE WORLD'S TRUST!
LOOK, WONDER WOMAN--
--I DON'T CARE IF IT'S A WHO OR A WHAT THAT GETS PUNCHED FIRST, SO LONG AS WE GET THE HELL UP THERE! WE'RE RACING THE CLOCK!
BEETLE'S RIGHT! IT'S FOURTH AND GOAL... AND THE FATE OF THE WORLD RESTS ON THIS DRIVE.
THERE'S FIVE AND A HALF MILES OF MOUNTAIN BETWEEN US AND THE END OF THE WORLD...
...SO I'D SUGGEST WE GET A MOVE ON.
WRITER: MARK WAID
PENCILLER: SAL VELLUTO
INKER: JEFF ALBRECHT
LETTERER: BOB PINAHA
COLORIST: GLENN WHITMORE
ASSISTANT EDITOR: RUBEN DIAZ AND
EDITOR: BRIAN AUGUSTYN
PRESENT...

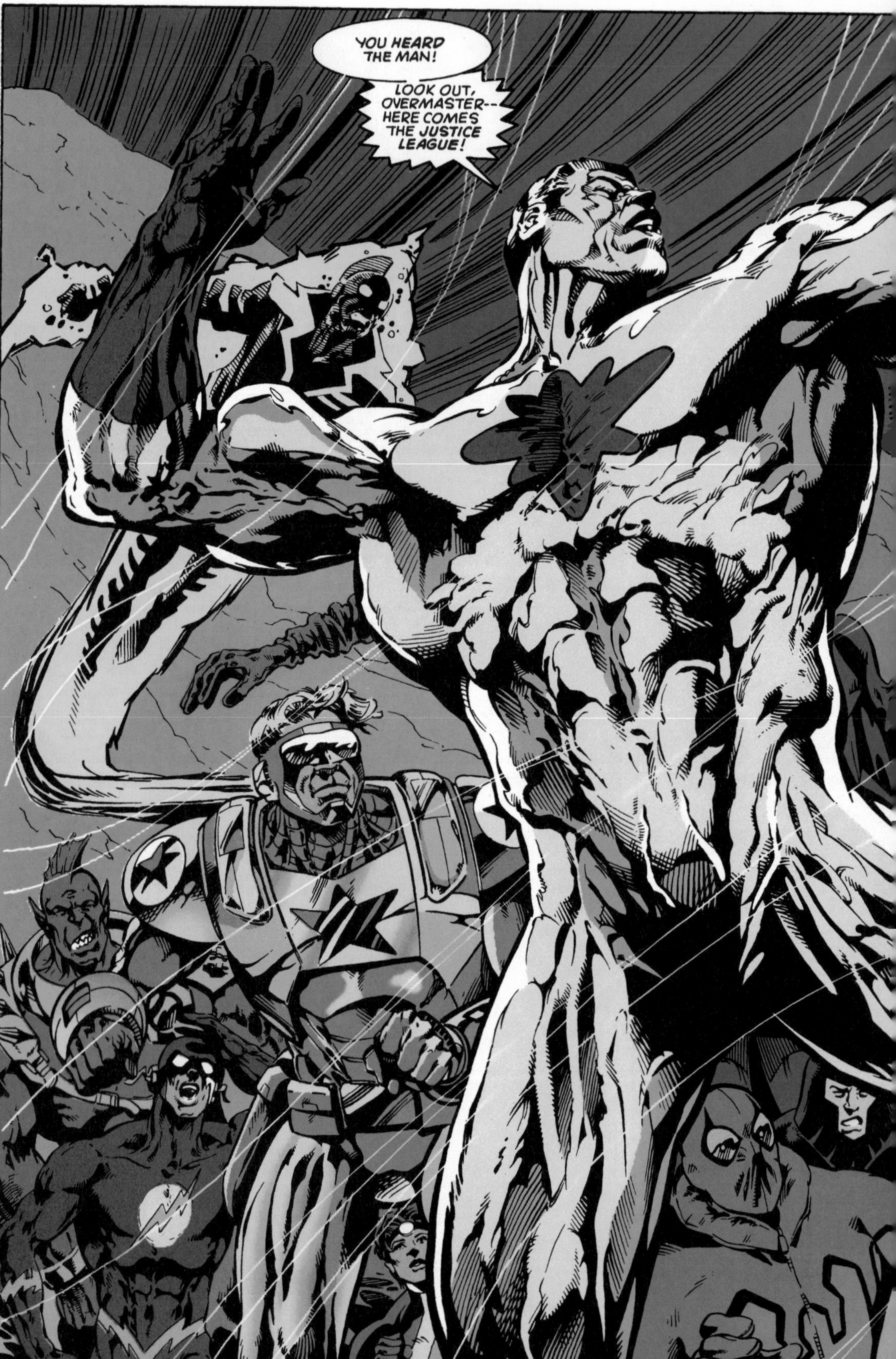
YOU HEARD THE MAN!
LOOK OUT, OVERMASTER-- HERE COMES THE JUSTICE LEAGUE!

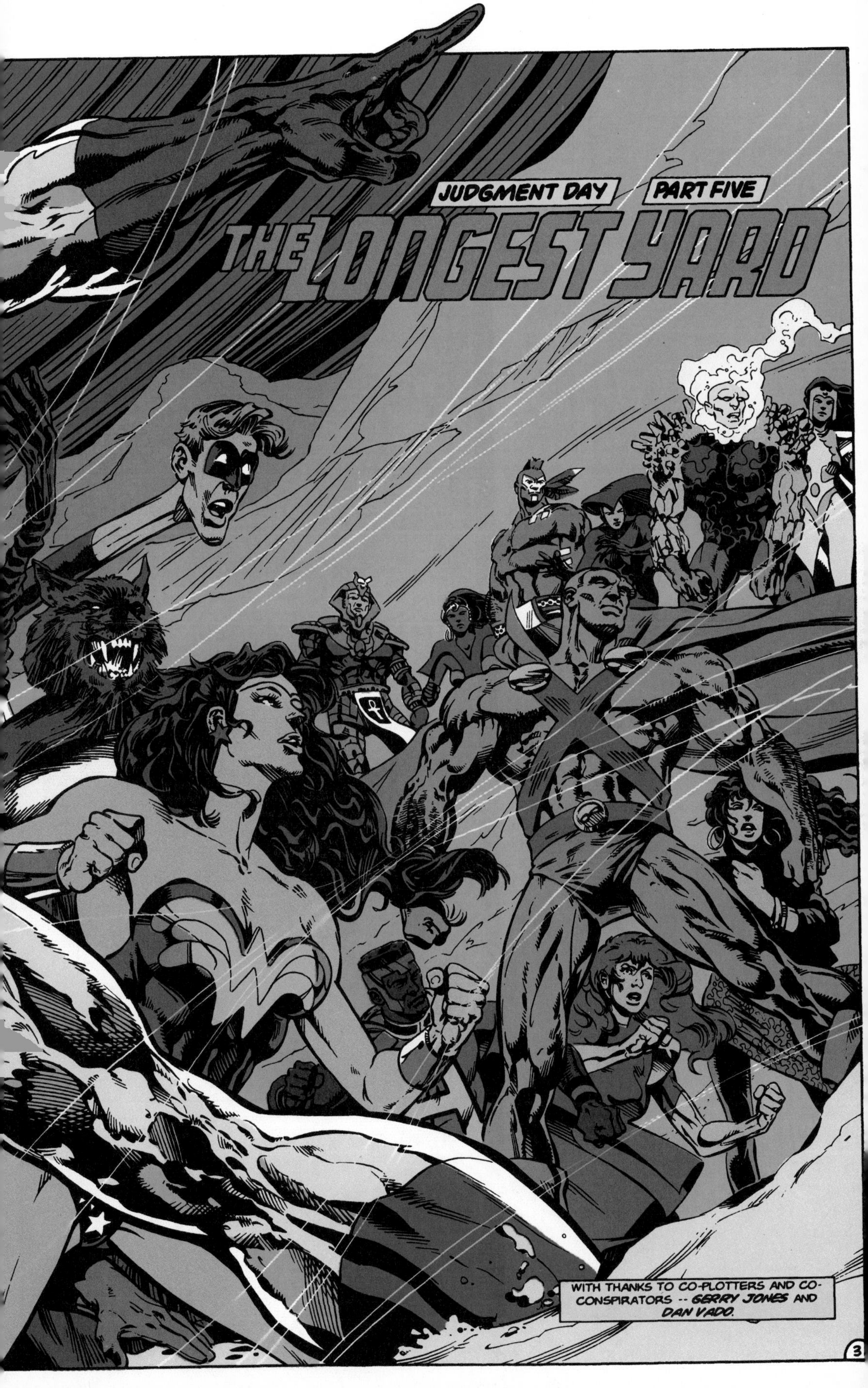

JUDGMENT DAY
PART FIVE
THE LONGEST YARD
WITH THANKS TO CO-PLOTTERS AND CO-CONSPIRATORS -- GERRY JONES AND DAN VADO.

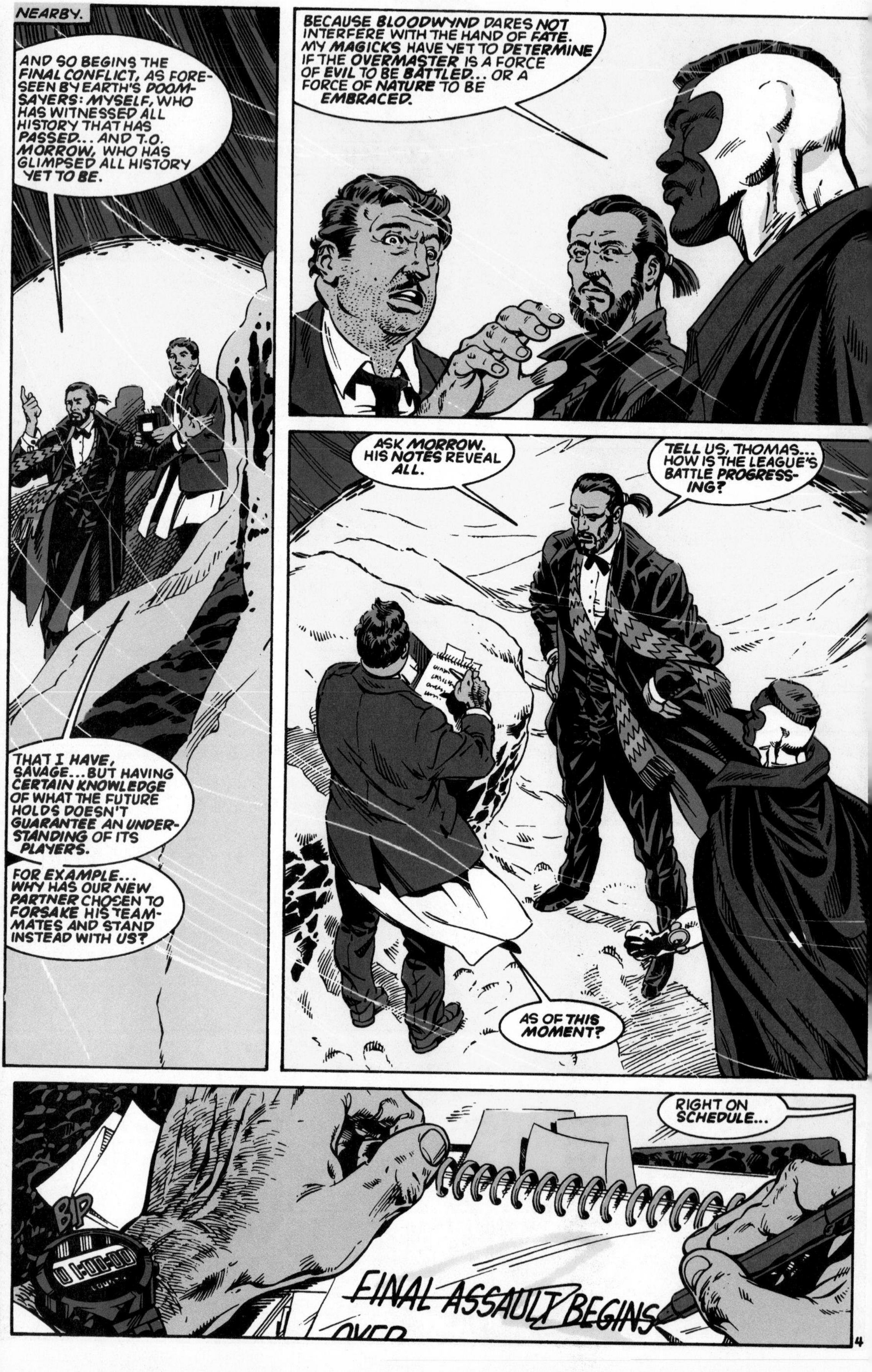
NEARBY.
AND SO BEGINS THE FINAL CONFLICT, AS FORESEEN BY EARTH'S DOOMSAYERS: MYSELF, WHO HAS WITNESSED ALL HISTORY THAT HAS PASSED... AND T.O. MORROW, WHO HAS GLIMPSED ALL HISTORY YET TO BE.
THAT I HAVE, SAVAGE... BUT HAVING CERTAIN KNOWLEDGE OF WHAT THE FUTURE HOLDS DOESN'T GUARANTEE AN UNDERSTANDING OF ITS PLAYERS.
FOR EXAMPLE... WHY HAS OUR NEW PARTNER CHOSEN TO FORSAKE HIS TEAMMATES AND STAND INSTEAD WITH US?
BECAUSE BLOODWYND DARES NOT INTERFERE WITH THE HAND OF FATE. MY MAGICKS HAVE YET TO DETERMINE IF THE OVERMASTER IS A FORCE OF EVIL TO BE BATTLED... OR A FORCE OF NATURE TO BE EMBRACED.
ASK MORROW. HIS NOTES REVEAL ALL.
TELL US, THOMAS... HOW IS THE LEAGUE'S BATTLE PROGRESSING?
AS OF THIS MOMENT?
RIGHT ON SCHEDULE...
FINAL ASSAULT BEGINS
OVER

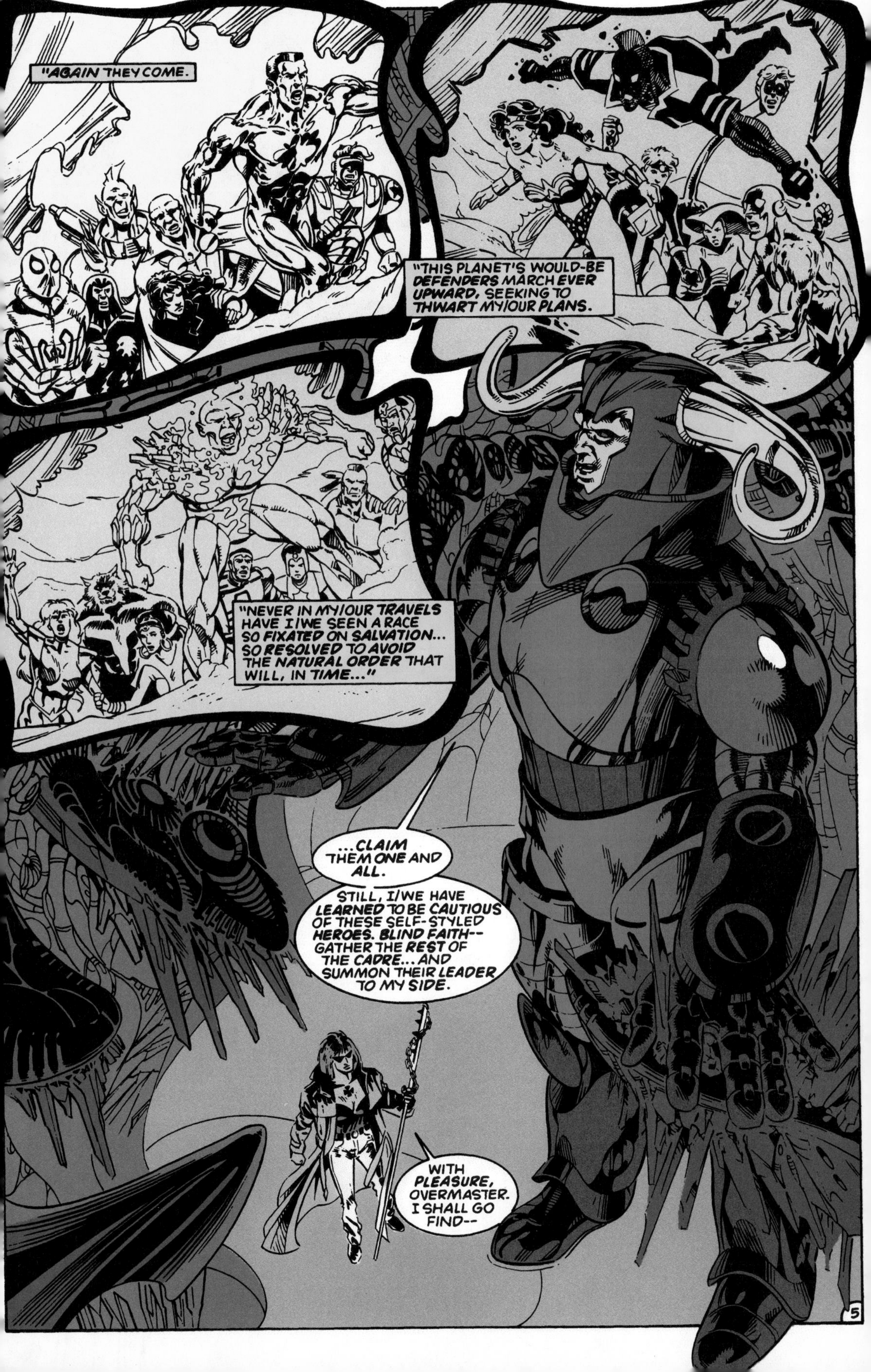
"AGAIN THEY COME.
"THIS PLANET'S WOULD-BE DEFENDERS MARCH EVER UPWARD, SEEKING TO THWART MY/OUR PLANS.
"NEVER IN MY/OUR TRAVELS HAVE I/WE SEEN A RACE SO FIXATED ON SALVATION... SO RESOLVED TO AVOID THE NATURAL ORDER THAT WILL, IN TIME..."
...CLAIM THEM ONE AND ALL.
STILL, I/WE HAVE LEARNED TO BE CAUTIOUS OF THESE SELF-STYLED HEROES. BLIND FAITH-- GATHER THE REST OF THE CADRE... AND SUMMON THEIR LEADER TO MY SIDE.
WITH PLEASURE, OVERMASTER. I SHALL GO FIND--
5

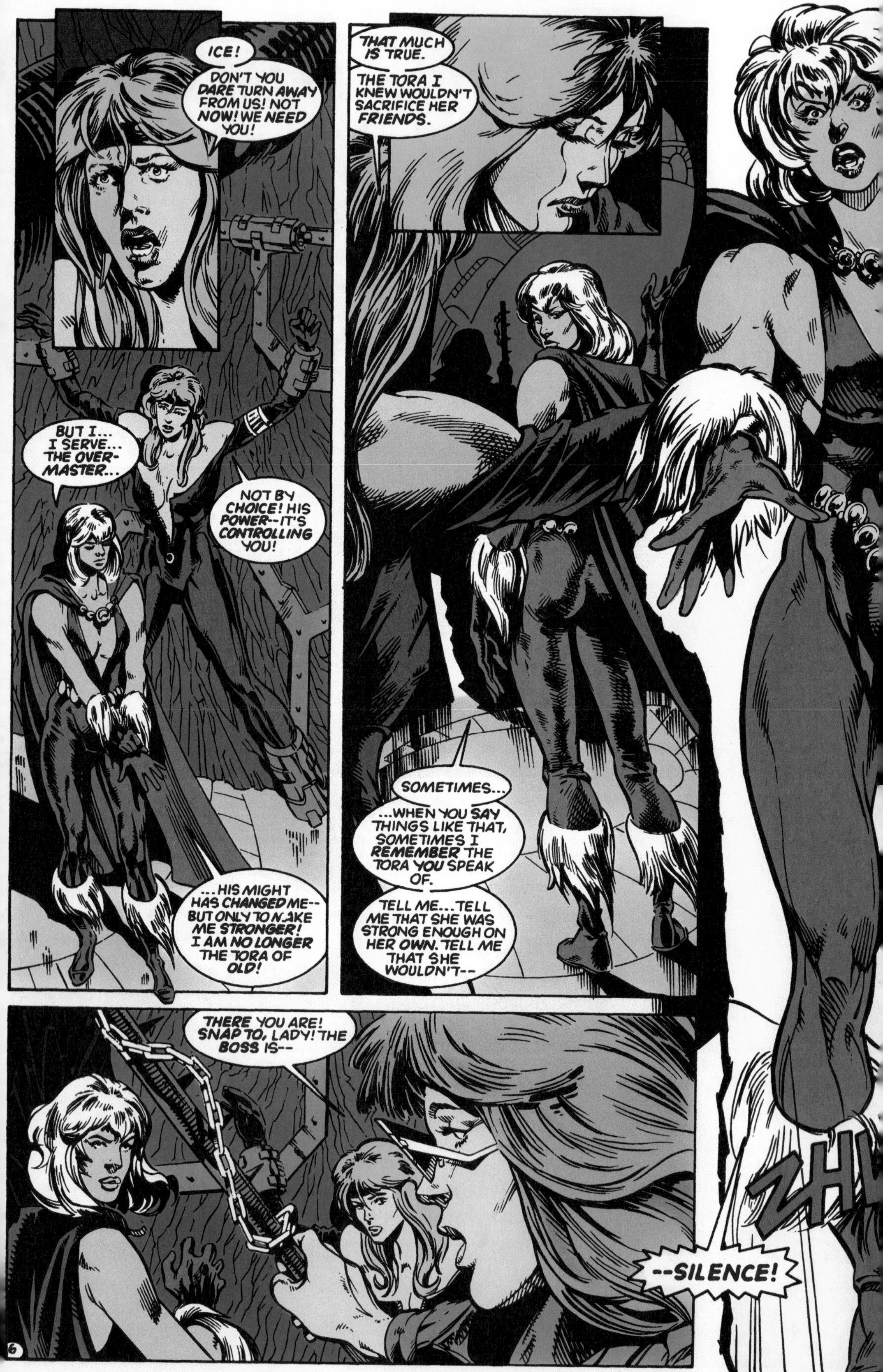
ICE!
DON'T YOU DARE TURN AWAY FROM US! NOT NOW! WE NEED YOU!
BUT I... I SERVE... THE OVER-MASTER...
NOT BY CHOICE! HIS POWER--IT'S CONTROLLING YOU!
...HIS MIGHT HAS CHANGED ME--BUT ONLY TO MAKE ME STRONGER! I AM NO LONGER THE TORA OF OLD!
THAT MUCH IS TRUE.
THE TORA I KNEW WOULDN'T SACRIFICE HER FRIENDS.
SOMETIMES...
...WHEN YOU SAY THINGS LIKE THAT, SOMETIMES I REMEMBER THE TORA YOU SPEAK OF.
TELL ME... TELL ME THAT SHE WAS STRONG ENOUGH ON HER OWN. TELL ME THAT SHE WOULDN'T--
THERE YOU ARE! SNAP TO, LADY! THE BOSS IS--
--SILENCE!

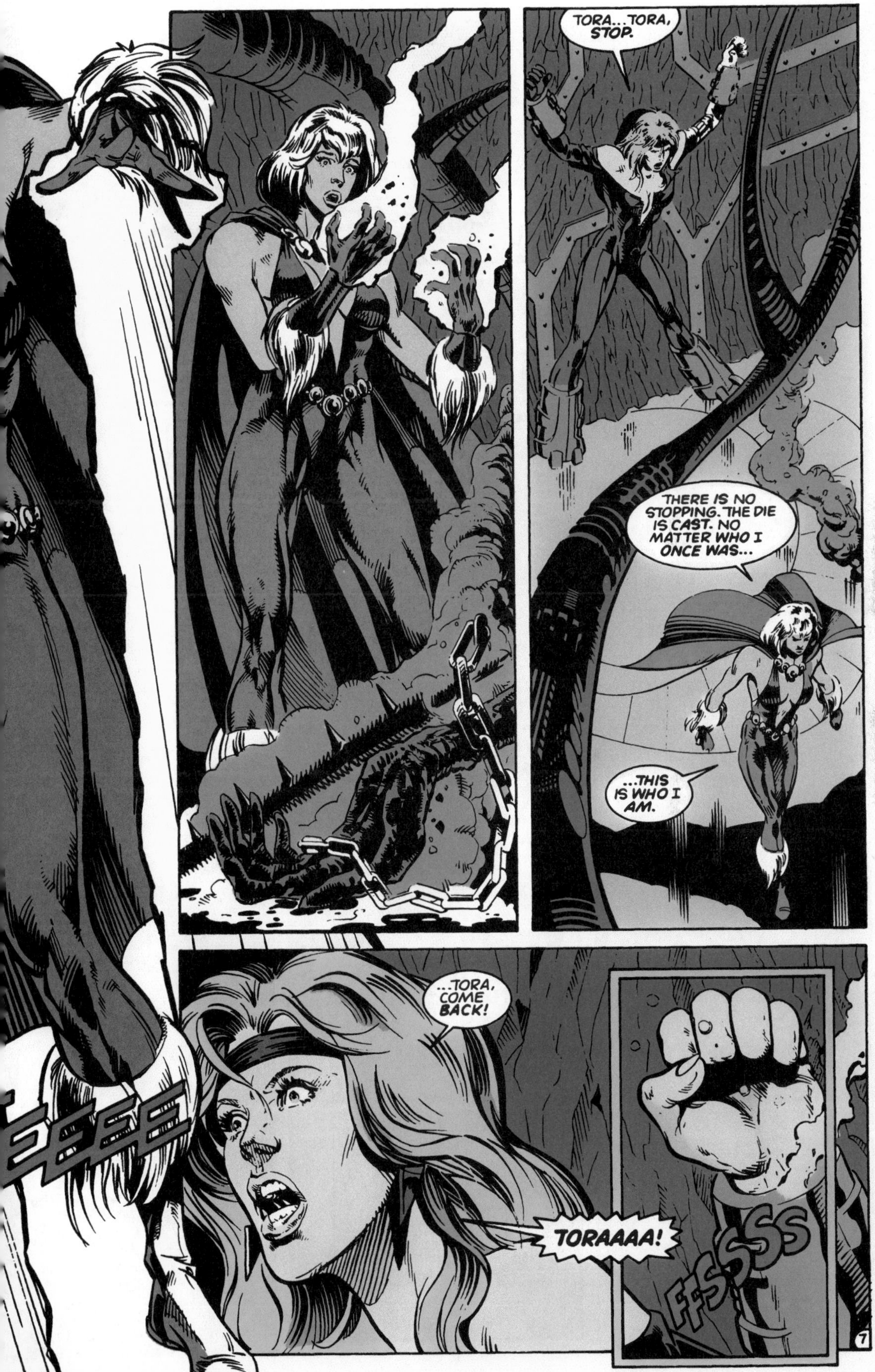
TORA...TORA, STOP.
THERE IS NO STOPPING. THE DIE IS CAST. NO MATTER WHO I ONCE WAS...
...THIS IS WHO I AM.
EEEE
...TORA, COME BACK!
TORAAAA!
FFSSSSS

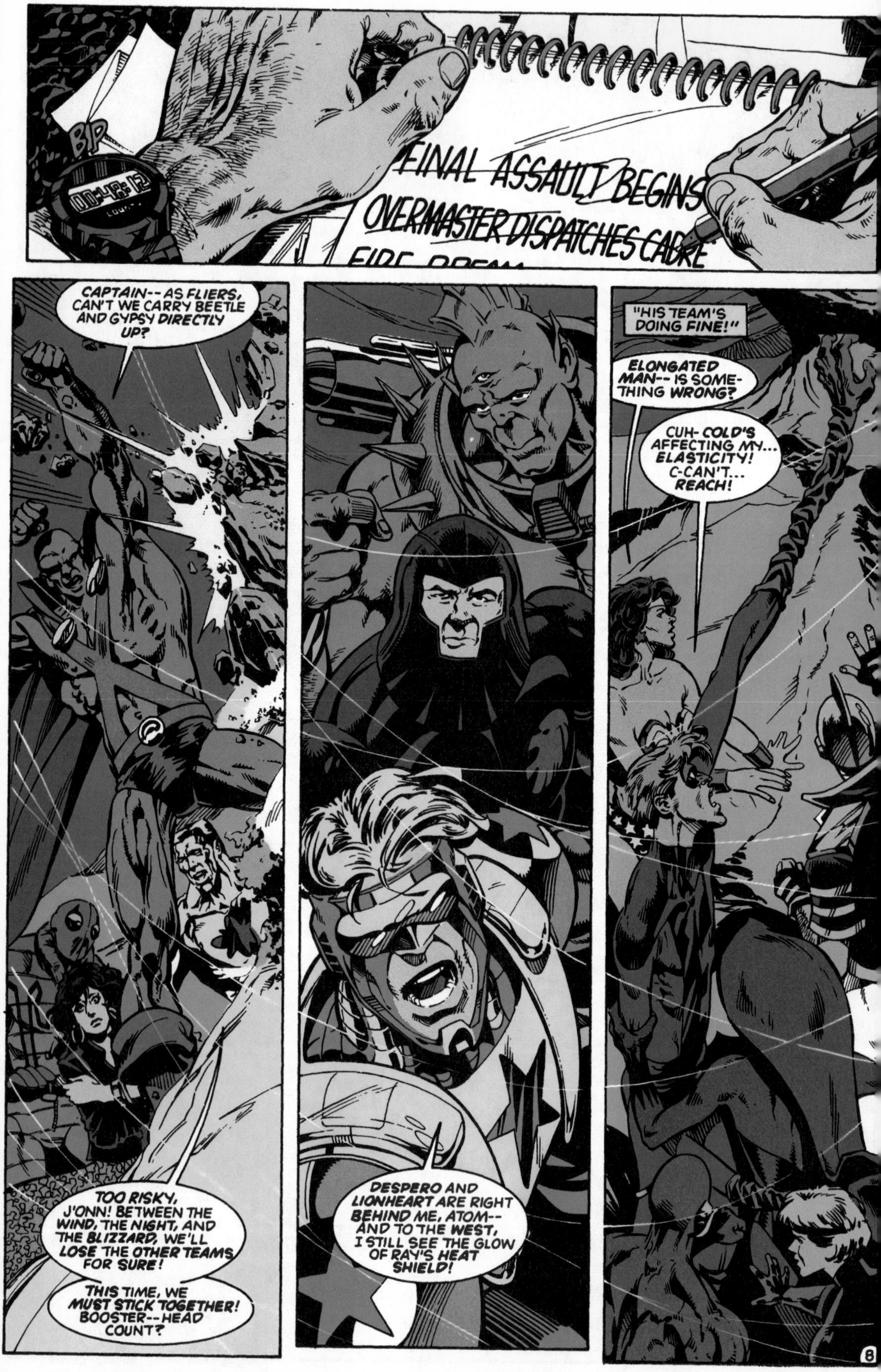
BIP
FINAL ASSAULT BEGINS
OVERMASTER DISPATCHES CADRE
CAPTAIN-- AS FLIERS, CAN'T WE CARRY BEETLE AND GYPSY DIRECTLY UP?
TOO RISKY, J'ONN! BETWEEN THE WIND, THE NIGHT, AND THE BLIZZARD, WE'LL LOSE THE OTHER TEAMS FOR SURE!
THIS TIME, WE MUST STICK TOGETHER! BOOSTER--HEAD COUNT?
DESPERO AND LIONHEART ARE RIGHT BEHIND ME, ATOM-- AND TO THE WEST, I STILL SEE THE GLOW OF RAY'S HEAT SHIELD!
"HIS TEAM'S DOING FINE!"
ELONGATED MAN-- IS SOMETHING WRONG?
CUH-COLD'S AFFECTING MY... ELASTICITY! C-CAN'T... REACH!
8

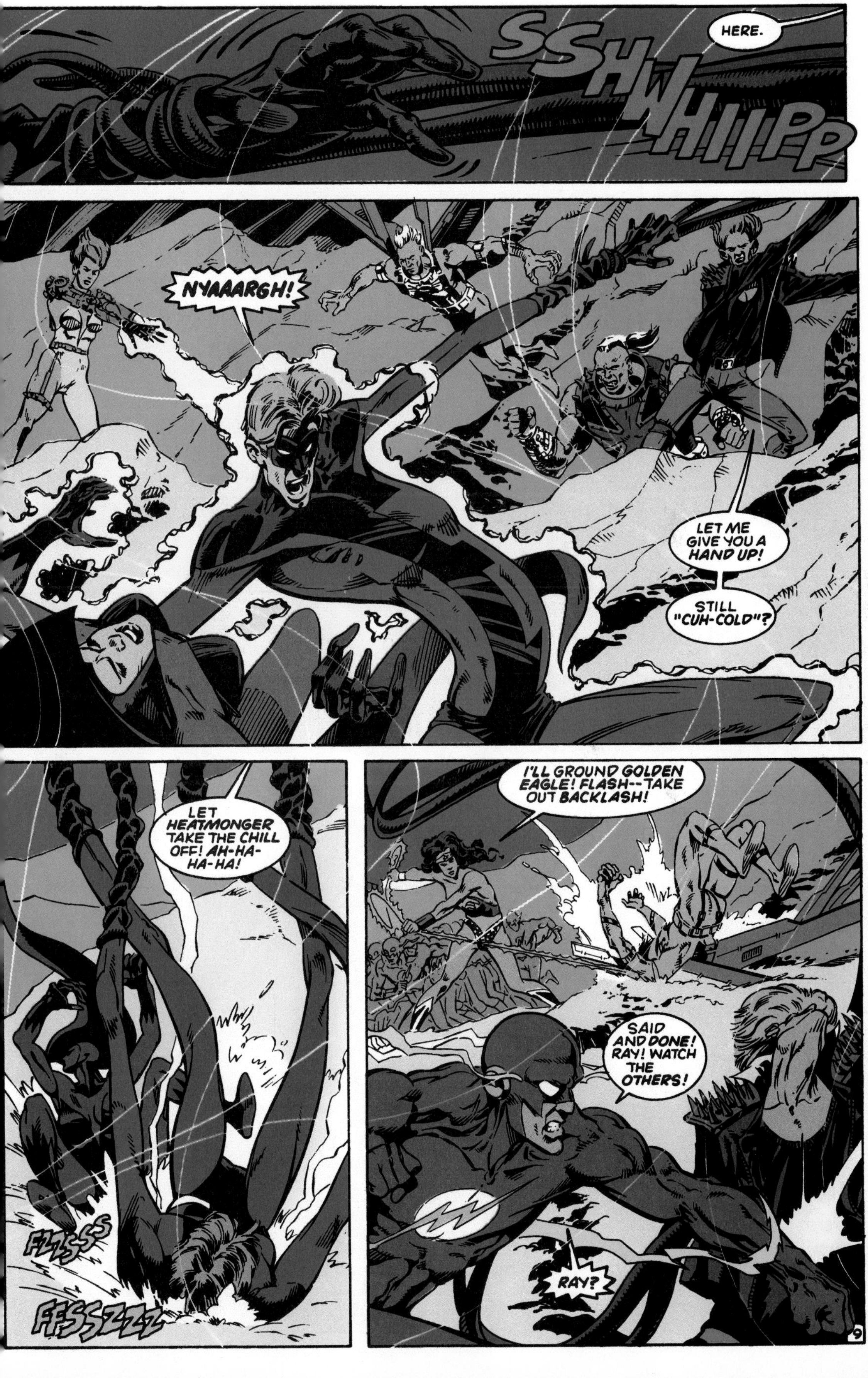
HERE.
SSHWHIIIPP
NYAAARGH!
LET ME GIVE YOU A HAND UP!
STILL "CUH-COLD"?
LET HEATMONGER TAKE THE CHILL OFF! AH-HA-HA-HA!
FZZSSS
FFSSZZZ
I'LL GROUND GOLDEN EAGLE! FLASH--TAKE OUT BACKLASH!
SAID AND DONE! RAY! WATCH THE OTHERS!
RAY?

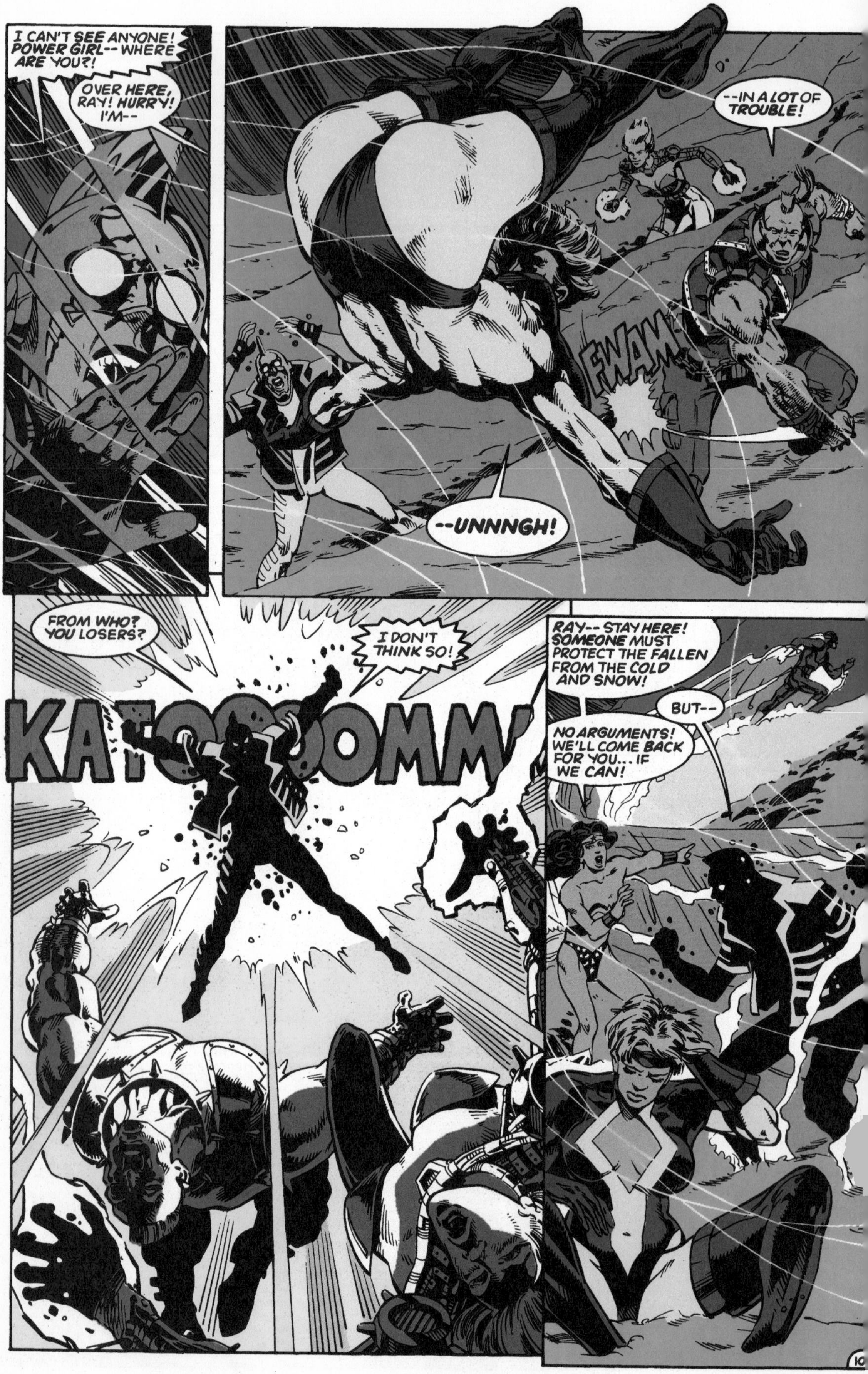

I CAN'T SEE ANYONE! POWER GIRL-- WHERE ARE YOU?!
OVER HERE, RAY! HURRY! I'M--
--IN A LOT OF TROUBLE!
FWAM
--UNNNGH!
FROM WHO? YOU LOSERS?
I DON'T THINK SO!
KATOOOOMM
RAY-- STAY HERE! SOMEONE MUST PROTECT THE FALLEN FROM THE COLD AND SNOW!
BUT--
NO ARGUMENTS! WE'LL COME BACK FOR YOU... IF WE CAN!
10

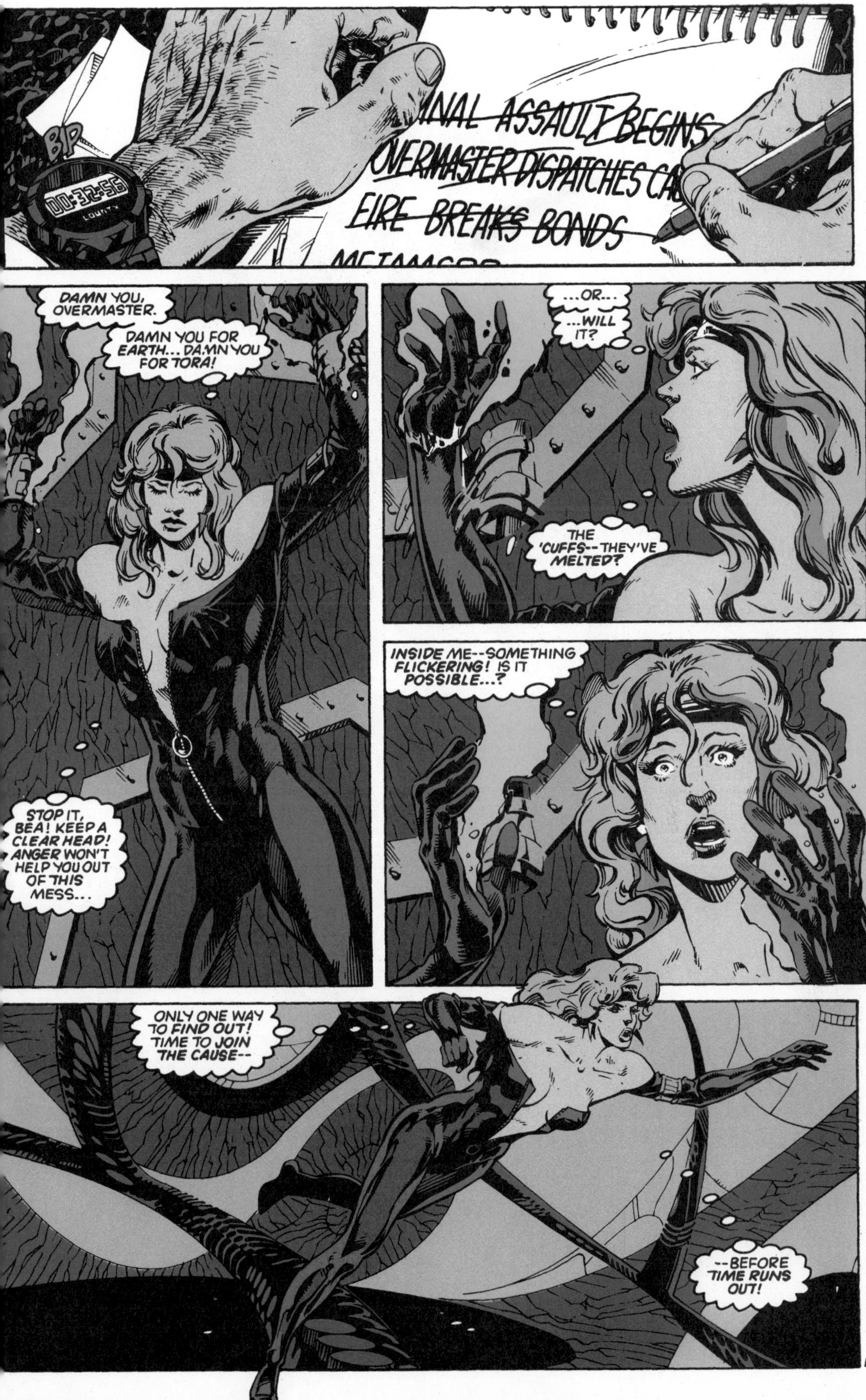

FINAL ASSAULT BEGINS
OVERMASTER DISPATCHES CA
FIRE BREAKS BONDS
BP
00:32:56
DAMN YOU, OVERMASTER.
DAMN YOU FOR EARTH... DAMN YOU FOR TORA!
STOP IT, BEA! KEEP A CLEAR HEAD! ANGER WON'T HELP YOU OUT OF THIS MESS...
...OR...
...WILL IT?
THE 'CUFFS--THEY'VE MELTED?
INSIDE ME--SOMETHING FLICKERING! IS IT POSSIBLE...?
ONLY ONE WAY TO FIND OUT! TIME TO JOIN THE CAUSE--
--BEFORE TIME RUNS OUT!

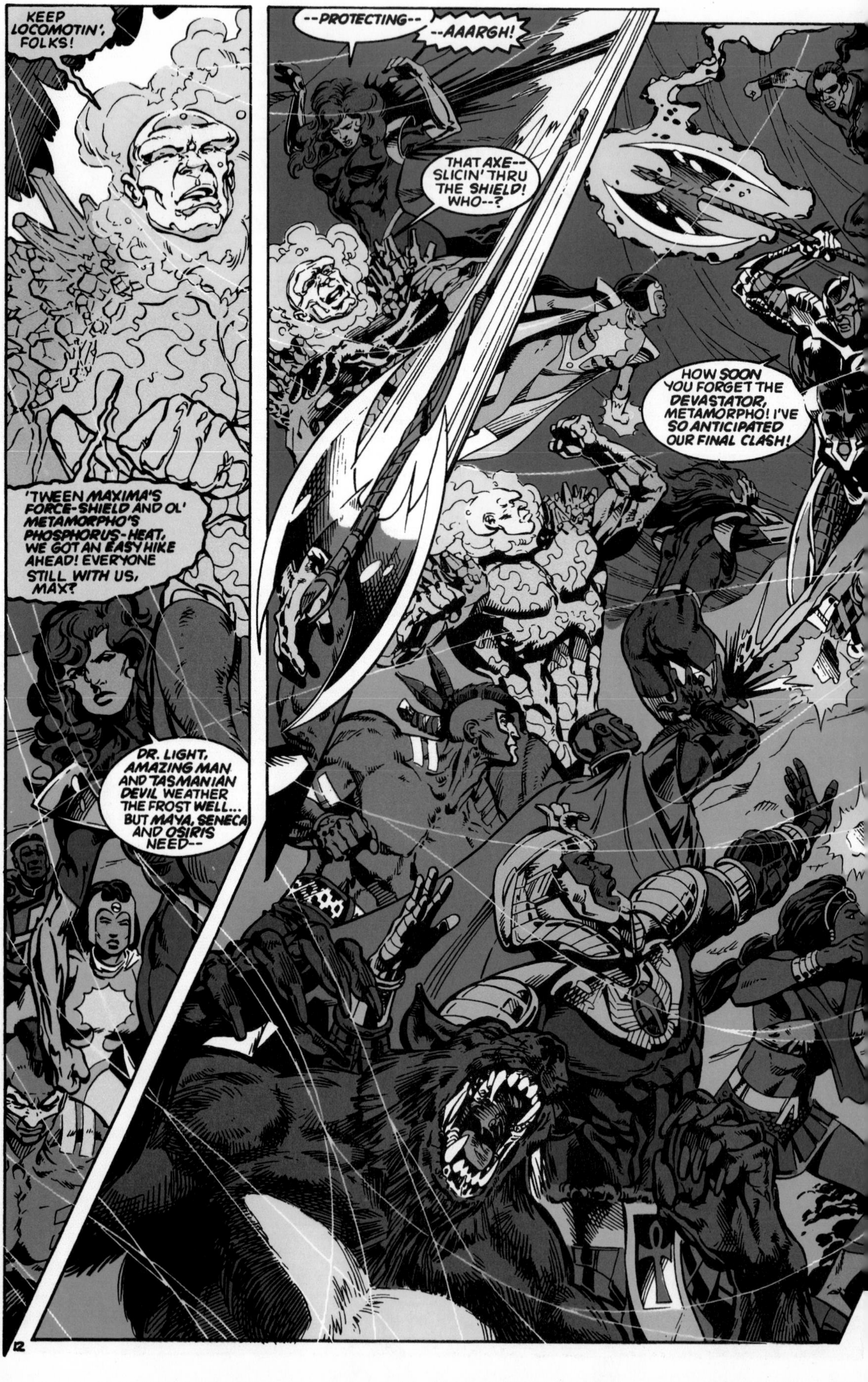
KEEP LOCOMOTIN', FOLKS!
'TWEEN MAXIMA'S FORCE-SHIELD AND OL' METAMORPHO'S PHOSPHORUS-HEAT, WE GOT AN EASY HIKE AHEAD! EVERYONE STILL WITH US, MAX?
DR. LIGHT, AMAZING MAN AND TASMANIAN DEVIL WEATHER THE FROST WELL... BUT MAYA, SENECA AND OSIRIS NEED--
--PROTECTING--
--AAARGH!
THAT AXE-- SLICIN' THRU THE SHIELD! WHO--?
HOW SOON YOU FORGET THE DEVASTATOR, METAMORPHO! I'VE SO ANTICIPATED OUR FINAL CLASH!

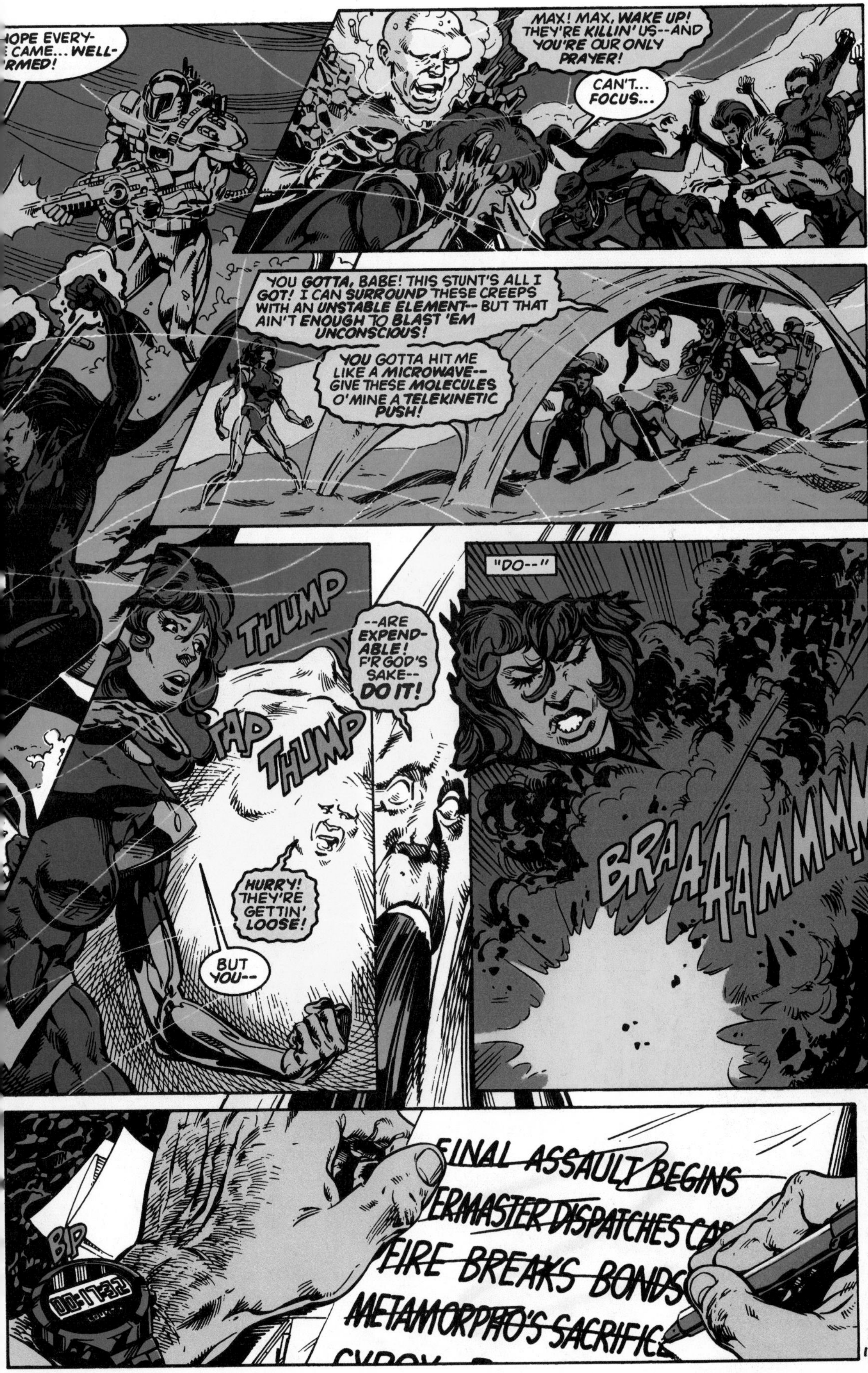
HOPE EVERY-
E CAME... WELL-
RMED!
MAX! MAX, WAKE UP! THEY'RE KILLIN' US--AND YOU'RE OUR ONLY PRAYER!
CAN'T... FOCUS...
YOU GOTTA, BABE! THIS STUNT'S ALL I GOT! I CAN SURROUND THESE CREEPS WITH AN UNSTABLE ELEMENT-- BUT THAT AIN'T ENOUGH TO BLAST 'EM UNCONSCIOUS!
YOU GOTTA HIT ME LIKE A MICROWAVE-- GIVE THESE MOLECULES O' MINE A TELEKINETIC PUSH!
THUMP
TAP
THUMP
HURRY! THEY'RE GETTIN' LOOSE!
BUT YOU--
--ARE EXPEND-ABLE! F'R GOD'S SAKE-- DO IT!
"DO--"
BRAAAAMMMM
BIP
00:17:52
FINAL ASSAULT BEGINS
ERMASTER DISPATCHES CA
FIRE BREAKS BONDS
METAMORPHO'S SACRIFICE

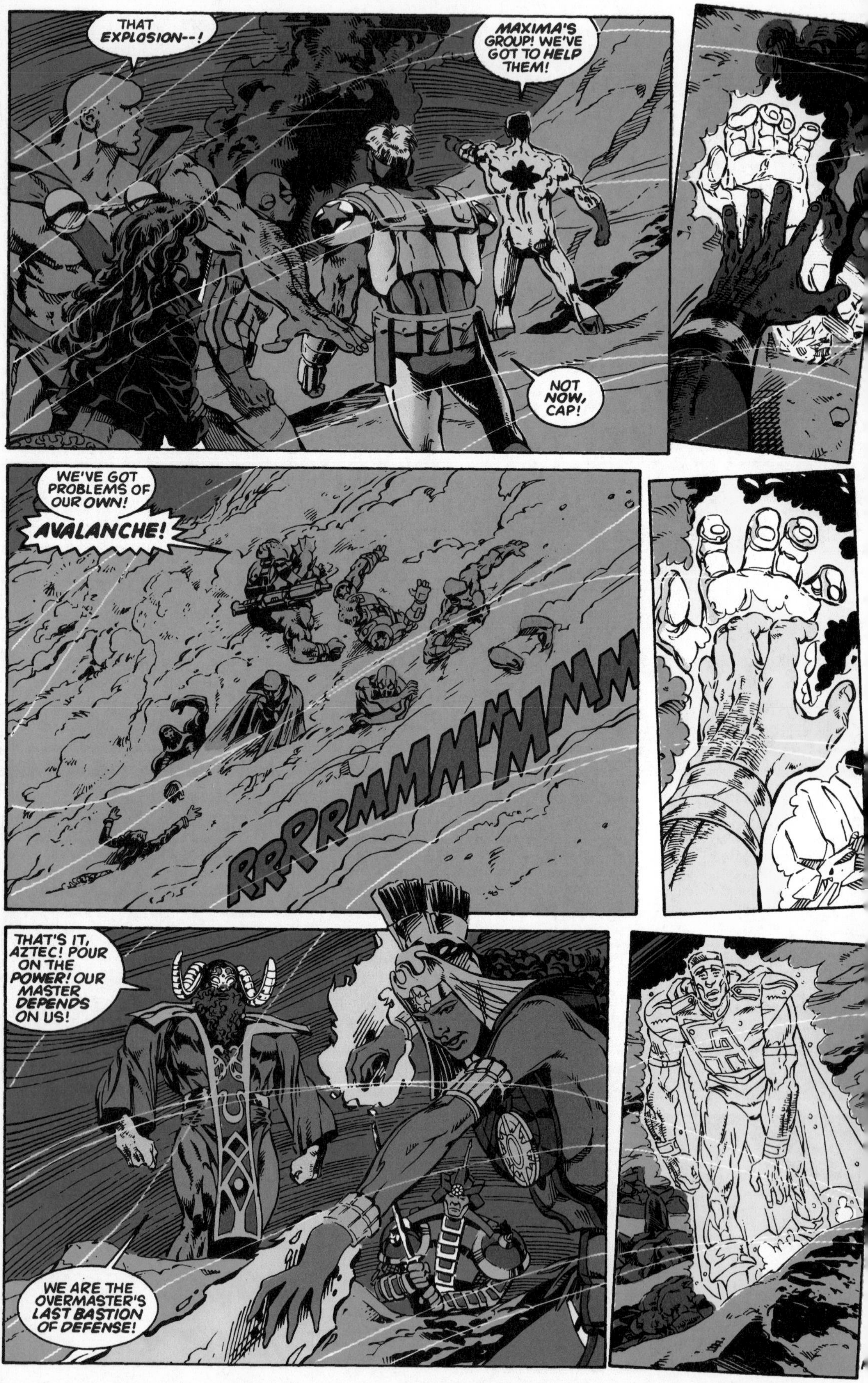
THAT EXPLOSION--!
MAXIMA'S GROUP! WE'VE GOT TO HELP THEM!
NOT NOW, CAP!
WE'VE GOT PROBLEMS OF OUR OWN!
AVALANCHE!
RRRRMMMMMMMMMM
THAT'S IT, AZTEC! POUR ON THE POWER! OUR MASTER DEPENDS ON US!
WE ARE THE OVERMASTER'S LAST BASTION OF DEFENSE!

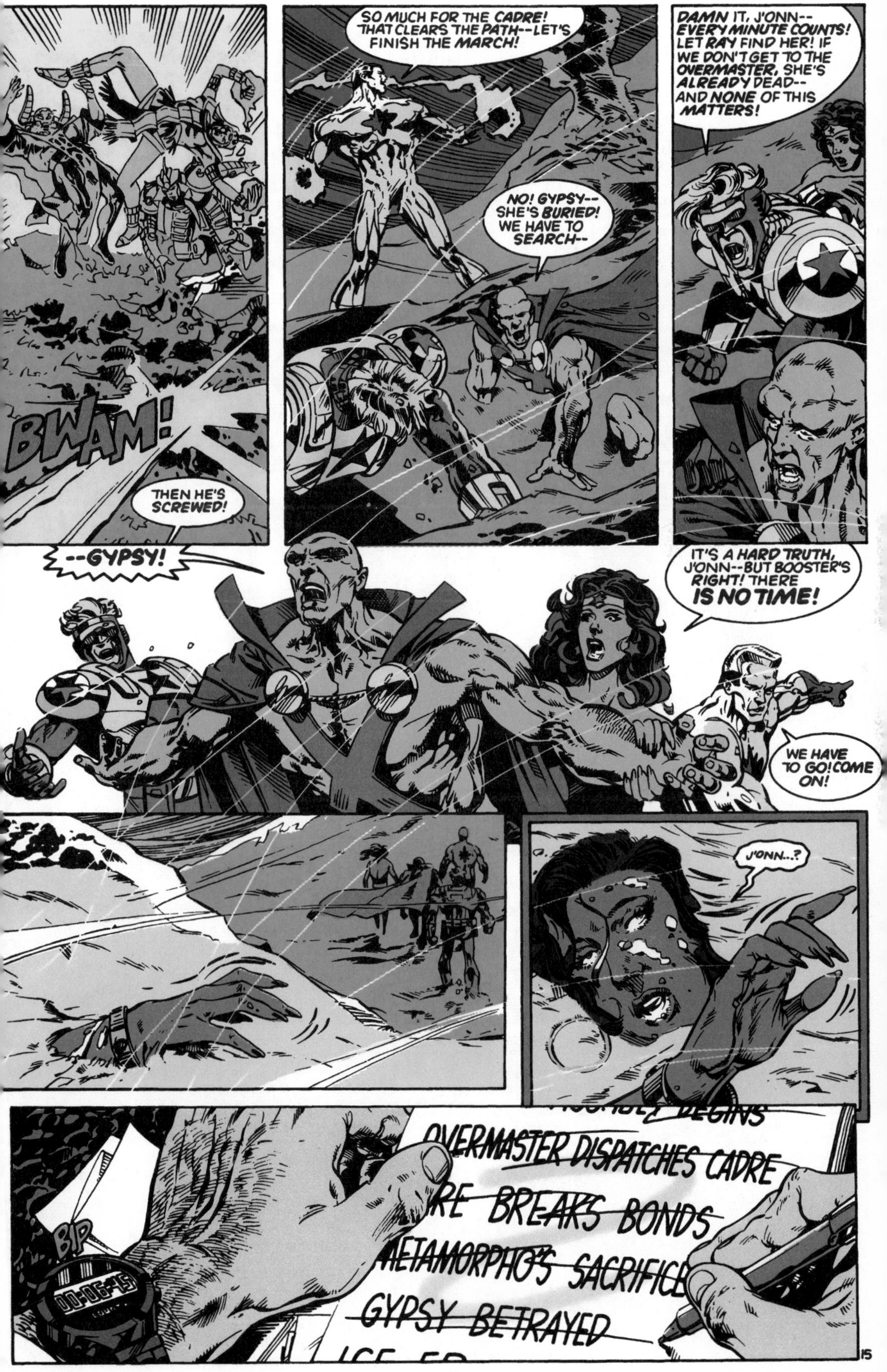
BWAM!
THEN HE'S SCREWED!
SO MUCH FOR THE CADRE! THAT CLEARS THE PATH--LET'S FINISH THE MARCH!
NO! GYPSY-- SHE'S BURIED! WE HAVE TO SEARCH--
DAMN IT, J'ONN-- EVERY MINUTE COUNTS! LET RAY FIND HER! IF WE DON'T GET TO THE OVERMASTER, SHE'S ALREADY DEAD-- AND NONE OF THIS MATTERS!
--GYPSY!
IT'S A HARD TRUTH, J'ONN--BUT BOOSTER'S RIGHT! THERE IS NO TIME!
WE HAVE TO GO! COME ON!
J'ONN...?
OVERMASTER DISPATCHES CADRE
BREAKS BONDS
METAMORPHO'S SACRIFICE
GYPSY BETRAYED
BIP
00-06-15

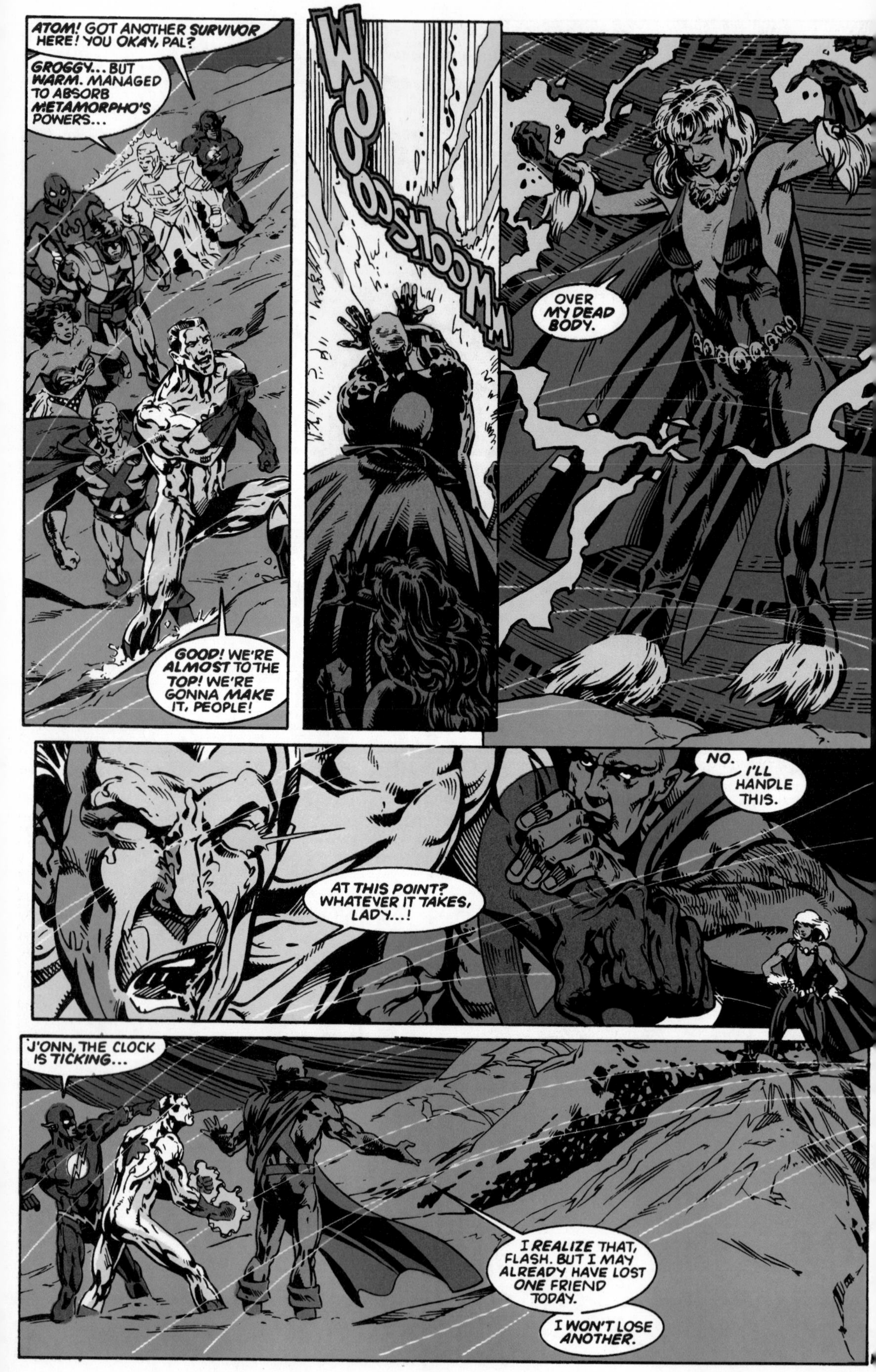

ATOM! GOT ANOTHER SURVIVOR HERE! YOU OKAY, PAL?
GROGGY... BUT WARM. MANAGED TO ABSORB METAMORPHO'S POWERS...
GOOD! WE'RE ALMOST TO THE TOP! WE'RE GONNA MAKE IT, PEOPLE!
WOOOOSHOOOM
OVER MY DEAD BODY.
AT THIS POINT? WHATEVER IT TAKES, LADY...!
NO.
I'LL HANDLE THIS.
J'ONN, THE CLOCK IS TICKING...
I REALIZE THAT, FLASH. BUT I MAY ALREADY HAVE LOST ONE FRIEND TODAY.
I WON'T LOSE ANOTHER.

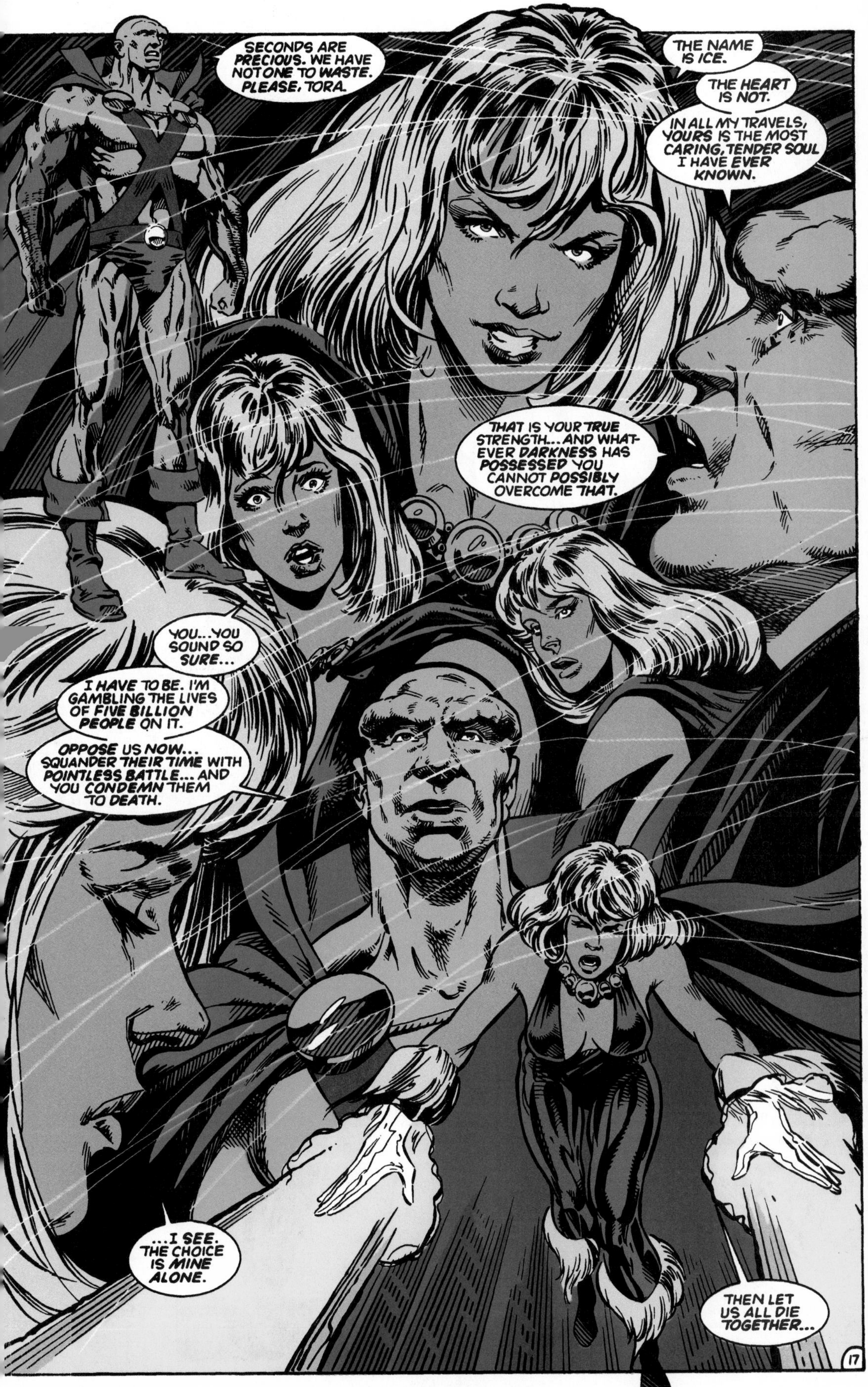
SECONDS ARE PRECIOUS. WE HAVE NOT ONE TO WASTE. PLEASE, TORA.
THE NAME IS ICE.
THE HEART IS NOT.
IN ALL MY TRAVELS, YOURS IS THE MOST CARING, TENDER SOUL I HAVE EVER KNOWN.
THAT IS YOUR TRUE STRENGTH... AND WHATEVER DARKNESS HAS POSSESSED YOU CANNOT POSSIBLY OVERCOME THAT.
YOU... YOU SOUND SO SURE...
I HAVE TO BE. I'M GAMBLING THE LIVES OF FIVE BILLION PEOPLE ON IT.
OPPOSE US NOW... SQUANDER THEIR TIME WITH POINTLESS BATTLE... AND YOU CONDEMN THEM TO DEATH.
...I SEE. THE CHOICE IS MINE ALONE.
THEN LET US ALL DIE TOGETHER...

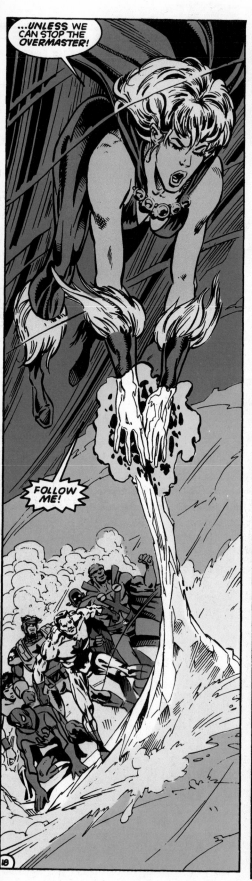

...UNLESS WE CAN STOP THE OVERMASTER!

FOLLOW ME!

BP 00:04:25

FIRE
~~DIAMOND~~
GYPSY
~~ICE FREE~~
OVERMAS...

I'M BACK, BEA. FOR GOOD---
--AND FOR ALWAYS!

WE'RE IN!

TORA! ARE YOU--?

YOU!

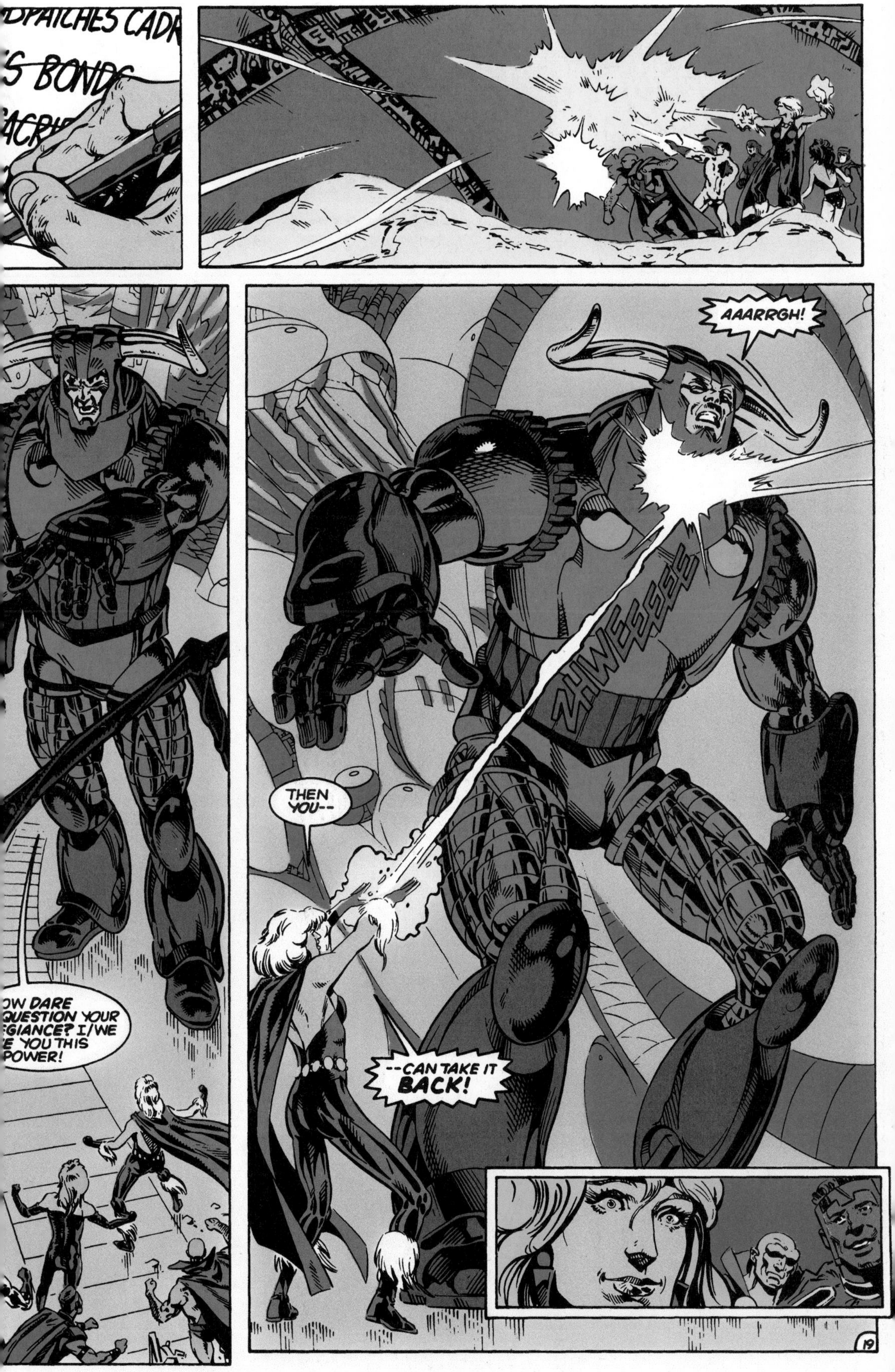

...DPATCHES CADR...
...S BONDS
...ACRI...
AAARRGH!
...OW DARE ...QUESTION YOUR ...GIANCE? I/WE ...E YOU THIS ...POWER!
ZHWEEEEE
THEN YOU--
--CAN TAKE IT BACK!

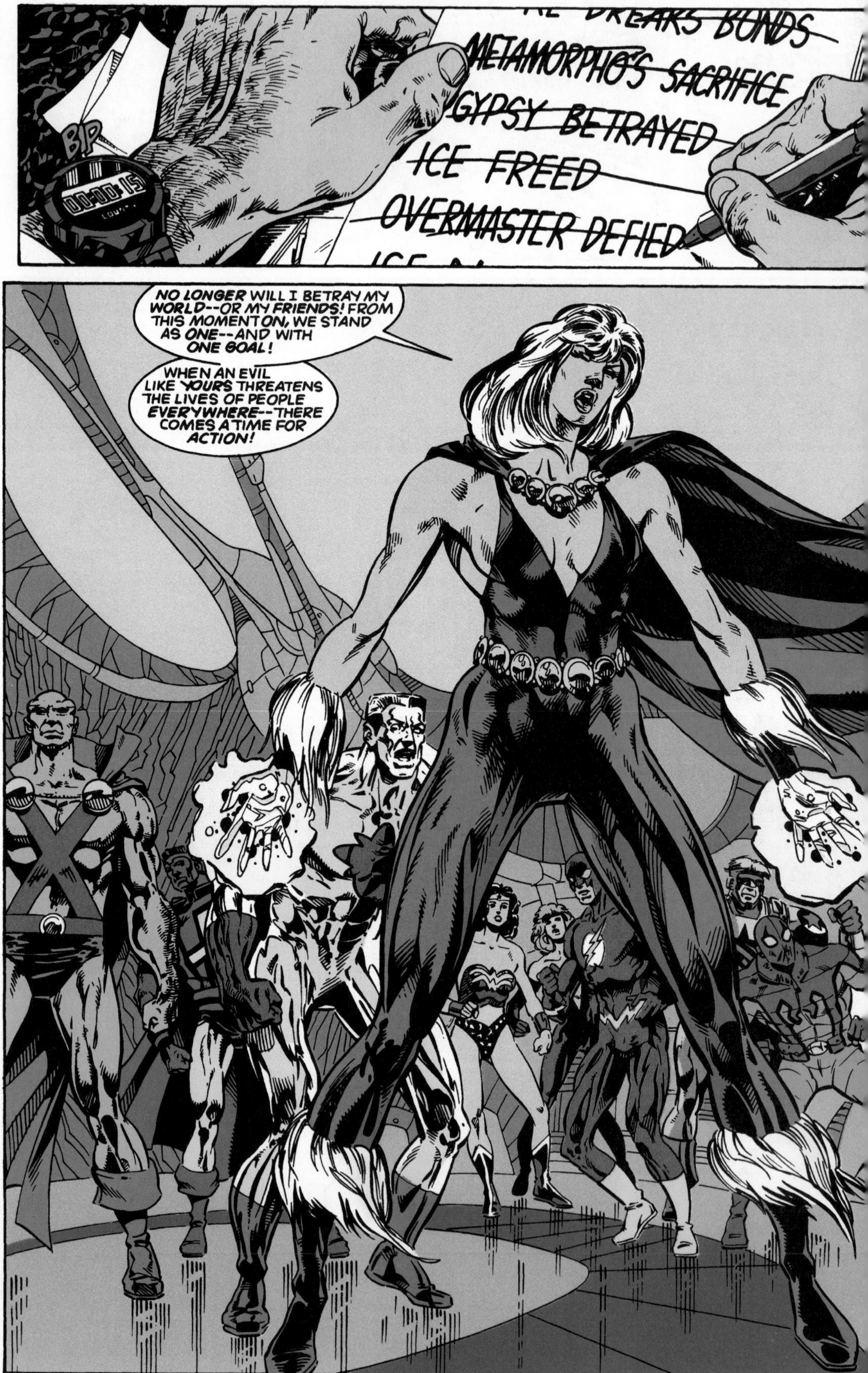

BIP
00:00:15
METAMORPHO'S SACRIFICE
GYPSY BETRAYED
ICE FREED
OVERMASTER DEFIED
NO LONGER WILL I BETRAY MY WORLD--OR MY FRIENDS! FROM THIS MOMENT ON, WE STAND AS ONE--AND WITH ONE GOAL!
WHEN AN EVIL LIKE YOURS THREATENS THE LIVES OF PEOPLE EVERYWHERE--THERE COMES A TIME FOR ACTION!

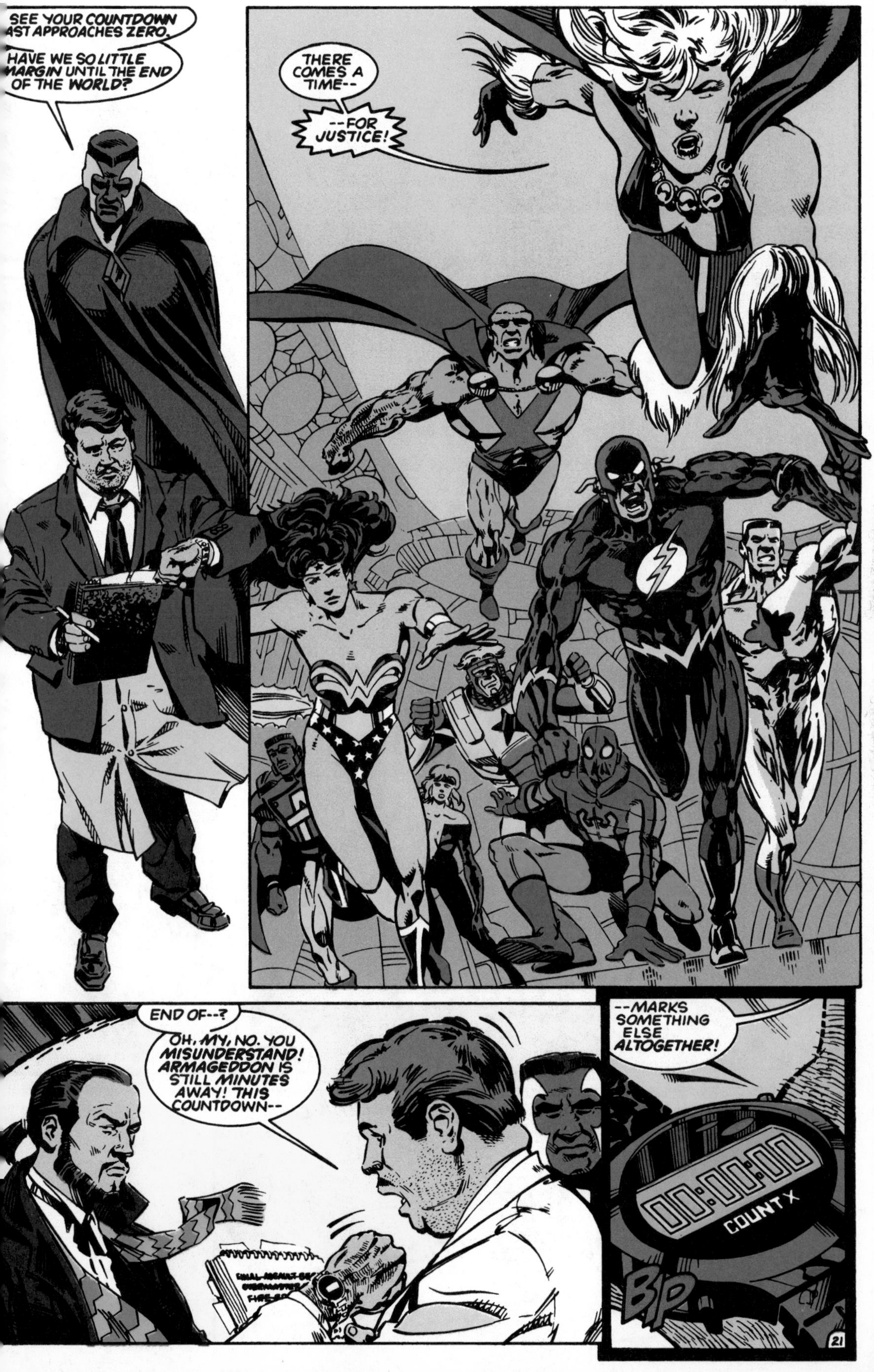
SEE YOUR COUNTDOWN
AST APPROACHES ZERO.
HAVE WE SO LITTLE MARGIN UNTIL THE END OF THE WORLD?
THERE COMES A TIME--
--FOR JUSTICE!
END OF--?
OH, MY, NO. YOU MISUNDERSTAND! ARMAGEDDON IS STILL MINUTES AWAY! THIS COUNTDOWN--
--MARKS SOMETHING ELSE ALTOGETHER!
00:00:00
COUNT X
BIP

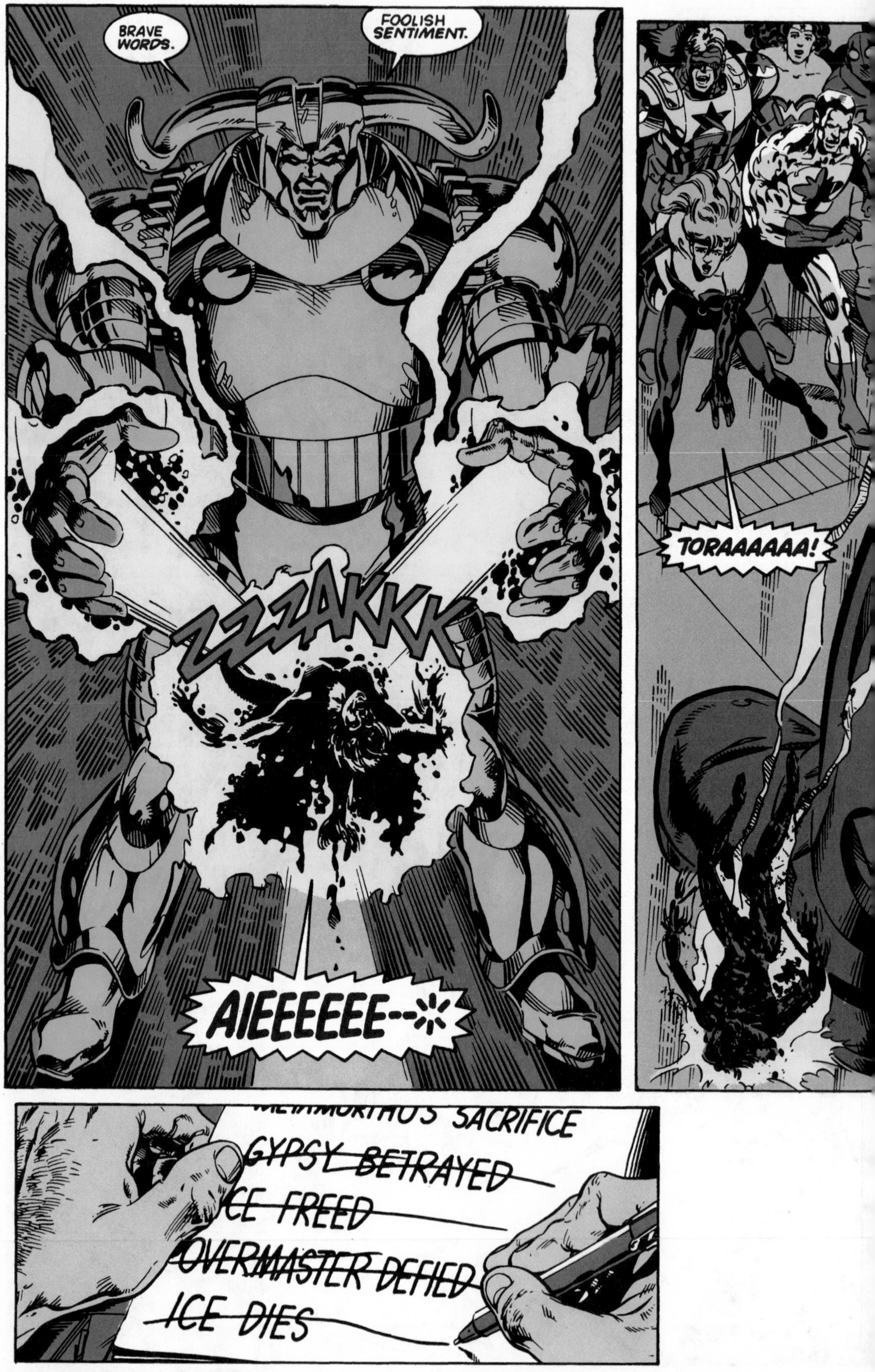
BRAVE WORDS.
FOOLISH SENTIMENT.
ZZZAKKK
AIEEEEEE--!!
TORAAAAAA!
METAMORPHO'S SACRIFICE
GYPSY BETRAYED
CE FREED
OVERMASTER DEFIED
ICE DIES

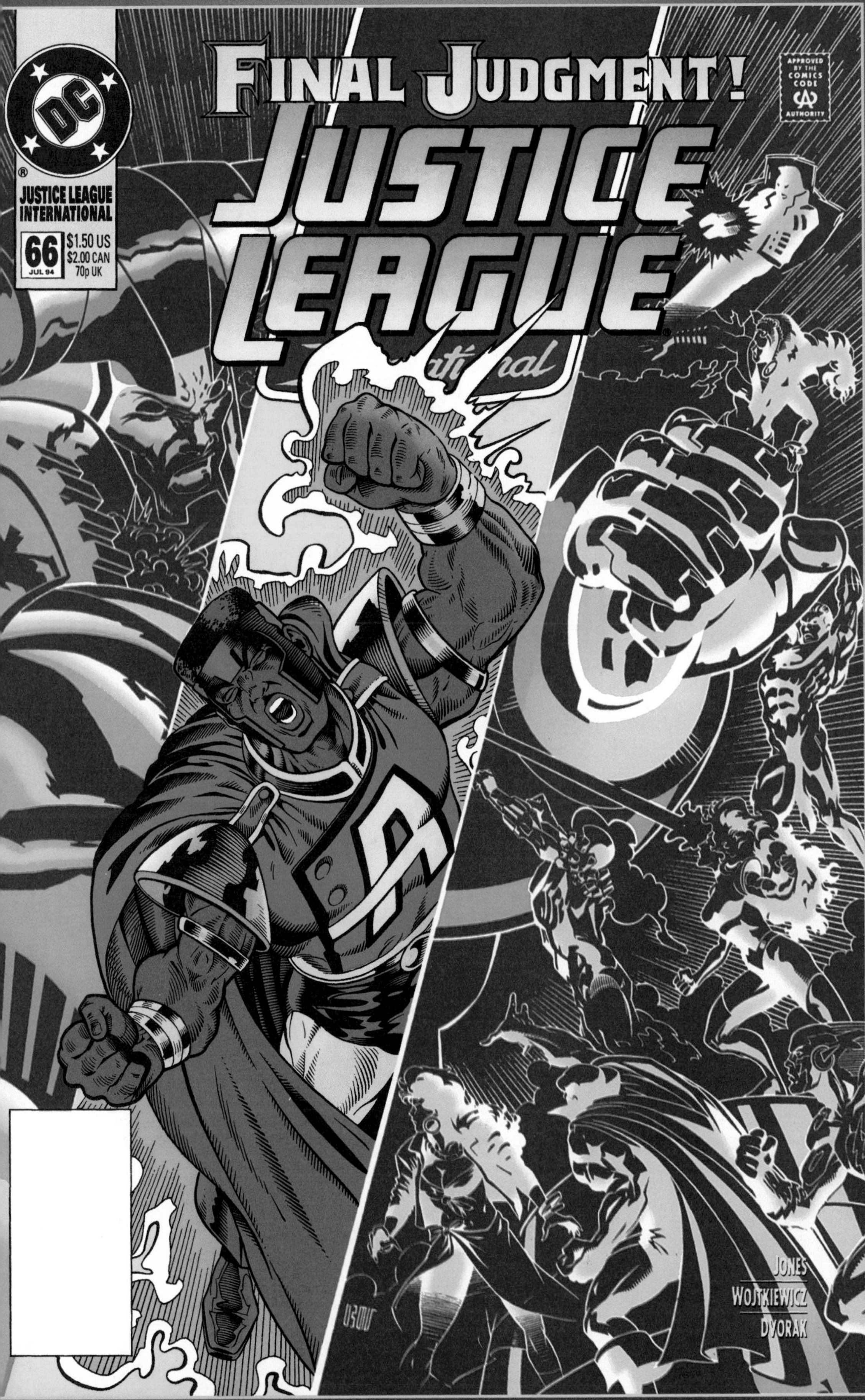

FINAL JUDGMENT!
JUSTICE LEAGUE International
DC
JUSTICE LEAGUE INTERNATIONAL
66
JUL 94
$1.50 US
$2.00 CAN
70p UK
APPROVED BY THE COMICS CODE AUTHORITY
JONES
WOJTKIEWICZ
DVORAK

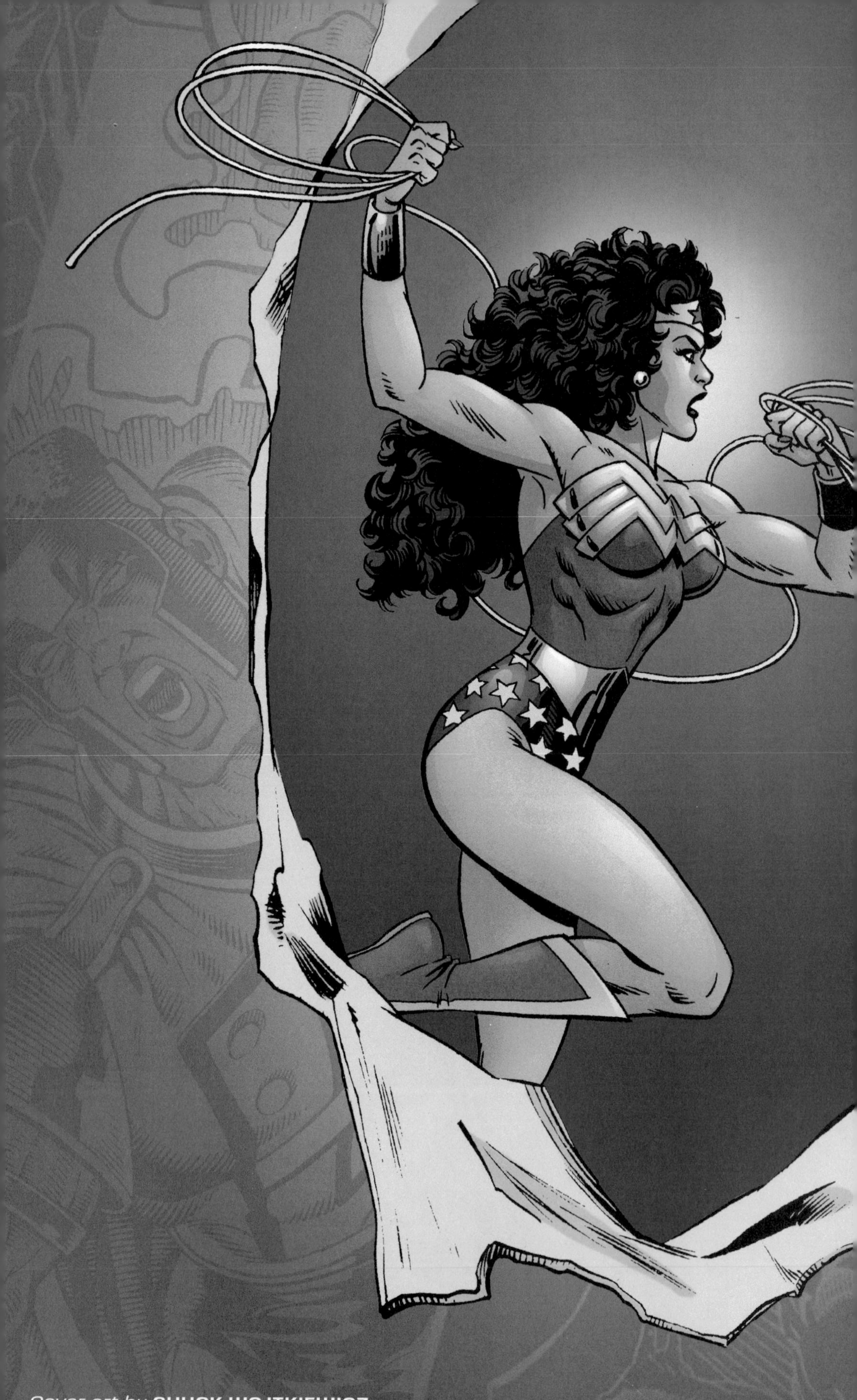

Cover art by **CHUCK WOJTKIEWICZ**

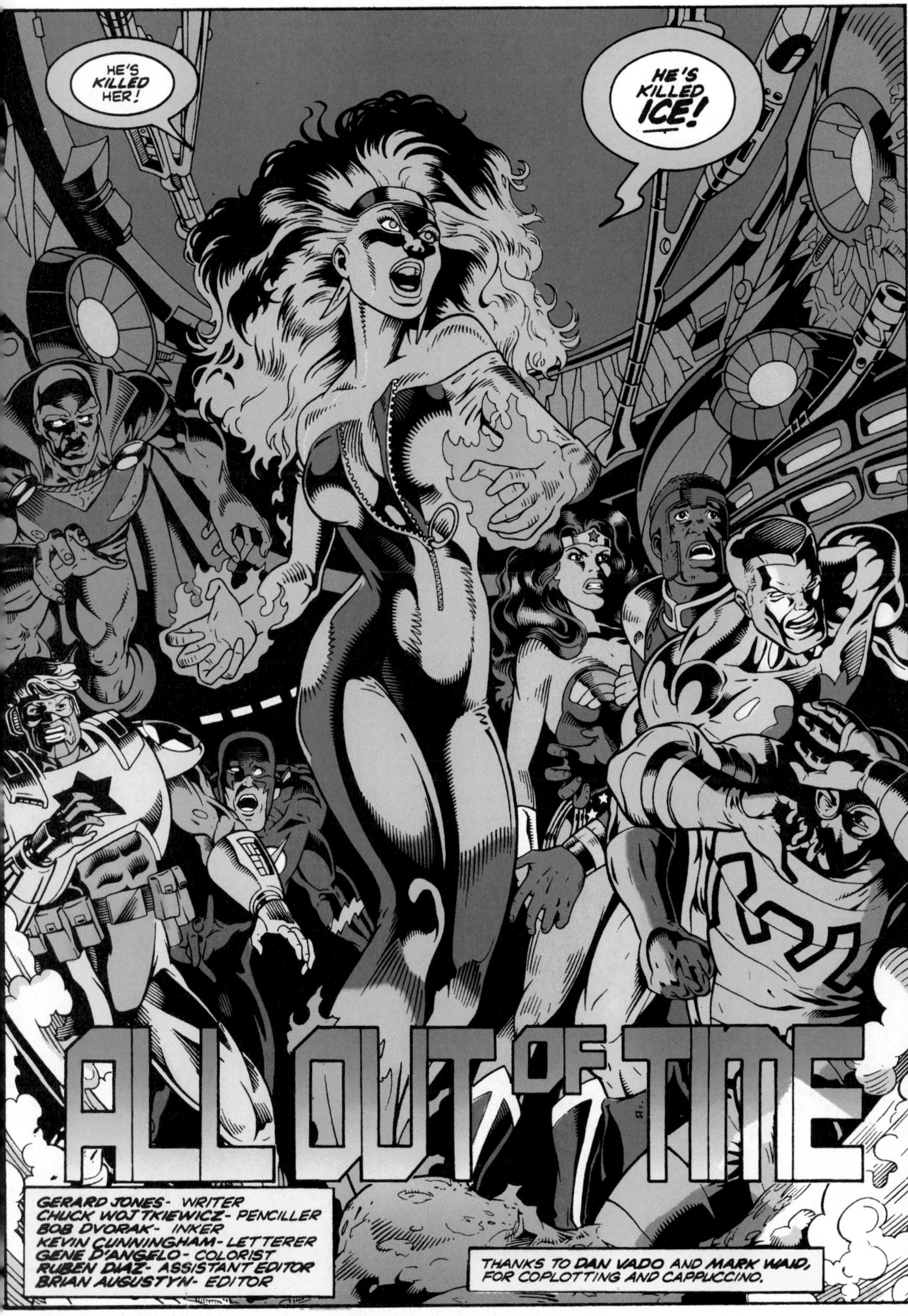
HE'S KILLED HER!
HE'S KILLED ICE!
ALL OUT OF TIME
GERARD JONES- WRITER
CHUCK WOJTKIEWICZ- PENCILLER
BOB DVORAK- INKER
KEVIN CUNNINGHAM- LETTERER
GENE D'ANGELO- COLORIST
RUBEN DIAZ- ASSISTANT EDITOR
BRIAN AUGUSTYN- EDITOR
THANKS TO DAN VADO AND MARK WAID, FOR COPLOTTING AND CAPPUCCINO.

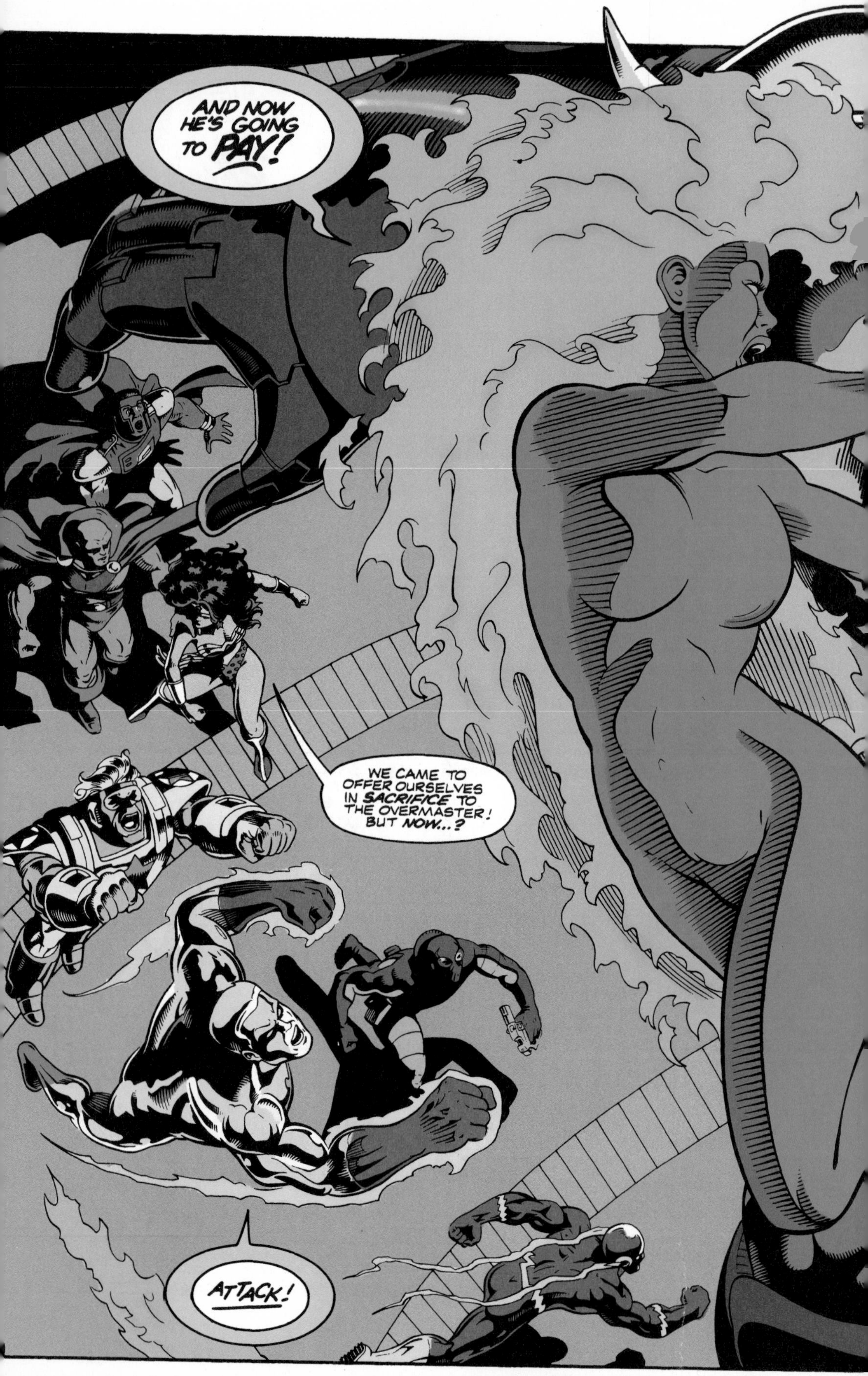
AND NOW HE'S GOING TO PAY!
WE CAME TO OFFER OURSELVES IN SACRIFICE TO THE OVERMASTER! BUT NOW...?
ATTACK!

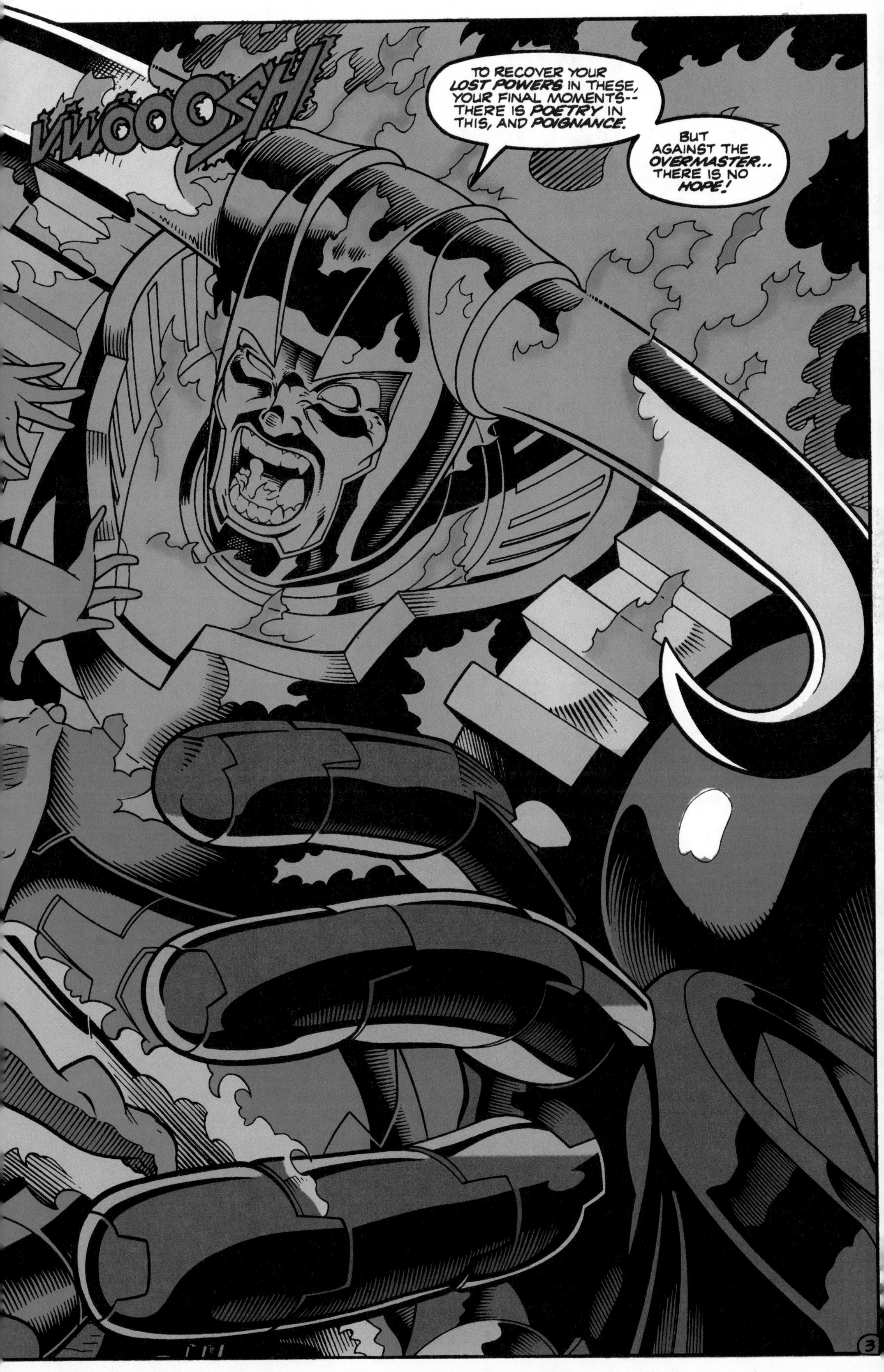

VWOOOSH
TO RECOVER YOUR LOST POWERS IN THESE, YOUR FINAL MOMENTS-- THERE IS POETRY IN THIS, AND POIGNANCE.
BUT AGAINST THE OVERMASTER... THERE IS NO HOPE!

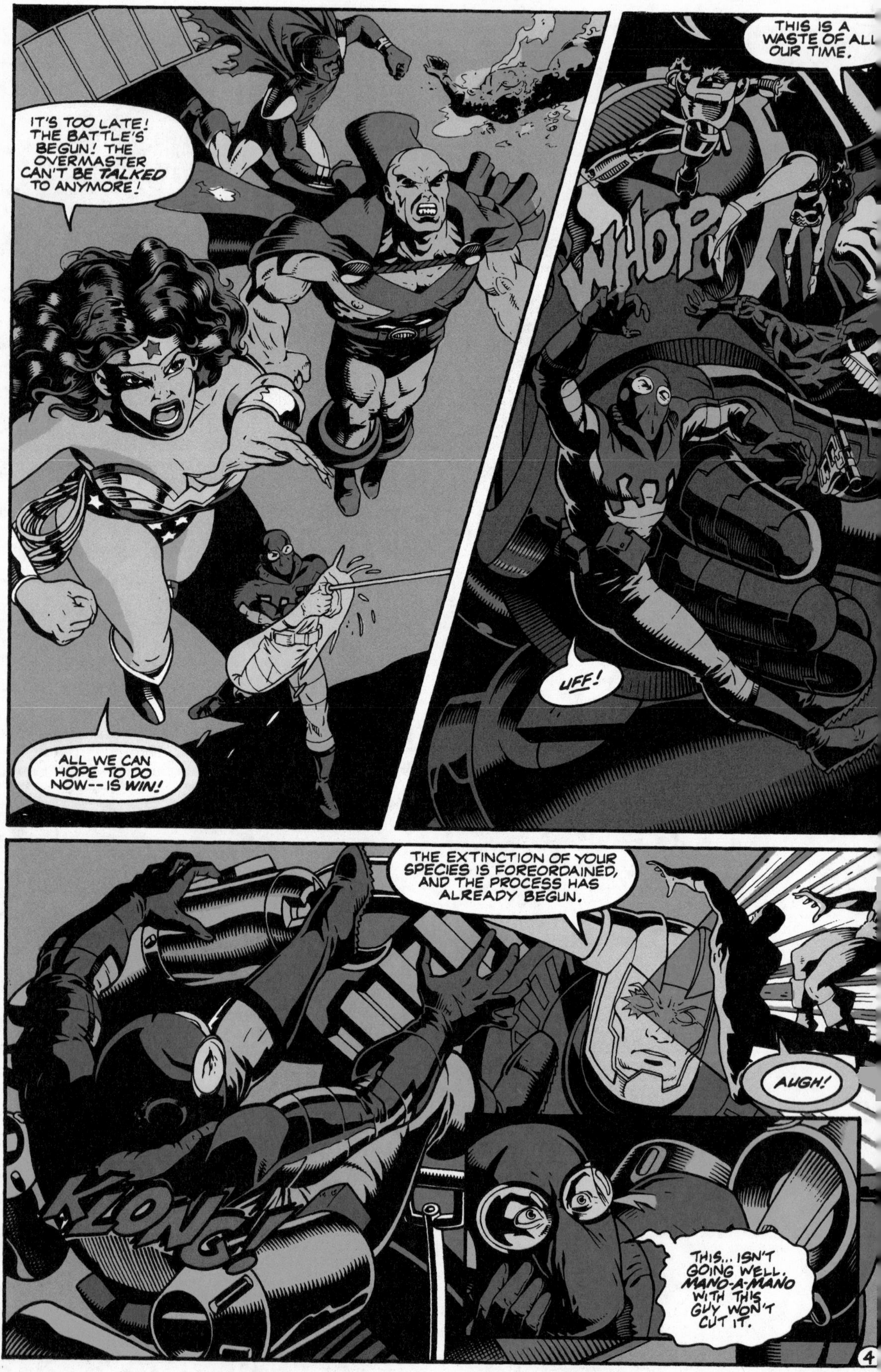

IT'S TOO LATE! THE BATTLE'S BEGUN! THE OVERMASTER CAN'T BE TALKED TO ANYMORE!
ALL WE CAN HOPE TO DO NOW--IS WIN!
THIS IS A WASTE OF ALL OUR TIME.
WHOP!
UFF!
THE EXTINCTION OF YOUR SPECIES IS FOREORDAINED, AND THE PROCESS HAS ALREADY BEGUN.
AUGH!
KLONG!
THIS... ISN'T GOING WELL. MANO-A-MANO WITH THIS GUY WON'T CUT IT.

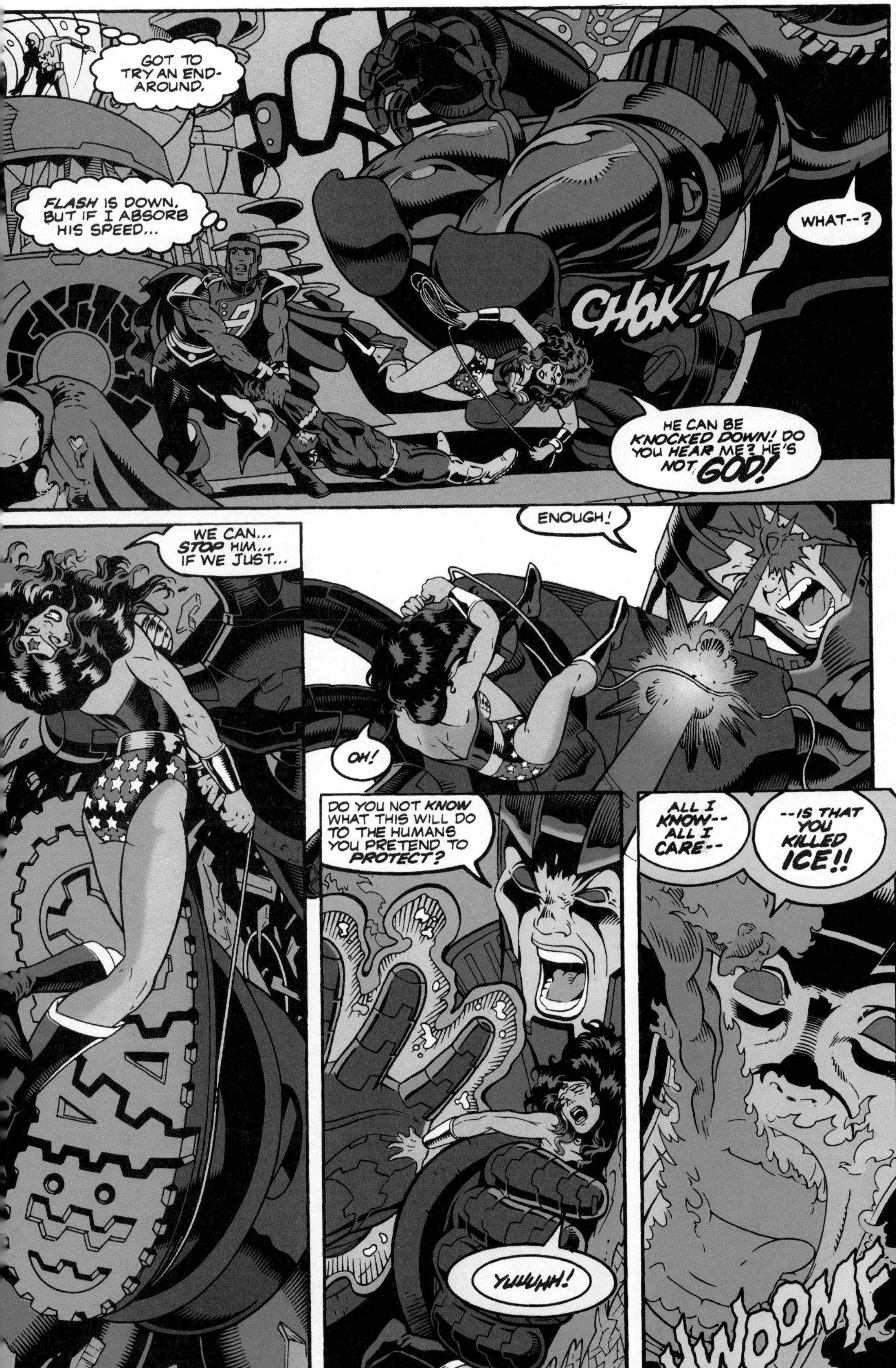

GOT TO TRY AN END-AROUND.
FLASH IS DOWN, BUT IF I ABSORB HIS SPEED...
WHAT--?
CHOK!
HE CAN BE KNOCKED DOWN! DO YOU HEAR ME? HE'S NOT GOD!
WE CAN... STOP HIM... IF WE JUST...
ENOUGH!
OH!
DO YOU NOT KNOW WHAT THIS WILL DO TO THE HUMANS YOU PRETEND TO PROTECT?
YWWWH!
ALL I KNOW-- ALL I CARE--
--IS THAT YOU KILLED ICE!!
HWOOM!

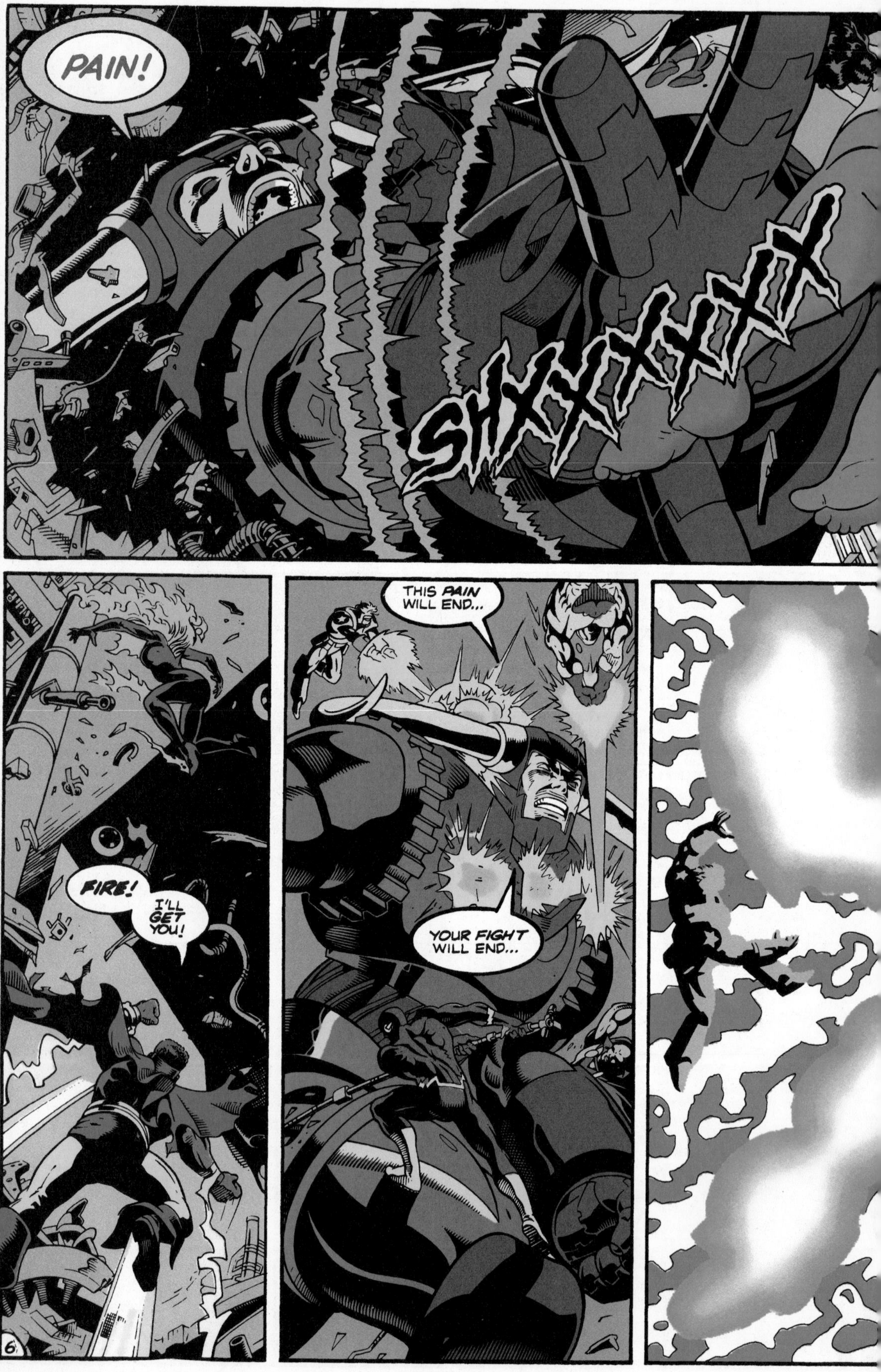
PAIN!
SHXXXXXX
FIRE!
I'LL GET YOU!
THIS PAIN WILL END...
YOUR FIGHT WILL END...

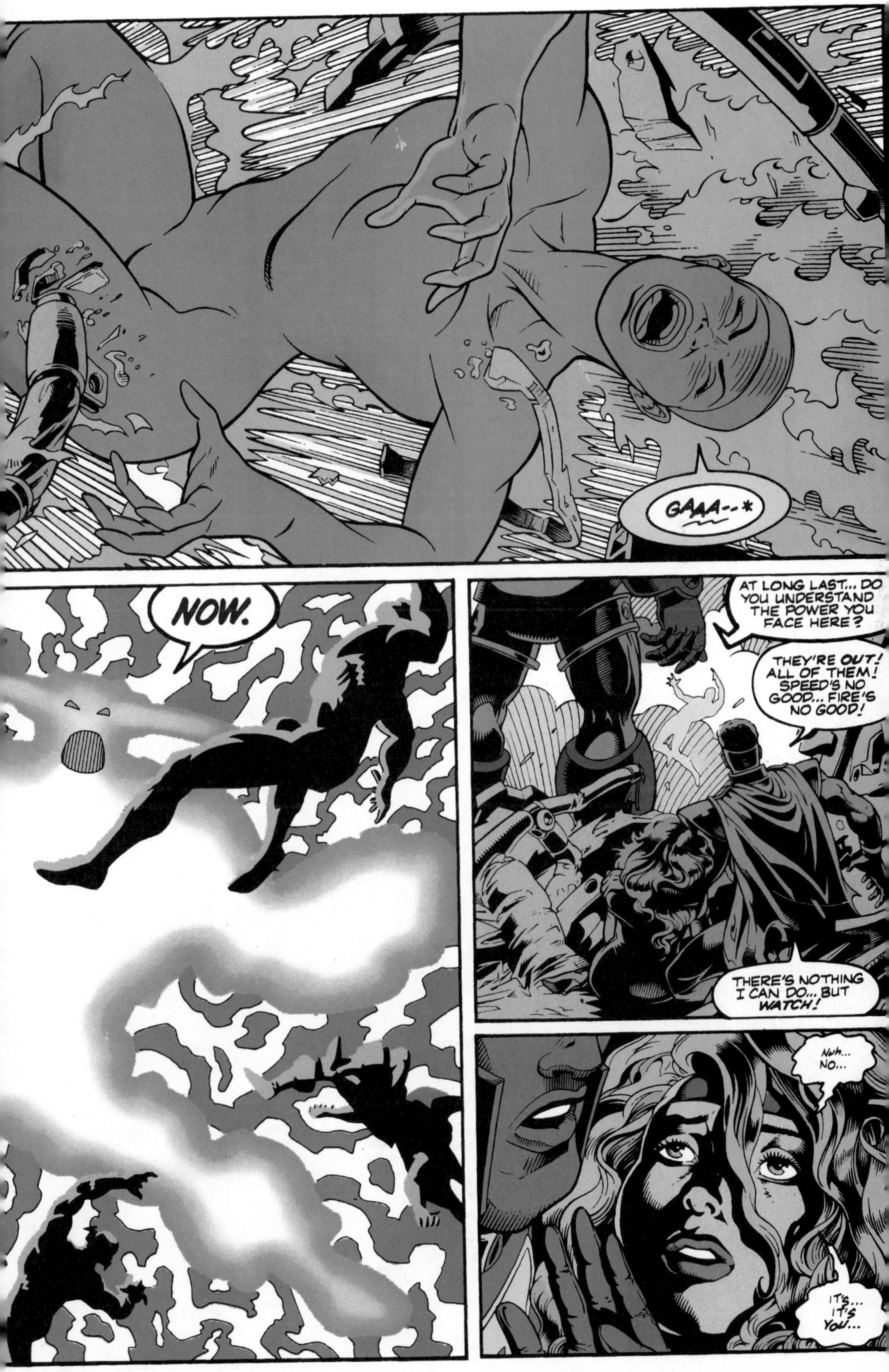
GAAA--*
NOW.
AT LONG LAST... DO YOU UNDERSTAND THE POWER YOU FACE HERE?
THEY'RE OUT! ALL OF THEM! SPEED'S NO GOOD... FIRE'S NO GOOD!
THERE'S NOTHING I CAN DO... BUT WATCH!
Nuh... NO...
IT'S... IT'S YOU...

THIS **MUST** BE THE WAY!

OR SO I **TELL** MYSELF.

BUT I FIGURE IF THIS SHIP IS MEANT FOR HEAVY IMPACTS LIKE *SLAMMING* INTO MT. EVEREST, THEN THE CONTROL ROOM MUST BE IN THE...

...CENTER. YEESH...GOOD **GUESS**, KORD.

NOW I HAVE TO FIGURE THIS MESS OUT-- OR MANKIND *DIES*!

NO...I CAN'T LET MYSELF EVEN THINK ABOUT IT!

JUST STAY COOL, STAY COOL, STAY...

ulp.

I THINK YOU SHOULD NOT **BE** HERE.

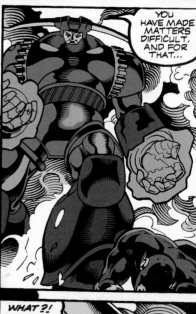

YOU HAVE MADE MATTERS *DIFFICULT*. AND FOR THAT...

WHAT?!

THE *WARNING FREQUENCIES*?!

THE *CONTROL ROOM*!!

8

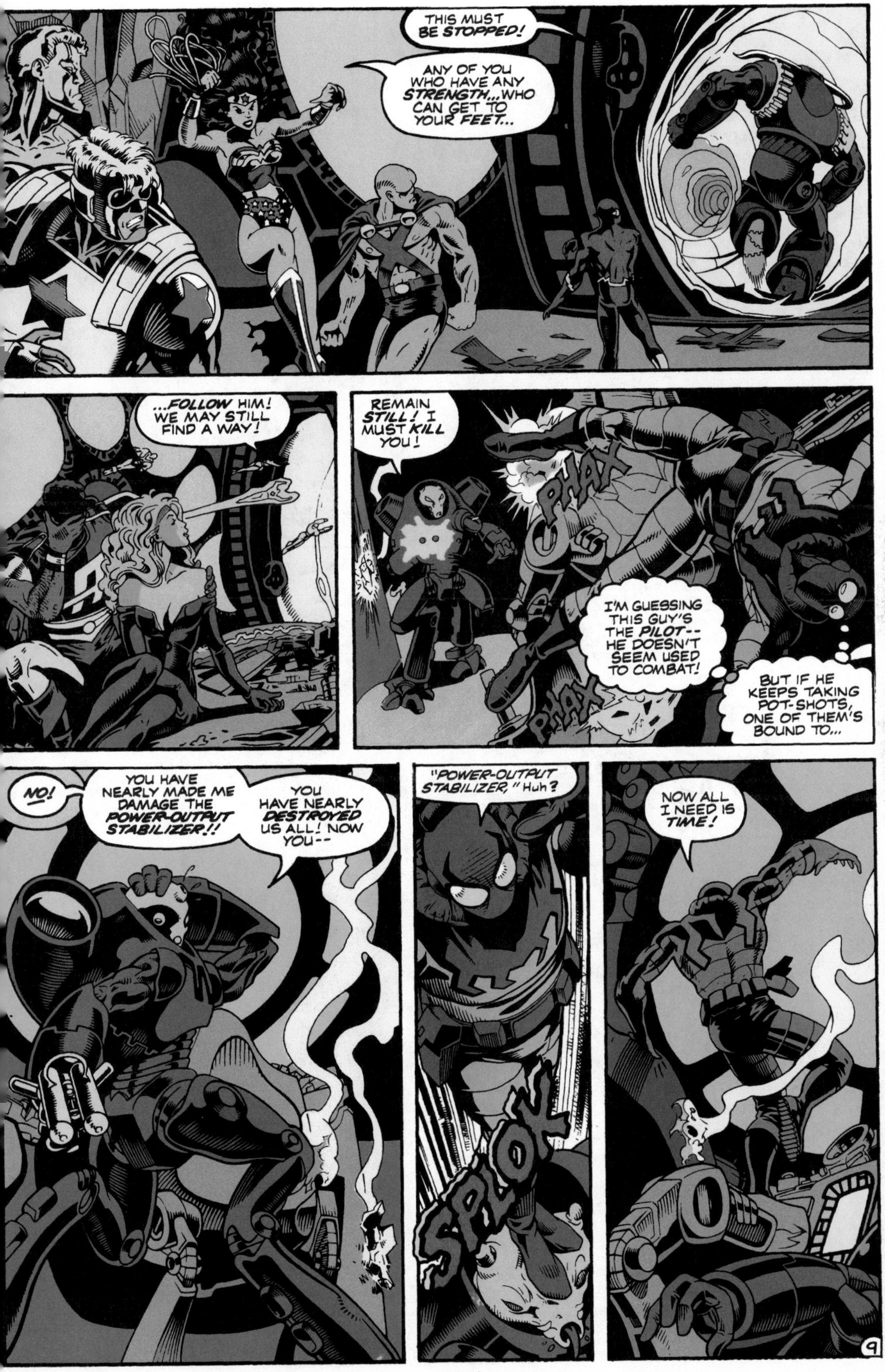
THIS MUST BE STOPPED!
ANY OF YOU WHO HAVE ANY STRENGTH... WHO CAN GET TO YOUR FEET...
...FOLLOW HIM! WE MAY STILL FIND A WAY!
REMAIN STILL! I MUST KILL YOU!
PHAX
I'M GUESSING THIS GUY'S THE PILOT-- HE DOESN'T SEEM USED TO COMBAT!
BUT IF HE KEEPS TAKING POT-SHOTS, ONE OF THEM'S BOUND TO...
PHAX
NO!
YOU HAVE NEARLY MADE ME DAMAGE THE POWER-OUTPUT STABILIZER!!
YOU HAVE NEARLY DESTROYED US ALL! NOW YOU--
"POWER-OUTPUT STABILIZER," Huh?
SPLOK
NOW ALL I NEED IS TIME!

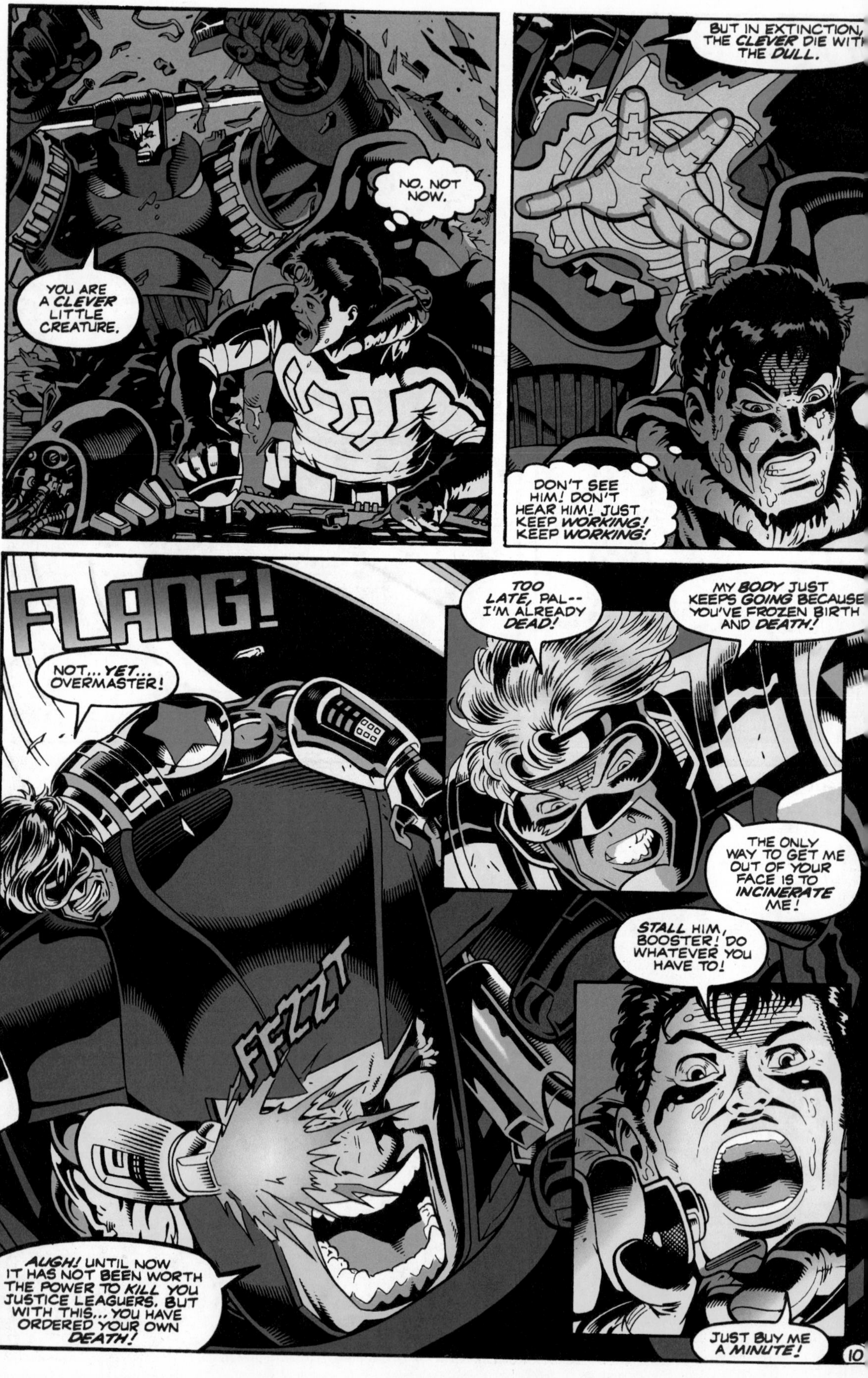

YOU ARE A CLEVER LITTLE CREATURE.
NO, NOT NOW.
BUT IN EXTINCTION, THE CLEVER DIE WIT THE DULL.
DON'T SEE HIM! DON'T HEAR HIM! JUST KEEP WORKING! KEEP WORKING!
FLANG!
NOT... YET... OVERMASTER!
TOO LATE, PAL-- I'M ALREADY DEAD!
MY BODY JUST KEEPS GOING BECAUSE YOU'VE FROZEN BIRTH AND DEATH!
THE ONLY WAY TO GET ME OUT OF YOUR FACE IS TO INCINERATE ME!
FFZZT
STALL HIM, BOOSTER! DO WHATEVER YOU HAVE TO!
AUGH! UNTIL NOW IT HAS NOT BEEN WORTH THE POWER TO KILL YOU JUSTICE LEAGUERS, BUT WITH THIS... YOU HAVE ORDERED YOUR OWN DEATH!
JUST BUY ME A MINUTE!

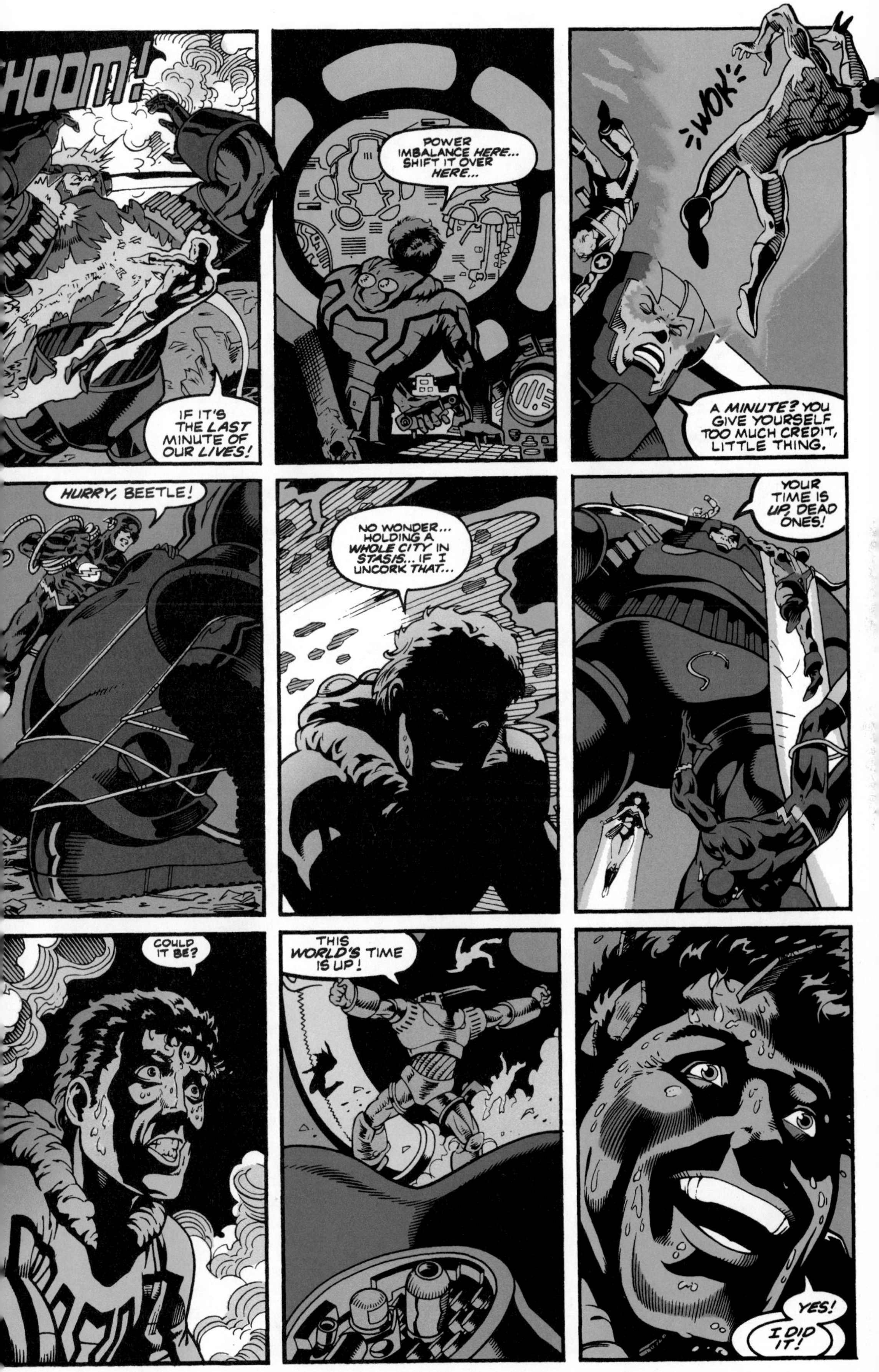

SHOOM!
IF IT'S THE LAST MINUTE OF OUR LIVES!
POWER IMBALANCE HERE... SHIFT IT OVER HERE...
WOK
A MINUTE? YOU GIVE YOURSELF TOO MUCH CREDIT, LITTLE THING.
HURRY, BEETLE!
NO WONDER... HOLDING A WHOLE CITY IN STASIS... IF I UNCORK THAT...
YOUR TIME IS UP, DEAD ONES!
COULD IT BE?
THIS WORLD'S TIME IS UP!
YES!
I DID IT!

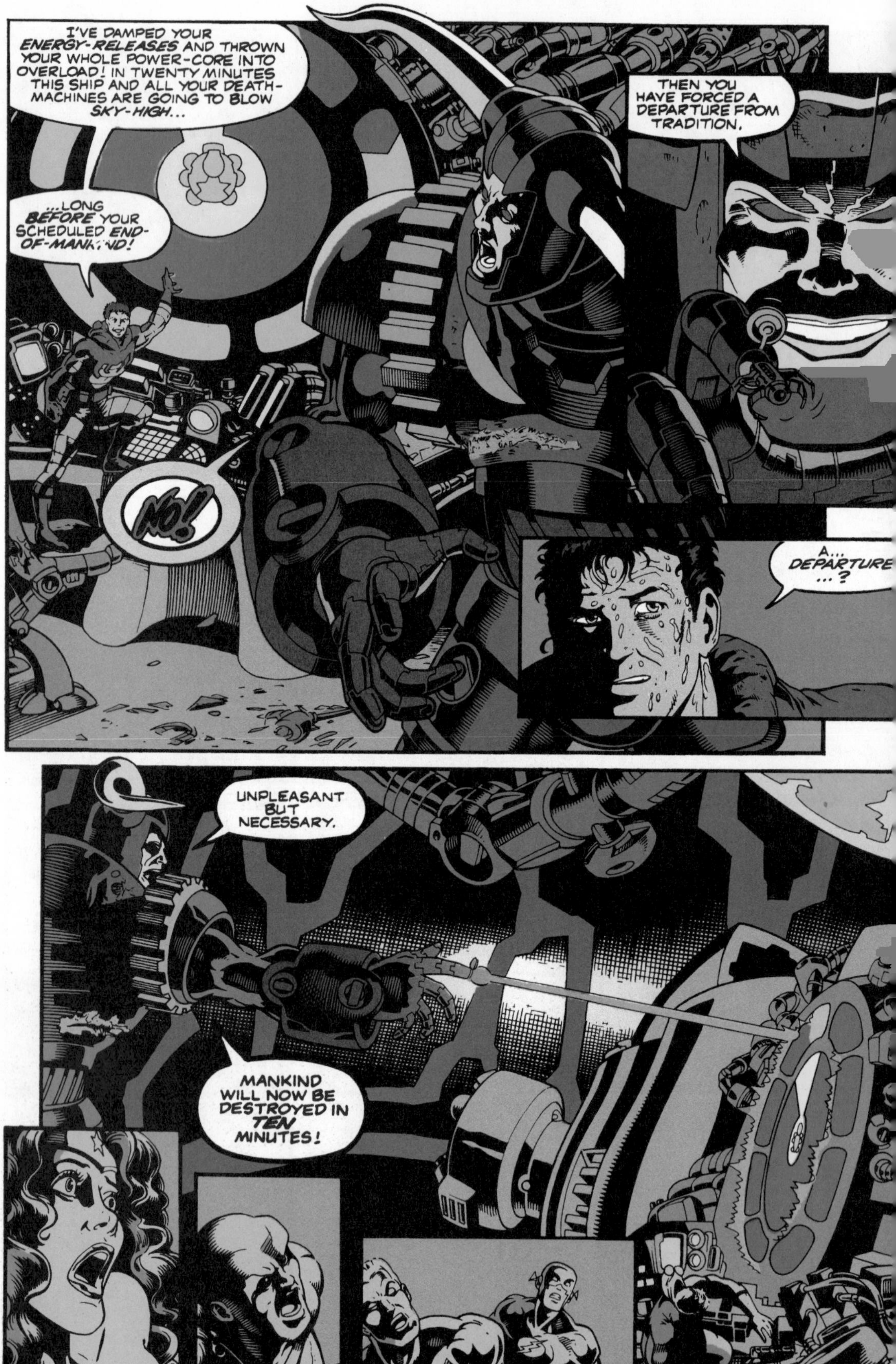

I'VE DAMPED YOUR ENERGY-RELEASES AND THROWN YOUR WHOLE POWER-CORE INTO OVERLOAD! IN TWENTY MINUTES THIS SHIP AND ALL YOUR DEATH-MACHINES ARE GOING TO BLOW SKY-HIGH...
...LONG BEFORE YOUR SCHEDULED END-OF-MANKIND!
NO!
THEN YOU HAVE FORCED A DEPARTURE FROM TRADITION.
A... DEPARTURE ...?
UNPLEASANT BUT NECESSARY.
MANKIND WILL NOW BE DESTROYED IN TEN MINUTES!

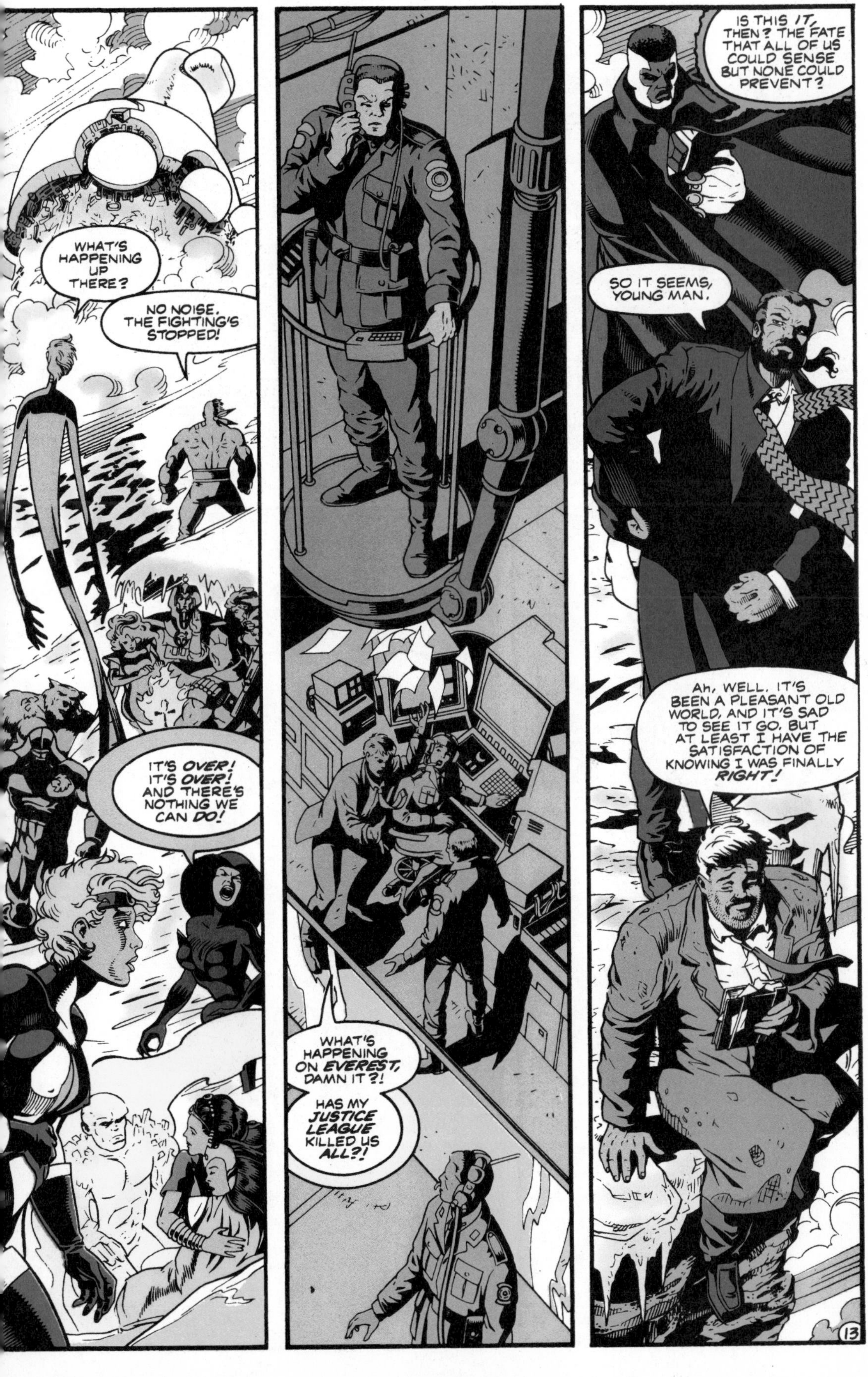

WHAT'S HAPPENING UP THERE?
NO NOISE. THE FIGHTING'S STOPPED!
IT'S OVER! IT'S OVER! AND THERE'S NOTHING WE CAN DO!
WHAT'S HAPPENING ON EVEREST, DAMN IT?!
HAS MY JUSTICE LEAGUE KILLED US ALL?!
IS THIS IT, THEN? THE FATE THAT ALL OF US COULD SENSE BUT NONE COULD PREVENT?
SO IT SEEMS, YOUNG MAN.
Ah, WELL. IT'S BEEN A PLEASANT OLD WORLD, AND IT'S SAD TO SEE IT GO, BUT AT LEAST I HAVE THE SATISFACTION OF KNOWING I WAS FINALLY RIGHT!
13

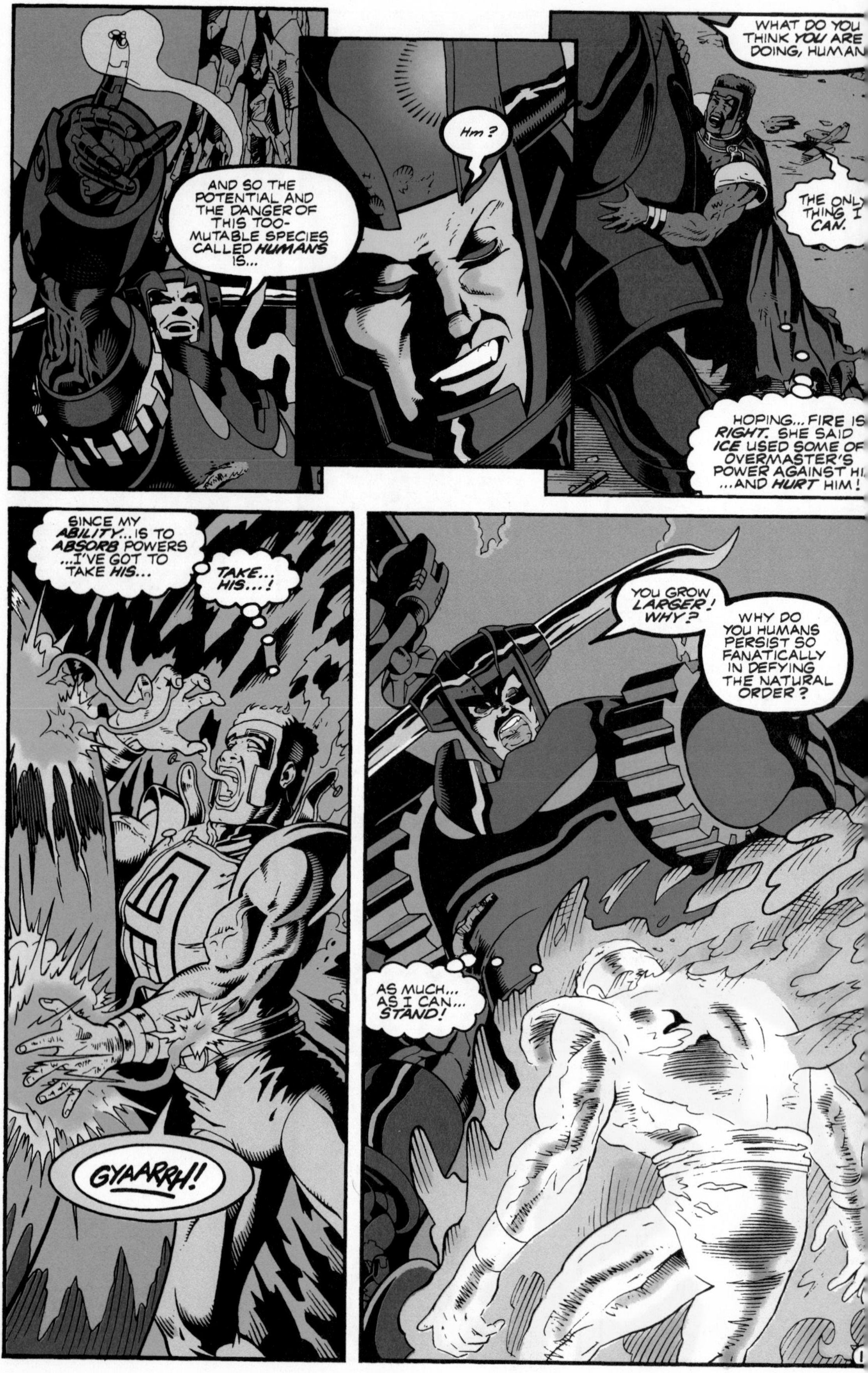
AND SO THE POTENTIAL AND THE DANGER OF THIS TOO-MUTABLE SPECIES CALLED HUMANS IS...
Hm?
WHAT DO YOU THINK YOU ARE DOING, HUMAN
THE ONLY THING I CAN.
HOPING... FIRE IS RIGHT. SHE SAID ICE USED SOME OF OVERMASTER'S POWER AGAINST HI ...AND HURT HIM!
SINCE MY ABILITY... IS TO ABSORB POWERS ...I'VE GOT TO TAKE HIS...
TAKE... HIS...!
GYAARRH!
YOU GROW LARGER! WHY?
WHY DO YOU HUMANS PERSIST SO FANATICALLY IN DEFYING THE NATURAL ORDER?
AS MUCH... AS I CAN... STAND!

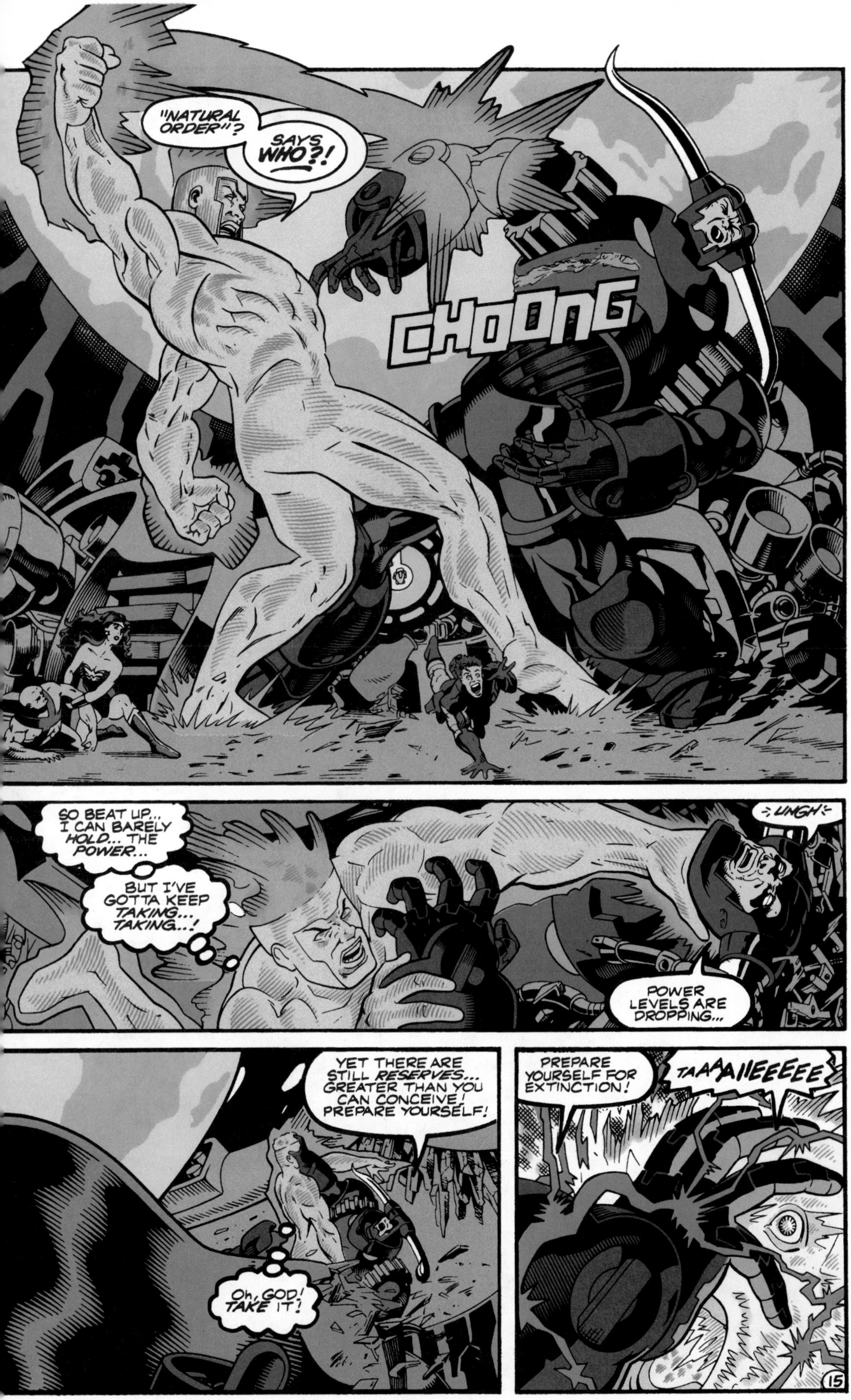

"NATURAL ORDER"?
SAYS WHO?!
CHOONG
SO BEAT UP... I CAN BARELY HOLD... THE POWER...
BUT I'VE GOTTA KEEP TAKING... TAKING...!
UNGH
POWER LEVELS ARE DROPPING...
YET THERE ARE STILL RESERVES... GREATER THAN YOU CAN CONCEIVE! PREPARE YOURSELF!
Oh, GOD! TAKE IT!
PREPARE YOURSELF FOR EXTINCTION!
TAAAAIIEEEEE

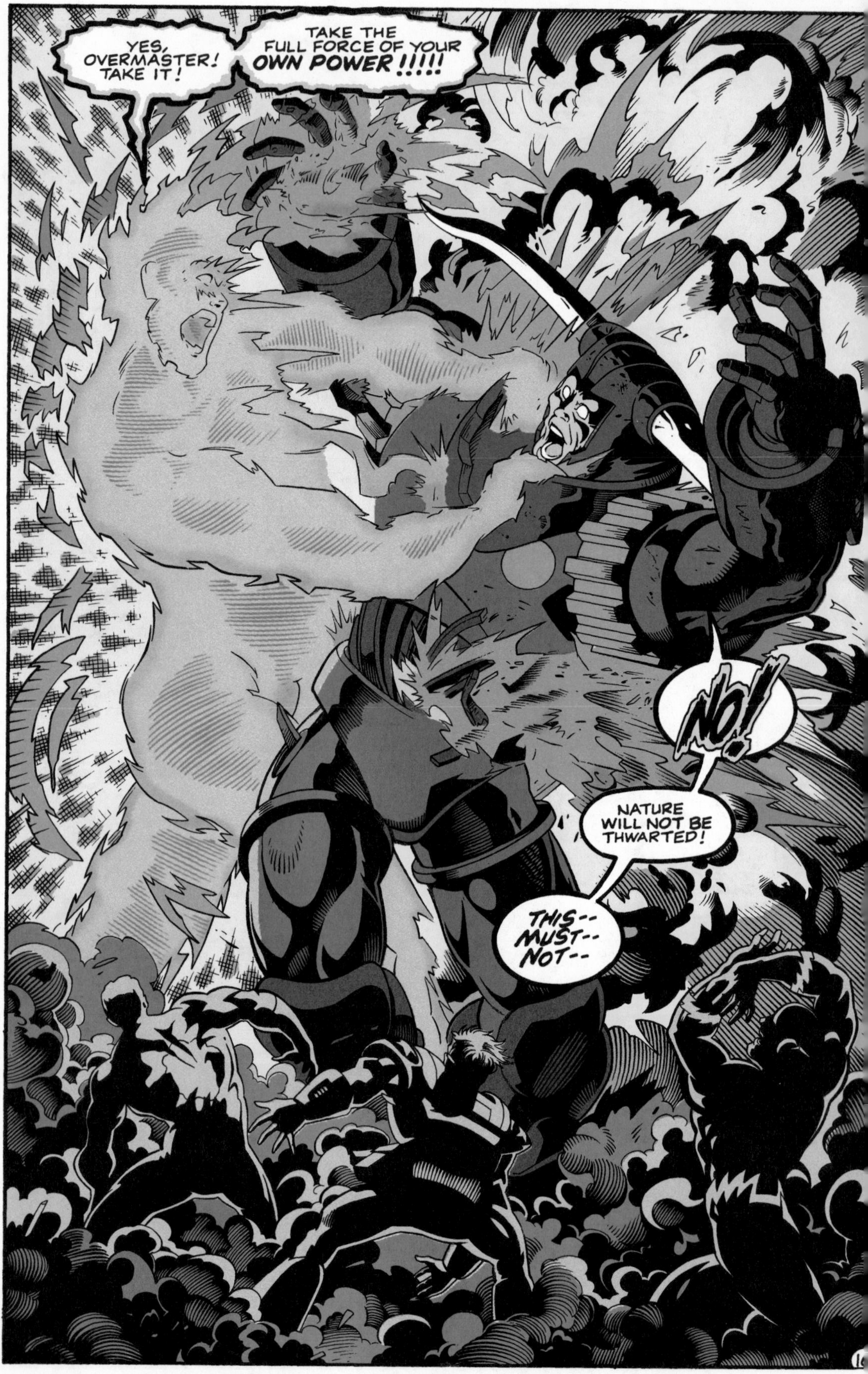
YES, OVERMASTER! TAKE IT!
TAKE THE FULL FORCE OF YOUR OWN POWER!!!!!
NO!!
NATURE WILL NOT BE THWARTED!
THIS-- MUST-- NOT--

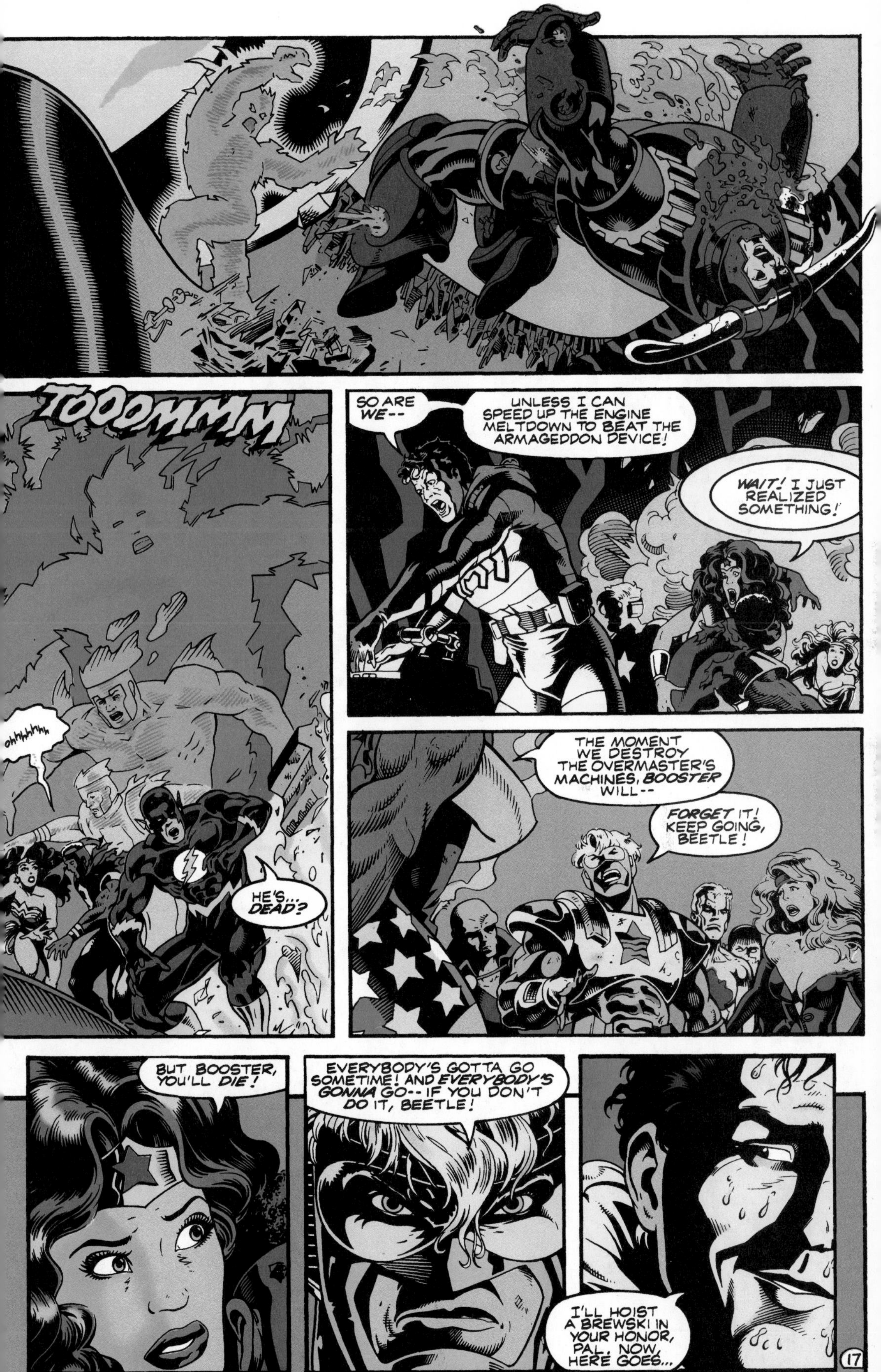
TOOOMMMM
ohhhhhhh
HE'S... DEAD?
SO ARE WE--
UNLESS I CAN SPEED UP THE ENGINE MELTDOWN TO BEAT THE ARMAGEDDON DEVICE!
WAIT! I JUST REALIZED SOMETHING!
THE MOMENT WE DESTROY THE OVERMASTER'S MACHINES, BOOSTER WILL--
FORGET IT! KEEP GOING, BEETLE!
BUT BOOSTER, YOU'LL DIE!
EVERYBODY'S GOTTA GO SOMETIME! AND EVERYBODY'S GONNA GO-- IF YOU DON'T DO IT, BEETLE!
I'LL HOIST A BREWSKI IN YOUR HONOR, PAL. NOW, HERE GOES...

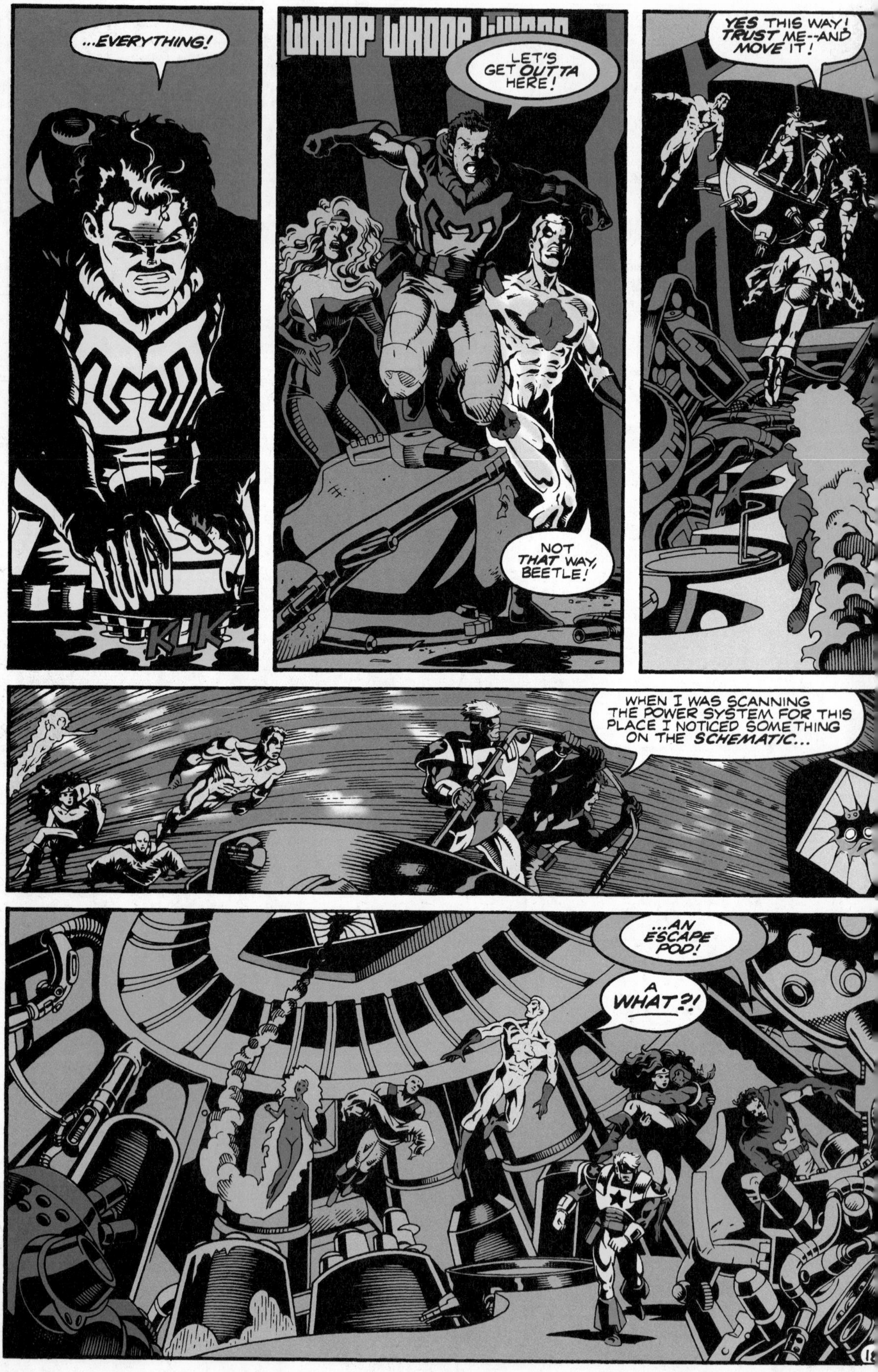
...EVERYTHING!
KLIK
WHOOP WHOOP
LET'S GET OUTTA HERE!
NOT THAT WAY, BEETLE!
YES THIS WAY! TRUST ME--AND MOVE IT!
WHEN I WAS SCANNING THE POWER SYSTEM FOR THIS PLACE I NOTICED SOMETHING ON THE SCHEMATIC...
...AN ESCAPE POD!
A WHAT?!

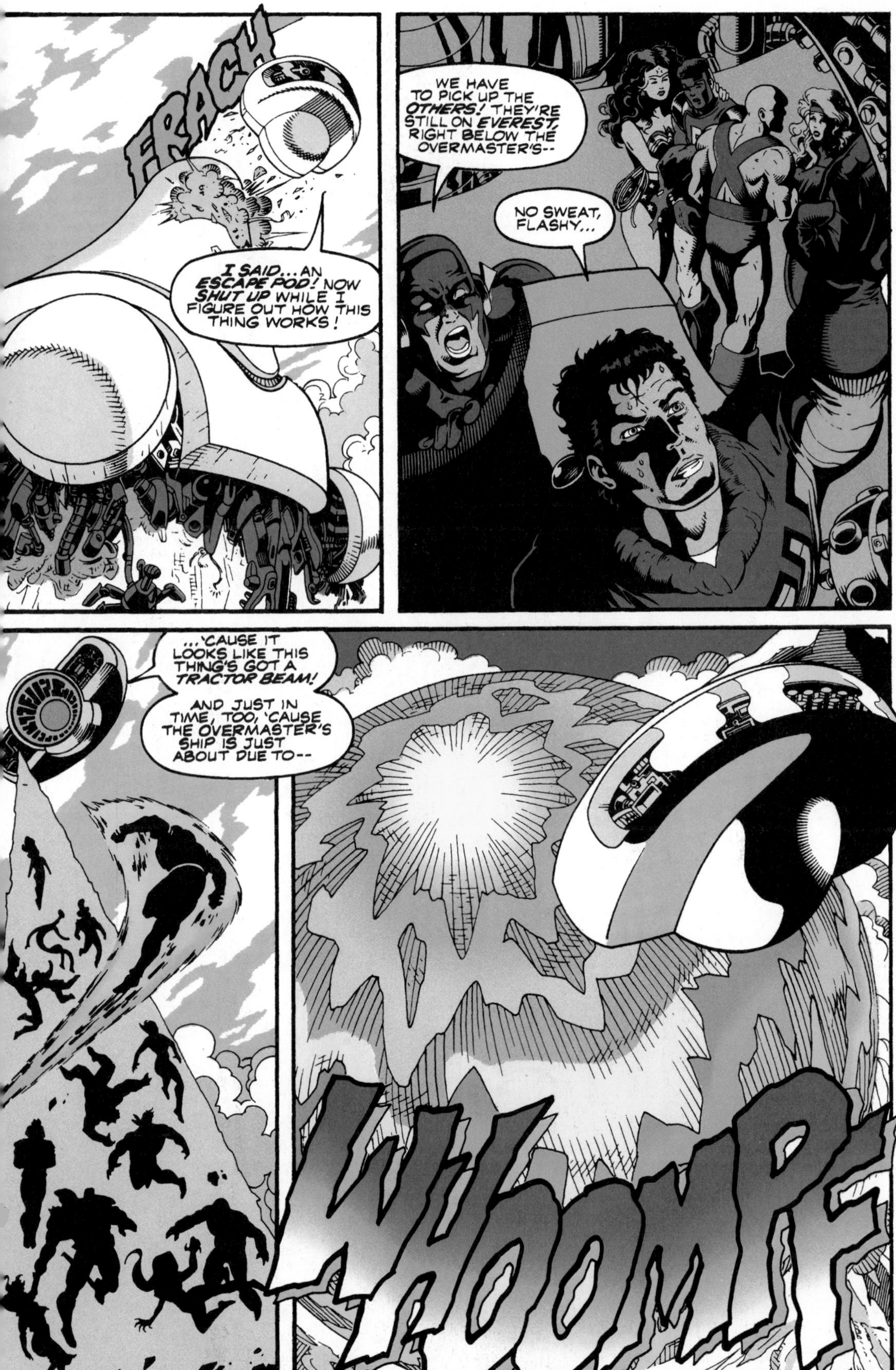
FRACH
I SAID... AN ESCAPE POD! NOW SHUT UP WHILE I FIGURE OUT HOW THIS THING WORKS!
WE HAVE TO PICK UP THE OTHERS! THEY'RE STILL ON EVEREST, RIGHT BELOW THE OVERMASTER'S--
NO SWEAT, FLASHY...
...'CAUSE IT LOOKS LIKE THIS THING'S GOT A TRACTOR BEAM!
AND JUST IN TIME, TOO, 'CAUSE THE OVERMASTER'S SHIP IS JUST ABOUT DUE TO--
WHOOMPF
19

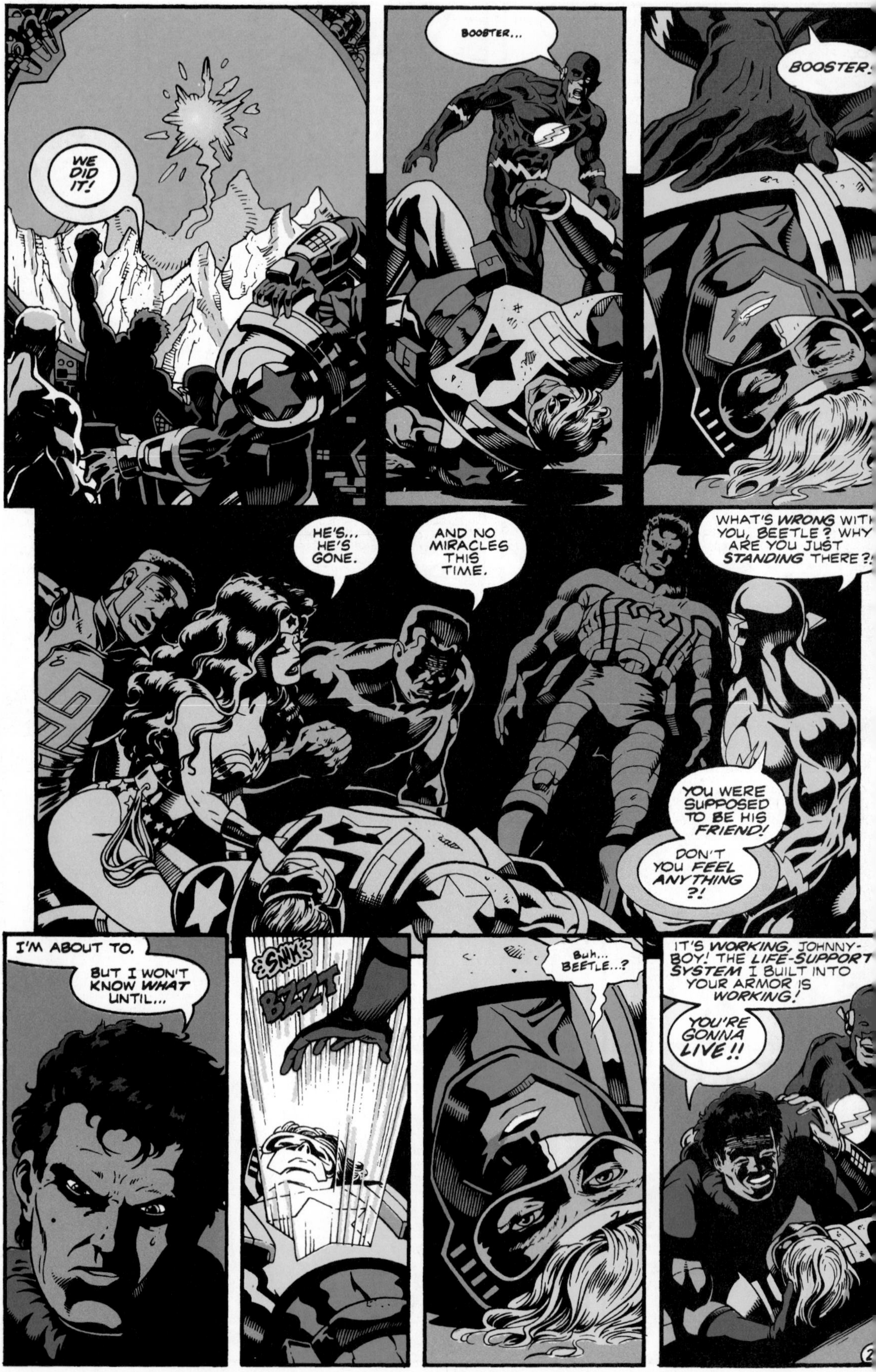
WE DID IT!
BOOSTER...
BOOSTER!
HE'S... HE'S GONE.
AND NO MIRACLES THIS TIME.
WHAT'S WRONG WITH YOU, BEETLE? WHY ARE YOU JUST STANDING THERE?!
YOU WERE SUPPOSED TO BE HIS FRIEND!
DON'T YOU FEEL ANYTHING ?!
I'M ABOUT TO.
BUT I WON'T KNOW WHAT UNTIL...
SNIK
BZZT
Buh... BEETLE...?
IT'S WORKING, JOHNNY-BOY! THE LIFE-SUPPORT SYSTEM I BUILT INTO YOUR ARMOR IS WORKING!
YOU'RE GONNA LIVE!!

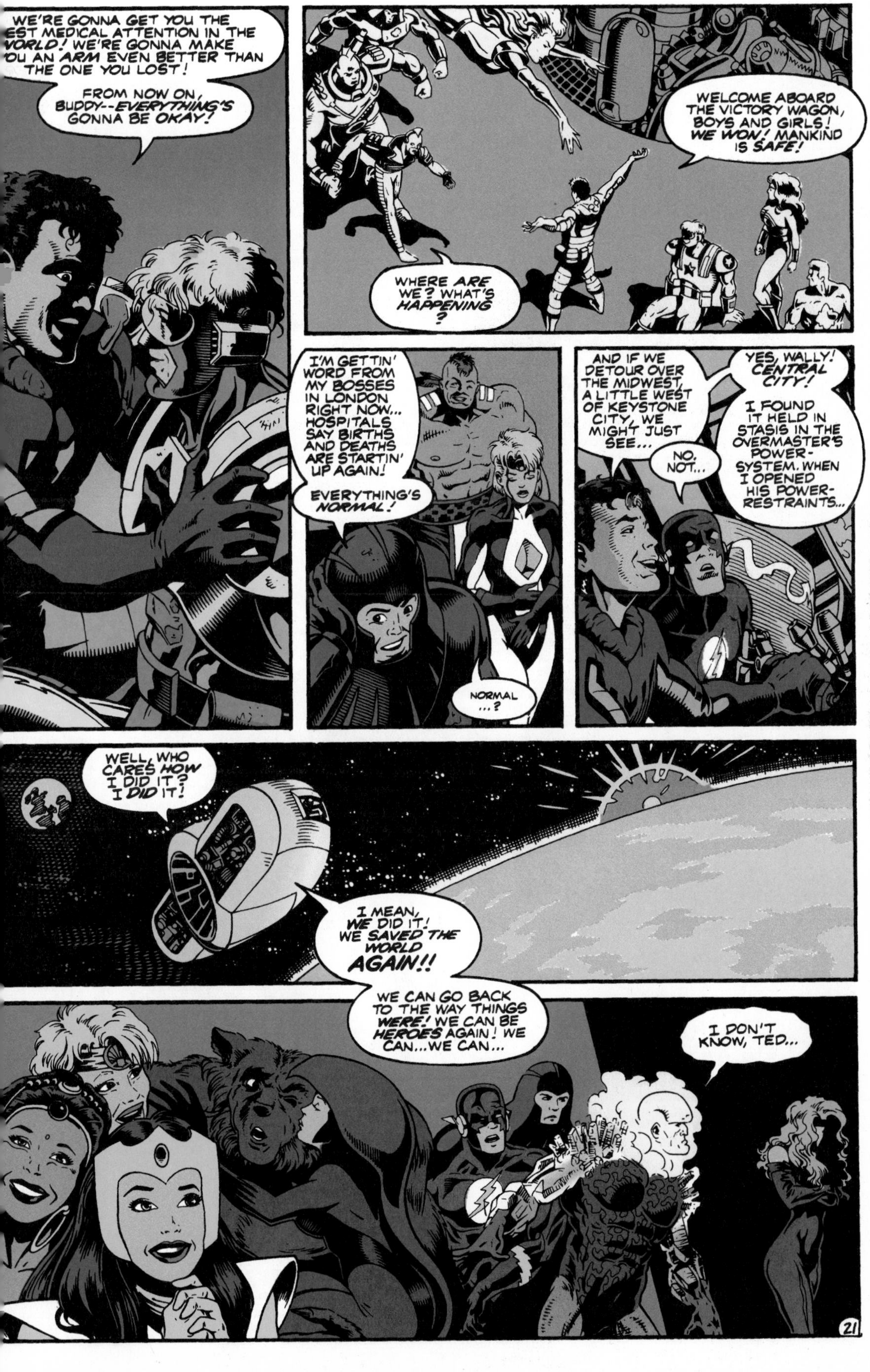
WE'RE GONNA GET YOU THE EST MEDICAL ATTENTION IN THE VORLD! WE'RE GONNA MAKE OU AN ARM EVEN BETTER THAN THE ONE YOU LOST!
FROM NOW ON, BUDDY--EVERYTHING'S GONNA BE OKAY!
WELCOME ABOARD THE VICTORY WAGON, BOYS AND GIRLS! WE WON! MANKIND IS SAFE!
WHERE ARE WE? WHAT'S HAPPENING?
I'M GETTIN' WORD FROM MY BOSSES IN LONDON RIGHT NOW... HOSPITALS SAY BIRTHS AND DEATHS ARE STARTIN' UP AGAIN!
EVERYTHING'S NORMAL!
NORMAL...?
AND IF WE DETOUR OVER THE MIDWEST, A LITTLE WEST OF KEYSTONE CITY, WE MIGHT JUST SEE...
NO. NOT...
YES, WALLY! CENTRAL CITY!
I FOUND IT HELD IN STASIS IN THE OVERMASTER'S POWER-SYSTEM. WHEN I OPENED HIS POWER-RESTRAINTS...
WELL, WHO CARES HOW I DID IT? I DID IT!
I MEAN, WE DID IT! WE SAVED THE WORLD AGAIN!!
WE CAN GO BACK TO THE WAY THINGS WERE! WE CAN BE HEROES AGAIN! WE CAN...WE CAN...
I DON'T KNOW, TED...

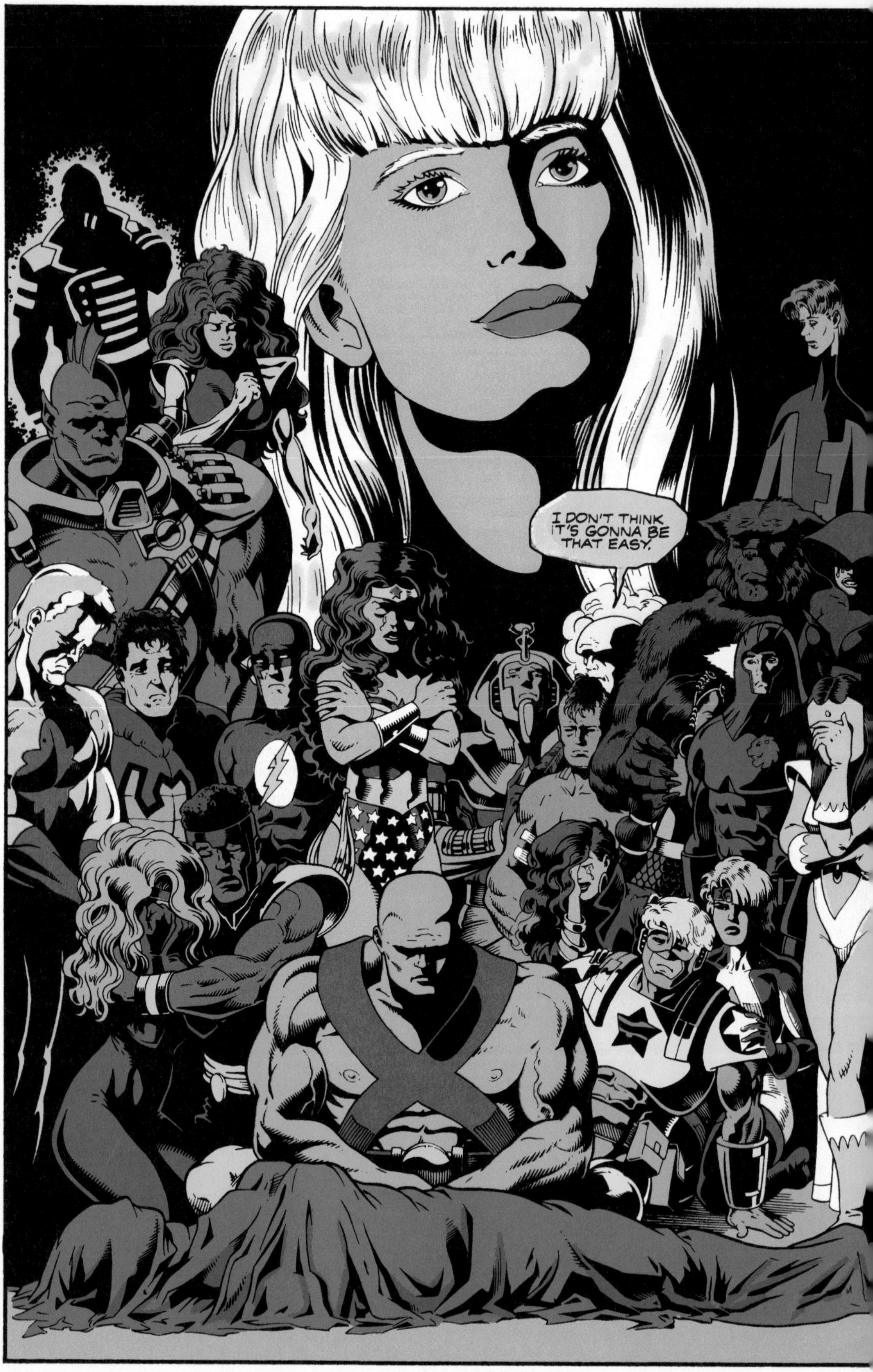
I DON'T THINK IT'S GONNA BE THAT EASY.

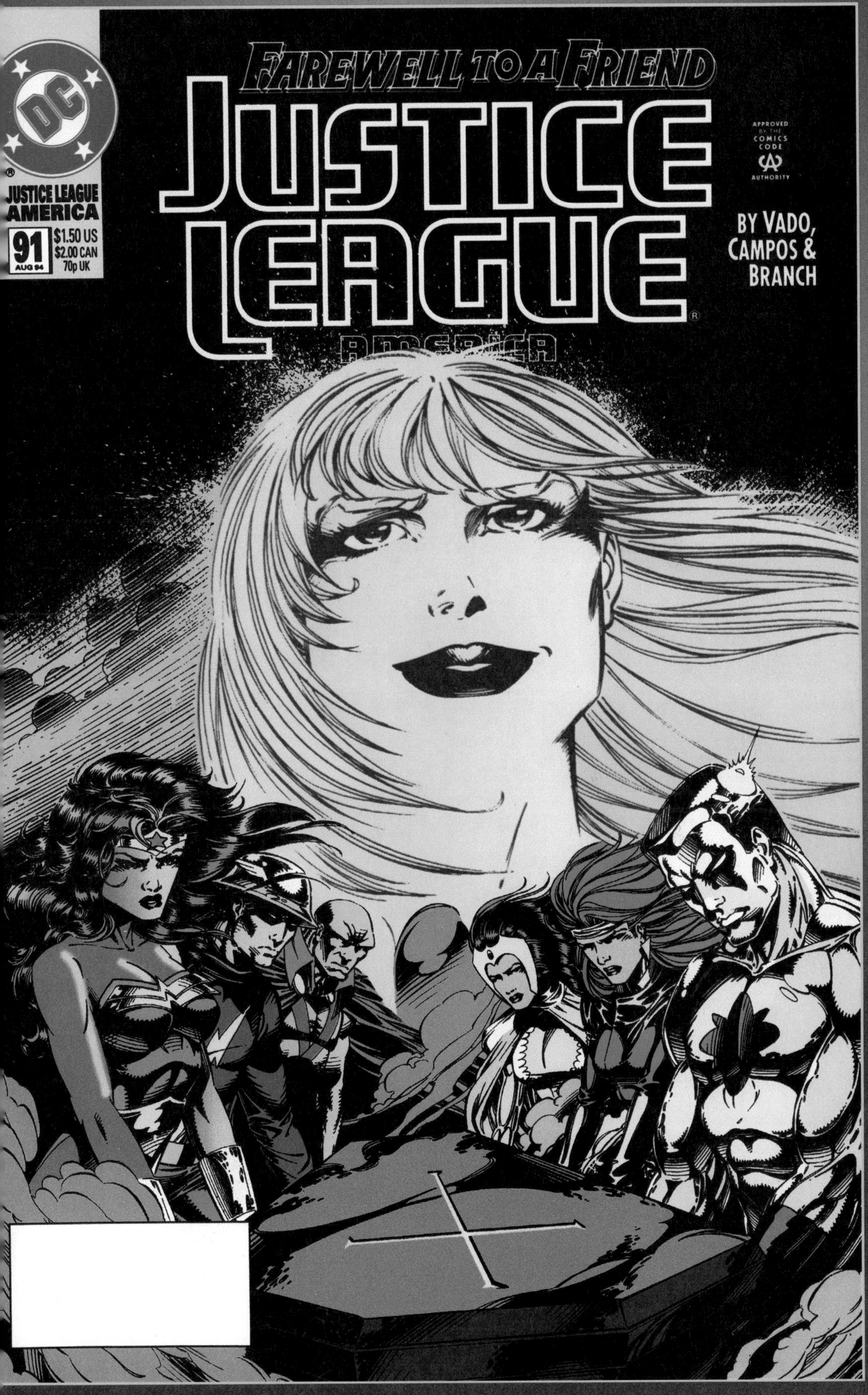

FAREWELL TO A FRIEND
JUSTICE LEAGUE
AMERICA
JUSTICE LEAGUE AMERICA
91
AUG 94
$1.50 US
$2.00 CAN
70p UK
APPROVED BY THE COMICS CODE AUTHORITY
BY VADO, CAMPOS & BRANCH

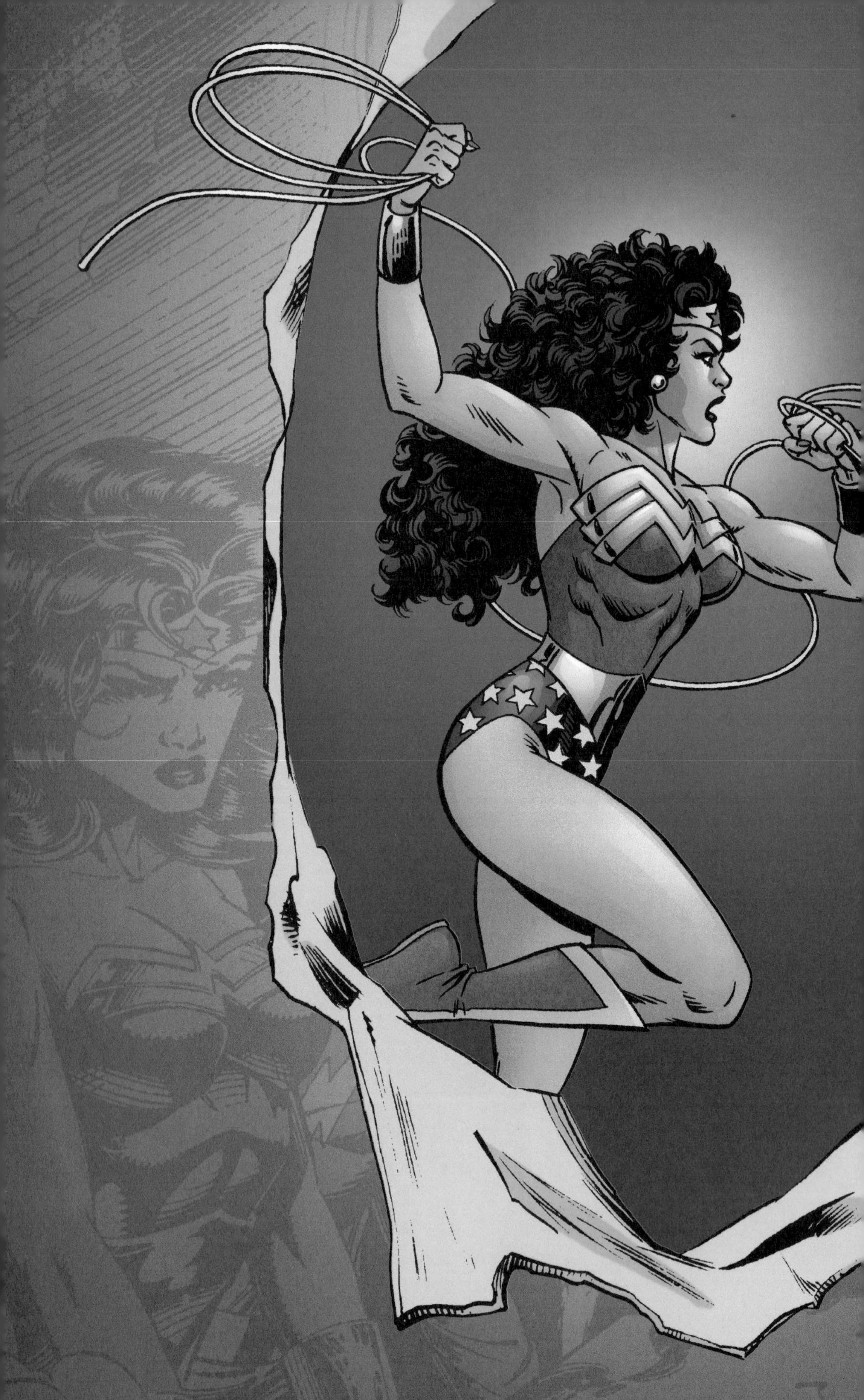

Cover art by **HOWARD PORTER**

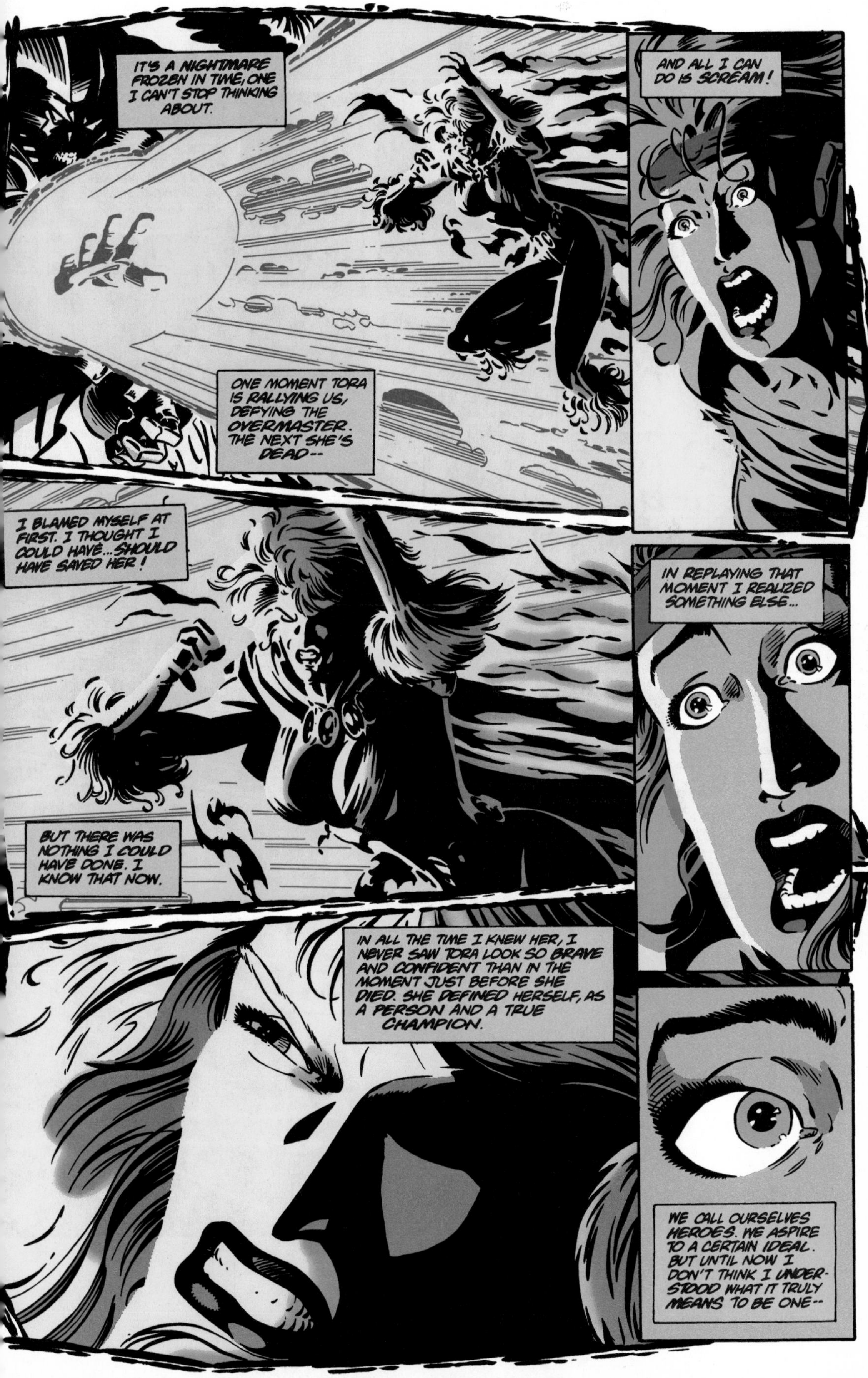
IT'S A NIGHTMARE FROZEN IN TIME, ONE I CAN'T STOP THINKING ABOUT.
ONE MOMENT TORA IS RALLYING US, DEFYING THE OVERMASTER. THE NEXT SHE'S DEAD--
AND ALL I CAN DO IS SCREAM!
I BLAMED MYSELF AT FIRST. I THOUGHT I COULD HAVE...SHOULD HAVE SAVED HER!
BUT THERE WAS NOTHING I COULD HAVE DONE. I KNOW THAT NOW.
IN REPLAYING THAT MOMENT I REALIZED SOMETHING ELSE...
IN ALL THE TIME I KNEW HER, I NEVER SAW TORA LOOK SO BRAVE AND CONFIDENT THAN IN THE MOMENT JUST BEFORE SHE DIED. SHE DEFINED HERSELF, AS A PERSON AND A TRUE CHAMPION.
WE CALL OURSELVES HEROES. WE ASPIRE TO A CERTAIN IDEAL. BUT UNTIL NOW I DON'T THINK I UNDERSTOOD WHAT IT TRULY MEANS TO BE ONE--

HEROES PASSAGE

WRITTEN BY
DAN VADO

PENCILS BY
MARC CAMPOS

INKS BY
KEN BRANCH

COLORS BY
GENE D'ANGELO

LETTERS BY
CLEM ROBINS

ASS'T EDITOR
RUBEN DIAZ

EDITOR
BRIAN AUGUSTYN

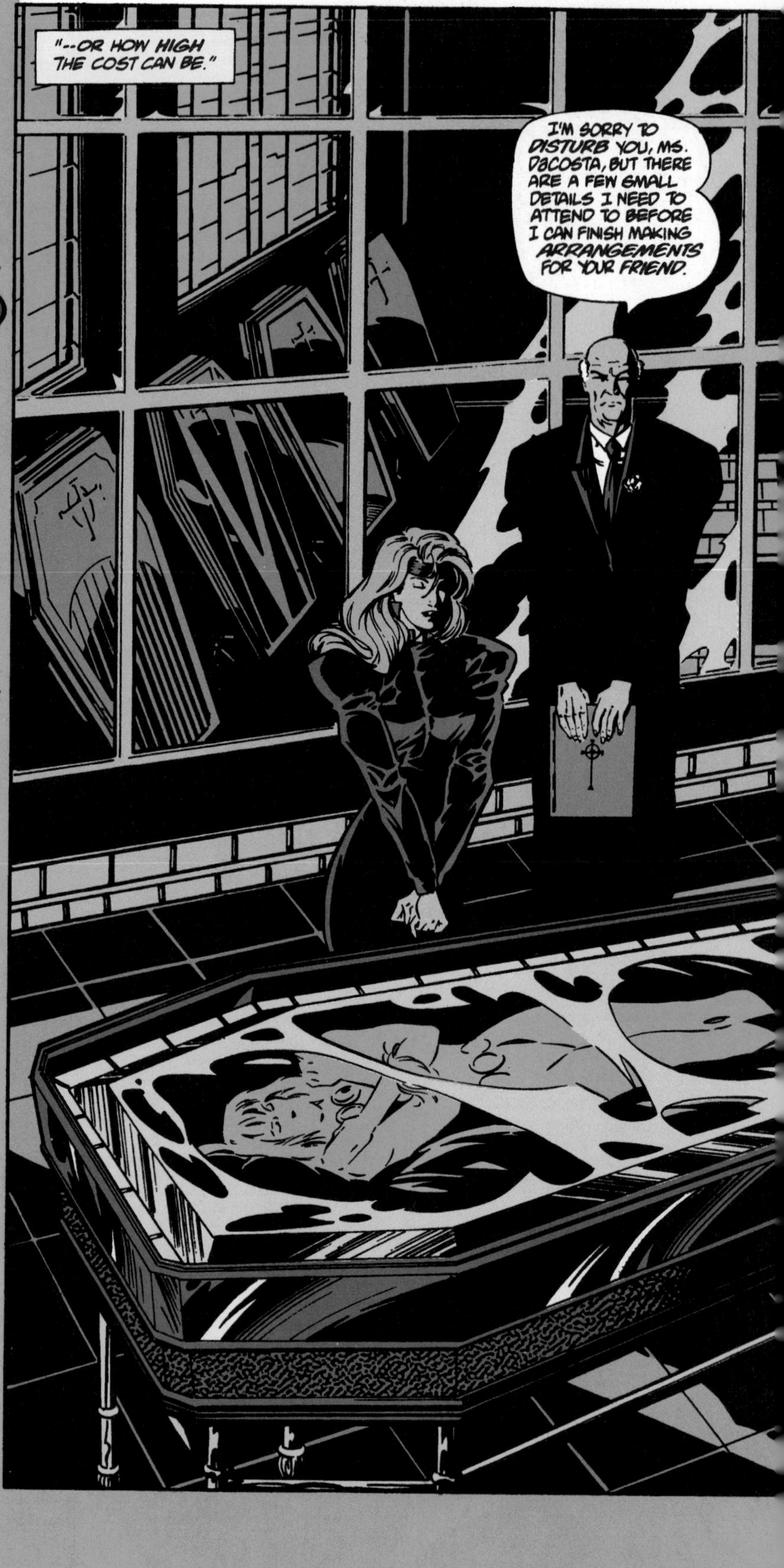
"--OR HOW HIGH THE COST CAN BE."
I'M SORRY TO DISTURB YOU, MS. DACOSTA, BUT THERE ARE A FEW SMALL DETAILS I NEED TO ATTEND TO BEFORE I CAN FINISH MAKING ARRANGEMENTS FOR YOUR FRIEND.

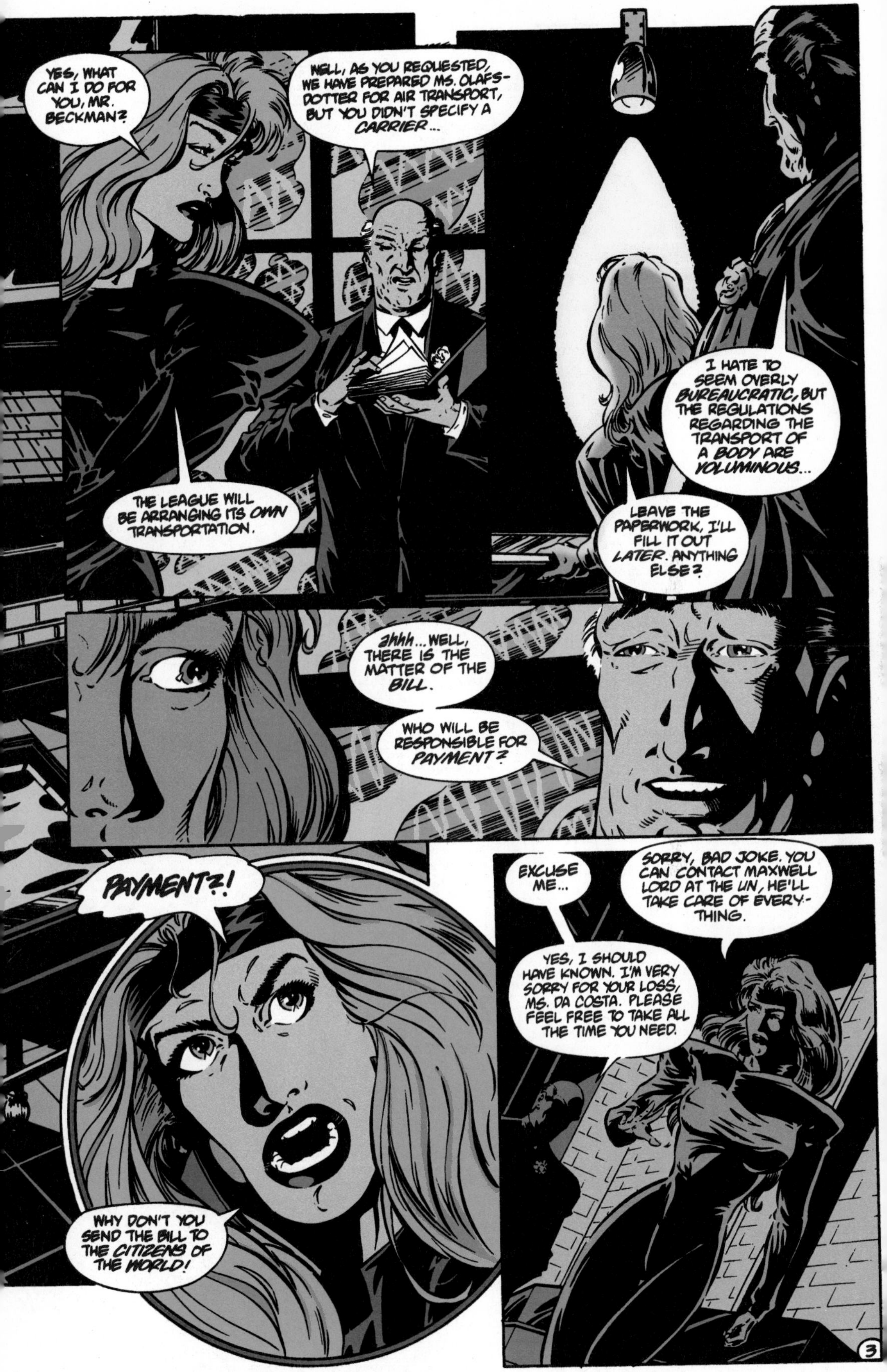
YES, WHAT CAN I DO FOR YOU, MR. BECKMAN?
WELL, AS YOU REQUESTED, WE HAVE PREPARED MS. OLAFS-DOTTER FOR AIR TRANSPORT, BUT YOU DIDN'T SPECIFY A CARRIER...
THE LEAGUE WILL BE ARRANGING ITS OWN TRANSPORTATION.
I HATE TO SEEM OVERLY BUREAUCRATIC, BUT THE REGULATIONS REGARDING THE TRANSPORT OF A BODY ARE VOLUMINOUS...
LEAVE THE PAPERWORK, I'LL FILL IT OUT LATER. ANYTHING ELSE?
ahhh... WELL, THERE IS THE MATTER OF THE BILL.
WHO WILL BE RESPONSIBLE FOR PAYMENT?
PAYMENT?!
WHY DON'T YOU SEND THE BILL TO THE CITIZENS OF THE WORLD!
EXCUSE ME...
SORRY, BAD JOKE. YOU CAN CONTACT MAXWELL LORD AT THE UN, HE'LL TAKE CARE OF EVERY-THING.
YES, I SHOULD HAVE KNOWN. I'M VERY SORRY FOR YOUR LOSS, MS. DA COSTA. PLEASE FEEL FREE TO TAKE ALL THE TIME YOU NEED.
3

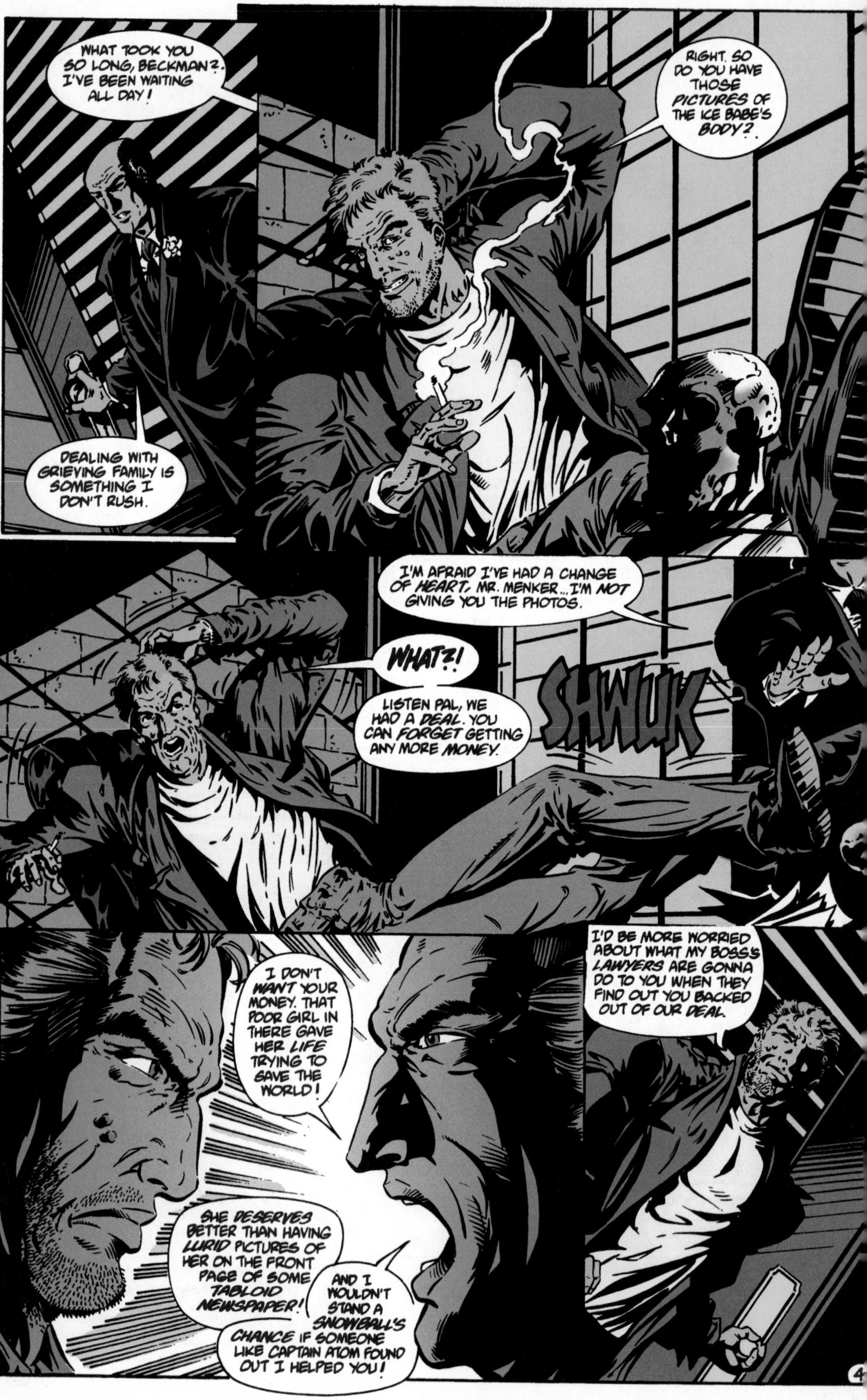
WHAT TOOK YOU SO LONG, BECKMAN?. I'VE BEEN WAITING ALL DAY!
DEALING WITH GRIEVING FAMILY IS SOMETHING I DON'T RUSH.
RIGHT. SO DO YOU HAVE THOSE PICTURES OF THE ICE BABE'S BODY?
I'M AFRAID I'VE HAD A CHANGE OF HEART, MR. MENKER...I'M NOT GIVING YOU THE PHOTOS.
WHAT?!
LISTEN PAL, WE HAD A DEAL. YOU CAN FORGET GETTING ANY MORE MONEY.
SHWUK
I DON'T WANT YOUR MONEY. THAT POOR GIRL IN THERE GAVE HER LIFE TRYING TO SAVE THE WORLD!
SHE DESERVES BETTER THAN HAVING LURID PICTURES OF HER ON THE FRONT PAGE OF SOME TABLOID NEWSPAPER!
AND I WOULDN'T STAND A SNOWBALL'S CHANCE IF SOMEONE LIKE CAPTAIN ATOM FOUND OUT I HELPED YOU!
I'D BE MORE WORRIED ABOUT WHAT MY BOSS'S LAWYERS ARE GONNA DO TO YOU WHEN THEY FIND OUT YOU BACKED OUT OF OUR DEAL.

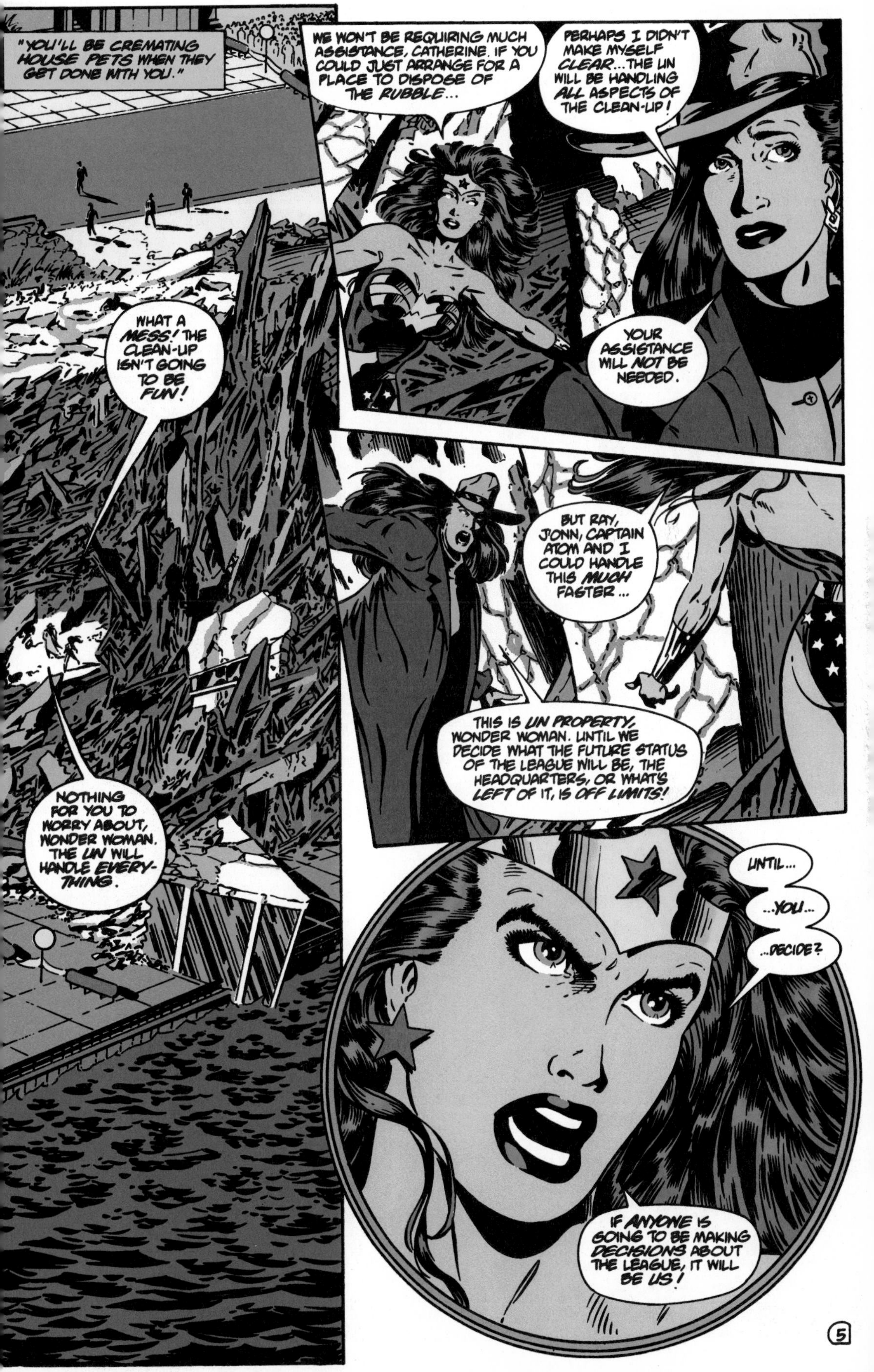
"YOU'LL BE CREMATING HOUSE PETS WHEN THEY GET DONE WITH YOU."
WHAT A MESS! THE CLEAN-UP ISN'T GOING TO BE FUN!
NOTHING FOR YOU TO WORRY ABOUT, WONDER WOMAN. THE UN WILL HANDLE EVERYTHING.
WE WON'T BE REQUIRING MUCH ASSISTANCE, CATHERINE. IF YOU COULD JUST ARRANGE FOR A PLACE TO DISPOSE OF THE RUBBLE...
PERHAPS I DIDN'T MAKE MYSELF CLEAR... THE UN WILL BE HANDLING ALL ASPECTS OF THE CLEAN-UP!
YOUR ASSISTANCE WILL NOT BE NEEDED.
BUT RAY, J'ONN, CAPTAIN ATOM AND I COULD HANDLE THIS MUCH FASTER...
THIS IS UN PROPERTY, WONDER WOMAN. UNTIL WE DECIDE WHAT THE FUTURE STATUS OF THE LEAGUE WILL BE, THE HEADQUARTERS, OR WHAT'S LEFT OF IT, IS OFF LIMITS!
UNTIL...
...YOU...
...DECIDE?
IF ANYONE IS GOING TO BE MAKING DECISIONS ABOUT THE LEAGUE, IT WILL BE US!

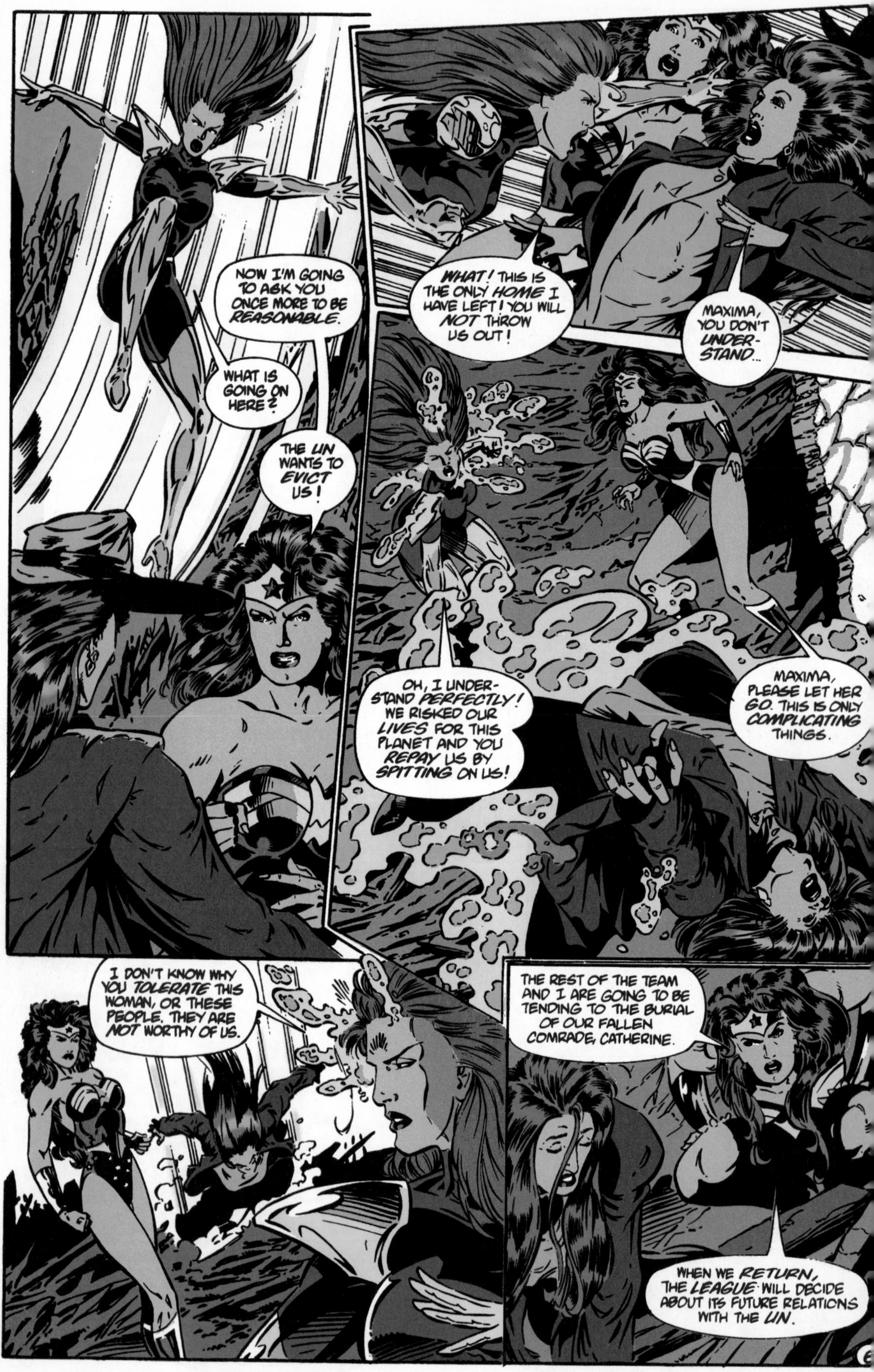

NOW I'M GOING TO ASK YOU ONCE MORE TO BE REASONABLE.
WHAT IS GOING ON HERE?
THE UN WANTS TO EVICT US!
WHAT! THIS IS THE ONLY HOME I HAVE LEFT! YOU WILL NOT THROW US OUT!
MAXIMA, YOU DON'T UNDER-STAND...
OH, I UNDER-STAND PERFECTLY! WE RISKED OUR LIVES FOR THIS PLANET AND YOU REPAY US BY SPITTING ON US!
MAXIMA, PLEASE LET HER GO. THIS IS ONLY COMPLICATING THINGS.
I DON'T KNOW WHY YOU TOLERATE THIS WOMAN, OR THESE PEOPLE. THEY ARE NOT WORTHY OF US.
THE REST OF THE TEAM AND I ARE GOING TO BE TENDING TO THE BURIAL OF OUR FALLEN COMRADE, CATHERINE.
WHEN WE RETURN, THE LEAGUE WILL DECIDE ABOUT ITS FUTURE RELATIONS WITH THE UN.
6

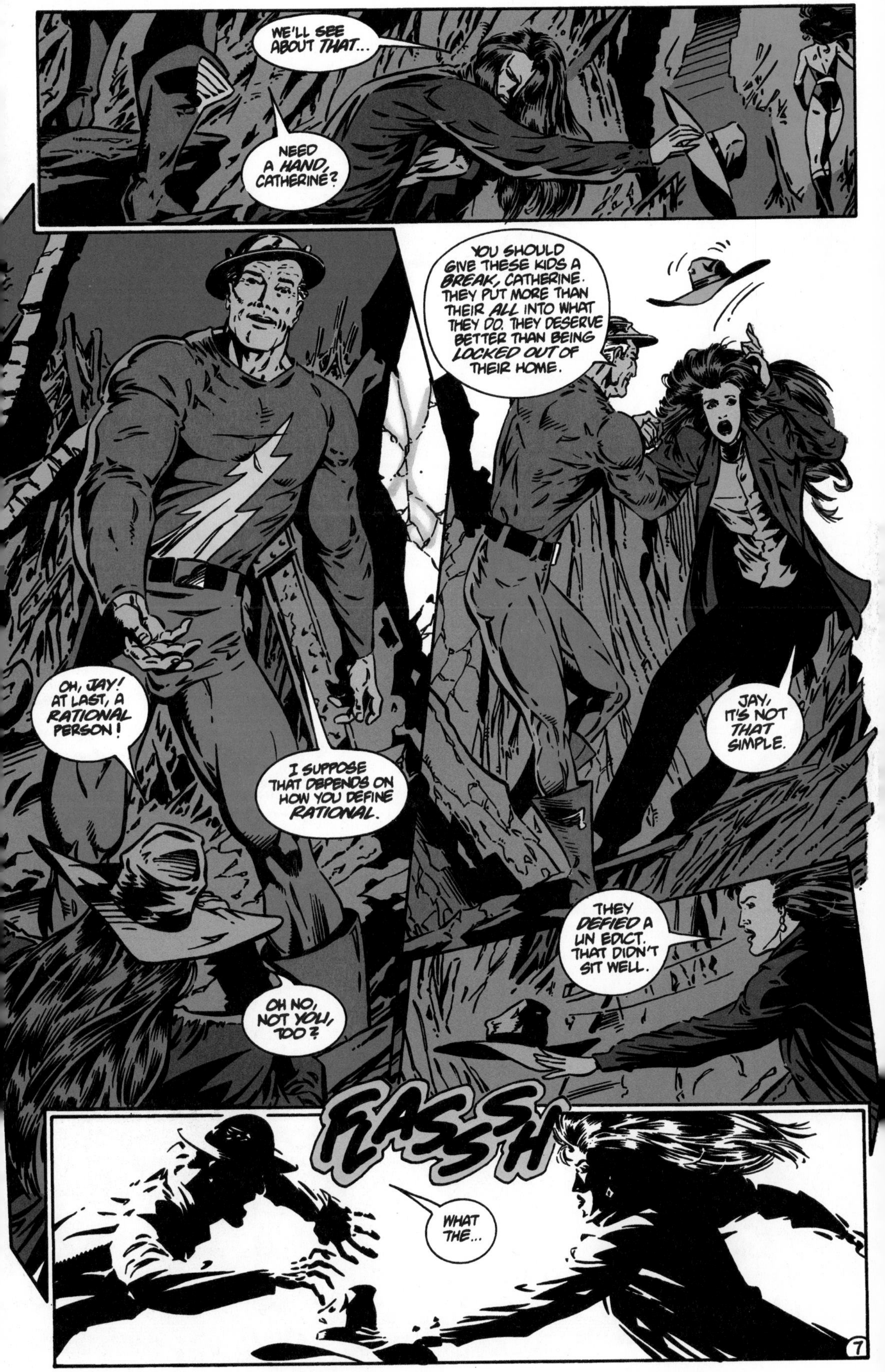
WE'LL SEE ABOUT THAT...
NEED A HAND, CATHERINE?
YOU SHOULD GIVE THESE KIDS A BREAK, CATHERINE. THEY PUT MORE THAN THEIR ALL INTO WHAT THEY DO. THEY DESERVE BETTER THAN BEING LOCKED OUT OF THEIR HOME.
OH, JAY! AT LAST, A RATIONAL PERSON!
I SUPPOSE THAT DEPENDS ON HOW YOU DEFINE RATIONAL.
JAY, IT'S NOT THAT SIMPLE.
THEY DEFIED A UN EDICT. THAT DIDN'T SIT WELL.
OH NO, NOT YOU, TOO?
FLASSH
WHAT THE...
7

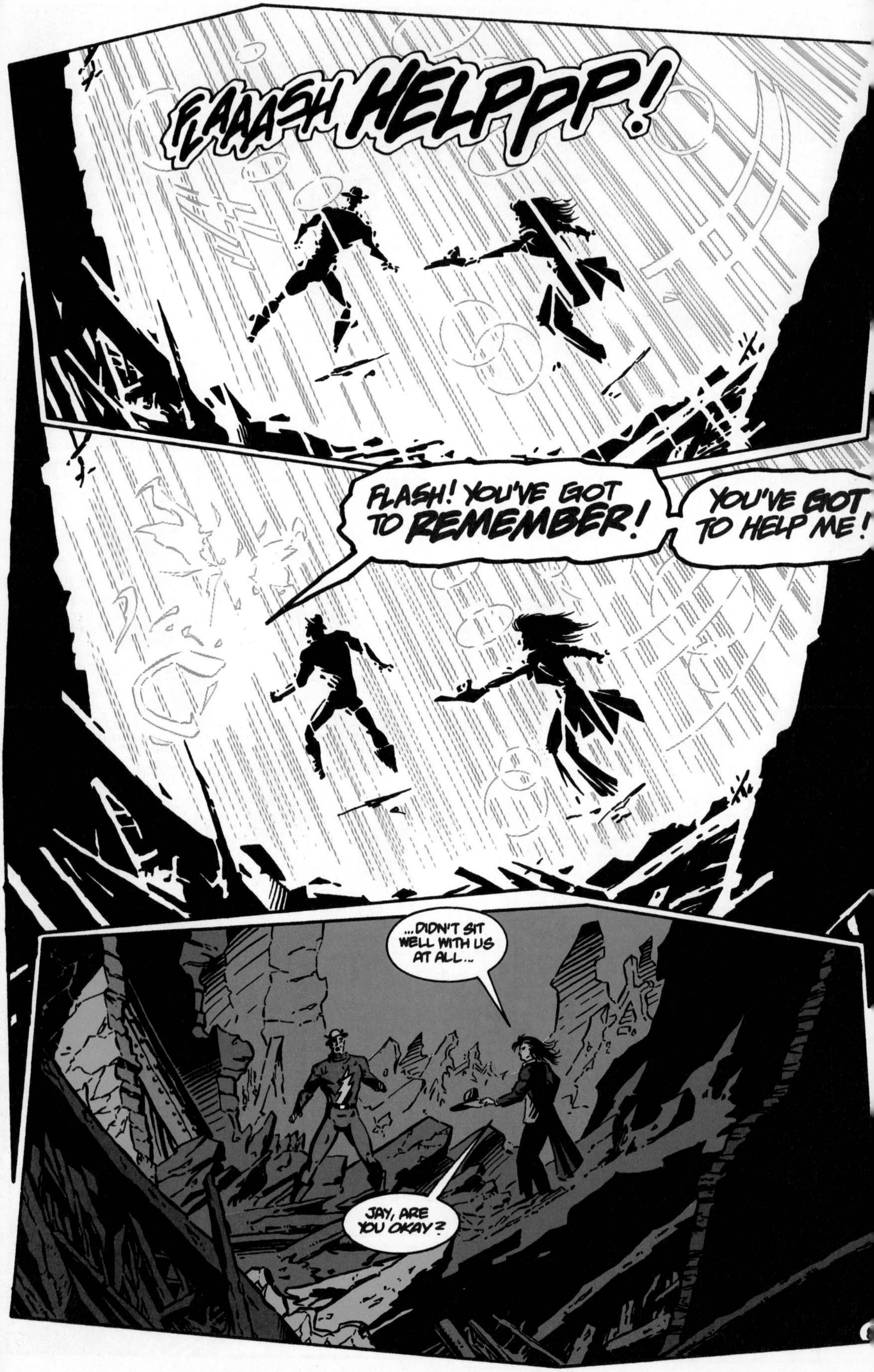
FLAAASH HELPPP!
FLASH! YOU'VE GOT TO REMEMBER!
YOU'VE GOT TO HELP ME!
...DIDN'T SIT WELL WITH US AT ALL...
JAY, ARE YOU OKAY?

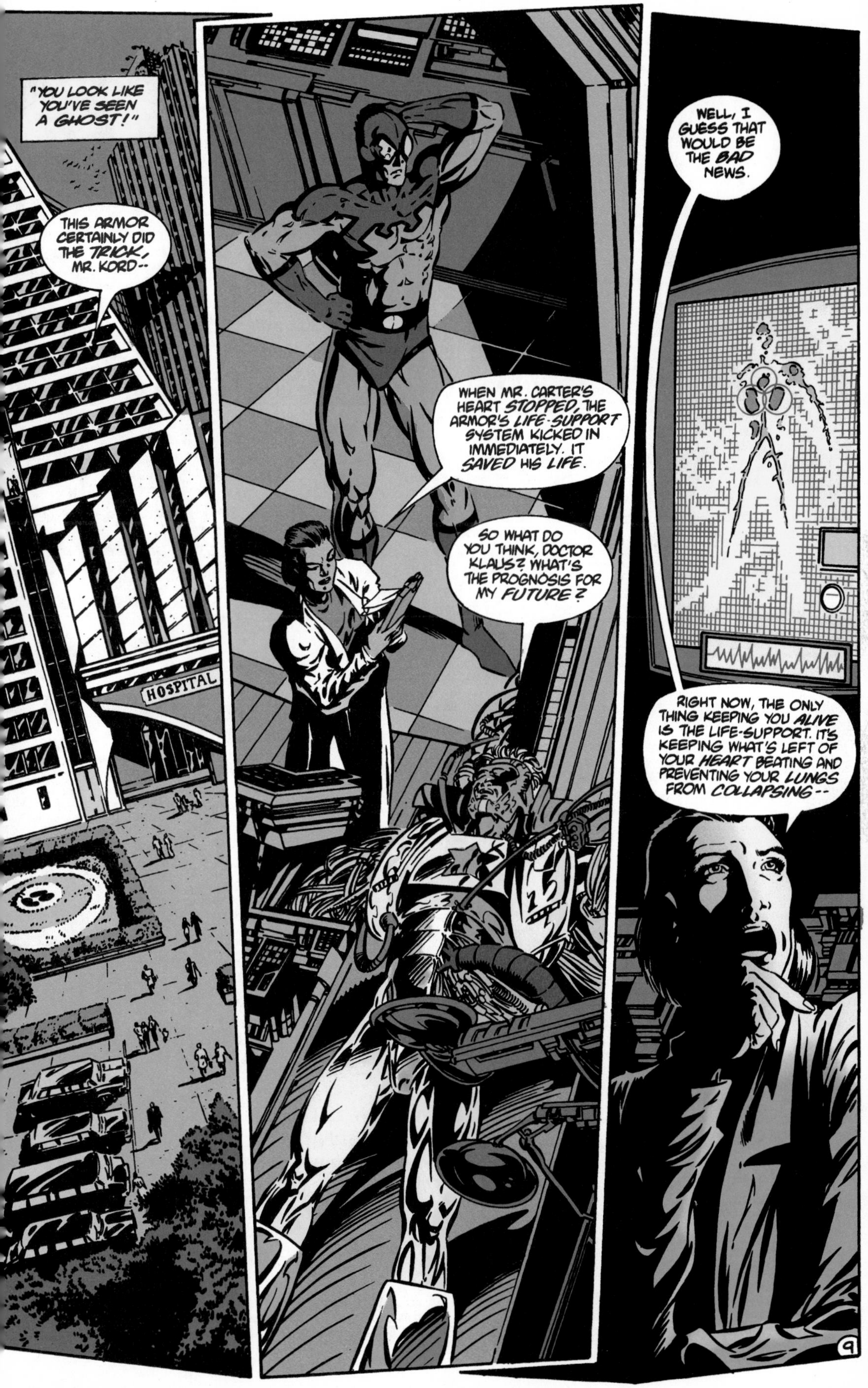
"YOU LOOK LIKE YOU'VE SEEN A GHOST!"
THIS ARMOR CERTAINLY DID THE TRICK, MR. KORD--
HOSPITAL
WHEN MR. CARTER'S HEART STOPPED, THE ARMOR'S LIFE-SUPPORT SYSTEM KICKED IN IMMEDIATELY. IT SAVED HIS LIFE.
SO WHAT DO YOU THINK, DOCTOR KLAUS? WHAT'S THE PROGNOSIS FOR MY FUTURE?
WELL, I GUESS THAT WOULD BE THE BAD NEWS.
RIGHT NOW, THE ONLY THING KEEPING YOU ALIVE IS THE LIFE-SUPPORT. IT'S KEEPING WHAT'S LEFT OF YOUR HEART BEATING AND PREVENTING YOUR LUNGS FROM COLLAPSING--

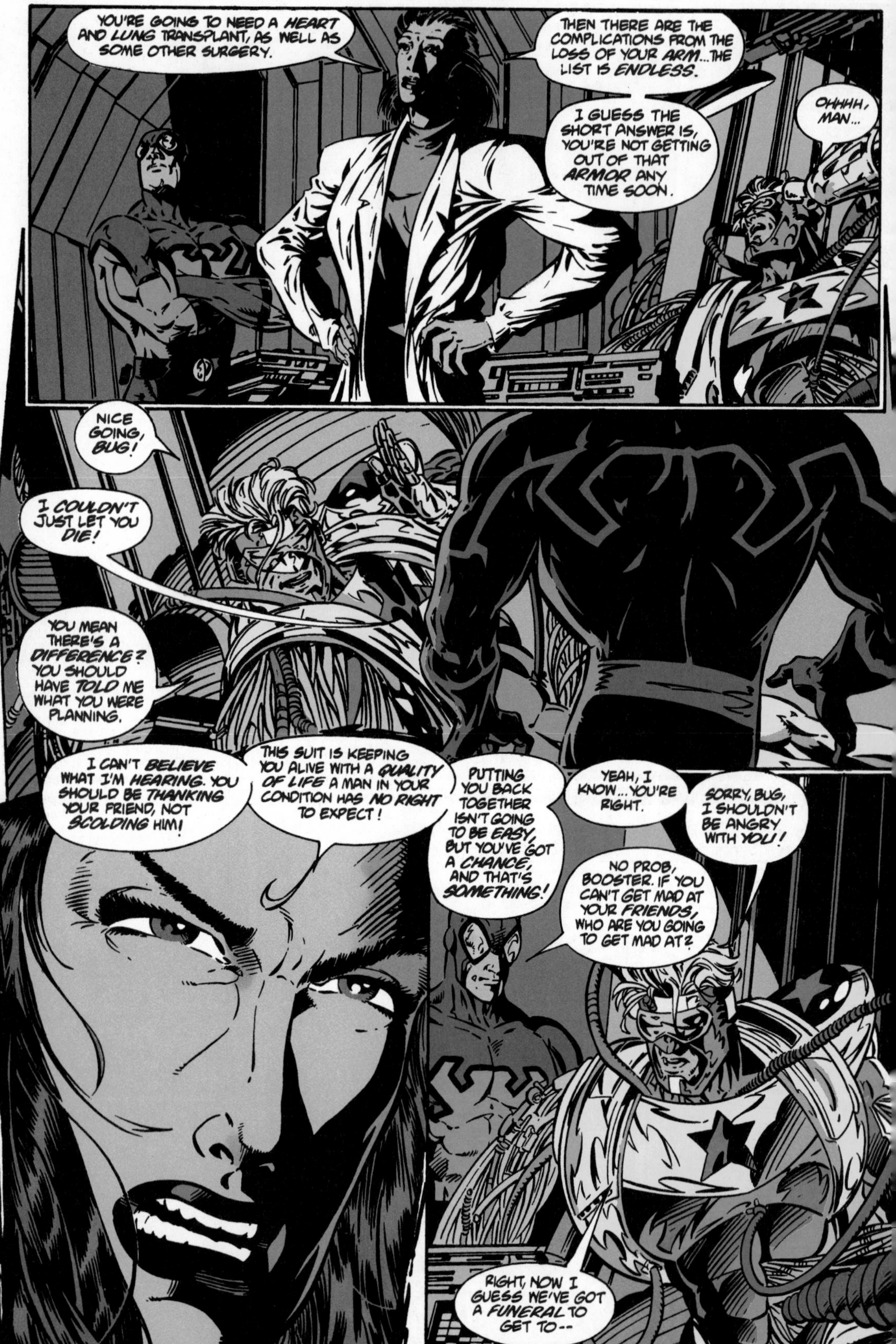
YOU'RE GOING TO NEED A HEART AND LUNG TRANSPLANT, AS WELL AS SOME OTHER SURGERY.
THEN THERE ARE THE COMPLICATIONS FROM THE LOSS OF YOUR ARM... THE LIST IS ENDLESS.
I GUESS THE SHORT ANSWER IS, YOU'RE NOT GETTING OUT OF THAT ARMOR ANY TIME SOON.
OHHHH, MAN...
NICE GOING, BUG!
I COULDN'T JUST LET YOU DIE!
YOU MEAN THERE'S A DIFFERENCE? YOU SHOULD HAVE TOLD ME WHAT YOU WERE PLANNING.
I CAN'T BELIEVE WHAT I'M HEARING. YOU SHOULD BE THANKING YOUR FRIEND, NOT SCOLDING HIM!
THIS SUIT IS KEEPING YOU ALIVE WITH A QUALITY OF LIFE A MAN IN YOUR CONDITION HAS NO RIGHT TO EXPECT!
PUTTING YOU BACK TOGETHER ISN'T GOING TO BE EASY, BUT YOU'VE GOT A CHANCE, AND THAT'S SOMETHING!
YEAH, I KNOW... YOU'RE RIGHT.
SORRY, BUG, I SHOULDN'T BE ANGRY WITH YOU!
NO PROB, BOOSTER. IF YOU CAN'T GET MAD AT YOUR FRIENDS, WHO ARE YOU GOING TO GET MAD AT?
RIGHT, NOW I GUESS WE'VE GOT A FUNERAL TO GET TO--

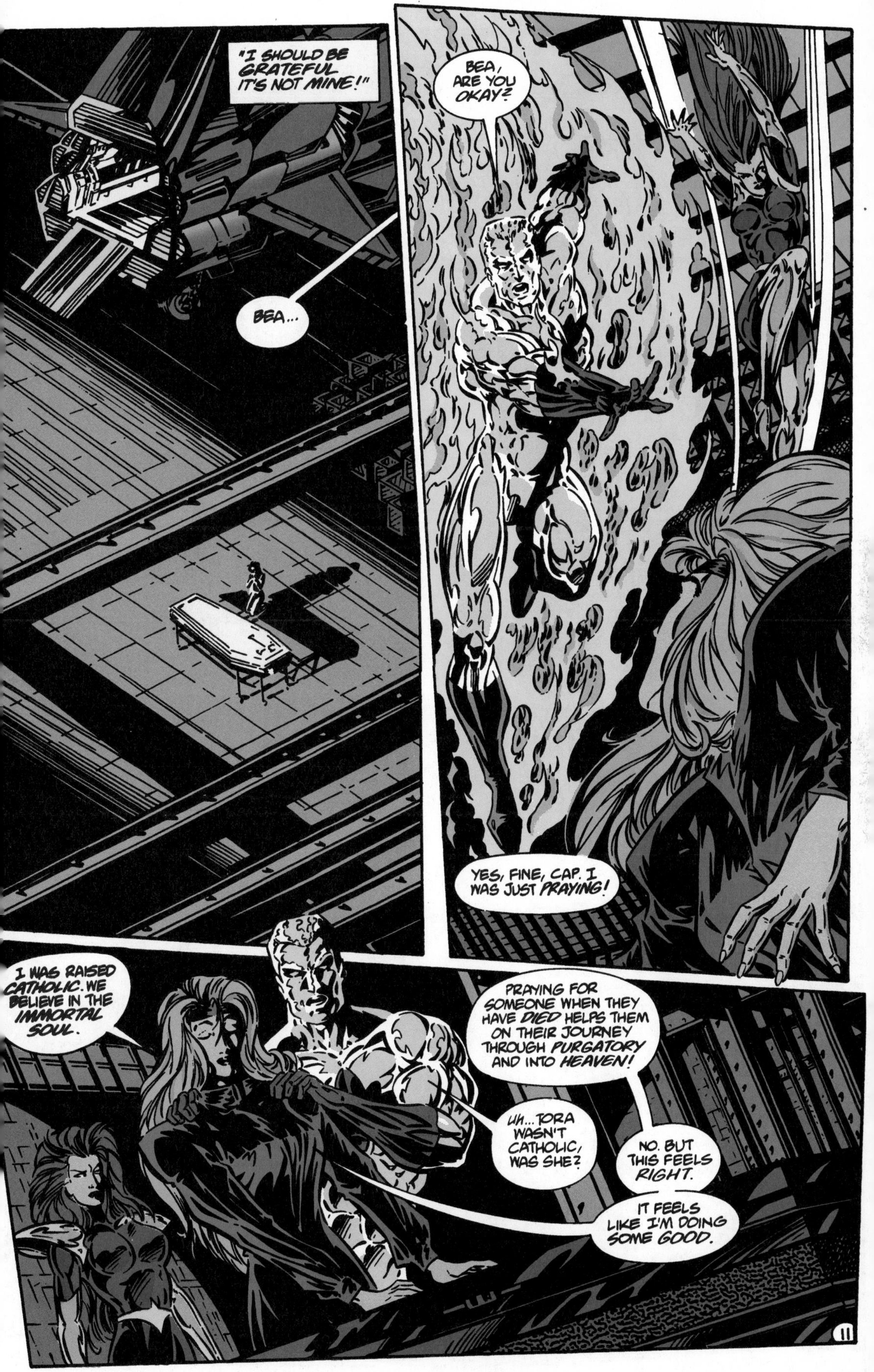
"I SHOULD BE GRATEFUL IT'S NOT MINE!"
BEA...
BEA, ARE YOU OKAY?
YES, FINE, CAP. I WAS JUST PRAYING!
I WAS RAISED CATHOLIC. WE BELIEVE IN THE IMMORTAL SOUL.
PRAYING FOR SOMEONE WHEN THEY HAVE DIED HELPS THEM ON THEIR JOURNEY THROUGH PURGATORY AND INTO HEAVEN!
UH... TORA WASN'T CATHOLIC, WAS SHE?
NO. BUT THIS FEELS RIGHT.
IT FEELS LIKE I'M DOING SOME GOOD.

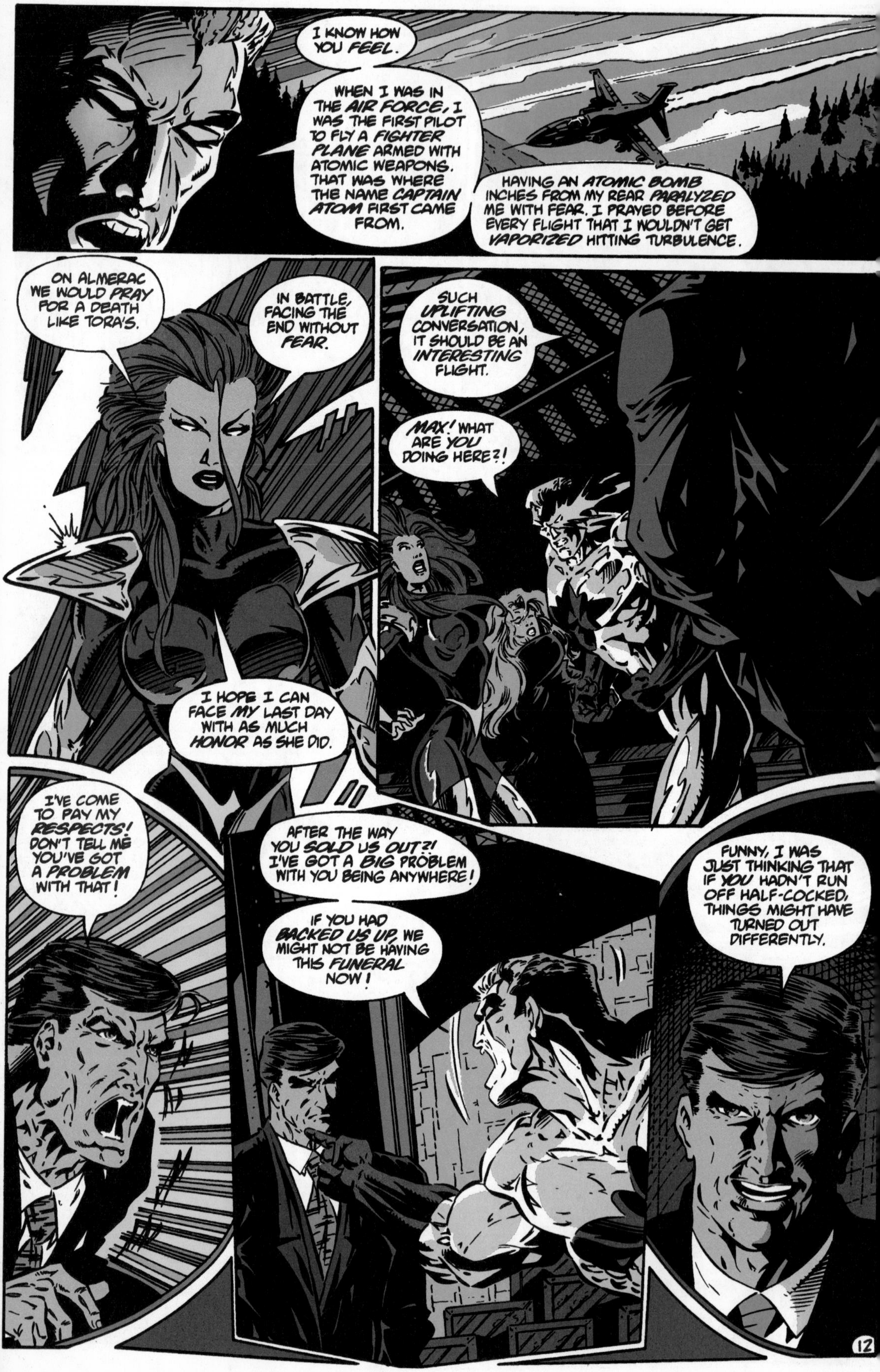

I KNOW HOW YOU FEEL.
WHEN I WAS IN THE AIR FORCE, I WAS THE FIRST PILOT TO FLY A FIGHTER PLANE ARMED WITH ATOMIC WEAPONS. THAT WAS WHERE THE NAME CAPTAIN ATOM FIRST CAME FROM.
HAVING AN ATOMIC BOMB INCHES FROM MY REAR PARALYZED ME WITH FEAR. I PRAYED BEFORE EVERY FLIGHT THAT I WOULDN'T GET VAPORIZED HITTING TURBULENCE.
ON ALMERAC WE WOULD PRAY FOR A DEATH LIKE TORA'S.
IN BATTLE, FACING THE END WITHOUT FEAR.
I HOPE I CAN FACE MY LAST DAY WITH AS MUCH HONOR AS SHE DID.
SUCH UPLIFTING CONVERSATION, IT SHOULD BE AN INTERESTING FLIGHT.
MAX! WHAT ARE YOU DOING HERE?!
I'VE COME TO PAY MY RESPECTS! DON'T TELL ME YOU'VE GOT A PROBLEM WITH THAT!
AFTER THE WAY YOU SOLD US OUT?! I'VE GOT A BIG PROBLEM WITH YOU BEING ANYWHERE!
IF YOU HAD BACKED US UP, WE MIGHT NOT BE HAVING THIS FUNERAL NOW!
FUNNY, I WAS JUST THINKING THAT IF YOU HADN'T RUN OFF HALF-COCKED, THINGS MIGHT HAVE TURNED OUT DIFFERENTLY.

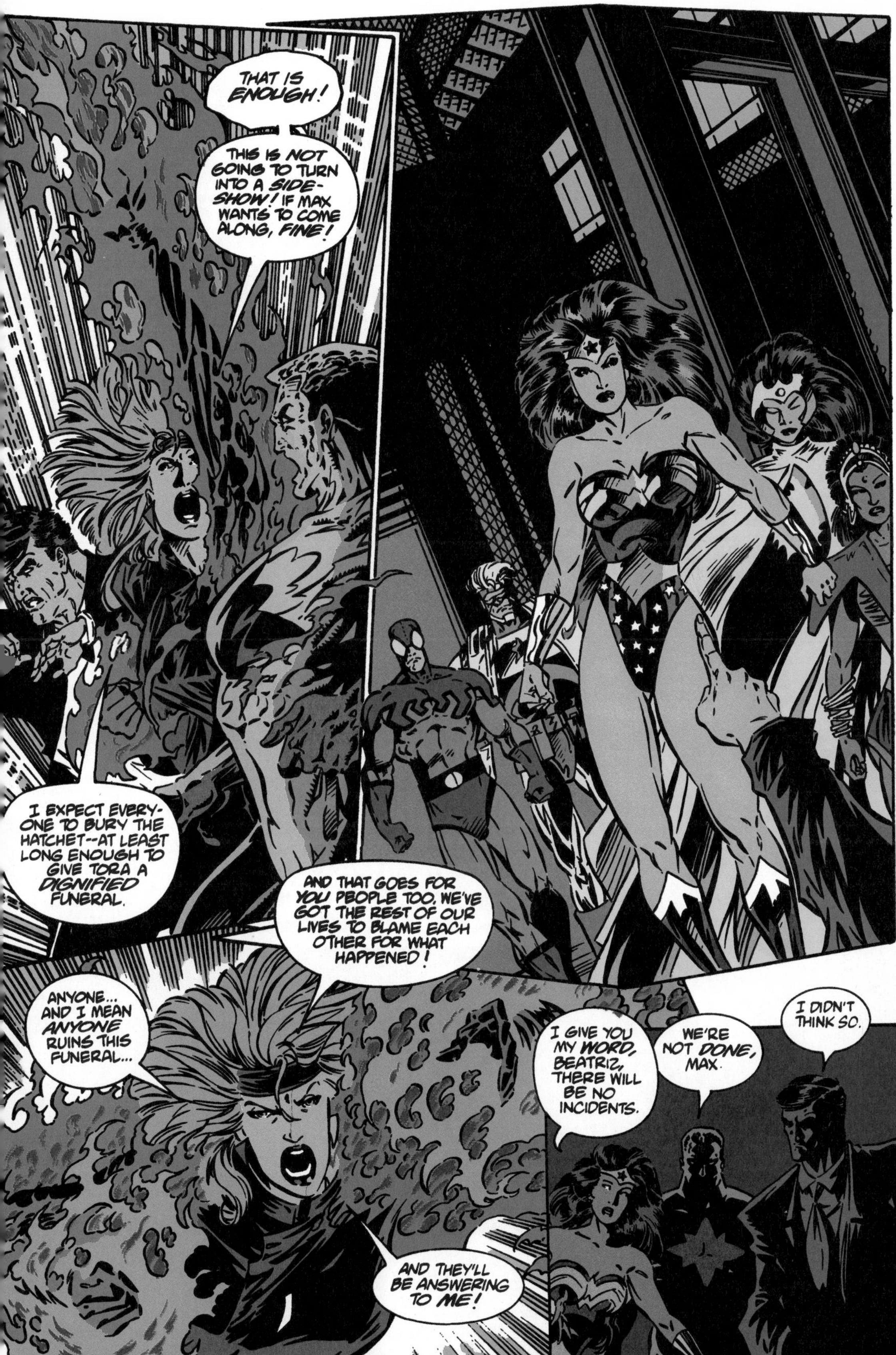

THAT IS ENOUGH!
THIS IS NOT GOING TO TURN INTO A SIDE-SHOW! IF MAX WANTS TO COME ALONG, FINE!
I EXPECT EVERY-ONE TO BURY THE HATCHET--AT LEAST LONG ENOUGH TO GIVE TORA A DIGNIFIED FUNERAL.
AND THAT GOES FOR YOU PEOPLE TOO, WE'VE GOT THE REST OF OUR LIVES TO BLAME EACH OTHER FOR WHAT HAPPENED!
ANYONE... AND I MEAN ANYONE RUINS THIS FUNERAL...
AND THEY'LL BE ANSWERING TO ME!
I GIVE YOU MY WORD, BEATRIZ, THERE WILL BE NO INCIDENTS.
WE'RE NOT DONE, MAX.
I DIDN'T THINK SO.

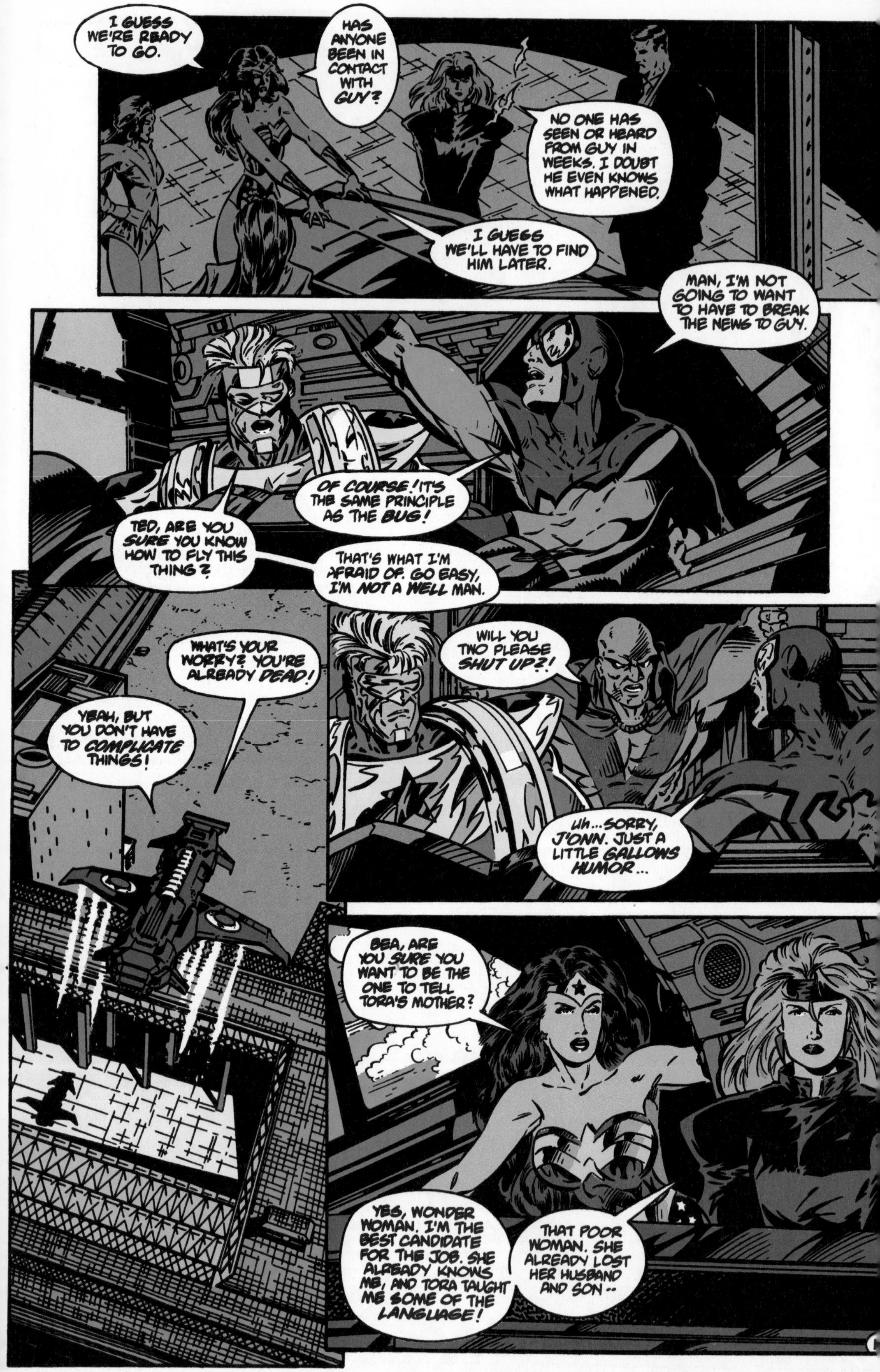
I GUESS WE'RE READY TO GO.
HAS ANYONE BEEN IN CONTACT WITH GUY?
NO ONE HAS SEEN OR HEARD FROM GUY IN WEEKS. I DOUBT HE EVEN KNOWS WHAT HAPPENED.
I GUESS WE'LL HAVE TO FIND HIM LATER.
MAN, I'M NOT GOING TO WANT TO HAVE TO BREAK THE NEWS TO GUY.
TED, ARE YOU SURE YOU KNOW HOW TO FLY THIS THING?
OF COURSE! IT'S THE SAME PRINCIPLE AS THE BUG!
THAT'S WHAT I'M AFRAID OF. GO EASY, I'M NOT A WELL MAN.
WHAT'S YOUR WORRY? YOU'RE ALREADY DEAD!
YEAH, BUT YOU DON'T HAVE TO COMPLICATE THINGS!
WILL YOU TWO PLEASE SHUT UP?!
Uh... SORRY, J'ONN. JUST A LITTLE GALLOWS HUMOR...
BEA, ARE YOU SURE YOU WANT TO BE THE ONE TO TELL TORA'S MOTHER?
THAT POOR WOMAN. SHE ALREADY LOST HER HUSBAND AND SON --
YES, WONDER WOMAN. I'M THE BEST CANDIDATE FOR THE JOB. SHE ALREADY KNOWS ME, AND TORA TAUGHT ME SOME OF THE LANGUAGE!

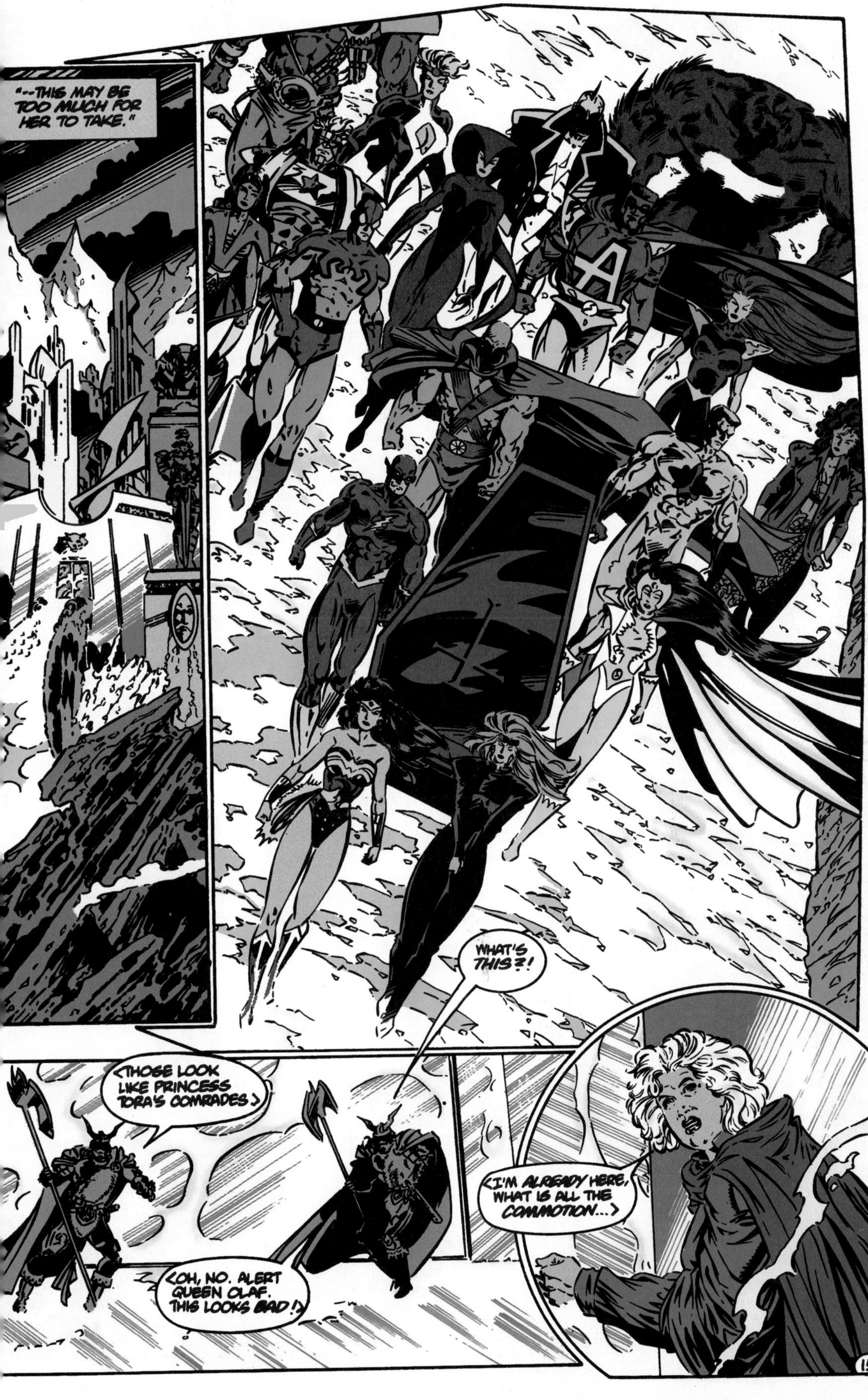
"--THIS MAY BE TOO MUCH FOR HER TO TAKE."
WHAT'S THIS?!
<THOSE LOOK LIKE PRINCESS TORA'S COMRADES.>
<OH, NO. ALERT QUEEN OLAF. THIS LOOKS BAD!>
<I'M ALREADY HERE, WHAT IS ALL THE COMMOTION...>

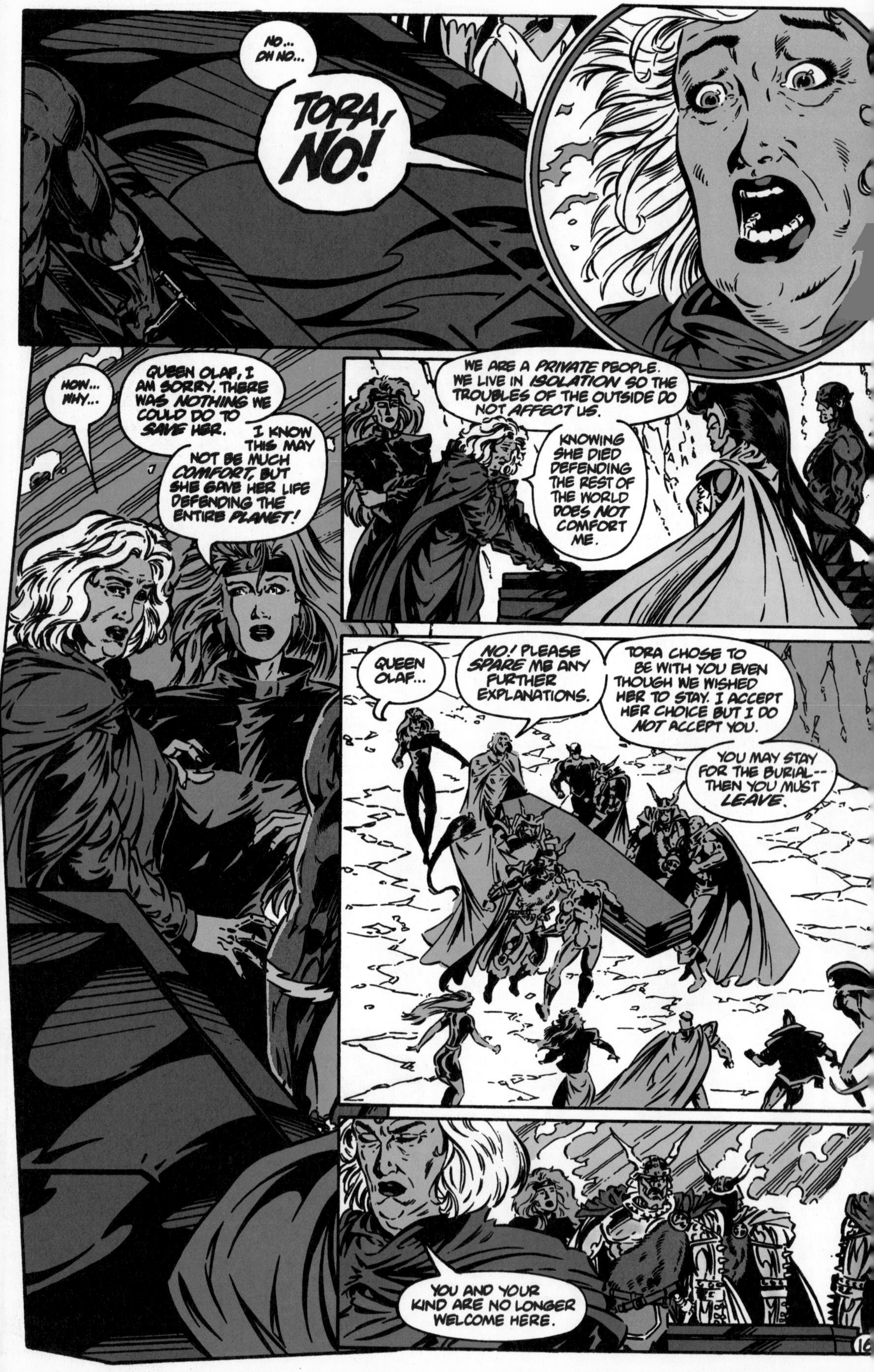
NO... OH NO...
TORA, NO!
HOW... WHY...
QUEEN OLAF, I AM SORRY. THERE WAS NOTHING WE COULD DO TO SAVE HER.
I KNOW THIS MAY NOT BE MUCH COMFORT, BUT SHE GAVE HER LIFE DEFENDING THE ENTIRE PLANET!
WE ARE A PRIVATE PEOPLE. WE LIVE IN ISOLATION SO THE TROUBLES OF THE OUTSIDE DO NOT AFFECT US.
KNOWING SHE DIED DEFENDING THE REST OF THE WORLD DOES NOT COMFORT ME.
QUEEN OLAF...
NO! PLEASE SPARE ME ANY FURTHER EXPLANATIONS.
TORA CHOSE TO BE WITH YOU EVEN THOUGH WE WISHED HER TO STAY. I ACCEPT HER CHOICE BUT I DO NOT ACCEPT YOU.
YOU MAY STAY FOR THE BURIAL-- THEN YOU MUST LEAVE.
YOU AND YOUR KIND ARE NO LONGER WELCOME HERE.

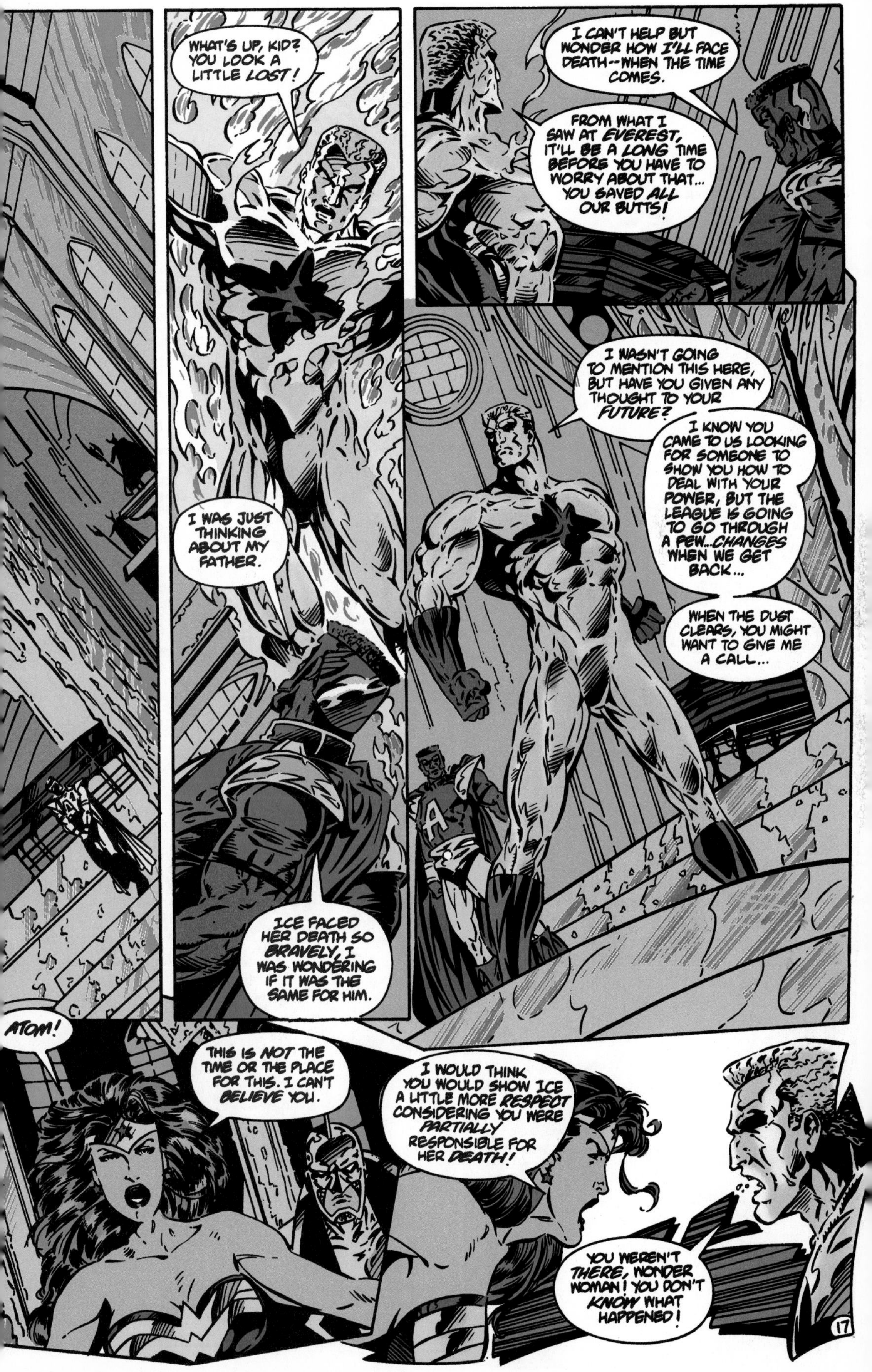
WHAT'S UP, KID? YOU LOOK A LITTLE LOST!
I WAS JUST THINKING ABOUT MY FATHER.
ICE FACED HER DEATH SO BRAVELY, I WAS WONDERING IF IT WAS THE SAME FOR HIM.
I CAN'T HELP BUT WONDER HOW I'LL FACE DEATH--WHEN THE TIME COMES.
FROM WHAT I SAW AT EVEREST, IT'LL BE A LONG TIME BEFORE YOU HAVE TO WORRY ABOUT THAT... YOU SAVED ALL OUR BUTTS!
I WASN'T GOING TO MENTION THIS HERE, BUT HAVE YOU GIVEN ANY THOUGHT TO YOUR FUTURE?
I KNOW YOU CAME TO US LOOKING FOR SOMEONE TO SHOW YOU HOW TO DEAL WITH YOUR POWER, BUT THE LEAGUE IS GOING TO GO THROUGH A FEW...CHANGES WHEN WE GET BACK...
WHEN THE DUST CLEARS, YOU MIGHT WANT TO GIVE ME A CALL...
ATOM!
THIS IS NOT THE TIME OR THE PLACE FOR THIS. I CAN'T BELIEVE YOU.
I WOULD THINK YOU WOULD SHOW ICE A LITTLE MORE RESPECT CONSIDERING YOU WERE PARTIALLY RESPONSIBLE FOR HER DEATH!
YOU WEREN'T THERE, WONDER WOMAN! YOU DON'T KNOW WHAT HAPPENED!

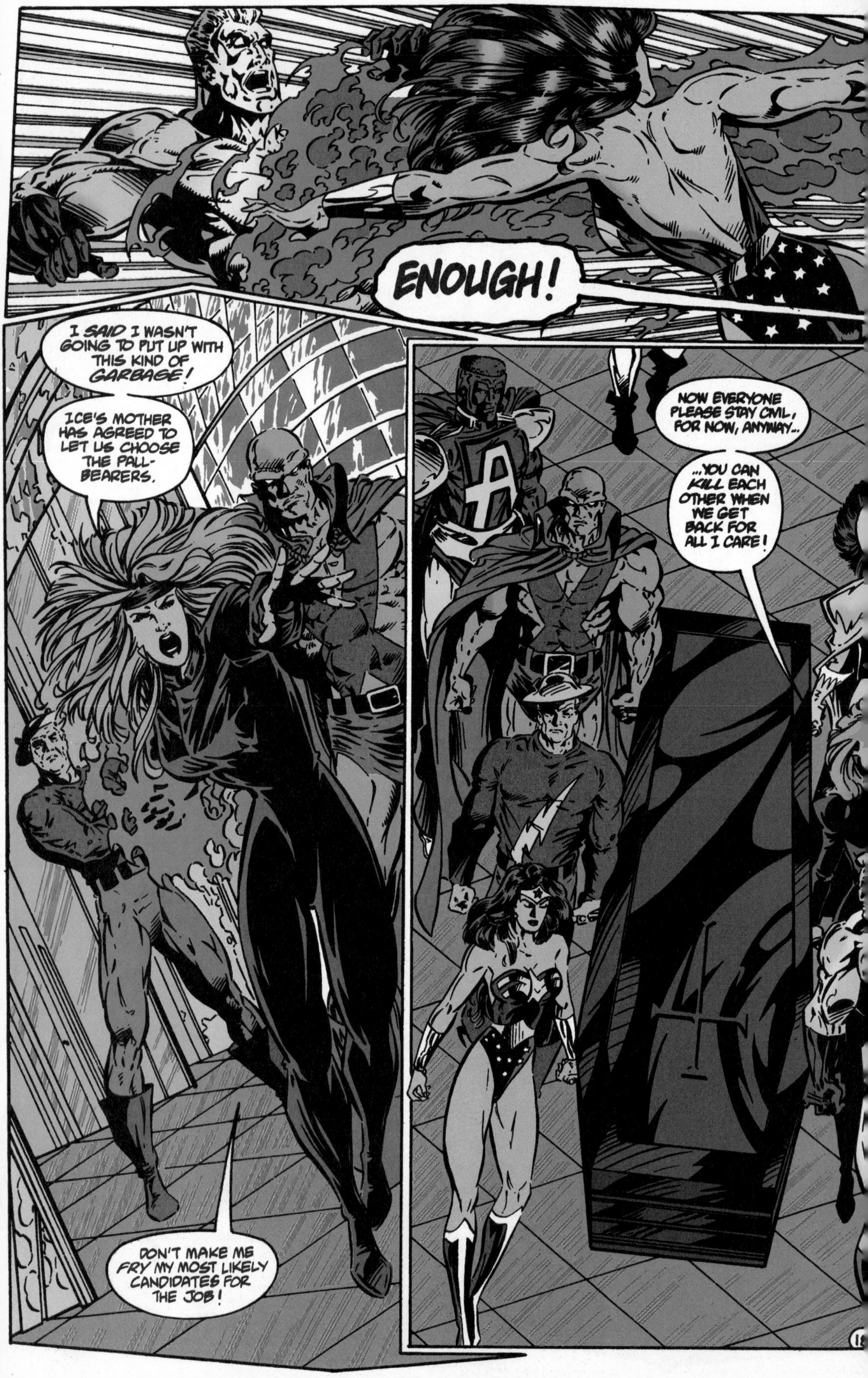
ENOUGH!
I SAID I WASN'T GOING TO PUT UP WITH THIS KIND OF GARBAGE!
ICE'S MOTHER HAS AGREED TO LET US CHOOSE THE PALL-BEARERS.
DON'T MAKE ME FRY MY MOST LIKELY CANDIDATES FOR THE JOB!
NOW EVERYONE PLEASE STAY CIVIL, FOR NOW, ANYWAY...
...YOU CAN KILL EACH OTHER WHEN WE GET BACK FOR ALL I CARE!

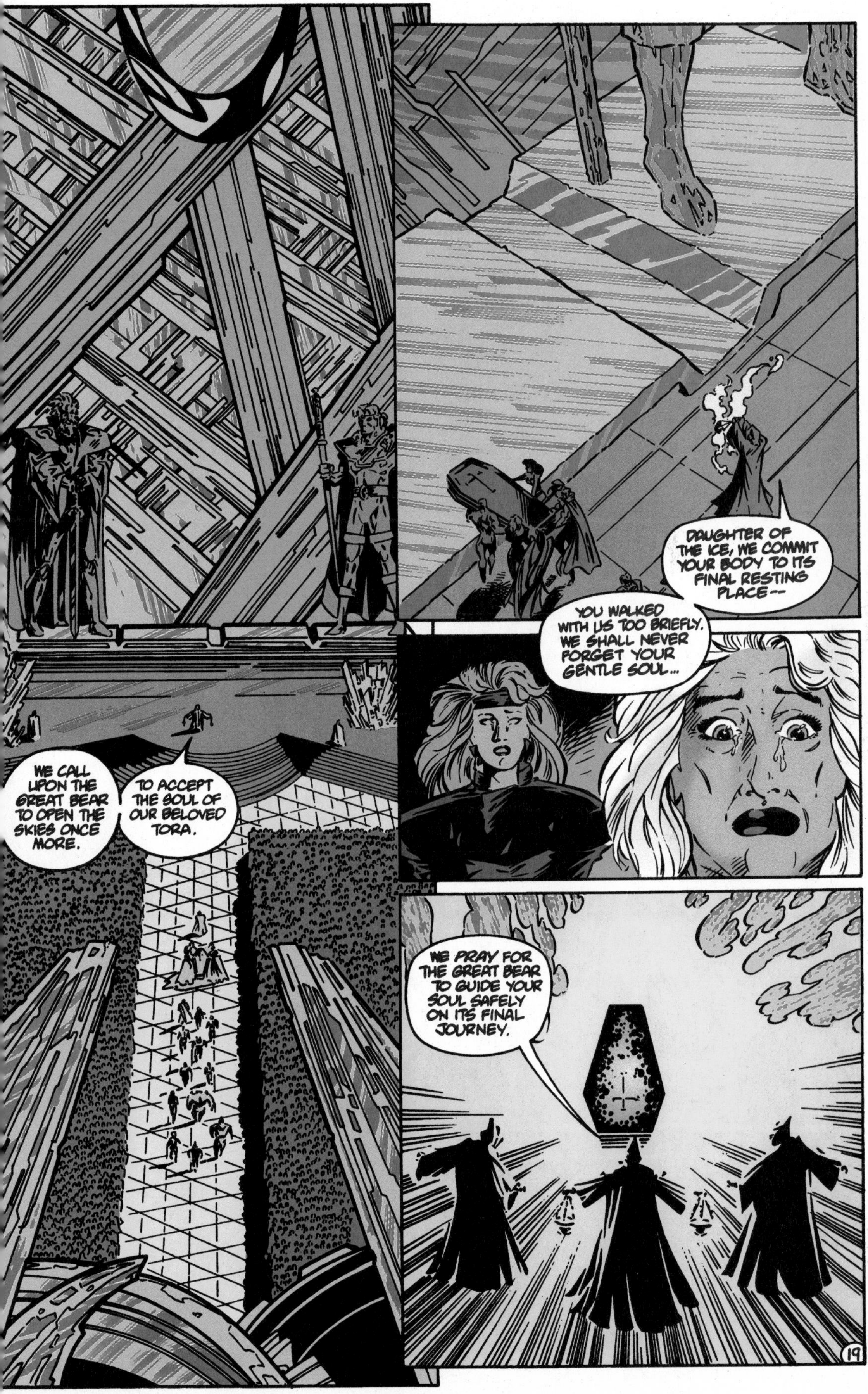
DAUGHTER OF THE ICE, WE COMMIT YOUR BODY TO ITS FINAL RESTING PLACE--
YOU WALKED WITH US TOO BRIEFLY. WE SHALL NEVER FORGET YOUR GENTLE SOUL...
WE CALL UPON THE GREAT BEAR TO OPEN THE SKIES ONCE MORE.
TO ACCEPT THE SOUL OF OUR BELOVED TORA.
WE PRAY FOR THE GREAT BEAR TO GUIDE YOUR SOUL SAFELY ON ITS FINAL JOURNEY.

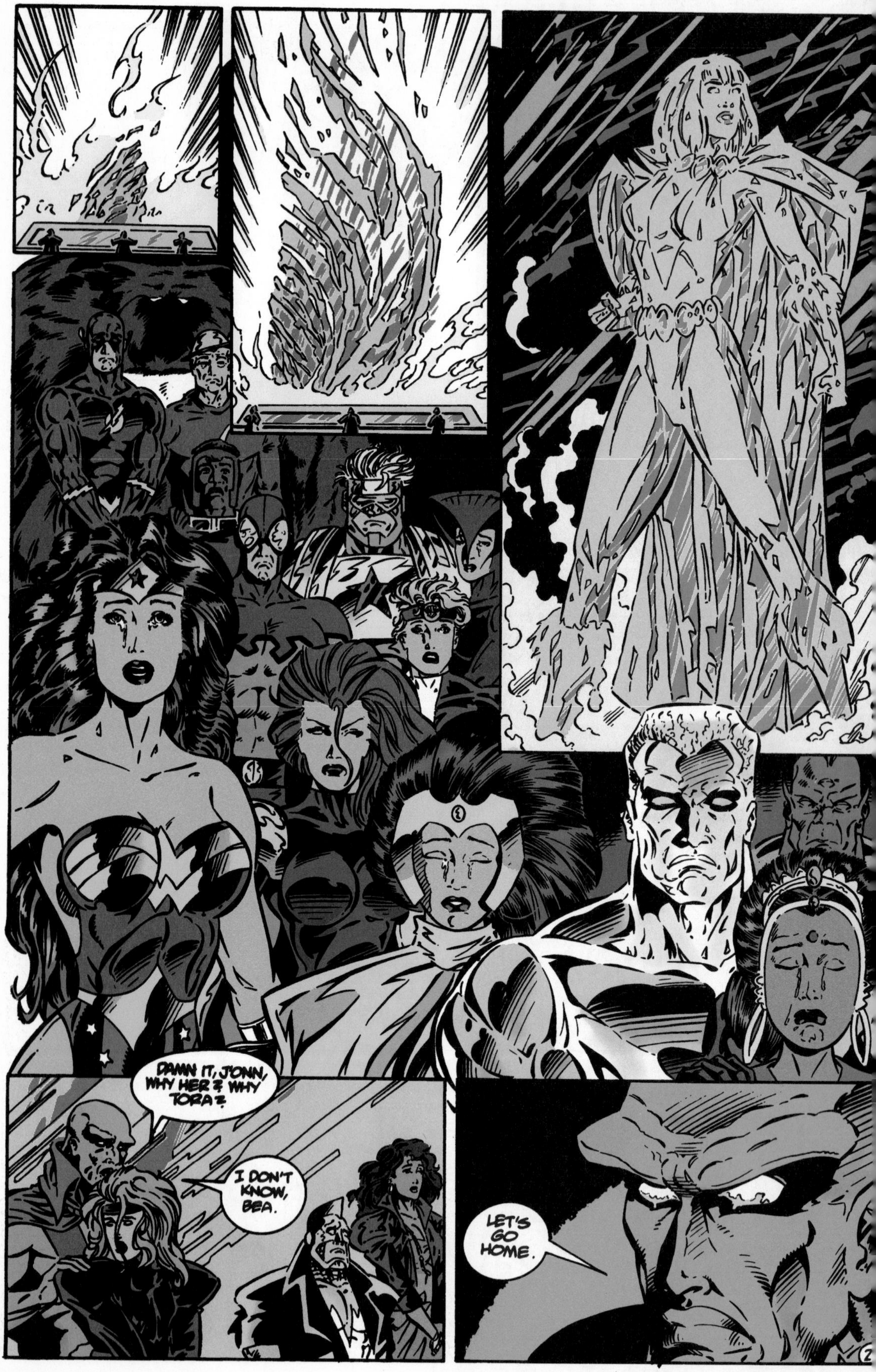
DAMN IT, J'ONN, WHY HER? WHY TORA?
I DON'T KNOW, BEA.
LET'S GO HOME.

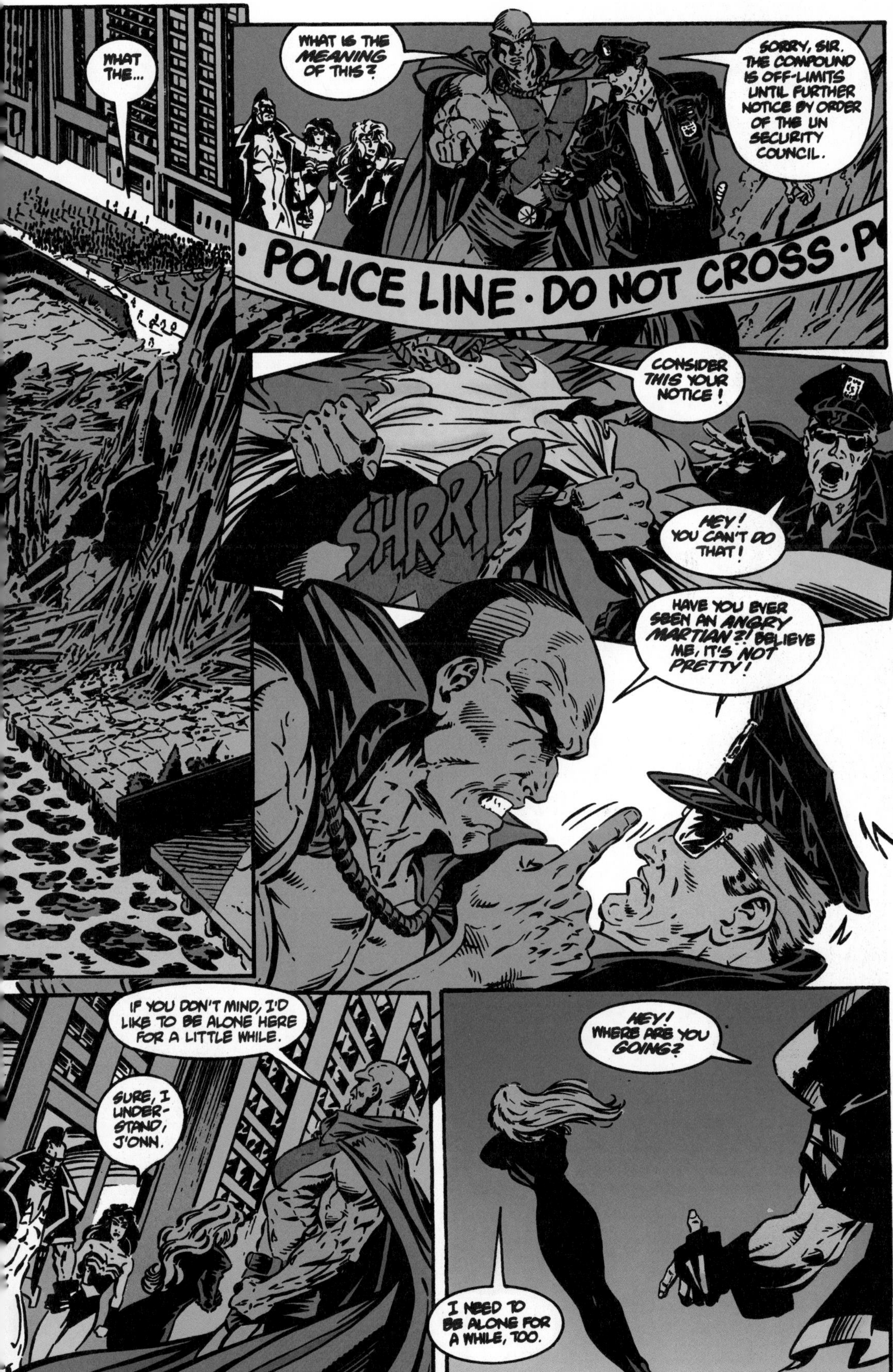

WHAT THE...
WHAT IS THE MEANING OF THIS?
SORRY, SIR. THE COMPOUND IS OFF-LIMITS UNTIL FURTHER NOTICE BY ORDER OF THE UN SECURITY COUNCIL.
POLICE LINE · DO NOT CROSS · P
CONSIDER THIS YOUR NOTICE!
SHRRIP
HEY! YOU CAN'T DO THAT!
HAVE YOU EVER SEEN AN ANGRY MARTIAN?! BELIEVE ME, IT'S NOT PRETTY!
IF YOU DON'T MIND, I'D LIKE TO BE ALONE HERE FOR A LITTLE WHILE.
SURE, I UNDER-STAND, J'ONN.
HEY! WHERE ARE YOU GOING?
I NEED TO BE ALONE FOR A WHILE, TOO.

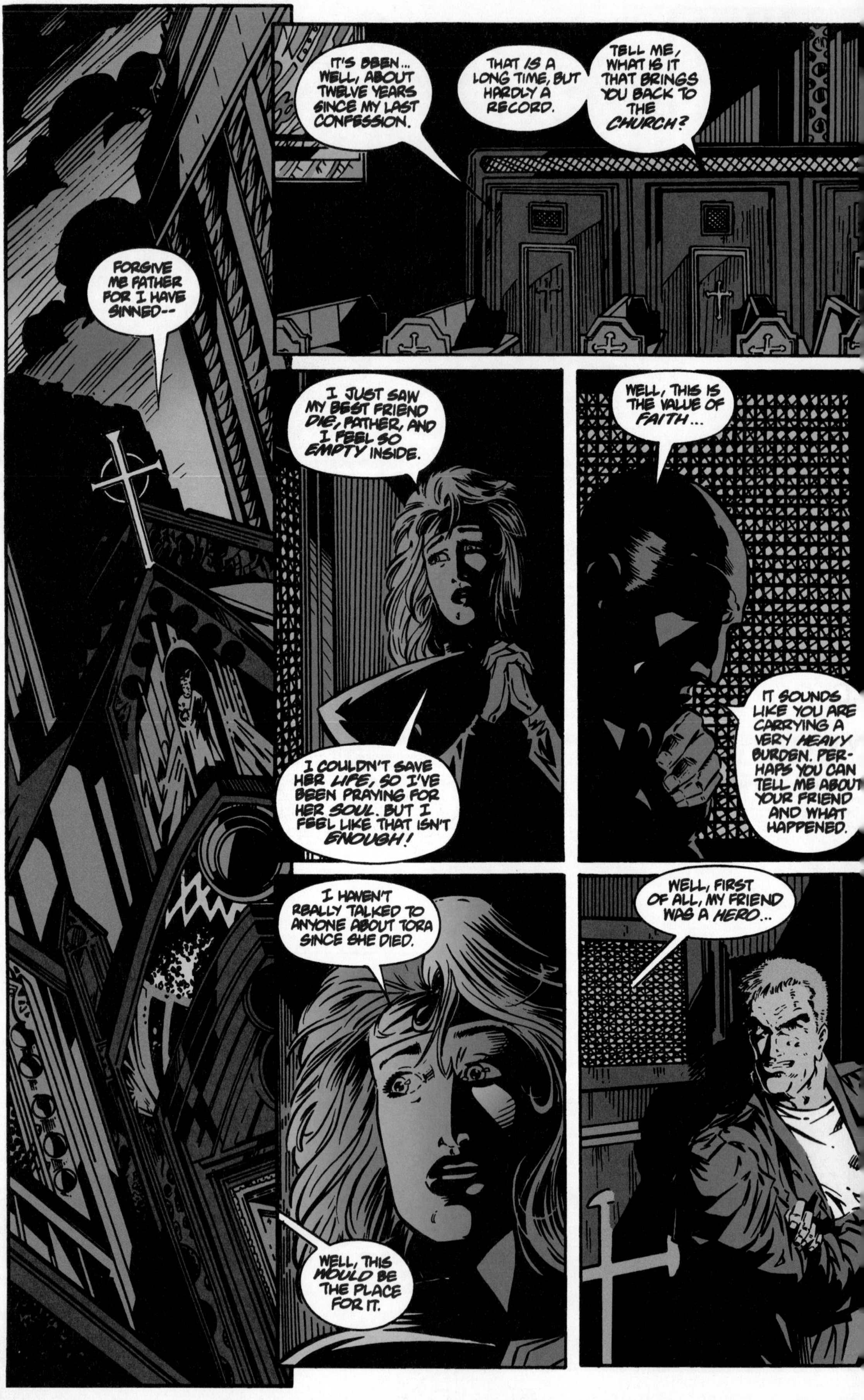
FORGIVE ME FATHER FOR I HAVE SINNED--
IT'S BEEN... WELL, ABOUT TWELVE YEARS SINCE MY LAST CONFESSION.
THAT IS A LONG TIME, BUT HARDLY A RECORD.
TELL ME, WHAT IS IT THAT BRINGS YOU BACK TO THE CHURCH?
I JUST SAW MY BEST FRIEND DIE, FATHER, AND I FEEL SO EMPTY INSIDE.
I COULDN'T SAVE HER LIFE, SO I'VE BEEN PRAYING FOR HER SOUL. BUT I FEEL LIKE THAT ISN'T ENOUGH!
WELL, THIS IS THE VALUE OF FAITH...
IT SOUNDS LIKE YOU ARE CARRYING A VERY HEAVY BURDEN. PERHAPS YOU CAN TELL ME ABOUT YOUR FRIEND AND WHAT HAPPENED.
I HAVEN'T REALLY TALKED TO ANYONE ABOUT TORA SINCE SHE DIED.
WELL, THIS WOULD BE THE PLACE FOR IT.
WELL, FIRST OF ALL, MY FRIEND WAS A HERO...

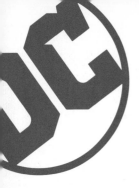

reg Rucka and company have created a
mpelling narrative for fans of the Amazing
nazon."– **NERDIST**

A) heartfelt and genuine take on Diana's
gin."– **NEWSARAMA**

C UNIVERSE REBIRTH

WONDER
WOMAN

OL. 1: THE LIES

GREG RUCKA
with LIAM SHARP

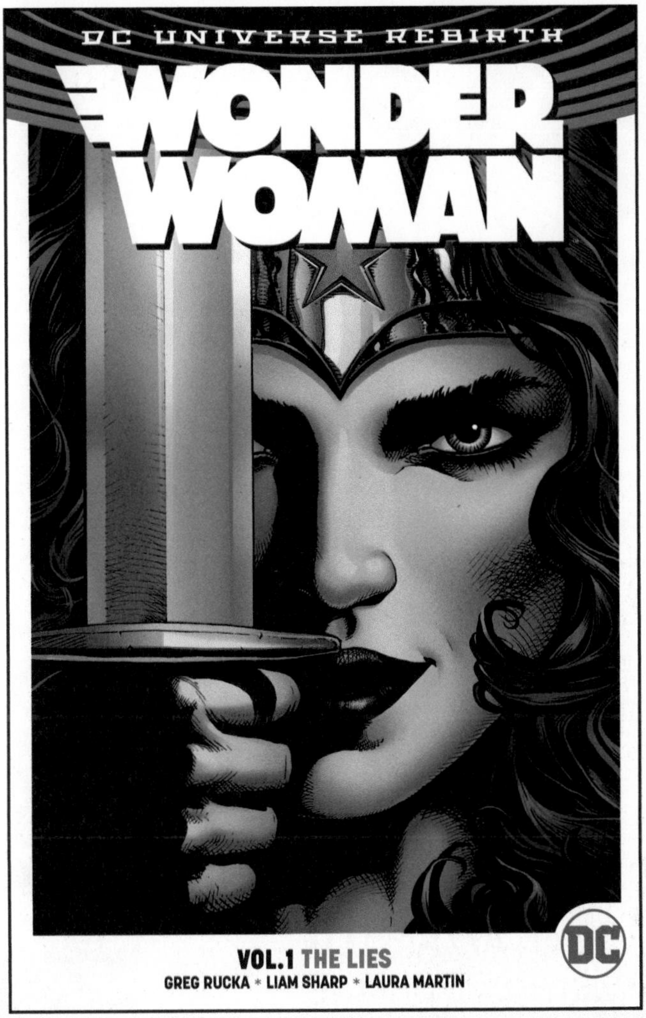
DC UNIVERSE REBIRTH
WONDER WOMAN
VOL.1 THE LIES
GREG RUCKA * LIAM SHARP * LAURA MARTIN

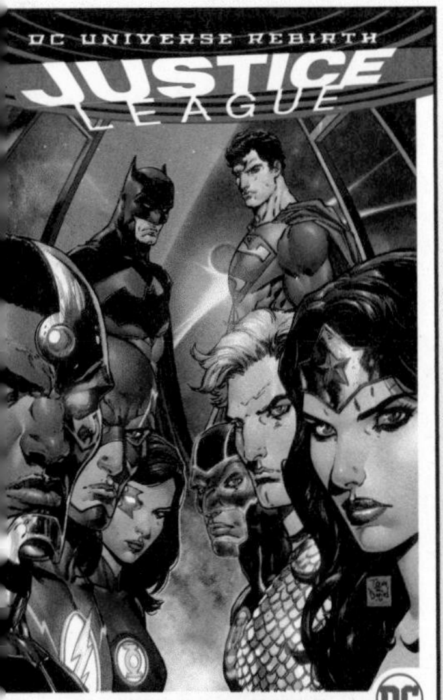
DC UNIVERSE REBIRTH
JUSTICE LEAGUE
VOL.1 THE EXTINCTION MACHINES
BRYAN HITCH * TONY S. DANIEL * SANDU FLOREA * TOMEU MOREY

JUSTICE LEAGUE VOL. 1: THE EXTINCTION MACHINES

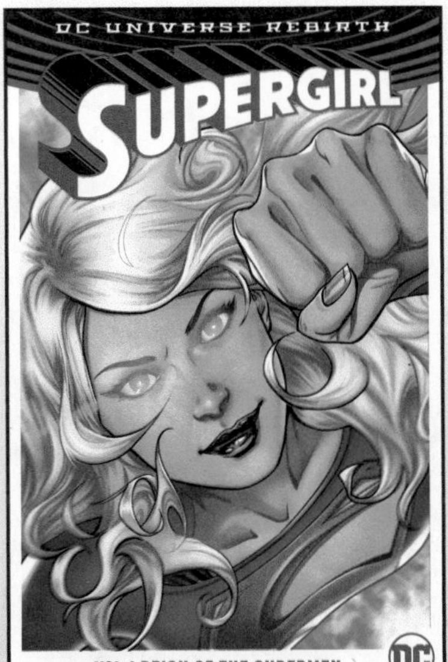
DC UNIVERSE REBIRTH
SUPERGIRL
VOL.1 REIGN OF THE SUPERMEN
STEVE ORLANDO * BRIAN CHING * MIKE ATIYEH

SUPERGIRL VOL. 1: REIGN OF THE SUPERMEN

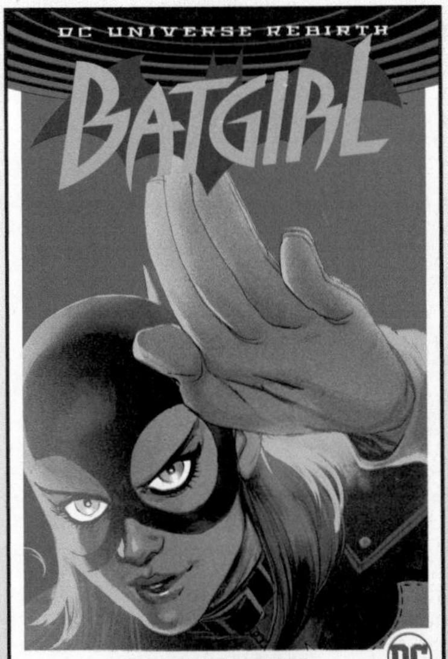
DC UNIVERSE REBIRTH
BATGIRL
VOL.1 BEYOND BURNSIDE
HOPE LARSON * RAFAEL ALBUQUERQUE

BATGIRL VOL. 1: BEYOND BURNSIDE

Get more DC graphic novels wherever comics and books are sold!

"Clear storytelling at its best. It's an intriguing concept and easy to grasp."
— **THE NEW YORK TIMES**

"Azzarello is rebuilding the mythology of Wonder Woman."
— **CRAVE ONLINE**

WONDER WOMAN
VOL. 1: BLOOD
BRIAN AZZARELLO
with CLIFF CHIANG

"EXPECT A LOT MORE WONDER WOMAN FANS AFTER A FEW ISSUES OF THIS BOOK."
— USA TODAY

THE NEW YORK TIMES BESTSELLER

THE NEW 52!

WONDER WOMAN

VOLUME 1 BLOOD

BRIAN *AZZARELLO* CLIFF *CHIANG* TONY *AKINS*

**WONDER WOMAN
VOL. 2: GUTS**

**WONDER WOMAN
VOL. 3: IRON**

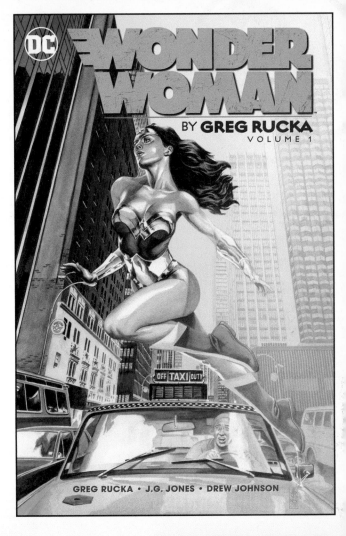

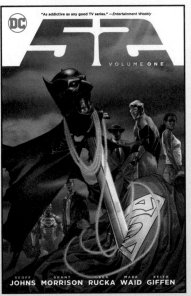
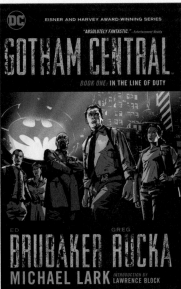
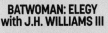

"Touch(es) on a sense of scale and complexity unique in comics, let alone any entertainment medium."
– **PASTE**

"A must-read for the first timer."
– **COMICSBEAT**

GRANT MORRISON
THE MULTIVERSITY

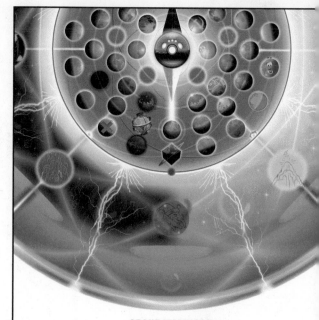

GRANT MORRISON

THE #1 NEW YORK TIMES BESTSELLER

IVAN REIS JOE PRADO JIM LEE DOUG MAHNKE FRANK QUITELY
CHRIS SPROUSE BEN OLIVER CAMERON STEWART

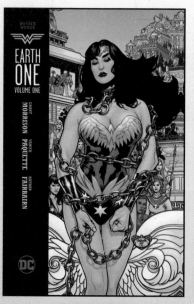

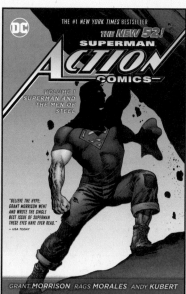

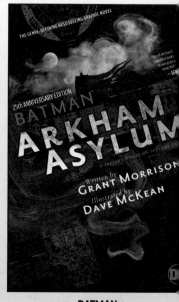

WONDER WOMAN: EARTH ONE VOL. 1
with YANICK PAQUETTE

SUPERMAN: ACTION COMICS VOL. 1
with RAGS MORALES & ANDY KUBERT

BATMAN: ARKHAM ASYLUM
with DAVE McKEAN